The Tyranny of the Left

BOOK I

GROWTH

Finbarr O'Keeffe

OK Publishing

Reading, England

First published in 2020

ISBN 978-1-8382408-2-0

For Mum & Dad

For Everything

'Democracy extends the sphere of individual freedom, socialism restricts it. Democracy attaches all possible value to each man; socialism makes each man a mere agent, a mere number. Democracy and socialism have nothing in common but one word: equality. But notice the difference: while democracy seeks equality in liberty, socialism seeks equality in restraint and servitude.'

Alexis de Tocqueville - 1835

Contents

Foreword

From 1917 to 1989, a mania swept the world. It was a form of bigotry that became, effectively, a new religion, a twisted and narrow mindset based primarily on hatred and resentment. It had incubated for some 150 years prior to that period, with regular explosions of violence, but it was in the twentieth century that it achieved its full realisation, and it resulted in the deaths of 150 million people while utterly destroying the lives of a billion more. Between 1932 and 1967, a span of just thirty-five years, this phenomenon killed ten times more than were abducted in the entire 300 year history of the Atlantic Slave Trade; wrecking the lives of fifty times as many people in just a tenth of the time. Remarkably, *astoundingly*, it is a prejudice that is rarely challenged and it remains as prevalent as ever, even after all that has happened. And it persists among those who regard themselves as the most intelligent, moral and tolerant members of our society. While slavery and imperialism have been all but banished, while racism, sexism and homophobia wither, this is the hate that will not die – it is the lesson that humanity stubbornly refuses to learn. Worse, at the time of writing, it is gaining considerable momentum once more. It is, quite simply, the most urgent issue that our society faces.

Introduction

'When we demonise our opponents, we abandon the possibility of peacefully resolving our differences, and seek to justify violence against them.'

Nelson Mandela. Cape Town, South Africa. 11 May 1999

By November of 1789, late in the first autumn of the French Revolution, Louis XVI had been dragged from Versailles to Paris, the new seat of French politics. The deputies of the Assembly soon joined him there and took up residence in the Salle du Manège, the long, honey-coloured building that previously housed the indoor riding school of the Tuileries Palace. Those politicians quickly became polarised with the conservatives drifting over to the right side of the hall while the more radical members congregated on the left. It was from that acrimonious division that the terms 'left-wing' and 'right-wing' originated, and it was the deputies of the left who were to seize control of events. Prior to the Revolution they had spoken loftily of virtue, equality, freedom and tolerance. Yet their deeds could not have diverged more sharply from their aspirations, for they tore France apart in an atmosphere of recrimination, persecution, intolerance and violence such as the world had rarely seen. The left-wing was thus born in an orgy of blood and hatred, forged in a cauldron of violent intolerance and insatiable state-sanctioned murder.* Yet, despite the horrors it unleashed, the cataclysm of the French Revolution had little impact on the left's

* The principles of left wing activism can be said to date back to at least the Gracchi Revolt of 133BC, the elections of the Tribunes of the plebs in 494BC, or even earlier. One could also argue that the historical Jesus, a committed anti-capitalist who railed against the elites of his day, was the epitome of a left-wing rabble rouser. But this study will primarily restrict itself to events from 1789 onwards - from which we can date not just the term but what we can legitimately label the modern movement.

assurance that it was on the side of justice and morality and, as a result, the disasters have kept on coming.

The events that have blotted the movement's copybook are not just limited to the heavy hitters which merit discussion in these volumes either, the totalitarian, almost dystopian, nightmares of Robespierre, Stalin, Mao and Pol Pot, for the left has gifted our planet with numerous other tyrannies. In Zimbabwe the regime of Robert Mugabe caused devastation with his unique blend of Maoism and racism. In Venezuela a few decades of socialist hegemony resulted in a collapsed economy, starvation, a gagged press, the crushing of political freedoms and spiralling death tolls under an effective military dictatorship. In Algeria the authoritarian socialist government saw the collectivisation of agriculture and the imposition of a state controlled economy that led to civil war, tribunals for 'economic crimes' and decades of bloodshed and repression. In Europe other socialist groups like Sinn Féin / IRA and the Red Army Faction of Ulrike Meinhof and Andreas Baader unleashed significant bombing campaigns, the latter blending their violence with strident anti-Semitism. The Italian Red Brigades of the 1970s and '80s were responsible for numerous assassinations, attacks, robberies and kidnappings. Sri Lanka was subjected to the murderous campaign of the Marxist-Leninist Tamil Tigers. In Peru there was 'Shining Path', the Maoist insurgent organisation which may have been the most vicious guerrilla movement in the world. In Angola the Marxist-Leninist MPLA, with Soviet and Chinese backing, committed atrocities in a civil war that dragged on for decades with a body-count in the millions. North Korea has suffered brutal suppression, purges of staggering profligacy and waves of famines with unimaginably horrendous death tolls. In Albania the regime of Enver Hoxha and the Party of Labour in the Socialist People's Republic was characterised by forced collectivisation, the brutality of his secret police and the imprisonment and murder of political opponents with perhaps 100,000 liquidated. This is not to neglect Romania under Ceaușescu, and his vile predecessors, Gaddafi's Cultural Revolution in his Great Socialist People's Libyan Arab *Jamahiriya* or the disaster of Ethiopia. In that bleak period the socialist rule of the Workers' Party of Ethiopia, established on the Soviet model, saw a one-party state, economic decline, thousands of political opponents killed or imprisoned and forced collectivisation which caused starvation on such Biblical levels that it inspired the Live Aid movement.

Tito's Yugoslavia was yet another state renowned for its severe repression and political violence. Its brutal secret police were modelled on the KGB and estimates suggest 100,000 died in the violent takeover that secured the single-party state. That embattled region suffered a second tragedy under the former leader of the Socialist Party of Serbia, the ex-Communist Slobodan Milosevic and his radical cronies like the prominent Green Party member, Radovan

Karadzić. They were guilty of a particularly gruesome genocide,* yet we have not even considered the various other despotisms of Soviet controlled Eastern Europe. Millions suffered under their yoke between WWII and the end of the '80s. Bulgaria, Hungary and East Germany were especially profligate with human lives, but they were far from alone in that region. There are plenty of other cases – Laos, the Philippines, Guatemala, Malaya, Mozambique, Chile, Nicaragua, Mali, Guinea, Zambia, El Salvador, Tanzania, Colombia, Zanzibar, Mexico, Somalia, Grenada, Eritrea, Nepal, Syria, Burma, Guyana, Namibia, Afghanistan and more, and the ingredients are usually the same: a crumbling economy, crippling oppression, wide-scale censorship and mass murder, frequently married with large scale famines.

Such examples, despite the frequency with which they occur, are usually brushed off by advocates as distortions that are wholly unrepresentative of their ideology. But the idea that they have nothing to do with the left is of course ludicrous. If these crises were aberrations of left-wing thought, then they would not keep happening. Yet they do. The fact that this cycle keeps repeating is damning evidence that they are less perversions of leftist ideals than a fairly predictable consequence of them, and the reasons why are quite obvious. Socialism attacks economic success and demands the compliance of the entire population. It thus moves swiftly from persuasion to coercion – censoring culture and the press, producing blizzards of propaganda, curtailing democratic participation and introducing a raft of thought-crimes. Both a secret police and the wider populace are encouraged to shop any dissidents while the punishments increase in brutality. Meanwhile, as it is impossible to maintain adequate levels of production and efficiency once incentives have been stripped from the workforce, economies flounder and shortages proliferate. Starvation frequently follows. The restrictions on free speech and cultural expression crush the human spirit too, so the population suffer physically, spiritually, intellectually and economically. The state regresses, quality of life disintegrates and technological development and cultural expression collapse. Put simply – socialism offers no carrot, so it must rely ever more regularly on the stick.

Yet in denying their movement's responsibility for these atrocities, the left increases the chances that they will happen again. Those who do not admit to mistakes will, after all, keep repeating them. This is why the movement is up to its old tricks again. They are censoring rivals, demolishing monuments, screaming hate at their opponents and launching physical attacks with increasing frequency. Yet while engaged in such behaviour they remain certain

---

* While the massacres in this study, most frequently not of biological or ethnic origin, may be more accurately termed ideocide or politicide, the term 'genocide' will be adhered to for purposes of narrative comprehension.

of their superior virtue. For the left seem largely oblivious to such salient facts. They have sallied on, blithely indifferent to their crimes, refusing to accept any blame for past or present misdemeanours. Indeed, the assurance of the movement appears, if anything, to have been bolstered in recent decades. Yet, by failing to accept and learn from the past, the activists continue spouting the same political and class prejudices that contributed to such disasters in the first place. None of this should be terribly surprising. It is *always* those who regard themselves as morally superior who commit the most terrible deeds, and that same conviction blinds them to the reality of their actions. The second decade of the twenty-first century saw ISIS raise the bar in human atrocities again, and they too regarded themselves as the most righteous people on the planet. Indeed, that is precisely why they felt justified in torturing and killing so many 'infidels'. So it is with the worst excesses of the left. The radicals go from hating certain sectors of society to gradually believing they deserve everything inflicted on them. It is an impulse that has driven every left-wing tyranny there has ever been.

But, despite this, the left tend to regard themselves as the tolerant and compassionate lot. It is a boast that does not stand up to scrutiny. If you are only tolerant of people who share your views, or whose lifestyles you empathise with, then you are intolerant. It's what the word means. And, while there is certainly much sympathy and decency on the left, it is hard to escape the impression that there is rather more hate. It is a hatred aimed at bankers, capitalists, Zionists, Tories, America, right-wingers, Etonians, landlords, 'white people' and a raft of other sectors of society. And those prejudices are not just limited to the extremists. They are common in decidedly moderate circles too. The *Guardian* columnist Charlie Brooker wrote

> 'I've instinctively hated the Tories since birth...The Conservative party is an eternally irritating force for wrong that appeals exclusively to bigots, toffs, money-minded machine men, faded entertainers and selfish, grasping simpletons who were born with some essential part of their soul missing'.[1]

Now, Brooker is a comedian, of sorts, so his comments should not really be taken literally, but these views have gained a broad cultural capital. Yet imagine how Brooker or his *Guardian* colleagues might have reacted were someone to have published identical sentiments about Muslims, women, homosexuals or black people; if one had sneered at 'plebs' the way he does at 'toffs'. They would explode with indignant rage, whether it was done for comedic value or not.

Yet there is little acceptance of this. The activists have persuaded themselves that their hatred is simply an expression of their compassion. They truly believe their rivals *must* be evil and thus deserve the scorn that is heaped on them. Indeed the abuse itself becomes a moral act - one so rewarding that any hysterical claims directed at their 'enemies' are readily believed. The sixteen year old Ivo Delingpole related a first-hand account of what it is like to belong to one of the groups singled out as a target. As an Etonian he self-consciously admitted to being 'possibly amongst Britain's most hated' and also reported how students are unable to wear their uniforms into Windsor 'for fear of being mugged'.[2] These, it should be remembered, are schoolboys, who become the objects of loathing and risk physical attack simply by donning their uniforms. Yet what chance do they have when even respected left-wing writers like John le Carré describe Etonians as a 'curse on the earth'? Hatred of this sort is not just common on the left, nor even merely tolerated. It is widely celebrated. The problem is not just that the left is so prone to bigotry. It is that they have such *pride* in their prejudice. Hatred is, of course, the worst possible basis for politics, yet it is the very lifeblood of the left. Hating people on an economic basis, professional grounds, political affiliation or social class is just as ludicrous as despising them on the basis of race, nationality, gender or sexuality. Yet while the militant left remain proud of their hatred, their bigotry has arguably killed more people than anything else in history, including the Black Death. It is this correlation between current intolerance and past atrocity that forms the basis of this study – and the parallels are striking.

A textbook example to illustrate this phenomenon can be found in the Twitter account of Another Angry Woman. She described herself, under the profile picture in which she made a concerted effort to display her hairy armpits, as 'Anarchist, Feminist, Queer, All Angry', while also announcing that 'bigots shouldn't be allowed fucking anywhere'; yet she then went on to add, without the slightest trace of irony, a slew of bigoted asides:

> 'Men are pathetic. They expect everyone to treat their every utterance like a proud parent looking at a toddler's first shit in the potty'; 'A cop could be a puppy-rescuing all-round nicey but the role he occupies means he's still a bastard'; 'The police are not reasonable humans'; 'And yet there's still no media discussions about white culture and how it breeds violence, for *some* reason'; 'hahahaha today seems to be National Men Being Super Irrational Day'; 'This knee jerking is another example of why men make bad scientists'; 'fucking hell, why are men such fucking oversensitive dummy-chuckers?'; 'tfw [the face when] you see horrible old white dudes' names trending and u hope they've died but actually they've just been horrible again :((((((((('; 'Raindrops on roses & Thatcher is #stilldead. Bright copper kettles & Thatcher is #still dead. Brown paper packages Thatcher's #stilldead'; 'ooo Toby Young's trending! Did he die? Embarrassingly?'; 'The Met are lying, racist, murdering scum'; 'Corbyn isn't articulating the much-needed need for an uprising and execution of all those propertarian scum, simmer down comment ppl'.

So, bigotry is appalling, unless it's directed at the police, Tories, white people, the rich, or men, basically anyone who differs from Another Angry Woman. In such circumstances it's absolutely brilliant and you can pray for, or celebrate, their deaths, obviously.

She also readily believed all the allegations of child abuse levelled at certain Conservative MPs. After all, the accused were white, male and Tory, and thus clearly guilty. Her opinion on the issue was 'Whenever white men spring to the defence of other white paedos I always wonder what ~they~ have to hide'. In fact the allegations were later proven the fantasies of a compulsive liar and paedophile, Carl Beech, who was promptly sentenced to eighteen years for perverting the course of justice.* When consumed by prejudice though, as this rather nasty individual is, one will believe what one wants. It is little wonder that she also expressed admiration for the poet Sean Bonney and his maxim that 'When you meet a Tory on the street, cut his throat. It will bring out the best in you'. In characters like this we can detect the seeds of the demagogues who have inflicted such misery over the ages. They shamelessly vocalise the undisguised loathing and distorted ideologies of history's great tyrants and, despite the fact that she and her ilk would be repelled if someone suggested that 'black culture breeds violence', 'women are irrational and make bad scientists' or 'Muslims are not reasonable humans', they appear oblivious to the double standards they vocalise with such depressing regularity.

While she is an extreme case, these are depressingly common sentiments. They are shared by millions in the UK alone who consider themselves decent, compassionate people. Such statements are not limited to the Twitterati either, for examples can be found at the highest levels of government. Harriet Harman, the former Deputy Leader of the Labour party admits to 'having loathed the Tories in the Commons for decades'[3] while Aneurin 'Nye' Bevan, who was the Minister for Health in the Clement Attlee administration of 1945-51, was pivotal in the introduction of the NHS, and is widely regarded as the voice of the left in that period offered similar, and rather more enduring, sentiments. In his most celebrated quote, delivered at the Bellvue Hotel on 3 July 1948, he gloated how nothing 'can eradicate from my heart a deep burning hatred for the Tory party... So far as I am concerned they are lower than vermin'. Now, at the risk of invoking Godwin's Law, to the neutral observer, these sentiments appear indistinguishable from those expressed by the Nazis. They should send a wave of revulsion through any decent person. Yet while most regard the Holocaust as a natural, if not inevitable consequence of the Nazis' talk of Jewish 'vermin', the mass killings of the left are widely regarded as an aberration, even when borne of identical rhetoric.

---

* Tom Watson, Labour's Deputy Prime Minister, had also gone public to support the allegations and he pressured the police into launching an expansive and expensive enquiry. A number of innocent individuals had their lives ruined by his pursuit of the bogus claims.

On the left however, such inconvenient realities are ignored. For Bevan's quote is still fondly remembered, even celebrated. Indeed, it is so popular that it has been immortalised on a tee-shirt by *The Guardian*.[4] Satisfied customers left gushing comments like 'wear with pride' and 'Anyone with a heart should wear one'. This then is the paradox ingrained in the militant left, and even the moderate *Guardian* reading left: it is a movement that avers to oppose prejudice, yet it frequently celebrates its own brand of bigotry and hostility. While claiming to be concerned with aiding the oppressed it seems, in practice, more preoccupied with simply bashing the rich and successful.

There is hatred at the heart of the left then, and it is further fuelled by irrational fears about their opposition. Political rivals are regularly labelled 'evil' or 'scum', ludicrous tales of their malevolence are accepted without demur, and the radical's view grows ever more deranged and hysterical. But once one has identified their opponents in such sweeping, negative terms, it becomes far easier to dehumanise them - to deny them the respect and consideration normally accorded to fellow human beings. The movement continually launches witch-hunts, both against their 'enemies' and their peers, which results in behaviour like that seen outside the Tory party conference in 2015. As people entered the venue a raucous group of agitators hurled projectiles and insults like 'pig' and 'scum' in their direction. They even spat on them, a form of abuse unimaginable from campaigners of any other stripe. If groups of women or Muslims entering a conference were spat on and abused by a mob then the outcry would be enormous. Yet the left continually behave in the most appalling fashion with impunity. At the following year's conference in Birmingham, sturdy barriers were erected to defend the delegates from the shower of expectoration, but a large crowd still gathered to brandish signs declaring 'Tory Scum, Get Out Of Brum', 'Cull The Tories' and 'The Only Cuts That We Need Are Tories On The Guillotine'. These scenes are repeated annually, but protests of this nature are never seen at the Labour party conference. Intolerance and hatred of this kind is strictly a one-way street.

There was a similar attitude on display during the death and funeral of Margaret Thatcher. That event proved the catalyst for this study, and it made one wonder who the 'nasty' party really were. Now, many people clearly disagreed strongly with the former Prime Minister's policies and disliked her intensely, as is their right. But this in itself provides no adequate explanation for the events that unfolded that spring. It was one thing to witness the vitriol and gloating that flooded the internet or the public celebrating, as revellers cavorted wildly around bonfires. One shudders to think of the distress that caused to Lady Thatcher's grieving friends, family and grandchildren. But the spectacle of people picketing, jeering and booing at the former Prime Minister's funeral was quite another. To joke over the death of an individual is fine, to use humour as a release is something that should always be protected. But to use the demise of a distinguished leader to justify such unrestrained malevolence is quite another. How on earth such people could claim to hold the moral high ground while behaving in such a repugnant manner was simply bewildering. One assumes these are individuals who *abhor* the actions of the Westboro Baptist Church. Yet they felt justified in aping the behaviour of people they would, under normal circumstances, be repelled by. This then is the level that many on the left are sinking to, though, as this study will demonstrate, they have regularly plumbed depths from which their rivals would recoil.

Another favourite epithet of the left, one regurgitated for around ninety years now, is to label all opponents as 'Fascists' or 'Nazis'. In 1944 George Orwell recalled how he had heard the term 'Fascist' applied to 'farmers, shopkeepers, Social Credit, corporal punishment, fox-hunting, bull-fighting...Kipling, Gandhi, Chiang Kai-Shek, homosexuality...Youth Hostels, astrology, women [and] dogs...'[5] Lee Harvey Oswald gunned down the American President because he believed JFK was a fascist, but Robert Conquest recalled an even more egregious example. In the 1970s he met four Norwegian professors who had either fought in the resistance against the Nazis or been imprisoned in concentration camps. Yet, after opposing a recent disruption at the university, they had been listed as 'Fascists' in the student handbook. The tag has recently come into vogue again and David Lammy, the race-baiting Labour MP, felt justified in announcing that Boris Johnson and Jacob Rees-Mogg were both Nazis for supporting Brexit. Having had time to ponder the issue he declared that he hadn't gone far enough. Rational observers wondered how much further you could go. It is the sort of hysterical rhetoric that stokes up hatred and encourages division, giving radicals licence to attack their rivals with a clean conscience. For the widespread acceptance of left-wing hatred makes their activism far more dangerous.

This was crudely displayed during the riots at UCA Berkeley, California, on 1 February 2017. With the cameras rolling, the violence, intolerance and censoriousness that have marred the movement for centuries were showcased for the whole world to see. Puffed up with their own virtue, large numbers of students and 'anti-fascist' protestors smashed property, set parts of the university on fire and viciously attacked and pepper-sprayed bystanders. Their intent was to prevent the flamboyant conservative commentator, Milo Yiannopoulos, from giving a talk on the campus. In doing so, the protestors hoped to shut down dissenting opinions in the very place where the free speech movement began under Mario Savio in 1964. The irony was doubtless lost on all those taking part. There is now little tolerance for free speech on the radical left though, as this study will show, there never has been. But the riot was not just a moral shambles, it was an intellectual one too. For while the protestors labelled Yiannopoulos a 'Nazi', a 'fascist' and a 'white supremacist', he is in fact Jewish and gay, with a black husband. His real crime is to hold opinions contrary to those of the left, and to have a sense of humour, both unforgiveable transgressions to the guardians of moral purity.

Yvette Felarca, one of the organisers of the protest and a leading figure in the chillingly titled organisation 'By Any Means Necessary' (BAMN), appeared on TV a few days later in an astonishingly smug and unrepentant mood. She declared to have 'no regrets' about the riot, even claiming to be 'proud' of it, and promised much worse violence to come. She repeated the lies about Milo being a 'fascist' and a 'white supremacist', before bizarrely calling him 'homophobic' as well. Felarca also argued that responsibility for the violence and destruction lay with the university authorities for failing to cancel the speech. She criticised the left for being 'far too timid for way too long' and eulogised the use of revolutionary violence and militancy, claiming the riot should be 'the model' for the future of the movement. But while she celebrated their success in preventing him from speaking, the publicity led to Milo getting a slot on Bill Maher's television show. Instead of appearing in front of a few hundred students, he spoke to an audience of millions.

It is remarkable that so many could use violence to prevent the free speech of others while claiming to *oppose* fascism. After all, such behaviour is the cornerstone of fascism itself. It is also hard to comprehend how individuals like Felarca are persuaded that they hold the moral high ground by setting fire to a university. Sadly, such behaviour is typical of the philosophical kin of this arrogant, foolish and deeply unpleasant young woman. The modern extremist seems to believe that other people's free speech is violence while their own violence constitutes free speech. Felarca is the epitome of this type. Film soon emerged of her leading a mob against a lone protestor in Sacramento. She punched him several times before two large, burly men flung the man to the ground. They repeatedly kicked and stamped on him while he screamed 'Please!' Their victim did not retaliate or even attempt to defend himself. It would be comforting to believe that we are discussing just a tiny extremist clique here. But while the wider movement offered numerous justifications for what happened at Berkeley, condemnations were pitifully few and far between. Accounts and films of the rioting were reposted across the internet millions of times by gloating supporters.

The left is the movement of protest, but, as events at Berkeley illustrate, there has long been a culture that seems unable to differentiate between protest and riot. Large numbers feel they have a licence to resort to violence and destruction whenever the mood takes them, and there were similar scenes in London after the 2015 general election. The given reason for the protest was frustration over the existing political system. Yet none of the placards on display called for 'Electoral Reform Now!' They were plastered with slogans like 'Tory Scum!' and 'Cull the Tories!' The protests were about hatred, pure and simple. One activist even scrawled 'Fuck Tory Scum!' on the plinth dedicated to the women of WWII, desecrating a war memorial on the 70th anniversary of VE day. It was a relatively minor affair as such events go, but then it was in opposition to a democratic election with a healthy voter turnout. Such events do not normally inspire such venomous outbursts. Still, those present seemed furious at the fact that the Tories had won an election with 37% of the vote and demanded a different system, presumably oblivious to the fact that under Proportional Representation Britain would have ended up with a Tory / UKip coalition, or that Labour won the 2005 election with only 36% of the vote, a result that nobody had moaned about.

Naturally, thousands more took to Twitter and Facebook to condone, defend and celebrate the actions of rioters who resort to abuse and violence when democracy fails to go their way. Laurie Penny tweeted 'I don't have a problem with this...what's disgusting is that some people are more worried about a war memorial than the destruction of the welfare state'. Yet not only did she attempt to condone such horrendous behaviour, she also lied while doing so. The idea that the Tories are trying to dismantle the welfare state was a commonly expressed refrain in the election campaign of 1983. Yet it still appears to be in robust health several decades later.* Modern activists like Penny are presumably oblivious to the fact that they are repeating falsehoods that were common currency even before they were born. But faults of this nature are virtually inevitable when one's views are determined more by dogma and a polarising view of society than by any kind of rational, objective analysis. Penny's reaction, coming as it does from a doyen of the left, also helps explain the movement's propensity for violence. It is characteristic of a certain type of leftist to excuse any sort of transgression when carried out by one who has 'sympathetic' views. Despite numerous protestations to the contrary, the 'moral compass' of such individuals appears determined more by affiliation than any genuinely consistent values. As with that *Guardian* tee-shirt the left continually forgive traits in themselves that would have them calling for the police if committed by others. But when violence, anger and destruction are encouraged, they will only escalate.

This tendency is a slippery slope; if people feel free to physically and verbally abuse those they differ from, to spout hatred and to vandalise cherished monuments, and if others leap to their defence, then the door towards worse

---

* Such fibs generally revolve around the NHS. In the 2019 election, after it emerged the Tories were planning a trade deal to buy vital drugs from the US, the rumour went round that they were colluding with Donald Trump to privatise health. Scores of credulous voters lapped it up yet again. Indeed, Penny was among them, screaming about 'a lying racist shitclown who'll sell off our precious health service'. She them moaned about how Labour were 'something better, something positive', seemingly unaware that her rhetoric might undermine any claims to the moral high ground.

excesses has already been nudged open. More excuses and justifications will be found even as the crimes escalate in severity. The same tendency was evident in July 2012 when Kelsey, a twenty year old Minnesotan blogger, went public with a recent encounter. She had been out during the evening when overhearing a young man make crude, jokey comments to his friend about a drunk girl on the other side of the street. Some people have a sense of humour that revolves around making statements with a certain shock value. Many other people dislike such remarks, and both reactions are fine. We are not the same after all. The young man in question did not make the comments *to* the drunk girl, but about her, to his friend. Unfortunately, he did so within earshot of Kelsey. Now, even if she had turned around and remonstrated with him, her response would have been unacceptable in this writer's opinion. One does not have the right to force one's own standards of speech and humour (or lack of) onto others. But Kelsey did not turn around and rebuke him. She turned around and punched him hard in the face. Not yet satisfied she quickly posted pictures on the internet, proudly displaying her bandaged hand. She looked extremely pleased with herself while making gloating, triumphalist comments about her actions, and she got a huge reaction on the tumblr feminist community. Thousands of people gleefully responded with shrill congratulations. But imagine the reaction if a man had overheard a feminist conversation and, finding it disagreeable, elected to punch the woman in the face before bragging about the deed. It takes little imagination to conclude that the same people would have reacted with shock and anger, yet they will still tell you that they are motivated by the desire for 'equality'; staggering. The oft-quoted line 'I may disapprove of what you say but I will defend to the death your right to say it' originated from the biography of Voltaire written by Evelyn Beatrice Hall in 1903, and has been taken as a maxim by advocates of liberty and free speech ever since. It is not one that is now held by many on the far-left however. Perhaps their new slogan should be 'I may disapprove of what you say. So if you open your mouth, I will stick my fist in it'.

These double standards go to the heart of the movement. Those of the left aver to support the oppressed but, in fact, by throwing in their lot with the underdog all they have done is picked a side. Instead of opposing cruelty, injustice or corruption, they will largely excuse or justify those traits in certain people while condemning them furiously in others. They also consistently get away with behaviour that no one else would. The extremist group Class War displays an image of a vast graveyard. Above it a logo boasts how 'We have found new homes for the rich'. One barely needs to imagine what the response would be if UKip had produced a similar image that related to immigrants, or if Pegida had done the same with Muslims. The outcry would be enormous. Yet Class War activists like 'Will Plasmic' feel free to post sentiments like 'Torch the rich inbred fkn parasites', the sort of comments that would have anyone else prosecuted for a 'hate crime'. Their internet group is, by the way, well worth a look for those who may be curious. The self-regard, hypocrisy and sheer unbridled nastiness of their membership are truly something to behold. Yes, Class War is an obscure and marginal group on the lunatic fringe with just 19,000 members on their Facebook page. The regular posts on that site usually elicit only three or four spittle flecked diatribes from their demented followers. But they are still illustrative of a far wider malaise, and this sickness seldom meets any resistance.

It is a habit which can have the most appalling consequences. Throughout the twentieth century the left repeatedly turned a blind eye to the worst excesses of Stalinism and Maoism. They refused to accept their philosophical peers could be in the wrong, conjured excuses for their actions, and blamed the West for all the strife in the world. In 1983, for instance, the far-left newspaper, the Labour Herald, then co-edited by Ken Livingstone, ran an article praising the regime of the North Korean dictator Kim Il-sung. It described the state where huge numbers were being killed in purges or dying in famines as a 'model of successful, self-reliant socialist development'.[6] Many of the left's most erudite minds, like Eric Hobsbawm and E.H. Carr, acted as apologists and advocates for the worst left-wing tyrannies for many years. In fact, not only did such figures tacitly defend the Soviet regime, but when Robert Conquest warned them of the horrific truth, they attacked him with unbridled ferocity. When it transpired that he had been right all along they neither apologised nor demonstrated any regret for their bullying mendacity.

Jean-Paul Sartre was equally guilty, dismissing evidence of the Gulag and other Stalinist atrocities while wholesale accepting and vocally condemning reports on French misconduct in Algeria.[7] The impartial mind would realise that both could be criticised while the objective mind must concede that the civilisation of modern France, warts and all, is infinitely superior to that of Soviet Russia. But even while appearing oblivious to such errors many have somehow re-imagined the late twentieth century as demonstrating the failure of neo-liberalism rather than socialism; surely the most audaciously revisionist distortion of history there has ever been. To such people, it is not Stalin who is the most infamous villain of the twentieth century, it is Ronald Reagan.

These crimes have largely been forgotten, whitewashed from history, even though some of the apologists are still around today. Martin Amis wrote perceptively on this issue in *Koba the Dread*, contrasting the very different attitudes still held towards Nazi and Soviet horrors. The former Maidenhead hostelry 'Bar Soviet', which this writer used to frequent, was a striking example of this phenomenon. The establishment was generously sprinkled with Communist regalia, hammer and sickle symbols and large inspiring portraits of Comrade Stalin. As partying customers mingled, drank and happily passed the time there, no one batted an eye. Were someone to open a 'Bar Auschwitz' though, adorned with swastikas and prominent pictures of the Führer, it would provoke a rather different reaction; it would be unthinkable. In a similar vein, I recall a History lecturer at Reading University who had his entire office bedecked in Maoist and Soviet memorabilia. Gigantic flags of each regime completely covered the opposing walls. This was not considered remarkable. Yet had his study been clad in Nazi regalia he would have been sacked and arrested. There are plenty of similar examples. In the summer of 2019 Goldsmiths University held a summer camp pushing the manifesto of the Communist Party of Great Britain. It was attended by a number of speakers of dubious repute. In 2017 large retrospectives were held at the British Library and Royal Academy to celebrate the 100th anniversary of the Russian Revolution. One suspects such institutions will not repeat that process in 2033.

This too is a lesson the movement failed to learn, and the left went on to repeat the same mistake with the greatest blight the world could offer in the next century: Fundamentalist Islam. Their stance is rarely to *defend* Islamism per se, but they have refused to criticise it, and their silence served to tacitly condone the terror. The knee-jerk response is to blame Western aggression in the Middle East for the rise in Islamic terror, though this fails to explain the attacks in places like Belgium, Spain or France which played no part in any recent deployment. Jeremy Corbyn even refused to censure Islamic terror when there was an attack *during the election campaign* of 2019. Yet he moved with indecent haste to denounce Britain's role in allegedly provoking it. He went on to claim that he would continue to release terror suspects early if he got elected, refusing to withdraw the remark when a similar attack occurred just weeks later. But while the left has failed the moral test in condemning the worst aspects of fundamentalist Islam, it never hesitates to attack those brave enough to voice criticism.

It is not compassion that informs campaigners of this ilk then but an institutional bias and, frankly, cowardice. Such advocates aspire to be seriously committed and independent-minded campaigners who resist despotism. Instead, they frequently appear like brain-washed sheep who are terrified of rocking the boat of liberal conformity. In his excellent book, *What's Left*, Nick Cohen argued that, in its habit of pandering to groups like Hamas, the left has lost its way. Yet, in making this claim, he was mistaken. The movement did not meander off course at the start of the twenty-first century. It was maintaining an ignoble tradition that has been enshrined in its methodology since its inception, enthusiastically ploughing a furrow it has farmed with unwavering enthusiasm for centuries. It has *always* had a blind spot for the most brutal regimes the world can offer.

This is a profoundly inconsistent ideology then, with even the most influential thinkers advancing critically flawed theories.* Yet, on the left, there remains a deep well of assurance that their views are absolutely correct. Voltaire ridiculed this trait when arguing that 'doubt is not a pleasant condition, but certainty is absurd'. Yet certainty and double standards may be the defining traits of the left. This should imply a lack of intelligence – but this is certainly not the case. Alan Ryan interprets the phenomenon by suggesting that 'Marxism was never anti-intellectual...[analysts] conclude that Marxism is hyperintellectual, that Marxists overestimate the role of ideas in social and political life, and that they are overly concerned with intellectual correctness'.[8] Yet this belief merely gilds the assurance of the convert. The consequences of such faith can be disastrous. Driven by the certainty that their rivals are evil, the left can all too easily be persuaded into the most abhorrent acts. The tyrants examined in this study all had a deep well of hubris - an unshakeable belief in the morality of their cause. Their modern counterparts share this conviction - with the most committed activists demonstrating alarming levels of narcissistic conceit. It takes, after all, quite extraordinary arrogance for one to imagine that not only do they know how society should be ordered, and be damned what anyone else who lives in that society thinks, but that they possess the personal characteristics to drive though such changes. It is little surprise then that such individuals frequently express disdain for others.

However, just because those on the left brag about their virtue and morally lord it over others with a tiresome frequency, it does not follow that such conceit is justified. Of course there are many decent, thoughtful members of the movement. But much left-wing advocacy appears rather selfish, seemingly motivated by salving the radical's conscience and giving a boost to their self-esteem. This is why their activism tends towards making a public spectacle. Puffed up with righteous indignation, ever primed to sniff out offence from the mildest of transgressions to their own narrow, rather humourless worldview, to loudly advertise their own ethical, altruistic credentials while bullying those whose philosophy fails to align with the 'consensus' they have surrendered to themselves: such constitutes contemporary 'morality'. The traits most apparent on the left are not genuine compassion then, but narcissism, ostentatious sentimentalism and overt virtue signalling. After all, those of a genuinely altruistic nature would recoil from the viciousness of much of the contemporary left.

---

* Many of these revolve around the belief that man is shaped entirely by social forces. The most committed activists are persuaded that they can create an environment which will sculpt man into a utopian ideal – an ideal that happens to tally with their own outlook. This mistaken assumption, and arrogant attempt to play at God, lies behind numerous disasters.

Many 'progressives' do little more than put an 'X' in a box, sign an online petition or occasionally hector others for their 'incorrect' views. Yet such minimal activism persuades them to develop contempt for those with the 'wrong' opinions. It is a conceit starkly illustrated in the memoirs of Shami Chakrabarti. Not only did she call her book *On Liberty*, swiping the title of John Stuart Mill's seminal work (the equivalent of a band naming their debut album 'Sgt. Pepper'). She also had herself photographed on the cover blindfolded as the personification of justice; simply jaw dropping egotism. When putting pen to paper to record their political musings the likes of Chakrabarti, Laurie Penny, Renni Eddo-Lodge, Afua Hirsch, Maurice Strong and Caitlin Moran invariably focus most of their prose on themselves. Jean-Jacques Rousseau's autobiographical *Confessions* was, similarly, twice as long as any of the political tracts he wrote. And it was only ever two-thirds completed - a neat illustration of the self-absorption that plays such an integral role in leftist politics.

Yet the radical's conviction can be so overwhelming that it frequently resembles religious fanaticism - a trait that has even been noted by sympathetic voices. When Jon Cruddas, the Labour MP and policy chief of Ed Miliband, discussed the hard left of his own party he spoke of 'its absolutism, its purity'.[9] This should not come as a surprise. Numerous academics have noted how socialism serves the same psychological need as religion. Both, after all, provide a reassuring structure and a clear sense of moral purpose. Socialism has mainly prospered in societies where religion has gone into retreat - a trend that suggests it has come to fill not just a personal void, but a societal one too. But while socialism and religion offer rewards, they can also cause terrible damage. In both cases the greatest harm has been wrought by the fusion of political power and moral certainty. The sort of behaviour under discussion here is only possible when supported by fanatical belief. It is the conviction of the faithful that informs their controlling instinct – and that trait has proven terrifically damaging. It is no coincidence that only religion and the left have shed blood in the name of an idea. Only they have killed people for what they *think*.

But the connections between these phenomena go beyond the psychological, for they share numerous physical manifestations too. In some cases, as in the French Revolution where a 'Goddess of Reason' was worshipped at an altar, the allusions have been particularly overt, but scratch the surface and the influence of faith on Soviet and Maoist societies is just as evident. Both worshipped idols and sought to universally establish moral law by indoctrinating the population with a dogma enshrined in sacred, inviolable texts. The radical left is effectively a new religion: its converts love to proselytise, they predict Armageddon if 'sinners' do not convert to their manifesto, they express a distaste for wealth and materialism, regard themselves as morally superior to those who do not share their faith and often have a markedly poor regard for humanity. The movement sometimes resembles a cult too, in the peculiar adoration it bestows on its leaders, and the conformity it demands of its disciples.

There is, quite obviously, a great deal of complexity and diversity in left-wing thought. But certain opinions and characteristics are common enough to warrant discussion without the need for frequent and tiresome reminders that they are not universal. It will be considered sufficient to note such here without referring to the issue again. Even the most committed followers have noted its tendency towards ideological conformity and, in the *New Statesman* of 4 April 1970, Eric Hobsbawm listed the package of beliefs held by the progressive temperament in the previous century: 'natural philosophy, phrenology, free thought, spiritualism, temperance, unorthodox medicine, social reform, and the transformation of the family'. These have largely gone the way of the dinosaur, but the habit of the left to cleave to collectivist thought has not.

If one were to encounter today's 'progressive' one could be reasonably certain of predicting their opinions in a multitude of different fields: Immigration, the welfare state, Israel, climate change, fracking, bankers, Islam, gay marriage, the NHS, Nestlé, BLM, Rupert Murdoch, multiculturalism, monarchy. The similarity in stances held over such a disparate set of subjects is incredibly revealing about the culture which informs left-wing opinion. The fact that there is little connection between such a disparity of fields means the uniformity of thought can have no logical cause. It is almost entirely due to the cultural conformity demanded of the advocate. The net result of this is that radicals frequently view the world in starkly simplified, Manichean terms: that there are only two types of people on the planet, the oppressors and the oppressed, and that elites scheme to maintain their privileged status while fleecing the masses. As such, anyone involved in this conspiracy, or sympathetic to it, is undeserving of sympathy or compassion. Indeed, stern persecution of them is not only justified but necessary due to the entrenched power of their privileged position.

Such thinking then imagines vast conspiracies which encourage sweeping generalisations: the 'patriarchy', 'the 1%', 'the military-industrial complex', 'white male privilege', the 'System' or 'The Man'. It is a tactic that allows the campaigner to neatly divide the world into the virtuous and corrupt, the noble rebels and evil Empire of Star Wars, with themselves on the side of the righteous. But this rush to blame societal problems on an 'oppressor' is a product of what Kierkegaard considered the most dangerous of mental faults: laziness and impatience. Laziness of mind results in an unwillingness to face complex and unsettling concepts or ideas, while impatience leads to a rush to embrace comforting all-inclusive theories without due rigour and critical analysis. Such comforting binary thinking bears little relation to the most advanced left-wing thought yet, make no mistake, these simplifications exist, they are reassuring and seductive, and nigh on identical sentiments have been employed to justify genocide on numerous occasions.

The entire basis of a successful society is in 'live and let live'. It is in calmly listening to the concerns of others and attempting to reach an equitable compromise. But this is a test the left has repeatedly failed. The movement has long had a tendency to split the world into 'us' and 'them', existing primarily on a policy of divide and rule while loudly decrying the same trait in others. In identifying itself as the movement of protest, as the vanguard that represents the disenfranchised and oppressed against privileged elites, the left has also ensured that conflict is as essential to its survival as oxygen. A nemesis of some description is an essential component for the self-righteous. What, after all, is Batman without the Joker, or Luke Skywalker without Darth Vader? Elites, institutions and traditions must be continually attacked to feed left-wing activism. But that means that once its enemies have been defeated, new ones must be located, so the left always turns on itself – usually with even more fury than on its political opposition. It is a trait that defined the regimes of Revolutionary France, Soviet Russia, Maoist China and Khmer Cambodia. They all continued to conjure more and more foes for them to subjugate. This need for continual battle also explains the frequently hysterical pitch of radical activism. Decent human beings become monsters in the left-wing imagination, and monsters must be destroyed. Indeed, the act of killing such ogres transforms those committing the deed into heroes. The self-image of those covered in these pages is akin to St. George slaying the dragon. But the reality is different, and considerably less glamorous.

The increasing dominance of such thought is exacerbated as an entire generation has grown up in the poisonous climate of political correctness. It is to their enormous credit that so many young people have not just resisted this culture but have loudly mocked it too – a reaction which has been thoroughly merited. Nevertheless, many have become eager disciples of the creed, a new generation of Mao's little Red Guards who are every bit as intolerant as their predecessors. Not only are such traits becoming more common, but the influence of left-wing views in the arts is growing ever more pervasive. In culture, in education and online, the leftist view holds a position of clear dominance. To catalogue said phenomenon would be a herculean, impossible task, but to verify its existence one need only dip their toe in the pool of social media. It is not a step that is recommended. The waters are most unwelcoming and teem with social justice piranha, ever poised to sink their teeth into prey in a self-righteous feeding frenzy. And their appetite is insatiable.

It is ironic that even as society has moved to the right economically, it has, in stubborn defiance of this irrefutable fact, swung sharply to the left in the philosophical and cultural spheres. This process has resulted in an increasingly uncritical acceptance of the far-left's position and all its attendant prejudices.

The activists of the left are currently wielding an influence disproportionate to their number, and their bullying tactics are paying dividends as otherwise sensible people scramble to apologise to and appease the insatiable juggernaut of cultural Marxism. At such a stage one recalls the wisdom of Edmund Burke who averred that because 'half a dozen grasshoppers under a fern make the field ring with their importunate chink, whilst thousands of great cattle, reposed beneath the shadow of the British oak, chew the cud and are silent, pray do not imagine that those who make the noise are the only inhabitants of the field'.[10]

But make noise they most assuredly do. This modern culture is less about *having* more compassion, it is primarily in *advertising* it. It could be argued that the real difference between left and right is one of moral posturing versus realistic and manageable solutions, with those opting for the former path sneering at the latter's inferior morality. This trait has become so ubiquitous that even carrier bags advertise their virtue now. The result is a culture that feels determined to make a spectacle of itself, to shout its agenda at every opportunity, whether in the streets or online. Emotion must now be publicly displayed, must make a song and dance of itself, but this demonstrative behaviour and rising tide of anger bring to mind pre-Revolutionary France. That is not a road we should look to take again. The idea of restraint, of the 'stiff upper lip', widely portrayed as the most admirable trait through the Victorian age up until the 1950s or early '60s, has melted away and been replaced with a far more strident, demonstrative society. One need only compare the dignity of the Jarrow marchers of 1936 with the anti-government protestors of 2015 to see the transformation that has taken place. The mawkish display following the death of Princess Diana was perhaps the most notable evidence of this phenomenon. But what particularly marked the grieving that followed her demise was not just that it was public. It was the palpable fury directed at the Royal Family for failing to join in the unedifying spectacle.

The heart should inform the head but, in the realm of politics, it should not *rule* it. Taking the left-wing stance is, in many ways, resorting to the easy option. It is difficult to thoroughly examine an issue and attempt, after laborious and rigorous research, to reach a balanced practical conclusion, especially if that conclusion is problematic or uncomfortable in any way. But it is simplicity itself to mouth sympathetic sounding platitudes while being loudly critical of those whose opposition appears to lack compassion. That option then is far more common, but it does not follow that it has superior moral or intellectual integrity. Excessive emotive bleating does not strengthen an argument, it obscures it. It buries it in a mound of sentiment that swamps the ability to reach rational and objective conclusions. Emotion has come to dominate the thought processes of the hard left to such a degree that there is simply no room for further debate. The issue is settled, all that is required is to forward the same argument at an increased volume. The political sphere of the far-left then is one largely of emotion over reason. More than this, it is most commonly expressed in furious resentment. As we sink deeper into a more emotional age, so the rhetoric and activism of the left becomes ever more shrill, ever more strident and ever more dangerous. Politics should never be personal. Government is ideally a matter of cool, dispassionate and objective calculation. But many on the left prefer to make it an arena of the emotions. They should be reminded that anger and hatred are emotions too - for when an ideology is based on prejudice, directed at scapegoats, and is informed by fury, then hatred and retribution will inevitably follow.

The left has aimed at protecting the most vulnerable from abuse. But instead they have *magnified* it, creating new targets and contributing to an accusative, judgemental society with a predilection for persecution. It should be obvious that the way to combat abuse is not to become an abuser oneself, but, apparently, it is not. For all their talk of embracing diversity many on the left do anything but. They seek to crush diversity and enforce conformity. Diversity is welcomed only when it is cosmetic, when the differences are superficial: skin tone, body type, sexual orientation and disability. But such tolerance is merely skin-deep and any sort of diversity of *thought,* any real individuality, is to be legislated out of existence.

Many on the left seem to believe themselves free from the faults they are so judgemental of in others. But they are not. They are capable of being just as nasty, venal and petty as anyone. Yet their prejudices are bolstered by an internal morality that convinces them of their superior personal rectitude. This makes them oblivious to how poorly they can behave towards others. It informs and arms them, resulting in hair-trigger sensibilities, a propensity to resort to violence, and an utter absence of the shame or contrition which may, in other circumstances, restrain them. Decent and compassionate people can, after all, behave in a vile manner if they are persuaded that it is a rational and justified response. This is the history of the left in a nutshell. This study attempts to explain why the most 'moral' people are so frequently guilty of such dreadful crimes. But the truth is that there is a direct causal link. It is precisely *because* such people consider themselves virtuous, and their opponents irredeemably vile, that they can excuse or condone any 'excesses' in dealing with them. Their consciences, moral compasses and ideology are untarnished by even the most repulsive acts. They do not commit atrocities *despite* being self-righteous. They do it *because* they are self-righteous.

The left has made many valuable contributions to society and scores of decent people have positioned themselves under its banner, but they are not the focus of this study. For whatever its merits it has a dark side too, and it is the darkness which has triumphed whenever it has attained a monopoly in the political sphere. While the majority of left-leaning individuals are emphatically reasonable and decent, we should not be deceived over the threat posed by the minority; and not just because the moderates tend to express the same kind of hatred as the militants. Extremists only made up small minorities in Revolutionary France, Nazi Germany, Soviet Russia, Maoist China and Khmer Cambodia, as well as in Syria in the second decade of the twenty-first century. In every one of those cases, the bulk of the population sought nothing more than comfort, freedom and security. Yet it was the numerically inferior militants that held sway on every occasion. Fanatical minorities drive events. They do so because they care more ardently, more passionately, than the majority who simply want to go about their lives. And because those extremists wield such a disproportionate influence they need to be vigorously and vocally denounced whenever they rear their ugly, intolerant little heads over the parapet.

The movement has yet to learn, as Burke warned nearly 250 years ago, that its manifesto is one that favours destruction over construction. This failure has echoed down the ages with incalculable costs. The attempts of the hard left to unite societies have always divided them; plans to socialise economies have always crippled them; schemes aimed at reducing inequality have always increased poverty; efforts to consolidate agricultural production have led to severe shortages; and when they have advanced their political ideals the result has been censorship, oppression, the closing of minds, a precipitous rise in hate-fuelled accusations and the strangling of democracy and cultural expression. As states have become more left-wing they have inevitably become less prosperous and less free. Ideology has leaked from the political sphere to taint the professional, cultural, social and private worlds too. And there is not a single exception to this pattern to be found.

The purpose of this study is to trace the history of this mindset, and to illustrate how the traits which wreaked such havoc throughout history still prevail. An examination of the differences between collectivist states and liberal democracies helps us understand why there is such hostility to difference of opinion and freedom of speech in the former - for the crises of those states stem from that intolerance. Across these two volumes we will encounter a parade of apparently sensitive and intelligent folk. They are largely well-educated, middle class individuals, with a predilection for poetry, who brimmed with compassion. Yet their legacy bears little relation to their self-image. The story contained in these pages is one of monstrous arrogance, of deeply unpleasant people utterly convinced of their superior virtue, of the most ludicrous theories adhered to with religious fanaticism, of shameless levels of censorship and propaganda, of furious iconoclasms and unrestrained cultural vandalism, of startling hypocrisy and double standards, of hatred and intolerance, of suspicion and wild conspiracy theories born of hysterical fears, of never-ending feuds, of ever-greater restrictions on basic liberties, of violence and persecution, and of oceans of blood. And it is a tale that is far from over.

Chapter 1
Liberty, Equality, Fraternity

'The true and tragic lesson of the epic descent to the Terror, is the summons to vigilance against ourselves – that we should not assume that we are righteous, and our enemies evil, that we can see clearly, and others are blinded by malice or folly; that we can abrogate the fragile rights of others in the name of our own certainty and all will be well regardless. If we do not honour the message of human rights in the revolutions of 1776 and 1789, as the French in their case most clearly failed to do, we too are on the road to Terror.'

David Andress

That morning, in June 1775, seemed more like the depths of winter than a summer's day. It was overcast, a chill wind whipped around the buildings and driving rain poured from the sky. Yet sizeable crowds jostled for space as an ostentatiously liveried carriage clattered and splashed its way through the streets of Paris. After a long and laborious procession it was finally pulled to a halt outside the prestigious College Louis-le-Grand, on the Rue Saint-Jacques, an institution renamed after a visit from Louis XIV in 1681. There a hushed and expectant audience, lined up like soldiers, patiently awaited the coach and its occupants. The passengers, a young couple of noble bearing, huddled in the warmth of the carriage to shelter from the still pouring rain, but they smiled and waved happily to the waiting throng. On cue, an earnest young man of seventeen, bright, eager and meticulously dressed, stepped forward and dropped to a knee to deliver a pre-prepared address. The young man had practised his panegyric for days on end before perfecting it. His words were formal, but full of felicitations for a prosperous and happy future for the couple, and the rain did nothing to dampen his ardour and commitment. As his speech ended the carriage trundled off with the occupants smiling and nodding amiably at the warm reception they had just been given. It was, despite the weather, a decidedly sunny and optimistic event, but it was to have a macabre and terrible epilogue some twenty years later. For the young couple were the King of France, Louis XVI, celebrating his coronation that day, and his Austrian Queen, Marie-Antoinette, while the youngster who had given such heartfelt hopes for their reign was Maximilien Robespierre. In the Revolution to come that obscure schoolboy would rise to prominence and play a pivotal role in taking the heads of not just the King and Queen, but thousands of others in a blood soaked reign of terror.

Robespierre was far from alone in causing that mayhem, but his complicity is undeniable, and he is deservedly synonymous with the atrocities of that period. He was characteristic of that generation: full of conceit that his time had come while brimming with conviction in the moral purity of his cause. When he regarded the Old Regime he saw nothing but greed, corruption and decadence while he believed his peers epitomised progress, compassion and virtue. Such simplistic certainties would empower the 'oppressed' of France to show no mercy when they assumed the whip hand over their former tormentors. Robespierre then, as one who espoused and believed so ardently in virtue, while practising oppression and state-sanctioned murder on almost unprecedented levels, is singularly suited to this study, and his role will be discussed at length in due course.

France, and indeed the world into which he and his contemporaries were born, was changing rapidly. The remarkable scientific and philosophical progress of that period was encouraging more and more people to question the status quo. That process had really begun when the Renaissance and Reformation shattered the Middle Ages, before accelerating through the scientific revolution of the seventeenth century. In that period, the increased focus on observed and recorded phenomena had a profound effect on the application of philosophy. The era began with the father of empiricism, Francis Bacon and reached its apogee with Sir Isaac Newton. Both figures were revered by the *philosophes* and considered to be among the three English fathers of the Enlightenment. The other was the philosopher John Locke, who, like René Descartes and Baruch Spinoza, had found refuge in the United Provinces of the Dutch Republic, the state that had amazed the world in the seventeenth century. The incredible economic, trading, cultural, artistic, social, military and political triumphs of the Netherlands acted as a beacon in what began to seem like the dusty and archaic sovereign states that surrounded it.

Further inspiration was provided by Britain which, via the English Civil War and Glorious Revolution, was left with a balanced constitutional monarchy. For Britain's economic and trading triumphs in the eighteenth century outstripped even the Dutch example. These developments fed back into France where a flood of literature based on scientific observation and rational analysis employed 'reason' to challenge the political, spiritual and social make-up of the world in which they lived, particularly the twin 'superstitions' of religion and monarchy. It was in France that the Enlightenment, and the *philosophes* who shaped it, truly flourished. In that culture of scientific scepticism a new generation began to formulate novel conceptions on how to reconstitute their society, while a growing café and salon set absorbed and spread the ideas percolating at the time. Arguably the most significant writer of that period was Denis Diderot, whose *Encyclopédie* contained contributions from the likes of d'Alembert and Condorcet, but the most popular and successful figures were Voltaire and Rousseau. By the latter part of the century fresh ideas about how to reform and reconstitute society had been widely disseminated just as the French monarchy entered a period of crisis.

Yet the climate of logical appraisal and rational, evidence-based reasoning sweeping Europe went in tandem with a quite contrasting phenomenon: the cult of sensibility. This anti-intellectual creed, which spread rapidly from the 1760s, was largely a reaction against the pomposity and rigid formality of rococo grandeur. The movement celebrated that which was natural over that which was artificial. It romanticised the noble savage, favoured the heart over the head, cherished impulsiveness over careful consideration, worshipped nature and made overt displays of emotion, especially the shedding of tears, not just acceptable but fashionable. Indeed, it was a widely held view that emotion was only genuine when made public. These lachrymose displays of a 'feeling heart' signalled virtue in an overly sentimental age. The culture would play a significant role in the events to come. It helped turn the earnest advocates of morality and simplicity into the oppressive despots of Revolution.

In many ways the phenomenon shares traits with more recent developments like the environmental movement that started in earnest in the 1960s, a culture that gained ascendancy with the publication of Rachel Carson's *Silent Spring*. Her tome was largely debunked by subsequent generations but the movement has retained its popularity. Its legacy is partly one of an over the top romanticism of nature and uncritical view of 'indigenous' peoples by sectors of the left. Unabashed displays of emotion and sobbing have also become fashionable again. One need only think of television successes like Oprah Winfrey or the *X-Factor* which are reliably geared towards teary outbursts of some description. People now tend to advertise their 'feeling heart' on the internet, usually prior to pouring quite nasty abuse on an unsuspecting target, but the culture is far more widespread than that. The scenes witnessed in Britain after the death of Princess Diana would, for example, have made a big impression on pre-revolutionary France. The saccharine movement had a huge cultural impact, and perhaps its most striking visualisation is Jean-Baptiste

Greuze's painting *Girl Weeping over a Dead Canary* (1765). But *An Experiment on a Bird in the Air Pump* (1768), a stunningly realised work by Joseph Wright of Derby, managed to marry the fashion for sobbing children with the contemporary passion for science.

The cult's most famous exponent though was the man who, in large part, inspired the whole movement: Jean-Jacques Rousseau. The *philosophe* believed that man in nature was inherently good but was corrupted by civilisation. Yet while he was the movement's greatest celebrity others were venerated too and Benjamin Franklin, a noted man of science, made a huge impression during his time in France. His deliberately rough frontier-style of dress made him stand out when mingling with the perfumed wig and coloured silk and satin set, and he drew huge audiences wherever he appeared. Yet it was not just sentiment that became fashionable but a romantic, rather idealised, and wildly inaccurate love of nature too.

For Hobbes, the realist of the seventeenth century, the natural world was one where life was 'nasty, brutish and short' while in Maistre's analysis nature was 'red in tooth and claw'. In the wild, despite its physical beauty, existence is a constant struggle, and for the majority consists of a short life and a violent death. But for many in the eighteenth century, sheltered from such realities by the advanced civilisation which nurtured them, nature was re-imagined as a pastoral idyll. It was civilisation which came to be viewed with apprehension. The discrepancy between the popular perception and gritty reality was vividly captured at Marie-Antoinette's toy farm at Versailles. The serenity and picturesque beauty of that little enclave bear little relation to the smell and noise of a working farm. It was a period where image and 'feelings' would trump reality.

However, any inconvenient truths about the rather childish movement had little impact. In eighteenth century France this mindset fed into the antipathy directed at established elites. It drove a wedge between the two cultures: on the one hand, the rustic, virtuous peasantry, imbued with a feeling heart and possessed of a deep well of morality, and on the other the corrupt, greedy and decadent representatives of a regime whose time was up. It was not enough to just disagree with the vagaries of the system anymore. Political activism had to be wrapped in scorn and revulsion directed at any who were perceived to belong to it. In fact, opposing the Old Regime became the badge of virtue and morality. Righteous anger came to be, not only justified, but almost compulsory. When given full rein this attitude of rising enmity would come at a terrible cost. Denis Diderot, certainly among the most perceptive minds in a century crammed with intellectual titans, detected the crisis that was brewing as early as 1759. Noting the rise of prejudice and the way religious feeling was being converted into political oppression, he anticipated a steep rise in dogma and persecution. Committing his fears to paper he recorded that 'wherever there is a cult, the natural order of morals is overturned, morality corrupted. Sooner or later, the moment comes where the notion that hindered people from stealing an *écu* [a French coin] leads to a hundred thousand people having their throats slashed. Some compensation!'[1]

Against this backdrop of increasing melodrama and resentment, the Crown was struggling to deal with a series of mounting problems. Louis had enthusiastically embraced the cause of the American Revolution against the old enemy of England, but the aid he provided put the crown's purse under unbearable strain*. Their support also saw an influx of revolutionary ideas flood back into an already volatile France. The potential for crisis was heightened by the *ancien règime's* desperate need for reform. Though it was not true to say that the first and second estates of the clergy and nobility were exempt from taxation, it is undeniable that a vast majority of the burden fell on the third estate - largely made up of the poorest slice of the population. The system of revenue collection was also in desperate need of modernisation. The Farmers General and *seigneurs* abused their privileged status and the masses had valid grounds to be terribly aggrieved. The archaic system was fertile ground to nurture the developing sense of grievance which would play such a significant role in events to come.

The Crown had tried to push through reform. However, their attempts were thwarted when a series of finance ministers had their proposals blocked by, first the *parlements* (courts of law, not to be confused with the English parliament) and then the Assembly of Notables. Turgot, Brienne, Calonne and the unfathomably popular Jacques Necker all failed to pass the reforms needed to get the crown on any sort of secure financial footing, and it slid inexorably towards bankruptcy. In stubbornly determining to protect their privileges the aristocracy were sowing the seeds for their destruction - for modest reforms could have staved off the growing clamour for change. There was also widespread dissent over the enduring remnants of arbitrary despotism like the *lettres de cachet*. These could see anyone imprisoned indefinitely on the basis of the king's signature. They had provoked considerable opposition during the reign of Louis XV when the crown's shrinking finances encouraged the monarch to sell off blank signed *lettres* which allowed the rich and powerful to gaol anyone they felt had crossed them. In a nation becoming more educated, polarised and melodramatic, and one that was witnessing other states grow in liberty, the indignation with the current system and its representatives, and the desire for change, were becoming a tumult.

---

* The costs were estimated at 1.3 billion livres

There were certainly horrendous incidents that stoked hostility to the state, even if they were relatively rare. In August 1765 a roadside crucifix in Abbeville had been damaged in an act of drunken vandalism. Locals pointed the finger of suspicion at Jean-François de la Barre, a youth from the minor local nobility. He had been heard singing blasphemous songs and once refused to remove his hat before a religious procession. A search of his property revealed no evidence of the crime but unearthed two erotic novels and a copy of Voltaire's *Philosophical Dictionary*, which was on the Pope's Index of banned books. He was condemned to have his tongue pulled out and hand cut off before being burned at the stake though, in the event, after a lengthy trial, on 1 July 1766 he was given a more 'humane' punishment. De la Barre's tongue was pierced and he was beheaded before his corpse was burned. In 1768 three unfortunates, an apprentice, a colporteur and his wife were caught with copies of d'Holbach's *Christianity Unveiled.* All three were pilloried, flogged and branded. The apprentice was sentenced to nine years in the galleys, the colporteur to five years, and the woman to the madhouse for the rest of her life.[2] Such incidents fuelled resentment of the ruling elites and their perceived abuse of power, particularly in a society which was growing ever more secular and enthusiastic about intellectual freedoms.

Yet while there is little doubt about the inequities of the French system, or the desperate need for change, there is some dispute over the severity of living conditions. Many historians cite Arthur Young, the renowned English agriculturalist who was travelling in France and making a record of the nation in the years 1787-9. The most oft-quoted extract is from the Dordogne where he reported that 'All the country girls and women, are without shoes or stockings; and the ploughmen at their work have neither sabots nor feet in their stockings. This is a poverty that strikes at the root of national prosperity...It reminded me of the misery of Ireland.'[3] Yet this extract is not particularly illustrative of what he saw in France at all.

Young fawned over the richness, cultivation and irrigation of Lille recording that 'It was a sort of fairy scene to me'. He diligently recorded the 'prosperity' of Nantes, the 'magnificence' of Bordeaux, and the 'rural happiness' of the southwest. While he was open about the manifest improvements that could be made, and of how Montauban and Brittany were both destitute, the overriding impression is of a largely contented, ordered and relatively prosperous realm. In Languedoc, Young eulogised how 'Every soul is employed, and with such an air of cheerfulness, that the people seem as well pleased with their labour, as the farmer himself with his great heaps of wheat. The scene is uncommonly animated and joyous'.[4] It is also pertinent to note that while numerous aristocrats were huge landowners with extraordinary wealth, many were little more than impoverished farmers with extremely modest smallholdings. They were considerably poorer than the increasingly wealthy and numerous urban middle classes. This aspirational bourgeoisie were certainly not exempt from joining the nobility through marriage or the purchase of titles, both of which were becoming increasingly common, but it was they who would be the driving force behind the Revolution.

The *ancien règime* had also been doing much to improve conditions for France's poorest citizens. Louis's last government had banned torture, and a vast bureaucracy had worked to improve sanitation and healthcare in the provinces. Valentin Haüy's school for the blind had rescued and significantly improved life for many impoverished youngsters. The Terror would return those children to beggary and persecution. However, it is undeniable that the Old Regime was, overall, terribly antiquated, punitive and monstrously unfair. The grievances of the vast bulk of the population were legitimate and urgent. The impetus for revolt though came not from the impoverished peasantry but from the affluent bourgeoisie. The Revolution was emphatically not a class war of the proletariat, but its objectives were often dressed up in the *language* of class war and this allowed prejudice against certain sectors of French society to become the driving force of events over the next few years.

Yet, while the system was undoubtedly inequitable and archaic, it was peopled by scores of resolutely decent individuals. They deserved neither the opprobrium nor bloody fates that awaited them. While certainly more fortunate than the peasantry, if not necessarily the bourgeoisie who attacked them with abandon, they experienced their own share of suffering. One source which humanises the often demonised aristocracy of the period is the *Memoirs* of Lucie Dillon, later the Marquise de la Tour du Pin. Her writing offers a revealing glimpse into some significant events of that period. Lucie's account exudes wit, charm, warmth and dignity, but her own experiences hardly make her seem especially privileged. Her mother died when she was twelve, and her father sallied off to Tobago where he had been made governor. Lucie was left in the care of her despotic and tyrannical maternal grandmother, Lucy de Rothe, and her childhood reads rather like a stereotypical Roald Dahl novel. Her grandmother, a bitter and acidic woman, proceeded to squander Lucie's inheritance with wild abandon while treating her with frosty disdain. Her less than idyllic upbringing, almost utterly bereft of any love or warmth, was followed by the experience of the Revolution which saw her life descend into horror. She was financially ruined and was forced to live on the run in constant fear. Her children died one by one, while her father, and many of her closest friends were guillotined; so much for a gilded life.

While the impetus for revolution came from the urban elites, much originated with the aristocracy themselves, from what might today be termed the 'champagne socialists'. Principal among these was the playwright

Beaumarchais, born the son of a watchmaker before becoming an influential figure at the court of Louis XV. The writer, a huge admirer of Voltaire, captured the turning tide in social thought in Act five of his *Marriage of Figaro*, later adapted as an opera by Mozart. The plot of the play, which opened on 21 April 1784, revolves around a cast of scheming servants who triumph over their lecherous master, and the scene in which Figaro rebukes Count Almaviva (expunged from Mozart's version for being too shocking) caused a sensation.

> 'Because you are a *grand seigneur* you think yourself a great genius...nobility, wealth, rank, offices! All this makes you so high and mighty! What have you done to have so much? You've hardly given yourself the trouble to be born and that's about it: for the rest you're an ordinary person while I, damn it, lost in the anonymous crowd, have had to use all my science and craft just to survive.'[5]

Many regarded the theatrical Beaumarchais's self-appointment as the champion of liberty as hypocritical posturing, but whatever the truth of that his impact was undeniable. Years later Napoleon would remark that the Revolution began, not in 1789, but on the opening night of that play.[6]

Yet while opprobrium mounted against the nobility, respect for the monarchy had largely endured. This too, however, was about to be put to the test. Louis himself was regarded as a decent man and he viewed himself as a 'modern' one. He was intelligent but indecisive, wanted to be loved and was not really suited to, nor ever desired, the high office that was thrust upon him. Apart from his coronation he regarded the only happy day of his reign as the one in June 1786 when he had gone to visit the great (though ultimately doomed) engineering works at the port of Cherbourg and had got to show off his knowledge as a scientist, sailor and engineer. The king was also thrilled to stage the world's very first hot air balloon flight at Versailles when the Montgolfier brothers' device took to the air on 19 September 1783. Louis was a voraciously keen hunter and cut a fine, graceful figure in the saddle. Sadly he was less statesmanlike on his feet. The Marquise de La Tour du Pin described him as having 'the worst possible bearing. He looked like some peasant shambling along behind his plough; there was nothing proud or regal about him'.[7] While happy sailing or hunting he had little aptitude for government and was a weak, prevaricating king. Always susceptible to advice, he would listen to counsel, take one course of action, but later waver and change his mind, often after being advised by a separate source. He was not the man to guide France through the coming crisis. His wife was made of sterner stuff but, through little fault of her own, had far greater problems with the French populace, problems that would undermine the institution of monarchy itself.

The issues that faced Marie-Antoinette, and the ire she aroused, are well illustrated by the Diamond Necklace Affair of 1784. Some ten years prior to that date, Böhmer and Bassange, Paris's leading jewellers, had made a spectacular necklace of 647 diamonds for Mme Du Barry, Louis XV's mistress. It was valued at 1.6 million livres. However, the king had died before it could be sold and Marie-Antoinette, the only legitimate prospective buyer, was not interested. Yet the Queen was unwittingly drawn into scandal when Jean de la Motte, a lady of the minor nobility who had fallen on hard times, concocted a scheme in hopes of a lucrative return. Through an earlier affair with him she knew that Louis, Prince de Rohan, Cardinal Bishop of Strasbourg, was both ostracised at court and desperate to win the Queen's favour. So Jean enticed him with a series of letters purporting to be from Marie-Antoinette. They dangled the carrot of court acceptance and dropped hints about the necklace. When Rohan declared his enthusiasm for a meeting, Jean dressed up a young, blonde woman, Nicole Le Guay, in the kind of white muslin dress favoured by the Queen, and got her to approach Louis in the Grove of Venus at Versailles. There she pressed a single rose into his hands with the words 'You know what this means'.

Rohan was hooked. Soon afterwards de la Motte told him that the Queen desired the necklace and wanted him to act as her intermediary with the jewellers who, promised deferred payments, passed the necklace to de la Motte. Her lover, de Réteaux, promptly broke it up and began selling pieces of it in London. Time passed, the Cardinal never saw the Queen in the necklace and Böhmer and Bassange began pressing for payment. The scheme quickly unravelled and Rohan threw himself at the mercy of the King. Louis, furious at the light the affair shone on his wife, had him sent to the Bastille. At the resultant trial while Le Guay was acquitted, at least in part due to her repeated sobbing in court, the Cardinal was divested of his offices and Jean de la Motte was stripped naked, beaten by the public executioner and ordered branded with a V for *voleuse*, thief, on her shoulder. In the event she twisted to avoid the branding iron and the large V was scorched onto her breast instead.

Despite Louis's efforts the Queen's reputation suffered lasting damage. Though blameless she was seen as a spiteful spendthrift and was widely held responsible for the punishments. Many believed she had concocted the whole scheme to get her hands on the necklace for free. Provocative lies were, it seems, more interesting than the mundane truth. The fact that the Cardinal believed he had met her in a secret tryst in a garden also cast doubts on her moral impropriety, and a blizzard of salacious pamphlets spread baseless tales of her sexual exploits. Rumours of gambling, frivolity, pleasure-seeking, profligacy and ambition had dogged the Queen for years. Now the public was only too eager to believe any grist the rumour mill threw up. Under Marie-Antoinette the sombre, serious and restrained court atmosphere of Louis XV had given way to a more light-hearted culture that celebrated theatre and gaiety. But, despite the largely innocent, fun-loving nature of her new brand of court etiquette, it backfired enormously and caused great resentment. She revelled in a love of Rousseau, flowers and nature, as many of her subjects did, but as a Queen she wasn't supposed to. She loved to go to the theatre, but when she began to be met by frosty silences from the gathered crowds, or even hissing, she elected to stay away. She was obsessed by jewellery and clothes, as was much of her entourage, and she was consequently perceived as being avaricious, acquisitive and materialistic. Yet, paradoxically, when her fashion tastes changed to a more restrained, naturalistic style, she was lambasted for eschewing the standards expected of a Queen. The unfortunate consort, it seems, simply could not win. Sadly, we have changed little. Elizabeth II presents a stoic face of dignified duty and is, rightly, almost universally respected. Sarah Ferguson was a fun loving party girl, and was widely unpopular because of it. Royalty, it seems, always need to know their place.

Researching the story of Marie-Antoinette is a crushingly depressing experience. While perhaps no paragon of virtue, she was a decent woman who did little to deserve the years of torment that awaited her. Lucie Dillon, the Marquise de la Tour du Pin, who actually met the Queen and knew her well, paints an entirely different picture to those only too willing to believe whatever sordid rumours they heard. She described the Queen as being of kind intentions and full of interest, pity and compassion, going out of her way to take Lucie under her protection - and this was in 1787 when years of disastrous publicity may have made others bitter. The Marquise though, who was observant and an excellent judge of character, was brutally honest about the Queen's strengths and flaws in her later memoirs. 'This ill starred princess...was gifted with very great courage, but little intelligence, absolutely no tact and, worst of all, a mistrust – always misplaced – of those most willing to serve her.'[8]

Problems had begun almost as soon as she arrived at Versailles in 1770. She was a young Habsburg princess wedded to Louis as a child bride of fourteen years old. It was a period when animosity still lingered over France's alliance with Austria, a pact that had seen the motherland dragged into the Seven Years War of 1756-63 against Britain. That conflict resulted in France losing possessions in North America and India to their great rival, and saw the rise of Prussia under Frederick the Great. All of this had caused a great deal of resentment about the marriage alliance, fears which seemed confirmed when, at a firework display to celebrate the wedding, a stampede left 130 spectators dead. It was hardly an auspicious start, but it was personal animosity rather than political concerns that caused the greatest friction. A fantasy depiction of the Queen as the idle, greedy and vindictive 'Austrian whore' took hold, and the baying crowds who subscribed to it were ready to believe any salacious stories, however implausible they were. Her presence also increased paranoia about the prospect of Austrian influence ruled, as it was, by her brother, Joseph II.

That all lay in the future but, in the meantime, the mania contributed to seriously undermine the monarchy. Fired by moral indignation, no level of sneering, vituperative animosity seemed off-limits for the Queen's detractors, including copious amounts of shockingly graphic and often violent pornography. Scores of publications depicted her in assorted lesbian trysts with ladies of the court or being enthusiastically penetrated by any man within range. They were utterly fabricated, but all too readily believed by a credulous and judgemental public. The Queen was certainly aware of these pamphlets and also of the most famous book published about her, the fake autobiographical confession the *Essai Historique sur la Vie de Marie-Antoinette*. It described 'the cruel and lascivious life of Marie-Antoinette...barbaric Queen, adulterous wife, woman without morals, soiled with crime and debauchery'.[9] The tome was awash with tales of orgies, lesbianism, nymphomania and masturbation - the latter theme dredged up again in sickening fashion at the end of her life. She was viewed not just as 'a despicable prostitute' but increasingly as *Austrian* and of wielding an unhealthy influence over the crown. The widely held animosity for the Queen is the clearest evidence we have of a far wider phenomenon, and attitudes towards Marie-Antoinette give a foretaste of the waves of hatred soon to erupt all over France. The prevailing culture was not one of compassion for the needy. It was driven by resentment of the privileged. What increasingly dominated France was less a desire for constructive improvement than an ever more destructive rage. It was a situation more conducive to romantic idealism, adolescent petulance and rising hysteria than cool, dispassionate pragmatism. And there would be a dreadful price to pay.

Revolution

By the spring of 1788 the nation was at a crisis point. The clamour for reform was deafening and, having run out of options to repair the state's crumbling finances, Louis was left with no other choice than to call an Estates-General, France's administrative body that had last sat in 1614. On 8 August the King announced that it would meet on 1 May 1789. The localities of France were instructed to elect deputies to send to Versailles and also to draft manifestos of complaints, *cahier de doléances*, which would be discussed when it convened. Political clubs, largely based on existing debating and literary societies, sprang up all over France and that winter the nation buzzed with political activity. In a few frantic months a huge number of pamphlets were produced, with the most popular and urgent topic being the format the assembly would take. In its traditional form the Estates General consisted of three separate chambers which voted by block. This meant the first two estates could always combine to outvote the third. However, as there were approximately 100,000 members of the clergy, 400,000 of the nobility and some 25 million in the third estate, this was no longer considered acceptable. The widely held consensus was that the third estate now represented the nation. It was a view that now seems deeply ironic. For while they hoped to free the masses from the aristocratic yoke the activists simply doomed them to a far worse despotism – that of the Parisian bourgeois radicals, whose tyranny would make the depredations of the Bourbons seem like a mother's soft embrace. That, however, was all in the future and on 5 December, under considerable pressure, the monarchy eventually decreed that the number of deputies to the third estate would be doubled to 646. There would ultimately be 282 noble deputies and 303 clergy of the First Estate, though no decision was reached about whether votes would be counted by head or by chamber. That issue was still unresolved when the deputies flooded into Versailles the following spring.

The sort of anarchy that would come to characterise the Revolution was already evident through the winter of 1788-9. Locals were raiding the livestock of *seigneurial* estates and mobs forced terrified farmers to lower grain prices. A savage hailstorm had devastated crops on 13 July and it was followed by the worst winter in memory. Rivers froze preventing mills from grinding the meagre amount of corn that had been harvested. The whole nation was hit by terrible hunger. Rumours that the shortages were the result of an 'aristocratic plot' began to gain capital and, with the pamphlets condemning the privileged as parasites, they fed into a growing sense of persecution and prejudice. That winter France was gripped by a determination to seize the imminent opportunity and combat the ills besetting the nation. The Old Regime was increasingly characterised as evil, a belief that gave the deputies of the third estate a sense of self-righteousness and a conviction that they were on a sort of crusade. The redress they sought was thus impassioned and idealistic rather than reasoned and realistic.

Simon Schama summed up this ideology neatly in his seminal work *Citizens* in a remark that remains as relevant as ever. 'The illusion that new political institutions could provide sustenance where the old ones had not, rested on the belief that the parasitical agents of the old regime had deliberately used their power to engineer crises from which they might profit.'[10] It was not true then as it is not true now, but reality has never had much effect on righteous indignation. More than this, those speaking on behalf of the Third Estate widely came to believe that only they represented the people and, by association,

France. Perhaps the clearest statement of this intent was in the pamphlet from the Abbé Sieyès, *What is the Third Estate?* In its most famous extract it asked 'What has the Third Estate been until now? Nothing. What should it be? Everything. What does it aim to become? Something.'[11] The anger it subsequently directed towards its intended targets was chillingly redolent of the rhetoric espoused by Nazism. 'It is impossible to say what place the nobility and clergy ought to occupy in the social order. This is equivalent to asking what place should be assigned to a malignant disease which preys upon and tortures the body of a sick man'.[12] Such sentiments were only ever likely to result in one outcome.

As a result, innocent victims were targeted even before the Revolution began. In April 1789 a rumour circulated that Réveillon, a wallpaper manufacturer, intended to cut his worker's wages to 15 sous a day. In reality, he was a conscientious employer who paid 35-50 sous a day and had retained most of his staff through the winter, even when they could not work due to the severe weather. But the truth of this had little impact on the artisans and journeymen filled with retributive rage by the all-consuming politics of envy. Despite being a self-made man who had begun his career as an apprentice, Réveillon seemed exactly the kind of capitalist entrepreneur they despised on principle. A mob, some several hundred strong, descended on his factory brandishing sticks and shouting 'Death to the rich, death to aristocrats!' By the next day a crowd of 5-10,000 had gathered to hang and burn Réveillon. The manufacturer and his family just managed to get out with their lives, escaping to the Bastille, but his house and factory were destroyed in an orgy of violence before the riot, predictably, descended into looting. Réveillon was a decent employer, a man of science, innocent of the measures he was accused of, but social and financial prejudice saw him ruined. Mme. De la Tour du Pin had much to say on this event too. She called him 'a good man...famed for his generosity to charity',[13] and also claimed that when he was poor he had sold off many of his own possessions to pay a stranger's debt and return him to his family. However, the sort of prejudice extant at the time, not dissimilar to that aimed at bankers today, left no room for such shades of grey, no time for analysis or consideration. All that counted was the position Réveillon held in society. The flames of this paranoid class war would continue to be stoked by the revolutionaries and a similar attitude later turned on Antoine Lavoisier, one of the pre-eminent chemists of the era and a true Enlightenment man. Lavoisier, memorably immortalised in a stunning portrait by Jacques-Louis David, had spent an enormous sum of his own money attempting to improve some of the poorest farming land in France, in the Sologne, south of the Loire valley. He spent plenty of time and money eradicating malaria on his country estates, but as a Farmer-General and a representative of the state, none of that mattered. Any connection with the Old

Regime was poison and he, like so many others, would lose his head because of it.

The atmosphere, when the delegates began to gather at Versailles that spring, was one of tension and heightened expectation. They had an emotively charged conviction that they were tasked with winning the reforms France so desperately needed. This, it has to be said, gave them the mettle they needed to resist the attempts at repression and intimidation with which the established orders sought to restrain them. The courage they demonstrated in that regard was considerable, but their determination to push for reform would eventually come at considerable cost. For the noble intentions of the new delegates had already been warped by hate.

Among the crowd who thronged the palace that day was an unassuming, slight young man from the northeast who, like so many of the elected deputies, was a lawyer. Maximilien Robespierre had been born in Arras in 1758. His mother died when he was a child and his dissolute father abandoned the family, never to be seen again. The boy and his sisters were left in the care of relatives. A quiet and serious child, he proved academic enough to get noticed and won a scholarship to Louis–le-Grand in 1769 where that fateful encounter with the royal couple took place. At school he was introduced to a number of works which proved tremendously influential. *The Social Contract* by Jean-Jacques Rousseau had a particularly big impression on the pious youngster and, ultimately, on the course of the Revolution.

But his influence, on Robespierre and wider French culture, was rivalled by that of the Classics of Ancient Rome. Writers like Cicero, whom Robespierre admired, and Plutarch, whose *Lives* focused on moral instruction rather than historical analysis, were a perfect fit for the pious culture of pre-Revolutionary France. Yet this was, and remains, a deeply flawed genre. The writers of the early Imperial era focused on the values of the Republic, and scribes like Sallust and Livy lamented how republican virtue had been eroded by greed. But it was a period that none of them had lived through, and the romantic ideal of flinty, virtuous heroes they depicted was one that never truly existed. Yet in portraying a world where decency had been poisoned by a corrupt elite, they struck a chord with the smart set of Paris.

The most significant scribe was probably Tacitus who, in common with Rousseau, idealised the 'noble savage', the proud and honest tribes-people he saw as purer in spirit and possessed of superior morality to the decadent society in which he lived. The French read these tomes and saw their own world reflected in the pages. But both impressions were largely chimeras, and the work of Tacitus was moulded to fit a desired image. He even appears to have fabricated the brutal rape of Boudicca's daughters. The crime did not exist when he first covered the revolt in the *Agricola* but had been conjured from the ether when he revisited the event two decades later in the *Annals of Imperial Rome*. The change in emphasis appears to have been prompted by the intervening period the author had spent in the service of the Emperor Domitian. The serious corruption he witnessed left Tacitus bitter and hostile towards Roman civilisation, and it seems he inserted the scene to 'sex up' the account. After all, a spat over taxation between Roman governors and collaborators, which is what the Iceni were, was less likely to win the sympathy of his readership than a brutal violation by occupying soldiers.

Tacitus was a man with an agenda and his writing was distorted by the intensity of his political activism. It was certainly not the dispassionate record of fact imagined by his audience. He was effectively a self-loathing liberal of the day, the equivalent of the modern radical who sees all the flaws of Western civilisation but few of its benefits. His view of Rome was similarly pessimistic. Yet, in focusing on the avarice and larceny that surrounded him, he was blinded to the assets and triumphs of Roman civilisation, ones that appear obvious to us now. People who lived under the umbrella of Roman rule enjoyed security, comforts, peace and opportunities denied to those beyond its borders. Life was indisputably better with Rome than without it, and the Empire's achievements overshadow its faults by some margin. But Tacitus refused to accept this and his French readers were oblivious to these flaws. It didn't matter that it wasn't true. It was what they wanted to hear.

Jacques Louis David, the greatest French painter of the age, was another devotee of the genre. He too would play a significant role in not just the cultural, but the political life of the nation for some decades, and he later became a close associate of Robespierre. David immortalised the same themes in some of his most powerful art, initially in *The Oath of the Horatii* (1784) which incorporated themes from the cult of sensibility, and then, even more strikingly and memorably, in *The Lictors Bringing Brutus the Bodies of his Sons* (1789). It was a heart-stoppingly powerful visualisation of righteous, patriotic duty. The work depicted Lucius Junius Brutus, not the famous assassin of Caesar but the hero of the foundation of the Republic. Discovering that his sons had been involved in a plot to restore Rome's kings, the Tarquins, Brutus himself had ordered them beheaded. Completed, as it was in 1789, art has rarely been more of its time. Both paintings, steeped in the history of Republican Rome, also emphasised the virtue of sacrifice and duty above personal ambition. But, like the writers of old, David's goal was moral instruction rather than historical truth. The romanticism of the Imperial writers, who dreamed of virtue, patriotism, love of liberty, self-sacrifice and courage while surrounded by luxury, greed, conspiracy and corruption, spoke directly to the future shapers of revolution. Yet they had been wooed by a romantic, airbrushed image that bore little relation to the complexity and practical realities of politics. The consequences of such idealism would be significant.

Upon graduation, Robespierre took up practice as a barrister. The highly conscientious young man put principles before prosperity, focusing on defending the poor and forwarding the case for science against 'superstition'. His sensitive nature was revealed by his sister Charlotte in her memoirs in 1782. She recorded that her brother had agonised over passing the death sentence on a murderer. He lamented 'I know that he is guilty, I know that he is a scoundrel, but to have a man killed!'[14] He would become less squeamish over the next decade. Robespierre was a keen writer too, and in 1784 he released a paper which criticised cases where innocents suffered from crimes committed by their relatives. It was another principle he would abandon when assuming power. Yet he perceived himself as a noble defender of the meek and oppressed - a legislative Zorro, if you will. In defending the humble François Deteuf against a corrupt monastery the barrister spoke passionately to urge 'never, under any pretext whatsoever, let us watch the oppressor defy the cries of the weak, oppressed man. May magistrates never afford society this spectacle, meant to encourage crime and instil the innocent with fear'.[15] Yet the innocent would tremble with far greater fear when he rose to power. Robespierre had been exposed to the worst failings of the old regime, to greed, corruption, intolerance and oppression. But his mistake was in failing to realise that these were not symptoms of the current system. They were *human* failings. As such, his own political allies were as likely to be prone to them as his enemies, as he would succumb to them himself.

Critically, Robespierre regarded his views as inseparable from morality from an early age. The young lawyer gained entry to the prestigious academy of Arras in 1783 and the following year submitted a paper setting out the beliefs he maintained until the end of his life. 'Morals are more powerful than laws, so it is incumbent upon us to uphold them, to improve them, so as to bring about the reign of virtue on the earth, which produces happiness as the sun produces light.'[16] He increasingly clashed with the local magistracy and developed a deep aversion to wealth and the existing regime, going public with his concerns to ask

> 'why are these children, exposed to all weather, with no roof to cover them, suffering the horrors of hunger? It is because you live in sumptuous houses, where your gold commands all the arts to serve your soft way of life, and occupy your idleness. It is because your luxurious existence devours in one day the sustenance of a thousand men.'[17]

The young idealist was expressing a noble enough sentiment, but a tone of anger had entered his voice, and he was beginning to imagine that the only way to aid the poor was by attacking the rich. Robespierre carried his self-righteous piety into revolutionary politics, and as his confidence increased his tolerance for dissent of any kind diminished. This latter Robespierre reminded Hilary Mantel of the 'conviction of [Islamic] militants, their rage for purity, their willingness to die'.[18] Adam Gopnik, in the *New Yorker* on 5 June 2006, memorably described him as a 'mass-murdering nerd – a man who having read a book, resolves to kill all the people who don't like it as much as he does.'[19]

Robespierre's outspoken nature gained him notoriety and stood him in good stead when the time came for Arras to choose its deputies. He drafted a widely liberal manifesto which called for improved conditions for the peasantry and broader electoral representation. He was duly elected and the trim, fastidious little man joined the enormous crowds that thronged Versailles when the Estates-General finally met. Approximately half the deputies of the Third Estate were, like the man from Arras, lawyers. They were from the wealthiest 10% of the nation. It was enlightened men of reason who would go on to be the blood-soaked terrorists of the Revolution: lawyers, poets, scientists, actors, artists, librarians, left-leaning journalists and theatrical producers. It was from these professions that the most intolerant and violent of the radicals were drawn. The likes of businessmen, entrepreneurs, landowners and bankers were notably absent, as were peasants, artisans and labourers. It was a sociological pattern that would be repeated for the next two centuries.

Robespierre was clad in the somewhat old fashioned garb of brightly coloured silks, satins and knee breeches with immaculately powdered wig. He was also frugal in his tastes, having little appetite for food, sex or money. But, despite his distinctive garb, the young Arras lawyer was somewhat anonymous in the early days of the Assembly. All eyes were on significant figures like the wily Talleyrand, Lafayette, the hero of the American Revolution who had idolised and befriended George Washington, the king's cousin, the Duc d'Orléans and, most notably, Mirabeau. The Comte de Mirabeau was an imposing figure and a booming orator who crackled with charisma. A *philosophe*, historian and political commentator with numerous publications to his name he was rejected by his own class, but subsequently won election to the Third Estate at Aix-en-Provence. He was famously dissolute, profligate, acquisitive and capricious, and was a notorious lothario, despite a face badly scarred by smallpox. Mirabeau had been imprisoned twice by his own father but enjoyed wild popularity among the masses. An advocate for reform, and a shrewd political analyst, he was seen as a man of the people, a larger than life character. His brilliant intellect and sparkling eloquence had inspired devotion in a generation of readers long before the Revolution ignited in France. The Comte, along with many others, hoped to maintain the monarchy, albeit on more constitutional lines similar to England. He certainly had no interest in democracy or a republic, though few did at this stage.

Next to figures such as these, the unassuming, diminutive and softly spoken Robespierre initially made little impression. He was a bureaucrat who lacked charisma but who was rigorous and methodical to a fault. But these attributes made his carefully composed arguments compelling, and he couched them in the sentimental and emotive rhetoric of the time. It was an approach that would see him slowly but inexorably rise to prominence. By the summer of 1790 he would be one of the most significant figures in French politics, and Mirabeau was canny enough to pick Robespierre out of the crowd from the off. He observed that 'He will go far, he believes everything he says'.[20]

While the monarchy hoped the Estates-General would retain its old form, the deputies of the Third Estate were determined to reform it. It was Le Chapelier who first suggested that members of the other estates should be invited to join them (ultimately 150 of the minor clergy and 47 nobles would do just that) before, on 17 June, the Third Estate simply declared itself to be the National Assembly. It was a remarkably bold move. On 20 June, the deputies found themselves locked out of the Salle des Menus Plaisirs. The hall was being renovated for a *séance royale* – an address by the King, but to the suspicious members of the Third Estate, who had not been informed, it looked like a plot. They suspected they were being prevented from congregating so the Assembly could be dissolved. So, amid driving rain, Dr. Guillotin led them to a place of shelter, the du Vieux Versailles, an indoor court for Royal Tennis, now largely, and mistakenly, known as 'real tennis'. It was there that they pledged the historic Tennis Court Oath; that seminal moment in time where they vowed they would not be separated until a new constitution was agreed. When swearing the oath they saluted like Romans while their president, Jean Sylvain Bailly, perched on a table at the heart of proceedings, melodramatically placed his hand on his heart. Jacques Louis David famously captured the idealism of that moment, and, in that image, Robespierre was depicted clutching his heart with *both* hands; such pure virtue.

The optimism and accord of that day would not last long. In reality the deputies had vastly differing ideas about what form the new constitution should take, and the unity of that utopian gathering would be shattered with a violence that should have been a wake-up call to idealism. For now though, they were brothers in concord, brimming with optimism that reform must come and that they must be the ones to shape it. They were not alone, and many of the lower aristocracy and parish clergy had already begun to join them. The King met with the deputies, responded with some modest reform proposals and, to the smug satisfaction of the nobility, declared they must return to their separate orders or he would proceed without them. Following Louis's departure however, it was Mirabeau who seized the moment, rising to his feet to make full use of his stentorian tones to rally the representatives.

'Gentlemen, we are being dictated to in an insulting manner...I demand that you assume your legislative powers and adhere to the faith of your oath. It allows us to disband only after we have made the Constitution...Go tell your master that we are here by the will of the people and that we shall not stir from our seats unless forced to do so by bayonets.'[21]

When informed of the rebellion the furious Louis vowed to drive them out, but then quickly and characteristically capitulated. He ordered the other two estates to meet with the third in the National Assembly. The Revolution had truly begun; it would prove from that point on to be an unstoppable juggernaut.

The news swept Paris which was quickly aflame with revolutionary activity and tension. The electors of the Parisian deputies met at the Hôtel De Ville where they established themselves as an unofficial municipal authority. They quickly formed a militia, the National Guard. The Guard's service requirements of one day in four ruled out working men, so it too was a bourgeois force largely composed of lawyers, doctors and merchants. The gardens of the Palais Royal were opened to the public by the Duc D'Orléans and they became a great meeting point. Huge crowds packed in to congregate, discuss events and listen to impromptu speeches. Soon the gardens buzzed with stories that the King had yet again dismissed Necker, whose popularity yet endured, and that he was moving 20,000 troops in to close the Assembly and restore royal authority. As panic began to spread Camille Desmoulins, a school-friend of Maximilien Robespierre, clambered onto a table at the Café de Foy and, temporarily losing the stammer that afflicted him his whole life, gave a rousing call 'To Arms!' The cry was taken up, it echoed through the throng, and the next two days saw frenetic activity in Paris. The National Guard joined the growing multitude and, as uniforms could not be provided, it was agreed they should wear a blue and red cockade, the colours of Paris, on their hats. The crowd first converged on the Invalides where they seized 28,000 muskets, and then swept on to the Bastille which held 250 barrels of gunpowder in its vaults.

The Bastille was fortified, but the mob would not be denied. Two men, followed by others, clambered onto the rooftops of adjacent shops and managed to clear the moat where they hacked down the drawbridge. The crowd swarmed inside, but were held back by an inner door. A fierce and protracted siege lasted most of the day before the fortress capitulated. Around a hundred had died in the fighting with the majority of the victims coming from the attacking forces. Just seven prisoners were found inside: four were convicted forgers, two were lunatics, one of whom believed himself to be Julius

Caesar[*], and the other was the Comte de Solages, incarcerated by his own family for sexual depravity. The Marquis de Sade had been an inmate too, but had been transferred a few days before for shouting obscenities at people passing by.

Following its capitulation, the Bastille's Governor, Bernard-René du Launay, was marched through the streets to the Hôtel de Ville. He was regularly spat on and beaten en route before being set on in a frenzy. He was brutally hacked to death by bayonets and knives, then blasted with musket fire before his head was cut off with a fruit knife. The mayor of Paris, Jacques de Flesselles, was shot as he came out of the Hôtel before being decapitated in turn. Both men's heads were then stuffed onto pikes and paraded by deliriously celebrating crowds. When the mob grew bored they flung the heads in the Seine. That day, 14 July 1789, would become the most celebrated in the nation's history. When he was woken with the news the king asked his Grand Master of the Wardrobe, the Duc de la Rochefoucauld-Liancourt 'is this a rebellion?' The Duke replied firmly. 'No Sire, it is a revolution'.

Some astutely sensed what was coming even at this stage. The Comte d'Artois, the King's youngest brother, and the Prince de Condé, his cousin, fled first to Piedmont on 16 July, and then to the German Rhineland, establishing a base for what would prove a steady trickle of emigrées. The fact that a growing community, hostile to the Revolution, existed beyond French borders contributed to fears of counter-revolution. They would grow increasingly paranoid from that point. It was a mania inflamed by the path the Revolution had already begun to take. The spontaneous and violent contribution of the urban masses emboldened those who hoped to push for a more reformist agenda while cowing those with conservative inclinations. The successes that had been gained increased the sense of destiny felt by many of those taking part. They gave the far-left the political energy that would be necessary to defeat their opponents. But its dependence from an early stage on the support of the masses also had a critical effect on the language of revolutionary rhetoric.

It was considered necessary to enflame the anger of the mob so they could be employed as a lever of pressure in the political sphere. That required the language of politics to be that of indignant rage, and many of the most successful orators and writers of revolutionary thought expressed their sentiments with rising levels of fury. Their grievances were expressed not in cool and rational tones, but in terms of accusation. Yet when anger is directed

---

[*] Both were swiftly locked up again

at targets rather than at effecting positive reform, it needs retribution to sate it. It requires victims to be punished, and from the rising's earliest stages the revolutionaries spoke to excuse violence when it served their needs. Events that would have been greeted with outrage had they been committed by agents of the Crown were condoned or given licence. The rhetoric that powered the Revolution made subsequent government impossible, a trait that has bedevilled leftist thought ever since. A significant slice of left-wing oratory has always attempted to whip up the emotions and indignation of their audience, a process that, once started, is like an avalanche - impossible to abate or control. This trait is significantly worsened when the subsequent mob violence is condoned or excused, as it invariably is.

The royalist, Mounier, had already noted 'the evident satisfaction the crowd took from stringing up arbitrarily identified malefactors from the réverbères (street lamps) and from parading heads on pikes'.[22] When, nine days after the fall of the Bastille the *intendant* of Paris, Bertier de Sauvigny, and Joseph Foulon, his father-in-law and a minister in the post-Necker administration, were both tortured, battered to death and beheaded, with Foulon's heart cut out and carried to the council chambers, there was little squeamishness on display. In Elysée Lanstalot's *Révolutions de Paris* Foulon's murder was reported at having 'announced to tyrants the terrible vengeance of a justly angered people'.[23] Foulon was a 'cruel and ambitious man who only existed to deserve the hatred of men and to make the unfortunate suffer'.[24] This language stoked up the populace against the ambitious and the successful, making them legitimate targets of retributive violence. The rich were tyrannical, the poor were virtuous, and the latter could spill the blood of the former with wanton abandon. Anyone with affiliations to the old regime was, it seemed, expendable. When asked if their deaths were necessary Antoine-Pierre Barnave had quipped 'What, then, is their blood so pure?'[25] This sort of flippancy about violence, when couched in the language of virtue, would permit ever greater atrocities.

Robespierre was equally guilty of such sentiments and gave early indications that his attitude was hardening. He was becoming increasingly hostile towards and impatient with any who had the audacity to oppose him. He had already described the lynching of de Launay and de Flesselles as their 'punishment'.[26] And when the Assembly proposed that militias be employed to restore stability to the capital, Robespierre protested 'What has happened in this riot in Paris? General freedom, a little blood spilt, a few heads chopped off, of course, but they were the heads of guilty people...It is to this uprising that the Nation owes its liberty'.[27] This set a precedent in Robespierre's thought. If individuals who shared his views were accused of violence, vandalism, even murder, then he pleaded for clemency, even licence. But if his political rivals voiced an opinion he found disagreeable, or if he *suspected* they held views even mildly contrary to his own, then he ended up calling for their heads. Robespierre chillingly added further justifications. 'Do you want to calm the people? Speak to them in the language of justice and reason. Let them be sure that their enemies will not escape the vengeance of the law, and sentiments of justice will replace those of hatred.'[28] It should be quite obvious, to a less dogmatic mindset, that permitting vengeance will not reduce hatred - it will only encourage it. By condoning aggression and murder from the outset the revolutionaries had cleared the path for the coming nightmare.

Following the fall of the Bastille, Louis withdrew the troops from Paris and declared, unconvincingly, that he only intended to use them to restore order and protect the deputies. He accepted the National Assembly, reinstated Necker and was compelled to appear in the capital on 16 July. He showed his face to give a touch of legality to proceedings and to restore what authority he could, though he must have bristled at what felt like a humiliation, a capitulation. In front of a massive crowd, which gave him a rapturous reception, Louis was presented to Lafayette, the new commander of the National Guard, and Bailly, now mayor of Paris. Lafayette made a cockade that united the blue and red of Paris with the white of the Bourbon dynasty, and pinned it on the king, later making the same emblem part of the uniform of the National Guard. Yet the pomp of that day was hardly illustrative of the tense and paranoid fever that was gripping the nation. The French peasantry were consumed by deranged visions of bands of brigands or Austrians descending on them and a Great Fear spread like wildfire through the countryside. Many chateaux were looted and burned while aristocrats, tax collectors, middle class landlords, Jews, local clergy or owners of small factories were violently attacked. Militias were raised to warn other localities about the approach of the Austrians, but when they were spied crossing the fields they were mistaken for invaders themselves and the hysteria and rumours simply spread further.

Cooler heads prevailed at times. In Normandy on 28 July Mme. De la Tour du Pin attempted to reassure panicking locals that the Austrians could not have reached Guillefontaine, which they were reported to be burning, without advance word having reached them. Lucie rode to the town in question, but the enraged mob quickly decided that she was the Queen. Fortunately, a local locksmith who had recently seen the monarch was able to calm the crowd. Yet by the time she returned the rumour mill was already convinced she had been seized by the Austrians.[29] On 1 August Arthur Young was similarly dismissive of the hysteria, believing the peasantry were responsible for the violent outbursts attributed to brigands or Austrians. After all 'how could a troop of 800 banditti march through a country and leave their existence the least questionable...ridiculous.'[30] Yet a few days later the rumours simply swelled the number of brigands in the area to 1,600.

But while the peasantry feared external foes, the residents of Paris were filled with a dread of the enemy within. Fears of counter-revolutionaries and their nefarious plots became almost endemic. Arthur Young recorded evidence of this phenomenon too by recounting the tale of a mob in Alsace who were convinced the Queen was planning to blow up the National Assembly, march the army to Paris, and massacre the inhabitants. An officer who voiced doubts about the veracity of the story was angrily shouted down by those who confirmed that it was undeniably true as they had seen the report. As Young wearily sighed, 'Thus it is in revolutions, one rascal writes, and an hundred thousand fools believe.'[31]

As riots spread into the countryside, Lally-Tollendal proposed that municipalities be given the right to use force to restore order. Robespierre, again defending the rioters, opposed the motion, believing it would extinguish the love of freedom. He echoed Rousseau's belief that 'when the entire nation is in danger, when people plot against its freedom, when respectable citizens are proscribed, a thing which is a crime at other times becomes a praiseworthy action. Lenience towards conspirators is treason against the people.'[32] So, perceived as a virtuous act, radical violence is excused. But that is exactly why it tends to break out so quickly, why it is immediately defended, and why it continues to escalate.

Yet France's neighbours initially responded to events with enthusiasm. In Westminster, the Whig leader Charles Edward Fox proclaimed 'How much the greatest event it is that ever happened in the World! & how much the best!'[33] Britain's Prime Minister, William Pitt, the future nemesis of Revolutionary France, was more circumspect but still largely positive. 'The present convulsions in France, must, sooner or later, terminate in general harmony and order; and though the fortunate arrangements of such a situation might make her more formidable, it might also render her less obnoxious as a neighbour.'[34] Arthur Young, after initial reservations, concluded that, in respect of the depredations of the Old Regime, it was difficult to dispute the contention 'that a revolution was not absolutely necessary to the welfare of the kingdom. Not one opposing voice can, with reason, be raised against this assertion'.[35] Wordsworth's *Prelude* though is perhaps the most emotive celebration of events, and certainly the most enduring. 'Bliss was it in that dawn to be alive. But to be young was very heaven!'[36] Richard Price, the Welsh nonconformist preacher and essayist, sparked off a pamphlet war when committing his views to paper. He wrote that the Revolution was one 'in which every friend to man is now exulting...I have lived to see thirty millions of people, indignant and resolute, spurning at slavery, and demanding liberty with an irresistible voice, their king led in triumph, and an arbitrary monarch surrendering himself to his subjects.'[37]

Not all were convinced though. Edmund Burke, the shrewd Irishman whose brilliant oratory made him a formidable figure at Westminster, was far more hesitant to bestow praise. In a letter to Lord Charlemont of 9 August 1789 he commented on the outbreaks of violence witnessed thus far:

> 'if it should be character rather than accident, then that people are not fit for liberty, and must have a strong hand like that of their former masters to coerce them. Men must have a certain fund of natural moderation to qualify them for freedom, else it become noxious to themselves and a perfect nuisance to everybody else'.[38]

Burke's reticence, upon reflection, soon turned into outright hostility and he would be the Revolution's most consistent and formidable opponent. Yet it was a stance that would see him isolated for several years while events in France maintained a high level of idealistic support. Monarchs, unsurprisingly, were also less than enamoured by developments. Gustavus III of Sweden, later assassinated at a masked ball on 16 March 1792, divined the full implications almost immediately. He wrote to Baron Armfield on 19 August 1789 to reveal that 'The news from France has horrified me so much that I could not get to sleep last night until 4 o'clock. What horrible people! They are the orang-outangs of Europe'.[39]

The Assembly busied itself with attempting to draw up a constitution but, in the meantime, focused on drafting a Declaration of the Rights of Man and of Citizen. It was clearly inspired by the American model and Thomas Jefferson, in Paris for a spell, aided Lafayette with the text. The rather vague document asserted its commitment to guaranteeing freedom, property, the safety of the individual, resistance to oppression, and the sovereignty of the nation. It also declared that all citizens should be involved in drawing up new laws while positions and honours should be dependent on virtue and talent rather than birth. One clause was a direct quote from Rousseau. It declared that 'Law is the expression of the general will' - a theme that would have a huge bearing on future events. For the concept of 'general will' would prove contentious and profoundly consequential. The Comte de la Blanche pertinently noted that 'Nothing is more dangerous than to give people ideas of an indeterminate liberty while leaving to one side an account of their obligations and duties'.[40] They were words which would prove prescient indeed. The Declaration guaranteed the rights of free speech and association as well as freedom of religion and opinion. Yet, in the event, those who agreed to those principles would prove less robust in defence of them.

But for the time being the deputies focused on legislative changes and, by any measure, made remarkable progress. The Declaration was ratified on 27

August, but by that point the Assembly had already been swept up by the extraordinary events of 4 August. In a single session, where euphoria rode roughshod over all other considerations, they largely brushed aside the entire remnants of the feudal system. The deputies then tussled over the issue of whether the King should be permitted a veto on the Assembly's decrees. Some opposed the suggestion, some supported it, and in the end, on 11 September, a compromise was reached which allowed for a temporary veto. For the rest of the nation though, the priority was mostly the acute lack of bread. Rumours that food shortages were part of some 'aristocratic plot' circulated with increasing frequency and created an atmosphere of suspicion and accusation that would have appalling consequences. In Paris, the issue came to a head when stories began circulating about a wild celebration held at Versailles. It was said that, amid an orgy of consumption, those in attendance had trampled on the Revolutionary cockade. Mme. De la Tour du Pin was there though and attested that 'I have since seen this absurd story printed in serious history books, yet in reality this thoughtless prank consisted of one bunch of ribbons which Mme de Mouillé, a heedless chit of nineteen, had taken from her hat'.[41] There is no suggestion that, when faced with news of the bread shortages, Marie-Antoinette ever said 'let them eat cake', but the apocryphal fable is eloquent testimony to the gathering hatred directed at the court. It is likely that this most enduring of the many lies spread about the Queen gained currency at this juncture.

But the protests did not die down. On 5 October a vast crowd of fishwives bullied others in the market into accompanying them before a total of some 6-7,000 set off for Versailles to call for bread. Conspicuous among those who slogged through the rain that day was a striking woman, clad in a distinctive scarlet tunic, who brandished two pistols while sat astride an ebony horse. She was Théroigne de Méricourt, in reality, Anne-Joseph Méricourt, a woman who, like so many others, would be consumed by the Revolution she briefly joined. The National Guard decided to follow the women, ignoring Layette's protestations and dragging their commander along with them. The fishwives arrived about five in the afternoon and, granted an audience with the King, were promised all the bread in Versailles. Louis, who had prevaricated up to that point, also agreed to accept the Declaration of the Rights of Man and the August decrees. In doing so, he appeared to dampen the simmering tension that had bubbled through the amassed crowd. The National Guard arrived around eleven at night, and Lafayette met with Louis, but the chaotic scenes around Versailles quietened down as everyone found places to sleep.

The night was not as tranquil as it appeared though. It seems some groups had gathered together and became fired up as they discussed the Revolution deep into the night. They were conversations that inevitably focused on the mob's hatred of Marie-Antoinette. The quiet was disturbed in the early hours of the morning of 6 October as a large gang of armed women and National Guards burst through a gate and rampaged through the palace. They were intent on dismembering the 'Austrian whore' and the Queen barely escaped with her life. Mme. De la Tour du Pin's account evokes the terror and confusion of that day. She woke to cries of 'kill them!' while her maid, Marguerite, recounted seeing a wild-eyed man with a long beard, Nicolas Jourdan, a well-known model at the Academy, beheading the body of a Garde du Corps who had been killed by the rampaging mob.[42] The scene was one of complete mayhem as gangs, wailing like banshees, tore through the palace in an orgy of destruction. Lafayette attempted to quell the growing disorder, but it took the King's appearance on a balcony to mollify the mob. Yet the crowd only calmed down when he agreed to return to Paris with them. They called for the Queen to appear before them too and when she did she got some cheers, perhaps sarcastically, perhaps borne out of some grudging respect. Versailles was boarded up, and the huge crowd surrounded the King's carriage as it trundled on its way to Paris with the heads of two decapitated royal bodyguards dancing on pikes in front of the royal coach. On reaching the capital the royal family were housed in the dilapidated palace of the Tuileries. It was to become their virtual prison.

The pace of the changes won thus far had been startling, surprising even the most ardent of the activists of 1789. The revolutionaries had arrived at Versailles earlier that year optimistic and determined, and their rapid successes had a tremendous effect on them, giving them a sense of destiny that would take years to shake off. In Tackett's interpretation 'the experience that summer and the ensuing commitment to the new system of political values had all the impact and power of a religious conversion, with much the same intensity of commitment as in the Protestant Reformation 250 years ago'.[43] Many now felt that the Revolution was finished, but others would continue pushing for more and more change. It was this latter group that would increasingly gain ascendancy.

Alarmed at the murders and violence in the provinces many *intendants* and officials of the Old Regime abandoned their posts. Revolutionary municipal authorities began to take their place in national politics. France was divided into eighty-three departments with the new town governments frequently the direct heirs of the improvised patriot groups formed in 1788. But in Paris, the existence of parallel powers that competed with the official organs created by the National Assembly began to pose severe problems. The National Guards became ever more radicalised, as only the most fervently committed members stuck to the rigours of duty. They grew increasingly difficult to control. Sixty neighbourhood district assemblies had been created as electoral bodies for the Estates-General, but they refused to disband after the elections had taken place. They were subsequently instrumental in the formation of the National Guards and the storming of the Bastille, and established themselves in grass-root politics. They directed the surveillance of suspects and counter-revolutionaries and competed with the municipal government and Lafayette for control of the National Guard battalions. In May 1790, in an effort to undermine them, they were replaced by forty-eight sections, but they remained a force to be reckoned with.

The concentration of political activity in Paris had a profound impact, and playing a pivotal role in this process were the clubs. The most significant of these was the Society of Friends of the Constitution which, because it convened in the old convent of Saint-Jacques in the rue Saint-Honoré, became known as 'The Jacobins'. It rapidly acquired a semi-official status as the voice of the left in the Assembly. Its members included Barnave, the Lameth brothers, Alexandre and Charles, Pétion and Robespierre. Affiliate clubs sprang up in the provinces and quickly proliferated across the nation, reaching some 800 in number by June 1791. Membership fees were kept high, which excluded the rabble the deputies so romantically eulogised, but the bien-pensant liberals who debated there allowed the hoi polloi to cram into galleries to watch their debates.

Less than a mile to the southeast of the Jacobins was another influential new club. The Society of the Friends of the Rights of Man is usually known, after the district in which it was established, as the Cordeliers Club. Unlike the Jacobins its members were not deputies, and subscription prices were low, allowing a far more representative slice of Parisian society to join. The club was formed in opposition to the deputies' dismantling of the districts, and as such they never shared the Jacobins' deferential attitude towards the Assembly. The Cordeliers included a number of figures who would go on to play a significant role in events: Camille Desmoulins, Jacques-René Hébert, François Robert, Louis-Stanislas Fréron, Phillipe Fabre d'Eglantine and Pierre Gaspard Chaumette.

Among their number were two who would prove especially prominent, and, political sympathies apart, they could hardly have been more different. Georges-Jacques Danton was a gregarious and ebullient character, full of charm and humour, if somewhat intimidating and with plenty of rough edges. Often referred to as the 'Mirabeau of the mob' he was a similarly energetic lothario and was rarely without the company of a beautiful woman. Like the noble to whom he was often compared, he was far from stereotypically handsome, his countenance being badly scarred from a childhood incident when gored in the face by a bull. He was a recently qualified junior lawyer from a small town in

Champagne who had emerged through sheer force of personality, and he cut a towering and voluminous physical presence. He was no intellectual, but was a powerful and brilliant orator, and he quickly became the dominant figure in the politically active Cordeliers district.

Jean-Paul Marat, by contrast, had none of Danton's bombast or charm. He was a sinewy, furtive figure of brooding intensity who startled many of even his closest political allies. At forty-five in 1789, he was also the oldest of the revolutionaries. A doctor, scientist and pamphleteer, Marat's forte during that tumultuous period was in journalism, and none of his peers could match the spite and venom that poured from his pen. Marat famously wrote that 'in order to ensure public tranquillity two hundred thousand heads must be cut off',[44] a statement that neatly characterises the violence of his prose. He left no doubt about his intentions towards those affiliated with the old regime when declaring 'Tremble, you who have sucked the blood of poor, unhappy wretches.'[45] He also encouraged hatred towards bankers and financiers who 'build their fortunes on the ruin of others'.[46] Marat's paper was called *L'Ami du Peuple*, the People's Friend, an ironic title as, unlike Robespierre, he was rather scathing and dismissive about the mass of the population, preferring the idea of a revolutionary dictator. But presenting such an image allowed him to identify himself as a moral crusader, one who represented the downtrodden while denouncing his opponents as self-interested plutocrats. It was a stance that gave him *carte-blanche* to treat them as inhumanly as possible.

The Cordeliers' symbol was the eye of surveillance. It was fixed to all their publications and they urged their affiliates throughout the city to unearth hidden conspiracies and spy on the privileged classes. Paris, in particular, was entering a period of ever-greater division and suspicion. In Tackett's analysis, fear was the primary factor in the rising paranoia. 'Almost from the beginning, moreover, patriots had been beset with fear that the transformations were too good to be true, that those who had dominated society under the Old Regime would do everything in their power to turn back the clock and reverse the achievements of 1789.'[47] However, he failed to address the role that prejudice played in developing this fear in the first place, for the dread of counter-revolution bore little relation to reality. It was a fear driven by the imagination, and the imagination was informed by bigotry. Nearly all members of the nobility and Church, or all who failed to demonstrate sufficient ardour for the changes sweeping France, were suspect in this mindset, and not just suspect, but dangerous. It was the distrust so many felt towards their targets that allowed them to assume such dangerous proportions in their imaginations. Tackett also discusses the importance of rumour, but it was prejudice that encouraged so many to believe nearly every story that came their way. Mirabeau summed the situation up eloquently:

'In periods of calamity nothing is more striking to an observer than the widespread tendency to believe and to exaggerate the most appalling news. It would seem that logic no longer consists of calculating degrees of probability, but of giving credence to even the most unlikely rumours...We then resemble children, for whom the most frightening tales are always the most eagerly followed'.[48]

The hysteria of the Revolution is no defence for the crimes of the Jacobins, for it was a hysteria which was largely their own creation. It resulted in France becoming a surveillance state with denunciation an increasingly common feature of everyday life. Yet Tackett attempts to condone developments here too. 'In a state of crisis, it is easier to cope with anxiety – and it is perhaps more generally comforting – if a specific group or individual can be held responsible. But such fears had also been impelled by the evidence of very real conspiracies in July 1789.'[49] Yet those concerns were based on wildly exaggerated fears and largely non-existent conspiracies. These were then used as a pretext so the reformers could denounce and destroy any who might stand in their way. The modern left still use this tactic, though the justifications offered by Tackett do not exist today. We live in a period of unparalleled peace, prosperity and stability, but that paranoid behaviour still proliferates. It is not circumstances that inspire accusative cultures then, it is something within the particular psychology that expresses them. In the final analysis, it is undeniable that, while the Old Regime would have preferred to turn the clock back, the revolutionaries were far more ruthless in advancing their own agenda.

Sagan's interpretation differs slightly from that of Tackett. He concludes that ideological zealots share one psychological symptom – severe paranoia.[50] This, again, is a common left-wing trait. While those on the right have a tendency towards optimism: that man's ingenuity will find solutions to the world's problems; those on the left, particularly the far-left, have a more pessimistic, paranoid streak. The world is viewed largely in terms of greed and corruption, systemic racism, warfare and pollution - as a dying planet on the cusp of ecological catastrophe, one blighted by a fat cat culture determined to exploit, fleece and oppress the world's poor. Among the paranoid Sagan lists Savonarola, Robespierre, Rousseau, Lenin, Stalin, Mao, Pol Pot and Hitler, and a more charming bunch could hardly be found. It is the sort of mindset that convinces the radical that

'society is suffering from a life-threatening malady; if nothing is done about it, the death of society is certain; only extraordinary radical measures can save the social world. The most horrible aggressive acts are committed under a huge banner of morality: the Jews are exterminated so that society may be cleansed and restored to health; the King must die that *la patrie* may live'.[51]

Remember, these are not psychotic, unbalanced individuals we are talking about here. These are rational men, moralistic and virtuous to a fault, yet they make Ted Bundy, Peter Sutcliffe and Jack the Ripper look like rank amateurs. The current left, in its paranoid state, appears to see racism, sexism, misogyny, Nazis and homophobia everywhere it looks, distorting the most mundane comments or deeds into acts of horrendous oppression. A reaction of furious, outraged offence is considered the only appropriate response. Vocal denunciations follow and grovelling penitence is demanded from the transgressor. As such, the ideology remains fertile ground for the potential tyrants of the future.

In such a climate the language of revolution was becoming increasingly hostile, with political opponents viewed as, not just rivals, but evil. This demonization of the other was particularly apparent on the left. In the spring of 1790 Rosalie Jullien summed up the views of many on the nobility. 'The aristocrats are posing so many obstacles, using so many ruses, planning so many horrors, that the friends of humanity, truth, and justice can only view them with indignation and anger...All the devils of Milton are but angels compared to the devils of the aristocracy'.[52] The deputy Claude Frieaude, who called the nobility 'monsters' wrote 'Oh, how I now hate more than anyone else the aristocrats of our country.'[53] Mme. De la Tour du Pin recounts in her Memoirs how it had become commonplace for the aristocracy to be loudly abused as 'dogs'[54] when out in public. Similar venom was aimed at the refractory clergy who Jean-François Gaultier de Biauzat called 'unjust and evil'.[55] There were negative sentiments expressed on both sides of the political divide. But while the likes of Marat were exhorting their followers to bloodshed, the conservatives were primarily concerned with a fear of Jacobin violence. The radicals were 'brigands who...preached violence to drunken brutes',[56]and the *Gazette de Paris* urged the crowned heads of Europe to their rescue. These 'murderous men who thirst after blood'[57] were preparing a new Saint-Bartholomew's Massacre of the priest and nobles. It seems that, trapped amid that maelstrom of hate and fury that engulfed them, the diminishing forces of conservatism knew exactly what was coming. At this juncture the Revolution could certainly have progressed with a reformist agenda and in a peaceful manner. It was, after all, handily winning every argument. But the bigotry, suspicion and sheer hatred embedded in the radical left was creating a climate where violence would be the only way to allay their fears.

Yet, even while pouring out venom, the radicals of the time continued to preach lofty idealism. Robespierre was particularly guilty of this, and his comments on the freedom of the press illustrate the self-regard that was inflating into full-blown hubris.

'Incorruptible men, who have no other passion besides the well-being and glory of their country, do not dread the public expression of the sentiments of their fellow citizens. They know only too well that it is not easy to lose their esteem, when one can counter calumny with an irreproachable life and proof of disinterested zeal; if they are sometimes victims of a passing persecution, this is, for them, the badge of their glory, the brilliant testimony of their virtue; they rest assured with gentle confidence in the suffering of a pure conscience and the force of truth which will soon reconcile them with their fellow citizens.'[58]

As with so many of his sentiments, his later practice bore no relation to such principles. He voiced many democratic and egalitarian ideals though, supporting universal male suffrage and opposing the widespread prejudice directed at Jews and actors. Thespians were generally considered 'untrustworthy', but Robespierre believed the theatre had a valuable role to play in the Revolution. He suggested that 'the virtues of the actors will reform the stage, and theatres will become once more schools of high principle, good conduct and patriotism.'[59] His words hinted at the cultural control which has defined the left ever since.

Yet he also argued that 'you have been told things about Jews which have been vastly exaggerated and which often belie history. The vices of the Jews have their roots in the degradation into which you have plunged them.'[60] These were remarkably progressive views in a nation where anti-Semitism was, if not universal, then incredibly common. Robespierre loved a sound bite and summed up his views when declaring 'equality is the source of all that is good; extreme inequality is the source of all evils.'[61] This sort of simplistic platitude, almost the prototype of the archetypal 'Tweet', is still cherished by swathes on the left today. His views won him the admiration of François-Nöel Babeuf, a prominent agrarian (a believer in forced land redistribution) who was impressed that 'M. De Robespierre is not interested in making money. He is, and will always remain, the lawyer only of the poor'.[62] Babeuf, who was known, in reference to the proletarian hero of Republican Rome, as 'Gracchus', later collaborated with the Italian Filipo Antonio Buonarotti of Pisa, a descendant of Michelangelo, in writing *The Plebian Manifesto.*[*] Published in 1795 it was the first real communist proposal, calling for the abolition of private property and stipulating that the ambitious were 'a social scourge'.[63]

On 31 May 1791 Robespierre attempted to get the death penalty outlawed. He looked back to the Classics in making his case and referred to the twin despotisms of Tiberius and Caligula. 'Once tyranny had invented the crime of high treason, fanaticism and ignorance in their turn invented crimes of outrage

[*] Babeuf was guillotined in 1796 for his political radicalism – a fate he had previously advocated for many others.

against Divine Majesty, which could be expiated only with blood.'[64] But the Assembly sided with the proposal of Dr. Guillotin on the universal and 'humane' punishment of decapitation by machine. Previously only nobles had been beheaded, while commoners had been hanged. Now their fate would be the same. The moralistic, deeply pious and well-meaning Robespierre was also opposed to the slave trade. But with the deputies attempting to quell the slave rebellion in St. Domingue* this was considered a step too far for many of his contemporaries. Barnave warned that imposing the Rights of Man on the island colony may destabilise it and leave it an easy target for English annexation. Still, Robespierre, whose theorising frequently seemed immune to practical realities, brushed aside such concerns. In following Rousseau he was exhibiting the dangers of adhering to an inflexible ideology inspired by a utopian vision. There was little attempt to weigh up issues and find pragmatic, balanced solutions. By trying to impose his own philosophy on society, rather than reacting to circumstances, he would be unable to accommodate the philosophies or wishes of anyone else. All resistance was to be trampled. It was Robespierre's way or the highway, and the highway led to the guillotine.

Jonathan Israel, in arguing that true revolutionary idealism was high-jacked by Robespierre's clique, is in denial of many of these facts. He credits the likes of Brissot, Condorcet, Mirabeau, Lavoisier and Olympe de Gouges with campaigning for the abolition of slavery, yet claims that Robespierre showed little concern for the cause and actually evinced sympathy for white plantation owners,[65] though he does admit that the Jacobins embraced black emancipation in 1794. He records how Mirabeau, Claude Thierry and Anarcharsis Cloots decried the prejudice directed against the Jews,[66] yet chooses not to mention that Robespierre did the same, perhaps because it doesn't fit in with his argument. In fact, he not only failed to defend Robespierre but even commended Johann Gottlieb Fichte for his principles, despite his virulent anti-Semitism.[67] Israel also cited Mercier's claim that the philosophes intended a revolution in men's attitudes, habits, morality and way of life, while the radicals only sought a revolution in government to concentrate power in their own hands.[68] Yet it was Robespierre who made a concerted effort to use the state to create a *nouvelle homme*, a 'new man', a virtuous citizen in accordance with the values of the philosophes. In February 1794, in the midst of the worst excesses of the Terror, Robespierre spoke openly of this aspiration.

'We wish to substitute in our country morality for egotism, probity for a mere sense of honour, principle for habit, duty for etiquette, the empire of reason for the tyranny of custom, contempt for vice for contempt for misfortune, pride for insolence, large-mindedness for vanity, the love of glory for the love of money, good men for good

* Modern day Haiti.

company, merit for intrigue, talent for conceit, truth for show, the charm of happiness for the tedium of pleasure, the grandeur of men for the triviality of grand society, a people magnanimous, powerful and happy for a people loveable, frivolous and wretched – that is to say all the virtues and miracles of the Republic for all the vices and puerilities of the monarchy.'[69]

This sort of utopian idealism is maligned by Tocqueville as 'the politics of the impossible'.[70]

In Israel's theory, Condorcet, who eulogised the principle of the general will, was the thinker who epitomised the true values of the Revolution. Yet not only did Robespierre share many of his key beliefs but that philosophe played little active role in shaping events. It is certainly possible to write a detailed history of the Revolution without mentioning Condorcet. Could the same be said of Robespierre? In fact, in its early months and years, constitutional monarchists were more numerous than the democratic republicans who Israel asserts to be the bearers of true revolutionary principles. One must also ask if, as he claims, Robespierre and his cohort perverted the 'true' revolution, then why has every other significant left-wing usurpation of power ended up roughly the same? Israel firmly believes that Enlightenment idealism was the primary cause of the Revolution - but he also absolves that movement of any culpability for the consequences, a quite remarkable *volte-face*. Unintended consequences or not, the link between the utopian rhetoric of the leftist reformers and the calamity of the Revolution is undeniable. The repression that swept France has been demonstrated to be, not an aberration of left-wing thought, but a recurring theme of it. Such repercussions are not a distortion of those values then, they are a natural consequence of their forced implementation. Israel is attempting to have his cake and eat it, to accept credit for the good while dodging blame for the bad.

Enlightenment idealism had not just espoused liberty, equality and reason for decades but had also attacked the established order of society. So, when a physical attack on that order followed, it was a natural consequence of the ideals that had been expressed. Israel's central thesis then, for all his learned acumen, is flawed. The Revolution did not go 'off course'; it was based from the start on prejudice, on attacking all contemporary systems of government and any who had a whiff of privilege, without giving considered thought to what was to replace them. Any form of idealistic movement, when given free rein, will almost inevitably be hijacked by a minority of pious fanatics as their determination outstrips that of their rivals. Attempts to impose egalitarianism are also in vain as equality itself is a chimera. Men are not equal in intelligence, health, charm, contacts, appearance, strength, work ethic, ambition, confidence or any aspect that determines success or failure in the game of life, and imposing equality robs man of all the assets that allow him to thrive. Sagan concludes that equality was the event's great fault, the issue that 'broke the back of the liberal Revolution'.[71] Yet Israel is unable to perceive that, as Enlightenment idealism cannot be readily applied to an imperfect species, it must rely on compulsion. This erodes the very freedoms and equality it claims to advance and, as it tends to brook no dissent, the retribution swiftly moves from stern to violent. In arguing that the Revolution was diverted the historian is unable to perceive, with the benefit of hindsight, the true nature of events which Edmund Burke foresaw from the outset. Israel's tract, written from a left-wing perspective, puts one in mind of the reaction of a moderate Muslim who brushes off the actions of the extremists as having nothing to do with Islam. Israel's tome is brilliantly written and the product of a deep and sagacious mind, but it is evocative of all those members of the liberal intelligentsia who, for all their erudition, tied themselves in knots to brush off any criticisms of Stalin's regime for decades.

More to the point when the Revolution erupted in France it meant many different things to different people. By what right does Israel identify a narrow stratum of the political kaleidoscope in that period and proclaim that these were the Revolution's 'core values', particularly when that viewpoint was resoundingly defeated? Whose values were they? Not Mirabeau's, not Louis's, not Lafayette's, not Danton's, not Talleyrand's, not Napoleon's, not Robespierre's. Yet these were the individuals who primarily shaped events. A bewildering array of factions wrestled for control of France during that period, and none of them had a monopoly on the Revolution's values. The bourgeoisie had started the rising, but it had been 'hijacked' by the artisans, the people; those who had stormed the Bastille, dragged the King to Paris, and later deposed him in the melee at the Tuileries. Those who had started the Revolution quickly lost control of it. Pressure from below and from the left prevented the original revolutionaries from developing the sort of stable society that those in America, who remained firmly in control, managed to achieve. The Revolution needs to be judged, not on the views of a moderate reformist group of liberals with which one happens to agree, but on its results, and those are beyond dispute.

But the real reason for Israel's miscalculation is quite simple. He has neglected an aspect continually overlooked by the left – the *human* factor. As a result, he failed to separate the manifesto of the Jacobins from their *character*. The movers and shakers of that period rejected reason, evidence and experiment in favour of hysteria, prejudice, speculation, rumour and accusation. For all their egalitarian talk they were disciples of Rousseau, so feeling trumped reason. They side-lined cool calculation for impassioned hatred and replaced old superstition with new, a belief in a fantastical utopia that still endures. But, despite this, they truly believed that they *were* sons of the Enlightenment - that their worldview was an entirely rational and empirical outlook, one so inarguably correct that its opponents could be dismissed or removed. This delusion continues to bedevil the left and is as recognisable in the scientific certainty of modern-day activists as it was over 200 years ago.

The true paragons of Enlightenment values, Diderot, Voltaire, Condorcet, D'Alembert et al, would have looked at the actions of the Jacobins and found virtually nothing they recognised or admired, despite the numerous points of policy on which they agreed. For the fact is that hypocrisy and unpleasantness will run riot without a legislative structure in place to restrain them. When the administration comes under a monopoly of 'progressive' voices, those restraints are not so much loosened as discarded altogether, and an untethered radical is a dangerous beast indeed. In America, under more clement conditions, the notions of the Enlightenment helped forge a new society by shaping an existing legislative body. But the Jacobins would have a rather different, and considerably more malign, legacy.

For many of the deputies the restoration of stability and order had become the main priority, but Robespierre was increasingly seen as the chief roadblock to realising such ends. He eschewed practical concerns at every junction to argue in favour of revolutionary principles. He was the archetypal idealist, fired with such ideological zeal that he seems, and must have seemed to his contemporaries too, almost a caricature. Increasingly, in seeking to implement Rousseau's 'General Will', he was coming to view the will of the people as being indistinguishable from his own. But while he spoke for the people he did not consider it necessary to consult them. He increasingly portrayed the 'virtuous' people and the 'evil' counter-revolutionaries in simplistic, Manichean terms, a romantic idealism which he summed up in April 1791.

> 'It is the people that is good, patient, and generous. The people asks for nothing but peace, justice and the right to live. The interest, the will of the people, is that of humanity: it is the general interest. The interest of that which is not the people, of that which separates itself from the people, is mere ambition and pride.'[72]

As Sagan has noted of the Rousseauist conception 'This sinister 1984 mode of "doublespeak", wherein the interests of the people are piously invoked in order to oppress the people – so important for twentieth century ideological terror – was invented in France in 1789 – 94'.[73] Robespierre's idealism permitted him to see all his rivals as enemies of morality. But his belief in the correctness of his position would permit all sorts of horrors. As with so many others, Robespierre slid into tyranny not *despite* his idealistic views, but *because* of them.

Rousseau's vague assertion of the General Will was in itself a call to a one-party state, a contention that a single viewpoint was, not just attainable, but desirable. In his ideology all factions were a hindrance to its implementation, so it was essential 'that there exist no partial associations within the state'.[74] But, from a legislative point of view, the great failing of the French Revolution was its inability to allow for any diversity of political opinion. The drive towards unanimity was effectively enshrined with the Tennis Court Oath and culminated in the Terror. In contrast with the American Revolution which had allowed a political split that ultimately developed into the Democratic and Republican parties, the French model effectively aimed at a single-party state, a process repeated with disastrous consequences in Germany, Russia, China, Cambodia and Cuba.

Robespierre quoted a revealing line of Rousseau in the Jacobins: 'the people want what is good, but they do not always see it'.[75] He would have no qualms in deciding for them, but his faith that he was almost singularly dialled into the 'General Will' was particularly puzzling in light of the minimal contact he ever had with the masses. Robespierre had moved in to the Duplays' house in Paris, a residence which also housed three of their four daughters, a son and a nephew. They were a Jacobin couple who rented out property, preferably to Jacobin tenants, so he was seldom exposed to dissenting voices. The house, at 366 rue Saint-Honoré, was just doors away from the Jacobins and around the corner from the Manège and the Tuileries. Robespierre's whole world thus revolved around a tiny nexus of streets where he was kept well insulated from those he professed to represent.

Yet, despite his minimal contact with the masses, Robespierre shared Rousseau's view that the people were inherently good but corrupted by civilisation. He believed they could be improved by politics and genuinely felt his manifesto could forge a virtuous 'new man'. It was a critical error, and this too set a precedent. Middle class radicals evoked concern for the masses, but their real priority was with their own agenda, for when they imposed it, those same people would endure horrific suffering. The deputies stopped choosing policies suitable for the masses and attempted to force the population to fit their manifesto instead. It was an approach that largely resulted from a failure to understand or account for human nature, and it was shared by Robespierre, Rousseau and all the demagogues that came in their wake. But rather than accept they were wrong, they grew increasingly frustrated with those their philosophising was inflicted upon - people who were then blamed for the failures of their theorising. Yet the movement would refuse to learn these lessons.

On 19 June 1790 the deputies voted to abolish the hereditary nobility in France. It was an act of suppression that saw a surge in emigration. In the summer and autumn of 1791, following the King's failed flight to Varennes, it would turn into a flood. By the end of that year, around 10,000 had fled the new regime. However, the extent of migration, while alarming to the Jacobins, meant that counter-revolutionary activity in France was minimal. Simply put, the majority of those most opposed to the Revolution had left. It was a salient reality that had little impact on the paranoid delusions of the radicals. On 30 September 1790 the old sovereign courts of France were abolished and replaced with elected judges and tribunals drawn from the doctors, engineers and lawyers who peopled the revolutionary class. The deputies also began mobilising against the Church, suppressing the monastic orders in February 1790, voting to sell off Church lands in April, making the appointment of the clergy subject to elections and, at the end of the year, decreeing that all ecclesiastical civil servants must swear an oath of allegiance to the state; a pledge which most promptly refused. The clergy began to feel more and more of a persecuted class. The baroness de Barbier captured the fear and remarkable loss of liberty that increasing numbers were dealing with on a day to day basis. 'It is only the nobles who are forced to smile and be silent and submit to everything demanded of them, if they want to avoid being massacred as 'aristocrats''.[76]

The King was growing terribly disillusioned, both with the way he was being side-lined and with the ever-mounting attacks on the Church that he revered. Louis was increasingly pressured by Marie-Antoinette and other advisors to link up with forces sympathetic to his cause outside France, notably the Austrians with whom the Queen was already in correspondence. However, the monarchy's already gloomy prospects suffered a further blow when Mirabeau died on 2 April. He had been in consultation with the Crown while attempting to cement a constitutional monarchy, and such was his political acumen that he may have been able to navigate the treacherous political terrain of the period and placate both sides. He naturally hoped to benefit from the situation himself, but he was not purely motivated by ambition. At this juncture it may still have been possible to salvage an amenable solution to France's worsening crisis. But the monarchy's wariness of Mirabeau made it unlikely, and with him gone that faint hope began to diminish.

The breaking point came on 18 April 1791 when the royal family attempted to leave the Tuileries to take Communion at Saint-Cloud during Holy Week. Fearing that the King intended to flee, a huge crowd, including a sizeable contingent of National Guardsmen ignoring Lafayette's orders, packed around the royal coach, prevented it from moving and angrily abused those inside. After a terrifying stand-off, which lasted several hours, the royal party gave up and returned to what now felt like a gaol. Feeling that in this new land of liberty the King was the only one who was not free, plans were hatched to leave. On the night of 20 June a heavily laden Berliner slipped away from the palace, but its progress was slow. The next day, at Varennes, not far from the border, the

King was recognised, the National Guard summoned, and the royal party were dragged humiliatingly back to Paris in front of a huge, stony, and eerily silent crowd. When the Comte du Val de Dampiere attempted to salute the coach, the crowd dragged him away and hacked him to death.

Louis had left a note behind in the Tuileries detailing his distaste with the course of events. He was also clear that all the concessions he had made to that point had been granted under duress. But a complete rupture with monarchy was still considered too shocking, so enough deputies were persuaded that the King had been spirited away by 'evil councillors'. The Assembly voted to complete the drafting of the Constitution and presented it to Louis in July. The chastened monarch now accepted the terms, eventually signing it on 14 September, though the celebrations of 14 July had been far more muted than in the previous, inaugural, year. With the signing of the document came the announcement that elections were to be held for a fresh Assembly which would operate under the newly arranged constitutional monarchy. But, with many now unconvinced about the King's intentions, opposition began to mount.

The Cordeliers organised a large meeting and called on the populace to sign a petition calling for the overthrow of the monarchy and the establishment of a Republic. It was planned for 17 July on the Champ de Mars, the parade ground, now home to the Eiffel Tower, where the celebrations had been held on Bastille Day. The event attracted some 50,000 people though it was marred in the morning when the petitioners found two men hiding under an altar and, assuming them to be royalist spies, lynched them. Six thousand had signed the document when, late in the day, fearing the increasing tension and anarchy in the area, Bailly and Lafayette agreed to send in the National Guard to restore order. When the crowd pelted the soldiers with stones they opened fire and followed the barrage up with a bayonet charge. Dozens were killed. It was the first time the new Assembly had used force against the people and it ripped open a schism in the revolutionary generation. Israel, peculiarly, fails to mention the murders in the morning, the growing antagonism of the crowd or the stone-throwing riot on the arrival of the National Guard, instead maintaining that the 'scene was peaceful enough'[77] until Lafayette's arrival. But the divisions were undeniable. It was hardly a surprising development. Events had been characterised by animosity and suspicion since before the Revolution had begun, now France was about to feel the consequences of all that resentment.

The Jacobins had already become split in the wake of the Flight to Varennes, with 264 deputies, led by Antoine Barnave, leaving to form their own society. The Feuilliants, whose name was derived from the monastery where they took up residence, moved right across the street from the Jacobins. They were committed to defending the King's role in the constitution, as well as press freedoms, something the remaining Jacobins could no longer countenance. But now, with French politics beginning to be torn asunder by dramatic rifts, the Feuilliants were charged with complicity in the Champ de Mars massacre. Robespierre was principal among those who argued that no members of the previous administration, including himself, should be allowed to sit in the new Assembly. His real desire was to expunge the legislature of any vestiges of royalist support while believing, correctly, that he would still be able to influence events from the clubs. By the time the Assembly closed Robespierre had become a well-established figure. He had been given the nickname of The Incorruptible, and this epithet, and the ecstatic crowds that cheered and bore him aloft in the streets, greatly embellished the hubris that would propel him to historical infamy.

The most significant figure in the new Assembly, which opened on 1 October 1791, was Jacques-Pierre Brissot, who had risen to prominence in the Jacobins over the previous few months. A thirty-eight year old from Chartres, he was a brilliant journalist, author and orator. Brissot was well endowed with charisma and brimmed with, if anything, excessive confidence. He admired the artisans' love of liberty, but believed them ill-equipped for office, and argued the likes of merchants, capitalists and especially bankers should be excluded from the Assembly. The only people he considered to be ideal representatives were ones who were, predictably, rather like himself. His clique, which came to dominate, were sometimes known as the Brissotins but, as the majority came from the Gironde, an area around Bordeaux, they were more commonly referred to as the Girondins.

Other prominent members of the faction included Pierre Vergniaud, Armand Gensonné, Jérôme Pétion, the Marquis de Condorcet and Jean-Marie Roland, whose wife, Marie-Jeanne 'Manon' Roland, a brilliant and vivacious woman, was the knowledgeable hostess of their salon. Mme. Roland possessed a dazzling intellect, a remarkable memory, was extraordinarily well-read and spoke several languages. She was one of a number of female intellectuals who, denied a role in the politics of the day, was an active and influential figure anyway. Germaine de Staël, the daughter of Necker, was another. She was a reputable woman of letters who remained significant during Napoleon's regime, while Louise de Kéralio was a literary and political figure whose admission to the Academy of Arras had been celebrated by Robespierre. But arguably the most politically active woman of the period was Olympe de Gouges. She was dedicated to the equality of the sexes and argued in her *Declaration of the Rights of Woman and the Citizen* that 'women are born and remain free and equal to men.'[78] It was a suggestion that would prove a step too far for even her revolutionary peers.

While the Feuilliants were the largest faction in the new Assembly, the relatively small Brissotins wielded considerable influence over the majority deputies of 'the plain' who milled between left and right. An extremist clique, loyal to Robespierre, congregated in the seats high on the far left-hand corner of the Assembly and consequently came to be known as the Mountain, or the Montagnards. The feud that would develop between the Jacobin factions of Montagnard and Girondins would define the next year. Half the membership of the original Assembly had been drawn from the privileged classes of nobility and clergy. But that figure dropped to 10% in the new legislative body. Only newly ennobled aristocrats were deputies, none of whom had been connected to the old regime, and only clergy who were oath-takers were permitted entry. It was thus a far more radical assembly than the one that had preceded it. It is ironic then that the new body would be more torn by bitter factional strife than that between patriots and aristocrats in the earlier legislature.

The Feuilliants had drifted over to the right, the position previously held by the 'blacks', the forces of religious conservatism, but there was more to unite them with the Jacobins than there was to divide them. Neither left nor right favoured republicanism, though both were wary about the King, both opposed the Old Regime, the privileges of the nobility, the émigrés and refractory priests, and both were in favour of improved rights for free coloured people. Despite this, the Jacobins became convinced that the Feuilliants were traitors, up to their necks in a royalist conspiracy. Claude Basire declared that 'we are surrounded by conspirators. Everywhere plots are being prepared and we must continually denounce specific incidents that are, in fact, linked to the grand conspiracy, whose existence no one can doubt'.[79]

The monarchists and the Feuilliants now believed the Revolution to be finished, and both parties consequently faded from the political scene. The Gironde felt anything but. They sensed the true position of the King who had been fomenting for royalist support from Austria and émigré conclaves, and as such Brissot pushed for war to test the King's loyalties. However, Louis was in favour of war too as a successful one would reinvigorate his standing while an unsuccessful one would reflect badly on the revolutionaries. The Brissotins then seemed outmanoeuvred, something that Robespierre, who vociferously opposed the war, was acutely aware of. In the event, the coming conflict would be the undoing of both Louis and Brissot, its principal cheerleaders.

Those on even the moderate right continued to suffer setbacks. Bailly, worn out by attacks from the left, resigned and in the mayoral elections Lafayette was defeated by Jérôme Pétion, a close friend of Robespierre. The Feuilliants effectively disintegrated as a political force over the long winter of 1791-2 while food shortages and riots continued to ripple through the provinces. Monarchist societies, despite their support for the Constitution, were forced to disband when attacked by popular demonstrations or local authorities who threw around the charge of 'counterrevolutionary activity'. Yet leftist groups were given free rein to discuss their ideas, a privilege denied to those on the right. Freedom of speech applied to just one perspective and opposing views were met with intolerance, violence and suppression. The Jacobins continued to grow in influence, but the increasing monopoly of the left was to reap a bitter harvest indeed.

Monopoly did not mean unity though, far from it. A fissure had developed in the Jacobins with Brissot, Robespierre, and their attendant cliques, beginning to clash with ever-greater frequency. The personal animosity between the two recognised leaders of their factions was to grow to alarming proportions. Robespierre also became increasingly estranged from former friends like Pétion and Roland. Pétion had come to believe that Robespierre was 'imperious in his opinions, listening only to himself, intolerant of objections, never pardoning those who wounded his vanity, never admitting mistakes, denouncing irresponsibly while taking offence at the slightest criticism of himself'.[80]

However, the issue that really began the split was the war. Brissot pursued the policy while Robespierre opposed it, largely as he did not want either the aristocratic generals or the Crown to gain any leverage. But the prospect of conflict was now unavoidable. On 14 December 1791 Louis came to the Assembly to announce that the German princes had been given an ultimatum to disperse the émigré communities in their territories. The rulers of Trier and Mainz began to comply but Leopold II, the Austrian ruler, Holy Roman Emperor and brother of Marie-Antoinette, who shrewdly sensed how hopeless the French monarchy's position had become, threatened to mobilise troops against France. On 7 February 1792 Austria and Prussia concluded a treaty. A period of sabre-rattling on both sides ensued, which not even Leopold's death could interrupt, before, on 20 April, France formally declared war against the new Austrian ruler Francis II.

The war began appallingly for the French as their forces melted away in the face of the Austrian assault. They even turned on each other in the chaos. Théobald Dillon, the Irish born commander of a force in Tournai, took shelter in a peasant's cottage after his troops had retreated in disarray. But Dillon had removed his uniform coat and the paranoid, patriotic propaganda about spies and 'traitors within' convinced the farmer that he had caught an enemy of the Revolution. Dillon was subsequently dragged to Lille by a mob of townspeople and National Guards before being slashed across the face and bayoneted to death on the cobblestones. He was hung from a *lanterne*, and his left leg was hacked off and paraded around as a trophy before his body was eventually tossed on a fire.

The war was also to worsen the already severe food shortages and rocketing inflation, just as uprisings in the French West Indies resulted in soaring prices for sugar and coffee. The anti-capitalist rhetoric which had been at the heart of the narrative could now be ratcheted up another notch. It was a culture that helped fuel the rise of the sans-culottes, literally, those without breeches, whose name referred to their taste for the long trousers of the working-class man. The ostensibly proletarian movement quickly became a potent force in political activism, and sartorial choices grew in importance. In February 1792 Brissot wrote an article expressing his support for the concept of the red Phrygian liberty cap, or *bonnet rouge*, allegedly worn by freed slaves in ancient Rome. On 15 March several members of the Jacobin club arrived wearing the headgear and the fashion spread like wildfire. Actors in a major Paris theatre donned the bonnets after a performance of *The Death of Caesar* before placing a cap on the bust of Voltaire in the theatre's foyer. Robespierre was never a fan of the fashion, but the sans-culottes took to it enthusiastically. In October 1790 Brissot had also published a lengthy piece in the *Patriote Français* promoting short, deliberately rough haircuts. Image has remained pivotal to the movement and both these severe trims and the consciously scruffy appearance of the sans-culottes evoke visions of the styles favoured by many on the left today. The sections and clubs both played a significant role in rallying the sans-culottes for the large scale street protests which started breaking out with increasing regularity.

Only seven deputies had opposed the war but, when the effort started to go badly, it was predictably blamed on conspirators and counter-revolutionaries. It could not be the fault of the people who had started or orchestrated the conflict, naturally. Suspicions grew that the King was in league with the Austrians, and on 23 May Brissot and his colleagues announced this 'plot' in a series of speeches to the Assembly, though he assured the delegates that the traitors were too canny to leave any actual evidence of their machinations. The plot was said to be masterminded by the Austrians, the King's advisers and, particularly, and predictably, the 'Austrian whore' herself, Marie-Antoinette. Jullien declared that only a 'crass imbecile' could doubt the evidence of this 'barbarous plot'.[81] It was more luck than judgement that on this occasion the Brissotins happened to be partly right, though in reality the plot consisted of a few desperate but ineffectual letters from the royals.

In the increasingly tense and desperate situation in which they found themselves, the royals *had* begun communicating with the Habsburgs, but there was certainly no large scale conspiracy. And what plotting there was had been driven by the revolutionaries. For Marie-Antoinette in particular, after the years of horrendous abuse she had suffered, her antipathy for the French politicians was well merited. Louis had also openly refused to sanction the

Assembly's measures against non-juring priests, which included exiling any who refused to take the oath, or their request to bring 20,000 National Guards to the capital. A reputation of the King as 'monsieur veto' took hold and his position became ever more precarious. In the increasingly tense climate Louis dismissed his Girondin ministers and replaced them with ones of a more conservative hue, a move which sparked even more opposition.

A huge protest against the king's dismissal of the ministers and his use of the royal veto was arranged for 20 June 1792, the third anniversary of the Tennis Court Oath. The first real display of people power since the storming of the Bastille, it would set the scene for the drama of the coming months. Thousands poured into the streets, a very great many of them armed. Invited into the Assembly the mob cursed the Feuilliants, many of whom left, before departing for the Tuileries where they swarmed into the palace, cornered Louis on a windowsill and taunted him over his policies and commitment to the war effort. A liberty cap was thrust on his head and he was forced to toast the nation with some red wine the mob had swiped from his cellar. The King's composed and dignified reaction mollified the protestors and, evidently satisfied, they began to drift away. But the monarchy was critically undermined by the event, and nervous politicians began to abandon the Assembly. By August only about a quarter of the near 800 deputies remained.

The protest sparked considerable debate about the role of the King and the rights and wrongs of the day's events. Paris was becoming ever more divided while the deputies of the left grew more convinced than ever that the King was impeding the war effort and conspiring with the Feuilliants. They were determined on removing Louis and crushing their opposition. Lafayette rushed back from the front and denounced the events of 20 June. He called for the prosecution of the Jacobins and a return to law and order. But the royal family did not trust the hero of the American Revolution at all. After all, had he not made his reputation by fighting a war against monarchy? As for the left, the remnants of Lafayette's reputation had been destroyed by the Champ de Mars massacre for which he, and Bailly, were roundly blamed. He cut an utterly isolated figure. Revered at the start of the Revolution, he was now widely reviled.

Robespierre spotted an opportunity and arranged a temporary truce with Brissot to undo the Constitution he had previously defended. He also conveniently re-evaluated the conflict he had opposed as a 'war of liberty', totally different to a war of intrigue fought between tyrannous powers. Naturally, there was no suggestion that in altering his policies his previous position had been in error in any way. Robespierre's gift for semantics and justifications was only just taking flight. An action that was an atrocity when committed by monarchy was one of nobility when the perpetrators were 'free'

Frenchmen. The bodies would pile up just the same though, and in the lands they 'liberated' the French would impose their own style of government on the locals before helping themselves to whatever they fancied as the spoils of war. And when spoiling themselves, their generosity knew no bounds.

Sporadic outbursts of sectarian violence had been a feature of the last few years: In Nîmes, in the spring of 1790, some three hundred Catholic supporters had been killed while in La Glacière in October 1791 sixty Catholic citizens were brutally murdered by extremists. Now, in the domestic theatre, violence began to spiral again. In March Jacques Simmoneau brought soldiers into Étampes to protect the free market in foodstuffs from rioting mobs, but the soldiers refused to obey his orders and the crowd turned on him, shooting and stabbing him to death before battering his body to cries of 'Vive le Nation!' At Les Vans in the Ardèche on 12 July the Comte de Saillons had been arrested with four companions. A massive mob ripped them from their gaol cells, butchered them, decapitated them, and paraded their heads on pikes. The next day, at Jongeuse in the same department, a counter-revolutionary priest and nobleman were killed by a mob largely comprised of National Guardsmen. In the same month a dozen officials were murdered in Toulon, two priests killed in Bordeaux and six suspects done away with in Marseilles. In Ardèche battalions of volunteers had butchered several hundred potential rebels and torched nearby villages suspected of complicity. As the violence spread to neighbouring provinces there were scores of lynchings. Attacks against the rich still proliferated too. Lally-Tollendall had witnessed one such assault on his friends, the Listenay family. He described Mme. Listenay and her daughters fleeing from the Château de Sauilay as it burned. The Chevalier d'Ambly was dragged to a dunghill, his hair and eyebrows were torn out and acquaintances of theirs were suspended over a well while the crowd debated their fate. A climate of hostility had long been encouraged. Now it was being released, and events like these were becoming ever more frequent.

Brissot had effectively ignored the king's veto and called in a Federal army of revolutionary troops from all over France. They came flooding into Paris during July and began conspiring with the sans-culottes, National Guard and other extremist political elements to remove the monarchy. On 30 July a sizeable contingent of armed workers arrived from Marseille and Provence. As they marched into the city they sang the *Song of the Army of the Rhine*, composed on 25 April that year in Strasbourg by Claude Joseph Rouget de Lisle, a young officer in the engineer corps. They made quite an impression and the song was eventually renamed *La Marseillaise* in their honour. Today it is widely regarded as the best, most rousing of all national anthems, but its lyrics are especially pertinent for that moment in time. 'The bloody standard of tyranny is raised against us...They are coming to butcher your sons and your wives. At arms citizens! Form your battalions! We march, we march so impure blood may water our soil.' The rousing and emotive timbre of that chorus can only have inflamed the righteously informed bloodlust that was beginning to grip France.

Much overblown propaganda has been spouted ever since about the troops of the Marseillaise and how they saved the Revolution. In fact, they accounted for a relatively small contingent of the forces which descended on Paris that summer, but as they were working men, as opposed to the bourgeoisie who made up the greater part of the total, they fitted the image the revolutionaries wanted to project. So their role was greatly romanticised and exaggerated. A young officer in the royal guards saw them otherwise as 'five hundred fanatics, three quarter of them drunk...followed by the dregs of the people.'[82] The National Guard from Marseilles were more radical than many of their colleagues, and between February and April of that year they had ruthlessly eliminated counter-revolutionary elements at Aix, Arles and Avignon, ending up lording it over Provence. Their role was inflated, not because they were indispensable to the Revolution, but over reverence for their brutality. In the twisted minds of the revolutionaries, it was a reflection of their virtue.

It is also likely that their role has been magnified because, even as they made such a triumphal, passionate entrance to the city, the Jacobins was in the process of receiving the Brunswick Manifesto, which had been issued by the commander in chief of the Prussian army five days earlier. It promised retribution should any harm befall the royal family, and the timely arrival of a large number of patriotic troops appeared fortuitous indeed. But if Brunswick hoped to save Louis, he doomed him instead. For the revolutionaries now felt they had nothing to lose. Forty of the forty-eight sections had signed a petition which demanded the King's removal. It was delivered to the Assembly by Pétion while a further petition, signed on the Champ de Mars on 6 August, ran to fifty-five pages. But, with the Assembly still divided on the issue, the impetus came from the Cordeliers and the sections. An Insurrectionary Commune, including Danton and Desmoulins, was established and met in the Hôtel de Ville. In the early hours of 10 August the bells of the Cordeliers church sounded the tocsin to draw out the activists. Revolutionary troops and sans-culottes swarmed onto the streets. It was to be one of the most pivotal days in history.

The Terror

Arthur Young, who had previously defended the Revolution, later altered his position and joined the growing tide of opposition to events in France; those who watched the crisis unfold with mounting horror while slowly waking up to the fact that Edmund Burke had been right all along. Young justified his abrupt change of heart by claiming that

'the same principles which directed me to approve the Revolution in its commencement...led me to detest it after the 10th of August...The Revolution before the 10th of August was as different from the Revolution after that day as light from darkness, as clearly distinct in principle and practice as liberty and slavery.'[83]

It is difficult to dispute these assertions. Violence had been a feature of the Revolution since its outset, but it had been sporadic, sparse even, certainly in comparison with what was to come. It really did all change on 10 August 1792. It began with the carnage of that day, and was to explode again in the bloodshed of the September Massacres that swiftly followed. From that autumn executions became an increasingly common feature of a punitive and repressive state, while from the following spring it was joined by the holocaust of the Vendée and the unbelievable atrocities perpetrated in Lyon and other parts of France. Finally, the Terror was unleashed on the nation - almost a full year of quite sickening slaughter. The scale of the horrors that France endured in that two year period are almost impossible to comprehend, and they all began on that summer's day in 1792.

The causes of the explosion of violence that swept France are complex, but it can be no coincidence that this sudden escalation happened following 10 August when those representing the right were driven from the political sphere. It is also undeniable that the characteristics directly responsible for the disaster mirror those that yet mar the political left: that certainty of conviction, the violent hatred for their political rivals, the tendency towards rage in protest and revolt, the determination to snuff out contradiction, the preference for insults and denunciation over debate, and the belief that they were engaged in a moral crusade. The activists were also primarily middle class, educated and virtuous to a fault. This was the calamitous cocktail that was to devastate France and much of the continent.

With the monarchy critically undermined the remaining right-wing deputies drifted away from the Assembly and the left were no longer constrained by conservative elements. There were moderates remaining on the left too, decent people who genuinely sought to improve the quality of life in France, but they would prove powerless to resist their radical brethren. The net of persecution was to be considerably widened under the new regime. While initially it had been aristocrats and the clergy who were the primary targets, now any who failed to conform to the new political landscape were considered suspect. This was to include not just 'counter-revolutionaries', but increasingly anyone who was lukewarm about developments. Around 80% of the people who would die in the course of events would be drawn from the peasantry and urban working classes, those whose rights the Revolution was supposed to advance. The new authorities brought inflation, food shortages, war, repression, intolerance, fear, censorship and retributive justice. The disgruntled populace protested these developments and were killed for their impertinence in a manner and on a level unimaginable under the old regime. Once the left attained a monopoly of the political sphere the consequences were all too apparent: factional strife, vituperative recriminations, accusations and denunciations, with violence and bloodletting on a scale that chills the soul.

Around 20,000 armed revolutionaries descended on the Tuileries palace that morning, with about 900 loyal Swiss Guards prepared to defend it. Unknown to both sets of belligerents their stand-off was academic. The King and his family had already been persuaded to abandon the residence at about 8.30 that morning and were sheltering in the confines of the Assembly. Accounts differ as to which side fired first, and in the final analysis it hardly matters. The Swiss Guards were certainly the *effective* side in the early stages, and their discipline and training were evident as they unleashed volleys into the besieging forces. They caused terrible carnage, but as their ammunition ran low they began to retreat, the mob swarmed after them, the withdrawal turned into a rout, and the true slaughter began in earnest.

As the Guards fled in disarray their protagonists deliriously set about them. The palace and surrounding area descended into a scene of chaos and savagery as the Swiss troops attempted to escape and discard their uniforms. But they were pursued and set upon by large numbers of frenzied attackers. Domestic servants were swallowed up by the carnage as mobs rampaged through the palace, cornering their victims or dragging them from hiding places before they were hacked, clubbed, battered and butchered in an appalling orgy of violence. Their bodies were stripped and mutilated, limbs hacked off and genitals severed before being stuffed into gaping dead mouths or thrown to dogs to eat. The carnage ranged over a wide area and there was horrible butchery in the Place de la Concorde.

Mr. Twiss, an English visitor to Paris, described the scene in the aftermath of that morning's events. He found the bridges, streets and gardens in a wide area around the Tuileries littered with bodies and the walls splashed with blood. So much was spilled that it had collected in large pools in the gravel while drunks, sans-culottes spattered with gore and crazed looters clad in Marie-Antoinette's dresses ran amok through the streets.[84] Marie Grosholz, later famous as Madame Tussaud, reported the same grisly scene. Inside the Tuileries the carnage was even worse and corpses were piled up in the blood-smeared rooms and staircases of the palace. Thus ended the monarchy in France. Yet Robespierre called it 'the most beautiful revolution ever to honour humanity'.[85] Around 1,000 died in total, in the region of 600 Swiss Guards and 400 of those who had stormed the residence. The events of that day confirmed what had begun on 14 July 1789. Whenever due democratic process did not give the left the result they wanted the recourse to violence would follow almost immediately. It was a feature that would be repeated time and again over the coming months and years.

The reaction overseas was revealing about the culture of radicalism: its blindness to atrocities carried out by its ideological brethren and its willingness to condone actions it would have furiously condemned if perpetrated by others. A large celebration was held at White's Hotel in Paris on 18 November 1792 where British, Irish and Americans gathered. Following the deposition of the King and the horror of the September massacres, even while majority opinion swung away from the Revolution, much of the intellectual and literary elite of Britain, Ireland and America remained supportive and keen to build bridges between themselves and the Jacobins. Charles James Fox continued to be an ardent enthusiast of the Revolution long past this point too. A strong vein of feminist support also endured. Olympe de Gouges and Helen Maria Williams, who were both committed to democracy and black emancipation as well as women's rights, were vociferously supportive of the Revolution, as were Mary Wollstonecraft, Charlotte Smith and Etta Palm d'Aelders. Just as they would later do with Stalin, the liberal 'intelligentsia' continued to endorse the regime long after it was guilty of the most horrific crimes.

Following their overthrow the monarchy was suspended and the royal family incarcerated in the Temple prison. In the wake of 10 August effective power resided not with the Assembly but with the Insurrectionary Commune. The new body, though dominated by the Cordeliers, had close links with the sections and the Montagnards. It reflected the alliance of radical militants, sans-culottes and artisans who had been instrumental in the battle of the Tuileries. Militant agitation and the language of class conflict may not have caused the Revolution, but it took over, and played a significant part in the rising levels of bloodshed. On 12 August the Paris Commune was joined by Robespierre. It promptly issued demands that the Assembly set-up a Revolutionary Tribunal to try the 'criminals' who had opposed the overthrow of the monarchy. It was established on 17 August, a guillotine was erected on the Place du Carousel in front of the Tuileries and on 21 August it claimed its first victim, Louis Collot d'Angremont, secretary of the administration of the National Guard, who was accused of conspiring in the monarchist 'plot'. A royalist journalist, du Rozoi and the *intendant* of the King's civil list, Arnaud de la Porte, swiftly followed. The Tribunal, tasked with pursuing suspected enemies of the Revolution, was granted extraordinary powers to bypass due legal process. In August 1792 a true revolutionary police state was created in Paris, and it came under the insistence and the aegis of the political left.

The clampdown on freedoms began almost immediately. Within weeks every organ of the royalist press had been shut down by the Paris Commune and their printing presses distributed to papers which had their political seal of approval. The activists' talk about freedom of the press and their opposition to censorship had been just that, talk. Such rights applied only to themselves. In November 1793 Chabot spoke in the Jacobins and left no illusions about the depth of their double standards.

> 'The freedom of the press was necessary against tyranny and the nation approved this liberty; but that this same nation can instinctively distinguish the true limits of this liberty is proved by its approval of the smashing of the presses of Gorsas and other [Gironde] counter-revolutionary journalists. The freedom of the press is necessary for the support and defence of liberty; those are its limits...this freedom should not degenerate into a licence which might destroy it.'[86]

Their determination to expunge any trace of inconvenient views from the cultural and political spheres knew little bounds. The arts were a particular area of contention in this period. The Feuilliants had promoted freedom of the theatre, a policy virulently opposed by Louise de Kéralio, a leftist Rousseau disciple. She derided the light entertainment available as 'immoral' and pressed for theatre management to eliminate insignificant and frivolous entertainment in favour of patriotic dramas. She joined the sans-culottes' drive for uncompromising popular censorship. It resulted in the theatre becoming an organ for leftist propaganda from that point on. It was a profoundly censorious and puritanical streak that came to be shared by the majority of radicals on the far-left, Robespierre and Marat among them.

Brissot also stamped down on freedom of the theatre and the press. He particularly opposed any pamphlets that were either pro-royalist or pornographic. The Commune issued a directive which declared that theatrical performances had 'a powerful influence on the morale of peoples, they needed to be incorporated into the scheme of public instruction'.[87] Such sentiments had already been apparent on 30 June 1790 when the Théâtre de la Nation premiered *Barnevelt*, by Lemierre, a drama about Oldenbarnevelt's downfall in the Dutch Republic in 1618. The audience dutifully, if embarrassingly, gave wild applause to its most republican moments while a defiant monarchist spectator, who hissed at such interludes, was hounded from the arena for refusing to conform. A play by Jean-Louis Laya, *Amis des Lois*, saw its opening on 2 December disrupted by scuffles as members of the Commune attempted to shut it down due to its unflattering portrayal of Robespierre.

Even conversation began to be monitored; the familiar 'tu' as an address came to replace the formal 'vous', a move that had been advocated by leftist intellectuals like Louise Kéralio since 1790. Out went Monsieur and Madame and in came 'citizen'. Failure to comply would almost inevitably provoke suspicion or even physical assault. Anger was also directed at icons of royalty and paintings and statues of past kings were torn down or demolished. Busts of those previously lionised but now tainted with royalist associations, like Lafayette, Bailly and Necker, were smashed, and statues of Brutus or Rousseau erected in their place.

Attacks against any who failed to conform to the revolutionary 'consensus' continued spiralling. François Suleau, a student with Robespierre at the Louis-le-Grand who was a royalist and editor of *Actes des Apôtres,* was killed by a mob after being pointed out to the sans-culottes by Théroigne de Méricourt, the woman whose attire had made her so conspicuous when the fishwives had descended on Versailles. She was a republican campaigner for women's rights but not, evidently, the rights of anyone with an opinion that differed from her own. The duke of La Rochefoucauld was another of the victims. He had played an important role in supporting the early revolution and was a close friend of Franklin, Jefferson and numerous significant philosophers, but as president of the department of Paris he was now regarded by the militants as not revolutionary enough, and was butchered in a frenzy of violence.

The surveillance organs of the sections and the Revolutionary Tribunal went into overdrive and more than a thousand people were incarcerated on shaky pretexts. No evidence was required and large numbers of priests and the personal servants of the royal family were gaoled, as well as many who had opposed the protest of 20 June or the prosecution of Lafayette. The latter had subsequently gone into exile on August 19, crossing over the frontlines and falling into the hands of the Austrians who promptly imprisoned him. The hero of the American Revolution would not be released for several years. Counter-revolutionary suspects, when arrested, were frequently pelted with mud and punched by baying crowds that gathered to witness their humiliation, but worse was to follow.

The Austrians and Prussians were rolling back French forces on the frontiers, and when the Duke of Brunswick entered France on 19 August, and Verdun fell shortly afterwards, the paranoia in Paris began to reach fever pitch. In the increasingly hysterical atmosphere Danton warned of fifth columnists at home. Rumours began to spread of counter-revolutionaries in the prisons who would whip up the other inmates and break out to massacre Parisians after the troops left for the front. Marat was characteristically blunt and graphic, urging 'good citizens to go to the Abbaye, to seize priests, and especially the officers of the Swiss guards and their accomplices and run a sword through them'.[88] Danton's friend, the poet and playwright Fabre d'Eglantine called for 'the blood of traitors to be the first holocaust to liberty, so that in advancing to meet the common enemy, we leave nothing behind to disquiet us'.[89]

The September massacres that followed were certainly organised, relatively rigorously too, though direct culpability has never been verified. Whether it was Danton, Robespierre, the Commune or the sections is open to conjecture, and suspicion has fallen on all of them. The only thing that can be said with confidence is that the impetus and the perpetrators came from the left, for that was all that remained of French politics. And whichever hands directed events the killings themselves were carried out by the hard left sans-culottes activists. Tribunals were hastily assembled to give the slaughter a veneer of legitimacy and, while there were many acquittals, around 1,400 people were put to death out of some 2,700 who stood before the magistrates. The whole process happened in just a few days, sufficient testimony to the perfunctory nature of proceedings. Hearings, such as they were, were brief and arbitrary and 'sentences' were carried out on the spot. However, despite the brutality, the fact that tribunals and acquittals were involved suggests the killings were not part of some blood-crazed frenzy but were committed in an atmosphere of calm, rational and methodical calculation – a realisation that makes the crimes even worse.

The Massacres began when twenty-four priests, being conveyed to the Abbaye on 2 September, were herded into a garden, subjected to a prolonged assault and hacked to death by a variety of implements. Nineteen of them were cut into pieces. Later that evening a further 122 were condemned at the Abbaye, swiftly dragged outside and murdered with pikes. Another 150 priests were killed at the Carmelites, some shot while others were bludgeoned and stabbed to death. At the Bicêtre 162 were killed, forty-three of whom were under eighteen. The youngest was just twelve years old. At La Salpêtrière over forty prostitutes were physically humiliated and sexually molested before being brutally slain. Similar grisly scenes were repeated at numerous makeshift prisons scattered throughout Paris.

Few of the victims were overtly political, and many of them were drawn from the weakest and most disadvantaged classes of society, though some, inevitably, came from rather more privileged backgrounds. Marie-Louise, the Princess de Lambelle, the best friend and court favourite of Marie-Antoinette, and subject of many of the salacious but spurious lesbian rumours that had swirled around the Queen, was held at La Force. She was ordered to swear an oath of loyalty to liberty and equality and one of hatred to the King, Queen and monarchy. She accepted the first but refused the latter. Her defiance was just the excuse the mob was looking for. A crowd armed with axes and pikes hacked her to death, stripped off her clothes, and mutilated her genitals before decapitating her. Some reports suggest that she was raped and her breasts were cut off too. Yet this was still insufficient to satisfy her butchers. They stuck her head on a pike and headed off to the Temple where they waved their trophy triumphantly outside the window to the Queen's cell, calling for her to kiss her friend on the lips. Marie-Antoinette, when confronted with the gory spectacle, was so overcome that she fainted.

David Andress cites some contemporary accounts of the massacres which go into horrific details. One woman, hacked about the head, tortured and tormented as she was pushed around, was finally set on by a mob stabbing at her with pikes and sabres in such a frenzied assault that her corpse was left unidentifiable as even a human body, just an indistinct and shapeless red mass. Another woman was left naked and exposed for hours before suddenly having her head hacked off and genitals mutilated. A carriage was seen trundling through the streets with various body parts carefully arranged like a macabre work of art. It ferried a dancing revolutionary who wielded a head on a pike in wide, swooping arcs, while a colleague of his brandished intestines that had been ripped from another victim.[90]

The Commune made no attempt to pursue the killers and the violence quickly spread to the provinces. Politicians and journalists had done much to provoke the masses that September. But while exhortations are easy to find there is little evidence of condemnation in either press or private correspondence. A line had been crossed, and the supine or even supportive response of the Commune served to rubber stamp the horror. When it came to the protection of revolutionary principles it seems that anything was justified, and no amount of blood was considered excessive. But the fact that so much killing was done methodically, under the illusion of just cause rather than in the heat of passion, makes events even more chilling to this writer. The culprits of those terrible crimes were armed less with pikes and halberds than with ideology. It was their political convictions that justified their actions and girded their sinews, however much it was dressed up in patriotism and condoned as necessary for the survival of the nation. In reality, innocents died over a delusion. Robespierre brushed off the murders in his usual fashion, declaring that the priority should be to 'weep instead for the hundred thousand victims of tyranny'.[91] As Ruth Scurr points out, in doing so he was glossing over 'the deaths of forty-three frightened children at the Bicêtre reformatory'.[92]

These sorts of justifications litter Robespierre's musings. He had famously asked 'Citizens, do you want a revolution without a revolution?'[93] He appeared to give carte blanche for all manner of transgressions when announcing 'The

Revolution is illegal; the fall of the Bastille and of the monarchy were illegal – as illegal as liberty itself'.[94] His earlier tacit support of rioting had already shown he was not particularly squeamish about death if it served the Revolution, or, at least, if it served his own definition of what that revolution was. It was his utter faith in the moral righteousness of his cause that allowed him to take that step, and he maintained his belief in the virtue of his actions, borne, as they were, out of nobility of purpose, until the very end of his life. The imposition of revolutionary measures superseded all other considerations. Faith in it was so strong that the ends justified any means of getting there, and so virtue became indistinguishable from vengeance. He was particularly scathing when the victims of revolutionary violence were wealthy. But for all his moralistic posturing Robespierre gives the impression that his political theory mattered more to him than people did, and his hatred of the rich was pathological.

By this point in events the star of the Incorruptible was very much in the ascendancy, and the prim little man who exuded piety and dedication had become an unlikely sex symbol. But there is no evidence which suggests he ever acted on his newfound desirability. In fact, as far as the historical record is concerned, he may well have died a virgin. Whatever the truth, he was certainly far removed from the insatiable libido of Danton. Condorcet said of Robespierre that 'he says he is the friend of the poor and the weak and he attracts a following of women and the easily led...Robespierre is a priest and will never be anything else'.[95] Not all were won over so easily however. Olympe de Gouges wrote 'I resent and detest you...your twitching eyelid exposes the turpitude of your soul, and every hair on your head is criminal'. She accused him of wanting to climb to power on the bodies of the Brissot faction but presciently noted that his 'throne will be the scaffold'.[96] Manon Roland was sharply critical of Robespierre too, seeing not virtue, but intolerance. 'I know excellent citizens who have opinions contrary to yours, and I have never found you to be esteemed the less for seeing things from a different point of view. I have bemoaned your prejudices...and in this interval you raise public opinion against those who do not think like you.'[97]

Mere weeks after the Massacres of 2 – 6 September, the fears of the culprits were proven groundless. On 20 September, at Valmy, the French army sent the Prussians, the vaunted military machine of the late Frederick the Great, packing. Dumouriez, the leading general of the revolutionary army in the wake of Lafayette's defection, called it their 'Thermopylae'. The German poet and intellectual, Goethe, among the Prussian forces who melted away that day, noted 'From this place and from this day forth commences a new era in the history of the world'. He was more right than he knew. The new French Assembly was convening that very day and it would prove to be revolutionary in every sense of the word.

It had been necessary to elect a new body, now under the title of the National Convention, as the overthrow of the monarchy had made the existing constitution redundant. As a result of widespread intimidation, just six per cent of those eligible to vote in the elections had done so, and the result was a far more militant assembly than any which had sat before. The Feuillants and anyone else with royalist connections had been expelled, so the new body was no reflection of the diversity of French life. It was a radical government bent on retribution. The Convention would spend nine months wrestling with a new constitution before immediately suspending it and continuing to rule by fiat for another two years. It immediately set about establishing its credentials though, and on 21 September, the day after it convened, the monarchy was formally abolished and the Republic declared. For those taking part it was not just the start of a new legislative body but the birth of a brand new France.

Among the new deputies was the Englishman Tom Paine, who gained entrance by virtue of his reputation as the nemesis of Edmund Burke. He was joined by the youngest of the revolutionary class, Louis-Antoine Saint-Just, who was just twenty-four years old when taking his seat in the Convention. Saint-Just, another radical poet with a passion for drama and virtue, hailed from Artois. He cut a striking figure – instantly recognisable by a large hooped earring and dark luxurious locks that cascaded over his shoulders and framed a strikingly beautiful visage. In appearance, he somewhat resembled the New Romantics of the 1980s, and the strutting youngster would not look out of place in the line-up of Duran Duran or Adam and the Ants. Saint-Just would soon make an impression politically too, and he effectively became Robespierre's right-hand man. The two shared similar romantic notions of virtue, both loved the works of Rousseau, and they formed, not just a close political bond, but a genuine friendship. It would have significant repercussions for France. The Montagnards were joined by Danton, Marat, Desmoulins, Collot d'Herbois, Billaud-Varenne, and the partially paralysed Georges Couthon. They now came face to face with the Girondins for the first time in the Assembly.

The feuding in the Convention was now effectively left against left. Like religion, where the friction between Catholic and Protestant or Sunni versus Shia is more volatile than with any foreign agency, it was more vicious than it had ever been when it was left against right. While there were decent, realistic and moderate deputies of the left, they would prove powerless to resist their more radical brethren or to heal the divisions in their ranks. For the enmity between Montagnard and Girondin would soon reach boiling point. Yet the split was determined more by a sense of morality than any clear divisions in policy. Brissot was expelled from the Paris Jacobins on 12 October 1792 as the rift in the Assembly widened into a gulf. But while both sects would be equally guilty of shocking levels of vitriol, the Montagnards would ultimately prove more ruthless than their rivals.

The leading Girondins criticised the Montagnards for their role in the September Massacres and were convinced they had been targeted in that period. After all, the Commune's surveillance committee had searched Brissot's flat and issued arrest warrants for both he and Roland. They now, not unreasonably, feared for their lives. But their opposition regarded themselves as impeccably virtuous. Rosalie Jullien, the wife of a staunch Montagnard, was dismissive of the Gironde, asking 'How could such good individuals have become so vile?'[98] Robespierre, in terms reminiscent of the contemporary left, also saw the division as between 'the party of good citizens and the party of evil citizens, those who represent the French people and those who think only of their ambition and personal gain'.[99] But Louvet took an opposing stance. He declared that the Gironde were 'composed of philosophers' while the Mountain consisted of 'thieves, robbers and murderers'.[100] Morality was increasingly determined by political affiliation. Politically, both sects endorsed the abolition of the monarchy, supported the general principle of popular sovereignty, the repression of emigrant nobles and refractory priests and continued commitment to the war. But while the Mountain romanticised and glorified the people, the Brissotins were far warier, almost repelled by the mob.

Robespierre believed in the inherent goodness of the people, but that they had been corrupted by centuries of poverty and ignorance. He was equally convinced that as civilisation had eroded their natural virtue they would have to be suitably educated to regain it. But it never occurred to him that civilisation may have played a role in mollifying some of mankind's wilder instincts. His absolute distrust of monarchs also reveals an inability to take a nuanced and objective view, for while there had certainly been bad kings, there were plenty of good ones too. The institution of monarchy had simply been the best attempt to order society that earlier generations had been able to construct. Those states relied on great displays of power to persuade their populations into obedience, and this in turn allowed for the co-operation on which their achievements depended: a litany of triumphs from Ancient Egypt to Tsarist Russia.

The organisation, financing, security and stability of the monarchical system provided the platform for the Great Pyramids, Mozart's symphonies, and nigh on everything in between. Any evaluation of the flaws of that system must acknowledge those accomplishments too. The role played by kings facilitated the astonishing progress of not just European states, but also Asian ones like China, India and Japan which operated under remarkably similar systems. For what really mattered was not the titles of various offices in the administration but the behaviour of the people who filled those positions. In the changing world of eighteenth century France it is true that monarchy had outlived its time. Yet the difference between the reality of the institution and its perception, especially in the fevered minds of the revolutionary class, is stark indeed. If Robespierre had read the *Basilikon Doron*, written in 1599 by James I for his eldest son Henry, and thus intended as a personal letter rather than an article of public propaganda, he would have learned that kings rarely regarded their position as a privilege. It was more often viewed as an awesome responsibility, and many cared deeply for how the role affected their subjects. A perusal of that text gives the impression of kingship as a thing far removed from the tyrannical despotisms that the revolutionaries perceived them to be. Yet Robespierre's conviction that he knew best, and that his motivations were pure, would create a tyrant worse than virtually any king who had ever lived.

On 20 November the correspondence between Mirabeau and Louis was revealed after being unearthed in a secret compartment in the Tuileries. It destroyed the reputation of the Comte with the revolutionary class, and the former doyen of the radicals was unceremoniously slung out of the Pantheon. It also acted as the prelude to, and the pretext for, the trial of the King. He was to be accused over the flight to Varennes, his apparent perjury when agreeing to the constitution of 1791, and of conspiring with the émigrés to undermine the Revolution. Other charges of bribery, corruption and a desire to reinstate his tyranny were thrown in too. On 11 December Louis was called to the Convention as a pre-trial witness and was accused, with no trace of irony, of being 'responsible for shedding French blood'.[101] The Gironde largely favoured clemency or exile, but the Montagnards sought his death. Tom Paine also argued in favour of sparing the King's life. The radicals had been star-struck by Paine's arrival, but they turned on him bitterly for siding with the Girondins and advocating humanity and clemency at the trial.

Louis's chief defence lawyer was de Malesherbes, the great-grandfather of Alexis de Tocqueville, who would write with such clarity on the democracy that the revolutionary class desired, but failed so conspicuously to attain. It was at the king's trial that Saint-Just first made a mark when eloquently calling for the death of the tyrant.

'Some day men will be astonished that in the eighteenth century humanity was less advanced than in the time of Caesar. Then, a tyrant was slain in the midst of the Senate, with no formality but thirty dagger blows, with no law but the liberty of Rome. No one can reign innocently...the king must reign or die. He was the murderer of the Bastille, of Nancy, of the Champ de Mars, of the Tuileries. What enemy has ever done more harm?'[102]

Saint-Just, conveniently forgetting that it was revolutionary aggression that had shed blood in every example he listed, would soon outstrip Louis in the 'harm' stakes by a country mile. But such thoughts did not seem to occur to the revolutionaries, and Robespierre also spoke to justify his change of heart.

'For myself, I abhor the death penalty lavishly imposed by your laws, and I feel neither love nor hatred for Louis, I hate only his crimes. I have asked for the abolition of the death penalty...it can be justified only in cases where it is necessary for the safety of individuals or society. But Louis must die because the homeland must live.'[103]

The verdict was close, but in the final analysis it was a formality. On the evening of 20 January 1793, Louis was granted time to say his farewells to his family, when this decent man spent most of his time comforting *them*. The next morning he was taken to the place de la Révolution (today the place de la Concorde) where the guillotine had been set up. The streets were lined with soldiers, four deep, and 1,200 guardsmen accompanied Louis's carriage to the scaffold. He spoke with dignity and composure to the assembled throng. 'I die innocent of all the crimes of which I have been charged. I pardon those who have brought about my death and I pray that the blood you are about to shed may never be required of France.'[104] His last wish was to be in vain - for the nation which he had been invested to protect was about to descend even further into the abyss.

There were immediate repercussions to the execution; some rather more consequential than others. Louis-Michel Lepeletier, an aristocrat by birth, was another lawyer and former president of the Paris *parlement* who had sided with the Mountain after joining the Convention. He was among those who voted to execute Louis and on the evening of 20 January was celebrating with friends at a restaurant in the Palais-Royal. It was there that Pâris, a former royal bodyguard, approached the table and plunged a huge knife into his chest, conferring on him the dubious honour of being the first martyr of the Revolution. The Montagnard deputy, Jacques-Louis David, produced a painting to commemorate the event. It transformed the spectacularly ugly victim into a figure who was matinée idol handsome, though it was later destroyed by Lepeletier's royalist daughter. David's stunning visual airbrushing was, however, not the only propaganda inspired by the incident. Lepeletier's last words were 'I'm cold', but they were recast by the Montagnards who claimed that he had gasped 'I am content to spill my blood for my country; I hope it will soon serve to consolidate liberty and equality and to reveal their enemies.'[105] France would soon get the opportunity to test those principles on a far wider stage.

The revolutionary army had followed up their success at Valmy and the liberation of Verdun with victory at Jemappes on 6 November. Soon afterwards they occupied Mons and Brussels. A policy of liberation began to morph into one of occupation, based on requisitioning, steep taxation and indemnities. Rather than liberating the Belgians the revolutionary government imposed French sovereignty over them instead. But the execution of the King provoked enormous revulsion and just ten days after the blade had fallen, following weeks of deteriorating relations, France declared war on Britain and the Netherlands. In March they declared war on Spain too. The widening of the military front had disastrous consequences. On 2 March 1793 the Austrians shattered the French forces at Maastricht, and on 18 March they were driven from Belgium following a crushing loss at Neerwinden. In the wake of the defeat Dumouriez planned to march on Paris and overthrow the revolutionary government, but his plan failed and he defected to the Austrians. In the same week the Vendée exploded in revolt against the Republic.

Dumouriez had planned a coup as he blamed the run of defeats on the government's poor handling of the war effort. The Convention though saw it not as an attack against their personal competence but, naturally, a traitorous assault on France itself. The revolutionaries' actions were creating enemies everywhere, but in their own imaginations they were blameless for the opposition they were provoking. They were merely beset by traitors. Their solution was more of the same; repression and bullying on a scale as yet untested. It would have calamitous consequences, and the profound irony is that when the counter-revolution finally erupted, it came not from the aristocrats, clerics, émigrés or royalists the Jacobins feared, but from the very peasant classes they claimed to represent. While the advocates of 'virtuous liberty' had been enthusiastic in promoting peasant revolts, they could not comprehend the backlash when accused of despotism themselves.

The Vendée was a considerable area to the west of France with Nantes at its centre. In that part of the country the nobility and clergy were not despised or resented but formed an integral part of the community - so revolutionary doctrine fell on stony ground. A draconian deportation law of August 1792 against refractory clerics had replaced the area's Catholic priests with a new breed of constitutional clergy. They were largely unwelcome. Resentment at the authorities had already been bubbling away prior to such impositions, and it increased significantly when Louis was beheaded. But it was the attempt to wring yet more conscripts from the region to fight in the ever-widening revolutionary wars that finally ignited insurrection.

On 11 March a huge mob, angered by the arrival of recruiting officers, descended on the town of Machecoul and set about anyone associated with the administration. They stabbed the commanding officer, Maupassant, through the heart as his troops fled, while the constitutional priest, Le Tort, was dragged from his church and bayoneted in the face for ten minutes. In all forty men were murdered and 400 rounded up as prisoners and marched to the Calvairienne convent. There they were ordered to dig ditches. They were tied together in long rows with ropes passed under the arms, a method known as rosaries, before being shot and falling into the graves they had prepared. The revolt quickly developed into a full-fledged civil war and, apart from the revolutionary wars, consumed more lives than any other aspect of that terrible period. The Republican forces were unused to fighting in rural communities where it was impossible to tell friend from foe, and many of the missives from the troops are redolent of those produced during the Vietnam War.* The Abbè Bernier summed up the feelings of many of the rebels when announcing 'You have introduced atheism in the place of religion, anarchy in the place of laws, men who are tyrants in place of the king who was our father. You reproach us with religious fanaticism, you whose pretensions to liberty have led to the most extreme penalties'.[106]

But such complaints fell on deaf ears. The revolutionaries, assailed by disasters on all fronts, and blind to their own incompetence, perceived just one cause: conspiracy. Inspired by paranoid delusions of counter-revolutionaries, their answer was yet more repression, more surveillance, more killing. Robespierre's notebook reveals his chief priorities in that period: 'supervision of the press, punishment of conspirators and direction of public opinion'.[107] The effects of such punitive views were to be felt throughout France. On 11 March a new Revolutionary Tribunal was set up in Paris with Antoine Fouquier-Tinville named public prosecutor. Representatives were sent out to the provinces to ensure the regional Communes complied with the State's sovereign will. Those Communes were equipped with committees of surveillance and all citizens were encouraged to denounce anyone they suspected of uncertain loyalties. On 6 April a Committee of Public Safety was set up; it would become, in light of its role in repressing and executing ever greater numbers of French citizens, perhaps the most ironically named organ in human history. Danton proclaimed 'let us be terrible so that the people will not have to be'.[108] As the regime tightened its grip the nature of their rule, and the culture of class hatred they had encouraged, created ever more severe consequences, even as war and the inefficiency of the new regime resulted in further shortages.

Food riots had begun in February, and the government's attempts to alleviate the situation by printing paper money, assignants, only led to inflation which rapidly pushed up prices. Large demonstrations called for a 'maximum' to be imposed on the price of bread, and grocery shops and warehouses were

---

* When facing similar conditions in the Peninsular war some fifteen years later the citizens' army referred to the enemy combatants as 'la petite guerre', *'guerrilla'* in Spanish, coining an enduring new phrase.

attacked by radicals dubbed the Énrages (the furious). They were an extremist group to the left of the Mountain, characterised by red liberty caps and large bushy moustaches, and they raised the level of violent animosity sweeping France to unprecedented heights. They were not organised in any way and had no leadership to speak of, but the movement still threw up some significant figures, like Jacques Roux who blamed the financial situation on 'profiteers'. Roux, along with his compatriot Jean Varlet, a well off man supported by a generous inheritance, cried that 'Monopolists, hoarders and speculators should be punished by death, and if the government refused to institute these penalties, then the people should themselves launch a new round of massacres against the "blood-suckers"'.[109]

Varlet, Roux and others inflamed crowds with their emotive speeches, contrasting the nobility and decency of the sans-culottes with the duplicitous, avaricious and pompous rich who lived off the toil of the urban proletariat. They called for heavy taxation and seizures of property, favouring a renewal of violence as the answer to the Revolution's political problems. They even attacked small shopkeepers, as well as large scale capitalist speculators. But while it was easy for radicals to pin the culpability on capitalist scapegoats, the problems were largely self-inflicted. They seemed entirely unprepared to accept that it was not greed and hoarding that were driving up prices but war, disruption to trade, and the fact that incentives had been eroded under the new regime. While the Énrages claimed to defend the poor from capitalist exactions, bankers and big merchants, they were really driven by prejudice, anger and a shaky grasp of economics. Their ideas were simplistic, lazy caricatures aimed at fostering resentment and division, but the Jacobins would broadly adopt them in the summer of 1793. For the culture of revolutionary anger was now expressed in an aversion to, not just nobility, but wealth, aspiration and success of any kind - to exactly the type of meritocracy the revolt was initially designed to create. It would merely worsen the problems of inflation and food shortages which beset the creaking revolutionary economy, and Robespierre's speeches increasingly pandered to such sentiments.

'It is the people who are good, patient, generous...The rich and powerful thirst after honours, wealth and sensual enjoyment. The interest and desire of the people is that of nature itself, of humanity; it is the general interest. The interest and desire of the rich and powerful; is that of ambition, pride, greed and the wildest fantasies of passions that are fatal to the happiness of society as a whole. The abuses that have ravaged society were always their doing. These men have always been the scourge of the people.'[110]

The Énrages began calling for the arrest of the leading Girondins. Their demands helped to further polarise the Convention. Brissot had warned of the activities of these levellers 'who want to level the talents, the knowledge, the virtues because they possess nothing of these'.[111] On 1 April 1793 Jérôme Pétion also cautioned the bourgeoisie on the coming cataclysm. 'Your property is threatened, yet you close your eyes to this danger. War is being stirred up between the haves and the have nots, yet you do nothing to avert it.'[112] The sentiments of the Énrages quickly turned into excuses for robbery, intimidation, appropriation, violence, incarceration and murder, and such incidents spread rapidly. Radicals in Marseilles were extracting reparations and levying indemnities on the rich in a wide area as early as 1792, while in 1793 a Terror was enacted on the prosperous inhabitants of Salon. A climate of violence predominated: forced loans were extracted, property pillaged or destroyed and the bourgeoisie locked up or executed. More and more people began taking the law into their own hands and many were imprisoned on the basis of their income alone.

In the seething tension that assailed revolutionary France that spring Pierre Vergniaud commented memorably and presciently on 13 March: 'So, citizens, it must be feared that the revolution, like Saturn, successively devouring its children, will engender, finally, only despotism with the calamities that accompany it.'[113] That violence went hand in hand with another steep rise in censorship. Just days before he spoke two Girondin printing presses had been smashed by revolutionaries whose commitment to freedom of the press extended only to those they agreed with. On 29 March the Convention passed a draconian decree stating that anyone printing royalist propaganda would be sentenced to death. As a result, the former prior of the Abbey of the Trinity at Clissou, André-Jean Saint-André, who had penned a pamphlet urging the people to revolt and restore the monarchy, was guillotined on 21 April along with one of Dumouriez's colonels. Plenty more were to follow. The strictures also clamped down on pornography and made it illegal for anyone to display pictures of the royal family in their own homes. The developing culture of anti-royalism soon saw the site of the abbey at Saint-Denis, the resting place of France's kings and queens, ransacked. The remains of former monarchs were unceremoniously flung in a pit.

More press restrictions followed. In Cambrai it was asserted that 'those who hold different opinions is not a good citizen'.[114] All journalists or writers hostile to the regime were shut down immediately. The few remaining freedoms of the stage were strangled too. Theatres staging the 'wrong' sort of plays were closed and their directors arrested. On 27 September Pierre-Yves Barré, who had staged *La Chaste Suzanne* at the Vaudeville, and several of his leading actors were imprisoned while Voltaire's *La Mort de César* (1733) was revived at the Théâtre de la République with a 'better' ending appended by the politically suitable Louis-Jérôme Gohier. By mid-March 1794 the Comité d'Instruction

Publique demanded the compulsory submission of all scripts to the censor for approval. Paris theatres were ordered to present weekly performances of tediously worthy republican tragedies like *Brutus, Guillame Tell* and *Gaius Gracchus* which glorified revolutionary zeal and the virtues of liberty's champions.

By that point the violence and tyranny in France had spiralled out of control. It was in the volatile spring of 1793 that Théroigne de Méricourt, while speaking up for the Girondins on the Terrasse des Feuillants, attracted the attention of a group of market women who supported the Mountain. They decided to register their displeasure by giving her a savage beating. Théroigne was stripped before being battered senseless. They might have killed her, but the attack was interrupted by a male bystander, with some saying her saviour was Marat. The victim recovered consciousness but the damage inflicted was of such severity that she never recovered her mind. She was committed to La Salpêtriére where she spent the next twenty years. By 1810 she lived naked in a dark cell, refusing any clothing, drinking from puddles in the courtyard and rambling incoherently on the Revolution, forever stuck on the topic she was debating when the vicious, unprovoked assault robbed her of her faculties.

That horrific attack was a symptom of a far wider culture. The Girondins were increasingly isolated against the unholy alliance of Mountain, Énrages, Commune, sections and sans-culottes. As a result, they opted to go on the offensive. They decided to focus their attack on their harshest critic - the most militant member of the opposition, the 'People's Friend', Jean-Paul Marat. The Gironde prepared a dossier listing his many calls for violence against members of the Convention. Marat was briefly arrested but quickly acquitted by some sympathetic judges before being chaired by a massive and euphoric crowd. But the attempted prosecution meant they had broken the principle of immunity for members of the Convention. It would soon be turned back on them.

On 15 April the Paris sections presented a petition demanding the expulsion of twenty-two Girondin deputies. That night Robespierre gave an impassioned speech in the Jacobins, forgetting his earlier defence of freedom of the press while bristling with violent intent. 'I demanded that the factions in the Convention cease to slander the people of Paris, and that journalists who pervert public opinion be reduced to silence...I demanded that the people make an effort to exterminate the aristocrats who are everywhere.'[115] The Gironde's reputation had been marred by the defection of Dumouriez, with whom many of their leadership had been close. They had also resisted the King's execution and expressed reservations about the imposition of the 'maximum', a fixed price on foodstuffs. As it transpired later, when the measures were passed, they were proven entirely correct to do so, but reality rarely affects such arguments. They were swimming against the tide, they were opposing a sans-culottes' *cause-célebrê*, and hysterical and emotive shrieking is always hard to compete against with rational argument. The policies of the Gironde may well have alleviated the crises created by the extremists but, propelled by hatred and conviction, the radicals would continue to drive France ever closer to the brink.

Faced with a political obstacle the Jacobins resolved, yet again, on violent insurrection rather than any appeal to democracy. On 31 May a huge crowd of petitioners besieged the Convention. The vocal contingent of Énrages in the Paris Commune had already persuaded an armed force of sans-culottes to agitate for a revolutionary programme. It included a punitive tax on the rich and the arrest of the Girondins; now they sought to impose it on the Convention by a show of force. The radical factions briefly united that summer, a concord illustrated by the addition of a new motto to Marat's paper. It declared 'let us tax the rich to subsidise the poor'.[116] It was a policy wholeheartedly endorsed by the Énrages, despite the fact that they were largely champagne socialists. Many, like Claude-Emmanuel Dobsen and J.B. Leys, were lawyers, while Louis-Henri Durorre had noble roots and an income of 20,000 livres a year. The deputies remained stubbornly unbowed by the pressure, so on 2 June the radicals prepared an even greater show of force. Around 80,000 thronged the Tuileries while Hanriot, of the National Guard, surrounded the Assembly with cannon. This finally forced the acquiescence of the Convention and persuaded them to hand over the Girondins. Twenty-nine deputies were placed under house arrest.

The hard left had engendered an anti-democratic and unconstitutional seizure of power. They would impose an increasingly severe dictatorship from that point on. The new regime demonstrated a staggering intolerance to any form of political non-conformity. The only acceptable response to their diktats was enthusiastic subservience. Any kind of resistance, questioning, or even apathy, would be met with startling brutality. The illegal nature of the insurrection sparked Girondin support in other parts of France, particularly Bordeaux, Marseilles, Toulon, Caen and Lyon where the Jacobins had been running a mini police state by imposing house searches, forced loans on the rich, spiralling arrests and the closure of opposing journals and societies. With France ripe for rebellion, the majority of the incarcerated Girondins leadership quickly slipped their bonds with many heading for refuge in Caen. There were even signs that a 'federalist' army may mobilise in the provinces against the dictatorship of Paris. In Lyon, Joseph Charlier had announced that 900 moderates must be found for the guillotine though a federalist rising imprisoned him before the threat could be carried out. In the event, the disparate nature of the areas resisting the regime, coupled with the severity of Jacobin oppression, prevented a truly widespread insurrection taking place. While dissent bubbled away, with terrible consequences to come, particularly in Lyon and Toulon, the federalist cause failed to inspire any real enthusiasm for war, bloodshed or martyrdom, qualities not lacking in those of a left-leaning persuasion. The federalist backlash ultimately failed because it lacked the determination and fanaticism exhibited by the Parisian radicals and their provincial kin.

On 24 June, with repression and despotism becoming ever more severe, Ducos declared it a scandal that the Brissotins had been illegally ousted from the Convention - the move of a tyrant or a Cromwell. He was appalled that no indictment had been issued detailing the charges against them, but Robespierre brushed off the idea that they should adhere to some sort of legal procedure. Such details were unnecessary: 'the people' had spoken. 'Someone here pretends we need a report as if the crimes of the detained were not known!...The Constitution will rally all France around us despite the clamours of the malicious 'factieux''.[117] In fact, not only was Robespierre about to suspend that same Constitution but posterity has proven that the 'crimes' of the Brissotins were nothing more than a tissue of lies, allegations and malicious rumour. The accused were guilty of nothing more than being the political opposition to the radical left, and for suggesting some practical policies in the face of increasingly extremist theorising. Yet, even as Robespierre spoke, Legrende threatened anyone who interrupted him with prison.

In the atmosphere of agitation now tearing France apart, Charlotte Corday, an attractive woman of twenty-five, arrived in Paris on July 13 and made her way to Marat's house. Corday, a Republican immersed in Rousseau and the standard Roman histories, had travelled from her home in Caen where a letter had been widely circulated. It read 'let Marat's head fall and the Republic is saved...Purge France of this man of blood...Marat sees the Public safety only in a river of blood; well then his own must flow, for his head must fall to save two hundred thousand others'.[118] Corday bluffed her way into Marat's quarters where, as was his practice, he was working in a cool bath. It was the only way to alleviate the psoriasis with which he was inflicted, a terrible skin condition that flared up in the summer heat. She claimed to have a list of traitors from Caen for his perusal and handed him a slip of paper. Without even looking at its contents, he replied 'Good, I will have them all guillotined'. At that point she slipped out the knife she had concealed in her skirt and plunged it deep into the Friend of the People's chest, severing his aortic artery and killing him almost immediately. Corday made no attempt to escape and was brutally interrogated to determine the scale of the conspiracy. After all, the suggestion that a slip of a girl could have acted independently was inconceivable, and all concerned knew there were counter-revolutionaries everywhere. The court even ordered that she be given a vaginal examination to prove that she was a whore; though, in the result, it revealed her to be a virgin instead.

Even as she was being cross-examined the revolutionary propaganda machine was amped up to eulogise the man whose poisonous pen had contributed so much to the carnage engulfing France. Streets and buildings across the nation were renamed in Marat's honour, his heart was embalmed and hung in an urn in the Cordeliers to inspire the members to follow the example of his 'virtue', and Jacques-Louis David organised an elaborate funeral service. The bath in which he was slain was borne aloft in the procession. Initially buried under a willow tree in the garden of the Cordeliers, his remains were moved to the Pantheon on 25 November 1793. David also produced a painting to commemorate the occasion. It is the single most stunning work of art of the period. Thankfully, unlike his tribute to Lepeletier, it survived the tumult of those years. It is a similarly airbrushed piece with Marat's psoriasis photoshopped out of existence. Instead of a list of traitors awaiting the guillotine, his desk is strewn with the generous bequest the saintly Marat was sending to a woman in need, and a letter from Charlotte Corday begging for his aid. Marat is depicted lying in repose enveloped in white sheets. He has the appearance of Christ gently lowered from the cross, his face frozen in an expression of tranquillity, as though a sigh has just left his body. The painting, which David finished in October, retains its mesmerising emotive power to this day and is eloquent testimony of how the revolutionary class perceived themselves. For all the bloodthirsty, divisive hyperbole they never tired of expressing, their self-image was one of virtuous, self-sacrificing martyrs, figures of pure nobility. Having failed to unearth evidence of any conspiracy, the authorities swiftly guillotined Charlotte Corday on 17 July. In November Adam Lux, whose sole crime was to publish a poem comparing her to Brutus, suffered the same fate.

The mantle of Marat was enthusiastically taken up by Jacques-René Hébert, already a figure of enormous significance in the Commune and, increasingly, in the Cordeliers too. He adopted crude and colourful working-class vernacular for his newspaper, *Père Duchesne*. It was named after a bad-tempered, foul-mouthed, pipe-smoking cartoon figure who was effectively the paper's mascot, a sort of socialist Andy Capp. Hébert's venomous prose made even that of Marat seem moderate in comparison, and it stoked up an ever more volatile political cauldron. His journal simplistically divided France into good and evil, honest patriots and malign conspirators, virtuous common folk and aristocratic counter-revolutionaries.

The situation seemed more critical than ever. Austrian, Prussian and English armies were pushing back French forces on the frontiers, and the spectre of federalist reprisals was rippling throughout France. Cities like Marseilles and Toulon were now in negotiation with the English to bring in supplies while the insurrection in the Vendée rumbled on. Danton believed that in such dire circumstances it was more desirable to mollify the factionalism splitting France. He recommended conciliation rather than escalation and resisted calls from the Commune for the trial of Marie-Antoinette. With Austria at the gates, her value as a hostage far exceeded her utility as a corpse. He looked for political settlements with the federalists and the Vendée, and opposed the economic policies of the Énrages and the Commune which called for extensive price controls and poor relief funded by swingeing forced loans on the rich. Danton's humanity and humour were part of a growing rift with the pious zealots of Jacobinism, and it was increasingly apparent that he had little in common with them. Georges-Jacques valued life, good company, drink and intimacy with women. Robespierre and co. prized virtue, the Revolution and inflexible idealism. Life seemed almost incidental. Growing increasingly estranged from the radicals, who were now driving events to ever further extremes, Danton was removed from the Committee of Public Safety on 10 July.

The Jacobins were not interested in seeking concord with any rivals, they preferred to focus on eliminating them, and a raft of new measures were rolled out to that effect. On 27 July Robespierre was elected to the Committee for Public Safety for the first time and, together with Saint-Just, Collot d'Herbois and Bertrand Barère, they were to seize an increasingly firm grip on events. Under their aegis it would become a terrible organ of repression. The representatives-on-mission, now dressed in flamboyant uniforms designed by David, were granted increased powers to extend Jacobin authority in the provinces. The Montagnards also employed their propaganda machine, focusing on the death of Marat to restore the public sympathies that had ebbed dramatically following their purging of the Girondins. A revolutionary army was created and sent out into the provinces to enforce the Convention's increasingly draconian measures. The creation of the army, which numbered 40,000 by the end of the year, would eventually allow the Revolution to secure its borders and crush the Vendéan revolt. It was an avowedly political force established to support and enforce the Jacobin manifesto. The Montagnards had created not just a police state but a military state, one demonstrably more punitive than the *ancien regimé*.

In addition to these developments a 'Law of Suspects' was passed on 17 September 1793. The exact nature of its implementation was left to the regional surveillance committees. They had been purged so that only radical patriots remained, and there was to be no appeal against their judgements. The law made identity cards compulsory and decreed that anyone could be arrested or put to death if 'either by their conduct, their contacts, their words of their writings, [they] showed themselves to be supporters of tyranny, or federalism, or to be enemies of liberty'.[119] There was no trace of irony intended by that last phrase.

Between August and October the number of inmates in Paris's prisons doubled. Collot d'Herbois illustrated the growing double standards when declaring that 'the rights of man were not made for counter-revolutionaries, but only for the sans-culottes'.[120] As the political climate grew ever more hysterical the punitive and vengeful policies of the Énrages proliferated. Their reforms were already causing rising economic turmoil, but they proved oblivious to such evidence. Jacques Roux appeared in the Convention on 25 June to proclaim that the 'commercial aristocracy [were] even more terrible than the nobility'. He called for war against the rich who he described as 'vampires'.[121] Maximum prices were imposed on foodstuffs with predictably disastrous results. Hordes descended on the shops and emptied them while suppliers refused to replace stocks until sufficiently remunerated. The hysteria became even greater on 2 September when word reached Paris that Toulon had opened up its harbour to the British navy under Admiral Hood. The Énrages, using the news that the enemy were now on French soil, whipped up angry mobs. They filled the streets for several days of wide-scale protests and descended on the Convention. It was under this pressure, in a heated meeting in the Jacobin club on 5 September, that Claude Roger claimed historical immortality by declaring that 'Terror must be made the order of the day'.[122]

The Terror would be the official policy of the regime for nine months. In that period approximately 17,000 were to be guillotined, mostly in the provinces. Many more died in custody or were lynched without trial, casualties which swelled the total to around 40,000. By December federalism and the Vendée rebellion were in retreat and France was winning the war effort, but the Terror would only continue to increase in severity. Many historians have defended the revolutionaries by claiming that the experiences of war forced them into ever more brutal methods of imposing their regime. Yet this is to ignore the fact that less oppressive methods, which may have proven more effective, were not even considered, never mind tried, and that the war was both started, and greatly extended, by the revolutionaries themselves. As such, they were the instigators of the situation, not the victims of it. The deputies were blaming everyone but themselves and conjuring phantoms to exonerate their failings. Their victims were nigh on universally innocent; individuals who posed no real threat to them or to anyone else. It does no credit for those with the benefit of hindsight to repeat their failings.

McPhee is one among many who seems guilty of this malaise. In his interpretation 'It was the desperate nature of the crisis of mid-1793, and the lack of resources or institutions to deal with it, that *forced* the deputies into *reluctant* suspension of civil liberties they would normally have seen as untouchable'.[123] The emphasis in McPhee's quote has been added as it seems to me that, in contrast to his conclusions, the radicals of the left enthusiastically embraced the opportunity to destroy their enemies. It is also undeniable that the atrocities committed by the Jacobins increased, not at the time when their status was threatened, but when their position was at its greatest strength. McPhee goes to extraordinary lengths to excuse the Jacobins, but the logic he applies may just as easily be used to justify the Holocaust. After all, Nazi Germany faced a situation on the Russian front easily comparable to the threat posed to Revolutionary France, and the existence of 'internal enemies', largely created by their own animosity, could be viewed as similarly threatening to their regime. Yet no one would offer such rationales. The Nazis' crimes were on a far greater scale, but the principle, to me, seems little different. Many states throughout history have faced crisis points and have not responded as the Jacobins did. Circumstances do not exculpate their guilt.

The Law of Suspects and the greatly increased powers of the Committee of Public safety led to the swift incarceration of 7,000 inmates in the now fifty places of detention In Paris, largely on the flimsiest of charges. There were 177 executions in just the last few months of 1793. The rule of law had been elbowed aside in favour of the personal whims of a 'moral' minority who felt their conduct to be unimpeachable. New revolutionary committees soon emerged as watchdogs. The Sociétié Populaire et République of the Paris section Droits-de-l'Homme, inaugurated with a bust of Marat in the hall, met daily to monitor activities in the area. It imposed 'patriotic' attitudes and 'correct' behaviour, and all were free to denounce suspects to its committee. It is the sort of organisation that brings to mind the religious police of contemporary Iran. Such societies proliferated and they strove to suppress monarchists, aristocrats, moderates, federalists, capitalists, traders, prostitutes, theatres and gambling. Pierre Gaspard Chaumette, who was publicly puritanical but privately a vigorously practicing homosexual, was particularly keen on clamping down on prostitution as a corrupt vestige of the *ancien regime*. He personally oversaw the arrests of scores of girls, a number of whom were destined for the guillotine. The quality of their trumped-up charges are illustrated by the trial of Eglé. A prostitute arrested for publicly criticising the new regime, she was also accused of having lesbian relations with Marie-Antoinette. Eglé dismissed her accusers by snorting that 'me who earned my living on street corners and would never have even made the humblest maid in her kitchen; that's really worthy of a bunch of crooks and imbeciles like you'.[124] For the high crime of pithily expressing such disparaging sentiments she was duly guillotined. The charges would be equally spurious when levelled at the most famous individual to fall under the blade in that period; the Queen herself.

The surviving members of the royal family had already experienced the full gamut of Jacobin hospitality since Louis's execution. Among the charges the Queen faced was that she had attempted to indoctrinate her eight year old son,

Louis-Charles, in royalism rather than Republicanism. He had been taken from her, dressed as a sans-culotte, had a red cap of liberty thrust on his head and was given a toy guillotine to play with in his cell. As the gaoler had dragged her son away he had shouted 'Don't be uneasy – the nation, always great and generous, will take care of his education'.[125] Hébert claimed that the boy had recovered his health since being separated from his mother and that he was better off under their care. In fact, he was kept in a dark, dank cell, full of his own excrement. Covered in insects and fleas, he came down with tuberculosis and in such squalid conditions he died, a lonely and frightened child, on 8 June 1795. He was just ten years old. One mercy is that at least his mother did not live to see his terrible fate.

Marie-Antoinette's trial, ostensibly centred on her alleged immorality and greed, simply regurgitated the fictions from a thousand pamphlets and pornographic comics, while Hébert and Fouquier-Tinville added some of their own for good measure. It is quite striking, given all the lies spread about her and the indignities heaped on her for years, that the authorities managed to plumb new depths that are hard to credit even now. The Queen was only thirty-eight when brought to the dock, though she appeared twenty years older, but she endured the trial with dignity even while scores of sans-culottes in the galleries bristled with contempt. She demonstrated remarkable resolve in the face of such hostility and certainly wanted no pity. Marie-Antoinette commented with some determination: 'I was a queen and you dethroned me – I was a wife and you murdered my husband – I was a mother and you have torn my children from me – I have nothing left but my blood – make haste to take it.'[126]

She lost her composure only once, briefly, when Hébert unveiled a confession he had forced Louis-Charles to sign. It declared the child's mother and aunt had enjoyed incestuous relations with him, masturbating the boy as he lay between them in the Queen's bed. She recovered to state that she would not lower herself to answer 'such a charge against a mother'.[127] Unlike the King who went to the scaffold in an enclosed coach with soldiers lining the streets and the shutters on every building closed, his wife was transported in an open tumbrel where she was exposed to the crowd who hurled abuse and spat on her from the balconies. David quickly sketched her as she was ferried to the guillotine on that 16 October, capturing the tragedy of her resolve and resignation in a few deft lines. Her last act was to apologise to her executioner when she stumbled slightly and stepped on his toe. Hébert revelled in her execution, particularly the visible fear she exhibited right at the last. In *Le Père Duchesne* he gloated of his joy at seeing the Queen's head 'separated from her fucking tart's neck'.[128]

Hébert, who couldn't get enough of such scenes, had also been calling for the trial and punishment of the Girondins for some months. While some, like

Brissot, had been rearrested and returned to Paris, those still at large were declared traitors in absentia and could thus be executed without trial. When the Girondin journalist Gorsas was caught slipping in to the capital to visit his mistress, he became, on 7 October, the first revolutionary deputy to be executed, having been prevented from speaking at his trial or on the scaffold. The Girondins were accused of orchestrating the federalist uprisings, of complicity in the Vendée rebellion, were linked to the assassination of Marat and were said to be agents of the British Prime Minister Pitt, all groundless indictments. Even as the charges were announced on 3 October by Jean-Pierre Amar the doors of the Convention were locked and a further seventy-five deputies who had protested the coup were arrested. They would remain in La Force prison for a year.

In these, as in all revolutionary trials that followed, the prosecutors were portrayed as wholly virtuous and selfless while the defendants were characterised as corrupt and avaricious. Robespierre drew allusions between the trial of the Gironde and the Catiline conspiracy. He portrayed that event as a first century BC attempt by an aristocratic faction under Catilina to seize power, and of the prompt and severe action taken by Cicero to foil it and save the Republic. Naturally the Incorruptible rather immodestly perceived himself as occupying the just and honourable Ciceronian position. In fact, Catalina's rebellion, though it had some noble backing, was largely a populist revolt with plebeian support that aimed to overthrow a corrupt oligarchy - the aristocratic faction's dominance of Rome. Cicero, lauded by the Incorruptible, was a brilliant advocate, but a man largely without principles or a spine. But then reality has never been a strong point for idealists.

Brissot and Vergniuad, in particular, employed the full range of their rhetorical brilliance when allowed to speak in their defence and made a mockery of the accusations. Robespierre responded with alacrity and used the Committee of Public Safety to change the rules of the Revolutionary Tribunal. The presiding judge was allowed to terminate proceedings after three days if the jury agreed that they had been suitably 'enlightened' to the facts. Their compliance was immediate, and the unanimous verdict of guilty swiftly followed. On the announcement of their sentence one of the defendants, Charles Dufriche-Valazé, stabbed himself in the chest and expired on the spot. Fouquier-Tinville ordered his corpse to be guillotined anyway, and it was. On 31 October the remaining Girondins defiantly sang the Marseillaise on the way to the scaffold where their twenty-two heads fell in just thirty-six minutes.

Many more fell under the blade that autumn. Olympe de Gouges had written a *Declaration of the Rights of Women* early in the Revolution, but after expressing humanitarian sympathy for the King she had been slung in gaol. On

4 November she was dragged out again and beheaded. She had bemoaned the fact that

'an arbitrary law worthy of the Inquisition, that even the *ancien régime* would have blushed to implement, imprisons the *esprit humain* and has wrested my liberty from me in the midst of a free people. Is not liberty of opinion and the press consecrated as the most precious patrimony of man in Article VII of the Constitution?'[129]

Just four days after she implacably went to the blade the King's cousin Philippe-Égalité, the duc d'Orléans, who had been such a friend to the reformists in the early days, also went to the guillotine. Manon Roland's trial consisted of little more than a cursory mention of her husband, her role as the hostess of the Gironde salon and her 'unnatural' female interest in politics. The irony of her being tried by a panel of her intellectual inferiors would no doubt have been lost on the tribunal. On hearing the news on 9 November, two days after her execution, her husband emerged from his hiding place in Rouen, stepped out into the countryside, wandered down a lane, found a beautiful spot in the shade of a magnificent tree, and committed suicide. Jean-Sylvain Bailly had administered the Tennis Court Oath but, as the mayor of Paris, he was considered responsible for the Champ de Mars massacre, and was guillotined on 11 November. His execution took place on a specially erected scaffold on the site of his crime in freezing rain before a massive crowd who hurled insults and spat on him, all of which he took stoically.

On 29 November Antoine-Barnave, the Feuillant leader who had guarded, and flirted with, Marie-Antoinette on the royal family's escort back from Varennes, suffered the same fate. On 8 December the last great 'official' mistress of Louis XV, Marie-Jeanne du Barry, also went to the guillotine. She was rumoured to have been a prostitute whose talent for arousing the ageing monarch had won her political influence before she had been forced into a convent on the King's death in 1774. Now, aged fifty, she was dragged out again and executed, effectively for the crime of owning jewellery. A grisly fate awaited the remaining Brissotins as well. Guadet, Salles, Birotteau and Barbaroux were eventually caught near Bordeaux and guillotined in the city along with six members of Guadet's family accused of hiding them. Pétion and Buzot, Manon Roland's former lover, fled into the countryside on hearing of the arrests but, finding all avenues of escape closed off by the Montagnards sent to apprehend them, committed suicide in a field. Their bodies were only discovered some time later, half eaten by wolves. Condorcet, in hiding near Paris, was eventually captured in March 1794 but allegedly took poison and died in his cell.

It was not all a relentless cascade of slaughter of course, and the revolutionaries made clear their intent to rewrite the world they inhabited in every way imaginable. On 20 September Gilbert Romme unveiled his new calendar, one that utilised a decimal system and drew its names from nature and rustic virtue. It consisted of twelve months of thirty days each with the 'spare' five or six days given over to public festivals. Months were in turn divided into three weeks of ten days, with just one day of rest. It was Philippe Fabre d'Eglantine who named the months to reflect the year's natural cycle, so Germinal = budding, Prairial = meadows, Thermidor = heat, Brumaire = fogs, and so on. Days were to be renamed too and in a foretaste of the Soviet era were given names like sickle day and plough day. It was backdated to 22 September 1792 so the day after the monarchy was abolished became the first day of year I of the Republic – the new founding event that supplanted the birth of Christ.

Rather more enduring was the metric system of weights and measures which, after five years of study and hearty endorsements from the likes of Condorcet and Talleyrand, was finally adopted on 7 April 1795. There were other genuine efforts at reform, particularly through Year II (September 1793 – September 1794). Illegitimate children were to be considered equal in the eyes of the law, primary schools were to be set up across the nation to educate the poor and ten million livres was to be provided for a raft of welfare programmes. Under this system of social security they aimed to create a welfare state. It included measures to provide relief in cases of severe economic distress while making provision for medical benefits, old-age pensions and special grants for large families. Property seized from victims of the Revolutionary Tribunal was to be distributed among the masses, and on 4 February 1794 a decree was passed abolishing slavery in the French colonies. Measures were also taken to improve the social rights of women while continuing to restrain their political rights. The Convention abolished the radical club of Revolutionary Republican Women who had been harassing working women in the marketplace, bullying them and forcing red caps on their heads. Men, whose activism was, it need not be said, far more extreme, escaped any such legislation.

However, despite their announced good intentions, most of the proposed measures were never actually implemented. Such policies were usually left to the representatives-on-mission. While some, like Gilbert Romme, worked assiduously to improve conditions in their locale, most prioritised the persecution of their enemies instead, real or imagined. There was, as ever, a clear discrepancy between the idealistic rhetoric and the punitive actions of the left. De-Christianisation spread rapidly from this point too. Perhaps the greatest instigators of that policy were Joseph Fouché and Pierre Gaspard Chaumette, representative-on-mission in Nièvre. They began ransacking and closing churches in September while advancing the cult of Reason. Not satisfied with obliterating any traces of Christianity from their calendar the militants began to remove Christian references from place names the way they had already done with those linked to royalty. But a new religion arose to replace the old. Celebrations were held in Notre Dame in honour of a statue of liberty and a 'Goddess of reason', while sans-culottes knocked the heads off Gothic saints carved on the cathedral's exterior. Throughout the country, sweeping changes were wrought by urban militants who expended more energy denying spiritual comfort to the peasantry than they did catering to their material needs.

Amidst this reformist zeal, Robespierre proposed a raft of policies aimed at the 'regeneration' of France and its people. Children would be removed from their parents for six or seven years to receive their 'education' – a schooling that would consist of indoctrination in revolutionary ideals. It was a scheme of social engineering that revealed a desire to control every aspect of people's lives. His system was all-encompassing, including civic study, physical exercise and manual work, as well as clothing and food. The programme is eerily reminiscent of those practised by modern Communist states and Nazism, in particular Hitler's youth movements. Jacobin culture aimed to build a new public morality. It brimmed with idealised depictions of domesticity and the purity of rustic labour - the sans-culottes family gathered nobly round their plough. These too were precedents of the sort of imagery favoured by Soviet Russia, Nazi Germany and Communist China, as well as the brochures distributed by the environment movement which dream of an idyllic, bucolic, 'sustainable' lifestyle.

Robespierre's manifesto was rejected, but his determination to transform the nation and its citizens was unaffected. In June he had proclaimed that 'There must be one single will – *une volanté une*.'[130] In Rousseau's theoretical model individual will had to be subordinated to the general will. In reality, that will rested in a small clique of elected representatives and their hand-picked agents. They ensured that any who queried their approach were excluded from the political community. It was, as Andress cites, 'a formula for an ever-narrowing definition of political purity and legitimacy, in a political climate that already assumed the worst of all opposition'.[131] In their pseudo-religious assurance the Jacobins were convinced they alone had the right to hold a political opinion; a strange sort of 'liberty' indeed. Their coercive, totalitarian utopia would, in consequence, turn out to be less of an idyll and more of a Hades. The price of liberty was to be freedom. Only conformity to the diktats of their political masters would 'free' the French. There were to be only republican ministers, republican newspapers, republican representatives and republican government. Saint-Just left nothing to the imagination when outlining how anything less than demonstrative zeal for the government was to be considered a crime.

'There is no prosperity to hope for as long as the last enemy of liberty breathes. You have to punish not only the traitors, but even those who are indifferent, you have to punish whoever is passive in the republic; and who does nothing for it. For, since the French people has manifested its will, everything opposed to it is outside the sovereign; all that is outside the sovereign is the enemy.'[132]

Events in the provinces showed that plenty were prepared to prove their virtue by getting blood on their hands. Nowhere was this more apparent than in the Vendée. The rebels had waged a successful guerrilla war against the state's professional army, waiting behind hedgerows for the Republic's columns to advance before decimating their ranks and melting back into the villages. They viewed their war as largely defensive and, after initial massacres, prisoners were usually released. In October the rebel general Charles-Melchier de Bouchamps had freed 5,000 Republican prisoners of war, but their rivals would prove less lenient. Government forces began turning the tide. After inflicting a shattering defeat at Sauvenoy on 23 December 1793, they showed no mercy, bayoneting and shooting rebel prisoners in their hundreds. Over 200 prisoners were executed at Angers in December, and 2,000 at Saint-Florent. Schama recounts how others 'were brought from the crowded prisons at Nantes and Angers to places like Pont-de-Cé and Arvillé where three to four thousand were shot in one long, relentless slaughter'.[133]

Worse was to follow in Nantes itself. It is alleged that Jean-Baptiste Carrier liked to indulge in night-time orgies with female prisoners, but he is rather more notorious for what he got up to after daybreak. Carrier decided to supplement the guillotine with boats adapted into *noyades*. They were crammed full of prisoners, bound hand and foot, before specially prepared planks were removed or broken allowing water to rush in. As many as 5,000 were drowned in this fashion in the Loire. Couples were also stripped naked and tied together in pairs before being flung in the river in what were dubbed 'republican marriages'. On 17 January 1794 General Turreau ordered six 'hell columns' to march through the region, burning every building they came across and bayoneting every suspect they found: man, woman or child. Large numbers of rural women were raped, bayoneted with their children, and then mutilated. On 23 January at Gonnord 200 elderly people, mothers and children were forced to dig a pit and kneel in front of it before being shot; tumbling into the mass grave they had just dug. Thirty children and two women were then flung in the pit with them and buried alive. The Committee of Public safety had decreed Turreau's mission to be 'good and pure...Exterminate the brigands down to the last one, that is your duty'.[134] It is estimated that, in total, a quarter of a million people died in the ulcer that was the Vendée.

On 17 October, the representatives-on-mission, who had been chased out of Bordeaux by the city's youth, returned with 1,600 soldiers. One of the representatives, Jean-Lambert Tallien, was scathing about the 'hypocrisy' of the locals' contrition, and he and his colleague, Claude-Alexandre Ysabeau, placed the city under martial law. Any confirmed rebels were executed without trial while a Surveillance Committee was established to enforce sans-culottes' orthodoxy throughout the administration. Only 104 executions took place before the next spring, but fines levied on the rich were numerous, and Tallien and his mistress enjoyed a notably luxurious standard of living. In Marseilles, Fréron and Barras acquitted almost half of the 974 suspects who appeared before the Revolutionary Tribunal, but still presided over a regime characterised by carnage and repression. Lyon, however, would prove to be a particularly disagreeable place when the federalist revolt collapsed on 9 October. Robespierre wanted 'these monsters unmasked and exterminated'.[135] He was to get his wish. Couthon declared that the houses of the rich and those associated with the rebellion should be destroyed, leaving only the residences of the poor. He had demolished 1,600 buildings, paid for by a 6 million livres tax on the rich, before the Convention, disagreeing with the waste of property, recalled him.

He was replaced by Joseph Fouché and Collot d'Herbois, an actor who had failed to enthuse the population of Lyon when performing there in 1782. As Schama acidly noted 'a good portion of them were about to learn the penalties of tepid applause'.[136] Collot, disappointed that 'only' thirty executions had occurred in October, resolved to 'improve' the situation. He imposed new measures, denunciations poured in, and the guillotine went into overdrive. In December thirty-two heads were collected in twenty-five minutes, a week later they decapitated twelve in five minutes. This was still not considered enough, so mass shootings took place to speed up the process. In a field by the Rhône men were tied together in groups of up to sixty and blasted by grapeshot. It was a horrendous spectacle. While the tactic was designed to speed up the pace of executions, the grapeshot was terribly inefficient. Men lay wounded and groaning for long periods while they were laboriously finished off with pikes, bayonets, sabres and rifles. On 4 December 113 were executed in a day while 209 were killed on 7 December. In a 'humanitarian' move firing squads eventually replaced the use of grapeshot and cannon. In all 1,905 died in that brief period in Lyon.

Through September and October the military position continued to improve with Republican forces scoring triumphs on all fronts against the Austrians and English. French forces won victories at Hondschoote near Dunkirk on 8 September, in the south at Peyrestortes, near Perpignan, on 17 September, and at Wattinges in the northeast on 16 October. The siege of Toulon, which had lasted three and a half months, was lifted on 17 December with the capture of 'Little Gibraltar', broken in a single day by the brilliant action of a swaggering young artillery commander named Napoleon Bonaparte. It was the operation that would launch his stratospheric career, and the victorious commander was promoted from captain to brigadier-general in just four months. Over 1,000 were executed in Toulon in the following two months.

With both internal and external threats to the Revolution abating, Danton and Desmoulins advocated relaxing the oppressive measures, but a cacophony of voices called for ever more terror. Both Georges-Jacques and Camille had been growing increasingly disenchanted with the direction events were taking and felt estranged from the new generation of rabid militants. Danton had even left Paris in September to retreat to the country for an extended break. He appeared to be slowly waking up to the reality of what the Revolution had become. He did not return until 21 November (1 Frimaire) at which point Hébert tried to have him expelled from the Jacobins. The Hébertistes were increasingly at odds with Danton's faction, now commonly known, by virtue of their moderation, as the Indulgents. Camille Desmoulins, on the announcement of the guilty verdict against the Gironde had cried 'My God. My God! It is I who kills them'.[137] He became more outspoken in his opposition to the Terror exclaiming that 'you want to remove all your enemies by means of the guillotine! Has there ever been such great folly? Could you make a single man perish on the scaffold, without making ten enemies for yourself from his family or his friends?'[138]

Robespierre's response, delivered on Christmas Day 1793 was chilling. He believed that 'the state is obliged to defend itself against the factions which attack it. Revolutionary government owes good citizens the protection of the state; to the enemies of the people, it owes only death'.[139] The very virtue that inspired him in his political stance had transformed the Incorruptible from the squeamish opponent of the death penalty into a cold, mass-murdering fanatic. On 5 February, in his Report on the Principles of Political Morality as a guide to the Convention, he went even further. As the threats to the Revolution continued to recede, he talked of his desire to transform the character of the French people, suggesting that 'in place of an easy-going, frivolous and discontented people, we would create one that is happy, powerful and stout-hearted...[replacing] the vices and follies of the monarchy by the virtues and astounding achievements of the republic'. Saint-Just spoke similarly on 26 February and his words are illustrative of the peculiar notion of liberty held by the radical Jacobins.

'A state in which such institutions are lacking is but an illusory republic. And since everybody interprets liberty as meaning the independence of his passions and his avarice, the spirit of conquest and selfishness is established between one citizen and another, and the individual idea of his own liberty formed by every man according to his interests leads to the slavery of all.'[140]

The Jacobins were not interested in freedom if it differed from their own conception of virtue. What was necessary was indoctrination and coercion, the sublimation of individuality to the needs of a radical interpretation of the General Will. Robespierre found further justifications for the use of the guillotine which seemed to thirst for ever more blood.

'If the basis of popular government in peacetime is virtue, its basis in a time of revolution is both virtue and terror – virtue, without which terror is disastrous, and terror, without which virtue has no power...Terror is merely justice, prompt, severe and inflexible. It is therefore an emanation of virtue, and results from the application of democracy to the most pressing needs of the country.'[141]

The left was splintering into an ever more bewildering array of factional rifts, but none were more bitter than that which opened between Danton's Indulgents and the Hébertistes. On one side were Danton, Desmoulins, Fabre d'Eglantine and Pierre Philippeaux while on the other were Hébert, Ronsin, Vincent, Collot d'Herbois and Billaud-Varenne. Robespierre was appalled by Hébert's atheism and his attempts to impose de-Christianisation. He had been a close friend to both Danton and Desmoulins for years, but he took a largely neutral stance. Yet it was far from the only rift that opened in that period. The Jacobins, having successfully removed the Girondins, were now finding the mob violence that had ushered them into power an inconvenience. They began to move against the Commune and sans-culottes they had sided with just months before, turning on the common people whose 'virtue' they had praised since the Revolution began. While they had played a pivotal role in allowing them to liquidate their rivals, the political elite increasingly perceived the sans-culottes, in their contrived, almost theatrical garb, as bearing little relation to the genuine working man they so consciously aped. Such were their justifications at any rate. In truth, the revolutionaries were finding the reality of the common man did not quite match the idealism of their Rousseau tinged imaginations. But, while glimmers of uncomfortable reality were intruding on their theorising, it had little impact on the certainty they held in their mission.

In this increasingly divisive atmosphere, a massive protest was organised by Roux and Varlet on 4 September. It culminated in a march on the Convention demanding action against 'the rich'. It was effectively a challenge to the Mountain, and the event demonstrated their inability to control the sans-culottes. The realisation brought home the necessity of dismantling the movement as a revolutionary force. The Énrages, in ambitiously pushing their case further, had overplayed their hand. Roux was condemned as a rebel and both he and Varlet were arrested. Roux deprived his accusers of sending him to the guillotine by stabbing himself five times in the chest in front of his judges, while Varlet, after spending a year in prison, ultimately survived the Terror.

Further measures were now enacted to neuter the mob and a new law of 4 December (14 Frimaire) brought regional control under the direct supervision of the Committee of Public Safety. It curtailed the authority of the representatives-on-mission and replaced them with vigorously vetted agents. It also made the sections answerable to the Convention rather than the Commune and limited them to two meetings a week. Robespierre's Committee was now the only official organ of state-sanctioned activism. Robespierre then sneered at the positions of both Indulgents and Hébertistes, intoning that 'one wants to take us to the Tropics, the other to the Arctic'.[142] He clearly regarded his own position as being altogether more temperate. Few would agree. The Incorruptible addressed the Convention to denounce 'moderation' and 'excess', but praised virtue. Effectively he was announcing that he was right and anyone who disagreed with him was simply wrong. There would only be one fate for those who failed to conform.

Appalled by the moderation of his rivals Hébert denounced both Danton and Desmoulins as Brissotins and cried that they were ripe for liquidation. Danton, partly because he was now attempting to halt the Terror, had lost control of the Cordeliers to the Hébertistes. It prompted Desmoulins to start a new newspaper, *The Old Cordelier*, dedicated to the club before Hébert's faction took over. It would prove a significant move. Desmoulins was no orator and had never been given any serious political role, but he was a provocative and dazzlingly brilliant journalist. In the first two issues he called for an end to the Terror, suggesting a 'committee of clemency', while currying Robespierre's favour by opposing de-Christianisation too. But in the third issue, published 15 December, he drew the ire of his former friend. Camille published a piece reputed to be an extract from Tacitus. In reality, it was a thinly-veiled swipe at the Incorruptible. The translation recorded in Hilary Mantel's *A Place of Greater Safety* is worth reproducing at length:

'As soon as words had become crimes against the state, it was only a small step to transform into offences, mere glances, sorrow, compassion, sighs, even silence... It was a crime against the state that Liborius Drusus asked the fortune tellers if he would ever be rich...It was a crime against the state that one of Cassius' descendants had a portrait of his ancestor in his house. Mannercus Scaurus committed a crime by writing a tragedy in which certain verses were capable of a double meaning. It was a crime against the state that the mother of the consul Furius Germinus mourned for the death of her son...It was necessary to rejoice at the death of a friend or relative, if one wished to escape death oneself.

Was a citizen popular? He might start a faction. Suspect. Did he try instead to retreat from public life? Suspect. Are you rich? Suspect. Are you – to all appearances – poor? You must be hiding something. Suspect. Are you melancholy? The state of the nation must upset you. Suspect. Are you cheerful? You must be rejoicing at national calamities. Suspect. Are you a philosopher, an orator or a poet? Suspect.'[143]

Their friendship had been strong enough that Camille did not immediately face persecution for publishing this obvious swipe. But Robespierre supported Camille's expulsion from the Jacobins on 10 January 1794 and relations between them certainly cooled from that point.

By February the Maximum fixed price was collapsing as the civil war led to spiralling costs, especially of meat, sugar, eggs and butter. The authorities began to realise that intimidation only encouraged hoarding and that profits needed to be protected to fuel the free market. But these pragmatic concerns were not what the radicals wanted to hear. They demanded retribution and lower prices, failing to realise the conflicting nature of their demands. The Hébertistes increasingly pushed for a more vigorous use of the revolutionary army, severe repression against grain hoarders and merchants, and ever more surveillance to weed out the agents of foreign powers who were undoubtedly manipulating the crises. In early March, frustrated at the lack of governmental action, the Hébertistes proposed an insurrection against the Committee of Public Safety, inadvertently giving the authorities the opportunity to move against them.

Hébert and his supporters were arrested on the night of 13 – 14 March, accused of planning an uprising and charged with profiteering, largely to diffuse their support among the artisans of Paris. They were prosecuted en masse, with a number of other figures accused of corruption. The trial was the usual travesty, with the forces of the Republic throwing in a random assortment of handy targets. They were accused of plotting to starve Paris and overthrow the Convention by opening the prisons. No written evidence was produced, but a string of witnesses gave convenient testimonies. The trial ran for three days, from 21-24 March, when the jury announced that they had heard enough to proceed to the inevitable guilty verdict. Requests to call defence witnesses were rejected out of hand and the executions were scheduled for that very afternoon. A massive crowd rammed the Place de la Révolution. They exploded with glee when Hébert, whose invective had sent so many to the guillotine, and who had gloated at the fear he sensed in Marie-Antoinette, lost his nerve when confronted with the same fate himself and was dragged screaming to the scaffold.

With his faction gone there seemed little reason to move against the Indulgents, but some of Danton's associates had been accused in the wide-ranging web of corruption used to ensnare the Hébertistes and such action followed with undue haste. Just five days after Hébert's execution the arrest warrant for Danton was signed in the Committee of Public Safety. Saint-Just, it seems, was the instigator of the indictment and was keen to prosecute Danton himself. But he was persuaded that it was wiser to stand aside as the wily orator may rip him to shreds in front of an audience. Saint-Just acquiesced but, in a fit of juvenile pique, flung his hat in the fireplace before storming from the room. Couthon, Collot d'Herbois, Billaud-Varenne and Marc Vadier were also instrumental in persuading Robespierre to issue the warrant, though a seemingly innocuous incident may have already inclined him. Danton had laughed at Robespierre's pursuit of virtue and snorted that there was no virtue more substantial than what he showed his wife every night. The Incorruptible found Danton's bawdy and blunt-spoken tavern humour distasteful. The prudish and puritanical Robespierre, determined to maintain his air of pious superiority, grew alienated from Danton and perhaps felt his old colleague was now treating his revolutionary values with contempt. Given his predilection for sanctimonious posturing, that should come as no surprise.

In the early hours of 31 March Danton, Desmoulins, Philippeaux, Fabre d'Eglantine and Delacroix were arrested. Imprisoned in the Luxembourg, Danton met Thomas Paine, another legendary figure of the revolutionary class who had fallen foul of the militants. To add insult to injury, Desmoulin's beautiful young wife, Lucile, was flung in prison on the pretext of being involved in a plot on the prisoners' behalf. The Indulgents' trial was yet another travesty of justice. Attempts were made to implicate Danton in a web of corruption and embezzlement, but no evidence was forthcoming and, despite the best efforts of scores of historians, none has been unearthed since. On the second day of proceedings Danton dominated the stage with a defence even more eloquent than Brissot had managed. He bellowed defiantly 'Against your accusation – for which you cannot provide proof, not even the hint of a proof or the shadow of a witness – I pitch my entire revolutionary career'.[144] Their arguments had already been so compelling that when the accused asked for defence witnesses they were removed from the court on the grounds that they had 'insulted' it. The next morning, 5 April 1794, the jury promptly reached their wholly predictable verdict of guilty and the defendants were executed before a vast, muted crowd that very afternoon. Desmoulins, inflamed by news of his wife's arrest grappled with his executioners and was dragged to his death with his shirt in rags. Danton, who had been growing cynical for months, had time for one last quip. An imposing figure, with a cranium to match, he swaggered up to the scaffold before announcing in confident tones 'Don't forget to show my head to the people; it's worth seeing'.[145]

A pall hung over the revolutionary class after the execution of the Indulgents. If even a giant of that generation like Danton could fall to the blade then surely no one was safe? Yet it also appeared that the Montagnards must have finally run out of enemies. With all rival factions obliterated it was surely now time to put the brakes on the Terror? But such was not to be the case; in fact the pace of executions was only to increase rapidly. It was a process greatly accelerated by the Law of 22 Prairial, enacted on 10 June 1794, though the rate of beheadings had been rising sharply anyway. The law, effectively shepherded through by Couthon and Robespierre, reduced the number of judges by a quarter and removed the counsel for the defence. Material evidence of guilt was no longer required, 'moral proofs' were now considered sufficient. Those accused no longer had any rights at all and the pace of tribunals accelerated rapidly. Couthon remarked that 'The delay in punishing the enemies of the *patrie* must be no longer than it takes to recognise them: it is less a question of punishing them than of annihilating them'.[146]

Robespierre's health was declining in this period even as his paranoia increased. His rapidly unravelling mental state had not been helped by two half-hearted attempts to assassinate him. On 23 May Henri Admiral had wandered the streets for a day before attempting to shoot Collot d'Herbois. He announced that he would have fired at Robespierre if he had found him. The very next day, sixteen-year old Cécile Renault had been caught sneaking around the Tuileries determined 'to see what a tyrant looks like'. When she was searched she was found to be carrying two knives and was quickly labelled 'another Corday'. Cécile was transported to her execution on 17 June (29 Prairial) with her father, brother and aunt. The concept of 'bad blood', guilt by association, which had so horrified Robespierre under the old regime, was, of course, permissible in defence of revolutionary principles. In fact, it would be taken to lengths that would have been unimaginable under the Bourbons. Sixty-one were executed that day including a tiny, underage servant girl to someone who had once been a Hébertist. Even the baying crowd found its limit and cried out 'No children!' It was a day that, in a microcosm, encapsulated how the utopian rhetoric of the Revolution had descended into an arbitrary, almost indiscriminate slaughter of innocents.

The family of Malesherbes, the personal friend of Rousseau and the man who had defended the King and offered to defend Marie-Antoinette, were also to fall to the principle of 'bad blood'. He had been languishing in Port-Libre, an institution used to detain a large number of formerly high ranking officials, like Lavoisier. Malesherbes, who was seventy-two, was accused on the flimsiest of pretexts. A piece of anecdotal evidence suggested that, when told by his sister that the vines on her estate were frozen, he had responded that he was glad. It meant they could not be used to make wine, and if the peasants had not got drunk then the Revolution would never have happened. This was deemed sufficient evidence for Fouquier-Tinville to denounce him as an arch counter-revolutionary. Malesherbes was forced to watch his daughter, grand-daughter and her husband, Chateaubriand, be executed before him. Fouquier-Tinville was not satisfied until he had executed the old man's seventy-six year old sister and two secretaries as well. Also guillotined that day was Jean-Jacques Duval d'Eprémesnil, who had led the *parlements'* resistance to royal authority in the late 1780s, activism that had paved the way for the Revolution. A few weeks later they guillotined Antoine-Laurent Lavoisier, the brilliant chemist who had discovered oxygen, while on 22 April Le Chapelier, a pillar of Feuilliant moderation was beheaded as well. Wives of earlier victims were another group who became disproportionately targeted. Beaumarchais, the author of *The Marriage of Figaro*, was in exile in Hamburg when he heard that his wife, daughter and sister had been imprisoned in Port Libre in Paris. They were among the lucky ones who had not yet been guillotined on 9 Thermidor (27 July) when the Terror was abruptly terminated.

The majority of those who had died with Cécile Renault were charged with having been part of the same foreign conspiracy she was alleged to have joined. Such plots were increasingly used as pretexts for mass executions in an atmosphere in which any pretence at judicial procedure had long been dropped. On 16 June thirty-seven inmates of Bicêtre prison were guillotined when it was suggested that they planned to break out, stab members of the Committee, tear out their hearts and cook and eat them. This ludicrous conspiracy theory gave the authorities the idea to execute 159 prisoners in the Luxembourg as 'agents of General Dillon', Lucie's father, who was guillotined himself on 13 April with Chaumette and the wives of Hébert and Desmoulins.

While Paris dominated events in those years there were plenty of tyrants active in the provinces too. Michael Kennedy, who has done more work on the Jacobin clubs scattered across France than anyone else, confirmed the impression one gets from a brief perusal of the facts when concluding 'One could spend a quarter-century scrutinizing membership rolls, studying tax records, and compiling charts and graphs, and still conclude that the Jacobins were basically middle class'.[147] The sort of doctors and lawyers active in Paris were just as numerous in rural France, and there were a significant percentage of bourgeois liberals prepared to shed blood in the name of virtuous liberty. In Arras, the former schoolteacher and cleric, Joseph le Bon, was responsible for some of the worst excesses of the period. He guillotined 298 men and 93 women in the town's square, just a few steps from Robespierre's old home. The Incorruptible commended him on 'the energy with which you have suppressed the enemies of Revolution'.[148]

As at the centre, with the rule of law effectively suspended, arrests and executions were dependant on the personal grudges and revolutionary zeal of the extremists who elbowed their way into positions of authority, or the hordes eager to join in the orgy of accusation. In Lille, le Bon called upon the locals to make denunciations 'on pain of being treated as accomplices...the guillotine is waiting imperiously to receive its prey'.[149] In the Loire department near Lyon, Claude Javogues, a lawyer in his early thirties, became especially infamous as a man of remarkable violence. He treated women particularly appallingly, grabbing their breasts or fondling them while berating them as 'sluts', 'cunts', and 'whores'. As refinement was considered a mark of aristocratic pretension, this sort of loutish and brutal machismo became depressingly familiar. In September 1793 he announced in Montbrison that 'blood would flow like water in the streets'. The regime of Javogues was characterised by prejudice and class hatred, and the successful were so brutalised that his policies damaged the livelihoods of the region's poor.

In Orange, a special commission had been formed at the behest of Etienne Maignot, which investigated an incident in the village of Bédoin where a liberty tree had been uprooted, and a red liberty bonnet taken from it and cast down a well. Maignot's response was to assault the village and burn it to the ground, guillotining thirty-five people and shooting twenty-eight more: men, women and boys. Another nineteen women were incarcerated and the surviving villagers forcibly repatriated elsewhere. The 'Popular Commission' set up at Orange operated under Robespierre's guidelines. There were five judges, no jury, and written evidence was deemed unnecessary. It adjudicated on only one offence, whether the accused was an 'enemy of the Revolution', and had but one punishment, death. Between 19 June and 4 August it tried 432 individuals. A hundred were spared the guillotine, mostly thanks to the benevolence of Roman-Fonrose, a sixty year old judge accustomed to more rigorous procedures under the Bourbons. Claude Payon wrote to him from Paris to admonish him for his stringent approach and the manner of his chastisement is revealing.

'Commissions charged with punishing conspirators bear absolutely no comparison with the tribunals of the Old Regime or even with those of the new. There must not be any forms; the judge's conscience is there to replace them. It does not matter whether an accused has been interrogated in such or such a manner...in a word these commissions are *revolutionary* commissions...they should also be *political* tribunals; they should remember that everyone who has not been for the Revolution has been by that very fact against it because he has not done anything for the *patrie*.'[150]

Political faith, like religious faith, requires no evidence or argument to support it; the testimony of a fellow believer, or just the conviction of the faithful, is sufficient proof in matters of life and death.

Back in Paris the leading revolutionaries were wading through the blood of their enemies while planning the moral education of the population. In Saint-

Just's utopian republic, one markedly similar to that envisaged by Robespierre, male children would be raised by the state from the age of five and fed on a vegetarian diet. His suggestions incorporated ideas pruned from Rousseau and Sparta, the latter of which he viewed as an ideal: a slave-state, where citizens were indoctrinated to suborn their individuality in service of the nation, a fascistic utopia similarly idealised by Hitler. Athens, which produced many of the greatest accomplishments in human history, and some of the most questioning and enquiring minds, was a society which Saint-Just and Robespierre considered distasteful. David also lionised the Spartan ideal, silkily rendering Leonidas at Thermopylae in characteristically romanticised fashion. Yet, in reality, the Sparta they idealised was a military dictatorship ruled by kings. It was the only *polis* to enslave fellow Greeks, while Athens was more of a direct democracy than the France they presided over. Such realities had little impact on the self-image of the converted. Robespierre busied himself planning his Festival of the Supreme Being, to be held on 8 June (20 Prairial), a ludicrously overblown extravaganza meant to counter the de-Christianisation which had swept France. It was designed to appeal to advocates of reason as well as Catholicism, and ostentatiously put Robespierre at its centre, to the ridicule of many in attendance. Thuriot, an old friend of Danton, on witnessing The Incorruptible descend like Moses, drily commented 'Look at the bugger; it's not enough for him to be master, he has to be God'.[151]

While the prisons filled to overflowing that summer executions continued to spiral ever upward. In April 244 had been executed, in May it was 339, in June the count reached 659 and it rose to over 900 in July. It is speculation, but one wonders how that total would have continued to escalate were the tyranny of the Jacobins not finally ended that month. The military situation had continued to improve dramatically in that period while the federalist and Vendée risings were long since over. The excuses they used to impose their despotism had evaporated, but their zeal was undimmed. The despots of the left were being driven, not by necessity, but by pure messianic absolutism. Claude Payon, who had replaced Chaumette in the Commune when the latter was arrested, had focused heavily on propaganda and revealingly announced in the *Anti fédéraliste* that he hoped Robespierre would 'centralise public opinion and make it uniform'.[152] But alarm was growing over the dictatorship which seemed increasingly threatening to any outside the small clique of radical militants.

Deputies like Barras and Fréron were already manoeuvring against Robespierre when The Incorruptible clashed with Fouché and had him expelled from the Jacobins. Fouché desperately sought allies and won over Collot, Billaud and Carnot. Jean-Lambert Tallien was also a member of the growing cabal as he, and his accomplice in Bordeaux, Claude Ysabeau, had been accused of being too lenient. Marc Antoine Jullien, just nineteen years old when attaining a significant position in Robespierre's patriotic network, had been sent to investigate. He was appalled to discover that only 104 executions had been carried out. Such clemency was largely due to the influence of Thérèsa Cabarrus, Tallien's captivating twenty-one year old mistress. Lucie Dillon certainly credits Thérésa with her salvation. She had threatened to withhold her affections from Tallien unless he produced permits for Lucie and her family to depart for America, and he promptly complied.

Lucie's account of hiding in Bordeaux, which has parallels with Anne Frank's diary, paints a terrifying picture of revolutionary France: the claustrophobia, the paranoia, the ever-present fear of detection and the inevitable fate that would follow. From her hiding place she could hear the drum-rolls that accompanied each execution and witnessed the iconoclasm of Bordeaux when all the great art and treasures of the city's churches were burned in a huge pyre in front of an actress posing as the Goddess of Reason. She also saw the crowds at the butcher's shop, patiently waiting for a few scraps of meat, meekly part to allow access for those who carried off healthy quantities of the finest cuts for the People's Representatives who continued to dine in conspicuous luxury. Such stories are eerily reminiscent of tales of the people's commissars who lived like gluttons during the siege of Stalingrad, even while their 'comrades' around them starved to death by the million and were driven to cannibalism. While Lucie's account is chilling, and profoundly moving, it is salient to remember that the touch of revolution was lighter in Bordeaux than nearly anywhere in France. How much worse must it have been in Lyon? When the youthful Jullien arrived, after Tallien had already voluntarily left for Paris, he discovered Ysabeau wallowing in Asiatic luxury. Jullien wasted little time in making amends sending Ysabeau back to Paris and executing 198 'aristocrats' within two months. It is little wonder that Tallien feared enough for his safety to join the growing resistance movement.

Yet even after everything that had happened, and oblivious to the plots that swirled around him, Robespierre was, right to the last, more convinced of his moral superiority than ever. By the summer of 1794 freedom of speech, freedom of the press and freedom of religion had been strangled. The population lived in fear of state spies, working undercover, who listened out for any incriminating speech. It was a nation gripped in a perpetual state of dread, and the material conditions of the populace were significantly worse than they had been just a few years previously. Nothing even remotely approaching it had existed in even the darkest days of the Old Regime. When Louis XVI had been confronted with rebellion he had dispersed his troops and attempted to agree a compromise. When the Jacobins sniffed resistance their response was brutality and repression on a level still difficult to contemplate.

When the Revolution had started there were just seven prisoners in the Bastille. By the summer of 1794 there were at least seven *thousand* inmates crammed into the prisons of Paris alone, and this even after the staggering number of executions that had taken place. There is no more telling evidence of the difference in severity between the two regimes. Yet Robespierre still seemed to believe that he presided over some sort of utopia, that France was far better off than it had ever been before. On 26 July (8 Thermidor), speaking to the Convention the day before the end, he gushed with moralistic fervour. 'Virtue is...this profound horror of tyranny, this sympathetic zeal for the oppressed, this sacred love of the *patrie*, this most sublime and most holy love of humanity...You can feel it at this very moment burning in your souls; I feel it in mine.'[153] He also referred, unbelievably, to the 'heavenly pleasure in the calm of a pure conscience'.[154] Robespierre continued to speak ramblingly of a conspiracy against him, but his refusal to name names was the last straw. To those now lining up against him, anticipating another purge, it provided the impetus to spur them into action. The conspiracy against Robespierre did not fully exist until created by his own paranoia.

The same evening of Robespierre's speech to the Convention, Collot spoke at the Jacobins to ask for a closer examination of the accusations he had made. He was met with a chorus of boos and catcalls from the Incorruptible's supporters. The next day in the Convention, 9 Thermidor, was the fateful one. Robespierre's enemies had worked feverishly through the night, winning converts and planning their assault. Saint-Just began proceedings in the Convention but was interrupted by Tallien and then Billaud who accused Robespierre of threatening the deputies with the law of 22 Prairial. The Incorruptible, he said, was 'always talking about virtue while defending crime...there is no representative of the people who wants to live under a tyrant'.[155] Robespierre attempted to speak but was drowned out with cries of 'Down with the Tyrant!' from the suddenly emboldened throng. When Vadier mocked Robespierre's self-pitying style the Convention roared with laughter. He attempted to respond again, but the words stuck in his throat and someone yelled 'Danton's blood is choking him!' Robespierre's response constituted the last words he would speak in the Convention: 'So you want to avenge Danton? Why then you wretched cowards did you not defend him?'

His arrest was proposed and seconded, and his brother Augustin, Saint-Just, Couthon and Lebas were detained with him. It was not to be quite so easy however. An insurrection was organised by the Commune to free him, and those arrested were all spirited away to the Hôtel de Ville. But by the time government troops arrived early in the morning most of Robespierre's defenders had drifted away. Inside the building Couthon proposed a decree calling the sections' troops to their assistance. It was decided, in a predictable case of extreme hubris, that it should be penned 'in the name of the French people' with whose will they still considered themselves synonymous. The Incorruptible had begun to sign it but had only got as far as penning the 'Ro' of his name. Next to his partly completed signature the document is spattered with blood. Government troops under Barras had rushed the building.

Lebas grabbed a gun and committed suicide; Augustin had hurled himself from a window and shattered a thighbone; Couthon's wheelchair had crashed down a stone staircase; Saint-Just stood frozen as if in a trance. Robespierre himself had taken a bullet in the face that had shattered his jawbone, though whether he was shot by the Convention's troops or it was a botched suicide attempt has never been ascertained. He was bandaged up and then left lying prone on a table in the Committee of Public Safety. The formerly immaculately attired deputy cut a bedraggled and pathetic looking figure as a steady stream of the curious came to gawp at and mock the fallen idol. On 28 July he was condemned at the Concierge before three carts and their twenty passengers began their long, slow procession through the jeering crowds at six pm. The executioner, fearing that it would interfere with the drop of the blade, ripped the bandage from Robespierre's face, tearing out a chunk of his jawbone in the process. The last sound he ever made was a blood-curdling scream before his sobs were cut short by the dull thud of the falling blade.

The Revolution did not end then, but it was the beginning of the end. The next day seventy-one Robspierreists and members of the Commune were guillotined, the greatest number to fall under the blade in a single day. The backlash lasted nearly a year as the Counter-Terror took hold and many who had ruthlessly presided over their locales now found themselves on the receiving end. For the floodgates of accusation and slaughter the Jacobins had opened could not easily be closed again. The consequences of this backlash would prove widespread and varied. When the now tarnished Marat's remains were removed from the Pantheon on 8 February 1795 the Gilded Youth, dandyish young men who repudiated the austere Spartan values of the Republic, seized his corpse and hurled it into an open sewer. Jacques-Louis David and Napoleon were both arrested, the latter as he had been close to Augustin Robespierre. But they were later released, the former to the relief of art lovers everywhere, and the painter ended up as the propagandist for Napoleon's regime as he had been for the revolutionaries. Jean-Baptiste Carrier was guillotined in December 1794 after a sensational trial which unearthed the true horrors he had unleashed in the Vendée. Fouquier-Tinville appeared bewildered when it was his turn to be sentenced to death in May 1795. The mild-mannered bureaucratic family man protested that he had only obeyed the law and done his duty, a sentiment and a stereotype that would become chillingly familiar through the twentieth century.

But the new authorities generally favoured clemency, and balanced justice began to return. The law of 22 Prairial was repealed, and the Revolutionary Tribunal scaled down. When Billaud, Barère and Collot were tried in March 1795 they were sentenced, not to death, but exile in Guiana. While Collot died of yellow fever in just over a year, Barère escaped and Billaud ended up as a comfortable farmer in Saint Domingue, living until 1819. On 8 September 1794 ninety-four accused Federalists from Nantes were put on trial. Just two months previously they would all have been speedily guillotined, but with evidence of the atrocities, corruption and violence of the authorities mounting, all were acquitted. When it came time to try those accused of the massacres of Nantes just three, including Carrier, were condemned, while twenty-eight were released. Cross examinations and evidence had made the difference, and the complete absence of any reprisals showed how unnecessary the bloodshed of the previous few years had been. It had been fuelled by the bigotry and paranoia of the radical left.

By February 1794 the Thermidoreans who ousted Robespierre's faction had lost their grip, and the French were regaining their senses, as if waking from a bad dream. They had swum with the tide of the Terror, now, epitomising the herd mentality all too evident in the human race, they were prepared and eager to swim in the other direction. The effects of that period could not be shaken off lightly however, and France would be convulsed by a series of revolutions that would last nearly a century: in 1795, 1799, 1815, 1830, 1848 and 1871. The political left would show their colours time and again in that tumultuous century. The Republican coup of 18 Fructidor (4 September) 1797 yet again revealed a tiresome trait: whenever the democracy they claimed to cherish produced a disagreeable result, and if they were in a position of power, the resort to violence was immediate.

The elections had returned royalist support. And the left predictably responded with military force, suppression and a brutal coup d'état, sending their political rivals into exile again. Their pronouncements in the wake of that bloodshed blamed the corruption of public opinion on the 'poison spread by a hundred journals'.[156] Simply put, the people had made the 'wrong' choice, rather like the left-wing commentators in the wake of the UK election of 2015 who, unable to comprehend why the electorate had rejected them, blamed it all on Rupert Murdoch. Riots erupted after that 2015 vote too; the only real difference being that they were limp and unsuccessful. The events of 1797 were rather more robust and well organised. A violent coup to purge the legislature was declared essential to preserve 'freedom'. The troops of Barras forcibly ejected 177 duly elected deputies while posters around the city denounced royalist intrigue and treason as justifying the actions of that day. The violence, it was said, had been necessary to save the Revolution, liberty and the Rights of Man, 'arguments' which were lapped up by a credulous public. The reality of a crude military coup that contravened all the ideals they had vocalised for years was airbrushed out of existence. The purged deputies were replaced, but not by elections. Royalists protested, and republicans retaliated with the usual justifications for their anti-democratic illegality. But had positions been reversed they would have been indignant with rage.

The new body was a repressive autocratic regime that imposed punitive measures on the aristocratic émigrés and the clergy. Nobles were given two weeks to leave the country or warned they would be executed and 160 were duly beheaded for nothing more than mild tardiness. Sixty newspapers were shut down, and forty journalists deported to Guiana, a virtual death sentence for those unable to escape. The regime grew increasingly bloated and authoritarian and rigged a series of elections before being overthrown by Napoleon in 1799, finally bringing the Revolution to an end. In the last thrash of its tail, in the terrible century that followed the events of 1789, the political left made an indelible mark once more, and the Communards of 1871 proved themselves the true heirs of the Jacobins. In 1789 the ossuarium of the church of Saint-Roch had been ransacked and the remains of the eminent philosophers and true preachers of enlightenment humanity: Diderot, Holbach, Helvétius and Marie-Thérèse de Geoffrin, were scattered about the church. The revolutionaries apparently preferred their demagogues of destruction to such individuals. Nearly a century later the Communards repeated the desecration of their progenitors so effectively that identifying the scattered remains proved impossible. That rising of 1871 left much of Paris in rubble, the Tuileries was burned to the ground, and the streets of the capital were littered with 25,000 bodies.

In light of his later actions, the speech Robespierre gave against the death penalty in May 1791 drips with irony:

'Even if you imagine the judicial order the most perfect, even if you find judges the most trustworthy and the most enlightened, you would still have to allow some place for error or for prejudice...If, in place of that powerful rigour, of that moderate calm which ought to characterise it, they put anger and vengeance; if they make human blood flow, blood that they ought to spare and have no right to spread; if they display to the eyes of the people cruel scenes of dead and tortured cadavers, then they alter in the hearts of citizens the ideas of justice and injustice, they cause to germinate in the bosom of society ferocious prejudices which then produce others in their turn.'[157]

Why was it then that, ultimately, these are considerations the revolutionary class felt did not apply to themselves, even as they became increasingly guilty of such excesses? The reasons for the Terror are incredibly complex but underpinning all other considerations is the deep reservoir of prejudice directed at certain sectors of society which demanded redress. All other factors grew out of this tendency, and its removal from the equation would make a repeat of events unlikely. But it was also the intense belief in their own morality that persuaded Robespierre and his ilk that they would be free from the faults to which others might succumb. That certainty and bigotry were informed by their conviction: that any who disagreed with them were so repellent that even allowing their opinions to be aired was intolerable. It informed the repressive, hectoring culture that permeated those bleak years of 'freedom' and 'equality'.

French politics was dominated by a loathing that impaired judgement and made compromise or discussion impossible. Their very certainty meant that, for all its grand rhetoric, the Revolution was largely unthinking and instinctive. The Jacobins readily believed any lies told about their rivals and, after those enemies were driven from the field they turned on their allies like uncaged beasts. But any criticisms directed at themselves and their peers were simply brushed aside. Robespierre is the epitome of the type. As his confidence developed in tandem with his success he became increasingly rigid and inflexible and grew ever more intolerant to challenges. He saw traitors everywhere, but it was his faith in his views that blinded him to the fact that the greatest enemy of French liberty was himself.

There were several points at which the Revolution could have proceeded in a peaceful and equitable manner, yet the radicals could not conceive those lacking their ardour were anything other than monsters. This irrational fear transformed the paragons of virtue into tyrants. Robespierre and his cohort had been armed with little more than vague assertions of equality, virtue, the natural goodness of the common people, class hatred, romantic notions of Rousseauist ideals, and a profusion of conceit. But his conviction became so all-consuming that he would, in a foretaste of Karl Marx, claim to be the repository of 'Historical Truth'.[158] It was the same faith that informed Saint-Just's dictum that 'the republic consists in the extermination of everything that opposes it'.[159] The results were seen in the Jacobins which was corrupted from a debating society into an echo chamber obsessed with denunciation, and they were apparent in the oppression and brutality that swept France.

Ultimately, as with the ideologues of the left today, the revolutionaries were not truly concerned with aiding the oppressed, their primary focus was on attacking and destroying the powerful. Their motivation was not compassion for the meek, whatever their occasional rhetoric suggested. It was on assaulting the established order. This is why the French Revolution took the course it did, why it became a force not for creation but for destruction, why it did next to nothing to help the downtrodden but consumed the elites and its opponents with zealous enthusiasm. But the Revolution did not just fail because it focused on resentment. It was also because its imagined alliance between middle class theorists and proletarian labourers did not exist. Its failures, both social and economic, disproportionately affected the most vulnerable in society, creating significant opposition to the regime, while proving a source of great frustration to the revolutionaries, and these twin factors were realised in rising levels of violence. In the perceptive analysis of Saint-Simon, who was imprisoned in that period but survived, it would all have turned out rather differently had the Revolution been led by the people who truly belonged to the modern world: the great new merchants, captains of industry and bankers. It is certainly not beyond the realms of possibility that such individuals would have focused on constructing a framework to improve the material conditions for the French people rather than on the twisted ideological concerns which occupied the Jacobins.

In 1792, on the fall of the monarchy, Robespierre had proclaimed 'It is not enough... to have overturned the throne: our concern is to erect upon its remains *holy equality* and the imprescriptable Rights of Man'.[160] Yet the desire to impose idealistic principles in government, despite a glaring lack of practical experience or prior experiment, is exactly what Burke warned against. It should act as a clarion call to all those who clamour for the same process today. The unshakeable conviction in their moral superiority permitted the Jacobins to demonise any who stood in their way and to justify increasing atrocities considered 'necessary' to fulfil their eminently laudable goal. But their somewhat vague theorising and lack of self-reflection blinded them to the costs of their actions. Their eyes were set firmly on the nirvana they were targeting, so the victims did not matter. They were like the 'cockroaches' of the Rwandan genocide. The Jacobins' virtue allowed them to be contemptuous of legal process and the right of others to hold opinions, and they even grew to resent those who failed to applaud their political vision with sufficient enthusiasm. Sagan talks of the 'moral rage'[161] that allowed the same people who favoured the abolition of slavery to partake in an orgy of guillotining their rivals, enemies and former friends.

The refusal to allow a plurality of opinion was the French Revolution's greatest failure. It was a disaster repeated in Soviet Russia, Nazi Germany and Communist China. It is not a feature of democratic societies in contemporary times, but one strongly suspects that much of the left wishes it was. One certainly gets that impression from the modern extremists' desire to gag anyone who fails to share the narrow tenets to which they cling with the adhesive stubbornness of a clam. On asking why the Revolution became violent, Schama pondered that 'it was perhaps Romanticism, with its addiction to the Absolute and the Ideal...its preference for passion over reason, for virtue over peace, that supplied a crucial ingredient in the mentality of the revolutionary elite: its association of liberty with wildness'.[162] More depressingly the psychology they inhabited and the precedent they set would be repeated again and again. As Sagan concluded, the French Terror 'was truly the role model, whether consciously stated or not, for all the left-wing ideological terrorisms of the twentieth century'.[163] However, the infrastructure and machinery of government available to the Jacobins' twentieth-century counterparts would enable the atrocities of their successors to dwarf those of the eighteenth century. In many ways, the Revolution was merely a dress rehearsal for what was to follow.

Chapter 2
The Philosophy of Revolution

'I am not wrong. I'll show you their pamphlets. Everything with them is "the influence of environment", it follows that, if society is normally organised, all crime will cease at once, since there will be nothing to protest against and all men will become righteous in one instant. Human nature is not taken into account, it is excluded, it's not supposed to exist! They don't recognise that humanity, developing by a historical living process, will become at last a normal society, but they believe that a social system that has come out of some mathematical brain is going to organise all humanity at once and make it just and sinless in an instant, quicker than any living process!'

Fyodor Dostoyevsky in Crime and Punishment: Summing up the Socialist Revolutionary mindset over fifty years before the Revolution

Jean-Jacques Rousseau

He recorded the moment in detail in a letter to his friend Malsherbes. He had been journeying, he wrote, the two leagues from Paris to Vincennes to visit his old friend Denis Diderot in prison, and his mind had been wandering as it does when one is strolling alone through the countryside. Then it hit him. It came to him in a flash, so sudden and overwhelming that he collapsed to his hands and knees, his limbs trembling, tears streaming from his eyes at the sheer emotional force of the revelation. He withdrew to recover beneath the shade of a large oak, resting his back against its broad trunk while he slowly began to regain his breath and equilibrium. It was his epiphany, his damascene moment. Suddenly everything was plain to him, revealed with a clarity and simplicity both startling and overwhelming. The revelation he had on that lonely road revealed to him the solution to the all-encompassing quandary he had been wrestling with for years, and he was to spend the remainder of his life moulding his thought and expression to fit the single, universal theory that came upon him in the euphoric rush of that moment. It was to him the single, defining event of his life and maintaining the cherished memory of that inner glow was to consume the rest of his days as much as the quest for it had occupied him until that pivotal afternoon.

Such melodrama was entirely in keeping with this strange, intense man, but if the peculiarities of his character are undeniable, so too is the significance and colossal influence of his thought. Rousseau's personality has been the subject of reams of historical discussion and analysis, and an examination of the writer offers a fascinating glimpse into the radical mind: the narcissism, the hostility to dissent and the willingness to dismiss practical realities in preference for idealistic flights of fancy. He shares many traits with Robespierre, who so related to his works and revered the man, and is another fascinating case study for the particular psychology under investigation in these pages: an individual inflated with a feeling of moral superiority, one who hoped to shape society according to his desires while restricting the harmless freedoms and frivolous pursuits of his peers, one who tediously vocalised his own virtue and lectured others about their supposed vices while being, in reality, a complete shit of a human being; that discrepancy between those who preach morality while practising vice which is at the heart of this study.

Yet he has proven to be one of the pivotal thinkers in history on the subject of democracy and, even more so, on education. It was he who popularised the veneration of nature and distaste for industrialization that retains its influence to the modern day, and he too who celebrated indigenous peoples, or what in his age were termed 'the noble savage', over the inhabitants of Western civilisation. He also embellished the idea that the poor are more virtuous than the rich and, just for good measure, effectively invented the modern autobiography and laid the foundations for psychoanalysis. Rousseau celebrated spontaneous feeling over conceptual thinking, an aspect of his thought that has had a colossal impact on Western culture and intellectual life. As Magee has argued 'he launched a tendency in Western thought and art that has remained powerful ever since, the longing to throw off the constraints of reason and give untrammelled expression to feeling and instinct. This way of looking at things often has a powerful appeal for the young.'[1]

If anyone can be said to have spawned the Romantic movement it was undoubtedly Jean-Jacques Rousseau, and his influence is just as apparent in the culture of the contemporary left, particularly since the 1960s when the thought he inspired came back into vogue. More immediately, of course, his influence had a profound impact on the French Revolution, and on that catastrophe's most significant figures. Rousseau's ideas seem very appealing at a superficial level, and it is easy to see why they won so many converts and have proven so enduring. But while his philosophy is undoubtedly attractive, and may have proven beneficial in people's personal lives, the consequences have been disastrous when his theorising has been applied to states.

However, even if his ideas do not seem so revolutionary today, it cannot be denied that he was one of the more unique thinkers of history. He differed sharply from the most influential philosophers of his day, and the same is true of those who had preceded him. While Hobbes argued that civilisation was necessary to restrain man's wilder instincts; Rousseau believed the opposite. He also fundamentally disagreed with John Locke about the role of politics. Central to Rousseau's conception of democracy was the forcible imposition of the general will. The Locke model was built around the protection and preservation of individual freedom. Essentially, since the late eighteenth century, political thought has polarised into two camps, those who have followed Rousseau, and those who followed Locke. In Bertrand Russell's analysis 'Hitler is an outcome of Rousseau, Roosevelt and Churchill, of Locke.'[2]

Geneva, which was not absorbed into Switzerland until after the Napoleonic wars, was still an independent city-state when Rousseau was born there on 28 June 1712. Rousseau's family had originally come from France but had fled the persecution of Protestants there. Jean-Jacques's great-great-grandfather, Didier, was the first to arrive in Geneva in 1549. It was, at that time, a Calvinist city and effectively an oligarchic democracy, a feature that shaped Rousseau's conception of political organisation. An examination of his subsequent life and thought is certainly a worthwhile activity, for while this study aims to explore the broad sweep of the leftist mindset it must also focus on individual case studies. The preachers of virtue should have their own moral compass put to the test, and if it fails, then their pronouncements may be dismissed as hypocritical posturing.

Rousseau's life certainly got off to an unpleasant start. His mother died of complications from the birth just a few days after his delivery. He subsequently lamented that 'my birth was the first of my misfortunes'.[3] It is undeniable that such an incident has a traumatic impact, one that endures for years, but Rousseau's life hardly seems as bleak as he frequently laments. Indeed his existence appears, to the neutral observer, somewhat gilded. His life was rather peripatetic, but it was no doubt stimulating, in both the activities in which he was frequently engaged and the company he kept. His existence was generally comfortable and he enjoyed the generosity of others at a level that seems scarcely credible. He maintained companionship until his dying day, despite alienating scores of friends and acquaintances, and he enjoyed remarkable success in his lifetime too. His was not a life without trauma, none is, but it was far from the hopeless experience claimed by the rather defeatist tone of his writing. His existence was unsettled, yes, but that in itself hardly explains the violent emotional state in which Rousseau lived it. The traumas of his life seem largely self-inflicted, though this in itself may indicate some incipient psychological condition which was undiagnosed at the time. The death of his mother and the reduced level of female affection in his formative years may have contributed to his later, somewhat odd, sexual proclivities. Still, genuine ordeals are few and far between.

Yet he recorded an extreme reaction to a relatively innocuous event that took place at an early age. The young Jean-Jacques was left alone in a room in which a broken comb was later discovered. He denied being responsible but was blamed for it and punished regardless. In his *Confessions,* composed towards the end of his life, he related this tale at length. The depth of feeling he still bore over the memory, where he maintained his innocence, is undeniable and profound. Could this be the incident that sparked his later paranoia; that resulted in his persistent belief of being secretly judged for crimes he had not committed? In Rousseau's own mind he saw this tale as the genesis of his hatred of injustice, but the memory clearly burned so brightly that he would always be far more concerned with injustices inflicted on himself than on others. Regardless, the intensity with which he related the seemingly minor incident decades later remains startling:

> 'As I write this I feel my pulse beginning to race again; these moments would always be fresh in my mind, even if I lived for a hundred thousand years. The first experience of violence and injustice has remained so deeply engraved in my heart that any idea that is at all associated with it brings back the emotions I felt at the time.'[4]

As such, Rousseau is informed more by emotion than reason at comparable points. More than this, it is the intense emotion of a petulant little boy who feels he has been wronged.

After the death of his mother, Suzanne, Rousseau was brought up by an aunt and by his father Isaac, a watchmaker. He had no real formal education but was taught to read by his father and given access to his mother's impressive collection of books. Isaac Rousseau, a relatively accomplished violinist, also introduced Jean-Jacques to music. It too would play a significant role in his adult life. His childhood was relatively idyllic and carefree, though trouble started for the young man when apprenticed to an engraver in Geneva. But his angst appeared to stem from the fact that he was expected to work and support himself, a burden that caused great bitterness. Rousseau rebelled from such indignities and was incredulous that he faced sanctions for his lateness, laziness and pilfering. As a result, at the age of sixteen, he ran away. It would become an habitual response.

An elderly priest named Benoît de Pontverre recommended a benevolent lady in Annecy, Francoise-Louise-Eléonore de la Tour, baroness de Warens, who might take him under her wing. When Rousseau met Mme. De Warens, who would play a massive role in his life over the following years, she was twenty-nine, and he was immediately enraptured with her. He appears to have had something of a mother complex and claimed that the love he felt for the woman he christened *Maman* (she called him *petit*) was pure. He admitted that he kissed her clothing and the furniture she had been sitting on when she was not around. However, when their relationship was consummated years later the experience made him uncomfortable and he appeared to regret it. He already seemed to be a somewhat sexually damaged individual by then though. When boarding with a pastor named Lambercier near Geneva, the pastor's sister, Gabrielle, had given a spanking to the then eleven year old Rousseau (he later claimed he was eight). The incident gave him an enormous sexual thrill, so evident that she became flustered and refused to administer the punishment again. In his later adolescence Rousseau took to exposing his posterior at women in the street, apparently hoping to repeat the experience, an activity that usually prompted laughter but on one occasion nearly earned him a beating.

Under Mme. De Waren's guidance Rousseau converted to Catholicism in Turin, though he would convert back to Calvinism years later. He used her home as a base and, while benefitting from her hospitality, several opportunities came his way. While in Turin, Rousseau worked for a while in the household of the comtesse de Vercelles who died five months after he started working there. However, at such a young age his paranoia at being the subject of conspiracies was already cemented into his psyche. Believing the other servants had acted in a plot to exclude him from the comtesse's will he petulantly stole a ribbon, but when caught he accused a maid, Marion, of stealing it and giving it to him. His indignation with 'injustice', which had festered since the incident with the comb, did not appear to extend to other people. Rousseau's conscience was troubled by the 'atrocious deed', yet he suggested that if M. De la Roque had taken him aside for a quiet confab rather than confront him in front of witnesses, then he would have confessed immediately. In Rousseau's mind it was the circumstances that were to blame, and his virtue remained unsullied.

He also seemed more troubled by how the incident made him feel than how it affected Marion. Both were dismissed and, considering Rousseau's admission that he remained a petty thief for life, it does not appear that he learned a valuable lesson. Just as he had blamed his engraving master for his own lying, laziness and stealing, so he now blamed inequality for his lifelong habit of pilfering. He also appeared rather proud that he stole because of his distaste for money, even boasting that he only ever swiped goods and never cash, oblivious to the fact that the loss of personal artefacts is more wounding than the loss of money. Such excuses do him few favours. He seems never to have got over the loss of his idyllic, and frankly spoiled, childhood, when he could do whatever he wanted.

Rousseau's education continued to develop under the tutelage of *Maman*, who was intelligent and a voracious reader as well as a music lover who held weekly concerts at her house. He found sporadic employment teaching music and his existence became even more nomadic. After a spell as a tutor to a family in Lyon, a role he admitted to being ill-suited for, he moved to Paris in 1742, finding lodging in the Hôtel St. Quentin on the rue des Cordeliers, near the Sorbonne and the Jardin du Luxembourg. He hoped initially to win his fortune by devising a new system of musical notation. But it was shortly after arriving in the capital that he met Denis Diderot, the most significant friend of his early years and foe of his twilight period. Then a struggling young man like himself, Diderot was destined to be one the most influential thinkers of the day and the *Encyclopédie*, of which he was the founder and driving force, would be among the most significant publishing ventures of all time. Rousseau was, by this stage, voraciously well-read, though he never truly mastered Latin and Greek, yet he was always rather stiff in company, lacking social ease and wit. Diderot was a far more volatile, confident character, flamboyant and charming, one whose eloquence and powers of persuasion were famed. Rousseau's abilities in this regard were strictly limited to his pen. In the social circles of Paris the gauche and tongue-tied Rousseau withered in the light of Diderot's radiant brilliance, but in the wider court of public opinion and that of posterity, it would be the man from Geneva who would score the emphatic and enduring triumph. Despite its ugly epilogue, Rousseau's move to Paris and his acceptance into the social set of the Enlightenment would prove to be his making. It was the launch-pad for the career that saw him achieve historical immortality.

His travelling was far from done though, and Rousseau next spent an extended period in Venice working as secretary to the French ambassador, Pierre-François, Comte de Montaigu. While there, apart from being enamoured with the beauty of Italian music, he also pondered on politics, the influence of another city-state having a significant impact on his thought. He ruminated on

> 'that great question, as to which is the best possible form of government, [it] seemed to me to come down in the end to this one; what is the nature of the government most likely to produce the most virtuous, the most enlightened, the wisest, and in short, taking this word in its widest sense, the best people?'[5]

It is a conclusion that echoes throughout leftist thought: that politics need not be arranged to fit the needs of the people; it is the people who must be shaped to fit the requirements of the idealised state. This controlling inclination, this desire to use politics to mould people into a form the political sculptor feels morally agreeable, is at the heart of left-wing idealism. It is a habit inherently coercive and inimical to freedom, and it is a trait that Rousseau developed into something of an art form.

After arriving back in Paris, Rousseau had another encounter that proved to be a milestone in his life. Returning to his old lodgings in the St. Quentin rooming house he met Thérèse Levasseur, a shy young woman in her early twenties who had been employed to do the laundry. She was neither attractive nor bright, but Rousseau claimed to be struck by her modesty and sweetness. She would be his companion until his death, thirty-three years later. It is revealing though that Jean-Jacques never wrote of her with anything approaching the warmth or passion of many other women he encountered. Even individuals like Mme Basile or Zulietta, whom he met only fleetingly, clearly enamoured him and the intense ardour he felt for them is apparent in his prose. But of Thérése, his partner for life who he eventually married, he admits that he 'felt no natural attraction towards the poor girl'[6] and even describes her as a 'substitute'. Rousseau's friends often wondered what he saw in the young woman who never learned to read and could not tell the time, count change or recall the months of the year. It appears that the writer kept her around for convenience, for her utility to him.

On returning to the capital, Rousseau became immersed in the intellectual life of Paris. He and Diderot frequented d'Holbach's salon and became friendly with d'Alembert and Friedrich Melchior Grimm. Rousseau contributed numerous articles to the *Encyclopédie*, mostly on music though he also penned a lengthy piece on Political Economy. It set the stage for the epiphany to come. In 1749 Diderot was imprisoned for writing *The Promenade of a Sceptic*, in which he effectively argued in favour of evolution, thus gazumping Darwin by over a century. But such an attack on the Church could not be tolerated and he was flung in the Vincennes. It was while walking to visit him, and casually flipping through a copy of the *Mercure de France*, that Rousseau had the revelation that set him firmly on his career as a writer. He noticed the Academy of Dijon offered a prize for the best essay on the question 'has the progress of the sciences and the arts contributed to the corruption or the purification of morals?' and the theory that would dominate the remainder of his life came upon him. So he claims at any rate. He resolved there and then to enter the competition. His success would change his life, and, arguably, the world.

In his *Discourse on the Arts and Sciences* Rousseau took the contrary, anti-Enlightenment view. While his contemporaries believed that progress and reason were improving humanity, Rousseau disagreed. His revelation was that civilisation had debased man, corrupting his natural virtue into greed and artifice. It was from that point that Rousseau started to develop his full political and social theory, but it would remain critically flawed at every stage. Those defects began in his study of antiquity. Rousseau had grown up on the Classics and devoured Plutarch's *Lives of Noble Greeks and Romans*, reading it frequently as a boy. The life of Lycurgus particularly resonated with him and had a noticeable impact on his later thought. But while such literature profoundly affected his conception of virtue, it also left him with a distorted perception of the ancient world. He argued that Sparta's durability was down to its ascetic primitivism, while Athens' civilisation resulted in despotism and decay. He posited a similar analysis on the fall of Rome: contrasting the Imperial period unfavourably with that of the rugged and virtuous Republic. But in doing so, he naively swallowed the source record's almost universal antagonism to Athens and sympathy towards Sparta. Rousseau rather meekly accepted the interpretation of Thucydides, effectively the Greek Tacitus who, admiration for Pericles apart, perceived his home *polis* in primarily negative terms.

Yet Athens produced a slew of great minds like Socrates, Plato, Aristotle, Demosthenes, Aristophanes, Epicurus, Themistocles and Solon. It also fostered the environment where thinkers like Pythagoras, Archimedes, Hippocrates, Diogenes, Herodotus and Euclid could thrive. The city which led the Delian League bequeathed a staggering legacy of magisterial buildings, theatre, politics, science, literature, learning and art which remains profoundly influential even today. Sparta, by contrast, produced great warriors and little else. While it had structures, it could boast of no architecture to speak of at all, and its citizens were conditioned in subservience to the state, pressured into a crushing uniformity. The only *polis* to enslave fellow Greeks, it could be argued that its citizens lacked liberties to such a degree that Sparta was little more than a slave state. Yet in Rousseau's thesis, the simple life of Sparta was considerably superior to the pretensions of the Athenians. This obsession with a form of primitive virtue morphed into an ever more censorious streak. He sneered that 'We no longer ask if a man has integrity, but if he has talent, nor whether a book is useful but if it is well written'.[7] Rousseau was already suggesting the arts and theatre should be employed for moral instruction rather than as forms of free expression.

By this point, along with scooping up the Dijon prize, Rousseau was beginning to win a notable reputation. He was, for example, immortalised in a portrait by Maurice Quentin de La Tour. But it was ironic, in light of his censorial views, that he was demonstrating talent as a playwright too. He had written a comedy for the theatre and an opera which both achieved a measure of success. His play, *Narcissus, or the Lover of Himself* was performed in December 1752 at the

Comédie Francaise. In the production, a young fop named Valère became so enamoured with himself that his sister had his portrait retouched to display him in a dress, whereupon he fell in love with the image and spent the remainder of the play attempting to track down the beauty. Such an overtly gender-bender theme perhaps revealed more about the state of Rousseau's mind and his unusual sexuality than he meant to, as well as offering insights into the depth of his self-absorption. But his opera, *The Village Soothsayer,* was an even more notable triumph. The plot concerned the tale of a country lad who preferred the love of a sweet shepherdess to a countess. It proved a huge hit when performed at Fontainebleau, garnering effusive accolades from both Louis XV and Madame de Pompadour. The king summoned Rousseau in expectation of awarding him a royal pension which would have set him up for life; instead, he fled, to the exasperation of his friends, particularly Diderot who chided him for not taking the money, if not for himself then to provide for Thérése. Yet he later complained bitterly about the opera 'which had not brought me any return or advantage of any kind commensurate with its success'.[8] Regardless, it was not the theatre where his real future lay and in 1754 he entered the Dijon competition again. Rousseau followed up his first effort with his *Discourse on Inequality* which expanded the ideas set out in his initial essay. This time, as he produced a paper double the permitted word-count for the competition, Rousseau had no chance of winning the prize, but he was unconcerned. He would publish the following year anyway, and his focus turned to developing his thinking into a more unified system.

The question the academy had proposed was 'What is the origin of inequality among men, and is it authorized by natural law?' Rousseau dismissed the academy's reference to natural law which was an implication that the status quo was natural and therefore right. In addressing the issue he first sought to imagine life prior to the formation of societies and to reconstruct the stages by which humans became human; the key word being to 'imagine'. His whole ideology was based on an illusion, a phantasm conjured from thin air, and his ultimate philosophical solution would prove equally fantastical. Rousseau's contention was that inequality was a product of civilisation, and that it had not existed in man's natural state, though what led him to this outcome is anyone's guess. The conclusion appears little more than a desire to maintain a consistent theme between his two discourses to date. There is certainly no empirical evidence to support such an assertion and neither is there any substantive logical reasoning to back his thesis. The fact that generations of academics have taken his nonsensical assertions seriously is simply bewildering.

Rousseau naively asserted that man in nature has little to fear from the wild animals he encounters. But in doing so, the picture he paints resembles a Disney film more than any form of recognisable reality. He cites as evidence the inhabitants of Venezuela who, he claims, one never hears of being devoured.[9] One suggests that this statistic, if it has any veracity at all, results from the relatively diminutive nature of the wildlife in the area. Rousseau also suggests that animals suffer fewer diseases than man and that the ailments of humans are largely self-inflicted.[10] It is an ironic conclusion in light of subsequent research. That data suggests most human illnesses resulted from the period in which people and animals cohabited and were passed from the beasts to us. He also remarks that savages 'have almost no disorders except wounds and old age'[11] without considering that when such tribes-people become ill they simply die. Living in civilisation at least affords some possibility that we may recover from our ailments, even in the disease riddled eighteenth century in which the author lived. Yet Rousseau perceived nature as being nothing other than a nurturing idyll where bones set naturally better than with a surgeon's aid and where both men and beast enjoy a robust nobility that civilisation does naught but strip them of.

Rousseau contended that primitive societies were free of the ambitious and competitive instincts that blight civilisation; that they were consequently bereft of the fierce, violent rivalries that characterise developed states, and that hierarchies were non-existent. His claim rests primarily on the fact that similar traits are not found in nature, so they would have been absent from man in his natural state too. Yet this belief contradicts all available evidence. In reality, hierarchies, inequality and fierce rivalries are apparent throughout the natural world: a wolf-pack is led by its alpha, a beehive has its queen, a troop of gorillas its silverback, a herd of elephants its bull and a pride of lions its regally maned king. Not only do hierarchies exist in the natural world but fresh challengers vie for the leadership of animal communities as dynasties rise and fall. Viewed in these terms the actions of man in civilisation are not an aberration against nature but an expression of it. In fact, the evidence suggests that progress has had a mollifying effect rather than a corrupting one. If, in the wild, a male lion, bull or rhinoceros encounters a rival they will fight, frequently to the death. But two random male humans, 'tainted' by civilisation and left alone in an enclosed space will almost certainly have a nice chat.

The evidence suggests that Rousseau's conception of man in his primitive, 'natural' state is also wide of the mark. The plains Indians of America, the closest contemporary equivalents to Rousseau's ideal were, after all, comprised of warring tribes presided over by chieftains whose position was reinforced by arcane, elaborate ritual and flamboyant headgear, not a million miles removed from the royal houses of Europe. Rousseau finds such behaviour and plumage distasteful when employed by monarchies yet acceptable as part of tribal societies. But his perception of the 'noble savage', a concept lifted from Tacitus, was a romantic fallacy in the time of the Roman writer too. Boudicca, for one, apart from being a collaborator with the Romans who rebelled over a tax dispute, butchered civilian women, impaled them on pikes and hacked off their breasts before sewing them into their mouths. Such actions denote her as a savage, certainly, but they are bereft of any nobility.

In Rousseau's time the concept of the noble savage had been popularised by the Baron de Lahontan. He had published a book of 'dialogues' between himself and a Huron Indian in 1704 which eulogised the innocent instincts and wise conduct of those who abided by natural laws. His effort was followed up in 1770 by Guillame Thomas Raynal's ten-volume *Histoire Philosophique et Politique des Établissements et du Commerce des Europeans dans les deux Indes*. This work, which was 'short on sound facts but strong on sentimental outrage at the evils inflicted on the world by Europeans',[12] bore little relation to reality but was lapped up by what was, by contemporary standards, a vast readership. The sentimentalised image of the 'virtuous' culture of the indigenous population was portrayed in sharp contrast with the acquisitive and tyrannical nature of the white, Western civilisation it came into contact with. Our contemporary 'progressives' then aren't quite as cutting edge as they would like to imagine.

More recent research suggests that Rousseau's speculative stone-age idyll bears little comparison to his rose-tinted view. It seems that, rather than the peaceful utopia of his imagination our ancestors were a touch more brutal, committing a genocide against the Neanderthals so savage and relentless that it drove them to extinction, an atrocity unmatched by industrialised slaughter. So much for his speculation that the onset of civilisation led to man 'committing more murders in a single day's battle and more atrocities in the sack of a single city than were committed in the state of nature throughout entire centuries over the whole face of the earth'.[13] It seems clear that, in the process of becoming civilized, man has refined his natural desires, not abandoned them. All the traits that Rousseau derides, those of ruling elites, fierce competition, vanity and violence exist in nature. The idea of them being creations of civilisation is absurd. Archaeology has revealed that cave-women constructed elaborate combs out of bone and ornate necklaces from beautiful stones. And the most lavish of these have been unearthed in the most commodious caves. Pride, jealousy and hierarchies were present millennia before agriculture and civilisation arose. Rousseau's theorizing has been based on conjured fantasies. Posterity has proven all his imaginings false, yet still, the influence of his writing endures.

Rousseau argued for another twenty pages that the condition of savage man is infinitely preferable to that of civilised man, but such assertions are just as full of holes. He appears to have paid little notice to animals that live in communities and seems persuaded that primitive man, clearly an evolved pack or herd animal, did not do the same. He strongly rebuked Hobbes and suggests that man in nature is capable of nothing but compassion and pity; only the corrupting influence of civilisation has seen him develop other qualities. He seems to have drawn these ideas from the speculative view of the dawn of man in Tacitus: 'Primitive man had no evil desires. Being blameless and innocent, his life was free of compulsions or penalties. He also needed no rewards, for he was naturally good.'[14] Yet civilisations arose because man strove so hard to change his circumstances. One wonders why this ever happened if life was the idyll that Rousseau claims. His imagination seems closer to the Biblical Eden than the desperate, dangerous and uncomfortable struggle for survival that archaeology is gradually revealing.

Germaine de Staël noted that Rousseau eulogised a condition of brutishness because he knew what suffering intelligence and sensitivity caused in the world. So was Rousseau's philosophy simply inspired by the fact that he didn't fit neatly into society? That would explain why he was wistful over the idea of sex as nothing more than a physical release, free from the jealousy and possessiveness of romantic love which continually bedevilled him. In Rousseau's conception, natural man was a creature of instinct who could feel pity but not thought. Yet it is peculiar that he failed to consider that this purely emotional creature could not feel anger and hatred too. Pity and compassion obviously existed, but to suggest that they were the exclusive qualities of primitive societies is ludicrous. Rousseau argued that the reason inequality does not exist in a state of nature is because the strong have no way of binding the weak to their service, it was only the development of advanced communities that allowed such a process to occur. In this he makes a compelling argument. But the fact that men co-operate to accrue the benefits of civilisation, and that such teamwork relies on an hierarchy of command, is what separates us from the savage. Rousseau's case is that this collaboration is injurious to us, which makes one wonder why he never set off into the woods to eke out an existence as a Wildman if he truly considered such a lifestyle to be the nirvana he claims.

In contrast to his claims, hierarchies are entirely natural, for they have formed in every type of social organisation there has ever been. Europe and Japan had no contact at all in the middle ages, yet both developed remarkably similar feudal systems. They were also supported by a warrior class operating on a similar code of honour – Chivalry in Europe and Bushido in Japan. Every company, school, charity, church, army, hospital, sports team, nation-state and club is organised around some sort of tier system. It is how people organise themselves. It is how *animals* organise themselves. And the left's enthusiasm for dismantling such hierarchies appears just another failure to acknowledge human nature. In reality, man needs to feel the security of belonging to a welcoming and protective group, but this instinct goes in tandem with a suspicion and hostility for rival factions. People look for both safety in numbers and potential enemies, just as animals do in the wild. Yet in Rousseau's thesis there is no hierarchy in nature, no conflict, either in the wild or in the primitive human societies he venerates.

Rousseau's speculations on how man progressed from the natural to the civilized state are far more convincing. As population numbers rose, and the demand for food grew, agriculture was developed to meet the need. Metallurgy emerged as well, so labour needed to be organised and enforced and, gradually, some people grew richer. Governments developed to protect the wealth of those who had it, and the minority came to lord it over the majority. Rousseau, in stating that 'it is iron and wheat which first civilized men and ruined the human race'[15] laments the development of farming. He simply cannot see it as an effective method of providing regular sustenance for the rising population, one stripped of the dangers and unreliability of hunting and foraging. Instead, it is viewed as some nefarious scheme to ensnare the populace in servitude.

It is a strange conclusion. The fact that civilisation burst forth so quickly following the development of agriculture seems compelling evidence that it gave man the freedom, security and time previously unimaginable in the struggle of scratching out an existence in his hunter / gatherer lifestyle. It also suggests that early societies were characterised by significantly increased levels of co-operation. Yet Rousseau describes the pivotal moment of transition, that of marking out property, thusly:

> 'The first man who, having enclosed a piece of land, thought of saying 'This is mine' and found people simple enough to believe him, was the true founder of civil society. How many crimes, wars, murders; how much misery and horror the human race would have been spared if someone had pulled up the stakes and filled in the ditch and cried to his fellow men: 'Beware of listening to this imposter. You are lost if you forget that the fruits of the earth belong to everyone and that the earth itself belongs to no one!'

Yet Rousseau was again forgetting that animals do precisely the same thing. Birds have their nests, badgers their sets, rabbits their warrens, foxes their lairs, and all are fiercely territorial about their property. Gerrard Winstanley's Diggers had preached the same line about common ownership and the rejection of private property a century before Rousseau. But after setting up a community on St. George's Hill, Weybridge, they reacted furiously when their own property was violated.

Rousseau claimed that once farming communities had formed competition developed between individuals: competition over potential mates and competition in dancing and appearance. Such contests led to pride and jealousy which, in turn, gave birth to rage, revenge and cruelty. This development placed some men at the disposal of others, resulting in greed and deceit. The veneer of civilisation was thus at the root of all the vices of modern man; the primitive, free from such ostentation, was noble indeed in comparison. Criticising the abundant failings in Western societies and the often rigid behaviour demanded by them is certainly warranted. Outright dismissing such cultures because of their inevitable human failings is not.

Yet Rousseau had belittled the restraint expected of people in developed societies in his first discourse when arguing that 'Suspicions, offences, fears, coldness, reserve, hatred, and betrayal will always be hiding under this uniform and perfidious veil of politeness, under that urbanity which is so praised and which we owe to our century's enlightenment'.[16] Such arguments, having been further developed, proved influential and certainly inspired Mary Wollstonecraft in suggesting 'a barbarian, considered as a normal being, is an angel compared with the refined villain of artificial life'.[17] In fact, the influence of these ideas remains as strong as ever. It is Rousseau who is the true father of the environmental movement, and the distaste for civilisation and revulsion for the market still define the alarmist eco-warriors. The likes of Extinction Rebellion who scream about the climate 'catastrophe' are all Rousseau's children.

While Rousseau had adhered to the theme he began in the *Discourse on the Arts and Sciences* he had expanded his argument considerably. He had also developed his writing style and the prose has a fluidity and confidence entirely lacking from his first effort. He had begun wrestling with the dilemma between freedom and equality too, one he believed he had resolved by the time he penned *The Social Contract.* In this second discourse he asserted 'For there is freedom...something which fortifies robust constitutions used to it, but which overwhelms, ruins and intoxicates weak and delicate people unused to it'.[18] He is right to go on to suggest that there is a considerable difference between liberty and licence, and that there must be some limitations on freedom. However, in opting to aim for equality over autonomy, he had made a fundamental error. Societies should offer equality of opportunity; but they must accept that inequalities of outcome are inevitable. Equality, if it is to be attained, must be *imposed*. This necessitates coercion, a culture that is stifling and suffocating at a level far beyond a state's reliance on the rule of law.

It seems to me that modern society has not created inequality, though it certainly reflects it. Rousseau regards ambition and competition as being entirely negative, yet those traits have been behind all the great achievements of humanity. Those aspects of civilisation he rails against then have not *created* the needs and characteristics that he abjures, they have *responded* to them. While he perceives human nature as being the by-product of civilisation, the reality is that civilisation is the creation, the end result, of human nature, the child of all its imperfections and manifest strengths; and what a dazzling progeny it is.

Yet just as his professional life was on the rise Rousseau's personal life started to go off the rails, and it all began so promisingly too. Another of his social circle, Louise d'Épinay, noticed how taken he was with a dishevelled cottage called the Hermitage on the edge of the Montmorency forest a mile from the main château on her estate at La Chevette. She promptly had the place renovated and offered it to him as a surprise. After a little persuasion he travelled ten miles north of Paris to the site and moved in on 9 April 1756. Once again Rousseau was living at the largesse of another, but he would yet again behave with remarkable ingratitude. Mme d'Épinay, memorably rendered in a fine portrait by Jean-Étienne Liotard around that time was, at thirty, fourteen years Rousseau's junior. She was something of a proto-feminist and a serious writer and thinker herself, having penned erudite articles on education and the role of women. Like *Maman* she was separated from her husband, but Rousseau's new patron was considerably wealthier than her precursor. This time though the writer felt no sexual attraction towards his hostess. Being somewhat angular and flat-chested she failed to arouse the ardour of the writer whose tastes gravitated towards rather more voluptuous figures.

The Hermitage itself was an attractive and spacious abode nestled in a beautiful garden in idyllic surroundings. Even accompanied, as he was, by not just Thérèse but her mother too, it promised the isolation that he craved. Rousseau had already been growing estranged from his Paris circle, unbeknownst to them, and the sections on this period in his *Confessions* are remarkably bitter. It was not simply that he was becoming philosophically removed from his former clique, though by taking up a position ever more counter to the Enlightenment, increasingly valuing feelings above reason and retaining a strong faith that saw him bristle at his contemporaries' atheism, such was certainly the case. It is likely too, that he had grown increasingly ill at ease in their company. The brooding and self-pitying Rousseau simply did not fit in with the witty repartee and banter at d'Holbach's salon. He also struggled to compete in the level of discourse there and bitterly resented the feeling of inferiority this bred in him. Rousseau's ego would simply not allow him to put up with such bruising blows to his self-esteem. Not having had the benefit of the formal education of his peers, lacking their command of Latin and Greek, and being far less eloquent with his tongue than he was with his pen, it is easy to see how this intense character became increasingly uncomfortable among his former friends.

One incident in particular captured the widening schism that was growing insurmountable in Rousseau's mind, even if Diderot and the others were oblivious to it. The other *philosophes* at d'Holbach's salon had allowed the abbé Petit to read aloud from a turgid tragedy he had written, growing ever more amused at the abbé's enthusiasm over his own feeble literary efforts. Rousseau fumed for a while before snatching the play from his hands and throwing it to the floor while bellowing 'Your play is worthless, your preface is crazy; all these gentlemen are mocking you; leave here and go back to being a vicar in your village'.

The sections of the *Confessions* where Rousseau described the disintegration of his primary friendships leave the reader shaking their head in despair. In attempting to argue his own side of the case the paranoid philosopher only undermines it with a frantic industry. Rousseau's friends in Paris missed him while he was away at the Hermitage and attempted to persuade him to return. But, in his fevered imagination, this was merely evidence of a vile conspiracy by which they hoped to drag him from his tranquil reverie. Rousseau complained about the hospitality of his hostess too. He resented Mme d'Épinay and moaned that 'she was fond of her friends, she was zealous in serving their interests, and since she spared herself neither time nor effort on their behalf, she doubtless deserved that they should in return be attentive to her'.[19] Some would call this 'friendship', but Rousseau appeared to bristle at the suggestion that he should be considerate towards people who had done the same to him. He began to view his situation as a form of bondage, and he bitterly resented it. Even when given free rein to paint events in a light favourable to himself he still comes across as a quite shocking ingrate. Mme d'Épinay's lover, Melchior Grimm, had warned her from the start 'If you refuse one single time to be at his command, he will accuse you of having begged him to live near you and of preventing him from living in his native land'.[20] It was to prove a most accurate forecast.

The drama really came to a head when Rousseau was introduced to his hostess's sister-in-law, Élisabeth-Sophie-Françoise Lalive de Bellegarde, the Comtesse d'Houdetot. Sophie, as she became known to him, was also estranged from her husband but was the lover of Rousseau's friend, Jean-François de Saint-Lambert, an army officer away campaigning in the Seven Years War. Lambert was a dashing, charismatic and lively character who exuded confidence, a sharp contrast to the withdrawn, moody, frail and overly sensitive writer. Sophie had an infectious personality, a wild, uproarious laugh, and frequently galloped around the estate in men's riding clothes. Her zest for life shone through and Rousseau's ardour quickly turned to obsession. The writer became utterly smitten with the woman, who was twenty years his junior, and began to pursue her with behaviour that would now be classified as high-level stalking. He admitted to habitually masturbating while walking the short distance through the woods to visit her. Flattered by the attention, though presumably oblivious to her prospective paramour's sylvan discharges, Sophie led him on somewhat, though there was never any question of her consummating their relationship. But Rousseau displayed little regard for the feelings of either his friend Lambert, his hostess Mme d'Épinay or the Comtesse de Houdetot herself, his preoccupation was with sating his own carnal lust. He had little regard for Thérèse either. He didn't just carry on his pursuit in front of her, he actually used his common-law wife as the go-between to ferry the letters fired back and forth with the object of his desire. Such behaviour was quite shockingly callous, revealing a heartlessness chilling in its indifference to her. Indeed, Rousseau's behaviour throughout the incident was far removed from the man of virtue he claimed to personify.

The fallout from the affair was quite spectacular and is rich in documentary evidence. Affairs were *de rigueur* at the time, but they were expected to be conducted with discretion, a concept with which Rousseau had only passing familiarity. His behaviour alarmed his peers and his circle buzzed with talk on his transgressions. Yet, in his addled mind, Rousseau cast his hostess, who had, not unreasonably, been attempting to find out the depth of the scandal taking place on her estate, as the villain. His paranoia of conspiracies convinced him she was guilty of sabotaging his non-existent love affair. In reality, it was the intensity of his pursuit, as well as the public repercussions, that had started to alarm Sophie. She distanced herself from him yet, despite being the one at fault, Rousseau recorded that 'My rage and indignation were indescribable'.[21] The letters that follow between himself and Mme d'Épinay are jaw-dropping. Rousseau replied to a polite enquiry thusly: 'I have nothing to say to you as yet. I am waiting until I am better informed, and sooner or later I will be. Meanwhile you may be certain that injured innocence will find a defender ardent enough to give the slanderers, whoever they are, cause for concern'.[22]

She replied politely again.

'My dear friend...I have just reread your letter; I am none the wiser, but it fills me with trepidation. You seem cruelly agitated. I would like to reassure you, but since I do not know the cause of your anxiety, I do not know what to say to you, except that I am every bit as wretched as you are and will continue to be so until I have seen you...Goodbye dear friend.'[23]

Yet his response seethed with hostility:

'The trust you speak of no longer exists, and it will be no easy matter for you to revive it. I see your present concern on my behalf as an attempt, quite simply, to extract from someone else's confidence some advantage that suits your own purposes; and my heart, ever eager to pour itself out to a heart that opens to receive it, closes up in the face of subtlety and guile. I detect your usual artfulness in the difficulty you find in understanding my letter. Do you really think me fool enough to believe that you did not understand it?'[24]

It is noteworthy that Rousseau could find room to boast about the purity of his heart amidst such furious paranoia. He goes on to state that if his suspicions are proven correct 'I would hate you until my dying day...I would never forgive you for this, I would become your irreconcilable enemy...I, who never did harm to anyone'.[25] She replied again, full of hurt and confusion, but also showed a willingness to forgive him.

Rousseau realised his error and reconciliation swiftly followed, but the damage had been done. Sadly, he failed to learn the lesson of his paranoia on non-existent conspiracies. His delusions did not abate, they only escalated. He then decided that the line 'only the wicked are alone' in Diderot's *The Natural Son* was an insulting reference to him. The diatribe in the *Confessions* that follows on his splintering relationship with his former friend appears, frankly, the product of an unhinged mind, though his subsequent writing proves that his faculties remained intact. One can only conclude that the fury that consumed him when committing the subject to paper was so powerful that it overwhelmed him. The whole affair unsurprisingly left Sophie rather less enthusiastic about socialising with Rousseau and she grew cold towards him. Feeling that he had done nothing to deserve such treatment Rousseau then, astonishingly, wrote to his still oblivious friend, Saint-Lambert, to ask him to use his influence to persuade Sophie to be more affectionate.

It was in this uncomfortable climate that Mme d'Épinay fell ill, or pregnant, depending on which source one believes, and announced that she would be leaving for Geneva to see Dr. Tronchin. As her partner, Grimm, was unable to accompany her and the destination was his birthplace she asked if Rousseau would care to be her chaperone. He appeared to regard the request as an outrageous impertinence, despite the hospitality she had shown him for years. The idea of inconveniencing himself for a friend was utterly alien to him. In fact, he admitted to laughing when she asked if he would join her on the journey. He even complained that the generosity she had shown him amounted to 'two years of slavery'.

Diderot wrote to Rousseau in an attempt to persuade him to go. He asked 'Will you find another such opportunity in life to demonstrate your gratitude?'[26] Diderot concluded his request in a manner designed to placate his friend, and to not appear too pushy, suggesting of his letter that 'if it annoys you, throw it into the fire and let us think no more of it than if it had never been written. I send you greetings, I send you love, I embrace you.' It seemed a reasonable, polite request but Rousseau commented on 'the trembling, the blind rage' with which he read it. He composed a furious response and marched up to the main house where he proudly read both letters out to Mme d'Épinay and Grimm. The couple were, unsurprisingly, speechless, a response he completely misinterpreted as surprise at his forthright, confident declaration. The self-obsession and delusion of his memoirs is frankly eye-watering and they make the incomprehension and despair of his former friends entirely understandable. Incredibly Rousseau still talked of his 'magnanimity', concluding 'This sacrifice, which my enemies were able to turn to their own advantage, and for which they had perhaps been waiting, has been the ruin of my reputation and has deprived me, through their efforts, of public esteem'.[27]

His refusal to take any responsibility for his plight, despite the stunning selfishness, paranoia and ingratitude of his actions, defies belief. In the wake of his unforgivable behaviour Rousseau's friends began to turn from him. In his addled mind he perceived this as them removing their masks and revealing their complicity at last, rather than such being the results of his own abominable conduct. He blamed the rupture on 'a heart, too loving and too tender, which, deceived by those it had believed to be of like temper, was forced to retreat into itself',[28] He had become convinced that a 'league' was conspired against him. But if such a convocation did exist it was entirely his own creation. One reads these passages in despair at the mania to which Rousseau had fallen prey. It was a malady that would taint the rest of his life. While Mme d'Épinay was away Rousseau wrote to assure her that their friendship was over but also informed her of his intention to stay at the Hermitage until such time as it was convenient for him to move on. Unsurprisingly her reply was now icy, and she suggested that he leave.

Relations never recovered between Rousseau and d'Holbach's clique, the group that had played such an important role in his life. Grimm, in particular, could not forgive Rousseau for his churlish ingratitude. He was fortunate indeed that Lambert's response was so restrained. He may very well have demanded a duel and one would not much fancy the chances of the hypochondriac writer against the flamboyant military hero. Rousseau rented a diminutive house in Montmorency from which he pestered Sophie with letters until she cut him off. His new abode had a small outhouse in the garden called the Donjon to which Rousseau retreated to write. But, before he completed the major works which would change his life, he clashed briefly with his former friends once more.

D'Alembert had written an article on Geneva for the *Encyclopédie*. It suggested the city state's ban on the theatre should be overturned. Rousseau, who strongly disagreed, believed that d'Alembert was being used by Voltaire who had moved to just outside Geneva. The great writer was, in defiance of its Calvinist principles, putting on plays at his estate in the suburbs. In Rousseau's perception, his birthplace was being perverted into Athenian decadence. In response to the article he wrote an open *Letter to D'Alembert*, which again praised the simplicity of Sparta over the ostentation of Athens and derided the theatre on principle. 'Far from learning moral truths, he asserted, audience members tended to admire clever rogues, laugh at virtuous people...and applaud performers whose profession is fundamentally degrading'.[29] He apparently saw no inherent contradiction in making such comments while remaining free to submit his own theatrical efforts. While his own plays were clearly morally laudable, he had no reservations about trying to suppress the output of others. In the published letter Rousseau also blamed Diderot for the failure of his attempt to woo Mme d'Houdetot and for Saint-Lambert discovering the truth about his machinations. It was not the fault of his own duplicity but the scheming of his friends.

The public slight earned him widespread rebukes, illustrated to some that he was determined to alienate all his friends, and was the final breaking point in his friendship with Diderot. The editor of the *Encyclopédie* committed his own thoughts on the relationship to paper, though not for publication. 'This man is false, vain as Satan, ungrateful, cruel, hypocritical, and wicked...Truly this man is a monster'.[30] Yet, having alienated or compromised all the important relationships in his life, Rousseau had a stroke of luck when an influential admirer, François-Frédéric de Montmorency-Luxembourg, the duc de Luxembourg, became his new patron. Rousseau and Thérèse moved into a villa known as the Petit Château on the Luxembourgs' vast estate while the house at Montmorency was restored. They would remain there for three years. While this time he managed, for the moment, not to alienate his hosts, Rousseau spent an extended segment of his *Confessions* bitchily sniping about the Luxembourgs' social circle, demonstrating the same characteristics that saw him alienated from d'Holbach's clique. In that same period though, in a blizzard of activity, he completed his three masterpieces: *Julie, or the New Heloise* in January 1761, *Émile* in October 1761 and *The Social Contract* in April 1762, two months before he turned fifty.

In *Julie*, Rousseau depicted his idealised society in a location called Clarens, a sort of communal hippy idyll. His rather naive economic theory was centred on a sustainable biosphere of rustic idealism. At Clarens the sun always shone and the workers sang as they gathered their crops, evoking the visual idealism that Soviet propaganda turned into something of an art form. *Julie* was the work which elevated and glorified sentiment and emotion above reason and self-restraint. It was essentially a love story - largely a wish fulfilment allegory of his relationship with Mme de Warens. *Julie* was a phenomenal publishing success and ranked among the biggest selling novels of the century. In Hegel's later terminology it captured the zeitgeist of the age of sentimentality, and it made its author a publishing sensation. Rousseau was inundated with gushing letters from scores of admirers and his reputation as a virtuous man of feeling was assured. The author later referred to its readership in order to boast, yet again, of the superiority of his morality, suggesting that it could not be enjoyed by one 'who did not have that sixth sense, that moral sense, with which so few hearts are endowed, and without which none can understand mine.'[31]

Rousseau's next published effort, *Émile*, has had a profound and lasting impact. Despite never raising children of his own and having only a brief, and notably unsuccessful career as a tutor, he elected to write a treatise on how to raise and educate a child. Rousseau thus became the first leftist philosopher who sought to direct human life from the cradle to the grave. He would not be the last. He admits that his impractical programme was 'fanciful',[32] but it remains a truly revolutionary work. However, *Émile* also sheds light on the most disturbing and difficult to excuse of the writer's manifest faults. He criticised the contemporary practice of swaddling new-born babies and handing them over to wet nurses. But he heartily endorsed breastfeeding and suggested that parents should spend time playing with their children. These recommendations have since become accepted practice, yet his scathing comments on those who 'abandon' their children to wet nurses contrast sharply with his own actions. Rousseau suggested that the duty of a father 'is to support and educate his own children. If a man of any natural feeling neglects these sacred duties he will repent it with bitter tears and will never be comforted'.[33] But, despite these words, it emerged that he had fathered five children with Thérèse and packed them all off to the foundling hospital with barely a backwards glance. More than this, the callousness with which he discussed the practice in his *Confessions* is chilling. He recorded how much Thérèse protested the decision, but her feelings on the subject were, naturally, immaterial. His justifications bear little relation to the public image of virtue and a 'feeling heart' he loved to project. 'I made up my mind to take it, blithely and without the least scruple...The following year the same inconvenience presented itself, the same expedient was adopted. I reflected no more deeply on the matter, the mother agreed no more readily.'[34] Rousseau defended the move on the grounds that he had no intention of marrying Thérèse. Such was his excuse at any rate. He also wallowed in the effect his actions had on him while remaining oblivious to the impact they had on the mother. Yet, having endured five pregnancies only to have the babes ripped from her unwilling arms, she was genuinely suffering, as, of course, were the children themselves.

But compounding such coldness is the fact that sending his offspring to the foundling hospital was a virtual death sentence. The mortality rates of these institutions were appalling. According to official records, 70% of foundlings in

1751 died in under a year[35] and it has been estimated that the total fatality rate hovered around the 90% mark.[36] Research also suggests that one of Jean-Jacques's offspring, a girl given up on 21 November 1746, was dead in under two months. Remarkably, Rousseau attempted to claim that, as the children had been formally deposited they had not really been abandoned at all. Yet, even more inexcusably, it emerged that both Mme d'Épinay and Mme de Luxembourg had offered to adopt his children. He refused. Given the opportunity for his offspring to be raised in ease and comfort he preferred the fantasy that they would grow up to be virtuous peasants. There is a significant disparity between what Rousseau practised and what he preached, but his immersion in these flights of fancy had become so complete that he appeared entirely removed from reality. He suggested that if those ladies of nobility had raised his children then 'I am sure that they would have been taught to hate and perhaps betray their parents; it is a hundred times better that they should never have known them'.[37] It was better for him perhaps, certainly not for his unfortunate progeny. But then ensuring situations suited Jean-Jacques was always his priority, no matter how he tried to justify his actions. He even appeared proud of abandoning his children bragging that 'This arrangement seemed to me so good, so sensible, so legitimate that, if I did not boast of it openly, this was solely out of consideration for their mother'.[38] Naturally, it was really Thérèse he was thinking of all along.

Émile was strongly influenced by the Socratic notion that true knowledge originated with asking questions rather than memorizing answers. However, it was deeply original in many aspects too, principally in suggesting that each person has a unique temperament that needs a certain amount of freedom to thrive. Rousseau's fixation with how childhood experiences shape adult personality, an issue that had concerned him for years, came to the fore and was the book's most notable breakthrough. He also recommended a vegetarian diet, claiming that 'the taste for meat is unnatural',[39] discouraged spanking, somewhat surprisingly, and argued that there should be no comparison or competition between children, even in running races.[40] This too is a popular notion now though, in twelve years of teaching, I can honestly say that students were always most enthused, motivated and energised when placed in competition with each-other. By contrast, nothing provoked a more negative response than attempting to motivate them to work as a team - for few people trust the judgement, ability or industry of others over their own.

Rousseau's political philosophy is evident on every page of the tome. He repeatedly compares town life unfavourably with that of the country, suggests that rural folk speak better than those raised in an urban environment and claims that 'peasants are generally shrewder than townsfolk'.[41] The conviction in his virtue is also apparent. Reading the book one gets the impression that it was written by an individual brimming over with love for his fellows, one whose main priority was the care and welfare of children; in short, a man who bears no relation at all to Rousseau. The disparity between the theory and practice of the man is immense.

Rousseau's central thesis was to allow the child to discover, actively, the world for himself, with his tutor to guide and respond to the student's enquiries. He also recommended keeping the child away from books until the age of twelve. It was this overall vision that inspired the movement of 'child-centred learning' which peaked in the '60s and '70s and which retains its advocates today. However, Émile's tutor constantly attempts to orchestrate situations so the student comes to the 'correct' conclusions. There is no suggestion that Émile has real freedom to discover the world for himself; every stage of his life is carefully managed to nudge him in the direction Rousseau desires. It is not a 'free' education but an entirely closed one, where he is to be kept sequestered from the rich, the cultivated and from female company until his tutor's indoctrination is ingrained. He suggests the child's teacher should 'guard them by means of this very taste from a dangerous idleness. Choose carefully their company, their occupations, and their pleasures; show them nothing but modest and pathetic pictures which are touching but not seductive, and nourish their sensibility without stimulating their senses'.[42]

The book was certainly a brave attempt to challenge the prevailing attitudes of the day, but it was frequently backwards-looking too. Rousseau eschewed medicine for tampering with nature and recommended a natural life and herbal remedies instead. He also opposed the idea of smallpox vaccination - the brainchild of Edward Jenner, which may have saved more lives in human history than any other development. While the medical profession was relatively primitive in his day, and frequently did more harm than good, the writer neglected the possibility of improvement through continued experimentation. His stance on this topic is redolent of the contemporary activists' aversion to new technologies like GM crops or fracking. Were Rousseau around now one suspects he would be an anti-vaxxer with a preference for natural, 'holistic' and herbal remedies, probably an advocate of homeopathy, strongly opposed to stem cell research and resolute in his belief that 'big pharma' was all part of some bloated conspiracy. He reveals an alarmist and Manichean worldview in some startling extracts: 'Nature showed me a scene of harmony and proportion; the human race shows me nothing but confusion and disorder...I behold the earth, and there is evil upon it.'[43] This interpretation reveals nothing of the desperate fight for survival in nature or the likes of earthquakes, tsunamis, volcanoes, floods and hurricanes that can strike without warning bringing 'confusion and disorder', or of the way that human societies function, for the most part, remarkably well.

Rousseau was dismissive of organised religion in a section titled the *Creed of the Savoyard Priest*, an aspect of the book that would cause him issues in due course. Yet he retained a deep and profound faith. He placed Christian concepts into a philosophical context and, while the movement he inspired tends to no longer share his faith, it does seem that left-wing dogma has filled a psychological need that religion used to sate: to have faith in a reassuring creed, to feel morally nourished by one's beliefs and actions, to be able to advertise one's virtue to others, and to convert one's fellows while admonishing 'sinners' who fail to conform. Both also share something of a binary outlook. With Christianity it is a choice between Heaven and Hell, but the modern activist has their own version of redemption or perdition. They frequently look to the future and envisage either a socialist utopia or the doomsday scenario of nuclear war or environmental collapse. In Blom's analysis the

'possibility of humanity's simply muddling through for millennia to come (the most likely scenario by far), avoiding some catastrophes while suffering others (some of them self-inflicted), is simply less instinctive to our theologically conditioned brains than the thought of salvation or damnation. So deeply ingrained are these cultural instincts that Rousseau's totalitarian utopia can seem more natural and sensible than Holbach's utilitarian tinkering. Utopians are always religious at heart'.[44]

Zamoyski has also theorised that revolutionary ardour replaced religious piety; the former serving the emotional needs left unsatisfied by the latter's crumbling authority.[45] His contention, that certain aspects of language, ritual, symbolism and customs were common from one culture to the other, is far from concrete proof. But it is undeniable that both movements have employed the rhetoric of virtue and piety to justify the destruction of their enemies. It also has to be conceded that both were guilty of levels of brutality and intolerance untouched by those they denounced. Tocqueville argued that since such activism was primarily concerned with the regeneration of the human race, rather than merely the organisation of the state, it inspired a proselytism which 'like Islam, flooded the whole world with its soldiers, its apostles and its martyrs'.[46]

Rousseau himself is clear on the psychological benefits that can accrue from surrendering to a dogma that salves one's conscience.

'I cannot understand how any one can be a sceptic sincerely and on principle...Doubt with regard to what we ought to know is a condition too violent for the human mind; it cannot long be endured; in spite of itself the mind decides one way or another, and it prefers to be deceived rather than to believe nothing'.[47]

Such a mental position is, no doubt comforting, easy, but this in no way validates it as an intellectual option. For while the pragmatists of the right are the children of Locke and the Enlightenment, the emotionally charged activists of the left are the progeny of Rousseau. The writer set a dangerous precedent when setting out his rules for life.

> 'I do not derive these rules from the principles of the higher philosophy, I find them in the depths of my heart, traced by nature in characters which nothing can efface. I need only consult myself with regard to what I wish to do; what I feel to be right is right, what I feel to be wrong is wrong; conscience is the best causist'.[48]

This is the sort of moral certainty that makes one immune to evidence and reason. More chillingly the influence of this passage is clearly visible in the speeches of Robespierre. It should come as no surprise that two individuals so puffed up on their own virtue should have ultimately proven such nasty pieces of work. The pompous, self-satisfied campaigner with the hair-trigger sensibilities is a common enough stereotype.

Rousseau's next offering, *The Social Contract*, was his vision of the ideally ordered society. It was effectively his magnum opus. The book opens with the most powerful line in his entire oeuvre: 'Man was born free, and everywhere he is in chains'.[49] That sentiment is a precursor of the Marxist call to arms: 'Workers of the world unite; you have nothing to lose but your chains'. Yet Marx never knew what it was to be a worker, and Rousseau's cry of indignation comes from a man who considered living rent-free in a stately home equivalent to slavery. One gets the impression that his philosophy is that of a spoilt child determined to run free and bristling with resentment when asked to behave. But, despite his high stakes opening gambit on freedom, Rousseau's true focus was on equality, even if he believed he had found the secret to effectively marrying the concepts. He hadn't though, and his failure in this regard would see him, despite the stirring power of his sentiment, immortalised as one of the greatest enemies of liberty there has ever been.

For millennia political philosophers have attempted to reconcile the desire for liberty with the need for authority: Machiavelli, Bodin, Hobbes and Locke, among others, have all struggled with the issue. Disagreement usually revolves over where to draw the line. Hobbes, who had a low opinion of human nature, recommended firmer control than Locke who sought to achieve the minimum of security while loosening man's leash more liberally. For Rousseau though, liberty was an absolute value and imposing restraints on such a characteristic was anathema. His solution appeared, to him at least, to reconcile all his concerns in one neat theory. The idea of uniting freedom and equality was Rousseau's most unique breakthrough but, idyllic though it sounds, the consequences of his theorising would prove devastating. Such repercussions are apparent in his threat that 'whoever refuses to obey the general will must be compelled to do so by the whole body. This means nothing else than that they will force him to be free'.[50]

Rousseau had ruminated on the general will, the *volunté générale,* in his article on political economy in volume V of Diderot's *Encyclopédie* some seven years earlier. It was a concept he had been formulating ever since he had been struck by that revelation on the road to Vincennes. Man feels free when he can achieve, or at least chase, his desires. However, if he could be persuaded to only desire that which is good for society, then freedom could be married with equality. What that meant of course, was that anyone who disagreed with this 'consensus' could simply be dismissed as irrational and ignored.

In Rousseau's conception it would be necessary to indoctrinate and control individuals so their desires tallied with the General Will - an approach that results in the stifling of independent minds. Rousseau's utopia would have condemned Galileo too. He envisaged a harmonious society with no agencies diverging from the common good. But this desire, anathema to any true lover of liberty, was taken up with relish by the extremist Jacobins and Mao's Red Guards as an excuse for all kinds of abominations. Rousseau's assertion that 'there should be no partial society within the state' would be music to the ears of Pol Pot, Stalin, Hitler and their contemporary ilk.

He remained frustratingly vague and elusive on what sort of decisions the general will might reach. As these would be dependent on the particular time and location of an individual state he refrained from even hinting at a specific example, leaving such conclusions up to interpretation. Damrosch argues that Rousseau cannot be blamed for the totalitarian states that followed in his wake, for the concept is an anachronism when applied to the Genevan. He also contends that what Rousseau had in mind was altogether different from the surveillance and thought control of a modern police state; but is it? It is true that the consequences of his philosophising bear little relation to his intent, but while those practicalities would not have occurred to Rousseau the principle which motivated them comes virtually unaltered from his work. If his theorising is faulty, and it is, then he can be held to account for the consequences.

He desired to impose an utterly untested theoretical model on a race which bore no resemblance at all to the citizens who would populate his idealised state. This fundamental error has been repeated time and again. Rousseau hoped to heal the ills of the world. But the plans he proposed, in their failure to recognise humanity's faults, are entirely ill-conceived. In consequence, they end up creating far greater problems than those they hoped to address. Modern Western democracies, while restraining man's wilder impulses, and encouraging and facilitating his creative, restless energy, have far more successfully combated man's inherent failings than any of the schemes proffered by the likes of Rousseau. Seeking to enforce a type of homogenous conformity does nothing to counter the faults of mankind. It only stifles his attributes, restraining him with the force of a straitjacket, and eroding his ambition, his motivation, the very freedom to express himself that defines him as an individual: that quality that Rousseau himself so revered. In his search for virtue he hoped to obliterate those seething tensions that can inflame man; but this is not possible, nor is it advisable. It is better by far to channel those impulses, to provide the outlet with which he can employ his energy productively. To do this means allowing the greatest possible freedom of speech, with economic and cultural liberties. To attempt to force man to comply with a bland template arbitrarily dictated by some well-meaning but misguided busybodies is to tether a stallion in a stable in preference to letting it run free.

Through Rousseau's social compact men, unequal in strength or intelligence, would gain parity through agreed convention. He believed that the general will would transform humanity, made selfish by the corrupting influence of civilisation, into a moral and altruistic race - for as the general will tended to the public welfare then it was always in the right. His conviction on this was unshakeable even though it is a long way from certain that a general will even exists. This writer contends that it does not, but to Rousseau there was no doubt. As such the state

'must have a coercive force of universal scope, in order to move and control each part in the manner most advantageous to the whole...the social pact gives the body politic absolute power over its members, and as I have said, it is this same power, directed by the general will, that bears the name of sovereignty'.[51]

The conclusion that Rousseau had arrived at was a totalitarian's wet dream. The writer went on to add that 'The general will is always in the right, but the judgement guiding it is not always enlightened. The general will needs to be shown things as they are, and sometimes as they ought to appear, to be taught which path is the right one for it to follow.'[52] One suspects this passage resonated strongly with Robespierre, the 'Incorruptible' memorizing it with particular zeal.

Rousseau went on to describe the Legislator who would guide the ignorant populace towards enlightenment (but most emphatically not Enlightenment). One can again imagine Robespierre's pulse racing while reading the extract. It is a piece written with pious reverence about the sort of chosen individual, with Lycurgus cited as an example, who can not only govern a state, but *establish* one for lesser men to follow in their footsteps. The extract in which Rousseau describes this process is worth reprinting at length.

'The man who dares to undertake the establishment of a people has to feel himself capable of changing, so to speak, the nature of man; of transforming each individual, who in himself is a perfect, isolated whole, into a part of a larger whole from which the individual, as it were, receives his life and being; of altering man's constitution in order to strengthen it; of substituting a morally dependent existence that we have all received from nature. In a word, he must deprive man of his own strength so as to give him strength from outside, which he cannot use without the help of others. The more completely these natural strengths are destroyed and reduced to nothing, the more powerful and durable are those which replace them, and the firmer and more perfect too, the society that is constituted.'[53]

It was effectively the first description of the 'New Man' which would echo through leftist thought. But Rousseau went further. When discussing the role of the state religion he asserted that if 'having publicly accepted these same dogmas, any person conducts himself as if he did not believe them, let him be punished by death'.[54] It is a brief mention, but it is undeniable that the writer has recommended the ultimate sanction for thought crimes. Robespierre certainly took him at his word, and the principles applied were to be repeated at far greater cost in the twentieth century. In the Legislator Rousseau has created not just a dictator but a totalitarian one committed to ensuring the citizenry's very thoughts and words conform to the general will. His influence is there in every despotic dictatorship that followed in his wake. The real-world consequences of his ideas undo all his noble talk of the sovereignty of the people which, in the final analysis, prove to be so much hot air. Such is Rousseau's true legacy.

When envisaging a society with a single will, one where decisions are always effectively unanimous, Rousseau was picturing a utopia of harmony. In his perception, 'virtue is nothing other than this conformity of particular wills to the general'.[55] The reality of attempts to build such societies has, of course, been very different. All the features which allow mankind to flourish: competition, ambition, and the influx of new, contrasting lifestyles and opinions, the ingredients that spark endless invention, are anathema to the man. It is interesting that the freedom to challenge and mock prevailing norms, something Rousseau thrived on as a thinker and writer, was to be expunged from the society he hoped to create. The likes of Rousseau never want their *own* liberties threatened. They just desire to direct other men, to decide what is good for them, what they should think, and who gets what from the communal pot. It is an inherently dictatorial mindset.

The student of philosophy may not be surprised then to discover the significant influence that Plato's *Republic* had on Rousseau's theory. The *Republic* is a fascistic fantasy that strips its citizens of any real individuality or opportunity to flourish, reducing the majority to drones in service of the state.

Plato's *Republic*, ruled by philosopher kings, was based entirely on the 'golden lie'. All inhabitants of Kallipolis, the city-state in his speculative work, were to be informed that they were born with various metals in their souls, either gold, silver or bronze and that their status in society was determined accordingly. Those with bronze souls were to be workers, those with silver were the soldiers and those with gold the guardians, the philosopher-kings. Bertrand Russell believes that Aldous Huxley plucked the idea for *Brave New World*, with its alphas and betas, directly from the pages of Plato. But that which seems a utopia to the likes of Plato and Rousseau is a dystopian nightmare to lovers of liberty. The priority of the state was in training the young to inculcate *virtue*. Yet his first move was to expel all poets and artists from his polis. He believed the arts had a powerful effect, so was determined to ensure they taught the *right* message. To Plato such activities were deceptions, and his state must be based on philosophical truth, an ironic proposition from the author of the 'Golden Lie'.

Plato, who had zero practical experience in the political life of Athens, based his system on the Spartan model. It is instructive that, besides Plato, Rousseau and Robespierre, there was another great admirer of Sparta. Adolf Hitler was inspired by that polis to indoctrinate boys into militarism while venerating the role of motherhood, and the Hitler Youth was a somewhat diluted version of the Spartan *Agoge*. Under Sparta's regime, boys from the age of seven were ripped from their mothers to be indoctrinated into militarism and blind subservience to the state's war machine. Yet Rousseau believed that state infinitely superior to the art, science and culture of contemporary Paris.

Novel tastes were to be unknown in Kallipolis, and the guardians were to organise the breeding of the ruling elite so that new citizens were born into the right class. Under this programme of eugenics abortion and infanticide were permissible, indeed compulsory, to avoid the spectre of any 'cross-pollination'. Yet Rousseau's enthusiasm for this work was unbridled and he called it 'the finest treatise on education ever written'.[56] He also shared Plato's desire to restrict the theatre, after all, savages do not put on plays. To this end he recommended a board of censors with sweeping powers. The task of that body was again the indoctrination of the populace. 'Put men's opinions to rights, and their behaviour will improve spontaneously.'[57]

Plato, as with all idealists of virtue, was fundamentally opposed to freedom of speech and commerce. Instead, he advocated censorship, suffocating propaganda and a coercive, all-powerful state. Like Marx, he believed that if one simply abolished the conflicts that politics are designed to address then harmony would reign. Plato is, via the pen of Rousseau, the antecedent of the modern left. He seems, with his rigid hierarchical structure, to have little in common with them, but his is not a hierarchy of wealth or hereditary primogeniture, it is a *philosophical* hierarchy. As such, its influence can be seen clearly in the Maoist and Soviet examples. There are, of course, significant differences in the manifestoes of Plato and his contemporary children, but there are a number of traits that have survived the circuitous route from antiquity to modernity: the dream of a utopia still lingers, it aims at a more virtuous, less avaricious society, and it is reliant on the population bearing scant resemblance to existing humanity. As such, the state is necessarily coercive and aims for unanimity in political thought. For well over two thousand years the allure of fiction, the appeal of fantasy in denial of human nature and the determination to impose such ideas on the population through deception, brainwashing and oppressive sanctions has stayed as strong as ever, even while all the other trappings have been cast off by the relentless march of history.

Rousseau discussed democracies, monarchies and aristocracies, but concluded *The Social Contract* by opting for an elective aristocracy as the best form of government. As much as he eulogised man in his primitive state Rousseau knew he could not return there. In fact, he went on record to state that the tribal societies of his time had evolved to the competitive stage and could not retreat to the innocent purity he believed had preceded them either. Yet he neglected to explain how the North American plains Indians, for example, had entered that stage of rivalry without, on the whole, developing agriculture or the smelting of metal - supposedly prerequisites for that process. Ignoring that rather significant oversight neatly allowed him to sidestep the issue of how all the available evidence contradicted his hypothesis without having to admit his theory was absurd. But then, perhaps he actually believed it. If so it seems strange that he suggested the primitive state existed as long as

'men were content with their rustic huts, as long as they confined themselves to sewing their garments of skin with thorns or fish-bones, and adorning themselves with feathers or shells, to painting their bodies with various colours, to improvising or decorating their bows and arrows; and to using sharp stones to make a few fishing canoes or crude musical instruments.'[58]

Sounds rather like the American Indians to me.

In drafting his philosophical vision, Rousseau had effectively created the emotional mindset of the left - the knee jerk antipathy to western civilisation and simplistic veneration of nature and 'indigenous' peoples. The economic blueprint of the movement would have to wait to be drawn up by Marx. Blom's summation of Rousseau's political solution is particularly memorable.

'Starting from a celebration of freedom, Rousseau created a dystopia of Stalinist severity, a state with censorship, sweeping police powers, and official propaganda, in which all dissidents are shipped off into 'exile' or simply killed while happy crowds of healthy peasants salute the great leader.'[59]

Despite his nods to pragmatic solutions, Rousseau's tract is the very definition of political idealism. It holds the blueprint for many of the crimes such utopianism has unleashed on the world. The 'monstrous paradox'[60] at the heart of his philosophising, that which aimed at freedom by crushing it, was, once released from Pandora's box, impossible to return to the obscurity it merited. All those who use the cause of egalitarianism as an excuse to limit the liberties of their peers are the true heirs of Rousseau. They are also the ideological brethren of the dictators he sired. In reaching for genuine liberty, in believing in the incorruptibility of his virtue and the purity of his goals, Rousseau had created the template for the worst tyrannies ever unleashed on the world.

But it would not be necessary for posterity to make a judgement as Rousseau's books sent shockwaves through his own era too. The criticisms of the Church and monarchy in *Émile* and *The Social Contract* were too much for the establishment of the time and a warrant was issued for his arrest. It prompted Rousseau to abscond from Paris. He claimed that he fled out of consideration for how his imprisonment would affect Thérése; that nothing would have persuaded him to run for his own benefit.[61] Odd, he never appeared to care much how his actions might affect her on any other occasion. He laid low for a protracted period before accepting an invitation from the great Scottish philosopher and historian, David Hume, to join him in England. Others had warned Hume to avoid the prickly Genevan but *Le Bon David*, as he was known, widely renowned as the most affable and gregarious man of the age, was confident that he could charm Rousseau. In England, Samuel Johnson took an immediate dislike to the visitor while Edmund Burke, the perceptive Irishman and one of the most brilliant politicians and polemicists of the day, met Rousseau a number of times and commented that 'He entertained no principle, either to influence his heart or guide his understanding, but vanity'.[62] Burke hit the nail on the head again. For, true to the warnings of the *philosophes*, Rousseau would prove too great an obstacle for even Hume's charm.

He was eventually sequestered at Wootton Hall and, though he insisted on paying a modest rent, was effectively living at the largesse of others yet again. He would once more prove to be characteristically and startlingly ungrateful. The grand house, in the midlands, at the southern end of the Peak District on the Staffordshire / Derbyshire border, thirty miles north of Birmingham, was sequestered in beautiful grounds which were themselves nestled in commodious woods. It presented the kind of rural beauty and privacy that Rousseau should have found ideal. Still he found reason to bristle at his circumstances. The somewhat inhospitable weather and his lack of English may have hampered his stay, but his host could not be blamed for these. Hume had not only secured comfortable accommodation for Rousseau but was attempting to arrange financial assistance for him too. But, despite the life of leisure he was living through the generosity of others, such overtures made the prickly writer ever more resentful.

Horace Walpole, son of Britain's first Prime Minister Robert Walpole, wrote a satirical article composed as a letter to Rousseau from Frederick the Great. The missive suggested that 'if you persist in racking your brains to find new misfortunes...I am a king and can procure them according to your wishes...I will stop persecuting you when you stop glorying in persecution.'[63] The letter clearly touched a nerve in its accuracy. Rousseau initially believed that d'Alembert was responsible, but when Hume and Walpole, who admired Rousseau and intended the letter to be a jest, informed him of its true authorship he decided the three of them were conspiring together. His paranoia convinced him that this 'triumvirate' were engaged in an insidious plot against him. In fact, such was Rousseau's mania that he soon concluded that Frederick the Great, George III, David Garrick, Adam Smith, James Boswell, Samuel Johnson, Diderot, d'Holbach and Voltaire were all involved in the conspiracy. Rousseau denounced Hume as a traitor who sought his downfall and had organised the conspiracy to that effect. D'Holbach had warned them that 'You don't know the man. I tell you frankly, you'll be nursing a viper in your bosom. I'm warning you, you will feel his bite.'[64] Hume lamented in a letter to Davenport, the owner of Wootton Hall, that 'You will be astonished as I was, at the monstrous ingratitude, ferocity, and frenzy of the man'.[65] The affair meant that even Rousseau's few remaining allies in France, like d'Alembert and Mme Luxembourg, now turned from him. Being well acquainted with Hume they realised the lunacy of Rousseau's vicious accusations.

After Hume published the long accusatory rant of a letter that Rousseau had sent him their relationship disintegrated in acrimony and Rousseau left Wootton Hall in April 1767. The servants were delighted to see the back of both him and Thérèse who they found to be unbearable guests. Rousseau left behind a bitter letter to Davenport before returning to France. He stayed in hiding for a period until learning that the authorities were no longer interested in pursuing him. He was free to return to Paris. In fact such was his rehabilitation that in 1770, the year he arrived back in the capital, *The Village Soothsayer* was performed at Fontainebleau at the wedding of the future Louis XVI and Marie-Antoinette.

He spent his last few years, before his death from heavy cerebral bleeding on 2 July 1778, working on his *Confessions*, a book of startling originality that effectively established the groundwork for psychoanalysis. Far from being a confession though, despite its frequent shocking admissions of the author's misdemeanours, the book is largely self-serving, a congratulatory tome that reveals and revels in Rousseau's triumph over the traumas and obstacles he endured. Of the incident where he accused Marion of stealing the ribbon, the blame was placed on the humiliating apprenticeship he was forced to endure, the secret yearning for girls that he couldn't have, and the public interrogation that he found so unbearable. In such ways, his own despicable actions were excused or blamed on the faults of others. Rousseau's tome is puffed up on its own self-importance and inflated with a sense of nobility, awash with the conviction that he has a 'feeling heart', the sort of nonsense that would have gone down well with his contemporaries. When it comes to other people though, the tone of the book grows increasingly bitter as Rousseau rails against practically everyone he encounters. Strange, then, that his political philosophy revolved around the concept of an unrealistic brotherhood of man. The book is, however, frank, shockingly original, and quite stunningly well written. It was a publishing sensation and proved hugely influential.

Rousseau's impact in the years after his death was simply colossal. We have already borne witness to his profound influence on the French Revolution, but the catastrophe that enveloped France did not diminish the impact of his writing at all. His legacy continued to be celebrated by the Romantics, those uniquely pompous, self-absorbed and entitled of young men. Rousseau, by launching the first great assault on the values of the Enlightenment, and in his glorification of uninhibited emotion, had become the acknowledged godfather of the movement. Lord Byron famously dragged Percy Bysshe Shelly on a pilgrimage to Switzerland in 1816 to tour the sites made sacred by their association with Rousseau. Shelley's future wife, Mary Godwin, the daughter of Mary Wollstonecraft, travelled with them and it was on that trip, at the Villa Diodati on the shores of Lake Geneva, that she first dreamt up the tale of Frankenstein. While there Byron became absorbed in reading *Julie*, thought deeply about the author, shared in Rousseau's veneration of nature, and later referenced him fondly in *Child Harold's Pilgrimage.*

The Romantics elevated emotion, and the stronger and more violent that emotion was, the more uninformed by thought, the better. Russell's summation of the phenomenon is probably still the best:

> 'The romantic movement is characterised, as a whole, by the substitution of aesthetic for utilitarian standards. The earth-worm is useful, but not beautiful; the tiger is beautiful, but not useful. Darwin (who was not a romantic) praised the earth-worm; Blake praised the tiger. The morals of the romantics have primarily aesthetic motives.'[66]

He went on to note 'The man of sensibility would be moved to tears by the sight of a single destitute peasant family, but would be cold to well thought-out schemes for ameliorating the lot of peasants as a class'.[67] It is a mindset that appears less virtuous and rather more self-indulgent than it would like to admit. Here we turn to Russell again. He concluded that 'the strongest passions are destructive – hate and resentment and jealousy, remorse and despair, outraged pride and the fury of the unjustly oppressed...Hence the type of man encouraged by romanticism, especially of the Byronic variety, is violent and anti-social, an anarchic rebel or a conquering tyrant.'[68]

There is, of course, nothing wrong with a love of nature, of emotion, compassion and sympathy (though wild conspiracy theories are another matter). But these, many on the left would be shocked to learn, are abundant in those who do not share their political inclinations. This would have surprised the Romantics too. They believed the poor possessed more virtue than the rich, they were a youth movement, embedded in revolt, they experimented with drugs, spurned the hierarchies and traditions of the societies in which they lived and eulogised the peasantry and the beauty of nature, the more dramatic the vista, the better. Byron, in tandem with many others, saw the world as being run by a cabal of Jewish Rothschild bankers, as well as the Baring institution. The similarities between them and the radicals of today, their direct philosophical descendants, are consequently striking; even the flamboyantly tousled and wind-blown hairstyles are somewhat familiar. This should not be surprising either. Rousseau also detested European civilisation, desired a system of enforced equality, hoped for oppressive cultural control and sneered at wealth even while enjoying a luxurious lifestyle. He seems almost indistinguishable from the most committed leftists who have followed in his wake.

Was Rousseau an evil man? Did he advocate brutality to his fellows? No, these are not accusations that can be levelled at him. He was troubled, certainly; selfish, weak and frequently deluded, though he probably hurt himself with his actions more than anyone else. What exactly happened to Rousseau is not entirely clear. It is evident that his youth led to him being a somewhat tormented character and that he descended into full-blown mania in his last few traumatic years. As to what happened in between, what seems likely is a somewhat self-inflicted spiral into isolation and melancholia. His guilt over both his mother's death and his unusual sexual peccadilloes seem to have combined with his social awkwardness and the lack of self-esteem he felt over his humble origins. Such traits were magnified by the fact that he spent so much time socialising with those who had an ease, education and confidence he found intimidating. These factors combined to create in him the paranoia that infested him with hostility and prickliness. Such characteristics would certainly have made his peers somewhat wary in his presence, especially considering the temper of this volatile, emotional man, and their reticence would have been picked up by him to further fuel his paranoia. Once started on this cycle, such traits would only continue to predominate until they became all-consuming.

It is regrettable that such a talented individual came to lead such a bleak and joyless existence, and it is entirely possible, if not probable, that he was prone to some psychological malady that the medicine of his time had yet to diagnose. Some form of depression or an inferiority complex perhaps, or some other equally debilitating ailment? One feels, not contempt for the car wreck that his life turned into, or for the raging pariah that he became, but only pity. Still, perhaps it was the intensity of his emotional life that allowed him to think and write as he did. Maybe, as with George Best, Amy Winehouse and Caravaggio, the demons and the talent were inseparable, the one propelled by the other. Such ruminations are speculative, even if based on the available evidence. All that is certain is that Rousseau was a tortured soul. But deeply troubled though he was, he was also a *cause* for trouble, and he inadvertently caused considerably more misery from beyond the grave.

An assessment of Rousseau's thought is thus far more challenging than any evaluation of the man. While Rousseau was not the progenitor of all the ideas he voiced, he certainly popularised them. As such, his impact is arguably more profound than many other, more original, thinkers. It is one of the great paradoxes of history that Rousseau, the man who may have done more than anyone to elevate the recognition and celebration of the individual, also contributed more than almost any other to influence and shape those societies most hostile to personal freedom and expression. For at the heart of his theorising was a critical flaw: Essentially he looked back to a past that never was and envisaged a future that never could be.

In addition to this, while he talked loftily of freedom, Rousseau's thought and expression was primarily concerned with equality. It appears that many people, impressed with the emotional force of his writing, the instinctive appeal of his ideas and the purity of his intentions have been blinded to the dangers inherent in many of his recommendations: the weaknesses in his reasoning, the lunacy of his suggestions and the likely consequences of any attempt to impose his implausible ideas. This should all have become apparent after the catastrophe of France in the 1790s. He has had many positive influences in the cultural and social spheres but attempts to apply his wistful and impractical suggestions in the political arena have been disastrous. That is hardly surprising; Rousseau was unable to operate in social settings, so how on earth could he be expected to devise a system geared to the social betterment of mankind, a phenomenon of which he had little understanding.

Yet his influence in fostering a culture of unthinking, automatic reverence for nature and lesser developed societies in preference to the West is undeniable - for Rousseau's fanciful ideas retain popularity while more robust solutions have fallen from favour. What *actually* works is that individuals be given liberty, within the law, to exercise their personal, philosophical, social, cultural and economic freedoms, while expecting reward for the industry, quality and success of their endeavours. The most successful societies have developed institutions to facilitate such an existence. The frequently vocalised distaste for money aired by the radicals also smacks of moralistic grandstanding, especially if, like Rousseau, they spend most of their life in conspicuous luxury.

His rhetoric in this regard is particularly ironic considering his attraction to aristocratic women, and in light of the fact that he barely associated with the artisan class at all. While the low-born Thérèse was his life companion, Rousseau's acquaintances noted that he behaved towards her more like a master to a servant, devoid of affection and frequently with sneering condescension. In his *Confessions* he admitted that 'from the very first moment I saw her until today, I have never felt the least spark of love for her'.[69] But, despite these inconsistencies, his claims that the rich hoped to fleece the poor simply increased class divisions and animosity. Voltaire was a sharp critic of the class hatred which ran through Rousseau's work and suggested his theory was 'like those famished wolves that reject all other food after once tasting human flesh, and thenceforth want only to devour men. *Voilá* the philosophy of a beggar who would like to see the rich robbed by the poor'.[70] But to really understand the consequences of Rousseau's legacy we need only look, not at his critics, but his admirers; and these include not just Robespierre but Lenin and Pol Pot too.

In Ryan's analysis, by 'thrusting the burden of original sin onto social organization, he paved the way for the utopian optimism of Marxism and other radical movements of the past two centuries'.[71] Such a belief stemmed from his contention that the human condition was imposed by social forces. It is perhaps the greatest irony of his work that, by attributing mankind's failings to nurture, Rousseau has neglected to account for the role of nature, the subject with which he was most obsessed. Yet it was by giving such ideas legitimacy that he popularised attacks against, not just particular aspects of society, but civilisation itself. More than this he introduced misty-eyed romantic and emotive idealism into the social and political arena at a new pitch, and those who followed him emulated the fury and indignation towards any perceived opposition, real or imagined, that had proven such a destructive force in his personal life.

Clearly social influences have a significant impact, but Rousseau's insistence on giving undue weight to such factors has resulted in an increasing tendency for the left to place dogma over the human condition; a feature which may be the movement's greatest failing. It is a trait that can be traced from Plato in an uninterrupted line to today. It led Robespierre to believe he could create a 'new man' through education and ornate festivals, one who would be as virtuous as he believed himself to be, in all his arrogant intolerance and paranoid fury.

Rousseau, like most preachers of moral rectitude, was far removed from the man of virtue of his imagination. Yet the conviction of his moral purity blinded him to his own faults while magnifying those of others.

Rousseau's impact has thus been profoundly damaging. His theories were based on miscalculations about how societies operate and a failure to understand human nature. As such, his solutions were disastrous. He popularised an irrational hysteria into political discourse – one based primarily on resentment and antipathy to progress, and he encouraged a juvenile petulance that preferred moral certainties and romantic platitudes to practical solutions. Despite the disasters unleashed by this trend, the volatile, knee jerk aversion to commerce and Western civilisation that he ingrained in the cultural psyche has never really gone away. Rousseau is, in a sense, the ultimate idealist who deals only in absolutes and extremes: extremes of freedom, extremes of passion and, ultimately, extremes of paranoia. He can legitimately be called the father of the left as he shaped its culture and sensibility, and this defines it as a movement more than its ever-fluctuating manifesto. In Isaiah Berlin's analysis

'Rousseau makes common cause with the outcasts, the rebels, the free wild artists. That is what makes him the founder of romanticism and wild individualism, as well as the founder of so many other movements of the nineteenth century – of socialism and communism...and anarchism, of almost everything, save what might be called liberal civilisation, with its fastidious love of culture'.[72]

The reliance on passion over reason and the simplification of the conflicts between the haves and have nots, and between progress and nature, still inform the movement today. It is dominated by an emotional culture that allows negative, and ultimately destructive, feelings room to breathe and proliferate. That springs largely from a misconception as Rousseau recommended basing politics upon rational, not emotional, conclusions. But regardless, it is what has *endured* most from his writing. The unique blend of imagined virtue and furious resentment that Rousseau specialised in, the culture that blamed society for the faults of its citizens and made angry demands for restitution, the ideology that claimed to love freedom and individuality while moving to strangle both: this was his true legacy.

Edmund Burke & Thomas Paine

The two men most frequently regarded as the fathers of radical and conservative thought were contemporaries of Rousseau who hailed from the British Isles. When the Genevan died in 1778 Edmund Burke, the Irish father of conservatism, was forty-nine while Thomas Paine, the Norfolk born pamphleteer, who was briefly Burke's ally before becoming his most bitter rival, was forty-one. At that stage Burke had a growing reputation as a writer and Member of Parliament. He was starting to make his name in the dispute brewing over the American Crisis. Paine, on that same divisive topic, had just caused a sensation with the publication of his first great work *Common Sense*. By the end of the century the mark left by both men would prove to be indelible. But, while it was the American Revolution that made them allies, it was the French Revolution that irreparably divided them.

To the contemporary reader Thomas Paine, who called for an extension to the franchise, frequent parliamentary elections, the separation of Church and State, the beginnings of a welfare system, the advancement of free trade and an end to the privileged ruling status of monarchy and aristocracy, can seem surprisingly modern. By contrast, Edmund Burke's stout defence of hereditary primogeniture, the rigid enforcement of state religion and those venerable institutions which, to most of us, now appear achingly archaic, seems dreadfully anachronistic. It would be very easy for the casual observer to label Paine as being on the 'winning' side of history. Yet to take such a stance would be a gross simplification of the war of words between them.

In the short term, of course, it was Burke who more clearly discerned the true nature and direction of the French Revolution. And although many aspects of Paine's ideal society have seen fruition, they came to be realised, as Burke insisted they must, gradually and incrementally. More than this, Burke wrote eloquently on the nostalgic reverence for the nation's heritage. Those institutions he cherished still exist, yet draped in the pomp and grandeur that characterise their traditions. The heritage of the nation and its institutions remain valued, they still help to define us, and one feels that were Burke to view us today he would recognise many vestiges from his own era with quiet satisfaction. Paine too would almost certainly exult at how so much of his vision for the future of the nation, and the world, has been realised. Burke and Paine still walk among us, and the intellectual and philosophical influence they wield is yet considerable. For all this though they need to be judged, not by the standards of our time, nor as part of some predestined pattern of progress, but in the context of the times in which they lived. For their political stances and significance are best understood in relation to each other, and in the fierce political debate that electrified their era and left such an indelible mark on ours.

Burke could be said to embody the spirit of 'compassionate conservatism'. It is a stereotype many on the left do not believe exists, but it is, in fact, incredibly common, though the vast majority do not share Burke's intellect or talents. While the Irishman came down resolutely on the side of order and stability he spent much of his life and career campaigning for the oppressed, even if he erred on the side of caution perhaps too frequently. He was also religiously and racially tolerant, for the standards of the day at least. He opposed slavery, worked tirelessly in support of the Indian subjects of British rule and was a staunch campaigner for the destitute Irish Catholics. He also opposed British policy in America and supported the right to self-determination of the colonists during the struggle for independence, the issue which, if only briefly, united him with Paine. But when it came to the French Revolution, he sensed almost immediately that this was an entirely different situation. He was its most outspoken critic from the outset, predicting that it would descend into anarchy and slaughter. His interpretation was soundly ridiculed by the vast majority who celebrated the apparent spread of Parisian democracy, but two to three years after penning his views in the classic *Reflections on the Revolution in France,* Burke was proven correct in every word. He gained a new level of respect for the depth and accuracy of his insight.

Paine, in contrast, was the proto radical of the period, the man who seemed to support every cause going. His nascent republicanism was incubated in England, but it was in America that his budding activism flowered into its full potential. Arriving there with the situation becoming increasingly tense he committed himself to advocating insurrection. The pamphlet he wrote in support of that cause, *Common Sense*, proved hugely influential in sparking revolution and transforming him into a significant figure in the reformist movement. Paine was a long way removed from the despots under discussion in these pages. He largely embodies the humanitarian side of the left, though his story shows that such individuals can get swept up in events and blinded to the faults of their allies. Upon arriving in France, just as revolution was in the air there too, Paine was almost lynched by a mob outside the Tuileries for the high crime of failing to display a revolutionary cockade on his hat. He laughingly brushed the incident off as 'over-enthusiasm', but perhaps it should have set a few alarm bells ringing. It is inconceivable that he would have been as blasé about a similar attack by royalists.

He was stunned when Burke, the man who had joined him in supporting the American cause, did not share his enthusiasm for events in France. *The Rights of Man*, his own withering response to the Irishman's *Reflections,* would prove one of the most controversial books of all time, and it ultimately led to impeachment and exile from his homeland. He appeared to never recover from the shock of the Irishman's 'treason', and certainly never conceded that Burke had been right, maintaining a notable hostility to his philosophical rival until his dying day, an antipathy that was entirely mutual.

But Paine's decency would see him oppose the execution of the King and recoil from the excesses of Robespierre's Terror. In doing so, he almost fell victim to the Jacobins himself, being imprisoned by them and missing execution by a whisker. Yet, following their fall, his enthusiasm for the Revolution was undimmed and he pursued the cause of war against England with relish, despite his frequent protests that war was only practised by kings and would vanish once monarchies were abolished. For all the criticisms that can be levelled at either man, both effectively demonstrate the better qualities their respective ideologies can produce. An examination of their lives and careers, and the times in which they lived, particularly in comparing the Tory 'terror' in England with its French counterpart, offers a fascinating insight into the formative stages of the contemporary left and right and, perhaps more than anything, is persuasive of the necessity of compromise.

Evidence from the early years of both men is sketchy at best, but it is certainly possible, in light of the illumination provided by the abundance of later material, to make some educated assumptions about their formative experiences. What is apparent is that the pair had deviated in a number of critical areas long before their official divergence in 1790, indeed, long before they had ever met. Even as young men it is possible to see the embryonic development of Burke as the staunch advocate and defender of the establishment, and Paine as the firebrand who would be its most virulent critic.

Burke was born in 1729 in Ireland, probably Dublin; Paine in 1737 in Norfolk. Neither were born to wealth, nor destitution. Paine was the son of a staymaker, Burke's father was a solicitor, but while the latter came from a more affluent family he would doubtless have witnessed poverty in Ireland on a greater scale than his counterpart, especially when visiting his Catholic mother's side of the family in Cork. Religious sectarianism was far more prevalent in Ireland, and while Enlightenment ideas were gaining capital in Britain they were far more sluggish in crossing the Irish Sea. O'Brien informs us that 'Burke had grown up in the first half of the century, when Montesquieu and Locke were in the ascendant, and enlightenment was felt to be fully compatible with tolerant forms of Christianity.'[73] Young Edmund was also profoundly influenced by the Penal Laws which were used to suppress the Catholic majority. They gave him a sharp lesson in oppression, one he remembered for the rest of his life.

While Burke then was made acutely aware of the consequences of poor government, it was Paine who likely had more access to the secular and political ideals of Enlightenment thought. For his part, Paine grew up in the shadow of the Thetford scaffold which appears to have made quite an impact on his young, impressionable mind. Keane believes that it probably left him with an aversion to the punitive retribution and overweening power of the state.[74] There is certainly evidence of this in Paine's writing. He laments how executions appear to primarily target the poor[75] and also comments that the 'effect of those cruel spectacles exhibited to the populace, is to destroy tenderness, or excite revenge; and by the base and false idea of governing men by terror, instead of reason, they become precedents.'[76] Much of Paine's determined opposition to state oppression was, it seems, formed at an early age.

While the reasons are not entirely clear, both men certainly emerged from their early years with markedly separate views on the accumulation of wealth. Keane cites the influence that the Dukes of Grafton may have had on young Tom. While relatively benevolent, the Grafton family exercised virtually undisputed control over the town of Thetford.[77] It was a sharp lesson about the power of the nobility, the malign influence of ostentatious wealth and the undemocratic nature of Britain at the time. What is certain is that Paine was left with a deep distrust of men of power and influence, and he was 'forever suspicious of men of wealth'.[78] Paine led a somewhat peripatetic existence and made overt gestures to show his lack of interest in money for the rest of his life, though, as we shall see, these were on occasion unconvincing.

Burke, by contrast, perhaps because of the poverty he had witnessed as a child, embraced and relished the finer things in life and strived for membership of the upper reaches of society. The beautiful Palladian house he eventually bought near Beaconsfield, Buckinghamshire, was sprinkled with a fine collection of paintings by Poussin, Titian and Reynolds and nestled in an estate some six hundred acres in size.[79] In a somewhat surprising extract from his *Reflections* Burke wrote 'for though hereditary wealth, and the rank which goes with it, *are too much idolized by creeping sycophants* [emphasis mine]...they are too rashly slighted in shallow speculations of the petulant, assuming, short-sighted coxcombs of philosophy'.[80] While the first comment is one that many feel may justly be directed at Burke himself, the latter sentiment could have been written squarely for Paine. Regardless, their conflicting stances on this issue had a significant bearing on their political positions.

When it came to religion both men were, unusually, raised by parents of different denominations. Paine had a Quaker father and an Anglican mother while Burke's father was Protestant and his mother Catholic. Interestingly, it was Burke, witness to greater religious persecution in his youth, who stoutly defended the place of organised religion in civil society while Paine was perhaps its most virulent critic. For Burke though religion could be defended on the basis of the culture of the indigenous inhabitants. Thus he campaigned on behalf of the Catholic Irish and Muslim and Hindu populations of India with equal vigour, while also defending the Protestant constitution of Britain. The issue of Burke's religious background has been the subject of much debate. O'Brien has taken Burke's silence on much Catholic persecution as evidence for his pro-Catholic views.[81] It's certainly possible that this was the case, but it is something of a reach to regard the paucity of evidence as evidence itself. O'Brien also claims that Burke was primarily motivated by guilt over his father's apostasy,[82] yet it is not certain that the Richard Burke who converted in 1722[83] was Edmund's father at all. According to James Prior the Burke family had been part of the Norman hierarchy since the time of Henry II and Edmund was descended from an Anglo-Norman with the surname de Burgh.[84] As such his family had likely formed part of the Protestant ascendancy since the time of Henry VIII. In contrast to O'Brien's detailed focus, Fennessy, in his otherwise superb study, makes one passing reference to Burke as a Protestant[85] and, while briefly acknowledging his Catholic links, does not consider the issue worthy of discussion, a disappointing oversight in an otherwise meticulous thesis.

The issue is, to me, yet unresolved. However, it is pertinent to note that Burke spent his whole career robustly defending the Glorious Revolution, an event that was not just embedded in Anglicanism but which overtly oppressed the Catholic faith. This fact alone leads me to doubt O'Brien's theory. However, while Burke was not shy about airing his views, going against the tide, and launching vigorous attacks against political heavyweights, he was also a canny and pragmatic operator who chose his battles carefully. One wonders if, for instance, he would have campaigned as vigorously on behalf of the Prince of Wales during the Regency Crisis if the heir to the throne had been the personal friend of Pitt instead of Fox. As a politician, Burke was always aware of the necessity of keeping his guard up when airing his opinions and this must be kept in mind when evaluating his work. He was also enough of an astute parliamentarian to keep the business of the house of Westminster out of any writing intended for the general public. Paine, by contrast, appeared constitutionally incapable of any discretion or deference at all.

Fennessy does feel that Paine's predominantly Quaker upbringing left him with an aversion to the likes of duelling and slavery[86] while Keane argues that he was likely impressed by the Quakers' philanthropy and appalled at their persecution.[87] Levin concludes that the Quakers' 'stark moralism deeply shaped him. He had a lifelong ingrained sense that the laws of justice are clear and simple, that they embody a preference for the weak over the strong, and that there can be no excuse for disregarding them'.[88] Burke, for his part, was also influenced by the same denomination, being schooled by a Quaker, Abraham Shackleton, and forming a lifelong friendship with his tutor's son, Richard.[89] Keane additionally reports on Paine's fleeting dalliance with the Methodist preaching of John Wesley, an experience that taught him the masses were a force to be communicated with, not excluded. He would also likely have been affected by the Methodist meeting in 1758 in Kent which 'was broken up by a club wielding mob assisted by forty soldiers'.[90] It was the sort of experience likely to heighten his already nascent republicanism and aversion to despotism.

The social and personal lives of both men also differed greatly, and this appears to result from a stark contrast in their understandings of human nature. Burke married Jane Nugent, a Catholic, in 1757, with the forty year marriage that lasted until Edmund's death being reportedly a happy one.[91] Paine was not so fortunate. In 1759, at the age of twenty-three, he married Mary Lambert, though she tragically died of complications from a pregnancy after less than a year. Keane claims that Paine showed little interest in women from this point.[92] He married again in 1771 at the age of thirty-four, to Elizabeth Ollive, his landlord's daughter. It was an ill-fated union that ended in separation in under a year with suspicions that it was a marriage of convenience. Whether a blind spot in human nature caused Paine's relationship problems, or whether his woes left him something of a damaged individual who had difficulties relating to others is unclear. But it seems evident that he was unable to read people in quite the same way as his rival, and this disparity profoundly affected their approaches to political philosophy.

Fennessy covers Paine's deficiencies in some detail, calling him 'a cold hearted man. There is always a certain artificiality in his references to sentiments and emotions'.[93] Calling him 'cold hearted' seems harsh; Paine repeatedly campaigned for the welfare of others, but he did appear to lack natural empathy. Yet one piece of evidence appears to support this view. It is eloquent testimony to the antipathy that developed between the pair, and a reminder of the latter's alarming lack of rapport. The Irish rebel, Theobald Wolfe Tone, made a record of his meeting with Paine in Paris in 1797, shortly after the death of Burke's only surviving son.

> 'I mentioned to him that I had known Burke in England, and spoke of the shattered state of his mind, in consequence of the death of his only son Richard. Paine immediately said that it was the *Rights of Man* which had broken his heart, and that the death of his son gave him occasion to develop the chagrin which had preyed upon him ever since the appearance of that work. I am sure the *Rights of Man* have tormented Burke exceedingly; but I have seen myself the workings of a father's grief on his spirit, and I could not be deceived. *Paine has no children!...*'[94]

This worrying extract suggests, not just a lack of compassion, but the unwavering faith Paine had in his political stance. It was a characteristic that ultimately led him to condone actions in his allies that he would have condemned in his rivals, and to blind him to many faults in his own theorising. By 1797 Burke's fears about the French Revolution had been manifestly realised, but there is no recognition of this in Paine's remark. In addition to this coldness he also seemed unable to relate to women, though reportedly fancying himself something of a ladies' man. The majority of women he encountered apparently disagreed with that image.[95] He was notoriously prickly too, Benjamin Franklin's daughter, Sarah Franklin Bach, wrote to her father on 14 January, 1781 'There never was a man less beloved in a place than Paine is in this, having at different times disputed with everybody'.[96]

Fennessy notes the impact that this characteristic had on Paine's work. 'As Paine saw it, all social evils are caused by a defective social system. Change the system, and you will get rid of the abuses. He was completely blind to the importance of passions, emotions, and sentiments in human affairs; and nothing could cure him of this blindness.'[97] The same could hardly be said of Burke whose philosophy may be neatly encapsulated in his belief that 'politics ought to be adjusted, not to human reasonings, but to human nature; of which the reason is but a part, and by no means the greatest part'.[98]

Burke's study of human behaviour was already well advanced at the start of his career when he published *A Philosophical Enquiry into the Origin of our Ideas of the Sublime and Beautiful* in 1756. The work examines, among other aspects, how the passions affect human reasoning[99] and how appearances of power can awe and cow those confronted with them.[100] A further thirty years of contemplation hardly dulled his edge in this regard. Burke was confident enough to note his talents in this area and declared that 'I can form a tolerable estimate of what is likely to happen from a character, chiefly dependent for fame and fortune on knowledge and talent, as well in its morbid and perverted state, as in that which is sound and natural'.[101] Burke's superiority in this department is perhaps best illustrated in his ability to discern the true nature and direction of the French Revolution. He held a clear edge when attempting to predict the consequences that politics would have on their respective populations. While Paine confidently declared 'the astonishment will be that it is marked with so few sacrifices',[102] Burke forecast that 'before its final settlement it may...be purified by fire and blood'.[103]

Each man's respective education also reveals much about their later divergence. Paine's schooling was comparatively moderate. He was educated at Thetford Grammar School primarily in mathematics, engineering and science, where results flow from sound, consistent principles, and he later confessed that the 'natural bent of my mind was to science [and] I had no disposition for what was called politics'.[104] In contrast, Burke had a more advanced education at Trinity College, Dublin, focusing on the Classics, History and Law, far more open to the minutiae of human behaviour. The influence of their respective educations on their conclusions is clear. Paine began with a principle he hoped to apply to every situation; Burke commenced with the people and their history and hoped to discern the best solution from his understanding of those criteria. In short, Paine saw things largely in terms of black and white, but for Burke, it was all shades of grey. This is why Paine hoped to replicate the American Revolution in France, Ireland and Britain, but Burke had very different approaches which considered the distinct circumstances affecting those societies. Paine also dismissed Latin and Greek as 'dead languages'.[105] One assumes that Burke, who generously sprinkled his polemics with classical references, would have disagreed.

It was Paine's interest in science though that opened the door to political theorising, the subject that would prove his true calling. 'To many in those circles, Paine included, it seemed obvious that the sciences were friends of liberty – providing indisputable proof of the rational foundations of the persistent eighteenth century fear of a Tory and royalist "conspiracy"'.[106] Around 1758-9 he gained the acquaintance of Benjamin Martin and James Ferguson, two renowned advocates of Newtonian science. It was through Ferguson and the scientific community that he met Benjamin Franklin,[107] a fortuitous encounter that would change his life. It was Franklin, impressed by the sincerity and rhetoric of the young activist, who gave him the letter of introduction which would establish him in America.

Paine's experience as an exciseman in Lewes was also pivotal. His career taught him about corruption and the greed of officials while his membership of The Headstrong Club heightened his burgeoning political activism. A visit to the locale reveals that Lewes is relatively unchanged from Paine's time, with the majority of its narrow streets still characterised by recognisably eighteenth century architecture. The White Hart tavern, where the club met, has changed little too and it is easy to visualise the intensity of debate in its cavernous, low ceilinged and gloomy rooms, illuminated by flickering light from spacious fireplaces. One of the pioneers of the club was William Lee, founder and printer of the *Sussex Weekly Advertiser,* a republican journal that trumpeted John Wilkes, among other issues. Paine was described by one contemporary, Thomas Rickman, as 'at this time a Whig, and notorious for that quality which has been defined perseverance in a good cause, and obstinacy in a bad one'.[108] Burke, by contrast, was a member of The Club, which met every two weeks at the Turk's Head tavern in Soho. Its rather more esteemed membership included Samuel Johnson, David Garrick and Joshua Reynolds, who immortalised Burke in portrait in 1774, another timely reminder of the very different social circles they mixed in.

Both men then were set on very different courses, but neither was treading an especially new path. Paine was swept up in the movement of enlightened political idealism which had been gaining momentum for a good century; while Burke was becoming a pillar of the establishment, even while he was a thorn in the side of much of it. Each would defend their corner with remarkable eloquence, but neither was to add anything revolutionarily new to the debate. The true calling of both individuals was as propagandists for pre-existing causes in a political atmosphere with some similarities to the Cold War, proxy wars and all.

It was arguably America that really forged both men though. Paine arrived in the Colonies with a string of failures behind him, both professional and personal, but he landed with revolution in the air, as he later would in France, and was in short order being feted as 'Common Sense'. He was the voice of the people who hobnobbed with the most significant figures of the revolt. It must have had a dizzying effect on him, and the experience, and its considerable success, appears to have fired him with a nigh on messianic zeal. It informed the rest of his life, something that can only have been reinforced when he arrived in France shortly before the Revolution exploded there. Even a sensible man may have felt the hand of providence in such coincidental circumstances.

Paine's almost religious belief in his political mission is encapsulated in a quote from *Rights of Man Part Two* (1792), 'The present age will hereafter merit to be called the Age of Reason, and the present generation will appear to the future as the Adam of a new world'. Burke, for his part, had spent years in the political wilderness for his principled stand on the American Crisis, only to gain a large measure of redemption. His opponents were forced to concede defeat and he entered office, albeit briefly. By that time, 1782-3, each man's philosophy was well developed and their confidence had been reinforced by the turn of events. They were on collision course, though that would not be apparent for nearly a decade.

The quite distinct philosophies of both men, which were firmly grounded in their religious beliefs, offer a tantalising insight into the development of modern left and right wing thought. Paine believed that creation itself was clear testament to God's existence,[109] but he was a Deist and any textual claims to religious knowledge were spurious for him. As such, his idea of the rights of man derived from the perceived 'natural' rights man enjoyed at the time of the creation.[110] Government, while a necessary evil, was an imposition on man's natural rights and must be resisted wherever there was a conflict of interests.

Burke had an entirely different, providential view. His own idea of 'natural law' was that the society man had evolved was entirely natural, and as such the likes of monarchy, aristocracy and commerce were enshrined in natural law. Burke believed, for instance, that the laws of commerce were the laws of nature and, consequently, the laws of God.[111] In the *Philosophical Enquiry* (1756) he alluded to a belief in the 'great chain of causes'[112] that seventeenth century conviction which viewed societal hierarchy as divinely ordained. According to Kirk, Burke's perception was based on Ciceronian natural rights though he refused to define them clearly as Divine intent could not be understood.[113] Paine's perception of progress was akin to that of Rousseau, and Levin suggests he concocted his philosophy 'as if all of human history had never happened'.[114] Burke's ideology is more effectively encapsulated by the maxim that 'we are standing on the shoulders of giants'.

While Paine saw history largely as an imposition then, Burke viewed it as part of man's natural development. As Paine saw man's simple and harmonious state plundered from him by a succession of tyrants who crushed his rights, Burke saw barbaric origins calmed by increasing levels of civilisation, that process which 'mellows into legality governments that were violent in their commencement'.[115] These profoundly differing beliefs laid the foundations for the divergence in political thought that defined their relationship. For Paine man's rights existed in the state of nature and civil society placed limits on those rights - for Burke the most important rights that man possessed were *provided* by the civil institutions of the society in which he lived.

Paine saw an idealisation of his free men when he met some Native American tribesmen in 1777. Keane records that 'he seemed magnetized by what he saw as the natural beauty, prudence, and intelligence of the Native Americans. He considered them fine human beings, unspoiled by modern civilization and the crooked ways of British despotism – examples of "the natural and primitive state of man"'.[116] What he made of their decision to later side with the English in defence of their king has gone unrecorded, but he still spoke warmly of their culture twenty years later in *Agrarian Law*[117] (1797). Paine did not wish to *revert* to that state, but he hoped that civilised nations would recognise the natural dignity and equality apparent in such societies.

To apply such standards to Western civilisation though, was, to Burke, a grave error. His view was that 'the primitive rights of men undergo such a variety of refractions and reflections, that it becomes absurd to talk of them as if they continued in the simplicity of their original direction'.[118] It was also, Burke recounted, 'a serious mistake if we draw a sharp distinction between the natural and the artificial in human affairs and thereby ignore everything that man does in the world as we seek to understand his nature'.[119] Civil society was as much a part of man as his original nature, for he had grown up in it and been shaped by it, just as he had moulded it in turn.

> 'Burke argues that to learn about man's nature, we need to understand man as he is and, to our knowledge at least, has always been: a social creature, living together with others in an organized society with a government. To imagine him as solitary and asocial is to ignore man himself in pursuit of an abstraction with little to teach us.'[120]

From a philosophical stance, Burke particularly opposed the malign influence of Jean-Jacques Rousseau, the man he called 'the insane Socrates of the

National Assembly'.[121] While Paine was not exactly a disciple of Rousseau, he was complimentary towards him[122] and they held many parallel beliefs. Both held that civil society was one where people achieved full rights and freedoms by a social contract through which they created their own laws. Burke, by contrast, unlike Hobbes, Locke and Rousseau, began, not with a state of nature, but with society itself, an aspect of Burke's thought that was quite original.[123] Different societies vary in numerous ways – but each has a social *order* which links people together in an enormous ever-shifting web of institutions, customs, traditions, habits and expectations, built up by innumerable interactions over many years.[124] This was the mortar that held society together. As societies shaped the individuals who lived in them, any political philosophy must start by taking the structures of that society into account. To dismiss or dismantle them wholesale was an egregious error.

While Paine felt that society inhibited man's freedoms, Burke believed that it protected them. Rather than choking off individual energy and aspiration it made social and economic advancement possible. Burke's entire system of belief revolved around protecting this structure. He saw it as a colossal collective achievement which must be treated with the utmost respect by would-be reformers. For Burke 'Politics was first and foremost about particular people living together, rather than about general rules put into effect'.[125] The complex interconnection of political and social groupings and customs, as well as the market, acted as checks and balances that have evolved over time, much as the systems inherent in nature have evolved too, though Darwin's theory was unknown in Burke's day. To wreck these systems, to start again, would be a disastrous error, though it was permissible to tinker with it, to allow it to similarly evolve.

Burke compared the constitution to an estate, handed down as a bequest by our forefathers. We should be permitted to make alterations to it, to knock down a dilapidated section and put up an extension or two, but our primary responsibility was to preserve it and pass it on to our descendants in turn.[126] He was not against reform, and fully supported the more moderate constructive events of the Glorious and American Revolutions. But he virulently opposed the violent, society breaking form of insurrection which ripped through France, and the differences to him seemed plain. He had supported the American Revolution as the colonists already had a working system in place. They simply desired the liberty to operate it independently. But the French sought to smash their institutions and replace them with nothing more than vague notions of 'liberty' – the sort of 'abstract reasoning' that Burke treated with contempt.

Posterity has proven him entirely correct in his conclusions, and his underlying principle is difficult to dispute: Man had a right to all that society has to offer, but he did *not* have a right to dismantle that society to the detriment of others.

As such, the restrictions that government put on man's natural impulses were wholly desirable. This was what he meant when he wrote to Charles Depont in the early days of the revolution, disputing Paine's vision of rights as he did so. True liberty 'is not solitary, unconnected, individual, selfish liberty...The liberty I mean is social freedom. It is that state of things in which liberty is assured by the equality of restraint'.[127]

Yet none of these disputes divided them as fiercely as did the aristocracy. Burke felt they played a vital role in fostering the deference which held society together, and he considered this culture of respect a far more potent societal glue than any legislation. One suspects that Burke would have found much to admire in *The Civilizing Process* by Norbert Elias. It contends that the aristocracy has long played a significant role by setting an example which filtered down to the lower orders - spreading civilisation and refinement through society to the benefit of all. While *The Civilizing Process* was unavailable in Burke's day, the chief text on the standards expected of the ruling class was *The Book of the Courtier* (1528) by Baldesar Castiglione. The central point of that tome was the rigorous behaviour expected of the aristocracy and the *example* they were supposed to set their peers. Membership of the elite sect was less a privilege and more an obligation, and the cultivation of refinement and nonchalance was a rigorously policed exercise. Burke is not known to have owned a copy of the *Courtier*, but Samuel Johnson and Joshua Reynolds, two of his closest friends did,[128] and it is inconceivable that he was not aware of the book. It was almost certainly discussed among them, and the great likelihood is that Burke at least borrowed a copy. But while he lauded the *institution* of aristocracy, the personnel could be an entirely different matter. He believed their role came with profound obligations, and he had nothing but scorn for those who failed to live up to their responsibilities.

Yet Paine refused to concede that the nobility were ever capable of good government. In one of his most famous extracts he sneered that 'the idea of hereditary legislators is as inconsistent as that of hereditary judges, or hereditary juries; and as absurd as an hereditary mathematician, or an hereditary wise man[129] ... I smile to myself when I contemplate the ridiculous insignificance into which literature and all the sciences would sink, were they made hereditary; and I carry the same idea into governments'.[130] For Paine it was *ability* that was the essential trait, not birth. Yet Burke, in defending the hereditary principle, was of the same opinion. He believed that government should be left to those best fit and able for the task, but he felt the hereditary principle allowed men to acquire and cultivate the requisite characteristics for government. In his *Appeal from the New to the Old Whigs* Burke outlined how it was necessary that our administrators be raised from birth to be educated and trained to assume command.[131] Burke quoted *Ecclesiastes*, chapter 38, verses 24-5,[132] to support his contention that wisdom was derived from leisure and he was overt about this principle in the *Reflections* too. 'You do not imagine, that I wish to confine power, authority, and distinction to blood, and names, and titles. No, sir. There is no qualification for government, but virtue and wisdom.'[133]

Burke could be as scathing as Paine of those he considered unsuited to govern, those whose backgrounds and ability had left them unprepared for the mantle of command, and he saw an abundance of these shortcomings in the French Assembly. The country squires or lowly judiciary were, in his mind, quite unfit for the task with which they had been presented.[134] Not only were they likely to get drunk on their newfound power and advance their own interests but he considered them 'Wholly unacquainted with the world in which they are so fond of meddling, and inexperienced in all its affairs, on which they pronounce with so much confidence, they have nothing of politics but the passions they excite.'[135] Paine's sentiments on the monarchy were almost eerily similar. 'The state of a king shuts him from the world, yet the business of a king requires him to know it thoroughly.'[136] Each felt that the preferred choice of the other was uniquely unfit to rule. Yet Burke's insight was on display again when he warned of what awaited France. With bonds to monarchy severed, and allegiance to the Assembly flimsy at best, the result would be 'some popular general [who shall become] the master of your whole republic'.[137] His remarkable foresight predicted not just the rise of Napoleon, but that the ensuing wars would match the campaigns of the League of Augsburg against Louis XIV and the War of Spanish Succession.[138] They lasted from 1689-1713, so Burke correctly forecast the duration of the Revolutionary and Napoleonic Wars up to the Corsican Ogre's exile on Elba, with startling accuracy.

Yet curiously, despite such willdly disparate stances, they held contrasting views on the difficulty of government itself. Burke often spoke gravely of the complexity and difficulty of running the ship of state, and warned of the perils of leaving such affairs to amateurs. In his *Appeal From the New to the Old Whigs* he commented that

'An ignorant man, who is not fool enough to meddle with his clock, is however sufficiently confident to think he can safely take to pieces, and put together at his pleasure, a moral machine of another guise importance and complexity, composed of far other wheels, and springs, and balances, and counteracting and co-operating powers. Men little think how immorally they act in rashly meddling with what they do not understand. Their delusive good intention is no sort of excuse for their presumption'.[139]

It is a passage, one feels, as relevant to Russell Brand today as it was for Paine over two hundred years ago. But while Burke saw government as a difficult task, best left to those qualified and experienced enough to administer it, those were not qualities *unique* to the aristocracy by any means. England was, after all, the Lords and Commons *together.* In his *Letter to a Noble Lord* (1796) Burke compared his own record and abilities in the political sphere favourably with both the original Duke of Bedford and the current incumbent. 'I cannot recognize, in his few and idle years, the competence to judge of my long and laborious life...My merits, whatever they are, are original and personal; his are derivative'.[140] They are lines that could almost have been lifted from Paine. Burke, immersed as he was in the Commons, was intimately aware that the politics of the eighteenth century were comprised of a delicate balance of vested interests. This complex web of social interactions, dependent on patronage, sinecures, appointments and associations, had to be taken into account before any sort of legislative steps could be undertaken, and the absence of formal political parties made affiliations even more fleeting.

Paine, in stark contrast to his antagonist, regarded politics as a far more straightforward affair where 'the Chiefs, in several offices...do little more than sign their name three or four times a year'.[141] The disparity in these stances can, of course, be explained by their respective experience in practical politics. Burke was thrust into the heart of British politics in all its pomp and titled tradition, all its carefully weighed compromise, and it clearly rubbed off on him. Paine was embroiled in rebellion and the excited spread of reformist ideas, but he rarely had to consider the consequences of his beliefs. His naivety was exposed when he finally entered the arena and spent just a brief period in a junior administrative position in Congress. The Silas Deane affair saw him booted out when he revealed evidence of the delicate transactions between America and France in an effort to expose a rival. John Adams, who knew of what he spoke, wrote that Paine 'is a keen writer but very ignorant of the Science of Government',[142] a sentiment which helps explain his similarly fleeting tenure in the French Convention. Burke, in stark contrast, spent thirty years at the coal face and must have bristled at being lectured on politics by a naive amateur like Paine.

Yet Paine believed Burke's argument on the complicated nature of government was merely a smokescreen to keep the masses disenfranchised while shielding the elites' vested interests. In his view, both despotisms and 'balanced' constitutions like England's, existed to enslave their populations while enriching themselves and propagating war, justifying a steady flow of taxation. He saw Burke as just the mouthpiece, the hireling of this cabal.[143] Burke mockingly suggested that:

'To make a government requires no great prudence. Settle the seat of power; teach obedience; and the work is done. To give freedom is still more easy. It is not necessary to guide; it only requires to let go the rein. But to form a *free government*; that is, to temper together these opposite elements of liberty and restraint in one consistent work, requires much thought, deep reflection, a sagacious, powerful, and combining mind. This I do not find in those who take the lead in the national assembly[144] ...It is this inability to wrestle with difficulty which has obliged the arbitrary assembly of France to commence their schemes of reform with abolition and total destruction.'[145]

Yet Paine was entirely serious when quoting Lafayette's view that 'For a nation to love liberty, it is sufficient that she knows it; and to be free it is sufficient that she wills it'.[146] One suspects though that Lafayette's experiences in France, and his lengthy incarceration in a dank Austrian cell, shattered his faith and caused him to revise this opinion.

Paine was absolutely determined to abolish titles, but he had grander ambitions too. Perhaps the most striking segment in all of his writing, and certainly that which was considered most inflammatory, was the extensive programme for a welfare state that comprised such a large slice of *The Rights of Man Part II*,[147] the section primarily responsible for seeing him convicted of sedition in his absence. He called for nothing less than the dismantling of the system of aristocratic privilege and an extensive programme of redistribution to provide for old age, the destitute poor and schooling for the children of the masses. He also suggested a huge reduction in military spending as a result of an alliance with France. It was a form of proto-socialism that relied on swingeing expropriation that effectively sought to dismantle the very edifice that Burke, with all his powers of persuasion, was determined on protecting. Yet, characteristically, Paine did not seem to consider the human cost such sweeping alterations might incur; what effect these radical reforms may wreak on a society centred on social distinctions that were to be annihilated.

Burke, one feels, would have had a field day in critiquing Paine's plan. It is somewhat regrettable that he chose not to go public with his opinions though, as it transpired, Paine's effort provoked such widespread opposition from other quarters that a reply from Burke would have been almost superfluous. Paine offered a somewhat mellowed welfare plan five years later in *Agrarian Justice*. He defended those who owned property, arguing that they were not to blame for the inequalities that civilisation had created,[148] but he did propose an effective ten per cent tax for restitution to those dispossessed.[149] His speculations here were in sharp contrast to Burke's writing on taxation in America and Ireland that forms such a significant part of his *Observations on a Late Publication* (1769). The Irishman's essay took thoughtful consideration of the human effects of such policies.

His more nuanced approach also contrasted with Paine's rather Manichean view of conflict. The radical frequently suggested that an end to the current system of government would see an end to war. Yet his argument, that commerce would replace combat as trade was simply more cost efficient,[150] is an opinion that seems hopelessly naive now. It is on a par with Sir Ralph Norman Angell's suggestion, in *The Great Illusion* (1909), that the interdependent relationships of Europe's economies made war between them unthinkable.

For Paine, war and greed were not aspects of the human condition, they were *against* human nature, and a republican system of government would see them simply vanish. In Burke's view they were entirely *within* human nature, and an established state was necessary to restrain man's wilder impulses. Posterity has proven Burke entirely correct in this regard, and Paine's inability to see that war sprang from man's nature, and not the current administrations, reveals his blind spot on this issue. However, Paine's argument that current levels of charity were insufficient to ameliorate poverty in society and that the state should pool resources to ease the burden on the poor[151] has gained far more widespread acceptance than Burke's perhaps excessive faith in the market.

Yet the two men did not disagree on everything. Both were enthusiastic in their support for free trade, advocated religious tolerance and were critical of the East India Company. Paine wrote of his horror at British rule in India[152] and reserved particular scorn for Robert Clive,[153] while Burke's protracted impeachment of Warren Hastings, Governor-General of India from 1773-1785, is one of the more noteworthy and well-chronicled events of his career. The corruption he believed Hastings guilty of was so severe that he spent the best part of fourteen years combating it and considered his efforts 'those on which I value myself the most'.[154] Neither had very much at all to say about women, particularly with regard to politics, which is why this section does the same, and both made frequent allusions to their distaste for Jews. Burke made several derogatory remarks about Jews in his *Reflections*[155] while Paine too was rather bluntly anti-Semitic in both *Rights of Man*[156] and *Rights of Man Part II,*[157] suggestive of just how prevalent such views were at the time. Burke did concede that there were 'respectable' Jews in his *Letter to a Member of the National Assembly* (1791), but of the rest he lamented that there were 'more than we can conveniently hang'.[158]

Both also opposed slavery, but their actions give an indication of Burke's sometimes excessive caution. Paine, despite his friendship with Joseph Kirkbride of Bordertown, Philadelphia, who owned three negro slaves,[159] and his close association with Thomas Jefferson, who owned considerably more, vocally condemned the practice almost as soon as he stepped off the boat in America. Yet Burke was noticeably more reticent. His *Sketch of a Negro Code* (1792) targeted reform rather than abolition, and, more revealingly, he lacked the nerve to publish it. The *Sketch* languished in a draw for more than a decade until the initiative had been taken by others, principally Wilberforce with the backing of Pitt.

Burke's view that the current status quo was ordained inhibited him from being able to visualise change in the way his rival could. But, while Burke believed that God's guiding hand had shaped society into the admirable state in which he lived, he had little to say on why this 'perfection' had been limited to Britain. If Christian providence was so indisputable then what explained the existence of such a vast Islamic empire, or of numerous eastern civilisations; if it was so universal then why the suffering of African slaves or his native Catholic Irish? While we have to separate Burke's private thoughts from his public announcements and admit to the influence his position played on his declarations, it is still apparent that there is little doubt in his public writing or private correspondence. The sincere religious belief that underpinned Burke's philosophy may have resulted in him being, in certain respects, as inflexible and dogmatic as Paine.

The dispute between the two men and the passion with which they forwarded their arguments can only really be understood in the intensity of the times in which they lived. The French Revolution was initially warmly received and for a few years Burke was something of a laughing stock, alienated by his uniquely critical stand. Yet as events in France became ever bloodier Britain grew increasingly alarmed, and gradually figures like Charles Edward Fox, the Whig leader who remained supportive even as the corpses mounted, were increasingly derided. The Revolution had a tremendous impact in England where a welter of reformist societies flourished - quickly countered by the establishment of an even greater number of patriotic clubs. The government stamped down on extremist agitation, but the era that was dubbed 'Pitt's Tory Reign of Terror' was a damp squib compared to what was taking place across the channel.

Paine, who had returned to England to agitate, was encouraged to leave and the government were careful to wait until he had fled before beginning proceedings, not wanting him to become another 'Wilkes and Liberty', martyred to the cause and a focus of reformist dissent. Paine was convicted in absentia, and the state's caution looked shrewd when his defence lawyer, Thomas Erskine, was given a rapturous reception for his robust and impassioned defence of freedom of speech.[160] Habeas Corpus was suspended, *Rights of Man* was banned, prosecutions escalated and in 1794 the treason trials of Horne Tooke, Thomas Hardy and John Thelwall took place. The limitations of the government's repression were exposed however, when the trials collapsed. The much-vaunted English 'Reign of Terror' then amounted to a handful of failed prosecutions, hardly comparable to its namesake in France.

The majority got behind crown and country at the time, but E.P. Thompson's seminal work, *The Making of the English Working Class*, suggests the reformists enjoyed the bulk of public opinion. He also claims their opponents, particularly after the Birmingham riots, were largely active because they were in the pay of the government.[161] He is simply wrong in these conclusions. In fact, patriotic societies and publications significantly outnumbered their rivals, while Pitt's government was so alarmed by events in Birmingham that they conducted a national defence review.[162] Yet accusations of this nature have endured in left-wing circles. It is incredibly common for contemporary advocates to dismiss their rivals as being in the pay of big oil or of having been brainwashed by Rupert Murdoch, allegations which are usually informed by assumptions rather than evidence. Paine lived up to this stereotype when accusing Burke of being 'purloined' by the royal purse. There is zero evidence to support this claim, but we do know that Burke refused a number of financial incentives when there was a whiff of any conflict of interest. Paine, on the other hand, willingly took several gratuities from the US government for services rendered, including a sizeable amount of cash and a farm in upstate New York from which he was able to draw a reasonable income.

Yet both writers were undoubtedly affected by the drama of these events. Paine was inflamed by the idea that the realisation of his political goals was a genuine possibility. Burke was motivated by the tangible fear that French excesses may yet swamp England and sweep aside all he cherished in an anarchic bloodbath. Circumstances sharpened and hardened the opinions of both. Burke's opposition to the growth of Enlightenment 'reason' had led him to develop an antipathy to its precepts and a formidable arsenal of arguments and rhetoric to deploy against it.* The threat to Britain presented an opportunity to deploy the resources he had been accumulating against a foe he had been training to contend with for decades. It is little wonder then that he took several months to polish and perfect his *Reflections*. This was the moment he had been dreading, but one he was unquestionably prepared for. Paine, by contrast, had been sharpening his quill and accumulating his own litany of pithy ripostes to the antiquated institutions he had been targeting since his excise days in Lewes. Both men had been preparing for the moment, both were

* He was, once more, right to be wary. The Enlightenment was a remarkable period that pushed mankind forward in numerous ways. But what alarmed Burke was how the movement exaggerated the impact of reason while neglecting the passions. It resulted in a belief taking hold - that as the laws of nature were being revealed as logical and unbending so too would the laws of man. Once these were divined the perfect, ordered society could be constructed around them. It was this splinter of Enlightenment thought that was seized upon by progressives of all stripes. The costs of that approach have been dreadful.

determined to bring their full powers to bear in pursuit of defending their respective beliefs and both, resultantly, left an indelible mark on political discourse.

The war that eventually followed the onset of revolution was the final bone of contention between them. Each man became the greatest cheerleader, the staunchest advocate for war on behalf of the state they represented, Burke for England, and Paine for France, as he had previously done for America. While Paine regarded war as the sole preserve of monarchy, he clearly believed it was an acceptable tool to wield *against* despotism. His presumption was that once victory had been attained the pacifist republican utopia would be realised. Yet the advocation of violence had long characterised his prose. Early in his career, in 1775, Paine had asserted that 'Liberty...was the only legitimate purpose violence could serve'.[163] When he had penned *The American Crisis*, and, to an extent, *Common Sense* (1776), he encouraged open rebellion against British rule. Now he hoped to foment war against his former home once more and his *Letter to the People of France* (1797) encouraged the French in their efforts against the English. While he initially took an aversion to Napoleon he came to rather admire him[164] and agitated for an invasion of England in 1796 and Ireland in 1798. He frequently hoped to stir up rebellion in the latter state, another event Burke had long opposed. Paine was, as late as 1806, still fervently endorsing the idea of a Napoleonic conquest of his birthplace.[165] But Napoleon's own views could hardly have differed more from Paine's. In 1796 he opined

> 'A republic of thirty million men! With our habits, our vices! How can it be possible? It is a wild dream, with which the French are infatuated, but it will pass like so many before it. They must have glory, the satisfactions of vanity. But as for liberty, they understand nothing about it'.[166]

It is more evidence how Paine's conviction blinded him to practical realities. He campaigned against despotism, yet tacitly supported the regime of Napoleon; he vocally opposed Pitt's 'reign of terror', yet brushed off the far worse terror of the Jacobins. On the coup in September 1797, which led to a censored press, house searches and a flurry of arrests, Paine wrote that 'The event itself is a matter of joy'.[167] Burke, on the other hand, felt so strongly on the issue of war against France that he dedicated his later years to campaigning for it, both in the Commons, and, after his retirement, in his extended *Letters on a Regicide Peace.* This then was the apotheosis of the divergence between them. The most extensive war Europe had ever seen would certainly have happened anyway, but the old sparring partners certainly did their utmost to ensure that no quarter was given by either side.

The many parallels in their lives lasted until their final days. In an almost eerie coincidence Burke, terrified that his tomb might be ransacked by invading Jacobins, requested that he be buried in an unmarked grave. While this plea was ultimately ignored after his death in 1797, a final ironic twist reserved that fate for his great antagonist. Ostracised in America, after the publication of the *Age of Reason*, just six people attended Paine's funeral in 1809. In 1819 William Cobbett had his body exhumed to be returned to England and given a fitting resting place. Yet his remains were lost and ended up, presumably, languishing in an unmarked grave. While this was an undeniably sad fate for a man whose impact continues to be so significant, we need no memorial to remember either man. Burke and Paine live on through their words, via the ideas they expressed with such persuasive clarity. They will continue to influence, to provoke and to astound future generations, just as they did their own.

Their legacies are certainly secure. Burke's warnings on the fate that awaited France were almost eerily prescient and the ability to make accurate forecasts was one he displayed throughout his career. He predicted the regicide of Louis XVI a year and a half before it happened and warned that the British government's attitude to America would result in rebellion, war and defeat. His insight into the human condition was also apparent when he noted that 'In this character of the Americans a love of freedom is the predominating feature...This fierce spirit of liberty is stronger in the English colonies, probably than in any other people of the earth'.[168] One suspects those are sentiments most Americans would agree with to this day.

Yet, despite the abundance of such material, Burke's *Reflections* is largely a persuasive tome, not an analytical one. As such it was written expressly to appeal to the emotions, primarily to the nostalgic loyalty of the propertied classes and the aristocracy. It is difficult to imagine anything better designed to rile the pragmatic sensibilities of Paine. The *Reflections* is not, by any stretch, a serious political tract, it is not a critique or a detailed analysis of Britain's constitution. It is aimed squarely at the layman and is more a romanticised, idealised account than a robust examination of the tripartite system. It reflects little of the intricacies and complexities of political life and glosses over any inherent weaknesses. No reference is made to Burke's frequent attempts to rein in the power of the monarchy or his opposition to Parliament's mismanagement of America, Ireland or India. The corruption and nepotism inherent in the system are airbrushed out of existence. It is a party political broadcast, softly lit and accompanied by soaring strings.

Paine, by contrast, held nothing back in presenting his political manifesto with all the rigour and detail he could muster. Considering the opposition that he provoked a touch more political prudence may not have gone amiss. Fennessy's interpretation is that

> 'Paine possessed that characteristic attribute of the born revolutionary – the absolute and unwavering conviction of the rightness and legitimacy of his revolution from the first moment of its existence, and the absolute wrongness of all who oppose it, no matter what their position or public authority may be. Again and again he states the issue in terms of black and white'.[169]

There was, ironically, no reasoning with Paine.

But while Paine's conviction blinded him to the myriad faults in the causes he championed Burke's faith in his blinded him to the realisation that he lived in a time of meteoric scientific, philosophical and economic change, and that a correspondingly rapid political development was a prudent reaction to the societal shift happening all around him. Both men accumulated enemies, and both were seen as rather arrogant in certain quarters, an accusation not entirely without merit. Both also fell out spectacularly with former allies, Burke with Fox, and Paine with Washington.

It is pertinent to note that two figures so revered today were largely reviled in their own time. The depth of the forces opposing Paine are apparent in his ruin in England, where he was public enemy number one after the publication of *Rights of Man*, and America, where he was widely demonised as an atheist for *The Age of Reason,* not to forget France where he spent the best part of a year in incarceration and missed death by a whisker. It is a profound irony that Paine fled English despotism for French liberty, and ended up being gaoled and almost executed in his place of refuge. Burke achieved a level of redemption after his spell as an outcast, even from his own party and friends, but his *Letters on a Regicide Peace* are still evidence of a man fighting a rising tide of opposition, despite the manner in which events had validated his views.

Essentially, Burke and Paine's disagreement happened because they held irretrievably conflicting views which were deeply embedded, and because of a misunderstanding on the part of Paine. Burke was arguably the more complex, nuanced thinker of the two, Paine something of a demagogue who had an inflexible template he attempted to apply to every situation. Theirs was a battle of pragmatist versus idealist. Burke attempted to approach issues with a more open mindset, though he was arguably as immobile as his rival when it came to the establishment triumvirate of church, monarchy and aristocracy. The central theme of each man's thinking was also markedly different. Burke relied primarily on experience and observation of empirical formula, while Paine chiefly employed reason and the application of logical analysis to situations, what Burke would have derided as 'abstract metaphysical speculation'. The flaws in both are apparent. Paine's use of logic allowed him to confidently assert that Mars and Jupiter teemed with life,[170] while Burke's reliance on precedent left him somewhat mired in tradition and unable to imagine or visualise the sort of radical changes that Paine advocated, changes that very much tally with the modern conception of how society should be ordered.

They were two flawed men, as are we all, but their assets outweigh their defects by some considerable margin. Both were unequivocally decent human beings, Paine's apparent lack of social empathy apart, and they believed in and campaigned for social justice and against despotic rule their whole lives. While they had markedly different ideas both valued virtue, despised and consistently opposed corruption and cruelty, and believed society should be based on merit. Both were concerned for the welfare of normal people, even if they had contrasting ideas about how it was to be secured. The fact that they shared such decency and so many values should send a salient message to the contemporary moralist: Your rivals are not the devils and enemies you believe them to be. A civil discussion between the two may have been fruitful and may have made each man realise that their rival had a point. It never happened, not after the publication of Burke's *Reflections* at any rate, but the fact that both men's manifestos have been so emphatically redeemed makes it clear that the most productive path to tread is the middle ground – that moderate reforms can be introduced while respecting existing institutions, and that these can be reached through civil and open discourse. We are living testimony to this as the most successful aspects of contemporary societies have been arrived at through an accord that Burke and Paine were unable to realise in their war of words.

If the most desirable outcome is for a compromise between such conflicting ideologies, views expressed with such lucid brilliance by these giants of the written word, then it is one that England, the nation that informed them, has largely been able to realise. Yet the birth pangs of that process, through the industrial age, were undeniably painful. It is perhaps no coincidence then that the England of the Industrial Revolution was also home to the man universally regarded as the definitive thinker in the pantheon of left-wing thought; a bearded and intense German of Jewish extraction whose resting place in London, marked by that imposing and unmistakable bust, is still something of a site of pilgrimage for radicals of all hues, a man whose name is synonymous with the movement he dedicated his life to: Karl Marx.

Karl Marx

While Rousseau had a disastrous impact on the world of political philosophy it has to be conceded that such consequences were unintended. One can reasonably assume that, were the Genevan informed of the catastrophes that followed in his wake, he would have been horrified. The same cannot be said of Karl Marx. The man whose name would inspire a movement of unparalleled fanaticism ardently craved such violent, convulsive eruptions. He looked back to the French Revolution as his template and desired with all his heart to see the bloodshed repeated, but on a much grander scale. More than this his arguments, which he haughtily forwarded as if they were irrefutable scientific facts, had been proven to be empty fallacies even before he died. His theory revolved around the 'fact' that as capitalism was necessarily competitive then rival industrialists must assuredly slash their workers' wages to gain an advantage over their competitors. As such, the workers of the world would inevitably see their relative incomes and standard of living plummet as capitalism continued to spread.

Even before his death it was apparent that this was a hollow theory. Workers' wages as well as their rights, representation and material comforts continued to rise, and have inexorably done so in the century and a half since. Marx also prophesied the middle classes would die out. Instead they have multiplied beyond all expectation. Yet, despite such damning and irrefutable evidence, his philosophising won millions of devotees and, though his name tends to be no longer referenced, the arguments he forwarded, and the culture of protest he inspired, still prevail among swathes of activists whose conviction remains unshakeable. If one wished to forward a case that no individual in history has had a more damaging impact or more harmful legacy than Karl Marx, then it would prove testing indeed to oppose.

Marx was born on 5 May 1818 in the historical city of Trier in southwestern Germany, the sprawling town that was briefly capital of the Roman Empire in the third century AD. His sisters recalled him as a 'tyrant' who drove them like they were his horses and forced them to eat the mud pies he prepared with his grubby fingers. But they put up with such indignities to hear the wild stories he entertained them with. These anecdotes apart, little is known about Marx's early years, but there is an abundance of evidence on the world and circumstances into which he was born. Hopes had endured that the French Revolution would 'turn good' right up to 1815. The effects of that tumultuous period then were still evident at the time of Karl's birth, particularly as Trier had come under the aegis of Napoleon and tasted French liberty before its return to Prussian despotism. This transfer was most keenly felt by the Jewish population of the area which, under the Emperor, had gained opportunities previously denied them, ones which were now cruelly and swiftly wrenched from their grasp again. The number of Jews in the predominantly Catholic city was tiny and in the post-Waterloo settlement they faced being returned to Trier's old 'society of orders' by which they had rather more obligations and restrictions than rights and privileges. Even though Marx's ancestors belonged to the more affluent sector of Trier's Jews, and included a significant number of rabbis, they still faced the prospect of becoming a persecuted minority once more.

Catholic Trier came under the dominion of the Protestant Prussian regime of Berlin but, despite the otherwise progressive nature of Prince von Hardenberg's Edict of Emancipation of 1812, Jews were still barred from working in any sort of government capacity. Karl's father, Herschel Mordechai, was the son of one rabbi and the brother of another, but was more ambitious than religious. As a result, in order to further his career as an attorney at the court of appeals, he changed his name to the more Germanic sounding Heinrich Marx and, in 1820, converted from Judaism to Protestantism. Heinrich was a staunch advocate of the Enlightenment. He was known to have read Voltaire and Thomas Paine's *Rights of Man*, and had few qualms about abandoning his family's faith. It was a secular and politically radical household that would play a hugely formative role in the development of young Karl. His mother and siblings would prove less influential though. Heinrich had married Henriette Presburg from Nijmegen in 1814. She was eleven years his junior and considerably more resistant about surrendering her Judaism. While Marx revered his father, he had little time for his mother largely, it seems, due to her lack of interest in politics. While she fussed over him his attitude to her tended to oscillate between frosty and hostile. He would have little to do with her while his siblings were effectively disowned from early in his life. Marx had bigger fish to fry than familial loyalties.

In 1830 he enrolled at the Trier *Gymnasium*, a university preparatory secondary school which, under Johann Heinrich Wyttenbach, had a notably leftist curriculum and a radical staffroom. One of the school's teachers was arrested with Karl's father, Heinrich, for raucously, and rather drunkenly, singing songs in support of the 1830 Revolution. The event doubtlessly influenced the youngster about the romanticism of protest, especially as he was an impressionable lad of fifteen. Wyttenbach himself, who was not just the headmaster but also Marx's History teacher, got arrested in 1832 at a demonstration in support of press freedom. Ludwig Simon, another member of the *Gymnasium* staff, ended up on the German National Assembly for Trier during the 1848 Revolution. The twin environments of home and school created the foundations for the youngster's political life. He would continue to grow in extremism for decades to come.

At the age of seventeen, Marx concluded in his final exams that 'The main consideration that must steer us in our choice of occupation is the welfare of humanity, our own completion'.[171] It is often claimed that Marx's writing focuses purely on scientific rigour - that morality plays no part in his conclusions at all. But while the topic is never overtly mentioned it informs his whole body of work. His distaste with the society in which he lived, and his contrasting attitudes to people from different walks of life, makes this clear. As Alan Ryan noted, 'Marx's professed indifference to moral considerations is hard to square with [his] evident hatred of the injustice and cruelty so visible in the early years of the industrial revolution'.[172] It seems that Marx decided to focus on a scientific bent to emphasise the objective nature of his theorising so he could argue that it was divorced from emotional, and thus irrational concerns. This is unconvincing though. One thing that Marx could never legitimately be described as is 'dispassionate'.

The intellectual culture of the time focused on a prevailing belief: as the laws of nature had been revealed by science, then the same empirical process could unveil the laws of man and society. It was also widely held that man was naturally good but oppressed by societal forces. In Berlin's summation of this conception

> 'Left to themselves, with no obstacles to obscure their vision and to frustrate their endeavours, men would pursue virtue and knowledge; justice and equality would take the place of authority and privilege, competition would yield to co-operation, happiness and wisdom would become universal possessions'.[173]

Marx's thought was still developing at this juncture, but he would soon fuse Jacobin politics with communist economics. He spent a rather drunken year at Bonn University, by which point both his political persuasion and the fiery temperament that propelled it were apparent. Marx was, at that stage, an aspiring poet and became president of the university's poetry club. But he was also an enthusiastic member of the Tavern Club, and he and his drinking buddies got involved in frequent brawls with the aristocratic Borussia Korps. In 1836 Marx was lucky to escape with his life when he engaged a member of the Korps in a duel, but he never grew out of this combative side of his nature. In 1851 he burst into the offices of a London based German-language paper whose editor had accused him of embezzling funds from the refugee committee. He challenged the man to a duel, and was still issuing challenges twenty years later when accused of complicity in the Paris Commune.

For his second year at university, Marx's father, who was concerned about his wild living, arranged a transfer to Berlin. He settled in quickly, and it would prove a transformative period. Marx got engaged to Jenny Ludwig, daughter of his father's aristocratic friend Ludwig von Westphalen, and wrote her Romantic poetry. He also, after initial resistance, fell under the spell of the philosopher who had held the seat at Berlin from 1818-31, and whose thinking still dominated the institution: Georg Wilhelm Friedrich Hegel.

Hegel built on and critiqued the ideas of Immanuel Kant who had questioned the validity of how our senses perceive the world around us. But Hegel went further and understood that both our perceptions and the objects they comprehend are interactive, or 'dialectical', a term that came to define his thinking. He argued that knowledge could only be understood as part of a historical process. As a result, Hegel perceived history as a developing mechanism in which every age must be understood, not just in relation to the preceding eras which shaped it, but also in light of the future, for the present contained the seeds which would determine subsequent events. He believed academics were neglecting their role by ignoring this aspect of the discipline. Historians must be able to analyse eras as an age in movement, as periods that act as the herald of the future. Hegel believed that as history unfolded man moved ever closer to the full consciousness which would prove the pinnacle of human development, that of 'Absolute Spirit'.

It was a conclusion that appeared to ratify what Marx had already envisaged - his adolescent dream of a collective utopia - and the concept eventually underpinned his theory of economic progress. Though he later came to refute much of the philosopher's theorising, or claimed to, it is clear that Hegel's thinking forms the framework for the system that Marx spent most of his life developing. Marx would not only envisage his theory as the inevitable unfolding of history, but he too believed that humanity would achieve full consciousness as part of a collective process. Until that moment of universal epiphany however, mankind was living under a 'false consciousness'. In a letter to his father he perceived Hegel's determinist view of history as 'the deed of spirit',[174] hauntingly close to later Nazi rhetoric. It seems apparent, in light of the fire and brimstone aspects of his writings, that Marx was also influenced by the philosopher's characteristically bleak take on philosophy and the inevitability of violent overthrow. This aspect contributed to Isaiah Berlin identifying Hegel as one of the six enemies of human liberty.* Marx, the most notable of his disciples, would significantly outdo him in that regard.

In 1838 Marx's father, who had been growing ever more exasperated with his son's failure to pursue a sensible career in law, along with his obsession with philosophy, atheism and political radicalism, died quite suddenly. Marx did not attend the funeral and, apart from chasing his inheritance, had little to do with his family from that point. An acrimonious dispute over that financial legacy would rumble on between Karl and his mother for years, but then Marx was

---

* It is little surprise that Rousseau also features prominently on that list.

notoriously dreadful with money. His father had written to him on 9 December 1837 to chastise his son on his spendthrift ways, lamenting how he 'spends in one year almost 700 taler...while the richest do not even spend 500'.[175] Despite such lavish spending Marx still owed not inconsiderable sums to a tailor, a dry-goods merchant and a book dealer, none of which he ever settled. In 1841 his university record noted that 'he has frequently been complained of regarding debts'.[176] This sort of wilful financial impecunity was a trait Marx never managed to break. Such issues caused him strife for decades, but he was always far more preoccupied with political concerns.

As his activism and immersion in philosophy intensified Marx became a leading member of the Young Hegelians - a group of intellectual radicals who regarded themselves as free thinkers united in hatred of King, Church and bourgeoisie. They combined a wildly bohemian lifestyle with ardent philosophical speculation, developing into a movement of outsiders and atheists which swept Marx along. The experience profoundly influenced his thought and temperament. The Young Hegelians believed that a catastrophe was imminent. This faith in a doomsday scenario remains a common trait among activists, the oppressive pessimism of the radical left being fertile soil for such ruminations. In Sperber's analysis, this springs from the devout atheists' transfer of their 'sense of the transcendent from God to humanity'[177].

Politically the Young Hegelians moved to the left, siding with the liberal opposition in Prussia and espousing democratic and republican ideals. Their activism led to them being excluded from academic life and forced into the murky world of underground publishing. Three figures in that circle stand out as particularly influential on Marx's nascent idealism. Eduard Gans was a friend of Alexis de Tocqueville and a Berlin professor of legal history. He had converted from Judaism to Protestantism while reinterpreting Hegel from a leftist stance. Ludwig Feuerbach also strongly affected Marx's thought, even though they never met. But probably the most influential to the fledgling firebrand was Bruno Bauer. The most radically far-left of all the Young Hegelians, Bauer was, by all accounts, a rather nasty piece of work. He was also an ardent anti-Semite and is widely regarded as one of the founders of the strain of anti-Semitism that would prove so costly in central Europe. All these factors coalesced into a volatile soup as his education drew to an end. Marx's dissertation, on the difference between the Democritean and the Epicurean Philosophies of nature, was submitted to Jena University in 1841. It bears the mark of all that had influenced him to that point, and he dedicated it to Ludwig von Westphalen with the inscription 'idealism is no illusion but a truth'.[178]

Upon completion of his degree and, firmly set on a course of political activism, Marx returned to his native area. But he was furious that his mother would not offer him an advance from the inheritance he was due on her death. His relationship with her and his siblings never truly recovered from the fallout. Bauer had also moved to the region and taken up a position at Bonn University, though his radicalism and atheism saw him speedily removed from the post. It probably did not help that during Easter weekend he and Marx drunkenly rode a donkey through town in a deliberate act of provocation. Denied entry into academia because of his radical tendencies, Marx quickly slid into political activism which aimed at subverting the Prussian state.

Bauer returned to Berlin while Marx remained in Bonn and began writing for a Cologne newspaper, the *Rheinische Zeitung* (The Rhineland News). In that period he came increasingly into contact with communist views which had been seeping into Germany. Ludwig Gall had been spreading the ideas of Fourier in Trier while in Berlin French utopian socialism had been disseminated through the poems of Heine and the lectures of Gans. Marx quickly developed a reputation as an able journalist, winning admirers among not just radicals but moderate liberals too. He was, however, quickly identified by the Prussian state as a dangerous subversive.

The *Rheinische Zeitung* was partly funded by an affluent Cologne jurist, Robert Jung, who recruited another young radical intellectual, Moses Hess, the son of a wealthy Jewish merchant and sugar refiner. Hess was a committed communist and follower of Henri de Saint-Simon, the man who had coined the motto 'From each according to his ability, to each according to his needs'. He regarded private property as evil, advocating its abolition and the imposition of collective ownership in its place. Hess was the first German to write a book of communist ideas, *The Secret History of Mankind*, a tome which McLellan describes as 'mystical and meandering, but [which] contained quite clearly the idea of the polarisation of classes and the imminence of a proletarian revolution'.[179] Both Hess and Bauer also worshipped the French Revolution and hoped for an encore. Hess was bowled over when he met Marx, gushing to Auerbach in a letter dated 2 September 1841 'Imagine Rousseau, Voltaire, Holbach, Lessing, Heine and Hegel united in one person'.[180] Hess had already converted Friedrich Engels to communism yet, despite his influence on the pair, they both eventually came to regard him as a tedious fool. Marx's new career was so successful that he joined the editorial team of the paper in October 1842, by which time, according to Isaiah Berlin, he was already known for his 'intolerance [and] dictatorial nature'.[181]

It was around that time that he began writing on socialism, a movement that had grown out of a French political climate fuelled by the still smouldering embers of revolution. It was characterised by the abortive revolution of 1830, itself unforgettably visualised by Delacroix's *Liberty Leading the People*. That painting extols the martial valour, virtue and glory of the rising as Liberty, breast exposed while dramatically heaving the Tricolour, exhorts the ragged but determined troops forward, over the barricades. Socialism informed the Chartist movement in England and fed off the doctrines of Robert Owen, Charles Fourier and Saint-Simon. It was also inspired by the radical egalitarianism of the French Revolution's extremist democrats and Ricardo's labour theory. Fourier hoped to create utopian communities which he believed would bring about a change in human nature that would liberate joy to an unprecedented degree. His *Phalansteries* were to be comprised of exactly 1,620 individuals. He seriously claimed that the realisation of these communes would result in the sea turning into lemonade, lions switching to a vegetarian diet and six moons orbiting the earth. Bizarrely his ideas appealed to sober thinkers, and he was read by John Stuart Mill and Karl Marx among others.

While virtually all socialist theorising has been wildly impractical it goes without saying that Fourier's ideas were almost singularly barking. Yet mainstream socialism was far more grounded. It was chiefly a response to the Industrial Revolution and gave rise to workers' associations and protests while broadly opposing property and inequality. Marx's peers had seen the optimism of the French Revolution give way to a new form of bondage and their distaste for the abysmal conditions of the working masses and the ingrained inequality of their society informed their activism. It was this 'social question', the debate on the condition of the proletariat that proved the genesis of Marx's communist ideas.

Marx was already beginning to diverge from the Young Hegelians' focus on atheism, a schism that ultimately led to an irreparable rift with the group. It was not that he did not share their inclination, but he did not hold the belief, as they did, that religion was the *cause* of mankind's ills. For Marx, it was just a symptom. Initially he laid the blame on the state and its officials, but he soon began pointing his finger at the capitalists. Relatively moderate in the early part of his burgeoning activism, an issue that led to friction with and estrangement from the more extreme Bauer, Marx was becoming more radical all the time. The Prussian authorities duly noted this and suppressed the *Rhineland News*. Marx promptly married Jenny and fled for the life of an émigré in Paris, a move that would significantly broaden his intellectual and political horizons. He worked on a repudiation of Hegel's *Philosophy of Law* which had defended monarchy, state and Church, and became more influenced by Saint-Simon, another of Berlin's six enemies of liberty.

Marx also absorbed Jean-Jacques Rousseau, particularly the *Social Contract*. His personal copy of that book was heavily underlined and annotated. The concept of the General Will particularly resonated with him. It encouraged him to envisage a future in which the state would perish. Marx was, at this point, coming to share with Rousseau the belief that civilisation had corrupted and debased man. His thinking eventually became far more developed than the

Genevan's, but that critical belief forms the kernel of both men's thought. They consequently envisaged an egalitarian society built on mutual co-operation and agreement. The pair shared more than just ideological similarities though. Both eulogised the common man, while seldom associating with them, and lauded the proletariat while harbouring a taste for the finer things in life, most notably a proclivity for aristocratic women: the blue-blooded Jenny von Westphalen for Marx and a whole raft of paramours in the case of Jean-Jacques. Karl was certainly more fortuitous in affairs of the heart though. His marriage to Jenny was one of true love which lasted their whole lifetimes, the odd hiccup apart, and saw them bear seven children, of whom three daughters survived to adulthood. It is their philosophical similarities which are more interesting though. In Marx's notorious pamphlet from 1844, *On the Jewish Question*, he added his own italics for emphasis and affirmed how Rousseau was entirely correct to state

> 'whoever dares to undertake the founding of a nation must feel himself capable of *changing*, so to speak, *human nature* and of *transforming* each individual who is in himself a complete but isolated whole into a *part* of something greater than himself...*Man* must be deprived of his *own powers* and given alien powers which he cannot use without the aid of others.'[182]

Marx and Jenny lived near Arnold Ruge at 38 rue Vanneau, a quiet side street in the Saint-Germain area of the Left Bank; and Karl thrived in the buzzing intellectual climate of Paris. There were significant French and German radical communities which forwarded a range of ideas. They varied from revolutionary struggle and subversive activism to the founding of voluntary communes organised around a quasi-religious zeal. At this point there were differing conceptions of what communism should entail: Étienne Cabet advocated a non-violent, utopian communism, believing that people should gather in communities where they wore the same clothes, ate the same food, and lived in identical communal dwellings under strict state censorship. Babeuf's followers preferred a despotic version identified by a dictatorship of the proletariat while Dezamy envisaged the abolition of the state, famously suggesting that an accountant and a register were all that would be necessary for the future communist society.

While their policies varied their goals largely overlapped yet, despite this, the lack of accord and co-operation between the factions was startling. Marx would prove particularly guilty of this bitter infighting, but his reputation was, for now, unsullied, and Heinrich Claessen, the Cologne liberal, compared him to Daniel O'Connell, the hugely respected figurehead of Irish nationalism. Claessen and several other members of Cologne's affluent bourgeoisie sent Marx a generous stipend to help support him through this tricky period. It was the same class that had financed the *Rheinische Zeitung*, and it was them that Marx would turn on most bitterly of all.

Some of Marx's most important works were composed during his time in Paris and he effectively developed the ideas that would sustain him for the rest of his intellectual life. In 1844 he wrote the previously mentioned *On the Jewish Question* which has alerted many observers to Marx's apparent anti-Semitism, a rather surprising position considering his background. Wheen argues that Marx attacks Judaism, as he attacks all religions, but not specifically the Jews. He abhors their exclusion from society on religious grounds and argues that, denied advancement by the state, it is not surprising that they take advantage of financial opportunities instead. He hopes for their full inclusion in society once religion is abolished. However it is hard to ignore comments such as 'We...recognise in Judaism the presence of a universal and contemporary anti-social element whose historical evolution – eagerly nurtured by the Jews in its harmful aspects – has arrived at its present peak, a peak at which it will inevitably disintegrate'.[183]

It also must be acknowledged that Marx's writings and correspondence were peppered with acerbic swipes directed at the Jews until his dying day. In 1875, in just one of numerous examples, Marx wrote scathingly to Engels about having shared a train carriage with a 'little Yid', an uncultured and greedy Jewish businessman, a stereotype which repelled him. Such comments have provoked much controversy and disagreement but, considering Marx's well-known antipathy to both organised religion and capitalism, it is hardly surprising that he voiced particular revulsion for Judaism. Marx was, rather like Benjamin Disraeli, frequently ironic about his own Jewish descent. It seems the pair regarded themselves as apart from, and rather superior to, the people with whom they shared common ancestral roots. Indeed it appeared to bolster their arrogance that they had 'transcended' the nauseating traits they saw as shackling those who maintained, for lack of a better term, a more traditional association with the culture of Judaism.

That paper was where Marx began to identify capitalism as the true problem and its destruction as the key to human emancipation. He identified capitalism with the Jews, and many suggest this explains the tone of his paper. It is pertinent to note though that the pamphlet is called 'On the Jewish Question' and not 'On the *Capitalist* Question'. It has also been argued that Marx's distaste was more cultural than religious or racial, inspired by what he saw as the grasping commercialism of Jewish communities. As such, the antipathy directed at a large sector of the populace was understandable, even justified; in doing so however Wheen, McLellan and other apologists miss the point. It is irrelevant whether his bigotry was inspired along racial and religious lines, or cultural and economic ones. All that matters is that it existed and it was a prejudice that came to underpin his entire philosophy. His work was based on the assumption that society's problem was the division between rich and poor, the former of which were subject to brutal generalisations. As a result, his answer to what assailed the state would prove to be violence, violence and more violence. For an ideology informed by hatred in such a way will always be too willing to move to the final sanction.

His conclusions led Marx to argue that religion was merely a by-product of the alienation identified by Hegel. His time in Paris cemented his break from, not just the Young Hegelians, who he began to regard as increasingly narrow and parochial in their outlook, but, increasingly, from Hegel himself. It was in his Hegelian analysis of religion, entitled *Introduction to the Critique of Hegel's Philosophy of Law* that Marx made his famous observation that religion was the 'opiate of the masses', by which he meant it helped soothe the pain caused by the forces which were truly detrimental to man's well-being. In 1798 Novalis had made the same observation suggesting that 'Their so-called religion works simply as an opiate' while in 1840 Heinrich Heine had made reference to 'spiritual opium'. Sperber claims that Marx had borrowed the phrase from Bruno Bauer,[184] one of many swipes for which he was ultimately given credit. What Marx targeted was less a criticism of religion and more an attack on its social and political position. His approach was influenced by Feuerbach's *Theses for the Reform of Philosophy* which was published in 1843. That work argued that Hegel's thought allowed theology to continue to prosper and that a real ideological framework must commence from more grounded, pragmatic concerns.

Marx became ever more convinced that philosophy must engage primarily with politics. He argued that Germany, while advanced culturally and philosophically, was politically backward and in urgent need of the sort of rising which had crushed feudalism in France. He further added that a German revolution must go further than that of 1789. The Prussian revolt should be led not by the bourgeoisie but by the artisan class - it should be a true revolution of the proletariat. It must, by necessity, be much wider, more far-ranging, and bloodier than the French Revolution which had only mobilised a small sector of the affluent classes. It is pertinent to note though that, while penning such thoughts, Marx socialised exclusively with the liberal intelligentsia and had barely met any working class people at all.

Apart from mixing in the circles of the radical bourgeoisie Marx also read widely, absorbing the political economy of Adam Smith and John Stuart Mill among others while further developing his own economic theory. He absorbed himself in the study of the French Revolution, eulogising its 'heroes' and the role class struggle played in social development. He additionally wrestled with the dilemma of why the Revolution had failed. But that failure was not its descent to the unrestrained slaughter of political opponents - it was represented in the eventual return of the Bourbons. The revolutionists' mistake, Marx concluded, was that they concentrated on what they wished to happen rather than what history would allow. To avoid its failings then it was necessary to deduce which features of society were to thrive and which would dwindle. All conclusions must be based entirely on this 'scientific' mode of investigation. Marx believed that the flow of history was determined by immutable laws which could be discerned to allow for the accurate plotting of later events. But history is a violently unpredictable beast subject to unforeseen developments in the environment, culture, technology and philosophy. The factors that conspire to shape historical development are bewilderingly complicated and cannot be accurately forecast through the application of higher algebra, as much as Marx fervently wished they could.

The effects of Marx's absorption in such issues are apparent in the *Paris Manuscripts* - also written in 1844, but not published until much later. In these tracts, Marx's conversion to communism was complete and his conception of the economics and effects of capitalism, which he attacked with relish, almost fully realised. In his analysis, the whole system of money and property was one of 'alienation', which resulted from the fact that workers could not keep the produce of their labours. He concluded that alienation was a curse inflicted on humanity by capitalism. It left workers feeling less than human. He also cited the influence of Proudhon: that 'communism is the positive expression of the abolition of private property', a feature he described as the 'universal aspect'[185] of the movement. In the communist society, not only would private property be abolished, but society would be based on collective and co-operative labour.

Yet the true concept of communism has frequently been misunderstood. In reality, socialism and communism are merely different sides of the same coin. Socialism advocated for the joint or state ownership of the means of production and exchange, with a more equitable distribution of the resultant bounty. Communism is the theoretical notion that once socialism has been ingrained in the populace for an adequate period, the need for a state disappears. It will simply wither away as the people begin to mutually share resources. The very idea of a communist state is an oxymoron, and none of the socialist states of the twentieth century actually regarded themselves as communist. But they all *aspired* to communism and believed that if they imposed their socialist principles for a sufficient period it would eventually come about. It was a pipe dream that Marx had inspired in them. He stated:

'This communism is...the true dissolution of the clash between man and nature and between man and man, the true dissolution of the clash between existence and essence, between objectification and self-confirmation, between freedom and necessity, between individual and species. It is the solution to the riddle of history and knows itself to be this solution.'[186]

Well, quite. Marx's true legacy is one of brutal oppression, political genocide and famines so monstrously damaging that, in comparison, they make Hitler seem no more threatening than a back alley hoodlum armed with a pocket knife. So much for communism as 'the riddle of history'.

Marx however, regarded the capitalist economy as not just dehumanising but fated to get much worse for the proletariat. Due to the competition inherent in the system, they must be reduced to ever more subsistence and degradation. Although his writing evolved and he developed this idea, he never really changed it. He was just twenty-six yet he would plough the same furrow with increasing fanaticism and obsession for decades. He would seek out evidence which supported his thesis while discarding any that contradicted it, and he sought to tear down all that man had carefully accumulated and start from scratch. One feels sure that Burke would have had a field day with Marx. Marx's worldview was wholly Manichean - expressed purely in terms of antagonism and conflict. He never considered the idea of an amicable solution to what he perceived as the world's ills. There was to be no suggestion of compromise or rapprochement, none of constructive development directed towards improving the material conditions, opportunities and freedoms of the working classes, just violence and destruction.

Yet, in painting his picture of what capitalism will create, Marx describes an alien world, one that bears no relation to the reality of what was to come. The bleak dystopian hell he envisaged is as far removed from the tranquil surroundings of most in the developed West as his idyll of utopian communal living diverged from the horrific reality of the regimes he inspired. Posterity has proven Marx's entire output to be almost entirely devoid of merit. But the ideas he popularised maintain a significant influence in leftist thought. The polarising language he employed and the distaste for the system and those who succeed in it still proliferate, as does the certainty of opinion that characterised their prophet, a confidence that proved groundless.

Such traits nurture the rage-fuelled rebelliousness which yet prevails, that which is still too quick to erupt in violent demonstration and which inspired Marx to continually pray for revolution and bloodshed. Marxism may have been officially debunked, but the principles and characteristics that defined his philosophy are indistinguishable from those practised by his radical descendants today. Little, if anything, has been learned from his manifest failings. In addition to this, despite his distaste for high finance, one becoming ever more pronounced, Marx never minded taking the proceeds of capitalist enterprises. He had no objection to being supported by others or of inheriting a bequest funded by capitalism. In fact, as we have seen, he stridently demanded his due of such income and, in the process, sabotaged his relationship with his own mother. Such traits have also endured. While vocalising their aversion to the capitalist system, the modern-day activists seem happy to wallow in its benefits and are loathe to surrender any of their own luxuries, even while furiously attacking the privileges of others.

1844 was a hugely important year in at least one other respect. While he broke with Arnold Ruge as he previously had with Bruno Bauer, and bitterly falling out with former collaborators would become another trait of the man, Marx made some new associations that year. He met the Russian anarchist Mikhail Bakunin for the first time, but by far his most important new acquaintance was Friedrich Engels. The historic meeting took place on 28 August at the Café de la Régence in Paris. They had met once before, briefly, but such was their immediate connection on this occasion that they spent the next ten days engaged in intense debate and almost universal agreement on every subject. In that frantic period, a life-long bond was forged. Both men came from comfortable middle class homes and had shared a youthful love for Romantic poetry, but it was in their political views that they truly found accord. The pair also complemented each-other in numerous ways. While Marx had a more secure philosophical footing, Engels was better grounded in the practical concerns of the working man. Marx was more accomplished at developing detailed and rigorous theoretical models while Engels could write more fluidly and produce finished work much more rapidly, though he was even more dogmatic than Marx.

Engels, a tall and fair Protestant, came from a Nordic background though he was born in Bardem, near Cologne, in 1820. As the son of a successful textile manufacturer, a mill owner with factories in Germany and Manchester, Engels was the archetypal champagne socialist in rebellion against daddy. Like Marx he had converted to Young Hegelian atheism, which caused a painful rift with his pious father. He moved in many of the same circles as Marx, associating with the likes of the Free Men in Berlin. Engels's father had sent him to Manchester for a spell but, in contrast to his hopes, the experience had only radicalised him even more. In Manchester, the hotbed of Chartism and trade unionism, the birthplace of the Anti-Corn Law League and the centre of the 1842 General Strike, scores toiled in misery while a tiny elite wallowed in conspicuous luxury. It epitomised all the issues that concerned the activists arguably more than anywhere else.

Engels poured his observations into a detailed analysis entitled *The Condition of the Working Class in England*, a book Marx regarded as truly admirable. The study proved to him that Engels's practical knowledge and experience of the subject was an invaluable boon to his own work. Engels would, he believed, prove a vital collaborator in avoiding the abstractions to which, in the 1790s, the previous generation of revolutionaries had fallen prey. While Marx agreed with the timbre of their views he felt it was essential to imbed radical ideas in a robust scientific framework. Such was what he set out to do. But in approaching it from a deterministic viewpoint rather than an open one, his conclusions were always likely to fall prey to the confirmation bias inherent in his theorising.

There is no doubt that conditions for workers were appalling at the time and that many states were, by contemporary standards, severely oppressive. Marx's motivations cannot be criticised in this regard at all. It is his solutions that are questionable. It is also worth remembering that much of the impetus for improving conditions for the poor came from fabulously wealthy philanthropists. These were precisely the people that Marx railed against, yet they, and the governments of the period, were responsible for numerous positive measures. They broadened the provision for education, significantly widened suffrage, improved working conditions and made drastic advances in sanitation - implementing large-scale engineering works on sewage treatment and the supply of clean water.* The governments of the time can be strongly criticised in many ways, this is beyond dispute, but they were undeniably improving.

Certainly pressure from leftist agencies played a part in stimulating some of these measures, but much was also motivated by genuine concern. The pattern begun in that period, aided by the moderate reformist activism that Marx repeatedly denounced for its timidity, has endured. It has been one of gradual improvement that continues to transform our world. While it is true that it is now the workers of the Third World whose conditions sometimes resemble those of Victorian labourers, the same process is seeing an inexorable rise in their standards of living too. Capitalism has been revealed as, not the oppressor of the masses, but their liberator; significantly improving rights and material comforts in the areas in which it has spread. The contribution of the Marxists has been rather less productive and considerably more damaging. While the issues that Marx was concerned with were certainly serious, he might have been better off agitating for the implementation of practical reforms designed to ameliorate the suffering of the masses. Yet he did not. Indeed, as we shall see, he actively hoped for the conditions of the poor to worsen. Instead of campaigning to improve their lot, he busied himself with somewhat wild, abstract theorising centred around a divisive view of society which focused little

---

* The work of Joseph Bazalgette in the 1860s was perhaps most noteworthy in this regard.

on helping the poor but heavily on attacking the rich. And he continually yearned for a violent and bloody uprising.

However, what frequently preoccupied Marx was neither aiding the poor nor attacking the system, it was in launching bitter assaults against fellow radicals. This activity engaged his passions more acutely than any other and became his top priority with dreary regularity. His first true collaboration with Engels offers an example and it set the stage for much of their later efforts. Engels swiftly dashed off fifteen pages which he contributed to *The Holy Family*, an acerbic swipe at the Bauer brothers, particularly Bruno. Marx's contribution swelled the finished product to some 300 ponderous pages. It was a typically vicious diatribe. McLellan describes the finished piece as consisting 'of hair-splitting and deliberate misrepresentation which distorted their opponents' articles to the point of absurdity'.[187] It was a snidey and derisive swipe at a former friend that reveals a notably cruel streak in Marx's psychological make-up and seems primarily motivated by intellectual snobbery.

Marx defended Pierre-Joseph Proudhon as the first thinker to have questioned the institution of private property, but he would later attack him too in a lengthy and pompous character assassination. At this juncture though he regarded Proudhon's *What is Property?* With its celebrated assertion that 'property is theft', another line frequently misattributed to Marx, as important a work as the Abbé Sièye's *What is the Third Estate?* But, though Marx's thought had developed considerably in Paris, his sojourn there was ended in January 1845 when he was expelled following a request from Count Arnim, the Prussian ambassador. He settled in Brussels where he wrote his *Theses on Feuerbach*, another criticism of a leftist rival, though a more measured one. It concluded with his most famous statement of intent: 'Philosophers have only *interpreted* the world in various ways, the point is to *change* it'.[188] This he most assuredly would.

Engels joined his friend in Brussels before the pair set off to Manchester and London where the younger man introduced Marx to the likes of Karl Schapper - the sort of professional revolutionary later eulogised by Lenin. Marx met other radicals in London, like the leading Chartist Ernest Jones, who was interested in co-ordinating a multinational group on the far-left, and it was to this end that The Fraternal Democrats were formed in 1845. Early the next year Marx and Engels, having decided to organise a Europe-wide network themselves, founded the Communist Committee of Correspondence. Engels proclaimed communism to be the contemporary form of democracy, though it is quite typical that he considered it unnecessary to canvass opinion before making such a unilateral declaration. The pair were joined in Brussels by Moses Hess who negotiated for funds with two pro-communist Westphalian capitalists: Julius Meyer, who owned an iron forge, and Rudolph Rompel, a linen wholesaler. It remains puzzling why businessmen would support the movement, but it is amusing to note that proto-communism was happy to be financed by a capitalist purse, even if the proposal ultimately collapsed, a failure that prompted Marx to write a furious letter to the pair.

The three years that Marx spent in the Belgian capital prepared him well for the Revolution of 1848. His new depths of extremism were revealed in a letter he penned to Koettgen in June 1846. Marx chillingly declared that 'it is necessary to support, in a single party, "everything" that helps the movement forward and not have any tiresome moral scruples about it'.[189] Yet the formation of a single party, or any real unified goal, would remain elusive. The most significant of the exiled German communists in Brussels were The League of the Just. The rather grandly titled artisanal group were inspired by the egalitarianism of the eighteenth century utopian Gracchus Babeuf, a writer who shared with Marx the belief that 'The French Revolution is the precursor of another, more magnificent revolution which will be the last', a view he had aired in his *Manifesto des Egaux* published in 1796. The League of the Just had established an international network and, in 1838, their leading light Wilhelm Weitling, a rather evangelical activist, published *Mankind As It Is and As It Ought To Be,* a pamphlet which derided the rich and powerful for causing all the injustice and inequality in the world. He recommended a range of egalitarian policies which he claimed would result in tranquillity and harmony.

Weitling, who compared himself to Jesus, prevaricated between warning of Armageddon and anticipating a return to Eden, a nirvana free from jealousy or hatred. When he visited London in 1844-5 he drew huge crowds of Chartists and agitators who he entranced with flowery language. He purred how 'We wish to be free as the birds in the sky; we wish to dart through life like them, carefree in joyful flight and sweet harmony'. But anyone expecting a peaceful campaign from this utopian idealist with a Christ fixation would be disappointed. He planned to recruit a force of 40,000 thugs and thieves, fired with resentment over private property, to violently overthrow the privileged establishment and herald a new age of peace and joy. He believed criminals were simply the product of society, so there would be no crime under communism. In Weitling's society everyone would wear identical clothes and dine in communal halls. He was of the view that 'Revolutions arise like storms and no one can chart their operations beforehand...The intellect has only a poor role to play and without emotion can do nothing...the greatest deeds are accomplished by the emotions that move the masses'. But Karl Schapper disagreed and believed that 'it is as easy to compel a tree to grow as to inculcate new ideas into mankind by force. Let us avoid physical violence: it is crude; and mankind does not need it...Let us view ourselves as leaves on the great tree of humanity and posterity will reap what our calm activity has sown'.[190] It is deeply regrettable that the sentiments of Weitling have proven rather more enduring on the left than those of Schapper. The appeals of such activism are, one supposes, like the 'Dark side' in Star Wars: quicker, easier, more seductive.

The fact that Weitling was a working class thinker gave him a significant amount of leeway from Marx who, by this stage, had still barely met anyone from a truly artisanal background. But, while Weitling made nearly all his political kin appear grounded and reasonable in comparison, he is sadly typical of the radical who talks of virtuous utopias while committed to startling hate and brutality. Yet he was invited to join Marx, Engels, Jenny Marx, Edgar von Westphalen and Moses Hess as a founding member of the new Communist Correspondence Committee. It would prove a brief marriage, but the organisation, effectively the progenitor of the Communist League, had a more lasting legacy. All subsequent Communist parties can be traced back to this little club with just eighteen members. It set the stage for what was to follow in numerous ways. 'Like most of its twentieth-century successors this communist cell asserted its authority by purging anyone suspected of deviation from official correctness. Inevitably, Weitling was picked out as the first sacrificial victim.'[191] It was Marx himself who turned on Weitling, disdainfully referring to him as 'ignorant' and humiliating him in a bitter and vicious manner. He mocked his preaching, which was compared unfavourably to Marx's own 'scientific ideas and constructive doctrine'. When Weitling responded that he knew more of the proletarians than his accuser did, a man who spent his time in libraries and drawing rooms far from the front lines of urban squalor, Marx exploded in a fury and had to be restrained. Shortly afterwards Marx also expelled Hermann Kniege after sneeringly referring to his 'childish pomposity'.

The same ire was directed at socialists beyond their little clique and *The German Ideology*, which Marx penned in Brussels, was a withering attack on the True Socialists, a movement of leftist German intellectuals. It included an extended diatribe aimed at Max Stirner - a relentless stream of juvenile taunts and sneeringly bitchy barbs - but Marx also developed some of his core ideas. He discussed the conception of a 'false consciousness' at length, an aspect of his thought that showed the enduring influence of Hegel. Yet for Marx, 'false consciousness' effectively meant anyone who disagreed with him. He described consciousness as merely a 'social product',[192] though while he was right in concluding that social forces play a part in forming character, he erred in claiming they monopolise the process. His greatest mistake though was in attributing the experiences that shape people to 'social forces' - for individual interactions are far more influential. It is not so much social forces that determine the world as social *relations*, and these will be present under any new system. Personal interactions are how humanity works. Yet Marx sought to tear apart the existing network without conceiving that the new society would operate on the same system of alliances and friendships, and rivalries and antagonisms that influence our behaviour in all spheres whether personal, professional or political.

The most profound breakthrough of the *German Ideology* was that Marx finally settled on the riddle of history that he had been struggling with for a number of years. He consequently laid out his conception of the tale of human development. Marx claimed that communities had gradually focused on the concepts of private property and bondage, a theory reminiscent of that of Rousseau's *Discourse on Inequality*. But he and Engels went much further. Their thesis claimed society was characterised by class struggle, by one stratum of people competing against the class above it until they were eventually overthrown. They also concluded that the engine of history was the means of production. In his words 'The hand-mill gives you society with the feudal lord; the steam-mill, society with the industrial capitalist'.[193] For Marx and Engels, economic activity was the driving force of history and it determined politics, ideas and the rule of law. They believed this theory did not just help them understand the past: it revealed the future too. For as the commercial age had overthrown the period of feudalism, so would the proletariat overthrow the capitalist. By 1850 Marx and Engels genuinely believed the fall of the capitalist system was imminent. Two centuries later, for all its faults, it appears more robust and beneficial than ever.

Yet Marx also believed the ascent of the proletariat would be the final stage of historical development – the equivalent of Hegel's Absolute Spirit – and it would prove an age of convivial harmony. Class conflict would cease and the world would melt into a tranquil brotherhood of equality. It was only the oppression of the ruling classes that caused the alienation, friction and crime that marred society. They regarded their theory as a matter of inevitable historical progression – an unavoidable scientific fact. Any who disputed it were simply irrational and could be dismissed. It was this theory that informed the cast-iron certainty of those who came after them: Gramsci, Kautsky, Lenin, Trotsky, Mao et al. They were persuaded that they were on the right side of history and the relentless march of progress would crush those who stood in their way.

Yet the theory was full of holes and their conclusion does not stand up to scrutiny at all. The suggestion that history is determined by the means of production rules out the influence of cultural, environmental and philosophical factors. While it is true that people frequently resent those doing better and agitate for that fortune to be spread, the idea of class struggle simply ignores the plethora of ethnic, racial and religious feuds that litter the historical record

- for conflicts between separate cultures and conflicting ideologies have always been far sharper than those of class origin. It is also abundantly clear that people struggle against individuals within their own class far more frequently than with those above or below. So it was ludicrous to suggest this friction would dissipate in his imagined future. For two million years man had been defined by ambition, inequality and conflict. Yet Marx somehow concluded this would immediately give way to co-operation and equanimity - a situation in stark contrast to everything and everyone that had preceded it. It is a peculiar conclusion to have reached. But to assert is as an unequivocal fact is frankly mind-boggling. It is incomprehensible how men of such obvious intelligence could spout such fatuous idiocy. Yet proclaim it they did, and with a confidence that makes the prime Muhammad Ali appear a trembling introvert.

But, while 1846 was proving such a pivotal year in developing their worldview, Marx's little clique suffered something of a rupture. Engels was living with a spirited, red-haired Irish proletarian woman named Mary Burns. Jenny von Westphalen claimed to share her husband's political leaning but her hostile and patrician attitude towards Mary, the only working class person she actually encountered, prompted Engels and Hess to confront Marx about his wife's behaviour. He responded with quite remarkable rancour. His relationship with Engels eventually recovered, but his bond with Hess was irreparably damaged. Yet, undaunted by the split, Marx carried on fomenting rifts with fellow leftists. Marx and Engels continued to denounce the True Socialists as vehemently as they had the Young Hegelians. They also dismissed Germany as a backward society, not yet divided into bourgeois and proletarian but consisting of petit-bourgeois, introducing a phrase that would become a common Marxist epithet. Marx penned a letter to Proudhon in May 1846 which was an acidly dismissive attack on the True Socialist, Karl Grün. He cast him as a 'charlatan' and a 'parasite'[194] and sneered that Grün 'tries to conceal his ignorance with pompous and arrogant phrases but all he does is make himself ridiculous with his *gibberish*'.[195]

Proudhon was deeply troubled by Marx's vindictive attitude and wrote to caution him that 'after we have demolished all the dogmatisms *a priori,* let us not of all things attempt in our turn to instil another kind of dogma into the people...let us not make ourselves the leaders of a new intolerance'.[196] Yet, on receipt of his missive, Marx attacked his colleague as well and penned a withering riposte to Proudhon's *The Philosophy of Poverty*. Marx's effort was called, not without some wit, *The Poverty of Philosophy*. He claimed that Proudhon did not understand either political economy or Hegel, and he attacked his individualism and clear opposition to collective organisation. Marx accused him of wanting to improve the system rather than destroy it, and seemed more angered by Proudhon's refusal to countenance revolutionary violence than anything else.

Engels displayed a similar level of combative arrogance when visiting the Paris branch of the League of the Just in August 1846. While there he bullied the members into driving out any remaining supporters of Grün and Proudhon. Marx then intimidated London's League of the Just to reform as a Communist League and to ritually denounce Proudhon, Grün and Weitling. The details of this relentlessly bitchy infighting bring to mind the French Revolution. The levels of denunciation suggest that, just as in France, if they were free to start killing each other over intricate points of socialist theory or alleged commitment to the cause, then they almost certainly would have. In this climate though, it is Marx who comes across as the prickliest of the bunch; a thin-skinned, shockingly arrogant intellectual snob who was, frankly, a literary bully. Little seemed to get him more energised and motivated than the opportunity to trash a socialist rival; for all other projects would be put on the back burner, and he pulled no punches when turning on an unsuspecting target. Though his efforts in this regard were limited to the pen rather than the sword, there is no denying the seething viciousness that lay behind his attacks. He only grew more hostile and isolated as the years passed.

But Marx's protestations about the evils of capitalism and the division of labour, which he considered just as ruinous as private property, never prevented him from keeping a full bevy of servants, even while beset by financial problems. The move to Brussels had brought the family a new maid, Helene Demuth, who would remain in their employ for the rest of their lives. It was an appointment that would ultimately cause considerable familial strife, yet other events seemed to be turning in their favour. In the wider economic picture, harvest failures were swiftly followed by a severe recession in 1847. Confidence in governments declined even as activism rose alarmingly. Liberal opposition grew particularly strident in Paris, Berlin, Rome and Budapest, and Marx threw himself into the surge in political activity. Most famously he would pen the manifesto for the Communist League, a tract which coincided with the revolutionary tidal wave that swept Europe in 1848.

Trouble began in the Swiss Civil War of 1847 which saw the radicals sweep to victory, an event quickly followed by risings in southern Italy in early 1848. At the end of February the monarchy was overthrown and a republic declared in Paris. From there the revolt spread rapidly throughout Europe with revolutions breaking out in Budapest, Vienna and Berlin. Marx was tireless in fomenting insurrection and hoped for a bloody workers' rising to destroy both capitalism and the Prussian monarchy. It was Karl Schapper though who gave the Communist League its new slogan, another one that Marx would swipe and that history would attribute to him: 'Workers of the world, unite!'

The Communist Manifesto, which rolled off the printing presses even as revolution exploded in Paris, is perhaps the most fortuitously timed pamphlet in history. It begins and ends with a threat: opening by announcing that 'A spectre is haunting Europe – the spectre of Communism',[197] it concludes when warning 'The Communists disdain to conceal their views and aims. They openly declare that their ends can be attained only by the forcible overthrow of all existing social conditions. Let the ruling classes tremble at a Communist revolution'.[198] While Marx contends that the idea of communism as a spectre is a 'nursery tale',[199] his later threats of violence and anarchy prove it to be an all too accurate description. His assertion that 'the history of all hitherto existing society is the history of class struggles'[200] is an appallingly simplified interpretation of history, but then such a binary approach allowed him to perceive the story of humanity as a feud between 'oppressor and oppressed'. Marx described free trade as 'naked, shameless, direct, brutal exploitation'.[201] He even concluded that 'the bourgeoisie has torn away from the family its sentimental vale, and has reduced the family relation to a mere money relation'.[202] Coming from a man who had abandoned his own family, apart from occasional and bitter efforts to extract cash from them, this was a remarkable conclusion. One hopes that his poor mother never read it.

The *Manifesto* was transparent in its aims. It repeatedly called for a violent revolt that must end in the 'removal' of the bourgeoisie. What this entailed was made explicit when Marx referred to their 'grave-diggers'.[203] It was rhetoric that would have the most appalling consequences in the next century. Yet Marx seemed untroubled by such outcomes. He did point out undeniable problems in the capitalist system: the periodic financial crises that can occur and the dehumanising labour undertaken by sectors of the workforce, yet he failed to identify any of the *benefits* that free markets can bring. It is also undeniable that menial labour and economic deprivation proved far more characteristic of the communist states he inspired. Marx expressed concrete certainty in the 'inevitability' of his conclusions. But that conviction was groundless, and, with the benefit of hindsight, they now appear ridiculous - to anyone who actually takes the trouble to read them that is.

Yet, having made clear the necessity of the destruction of society and its personnel, Marx then established the guidelines for a communist state. These included heavily progressive taxation and the abolition of private property as well as, incredibly, the abolition of inheritance – that which concerned him and supported him for decades. It also called for state control of all factories and the means of transport and communication as well as some form of agricultural collectivism and the merging of industrial production with education. Many claim the Soviets and Mao were mere despots who corrupted Marx's teachings and cared only for power. But in their suppression of the free market, their focus on indoctrination, their abolition of private property, their savage attacks on the bourgeoisie, their state run economies, collectivisation of land and reliance on a revolutionary vanguard they followed the old sage's dictums to the letter.

Marx grandly proclaimed that class conflict would melt away and that, as the state focused on oppressing the proletariat to protect the wealthy, then it too would dissolve. This would leave a harmonious community of equality and brotherhood 'in which the free development of each is the condition for the free development of all'.[204] It is ironic that the communists believed their society would be free of contemporary divisions when, in reality, no one held class hatred more fiercely than they did, and the utopian society they envisaged was to be established by unleashing those antagonisms in a violent upheaval. It is simply not the case, as many claim, that the communist regimes of the twentieth century failed to implement Marx's policies correctly. The truth is that he was just wrong in envisaging the consequences of such suggestions. Though why he believed an explosion of sectarian violence would create a utopia of peace, opportunity and equality is another matter.

Perhaps that is why, for all its learning and pomposity, one gets much the same impression reading the *Communist Manifesto* that one gets from reading a fairy tale – a simplistic black and white portrayal of villainy positioned against nobility. In tone, it is rather like Cinderella. Beautiful and virtuous, though impoverished, Cinders may be currently subjugated by the spiteful tyranny of the ugly sisters, but the day of reckoning is imminent and she is destined to live happily ever after in a perfect world of smiles and sun-drenched fields. Yet Marx applies such simplistic wishful thinking not just to a humble servant girl with dainty feet and a fair complexion, but to the whole of humanity. It is almost as if he is saying to the proletariat 'Don't worry brothers, you shall go to the ball!' It is no less than the Disneyfication of political philosophy, but shorn of the songs, heart and entertainment value.

The tone of the *Communist Manifesto* is one of relentlessly haughty arrogance and a disdainful impatience with any who might question Marx's conclusions. There is no suggestion that he is offering an argument or an interpretation, he is simply informing us of facts, of the way that the world has been up to now, and of the shape it will take in the future. After predictably taking an extended section to dismiss all other socialists as idiots, Marx ends with an evocation that acts as a bookend to the opening gambit of another writer whose best bits he swiped, Rousseau: 'The proletarians have nothing to lose but their chains. They have a world to win. WORKING MEN OF ALL COUNTRIES UNITE!'[205] It was, in light of the preceding pages, nothing less than a call to arms.

It appeared for much of 1848 that Marx's manifesto had been realised as soon as it hit the streets. The three days of barricade fighting in Paris and the declaration of the Second Republic had an electrifying effect on radicals across Europe. The authorities in Belgium quickly moved to stamp out rebellion in Brussels, and Marx fled to Paris where the former radical opposition now dominated the provisional government of the French Republic. He was joined there by most of the leading figures of the Communist League. By the second half of March, revolutionary war broke over the barricades erected in Berlin and Vienna forcing the monarchs to appoint liberal governments which allowed exiled German radicals to return home.

The activists of 1848 had been eulogising not just the outbreak of the French Revolution, its period of gaudy optimism, but also the grisly events of 1793. The ten-point programme of the *Manifesto* had been designed specifically for a revolutionary government, one modelled on the radical Jacobin phase of the Revolution. Sperber describes the rest of the document as 'a plan for revolution and civil war, based on the previous experiences of the Reign of Terror, the most radical phase of the French Revolution in the years 1793-94'.[206] Such sentiments fed into the activism of the time. Many of Marx's peers hoped that the seizure of capitalists' assets would create opposition which allowed them to take more severe measures. They genuinely hoped to replicate the Terror there and then. Naturally, Marx and Engels were dismissive of any conservative socialists who opposed violence.

That year must have been a period of some heady excitement for the radicals who, for all their faults, at least envisaged a better, fairer society to result from the bloody insurrection they craved. Their reasoning was faulty, and they genuinely hoped for things to get worse before they got better, but their intent was pure, though we all know where good intentions can lead. Yet, in the end, their ideological certainty blinded them to the fact that their actions could only ever result in disaster. No one was more culpable of such iron-clad stubbornness than Marx. It is strange though that, despite his obsession with industrialisation, he appeared oblivious to how it might transform violent insurrection, the nature of warfare and the punitive retribution of the state he hoped to establish. The Soviets would teach the world the lesson he was unable to learn himself. Marx had at least opposed the formation of the German Legion in Paris which hoped to establish the sort of revolutionary war popularised after 1789. Their aim, after liberating their homeland, was to march to Russia to spread revolution there. Marx's opposition though was not one of principle, but of practicality, and his belief that they were doomed to failure was ratified when their army, numbering 1,000, set off on April Fools' Day and was routed as soon as it crossed the border.

In the euphoria of that year though, his confidence was undimmed and Marx returned to Germany in the hope of establishing a newspaper and fomenting further revolution there. He arrived in Cologne which buzzed with radical agitation that spring. In scenes redolent of Paris in the 1790s the Communist League had mobilised thousands of workers to besiege City Hall demanding more jobs and lower taxes. However, the nation-wide network that Marx called for was not emerging, and the revolutionary activists had no real unity or effective operational organisation. It is ironic that the movement was critically weakened by the divisions that Marx himself had so enthusiastically fostered. Various leftist factions turned on each-other and denounced their rivals as insufficiently radical or revolutionary. Each clique was certain of its stance, so any sympathetic agencies that even slightly differed from them were furiously denounced. Andreas Gottschalk was head of the Cologne Worker's Association but also a True Socialist, the group Marx had so sneeringly derided for years. Gottschalk now paid him back in kind by denouncing the communists as a bourgeois farce. He appealed to his members to boycott them.

In early June Marx's *New Rhineland News* hit the stands. The language of the paper made it inaccessible to even the most literate of the working masses and the increasing violence of events saw Marx diverging ever further from any moderates. While a minor revolutionary figure in comparison to the members of the German National Assembly in Frankfurt and the Prussian Constituent Assembly in Berlin, Marx still played an influential, if provincial, role. He launched a veritable barrage of attacks against the monarchy and the state's administrative officials and military. He also criticised Germany's parliamentary bodies for their political timidity and failure to bring Prussia's monarchy to heel. In calling for a single German republic he was vocalising the rhetoric of French Jacobinism. And, while he had to phrase his more radical sentiments cautiously, he sarcastically denounced the Frankfurt Assembly as 'a republic of provincial philistines, far from all atrocities and crimes that soiled the first French Republic, free of blood and despising the red flag'.[207]

He regretted the fact that 'none of the chief culprits of the July monarchy [which had reigned in France from 1830-48] was bought to account'.[208] The grim nature of the language he employed leaves little doubt as to what he felt might constitute an acceptable 'account'. He made clear what form a revolutionary government should take in an article directed at Rudolf Camphausen, the new head of Frederick William's ministry. That piece should be perused by anyone who believes that Lenin broke with Marx's recommendations: 'The provisional political circumstances that follow a revolution always require a dictatorship and an energetic one at that. From the beginning we reproached Camphausen with not acting dictatorially, with not immediately breaking and abolishing the remains of the old institutions'.[209] Marx's other main target, following the formation of the united German republic, was war with Tsarist Russia. He hoped to emulate not just the excesses of the Terror but of the revolutionary war that swept east to accompany it. The deplorable consequences of such prior events did not deter his enthusiasm at all.

Yet despite his eagerness, these fractious revolts were doomed. In June the workers of Paris, finding conditions far worse than they had been in February, the inevitable consequence of all revolutions, rose in a violent upheaval. They were slaughtered in their thousands by the troops of General Cavaignac with bloodshed becoming an ever more frequent feature of the risings that marked that year. When the republican government had been subjected to fierce barricade battles from the working class population of the east of the city a significant majority of left wing thought lamented the development. Isaiah Berlin described this event as 'the first purely socialist rising in Europe...for the first time revolutionary socialism revealed itself in that savage and menacing aspect in which it has appeared ever since to its opponents in every land'.[210] Yet Marx and Engels celebrated the assault on the timorous moderation of the assembly. Marx was predictably dismissive about the large numbers of the Republican and National Guard killed by the rebels while wailing indignantly about those who lost their lives in the retaliation, a trait he would repeat in 1871.

As the revolutions imploded in a cycle of bitter infighting and frequent eruptions of violence the old elites moved to regain control. In July 1848 the Prussian authorities arrested Andreas Gottschalk. But Marx's attempt to take-over the Cologne Workers' association resulted in an exodus of its membership as the artisans fell over each-other in a flood to desert him. The nationalism of the leftists was again evident in their support for Schleswig and Holstein's secession from the Danish sphere of influence. The pressure the Tsar put on the Prussian authorities to back down over the issue only encouraged the radicals. In Cologne, Marx convened a chillingly titled Committee of Public Safety and both he and Engels called for a Red Republic. Fearing the resurgence of Prussian authoritarianism they encouraged the peasants of Cologne to clash with the soldiers. The city briefly ignited in violence before the authorities regained stability by imposing martial law. Marx was ultimately expelled again and his newspaper was closed down. The final issue, published on 19 May 1849 and printed in red ink, called for the emancipation of the working class and predicted a future revolutionary war with Russia.

Following its closure, Marx and Engels reputedly spent time travelling in Germany hoping to foment more violent rebellion. In the Palatinate Engels proved tactless and frequently abused his compatriots. His behaviour caused severe rifts with fellow leftists three times in six months. He allegedly mocked the insurgents as petit-bourgeois dilettantes whose military incompetence was staggering. Verbally Engels was every bit a match for Marx's acidic prose, though he did join in the fighting while Marx headed for Paris. However, the working class insurgents there had been defeated in June 1848, and in December Louis Napoleon Bonaparte, nephew of the great revolutionary general and emperor, was elected president of the Republic. The government was swiftly purged of Marx's radical friends. When France sent troops to Italy to aid in the restoration of the Pope, Prussian leftists staged a huge protest on 13 June 1849. But the authorities crushed the demonstration and the regime made it clear that Marx would not be welcome. The socialist dream that had burned so brightly for most of a year had been effectively doused. With few safe havens left for him on the continent Marx elected to move to London and arrived on 28 August 1849. Intending it to be a temporary stay he would, in the event, remain until his death over thirty years later.

The London Years

For much of the next decade Marx retreated from activism to focus on journalism and academia. He largely filled his days studying the great political economists in the library of the British Museum. His large brood found lodgings in a small flat at 28 Dean Street in Soho where they would live from 1850-56.* Wilhelm Liebknecht helped him settle in and testified to Marx's faith in phrenology. When he arrived, Karl gave his head a thorough examination, took him to a specialist and angrily denounced him as a 'philistine' for his sceptical reaction to the ordeal. Liebknecht also noted Marx's aggression in everything he did: debate, journalism and fencing, yet, despite regarding him as a bully, he was terribly fond of him.

Soho was becoming a meeting point for the exiles of the Revolution of 1848, and in the climate there Marx helped to reactivate the Communist League and establish a new German paper: *The New Rhineland News: Review of Political Economy*. Engels joined him in November and most of their political allies followed suit. There the plotting began again. In the spring of 1850 one Wilhelm Stieber, later Bismarck's secret service chief, infiltrated the communist HQ at 20 Great Windmill Street. He sent back a report detailing how a meeting, presided over by Marx, was dominated by a gleeful discussion of the murder of Queen Victoria and other crowned heads of Europe. Marx had closed the meeting by assuring the members that the blood of every European royal would soon be spilt. Some have poured scorn on this suggestion, but Marx had long been adamant that a violent overthrow of the established order was not just

* The blue plaque erected by the London Labour council at the address got the dates wrong.

inevitable but a cause for celebration. Such sentiments then were entirely in keeping with his character.

In his address to the Communist League of March 1850 Marx declared that to achieve their ends the workers would need to 'make the revolution permanent'. They must be organised and armed 'with flintlocks, muskets, artillery and munitions'. One of their three main tasks was to expand and deepen revolutionary violence: 'Far from opposing so-called excesses, examples of the people's revenge on hated individuals or public buildings connected with hateful memories, they must not just tolerate such excesses but take over the leadership of them'.[211] Both he and Engels praised the 'resolutely revolutionary' League which had 'participated energetically in the agitation...on the barricades and on the battlefields'.[212] The experience of 1848 had persuaded him that a *coup d'état* should be carried out by a small devoted band of revolutionaries acting on behalf of the proletarian revolt. It should come as no surprise that he regarded a radical and intellectual vanguard to be a prerequisite of revolution. After all, he himself was part of a radical intellectual elite that hoped to shape and direct the workers towards that same rising. It was this policy that was recommended by Trotsky in 1905 and adapted and put into practice by Lenin.

In the December 1849 edition of his paper Marx wrote a piece on the *Class Struggles in France*. He reflected on the events of the previous year and called for further revolution - hoping for a 'new proletarian uprising in France that will immediately coincide with a world war'.[213] He clearly relished the thought. Indeed, it echoed the sentiments he had expressed at the start of the year. On 1 January he had opined: 'Revolutionary uprising of the French working class, world war – that is the programme for the year 1849'.[214] While everyone else was celebrating New Years' Eve, Marx was hunched over his desk, furiously scribbling and advocating global conflict. As others dreamed of peace and prosperity, he craved the opposite. From this point on Marx saw a great European war as necessary, even desirable; the spark that would ignite revolution across the planet. He had always craved a violent uprising, but in light of the failures of the past year he now called for a *more* violent revolution, one that must be pursued until his enemies were destroyed.

Yet, failing such a cataclysm, Marx anticipated an economic crisis too – and he was optimistic that such a crash might be imminent. He opposed the moderate democrats who attempted to alleviate the suffering of the working class, and he hoped for the desperate conditions of the Victorian poor to worsen. Marx believed that if the removal of tariffs lowered food prices, as others suggested, then it would lower wages too. He claimed that increased mechanisation, such as that transforming the cotton industry, was leading to fewer jobs and lower wages while markedly increasing production. He held it responsible for damaging the hand-produced textile trade of India. Marx argued that free trade was impoverishing the working classes and undeveloped nations while enriching a small group of capitalists. But he welcomed these developments and was dismissive of protectionism. Marx preferred to foster antagonism between bourgeoisie and proletariat to hasten the onset of violent revolution. It is a telling reaction. The fact that he relished a decline in wages, opportunities and living standards puts into some context just how much Marx really cared about the poor.

But, if war and the prospect of economic disaster dominated his writing, his paper also featured frequent attacks on non-communist radicals. Gottfried Kinkel, who, unlike Marx, had actually fought in the German insurrection, was denounced for not provoking his captors into putting him in front of a firing squad; ironic sentiments from a man who had avoided the fighting and then, to borrow a phrase from Monty Python, 'bravely ran away'. Gottschalk composed a withering response to Marx's frequent cries for revolutionary violence:

> 'Why should we make a revolution? Why should we, men of the proletariat, spill our blood?...You are not serious about the liberation of the oppressed. For you the misery of the worker, the hunger of the poor has only a scientific and doctrinaire interest. You are elevated above such miseries and merely shine down upon the parties as a learned sun-god. You are not affected by what moves the heart of man. You have no belief in the cause that you pretend to represent.'[215]

Marx, in a rare show of restraint, did not reply. Perhaps this time the barbs were a bit too close for comfort. Such abstemiousness was rare indeed for the German. It was not just that he was volatile and acidic towards rivals in the radical community, but that he went to such extraordinary lengths to vent his spleen. Not satisfied with pillorying Kinkel, Marx also produced a lengthy character assassination sarcastically entitled *The Great Men of the Exile*. It was a densely written hundred pages of interminable venom that added a slew of revolutionaries to his targets, including Heinzel and Ruge. Ideologically, as he became more committed to communist radicalism, he grew increasingly hostile to the moderation of the petit-bourgeois democrats. Yet his intolerance continued to isolate him from potential allies. Invited to attend a meeting to create a refugee support committee Marx instead denounced the enterprise. The result was a predictable rift in the Communist League. After a meeting on 15 September 1850 where the four main players, in Robespeierrist fashion, all melodramatically asserted their willingness to die for the cause, August Willich and Karl Schapper split with Marx and Engels to establish two separate leagues, neither pair willing to share leadership with the other.

Marx's rump league now consisted of no more than a dozen or so members, aligned with a similarly sized clique in Cologne. The ideological differences between them were slight enough to be undetectable to the uninitiated but, as with the warring factions of the Soviet Union, the radicals reserved their greatest ire for their kin. To Willich and Schapper the splits were caused not by ideology but by the bullying and patrician behaviour of their former colleagues. As if to prove their point, when Kinkel joined Willich, Marx and Engels slighted them as 'the insufficiently revolutionary petit-bourgeois leftist and the excessively revolutionary communist extremist'.[216] It is an observation that makes one recall Robespierre's disdain with two sets of rivals, 'one who wish to take us to the tropics, the other to the pole'. Nevertheless, to Marx and Engels the disparate pairing of Willich and Kinkel became indivisible, regarded as a single entity in the letters that flew back and forth between the pair. Marx's rivals respected his intellect though. In Willich's post-revolutionary plans it stated 'Citizen Marx is called upon to present himself in Cologne within 48 hours and to take over the direction of finances and social reform...Disobedience of this order, any resistance or effort to argue, as well as inappropriate jokes, will be punished by death'.[217]

In the meantime, both sides denounced their rivals as police spies, and they favoured personal insult over any ideological scrutiny of their positions. Marx's condemnation of Willich as a 'lazy, greedy bum [who]...hangs around in a pub all day...where he can consume for free',[218] was especially ironic in light of the large number of unpaid tabs he had run up in inns. Marx and Engels were repeatedly attacked for having no real affinity with the workers; comments that were, it must be said, not entirely without merit. Willich and Schapper, by contrast, both mixed with the artisans with ease and won more working class support than their rivals who looked like, and were, rather lofty bourgeois Hegelian intellectuals. Indeed, both Marx and Engels *did* look down on the poor who they regularly called 'knot-heads'.[219] They drew a sharp distinction between them and the future workers of the communist society they hoped to inspire. It was this future class they spoke for - the 'new man' they aspired to create. Marx had been contemplating such a concept since at least 1843 when he had written to Ruge on the necessity for a 'reform of consciousness'.[220] As such his theorising was directed at the world he longed for rather than the one in which he actually lived.

Marx famously endured a period of relative penury in the early years of his London sojourn, yet this has been over-estimated by some biographers and, more to the point, was largely a consequence of his own incipient profligacy. Most historians cite the letter that Jenny wrote to Joseph Weydemeyer on 20 May 1850 as evidence of their financial straits. But this was a begging letter sent to a man who was never going to visit them to check the reality of their situation. As such, it clearly exaggerated the depth of their poverty, laughingly so at points. The letter cannot be regarded as an impartial or reliable source, unless one is examining the extent of Jenny's imagination. While the Marx clan certainly endured some hardships in this period, it was Karl's determination to maintain a bourgeois front that was at the root of their financial woes. He insisted, for example, on employing a secretary, the young German philologist Wilhelm Pieper, even though Jenny was qualified and willing to do the job. As a consequence of this extravagance Marx could barely afford to feed his children at times. It is also odd that Marx, who declared to hate the uneven relationship between master and servant or capitalist and worker, maintained not just a secretary during his years of greatest financial straits, but kept a full staff of domestic servants throughout his adult life. Not only was his secretary an excessive expense, the young man was also unreliable and incompetent. Engels often had to redo his work, yet Pieper maintained his position for most of the 1850s until Jenny finally took over the role.

Marx also frequently failed to pay the debts he owed to doctors, grocers, bakers and publicans while spending extravagantly in other areas. In one begging letter to Engels he asked for money to pay his wife's medical bills while glibly recounting the long trip to Germany he had just taken. Marx purred about the expensive wardrobe he had bought for Jenny so she could travel in style. Yet he appeared oblivious to how this might come across to his friend and found his creditors' indignation at such behaviour incomprehensible. He appeared to have no qualms about brushing off their appeals for him to settle debts while continuing to spend lavishly to keep up appearances. Like many radicals of his inclination, he was more generous with other people's money than with his own. Many of his debtors were never paid at all such as Dr. Freund who chased him for a considerable period to no avail. When he came knocking, Marx would hide in his study and send his children to deal with the enraged practitioner. Yet Marx was always conscious of social airs. Apart from his undisguised pride at having married a member of the lower nobility, he ensured his daughters had the right dancing lessons and ball-gowns. He also sent the girls to an expensive ladies' seminary where the tuition was geared towards preparing them to operate effectively in society, mainly so they could secure prosperous marriages. He would have been mortified at the thought of them getting wed to a prole. Yet with all his financial woes, his desperation to impress and his constant sponging off Engels, it never once occurred to Marx to get a job. He even wrote of his distaste of having to do a 'trade'.[221]

Jenny Marx travelled to the Netherlands in this period to beg Marx's maternal uncle, Lion Phillips, the founder of the electronics company that still bears his name, for money. He refused, but the attempt again illustrates the willingness of Marx to live off the proceeds of capitalism to afford him the luxury of fighting against it. It was capitalism that would rescue him from impoverishment too. He was significantly aided by Engels's decision to move to Manchester to take up a partnership role in his father's company. Upon arrival, he quickly settled into a lucrative position and provided financial support for Marx. But neither appeared troubled that they were living off the largesse of a mill owner, funded by the fruits of the capitalist system they railed against.

In the early 1850s the economic situation in Europe continued to improve and radicalism grew less appealing to the masses. As a result of the increased prosperity, Chartism effectively died as a movement. Following the familiar pattern of leftist antagonisms, and an unwillingness to compromise or co-operate, it had splintered into bitter rival factions. George Julian Harney abandoned the main movement under Feargus O'Connor, the firebrand Irish demagogue, to set up his own organisation which churned out publications like *Red Republican* and the chillingly titled *Friend of the People*. Marat would have heartily approved. Harney hoped to forge a 'brotherhood of man' but Marx and Engels, who had no time at all for such moderates, were dismissive about the project.

Marx claimed their bitterness and isolation were 'wholly in accord with our attitude and principles'. He disdained the 'system of mutual concessions, half-measures tolerated for decency's sake'.[222] Engels was even more scathing. He claimed to find tact 'irritating' and thought the concept of a party akin to a 'herd of jackasses'. He even boasted that he and his political partner 'spit on popularity...our position is completely independent of such ludicrous trifles. From now on we are only answerable to ourselves and, come the time when these gentry need us, we shall be in a position to dictate our own terms'.[223] He sneered at those 'ignorant curs' who dared to regard themselves of the same stripe as intellectual deities like Marx and himself.

Yet while disdaining the doltish conservatism of the English they still fervently hoped for a financial catastrophe to strike. In July 1851 Engels wrote to Marx to gleefully predict that 'Provided nothing untoward happens within the next six weeks, this year's cotton crop will amount to 3,000,000 bales. If the CRASH in the market coincides with such a gigantic crop, things will be cheery indeed. Peter Ermen is already fouling his breeches at the very thought'.[224] Marx and Engels awaited this crash with the enthusiasm of a child anticipating Christmas, relishing the prospect of the poverty, hunger, anarchy and violence that must inevitably follow. But ultimately their hopes were to be disappointed again. So Marx turned back to war as the likely spark for revolt, though what he really desired was chaos. To Marx, anything seemed preferable to peace, prosperity and stability.

It is an irony then, that the tranquillity of Marx's home life suffered a dislocation in the same period, and he found the experience most unsettling. On 23 June 1851 the family servant, Lenchen Demuth, gave birth to a son. Engels claimed paternity though it was later revealed that the true father was

Marx. It is not known if the child resulted from an isolated moment of passion or if the affair was rather more protracted, though Marx's genuine love for his wife is not in doubt. Demuth retained her employment in the Marx household so we must assume that the situation was settled amicably. The baby was quickly fostered which, at the time was almost a death sentence, though on this occasion little Freddy Demuth lived to a ripe old age and only died in 1929. He grew up to be a committed member of the Amalgamated Engineering Union and a founding member of the Hackney Labour Party but, as Marx never had anything to do with him and his true paternity was kept a closely guarded secret, he expired without ever knowing his father's identity. In his defence, it is likely that Marx's callous treatment of his son was in deference to the wishes of his wife. It would not be wise to draw any parallels with Rousseau here as Marx was undeniably a fantastic father, but this incident is nonetheless an intriguing coincidence.

It becomes more interesting when one considers the progenitor of the American left: Thomas Jefferson. He was certainly a remarkable man, but one of the more extreme of the Founding Fathers. Jefferson was a Virginia landowner who had something of a country squire's perspective. He idealised small scale agriculture while believing the entire United States could be sustained on an economy of yeoman farmers. He was also, like Thomas Paine, another advocate of 'Anglo-Saxon liberty', viewing the Americans as freeholders just as he believed the inhabitants of Britain were before falling under the Norman yoke. His republicanism was thus squarely in the tradition of the radicals of the English Civil War. Hamilton wanted a United States that was commercial and imperial – a centralised state focused on military effectiveness with the financial and revenue-raising institutions of the modern nation in place from the beginning. Jefferson preferred 'the political system of world republics, agrarian, democratic, ideologically hostile to commerce and industry'.[225] The final result was Madison's vision which sat somewhere between those extremes. That pragmatism resulted in perhaps the world's most successful democracy, while utopian and theoretical idealism tends to catastrophic disasters.

Jefferson certainly leaned towards that ilk, and there is much evidence of his rather extreme views. In 1786 he had remarked that 'the tree of liberty must be refreshed from time to time with the blood of patriots and tyrants. It is it's *(sic)* natural manure'.[226] Hamilton sought an accord with prosperous Britain rather than revolutionary France, which was a shambles. Yet the latter was the preferred option of Jefferson. His refusal to criticise or condemn the excesses in Paris damaged many of his friendships. It is also well known that the man most famous for penning the words 'We hold these truths to be self-evident, that all men are created equal, that they are endowed by their creator with certain unalienable rights, that among these are life, liberty and the pursuit of happiness' was a significant slave owner. It is clearly difficult to square poetic demands for freedom and equality with slave ownership. Jefferson did aver to opposing slavery while maintaining it. He did, however, believe that blacks were inferior to whites and that they should not live in the same society. He had a higher opinion of the American Indians but felt they had two options for the future – converting to farming or 'extermination', a phrase he employed liberally. Most pertinently though, when comparing him to Marx and, especially, Rousseau, Jefferson had five or six children with one of his slaves, Sally Hemings, who he allegedly first impregnated when she was just fourteen, and all the offspring were packed off as slaves themselves.

Apart from the hangover following the failed revolution of 1848, the improving economic climate, the dwindling support and the fragmenting of the likes of the Communist League, there were a number of other factors which help explain Marx's retreat from activism during the 1850s. In Cologne, Hermann Becker, known as 'Red Becker', the driving force behind the *West German News*, had collaborated with Marx until May 1851 when Cologne's Communist League were rounded up and imprisoned. When the prosecution offered fabricated evidence purporting to be the minutes of a meeting in London, Marx produced material proving the claims to be false and rushed it to the group's defence counsel. Yet, despite such efforts, seven of the eleven defendants were found guilty that November and sentenced to up to six years. The trial also destroyed the reputations of Willich and Schapper who were alleged to have conspired with the Prussian authorities. With no overseas' collaborators left Marx elected to dissolve the Communist League.

The aspirations of Europe's activists suffered another blow on 2 December 1851 when a coup d'état in France saw Louis Napoleon transformed from president to First Consul and then Emperor Napoleon III. This crushed the hopes of the radical community in London who believed that revolution must begin in France. Marx responded by producing *The Eighteenth Brumaire* which criticised the French individuals and tactics he had lauded just a few years previously. He now looked not to the past but to the future and a new type of violent revolution. This should not be a surprise. Marx had thrived on confrontation and denunciation in his writing, in his personal relations, and in the policies he advocated. History has taught us the wisdom of allowing such characteristics to dominate the political sphere, and Marx himself began to reap the harvest of the discord he had sown. From 1852-9 he cut an isolated figure. He wrote to Engels on the possibility of retiring from political life and ironically commented that he was no longer inclined 'to allow myself to be insulted by every party jackass'.[227]

In the meantime, he immersed himself in journalism with much of his work in the period appearing in the *New York Tribune*. But he also fell under the influence of a British politician called David Urquhart, a charismatic but rather unhinged Scotsman. Urquhart became obsessed with Islamic culture and truly believed that 'only the Turk is a gentleman and freedom exists only in Turkey'.[228] He was another who believed in the myth of Anglo-Saxon liberties, but his love of the Ottomans, coupled with his hatred of Russia, warped his judgement and drove him to some deeply peculiar conclusions; most notably that the Foreign Secretary, Lord Palmerston, was a secret agent for Russia. Yet this irrational conspiracy theorist won widespread support among radicals. His manic vision fitted their conception of the world. As such, they were prepared to lap up any wild theories that confirmed their own distorted views. Marx's incipient hatred of Russia made him particularly susceptible to this lunacy. While sceptical at first, he was soon convinced and became an ardent supporter of Urquhart. Marx wrote several articles on Palmerston's clandestine support of Russia and later collected his musings in a controversial pamphlet called *The Secret Diplomatic History of the Eighteenth Century*. This collection was the period's equivalent of a 'truther' website full of delusional conspiracy theories suggesting that 9-11 was an inside job. It was also quietly deleted from the canon when Marx's works were translated into Russian.

Marx came to believe that Palmerston was engaged in a lifelong mission to undermine the interests of Western Europe in service to his Russian master. It was a serious lapse of judgement to claim the overtly patriotic, strongly anti-Russian Palmerston was a puppet of the Tsar. If Marx could make errors as egregious as this in relation to his peers how on earth was he to formulate an objective view of events in some distant, uncertain future? Yet it was upon this assumed ability that his entire philosophy rested.

Even after the outbreak of the Crimean War which pitted Palmerston's government against that of Russia, Marx's paranoia allowed him to twist the evidence to fit the theory. He concluded the entire conflict was a ruse to mask Palmerston's corrupt alliance and regarded the serious problems the British encountered in their campaign as proof. He claimed they resulted from deliberate sabotage by the now Prime Minister to ensure the failure of his phoney war. Even the ultimate British victory failed to dent Marx's belief. In his collected pamphlets Marx claimed that Russia had subversively orchestrated every European disaster for the previous century and a half. He concluded that Palmerston had been a double agent of the Tsar for some twenty-five years before assuming office in 1859. Marx even claimed that Russia had been successfully bribing every notable Whig politician for over a century. He thus perceived the Great Reform Bill of 1832 and their opposition to the Corn Laws as cynically manipulative policies, even while they benefitted the slice of the population Marx claimed to represent.

Marx and Urquhart were convinced of the need to maintain the integrity of the Ottoman Empire in the face of Russian aggression. Such was his belief that Marx angrily denounced the Greek insurgents who rose up against the Ottoman yoke - precisely the sort of revolutionaries he had always sworn to defend. He naturally concluded that the revolt had been a Russian conspiracy, and he resisted those who advanced the case for liberal reforms in the Ottoman Empire. He also denounced the suggestion of equality between Christians and Muslims. Marx's belief in this nonsense informed his political writing for most of the rest of his life. As for Urquhart, his obsession with Ottoman culture and his conviction in their restorative properties later convinced him to treat his thirteen month old son to a Turkish bath. The experience promptly killed the child.

In 1855 Marx wrote to Engels of a 'VERY HAPPY EVENT'. It was the death of the 'inheritance thwarter', Jenny's uncle Heinrich Georg von Westphalen, whose demise he had been eagerly anticipating for years. He was less euphoric when suffering a deep tragedy of his own when his eight year old son Edgar died the same year, an event which affected him profoundly. His financial situation improved though. By 1856 a steady income from journalism and the stipends he received from Engels allowed him to move into a more comfortable, bourgeois residence at 9 Grafton Terrace in Kentish Town. The house was near Primrose Hill, at the foot of Hampstead Heath. He had no shortage of good subject material as the period between the Crimean War of 1853-6 and the Franco – Prussian War of 1870-71 was one in which the great powers tussled for supremacy. Marx's articles of the time focused on those issues as well as the likes of the Indian Mutiny of 1857 and the Opium War of 1856-60, though his Urquhart inspired flights of fancy still occupied much of his output. He came to believe the French Emperor consorted with the Tsar and Palmerston in some sort of malevolent triumvirate. When Napoleon III attacked the Habsburg's northern Italian possessions in 1859, Marx and Engels called for the other German states to rally in defence of Austria.

When a worldwide recession hit in 1857, that which would necessarily hit the poor the hardest, it was again celebrated by Marx. Engels had become an avid fox-hunter, riding in the Cheshire hunt with the future Duke of Westminster. He called it 'the greatest physical pleasure I know',[229] but he revelled in the chaos he saw around him, recounting his 'high spirits' at the 'truly delightful'[230] turn of events. It didn't last. The crisis began to ease by the next year and the hoped-for revolutions never materialised. Society did not collapse. There was no blood running through the streets. Poverty, destitution and chaos failed to take hold. Tranquillity and prosperity were restored, a situation they found most depressing. Had anarchy and violence exploded they would doubtless have behaved like giddy schoolboys on the last day of term. Instead, Marx joined a short-lived German paper called *Das Volk* (The People). It was produced by the communist artisans of the Workers' Educational Association and run by the likes of Bruno Bauer's younger brother Edgar and Wilhelm Liebknecht. Though its publishing run was severely truncated it brought Marx back into contact with London's artisan community.

It was a move that coincided with another of Marx's interminably bitter and acrimonious rows. The feud began at an Urquhart anti-Russian rally in May 1859. Karl Blind enjoyed an acidic little chat with Marx and passed on his conviction that Karl Vogt was in the pay of Napoleon III. Blind later went public with this theory, though he published his attack anonymously, and Vogt, believing Marx had penned the diatribe, rushed out a response. It denounced him as a revolutionary charlatan who sponged off the workers while hobnobbing with the aristocracy, a jibe that was stinging in its accuracy. Vogt also claimed that Marx was in the pay of the Austrian government and had betrayed German radicals to the police. Marx's reputation took a massive hit. Blind and the radical German exiles in London all disowned him.

Marx spent an entire year composing his retaliation, *Herr Vogt*, a wordy, exceedingly bitter riposte which weighed in at a hefty 300 pages. He attacked Vogt, who was accused of being sympathetic to Russia and, with references to 'sewers' and 'piss', was denounced in scatological terms as a skunk and a performing dog. But he also skewered anyone even tangentially associated with Vogt. As such the editor of the *Telegraph*, Joseph Moses Levy, was subjected to a protracted anti-Semitic tirade. Like that of a noxious schoolboy, it focused on mocking the size of his nose, a subject Marx concentrated on with embarrassing excess. He also berated him for changing the spelling of his surname from Levi. Considering how Marx's own parents had expunged any trace of Jewishness from their own family name this was a remarkable angle of attack. Marx never railed against the conditions of the poor with anything like the venom he did when he felt personally slighted. On this occasion though, Marx gained a measure of vindication when it was revealed that Vogt actually *had* been in the employ of Napoleon III.

The same period saw the gestation of a new militant party of socialist German workers, but while it was a movement inspired by his activism, and one that communicated with him frequently, it was led, not by Marx, but by his next bitter rival, Ferdinand Lassalle. The creator of German Social Democracy was a Silesian Jew who was a renowned lawyer. As a leader he was a romantic revolutionary through and through. A man of considerable intelligence, confidence and charisma, Lassalle was a great organiser but was also terrifically vain. He developed a reputation as a rabble-rouser and a superb orator and was strongly influenced by Hegel and Marx. But, predictably, he had a troubled relationship with both the latter and Engels.

Marx frankly detested him; he hated his extravagance and ambition and used his personal dislike to develop an intellectual and ideological loathing of the man. He was also likely jealous of the rapport that Lassalle had with the working man, something Marx never attained himself. Much of Marx's antipathy to his radical brethren though seems inspired by the fact that he desired to be the totemic figure of the revolutionary movement. As such, he despised and attempted to destroy every rival for that position. Such reasoning explains why Engels, who remained rather subservient to his colleague, the Robin to Marx's Batman, was the only significant figure in the movement he never fell out with.

Lassalle had arranged for Marx to contribute to his German newspapers. But, in their letters, Karl and Engels employed a plethora of anti-Semitic slurs to cast Lassalle as 'Isidor Berlin Blue Dye', 'Itzig', 'the little Yid Braun', and 'Jacob the Wizard'. In 1861, when Marx travelled to Berlin to be feted by Lassalle, he began to refer to him as 'the Jewish nigger'.[231] On that trip to Germany Marx also dropped in on his mother to pester her about an advance on his inheritance. He acidly confided in her how he believed his sister Emilia and her husband Johann Conrad had designs on her estate. As the couple were caring for Marx's mother, who had moved in with them, while his only contact with her was occasional angry demands for cash, his sniping was rather rich. She broke off contact with him again and refused to give him another advance. Considering the hostility he had treated her with for decades it is astonishing that his mother still had anything to do with him at all.

The next year Lassalle turned up in London to visit the Great Exhibition and Marx grudgingly felt obliged to return his hospitality. Yet both Marx and Jenny sneered at Lassalle's 'niggerlike'[232] characteristics and Marx, who accompanied him on trips to the British Museum, as well as further afield to Windsor and Virginia Water, grew enraged at his vanity and ostentation. His sartorial elegance, relaxed and louche flippancy, his extravagance, luxurious silk dressing gowns and expensive cigars all rankled with Marx who may have felt conscious of his own impecunious circumstances and the cheap stogies he habitually smoked. Whatever the motivations, from that point on, Marx became bitterly opposed to a man who should have been among his staunchest and most useful allies. Lassalle was certainly a strange character though; he was killed in a duel over a love affair two years after his visit to London, when he had merely smiled and refused to raise his pistol, perhaps persuaded of his invincible destiny.

Marx continued to have financial problems, though such were again caused as much by his own extravagance than any genuine poverty. He was ever more determined to put up the front of the respectable bourgeois gentleman he so averred to despise. His fiscal woes amounted to the likes of cancelling lessons for his daughters on the piano he had just bought for them. But some of his income from Engels did dry up at that point when the textile industry suffered from a severe cotton shortage following the outbreak of the American Civil War. Engels complained about feeling the pinch, but it is difficult to find much sympathy for the plight of a man who had so regularly celebrated the penury of others.

It is possible that Marx's strained circumstances contributed to the single brief falling out between the pair. In January 1863 Engels wrote to Marx to inform him of the death of his long term partner Mary Burns. As Friedrich had expressed deep remorse at the deaths of Marx's children and the case of smallpox endured by Jenny, and had not just financially supported him for years but had also taken a bullet for his friend over the pregnancy of Helene Demuth, he might have expected such sentiments to be reciprocated. But he was to be disappointed. Marx made a cursory reference to Mary's passing and then went on at interminable length about his own woes before concentrating on asking Engels for more money. Astonishingly Marx concluded by lamenting 'Instead of Mary, ought it not to have been my mother, who is in any case a prey to physical ailments and has had her fair share of life?'[233] Desiring the death of his own mother was a new low even for Marx, though he was soon to get his wish in that regard. Engels was furious at his friend's callousness though he was quickly mollified by Marx's subsequent apology.

Just a few months later Marx's financial condition changed quite suddenly. On 30 November 1863 his mother died and he finally gained the inheritance he had pursued so graspingly for so long. His correspondence at the time was rather cold, focusing on the financial implications with not the slightest suggestion of remorse or feeling at all. The amount he received was quite generous but Marx promptly received an even more substantial bequest from Wilhelm Wolff who died on 9 May 1864. Marx finally paid off his debts and moved to 1 Modena Villas, Maitland Park Road, in Belsize Park, North London. It was a fine building spread over four spacious floors and Marx appropriated the room with a grand view of the park as his study.

That same year Marx wrote to his uncle Lion Philips to boast how he had invested some of his new windfall by speculating on the stock exchange. He had made a killing, just like a good capitalist. The sheer joy he took from this speculative success virtually radiates out of the missive. Naturally he had to justify his crass hypocrisy by arguing that his real intent was 'to relieve the enemy of his money'.[234] Yeah, right. Having moved to a salubrious new address, regularly hosting extravagant dinner parties, taking frequent holidays at the seaside and strolling through the park in his freshly tailored new suits Marx was ever more living the bourgeois life he fiercely denounced from his oak lined study with its picturesque park view.

But Marx, who avidly supported both the North in the US Civil War and the 1863 Polish uprising against Russian rule, a leftist cause-célèbre of the time, was about to be drawn back into political activism. He anticipated the 'annihilation' of Russia and attended the July 1863 rally in London attended by workers representatives from many nations. There was unanimous support for Poland and firm opposition to the Tsar. George Odger, secretary of the London Trades Council, saw the potential that day and invited representatives back to another gathering on 28 September 1864 at St. Martin's Hall in Covent Garden. It was the first effective meeting of the International Working Men's Association (IWMA) which became famed as simply 'The International', though in light of the Second Socialist International of 1889 it is usually called the 'First' International. Its creation radically altered the character and history of European Socialism.

Marx attended that first meeting, was enthusiastic about the organisation, and was swiftly invited to sit on its General Council. He would, by sheer force of personality and not a little determination, become its leader in less than a year. It was an extremist organisation whose members regarded themselves as involved in implacable conflict with an entrenched enemy. At that first gathering they pledged to destroy, rather than reform, the current economic system. It was to be replaced with one where the workers seized the means of production and shared its profits communally – such would be the end of private property in all its forms. Marx himself opposed property ownership, except his own, naturally, but he hated the ownership of land even more. He despised landlords, haughtily referring to them as 'parasites'. Marx was invited to compose an address to the group and characteristically made doom-laden and wildly inaccurate predictions about the future of capitalism.

> 'In all countries of Europe it has become a truth demonstrable to every unprejudiced mind, and only denied by those whose interest it is to hedge other people in a fool's paradise, that no improvement of machinery, no application of science to production, no contrivance of communication, no new colonies, no emigration, no opening of markets, no free trade, nor all these things put together, will do away with the miseries of the industrial masses.'[235]

A 'truth demonstrable to every unprejudiced mind' and a 'fool's paradise' indeed.

But Marx did finally address some legitimate concerns of the workers. He proposed shorter working hours, limitations on the labour of women and children and, predictably, the annihilation of the Muscovite influence on Europe. The great inequality of the period, the lack of opportunity for advancement through legitimate means, the horrendous living conditions of the working classes and the almost complete absence of education, representation, healthcare and sanitation in Victorian Britain made their position on such issues entirely understandable. But his forecasts and solutions proved hopelessly wide of the mark. Marx's books should be little more than museum pieces. Yet, far from being consigned to the dustbin of history, his perspective still resonates. The combative nature in which left-wing activism was forged endures, even as the motivations for such radicalism have melted away.

The *Address* to the International had yet again ended with the slogan 'Proletarians of all countries unite!' Yet, no matter how many times Marx made this claim, he never seemed remotely interested in trying to 'unite' with the comrades he feuded with. The International was quickly, and inevitably, riven by factionalism. Even the small French contingent split into irreconcilable cliques of republicans and Proudhonists. Such internecine squabbling was at least as characteristic as their areas of mutual agreement, and it was probably much *more* illustrative of the mood of their meetings. Marx was hardly the man to heal such rifts. Although officially the German representative of the International, he had no real allies left east of the Rhine. The scant correspondence he shared with fellow Germans largely consisted of dismissive insults on the primitive state of the German people, and crude barbs on the alleged homosexuality of Lassalle's successor, Johann Baptist von Schweitzer. Despite its stated intent of international co-operation, Marx resisted any attempts of the IWMA to ally itself with any other socialist organisations.

He did have a rival for leadership of the International though, and it was a man who, in many ways, was his polar opposite. Mikhail Bakunin, the imposing Russian anarchist, was an instinctive and emotional campaigner famed for his bombastic oration, a world removed from the rigorous academic application that characterised Marx. Wheen memorably portrayed him as 'a hairy Russian giant, the very model of a thunderbolt-hurling revolutionist, all impulse and passion and pure will'.[236] He had come from a privileged, positively aristocratic background and had grown up on a prosperous estate before becoming immersed in the works of Hegel and Fichte, the latter yet another of Isaiah Berlin's enemies of liberty. But he had grown into a coarse and capricious activist, far removed from the diligent application of his rival. The pair diverged ideologically as well as personally, and Bakunin was dismissive of the 'communist dictatorship' favoured by Marx. Ideology is not something the man is renowned for, but in this one sense at least he was quite perceptive, believing that 'Communist states were no better than capitalist: authority would still be centralised in the hands of the few, and even if the state were run by 'workers' they would soon become as corrupt and despotic as the tyrants they had overthrown'.[237] Yet his impassioned wishful thinking was equally specious. Alexander Herzen, a friend and compatriot, who despised Tsarism and all absolutist government, said of Bakunin in his memoirs that he 'longed desperately to tear himself away from a land where every form of thought was prosecuted as evil-mindedness, and independence of judgement or speech was looked upon as an insult to public morality'.[238] It was, in light of the Russia that Bakunin and his fellow radicals helped to inspire, an ironic dream.

Despite Bakunin's lack of any kind of coherent theory and the utter absence of support in his lifetime, bar a dozen or so sozzled disciples who acted as his drinking buddies, subsequent generations of leftist intellectuals have re-imagined him as a visionary of almost unparalleled importance - the beating heart and moral compass of left-wing activism. Thinkers as 'eminent' as E.H. Carr and Professor Fritz Raddatz have sung Bakunin's praises and eulogised his importance and virtue. However, while a great rabble-rouser Bakunin was not a great thinker and relied purely on the egalitarian dream of smashing authority and freeing the oppressed, assuming that a fairer, happier society would simply spring from the ashes. Marx came to despise the intellectual emptiness of Bakunin's rhetoric, though he essentially believed exactly the same thing himself. The movement quickly began to splinter into factions who supported either the Bakunin line or that of Marx, and both men appeared too proud to let the other dominate the organisation. However, by the time the battle for leadership of the International was resolved, events had overtaken them.

In 1867 Marx finally finished and published the first volume of *Capital*. The book is, at heart, a rigorous attempt to give a detailed account in support of the theory the author had arrived at long before he began to write it. It is the economic equivalent of the tail wagging the dog. He had already decided that societal progress was dependant on the means of production, he had long since concluded that the driving engine of history was class warfare. Now he set out to prove it. The essence of *Capital* is that the proletariat is the only class that produces more wealth than it consumes, a surplus that was absorbed by others. It is a mistake to regard such circumstances as a deliberate conspiracy by entrenched elites, rather than a result of haphazard societal evolution. Regardless, one could simply counter Marx by suggesting that profit is an essential part of business and the capitalist exchange. The entrepreneur profits from his initiative and risk-taking in setting up his business and the worker profits from his labour and time. Yet, to Marx, this was a most nefarious exchange.

He was certainly a man of deep and profound intelligence, but his attempts at analysis were consistently undermined by theorising supported on a number of assumptions that were fundamentally wrong. Yet the conviction he had in his opinions blinded him to this. So he focused all his intellectual energy on proving that his pre-existing positions were correct rather than analysing his core beliefs or considering that his entire philosophical, historical and economic model may have been constructed on a bed of sand. This critical lack of self-analysis, characterised by his tendency to denounce critics rather than consider they may have a point, not only undermined his efforts but also imbued his disciples with a confidence in their position that was wholly unjustified. It meant the cycle of errors begun by Marx was to be repeated again and again at incalculable cost.

Capital made little impact on its release though and the Second Reform Bill of the same year, which effectively doubled the franchise by allowing for household and urban votes, contributed to the decline of radicalism in Britain. In its timeliness *Capital* is the polar opposite of the *Communist Manifesto*. Marx was absolutely right that there needed to be change, but by the time he finally finished his massive tome change was happening anyway, and it bore no relation to what he expected. History was already moving along and leaving him behind. While Marx argued that the current economic system must necessarily result in relative penury for the workers, what actually unfolded has been the polar opposite, a process that had already begun before the ink was dry on his magnum opus. To attempt to draw any allusions between Marx's forecasts and the subsequent reality would be the most ludicrous folly. As for the idea of 'alienation', that the factory worker doesn't get to keep the fruits of their labour and that this has devastating, dehumanising consequences, well, the same could be said about Rembrandt. As much as Marx bangs on about the 'torment' of the working man, we should remember that he did not share their labours or lifestyle for a single day of his entire life. It didn't take a genius to work out that life for the proletariat in Marx's time was unpleasant, but, additionally, it doesn't take 1,200 pages of algebra and repetitive waffle to conclude that the lot of the working man in capitalist nations has been infinitely preferable to those who toiled under the systems inspired by Marx.

Capital was advertised, and seized on by many, as finally giving the intellectual framework and foundation for international socialism. Such was the impression at any rate. Yet, in truth, for all the impressiveness of its nigh on impenetrable reasoning, the conclusions of the study were fallacious nonsense. However, the *image* of it proved enormously persuasive to those who wanted to believe. They seized it as irrefutable proof, brandishing it with the pride of one who claims to hold in their hand the cure for cancer. Unfortunately, not only had this tonic never been tested and never cured anyone, but posterity would reveal it to be a physic that would prove fatal to all those forced to imbibe it. Yet its advocates, even when exposed to the deadly reality of the palliative they had recommended, continued to administer it while angrily berating those who advised caution.

By 1867 the spendthrift Marx had blown his inheritances. He resorted to increasingly desperate appeals to Engels to restore him to financial health, entreaties which were soon answered. In 1869 Engels sold his interest in his father's company, paid off Marx's debts and secured his partner a generous annual salary for life. He then moved from Manchester to London in 1870, settling into a fine house at 122 Regent's Park Road. Engels arrived just as the European political scene was about to explode again. The roots of the crisis lay in Marx's homeland, specifically Prussia which had seen the rise of Otto von Bismarck. To Marx he represented the most repressive aspects of conservative, authoritarian rule. But, in a profound case of historical irony, it was the robustly right-wing Bismarck who became the first to introduce a welfare state. The step was vehemently opposed by the majority of socialists at the time, particularly Engels. Convinced it was a bribe that would dampen the prospects of revolution he fumed about the development in a number of articles.

Yet Bismarck also saw an appeal to German nationalism as the most effective way to galvanise support. In 1864 he launched a war against Denmark to reclaim the largely German duchies of Schleswig and Holstein, and secured a speedy and emphatic victory. Marx approved of German nationalism, but he felt the Prussian dynasty was an agent of the Tsar and an ally of Napoleon III. He was sure that Bismarck was not the man to unite Germany. Marx was to be proven wrong yet again. In 1866 Bismarck called for an end to the Congress of Vienna and demanded a united German nation-state in its place. He was opposed by Austria and maligned by Marx and Engels who believed him to be acting in allegiance with Imperial France. Wrong again! They expected Prussia to be crushed in the war against Austria and its allies. But to their surprise they swept their opponents aside in just six weeks.

Bismarck created a North German Federation under universal male suffrage and won many former revolutionaries to his cause. The leftists were again divided between those who recommended working within the new system to achieve long term goals and those who favoured short term working class activism. Marx belittled the leaders of both factions denouncing Johann Baptist von Schweitzer as a 'scoundrel' and Wilhelm Liebknecht as 'incompetent' and 'stupid'. He then, amazingly, criticised the leaders for their inability to put aside their differences and work together.

The Franco-Prussian War, that Marx had claimed would never take place, broke out in 1870. It sent the International into paroxysms of debate. Just as his predecessors of a century before had confidently predicted that the fall of monarchy would mean an end to war, Marx, his head full of utopian dreams, contended that in future 'the alliance of working classes of all countries will ultimately kill war'.[239] He continued:

'The very fact that while official France and Germany are rushing into a fratricidal feud, the workmen of France and Germany send each other messages of peace and goodwill; this great fact, unparalleled in the history of the past, opens the vista of a brighter future. It proves that in contrast to old society, with its economical miseries and its political delirium, a new society is springing up, whose International rule will be *Peace*, because its natural ruler will be everywhere the same – *Labour!* The Pioneer of that new society is the International Working Men's Association.'[240]

That same association was soon to dissolve in acrimonious rancour. For now, of course, Marx still celebrated the prospect of war. He suggested the future conflict would be between Prussia and Russia, and that it would lead to revolution in the vast latter state. He was, on this occasion, entirely correct. But, while he craved such an eventuality, its consequences would prove calamitous beyond measure. The war between France and Prussia had been provoked by Bismarck's skilful manipulation of the French. Bismarck hoped the declaration of hostilities would result in an explosion of nationalistic fervour in Germany. He had calculated so superbly that even Marx and Engels joined in the orgy of patriotism. Marx, enthusiastic as ever on the outbreak of war, declared in a letter to Engels that 'The French need a thrashing'.[241] They duly got it. Within weeks the French army had been decimated at Sedan and Louis Napoleon taken prisoner. The decisive victory resulted in German unification even as France began unravelling again.

When insurrection erupted in Lyon, Bakunin raced there and proclaimed himself leader of the Committee of French Salvation, declaring the abolition of the state and demanding the execution of anyone who disagreed with him. But when a platoon of National Guards descended on the town he promptly fled to Geneva. The capital began collapsing into anarchy. A Republic was declared in Paris and the city was assailed by revolutionary forces even as Bismarck demanded the cession of Alsace and Lorraine. The new republican government could not resist Bismarck's Prussia so signed an armistice in January 1871. The 'Iron Chancellor' ordered elections in France, demanding the formation of a new National Assembly before he would consider drawing up a treaty with it. When this Assembly convened it was in the face of significant opposition. That resistance was especially hostile to the president of the Third Republic, Adolphe Thiers, who had capitulated to Prussia while demanding reparations from the French people.

In March he attempted to disarm the Paris National Guard, a volunteer force with decidedly radical leanings. It refused, declared independence and deposed the provisional government. The rebels forced Thiers to flee to Versailles, and declared its own revolutionary committee of the people as the true government of France. Hastily arranged elections resulted in a new revolutionary government called the 'Commune' in honour of the body established during the dark days of the Revolution. A revolutionary wave swept up bohemians, idealists and romantics of all stripes in the sort of euphoria not seen since 1789.

The Communards had vague aims and no manifesto, they merely called on the people to govern themselves. They would become ludicrously lionised by the left though and the red flag they hoisted during that rebellion became the enduring symbol of the movement. Initially Marx decried the timidity of the rebels, damning them for organising a city-wide election for the Commune instead of marching on Versailles and butchering Thiers and his ministers. He was appalled when they allowed the National Bank to continue operating rather than looting its vaults. When reflecting on the Communards though he still said 'History has no like example of such greatness'.[242]

In June 1871 government troops besieged the socialist rebels and supplies began to run low. The old intolerances swiftly returned, and the Communards began to execute suspects. As in the Terror of the previous century, it was almost entirely innocents who fell victim to their regime. They horrified Europe by sending women into battle, shooting the Archbishop of Paris and wantonly burning much of the historic capital to the ground. Revulsion quickly mounted at the atrocities and the radicals were widely denounced as bloodthirsty monsters. But Marx's response was to write a piece called *The Civil War in France* which described the short-lived regime as 'the glorious harbinger of a new society'.[243] Marx claimed the rising was 'the greatest achievement of our party since the June revolt' while Engels called the Commune 'the child of the International intellectually'.[244] But, in expressing their kinship for the violent upheaval, both men had inadvertently given the impression that they were responsible. The association was to tar them both, particularly Marx who, after a lifetime of studious anonymity, woke up to infamy.

In *The Civil War in France* Marx chastised Thiers, with no trace of irony and something of a lack of self-awareness, as 'never scrupling...to fan a revolution, and to stifle it in blood...with class prejudices standing him in the place of ideas, and vanity in the place'.[245] It was entirely typical of both Marx and Engels that they celebrated the shocking violence of the Commune with the sort of gushing sentiment usually reserved for poets. One can almost picture Marx poised on a hilltop, silhouetted against a dramatic sunset, hair billowing in the wind, his hand clutching his heart as he extols the manly virtues of the revolt. But the reality was a rather squalid, vicious and poorly organised event.

The Communards were denounced far and wide as common murderers - the killers of innocent women and wanton vandals who destroyed much of Paris.

Yet to Marx, they were heroes battling oppression, martyrs whose sacrifice should be immortalised. When it came to political ideology, for Marx there was no room at all for humanity, a characteristic enthusiastically replicated by his heirs. The fact that they celebrated violence when committed by their political brethren was as predictable as the revulsion they expressed for their enemies. Marx claimed the Communards were nowhere near violent enough, but he virulently condemned Thiers for the level of force used in crushing the revolt. While the suppression of the Commune was shockingly brutal, this is still somewhat inconsistent. After all, both sides committed excesses and if Marx was prepared to encourage and celebrate violence, as he frequently did, he should not protest the consequences with quite such vigour.

The clampdown following the Commune of 1871 effectively sounded the death knell of the organisation that had become, in the public's mind at least, inextricably associated with it: the International. It had already been disintegrating over the irreconcilable differences between the French and the Spaniards, as well as the Germans and the English. But even more pivotal was the increasingly bitter rivalry between Marx and Bakunin, the latter of whom had taken up with Sergei Nechayev, a violent anarcho-terrorist who wrote incendiary articles that warned of Armageddon. Nechayev had reportedly murdered a fellow student in St. Petersburg just to prove he could. When a publisher later began chasing Bakunin for money he had been forwarded for a Russian language edition of *Capital*, it was Nechayev who wrote to the unfortunate man to threaten that he would be murdered unless he let Bakunin keep the cash.*

It was now Marx's turn to be on the receiving end of the sort of anti-Semitism he had been accustomed to dishing out. Bakunin claimed that Marx was the dictator-messiah of a wide-ranging plot of German and Russian Jews which, in collaboration with the Rothschilds, aimed at world domination. The two men, who both claimed to despise any form of hierarchy, fought tooth and nail to be recognised as the leading light of the International. But as much of a motivation for the International's end was that Marx was ageing and ailing and, unable to bear the thought of anyone else taking over the organisation, announced it would relocate to America, where it promptly fizzled and died.

The remaining years of Marx's life were ones of declining health and a significant reduction in writing and activism. He had worked tirelessly on the radical cause for decades so focused on trying to enjoy his twilight years and his newfound fame. In the *Communist Manifesto* Marx had attested that worker's labour is transformed into capital and ultimately impoverishes them.

---

* Nechayev served as the inspiration for Pyotr Stepanovich Verkhonevsky, the protagonist in Fyodor Dostoyevsky's 1871 novel *Demons*.

Decades later, in his *Address* to the International and in *Capital*, his argument had not changed a jot. But his expression had become more 'scientific' and detailed, focusing on the specific grains of carbon and nitrogen necessary to sustain the worker, and of how capitalism led to their depletion. For Marx the philosophy came first and the science, the evidence, must be moulded and selected to fit.

This trait reveals in him both a resistance to changing the core of his belief and a desire to convey his message as one of incontrovertible scientific truth. He was heavily influenced in the latter regard by the publication of Charles Darwin's *On the Origins of Species* in 1859. Marx frequently claimed that Darwin's findings on nature tallied with his own on human society. Such a conclusion gave him the confidence that his theories could be proved with a similar level of empirical veracity. Once introduced to Darwin through Engels, who bought the book two weeks after its publication, Marx became an enthusiastic advocate of his ideas. He wrote to Engels in 1862 on Darwin's reference to the Malthusian dictum that

'It is remarkable how Darwin recognises among beasts and plants his English society with its division of labour, competition, opening of new markets, "inventions" and Malthusian "struggle for existence". It is...reminiscent of Hegel, in the "phenomenology", where bourgeois society appears as the "spiritual animal kingdom", while in Darwin the animal kingdom appears as bourgeois'.[246]

Such ruminations reveal the single-mindedness of Marx's thought processes; everything had to neatly fit his theory.

What to make then of this man and his ideas? A columnist for the *New York World* met Marx in the wake of the Commune of 1871, at the height of his notoriety. Expecting a terrifying fire and brimstone vision of a maniacal demagogue, he was surprised to be greeted by a gentle, twinkly-eyed academic in tweed ensconced in a rustic study. Marx could certainly turn on the charm when he wanted and, in his personal life, was frequently regarded as warm and humorous. He was also, the odd slip apart, a good husband and doting father. He worked hard to provide opportunities for his daughters, ensuring they learned the piano and had lessons in French and Italian. He also encouraged their political activism, though they were indoctrinated in his own ideology from an early age. Indeed, Marx and his family only ever really associated with fellow socialists, with those whose political persuasion was 'correct', a practice that rather narrowed their world-view. His daughters ended up dabbling in radical journalism and obediently marrying French socialists. Marx spent many happy and carefree hours with his girls though. Eleanor, his youngest daughter, described him as 'the cheeriest, gayest soul that ever breathed, of a man brimming over with humour and good-humour, whose hearty laugh was infectious and irresistible, of the kindliest, gentlest, most sympathetic of companions'.[247] That American journalist though perceptively concluded that Marx was 'that most formidable of all composite forces – a dreamer who thinks, a thinker who dreams'.[248]

While he could be affable in his personal life, Marx was a quite different animal in the political sphere. For all the anecdotal evidence of his charms, it is difficult to escape the impression that he was the embodiment of a dictator. Marx's intolerance to opposing views and dissent, his determination to crush any rivals or opposition and the nigh-on messianic faith he had in his own political vision are all characteristic of the great brutes of history. Marx was confined to being a big fish in a small pond, but one does wonder how he might have behaved if he had ever attained any real power. One suspects that he may have proven far more despotic than the 'tyrants' he railed against. This desire to coerce others, to bend them to one's will, is particularly characteristic of the left's most ardent activists. Is it any surprise that such a mindset results in despots once the obstacles that restrained them have been removed?

On 30 March 1846 Pavel Annenkov had described Marx as 'the type of man who is made up of energy, will and unshakeable conviction.' He also recorded 'the firm conviction of his mission to dominate men's minds and prescribe them their laws. Before me stood the embodiment of a democratic dictator'.[249] Moses Hess commented regretfully on Marx's vanity which, unsatisfied with the wide-ranging plaudits he had received, demanded an incredible level of submission from everyone.[250] Bakunin also commented on his arrogance and, recalling their days in Paris, said of him 'I eagerly sought his conversation, which was always instructive and witty, when it was not inspired by petty hate which alas! was only too often the case'.[251] Bakunin concluded of Marx that 'He called me a sentimental idealist, and he was right, I called him vain, perfidious, and sly, and I was right too'.[252] In 1850 Gustav Techow reached a similar conclusion and said of Marx

> 'If he had had as much heart as intellect and love as hate, I should have gone through fire for him...I regret that this man, with his fine intellect, is lacking in nobility of soul. I am convinced that the most dangerous personal ambition has eaten away at all the good in him. He laughs at the fools who parrot his proletarian catechism, just as he laughs over the communists *á la* Willich and over the bourgeoisie. The only people he respects are the aristocrats, the genuine ones who are well aware of it. In order to drive them from government, he needs a source of strength, which he can only find in the proletariat...I took away with me the impression that the acquisition of personal power was the aim of all his endeavours.'[253]

Karl Schurz joined the chorus when commenting that:

'To no opinion which differed from his own did he accord the honour of even condescending consideration. Everyone who contradicted him he treated with abject contempt; every argument that he did not like he treated either with biting scorn at the unfathomable ignorance that had prompted it, or with opprobrius aspersions on the motives of him who advanced it...he denounced everyone who dared oppose his opinions'.[254]

In light of this, Marx's self-image, which he unveiled through the Victorian parlour game of Confessions, is revealing. He recorded that his favourite virtue in man was 'strength', his chief characteristic was 'singleness of purpose', his idea of happiness was 'to fight' and his idea of misery was 'submission'. Marx's favourite colour was, predictably, red, while his preferred motto was 'To doubt everything'.[255] What a pity he never applied that principle to his own philosophy.

The theories advanced by this intense personality were inherently destructive. Marx did not want to tackle the problems people faced or improve the world in which we live. He offered no constructive suggestions directed at the betterment of the state or soothing the conditions suffered by the poor. He simply wanted to wreck society and start again from scratch. In his Address to the Communist League of 1850 he declared that 'it cannot be a question of changing private property but only of destroying it, not of smothering class antagonisms but only of wiping out classes, not of improving existing society but of founding a new one'.[256] Ultimately, while Marx was right in believing that things needed to change, he was wrong in envisaging the direction and form those changes should take. Where he foresaw poverty and revolution what actually came to pass was peace and prosperity, a salient point to remember when considering the doomsday warnings of the modern left. While Marx perceived that radical alterations to society were necessary, in the event, a series of moderate reforms proved far more effective in enriching and emancipating the working man.

Those reforms, propelled by the capitalist system he despised, had begun long before he died. History had already moved on and left him behind. In contrast to his radical recommendations, the societies of Western Europe and North America focused on addressing practical concerns: the living and working conditions of their populaces, the issues of suffrage and the education of the masses, the health and welfare of their citizens, law and order, freedom of expression and access to culture. As a consequence, working conditions have improved beyond all recognition, and the wealth generated helped to pay for the welfare provision which alleviated those socialists' primary concerns. By gradually tinkering in such matters and focusing on incremental legislative changes those societies have witnessed remarkable improvements in both material conditions and the psychological well-being of those fortunate enough to live under them. Maintaining the balance between economic interests and humane concern will continue to get a return on its investment. This allows these benefits to spread to parts of the still-developing world.

The problem with extremist solutions is that of unintended consequences; that it is impossible to accurately envisage the effects of such revolutionary proposals. It was a ludicrous leap of faith for Marx to assume that his radical proletarian society would evolve into a nirvana of egalitarianism. The genuine results of his theorising are only too familiar to us now. The repercussions that have arisen every time the political pendulum has swung too far to the left or the right have always worsened their citizens' lives. For while people have frequently liked the *idea* of a purely left-wing state they have never once been able to bear the reality. Nations such as China, Cuba and North Korea have only endured because they persist in denying their populations any kind of democratic participation. As for the former Soviet states of Eastern Europe, on the very first occasion when the citizens had an opportunity to decide their fates for themselves, in the period from 1989-91, they threw off their socialist overlords. They dragged their leaders out in front of cameras, executed them on live TV and smashed down the walls that surrounded them. Socialist states have only ever thrived on effectively imprisoning their entire populations. The hard left is not in the habit of winning elections, or even of *allowing* elections. Its tendency is violent seizures of power, the suspension of democracy and the suppression of all political opposition; traits which formed the core of Marx's recommendations and which remain endemic among extremists. But, as Margaret Thatcher made clear, 'When people are free to choose they choose freedom'.[257]

Marx has been praised for accuracy in some forecasts of how capitalism would progress, such as predicting large corporations and cycles of boom and bust. But even here he has been credited with foresight he did not truly possess. The likes of the Dutch tulip craze and the South Sea Bubble revealed how markets can be affected by wild fluctuations long before he began writing. His conclusion on the phenomenon then was no forecast but merely an observation of past trends. The capitalist system had survived those ruptures. It would survive others. Regardless, even if we accept his insight in making such claims, he was still mistaken in every way that truly counts. He was, for instance, utterly wrong about the *effects* of such developments, on how capitalism would alter people's lives. And he was just as wrong, if not more so, in how he visualised the communist future. His prediction that the middle classes would become extinct was also woefully wide of the mark - for they multiplied beyond all possible expectation.

Marx was so consumed by his vision of the conflict between workers and capitalists that he also ignored a third factor – the state. He expected both capitalism and the state to fade. In fact they have found an accord, with one more equitably redistributing the fruits of the other without discouraging its growth. Critically, in defiance of his most central assertion, a period of bourgeois capitalism has, rather than encouraging revolution, proven to be a cast-iron deterrent to it. While he believed the free market's collapse was imminent, it was only just getting warmed up. He also predicted that the dictatorship of the proletariat would 'wither away', but it simply became ever more bloated, controlling, arrogant and violent. For the collectivist state is a disaster. It is prosperity that frees humanity, and where it has spread rights and freedoms have accompanied the myriad benefits it provides. Yet financial growth was what Marx most hoped to inhibit. From this pivotal miscalculation the rest of his theorising crumbles like a sandcastle washed away by the tide.

Marx perceived history as a progression through variously improving means of production, yet he saw communism as a fundamental break from all past society. But the suggestion that millennia of competition would suddenly, almost at the flick of a switch, transform into a culture of co-operation was frankly laughable. The idea that such an eventuality was a pre-ordained scientific fact though is simply dangerous, one laden with disastrous probabilities. Yet it is even more remarkable that Marx, as well as his entire class of peers, believed the communist society they hoped to create would be one of tranquil harmony. For their movement was defined more by the intensity of its furious and never-ending rivalries than anything else. It is astonishing that Marx could have reached such a conclusion when his own experiences were a constant reminder of that strife.

There are numerous examples which should have sounded alarm bells. In the 1860s, for instance, he looked to resurgent Irish nationalism as the potential spark for revolution. In hoping for an agrarian revolt where the Irish tenant farmers would seize the property of the great landlords though he alienated himself from the English workers who were competing with the Irish for jobs. This in itself is hardly surprising as the concerns of working men rarely featured prominently in Marx's thoughts. However, there was also considerable friction from the other camp, for the staunchly Catholic Irish opposed the radicals' atheism and their desire to carve up the Papal States. Such issues should have alerted the communists to the reality that their planned utopia of a brotherhood of workers would inevitably be split by deep religious, social, personal and national divisions. Yet they never let such inconvenient truths interfere with their judgement.

For Marx never wavered in his belief. And he was also sure that the new society would be more prosperous and successful than the old. His greatest mistake though was in defining history in the simplistic terms of class struggle. Such a sweepingly Manichean outlook failed to acknowledge that people compete far more frequently and bitterly with members of their own class than they do with individuals from other strata. Marx, of course, was rarely involved in a 'struggle' with either aristocrats or proletarians. With his peers it was another matter. Few got involved in fractious disputes with such regularity, and he attacked any rival to his position with a ferocity that would have put the most despotic tyrant or grasping capitalist to shame. The suggestion that this conflict would dissipate after a bloody revolution was preposterous.

It was this miscalculation though that convinced him the proletarian world would be a utopia and inspired him to agitate for dismantling all those aspects of society which galvanised humanity. He hoped to break that which worked and replace it with an utterly untested model based on a critically flawed assumption about how society operates. The result would be an equally divided state but one shorn of the motivations for people to strive for betterment. It would also lack the institutions that protected its citizens' liberties and of the pleasures that actually made life worth living. The failure to countenance such an obvious point undermined every sentence Marx ever wrote. It is remarkable that a mind of such deep intelligence could have reached these absurd conclusions after a lifetime of intense study. Yet this is a common malady of the left. It is their very intelligence, one supposes, that imbues such individuals with the arrogance to believe that they are right, no matter how much evidence piles up to contradict their hypotheses.

Even though his theorising was proven utterly wrong even before he died, the certainty with which he and Engels expressed their programme was employed by socialist regimes to practice the most brutal intolerance imaginable. Such is his legacy. This unjustified conviction in the cause is the chief reason why Marxism has proven such a delusional menace. The arrogance and impatience with even the most minor forms of dissent, epitomised by the likes of Lenin and Trotsky, mirrored those characteristics in Marx, the writer whose work and whose memory they worshipped with an almost religious zeal. Much of Marx's work was framed by a belief in conspiracies orchestrated by the ruling elites, such as his contention that the upper classes were attempting to foment antagonism between English and Irish workers. This paranoia over nefarious plots mirrors that of Robespierre and Rousseau and seems an inevitable result of one convinced they are battling against powerful legislative bodies, however ludicrous such concerns usually prove. His language about the state, capitalists and property holders was relentlessly divisive and provocative. They were 'parasites' and 'prostitutes', the state an 'abortion' and a 'monster'.

Marx was a man for whom politics was nearly everything. He did have a love for Shakespeare, but apart from that, there was little room in his life for art, contemporary theatre, music or culture. When he did frequent alehouses it was primarily to discuss extremist politics with fellow radicals. Such a man seems oblivious to the true priorities of life. Is he really the sort of individual to determine the type of state in which the rest of us should live? It is hardly surprising that he inspired the most humourless and rigid societies the world has ever seen, the ones most drained of true energy, culture, freedom, humour and the vitality of life - all those pious political paragons in their drab overalls overseeing grey and miserable societies where liberty and individuality have been crushed.

Marx may not have pictured the real bleakness of the communist states he inspired, but he would surely have recoiled from the consumerist society of twentieth century America. That coincided with the spread of communism, but bequeathed to the world Elvis, Scott Fitzgerald, Hollywood musicals, Disney, Marvel comics, The Muppets, Mark Rothko, Gene Kelly, Fred Astaire, John Steinbeck, Joe Louis, Muhammad Ali, John McEnroe, Dolly Parton, Stevie Wonder, Michael Jackson, Jazz, Motown, Rap, Hip Hop, Stanley Kubrick, Steven Spielberg, Star Wars, The Doors, The Beach Boys, Nirvana, Aerosmith and countless others that have enriched the world. All those deeply serious and earnestly pious agitators like Marx and his kin have done has been incalculably harmful to the human spirit and experience. The world would certainly have been a better place had they never been born.

Marx was not an evil man: most accounts of meetings with him extol his warmth, charisma and humour. The bitter way he fell out with his contemporaries is a reflection of the depth of his commitment to an ideological position rather than evidence of a particularly malicious personality. But this merely illustrates just how problematic the moral certainties expressed by the left can be. With Marx, it led a compassionate and intelligent man into bitter acrimony with fellows who should have been his comrades while advocating and celebrating dreadful sectarian violence. His faith blinded him to the gaping faults in his reasoning and led him to believe the most implausible consequences would result from his theorising. That certainty resulted in half the world stubbornly attempting to realise his dreams for a century that would prove the bloodiest in human history.

The conviction that underpins their ideology means the movement has refused to accept responsibility for such catastrophes while maintaining the polarising and aggressive activism that caused them. The movement has discarded many of the specific suggestions made by Marx but, regardless, whether his latter-day acolytes followed the letter of the Marx's law or not is irrelevant. He cemented the idea that society was split between a small elite and the teeming oppressed, and that class conflict and the destruction of the established system and its personnel was not just desirable but a scientific and historical inevitability. He gave the movement the confidence it needed to commit the atrocities it did while keeping the perpetrators' consciences clean. That culture dominated the totalitarian disasters that blighted the twentieth century and still wields a prevailing influence now. The ghost of Karl Marx can still be heard in the radical rhetoric favoured by the movement today.

While Marx was less politically active in his dotage he did not, of course, completely retire from the arena. Most leftists saw the Bulgarian Revolution against Ottoman rule in 1877 as something to celebrate. But Marx and Engels perceived the Balkan activism as, predictably, an organ of Russian power and influence. They stridently opposed events there. When the Tsar declared war on the Sultan it only acted to confirm his prejudices. The Russo-Turkish war, which saw the Ottomans massacre thousands of Christians in the 'Bulgarian horrors' polarised European opinion. Gladstone was with Russia, Disraeli against it. One hardly needs a psychic or crystal ball to determine which side Marx was on. Marx despised Gladstone as a pawn of Russia, despite the Liberal leader's efforts to alleviate the condition of the Irish peasantry, a cause that had become close to his heart. He did hope that defeat by the Turks would see revolution strike Russia, an eventuality that came to pass after crushing losses to Japan in 1905 and the central European powers in 1917. He also exulted when, in 1881, Tsar Alexander II was murdered by a suicide bomber. Marx called the terrorists who had carried out the attack 'brave people with no melodramatic poses, straightforward, realistic and heroic'.[258]

Marx had spent most of his life attacking Russia and its people - who he dismissed as 'clodhoppers'. Yet this attitude underwent a remarkable transformation in his dotage. He was surprised in his later years to find that, of all countries, Russia proved most receptive to his work and *Capital* became a bigger success there than anywhere else. This delighted him, though he never admitted to having been wrong about the place before. His *On the Critique of Political Economy* began to develop quite a reputation there and through the 1870s university students began taking his ideas terribly seriously. This was the period when young Russian noblemen, wracked with social guilt, became absorbed in socialism to placate their troubled consciences. These compassionate young men were primed to become the intolerant, murderous despots of the future.

It has long been claimed that Marx's theories identified Russia as an unsuitable location for revolution. Yet he claimed a major European conflict could cause a revolt just as reliably as a period of bourgeois capitalism. He did just that in 1874 when writing to Sorge to observe that 'The general situation of Europe is such that it moves to a general European war. We must go through this war before we can think of any decisive external effectiveness of the European working class'. In his introduction to the Russian edition of *The Communist Manifesto*, which he penned in 1882, Marx asserted that 'Russia forms the vanguard of revolutionary action in Europe'.[259] He declared that 'the present Russian common ownership of land may serve as the starting-point for a communist development'.[260]

In his correspondence of the time he was even more overt in these views. Revolution in Russia was, he said, 'historically unavoidable'[261], even stating that 'Russia must leap with a *salto mortale* into a anarchist – communist – atheist millennium!'[262] In fact, he specifically stated that Russia's peasantry could form the basis for a new society if the present ruling elites were 'eliminated'. He would be very much taken at his word. The local communists were certainly listening when he declared 'To save the Russian commune, a Russian revolution is necessary'.[263] He believed that the 1877 Russo-Turkish war would 'lead directly to revolution in Russia', and declared that

> 'I have studied her circumstances from original Russian sources, both official and unofficial, [and Russia] was already on the threshold of a revolution with all the elements ready. It will duly begin with constitutional games and then there will be a fine explosion! Unless mother Nature is particularly unkind to us then we will still experience this joy'.[264]

Revolution in Russia did not happen too soon for Marx, it happened too late.

Marx's last few years were not his happiest. He became more nostalgic as time passed and a Viennese newspaper reported that he 'prefers to direct his steps back into past days when romanticism was singing its last free woodland song, when...Heine brought poems into his study with the ink still wet'.[265] In 1881 his beloved wife died and as his health declined he travelled to spas to seek some respite from his ailments. But as Marx toured the French Riviera, Monte Carlo and Algeria he was dogged by unseasonal torrential rain and howling gales wherever he went. In early 1883 his eldest daughter, also called Jenny, died as well. It was the final blow. On 13 March 1883 Karl Marx died peacefully while sitting in his favourite chair. His burial was a quiet affair in the corner of Highgate cemetery attended by just eleven people.* When Engels spoke at that modest ceremony then, to declare that 'His name will endure through the ages, and so also will his work!'[266] it must have seemed like a hollow claim. Yet they may well be the truest words ever uttered about Marx.

Sadly posterity was not kind to his family either. Marx's youngest daughter Eleanor, an aspiring left-wing journalist, committed suicide in 1898. Tragically,

---

* That imposing bust was not added until 1956 when erected by the now defunct Communist Party of Great Britain

thirteen years later, his last surviving daughter, Laura, killed herself too. At her funeral in November 1911 a slightly built, balding man with an intense demeanour and a ringing East European accent spoke movingly to say that the ideas of her father would be gloriously achieved far sooner than people expected. His words would prove as prophetic as those of Engels from nearly thirty years before. For that obscure young man was named Vladimir Ilich Ulyanov, but the world would soon come to know him by the concise alias he had assumed: Lenin.

Chapter 3
The Soviet Nightmare

'You are on treacherous ground, comrade Trotsky. The doctrine of 'class truth' is the road of Plato's Philosopher Kings, of prophets and Popes and Stalins. For all of them, also, a man must be among the anointed order to know the truth. It leads in a direction diametrically opposite to that of socialism, of a truly human *society...beware, beware comrades, of anyone or any doctrine that tells you that any man, or group of men, holds a monopoly on truth, or on the ways of getting truth.'*

James Burnham in an open letter to Trotsky. 1 February 1940

Night had settled over Moscow when the Black Maria purred into Lubyanka Square. As the vehicle swept round in a wide arc its headlights briefly illuminated the grand open space, and the imposing buildings that flanked it, before it slipped down Varsonofsky Lane to the right of the NKVD's headquarters. It pulled to a halt in a secluded courtyard, almost invisible in the shadows behind the Lubyanka. The doors popped open and Grigorii Evdokimov was pulled from the back of the vehicle. He had always been a man of fragile appearance, a wispy, and rather weak, moustache the only feature that distracted from his large, nervous eyes. Yet now he seemed utterly broken. The former Trade Unionist and Deputy Chairman of the Petrograd Soviet was so unsteady on his feet as to be practically trembling, and his formerly wary expression appeared haunted. There were tears in his eyes as he was half escorted, half dragged across the courtyard towards a low, squarish building which had been newly, as well as roughly, constructed.

Inside the structure the concrete floor sloped down towards the far wall which was formed entirely from a series of large logs. The wood of that wall was pockmarked and splintered from what looked like a thousand impacts. The floor glistened wet. Its surface was streaked with red and spattered with small pools of gore. On one wall a hose was hung loosely from a crude bracket. Another had been casually dropped to the floor where it lay coiled like a hangman's noose. Evdokimov was ordered to face the far wall while the man who had barked that command casually pulled out a pistol and aimed it at the back of his head. The gun spat once and the fifty-two year old former revolutionist crumpled to the floor amid a shower of crimson.

His executioner appeared implacable. He wiped a few spots of blood from his face, but otherwise betrayed no reaction. It was just another day at the office. Evdokimov's body would be placed in a metal box and driven to the crematorium in Moscow. The ashes would later be dumped on a mass grave like the one at Donskoi cemetery. The floor would be hosed down and the next victim would be brought in. It was just one killing, one among so many that it ceased to matter to those who were carrying out the shootings, or to those who were commanding them. Perhaps the most famous quote attributed to Stalin is that 'a single death is a tragedy, a million deaths is a statistic'. He was of course, if he ever actually made such a comment, wrong, as he was in so many ways.* A million deaths are a million tragedies, but to suggest that the Stalinist regime was responsible for a million deaths would be the gravest of under-estimates. Tens of millions were to die under Soviet tyranny and Evdokimov, who was at least despatched quickly and cleanly that late August night in 1936, may be considered one of the more fortunate victims of the regime. While the French Revolution had ultimately failed, with Robespierre and his faction driven from power after little more than a year of carnage, the Soviets were to succeed. They would maintain their grip on the state for decades, and they were aided in their efforts by significant advances in bureaucracy, communications and the industrial capacity for slaughter. Stalin would become renowned as 'Genghis Khan with a telegraph'.

The British had their revolutions in 1649 and 1688 followed by two and a half centuries of gradual, relatively tranquil, reform. The American Revolution ignited in 1776 and the French, of course, in 1789, the latter followed by another hundred years of seismic political upheaval. But in 1914, as the world descended into a war unlike any that had preceded it, the great bear of Russia

---

* There is no clear evidence attributing the remark to him and the suggestion appears to be apocryphal, even if it is certainly consistent with his attitude

still creaked on under its ancient monarchy. Indeed, it was not just Russia's style of government that was archaic. The massive state still effectively operated under a feudal system and was primarily a backwards, rural-based economy that appeared positively medieval in comparison to its thrusting, industrialised neighbours in Western Europe. The incumbents of the Russian throne were the Romanov Dynasty who had lorded it over them since 1613. Russia's ruler went under the title of Tsar, or Czar, which had the same root as the German word Kaiser, both having taken their name from Caesar, the formidable Roman dictator whose name had come to mean 'king'. But as the guns thundered across Europe to signal the outbreak of World War I, Nicholas II, though he could not know it, was destined to experience something more profound than a titular resemblance to one of antiquity's greatest generals. He would share his bloody fate as well.

The prospect of revolution in Russia had been bubbling just under the surface for longer than anyone could remember. The state had been characterised by tentative reform and an ever-swelling tide of extremist activism for several decades before it finally erupted like an Icelandic geyser in 1917. For a time though, it seemed there was a good chance the nation may go through a period of moderate transformation that would soothe its development into a modern and prosperous state. Such hopes were ultimately to be thwarted through the combined efforts of the reactionaries and progressives. Their interference from opposite ends of the political spectrum would tear Russia apart, but it was primarily the radicals who were responsible for scuppering such hopes. In two decades the extremists killed nearly 20,000 people, including the Tsar and his prime minister, and their bloody activism resulted in moderate reformers being pushed aside by increasingly hardline reactionaries.

In 1861 Alexander II had emancipated the serfs, ending the system of slavery that had kept Russia's peasantry in bondage to the landowning class for centuries. The result was something of a fudged compromise. The arrangement was too radical for the landed gentry while insufficiently revolutionary for the masses of urban labourers who constituted perhaps 85% of the population. Instead of spreading prosperity it merely increased privation. The Tsar continued with a programme of modest reforms in the wake of this great legislation, the establishment of zemstvos, local assemblies permitting a level of self-government following, for instance, in 1864. But such measures were wholly insufficient to quell the rising clamour that demanded significant change. The regime was effectively attempting to hold back a creaking and bursting dam by hammering up a few planks.

The growing number of activists were certainly unimpressed by Alexander's attempts at reform. In 1881 he was assassinated while travelling to the Winter Palace in St. Petersburg. Ignaty Grinevitsky, on a suicide mission, approached his carriage while holding a bomb and killed them both in a massive explosion.

The group behind the attack were a radical organisation dubbed the People's Will. The killers hoped to inspire a mass uprising, but their optimism was to prove groundless. The new Tsar, Alexander III, horrified at the crime, put an immediate halt to any further reform, effectively snuffed out the zemstvos, and instituted a raft of repressive measures which hoped to crush revolutionary activism for a generation. The severe authoritarianism of Alexander's regime drove the radicals underground but could never extinguish their zeal for modernisation. That determination was only strengthened when a devastating famine in 1891, swiftly followed by outbreaks of cholera and typhus, served as a reminder of the urgent necessity for change. A huge relief operation responded to the crisis with figures like Leo Tolstoy and Anton Chekhov throwing themselves into the fray. Such efforts though were akin to treating a severed artery with a sticking plaster. Perhaps half a million died, the regime was blamed, and the revolutionary movement gained considerable momentum.

As with events in France over a century before, much of the responsibility for the impending crisis lay with the landed gentry's resistance to reform. And their stubborn intransigence only worsened with the turn of the twentieth century. Change would certainly have come anyway, but the sluggish pace of state-sanctioned initiatives, swimming as they were against the tide of reactionary resistance, made it ever more likely that it would be driven by the extremists rather than those of more temperate inclination. Those moderate reformers were frequently drawn from the liberal gentry, guilt-ridden sons of ex-serf owners motivated by the need to salve their consciences. Many among that class were monarchists who hoped for a paternal aristocracy which cared for the welfare of the masses. Characteristic of this breed was Prince Lvov, a close friend of Leo Tolstoy. He lived as a peasant for a considerable period before transforming his farm into a profitable venture and getting involved in local politics.

The great Tolstoy himself though was the most significant of the breed. He too worked as a peasant, dressing in a tunic and the sort of boots favoured by the serfs to labour with them in his fields. He supported land reform and opposed private property, referring to it as the 'great sin', but at the end of the day he would return to his manor house. There he would don evening wear and be served the finest cuisine from silver trays by staff clad in smart uniforms and white gloves. Tolstoy mixed influences as varied as Proudhon, Kropotkin and Schopenhauer with a pious Christianity. His faith singled him out from the majority of the reformists, and his sincere belief in non-violent protest later shaped the campaigns of both Gandhi and Martin Luther King. But Russia was destined not to follow his example.

Count Witte, the great reforming minister of the 1890s, had aspirations that largely tallied with this liberal class. He recommended the transformation of

Russia into an industrialised economy that encouraged and rewarded ambition while protecting civil liberties. It was, he warned, what was needed to stave off revolution. Russia had begun making significant strides in this direction already. But the atmosphere of fear that took hold after the Tsar's assassination ultimately threw that process into reverse and allowed the reactionaries to steer events. Repression thus came to take precedence over progress.

Regardless, while the liberal intelligentsia romanticised the peasants they were frequently alarmed by the brutal reality and some, like Chekhov and Maxim Gorky, grew deeply cynical about the state of the rural Russian. Dostoyevsky commented that 'none of us really likes them as they actually are but only as each of us has imagined them'.[1] Such antipathy was entirely mutual. In 1837 Belinsky, noting the smouldering hatred for the aristocracy that informed much of the violence of peasant life, predicted that 'The liberated Russian nation will not head for the parliament but will run for the tavern to drink liquor, smash glasses and hang the nobility, whose only guilt is to shave their beards and wear a frock-coat instead of a peasant tunic'.[2]

The urban factory workers also tended to look down on the peasantry, and it was around, and within, their ranks that the more radical wing of revolutionary activism had been gathering. The class that would determine Russia's future were largely a strait-laced lot who avoided vodka or womanising and preferred tea instead. The typical extremist of the period came from a privileged background and was well educated but adopted a consciously scruffy look of glasses with long hair for men and short hair for women. They were as disdainful of the liberal democrats as they were the members of the ruling elite. But they worshipped Gorky, the darling of the left, whose empathy with the urban worker and antipathy to the peasantry mirrored their own. The industrial proletariat represented the future, after all, while the rural labourer was a symbol of Russia's antiquated past. It was a mindset, as Orlando Figes noted, that was strikingly similar to that of Christianity:

> 'Take, for example, their rejection of the existing order as sinful and corrupt, or their self-image as the righteous champions of the 'people's cause'; or indeed their almost mystical belief in the existence of absolute truth...If only, they thought, they could bring about the people's liberation, then their own original sin – that of being born into privilege – would be redeemed'.[3]

Such individuals tended to think in moral absolutes and condoned and even funded terrorism, a tendency that wrought a terrible cost. It is estimated that 17,000 lives were lost to extremist violence in the last twenty years of the Tsarist regime. Their idealism rested entirely on an ideological dogmatism that encouraged furious intolerance. For such committed campaigners there was no room for either uncertainty or apathy, and both characteristics were greeted with equal scorn. They were utterly convinced they held the key to the world's future and, as a consequence, they neatly divided society into the forces of 'progress' and 'reaction', allies or enemies of the people. Yet despite their lofty-sounding goals they were really more concerned with finding a higher meaning for their own lives than aiding the peasantry. In fact, they held the masses in contempt. They sought not to help them but to change them, to mould them in their own image – to impose their own values on them. Indeed, their attitudes were frequently just as patrician as those of the Tsarist elite. The reality of the revolution to come was that Russia would simply shift from one privileged caste to another; but the coming rulers, those who considered themselves the most virtuous of reformists, were to prove significantly more violent and intolerant than the aristocrats they would replace. There was no question that the peasants or urban multitudes would be allowed to act with any genuine autonomy; the radical intelligentsia would decide what was in their best interests. They were concerned with the teeming masses of Russia the way a shepherd is by his flock. They sought to control and direct them just the same, and if they met any resistance from the people then they would force them to be free.

Unsurprisingly, in this political climate, the Russian literature of the period was heavily dominated by themes of social engineering, and it frequently acted as a form of moral instruction. Such books teemed with revolutionary heroes who epitomised the characteristics of the New Man: virtuous, incorruptible and self-sacrificing. Published in tandem with such tediously worthy fare was the revolution's manifesto, *Young Russia,* penned by Zaichnevsky in 1862. It called for the violent seizure of power by an elite dictatorship who were entirely committed to the revolution. They demanded the nationalisation of land, the extermination of enemies, suppression of any political opposition and for all children to be taken into the care of the state. It could hardly have been plainer about its intentions towards the imperial party:

> 'We shall kill them in the squares; if the dirty swine ever dare to appear there; kill them in their houses; kill them in the narrow streets of the towns; kill them in the villages. Remember anyone who is not with us is our enemy, and every method may be used to exterminate our enemies'.[4]

Similar sentiments were expressed in the influential work of Sergei Nechayev, the violent collaborator of Bakunin, who poured out hate-filled rhetoric which was highly valued by Lenin. In his *Revolutionary Catechism* of 1869 he made it clear that the activist must let no compassion divert him from his single-minded commitment to the cause. As their 'cause' was in the best interests of the people, so they claimed, then no other considerations, not law, nor morality, nor squeamishness, should make them hesitate from furthering their agenda. Any means were thus justified in pursuit of their revolutionary goals. The true

Bible of such individuals though was, naturally, Marx's *Capital.* Passed by the censor in 1872 it became the first foreign language version of the study, and it sold at fifteen times the rate of the German original. Marx's writing was seized on so eagerly because it told the activists what they wanted to hear, but it appeared to be rigorous, serious and objective enough to confirm the certainty they already held in their cause. It became almost ubiquitous. One student liberal lamented that 'Nobody dares to raise a voice against Karl Marx these days without bringing down the wrath of his youthful admirers'.[5]

This then was the situation facing Nicholas II when he ascended to the throne in 1894, and his reign got off to an inauspicious start. In 1896, just a few days after his coronation, he threw a celebration which attracted half a million people. A rumour about free biscuits and beer prompted a stampede which killed 1,400 people. Nicholas was not personally responsible, but he continued with his itinerary and entertained the French ambassador at a garish ball even as the bodies were being carted away, a seemingly callous indifference that shocked the nation. He elicited, in many respects, comparisons with Louis XVI, though he lacked his French counterpart's intelligence. Nicholas was a decent man but a weak and incompetent king and one ill-equipped to cope with the violently turbulent period into which the nation was about to descend. He was the wrong man in the wrong place at the wrong time. But, despite his utter lack of suitability for the task thrust upon him, Nicholas was a control freak who had a habit of dismissing his most able ministers whenever he felt threatened by them. Such characteristics were hardly propitious at the best of times, and the period in which he ruled was far removed from that.

The need for significant change in Russia was even greater than it had been in France and, if Nicholas himself was not cruel or despotic, his regime certainly was. His secret police, the Okhrana, operated a surveillance state that could reach quite remarkable levels of violence, even if there was a far healthier subversive press under the Tsars than their successors. The radicals who supplanted it would significantly outstrip it in every way, but it should not be understated just how distasteful Tsarist Russia was in the late nineteenth century. It was also a violently anti-Semitic state which had a long history of pogroms against its Jewish population. The obsession this issue held in the authorities' minds is perhaps best illustrated by the publication of the *Protocols of the Elders of Zion* in St. Petersburg in 1902. This forgery, produced by the Tsarist police, claimed to prove the existence of a worldwide Jewish conspiracy aimed at global domination and the subjugation of the Christian nations. The tome was regrettably lapped up by significant numbers of credulous bigots only too eager to believe it. Sadly, its influence is still felt today.

As the twentieth century dawned the extremists had formed themselves into two distinct political parties. The Socialist-Revolutionaries largely favoured reform based on agrarian lines, while the Social-Democrats claimed to represent the urban proletariat. The latter party had quickly splintered into two factions which were moving further and further apart: the Bolsheviks and the Mensheviks. But it would not be long before they got to play an active role in the political life of the nation. Conflicting interests in Manchuria and Korea and an incompetent and arrogant stewardship of the requisite diplomacy, much of it the culpability of the Tsar himself, resulted in a calamitous war with Japan in 1904. Russia swaggered into the conflict with an entitled air of superiority that was speedily checked by a series of devastating defeats. The regime had hoped that a show of strength and some patriotic celebrations would quell the growing calls for reform, but in the wake of their reverses such requests escalated sharply.

On Sunday 9 January 1905 Father Georgi Gapon led a huge crowd to the Winter Palace. They aimed to present the Tsar with a petition which called for the introduction of social policies to aid the suffering populace. Gapon naively believed that an appeal to the 'Father Tsar' would quickly result in reforms which would benefit the working poor, and 150,000 similarly inclined individuals hopefully joined his vast procession. But their faith turned to disbelief when the soldiers guarding the palace unleashed volleys of gunfire at the marchers. As the panicked hordes began to flee they were beset by Cossack cavalry charges which felled them by the dozen. Many children were among the casualties with perhaps 200 killed and a further 800 wounded. The snow on Nevsky Prospekt was dyed red by the slaughter on what came to be known as Bloody Sunday.

When the news broke of the massacre that had taken place that day the nation exploded in revolution. Strikes spread like wildfire and peasant revolts erupted all over the countryside. Large numbers of aristocratic estates were looted and burned. Soviets, or councils, were established primarily to direct strikes before swiftly taking the form of local workers' governments. Dissent soon spread to the military, and on 14 June it struck the Black Sea Fleet. A mutiny on the battleship *Potemkin* ended with the crew murdering their officers and running up the red flag. When the vessel was greeted by a huge, delirious mob in Odessa, Tsarist forces were ordered to fire on the multitude killing 2,000 and wounding 3,000 more. This action sparked an even greater wave of civil unrest and when, after a crushing defeat at Tsushima, the regime was forced to surrender to Japan, the first time an Asian power had defeated a European one since the time of Genghis Khan, the nation reached absolute crisis point.

Count Witte, who was brought out of retirement by Nicholas, informed the Tsar that urgent measures were necessary to stave off the threat of revolution and the Emperor was eventually compelled to announce a new manifesto and programme of social reforms. The resultant document, issued on 17 October, would transform him into a form of constitutional monarch by establishing a legislative Duma elected on a democratic franchise. In the wake of the legislation the crisis gradually began to abate, and the regime restored control by arresting and executing significant numbers of known activists. Father Gapon had fled to Geneva, where he briefly befriended Lenin. But in 1906, after a shambolic trial, the Socialist-Revolutionaries decided he was a police spy and hanged him. Some already foresaw what lay ahead and Nicholas Berdyaev warned what would become of the Marxist 'heresy'. Communists 'had projected onto fallible human beings godlike powers that would enable them to overcome their human fate. In doing so...the Communists had created demons they would not be able to control.'[6] He was entirely correct, but revolutionary arrogance would brush aside such concerns.

Despite the Tsar's measures, writers like Boris Pasternak and Maxim Gorky were now even more confident that a full revolution would not be long in coming. Yet Nicholas had no intention of surrendering his authority and the Duma, when called, was effectively handcuffed. Petr Stolypin instituted an ambitiously reformist programme, but his efforts were blocked by the established order, ever more determined to impose repressive measures after the shock of 1905, and he was politically isolated. On 1 September 1911, at the Kiev Opera, Stolypin was shot during the interval. He died a few days later. Perhaps Russia's best chance of peaceful reform died with him. Dissatisfaction continued to spread through the army, which practised a form of military serfdom on the troops. It would prove the crucial factor that would finally break the monarchy.

The Crown was further undermined by the population's distaste for the Queen. The Empress Alexandra was roundly disliked for her aloofness from the Russian people. As Orlando Figes said of the deeply unpopular Tsarina 'Alexandra liked to compare herself with Catherine the Great. But in fact, her role was much more reminiscent of Marie Antoinette'[7], a portrait of whom hung over her writing desk in the Alexander Palace. Alexandra was addicted to mysticism and the supernatural and, as such, was particularly prone to the appeals of a charismatic charlatan like the 'mad monk' Rasputin, the mystic who could apparently alleviate the haemophilia of the Tsarevich Alexei, the heir to the throne. The fact that she was a mother, consumed with anxiety over the health of her only son, significantly magnified her innate susceptibility to such an enigmatic con-man. She became persuaded that Rasputin had the power to save the boy's life and his position at court grew increasingly unassailable. But the public were less impressed and the Empress was widely dismissed as a slut. Rumours spread that the Tsarina and her lady-in-waiting, Anna Vyrubova, engaged in wild orgies with Rasputin, as well as each-other. History was already beginning to repeat itself, a trend that was destined to continue.

As the First World War approached then the situation was decidedly precarious. It was soon to worsen significantly. The Tsar himself elected to take charge of the war effort, but it was a disaster which reflected poorly on him and served to further revolutionise the troops. It hardly helped matters that he left his German wife in charge of the administration while directing affairs at the front. Her heritage was only ever going to encourage rumours about traitorous collusions with the enemy, even if the reality was that, while German-born, she had spent most of her life in England and spoke with a cut-glass home-counties accent. Yet stories continued to spread about Alexandra and there were calls for her to be locked up in a convent. Lurid tales of the greed, licentiousness and duplicity of the ruling elites, ever seen as colluding in the oppression of the people, are predictably seized on by revolutionaries of all stripes. As usual, they were naught but lies, yet reality has little effect on such speculations.

It was widely believed that Rasputin was pulling her strings while plotting a German victory and the subjugation of the people. His murder on 16 December 1916 by the transvestite Prince Felix Yusupov happened far too late to have any real effect on the looming disaster and, in reality, would have made little difference anyway. The rising tide of revolutionary activism was now irresistible. With the military situation worsening, food shortages taking hold and faith in the regime having dissipated, the dam was about to break. Striking workers took to the streets in February 1917 demanding 'Peace, Bread and Land!' The bread shortages that hit Petrograd (St. Petersburg had been renamed during the war as its original appellation was considered too German) were largely blamed on 'speculators' and 'capitalists'. Perhaps the people vocalising such opinions hadn't noticed that there was a war going on.

On 23 February 1917*, International Women's Day, a protest took to the streets to call for equality. Large numbers of workers downed tools to join in the demonstration. Emboldened by the authorities' supine response, more and more people joined the throng over the following days to call for revolution. On 26 February, by which time 200,000 swarmed through the capital's streets, soldiers drafted in to deal with the strikes fired on the crowds. The incident stiffened the resolve of the revolutionaries and shocked the troops who increasingly sided with the protestors. Mutinies began to break out in numerous locations and the revolution had its 'Bastille' moment when the mob stormed the Peter and Paul Fortress, the symbol of Tsarist despotism, on 28 February. The parallels were perhaps closer than they would have liked; the dreaded dungeon contained just nineteen prisoners, all soldiers who had been incarcerated the previous day. By now though the revolution was irresistible; a meeting at the Tauride Palace on 27 February declared itself a Committee of Worker's Soviets and it quickly won the support of the military. Nicholas II, his

* In 1917 Russia still used the Julian calendar which ran 13 days behind the Gregorian version which the revolutionaries adopted on 31 January 1918.

authority having eroded and bereft of any remaining support, was forced to abdicate on 2 March 1917.

While the military had pledged itself to the Soviet, it was the Duma, who met in the opposite wing of the Tauride Palace to the workers' council, which formed the Provisional Government that hoped to shepherd Russia through the crisis. The Soviet agreed to support it as long as its demands were met, though the army would take its orders only from the workers' delegates. The new legislative body announced it would run affairs only until elections could be held and a Constituent Assembly established. They could hardly come soon enough. The body was unused to assuming such awesome responsibilities and its commitment to maintaining the war effort only added to the formidable nature of the task it faced. Attempting to administrate the world's largest nation state, during a period of political turmoil and crippling shortages while waging the single greatest conflict in history, was always going to present the new authorities with challenges that would be essentially insurmountable. Two prime ministers presided over the Provisional Government during its eight months of life, yet neither Georgi Lvov, who assumed the role in March, nor Alexander Kerensky, who replaced him in July, could truly rally the support of the people. As with all revolutions while the populace optimistically expected things to get better, they inevitably got worse. Disillusionment with the new regime swiftly set in and the Provisional Government had to withstand violent upheavals from the left in July and then the right, under General Kornilov, in August. It survived the traumatic summer but had been forced to arm the left-wing radicals to help it resist the Kornilov Revolt and they, with a characteristic distaste for democracy, became determined to seize power before the impending elections took place.

The most violently dangerous of such groups were the Bolsheviks, the faction led by Lenin who had assumed total control after returning from exile in April. By the autumn the Provisional Government could rally barely any support from the apathetic population and on 25 October a second Revolution took place, this one even more seismic than the first. The Bolsheviks overthrew the liberal regime in an armed coup and set about establishing the world's first socialist state. Such was their determination not to relinquish control that they would go on to commit atrocities which remain almost incomprehensible to this day. While the Provisional Government had granted sweeping press freedoms, embraced the concept of democracy, arranged elections, hoped to strengthen the economy and been restrained in its use of force against its opponents, the new administration veered dramatically in the opposite direction. Any sort of tolerance, liberty or democracy were anathema to the Bolsheviks from the outset. Their reliance on severe oppression, stifling limitations on freedoms, suffocating censorship, control of the press, the termination of any democratic process and arbitrary and unrestrained violence would be immediate. That unique blend of indignant certainty practised by the left, rivalled by only the most fanatic of religious fundamentalists, was about to achieve its most unrestrained expression yet and was then to be unleashed on the Russian people.

Lenin

Vladimir Ilich Ulyanov had been born on 10 April 1870 in the provincial town of Simbirsk. In 1924 the obscure little urban sprawl, which straddles the Volga River, was rechristened Ulyanovsk in his honour, a name it still bears today. Vladimir had both Jewish and Mongolian ancestry and his father, Ilya Nikolaevich Ulyanov, held a respected and lucrative profession as inspector of the province's schools. His mother, Maria Alexandrovna Ulyanova, had inherited a share in a sizeable estate at Kokushkino, near Kazan, after Vladimir's maternal grandfather had taken up with Yekaterina von Essen – *née* Grosschopf. She was his own late wife's sister, as well as a widow with a substantial legacy. By taking on the estate they became substantial landowners with responsibility for forty peasant families. Young Vladimir's grandfather passed away just two months after he was born and Maria, with her sisters, became joint shareholders of the property. As a state councillor, Ilya was entitled to be addressed as 'His Excellency', a fitting title for the family's new lifestyle. Their position was such that young Vladimir would automatically attain noble status on reaching maturity. The family also employed a cook, a nanny and numerous labourers to look after the estate. Vladimir's childhood summers were spent playing happily at the estate in Kokushkino. His parents sipped lemonade on the manicured lawns as the peasants toiled and sweated in the fields. Such was the background of the great revolutionary.

The family had another home in the prosperous part of Simbirsk where they retained a full bevy of servants. It was a politically progressive household with both parents steeped in education and little Vladimir, who showed promise from an early age, was encouraged to pursue academia. He won admission to the prestigious Classical Gimnazia in Simbirsk where, in a bizarre historical coincidence, his headmaster was Fedor Kerensky, father of Alexander, the future prime minister of the Provisional Government who would briefly become his political rival. He was schooled in the Classics though his own preferences were already heading in a different direction. As a boy his favourite book was *Uncle Tom's Cabin* by Harriet Beecher Stowe, and he played with toy soldiers clad in the blue uniforms of Lincoln's Union army which fought to free the slaves.

His childhood idyll was fated not to last though. In 1886 his father died quite suddenly, and his elder brother, Alexander, fell in with radicals at the university in St. Petersburg. They were all the sons of squires and Ulyanov became involved in a plot to assassinate Alexander III, promising to make the group's bombs. But the scheme unravelled in farce and all the conspirators were swiftly apprehended. Alexander freely confessed his guilt, and on 8 May 1887 was hanged. Social ostracism followed as the surviving Ulyanovs were shunned by the society that had formed their whole life up to that point. At the age of sixteen a piece of steel entered young Vladimir's soul.

He had already been leaning towards radicalism, but his brother's demise cemented the young man on an extremist path. He quickly became immersed in the writing of Nikolai Chernyshevsky and in particular his dismal novel *What Is To Be Done?* Young Vladimir was so taken with this turgid tome that he read it five times in one summer, a feat which prompted Martin Amis to remark that 'To read this book once in five summers would defeat most of us'.[8] Chernyshevsky, who had been in frequent communication with Karl Marx, supported democracy, industrialisation and women's rights. He virulently opposed Russia's autocratic system of government, favoured agrarian socialism and hoped for the imposition of a classless society. *What Is To Be Done?* set out the template for the ideal commune where everything was to be shared, including lovers. Communities inspired by his writing subsequently sprang up and idealists flocked to them. But the enclaves soon descended into bitter rows over property and sexual partners. Suitably disillusioned by inconvenient realities, the chastised students quickly returned home, yet its influence lingered. The book's idealised group of activists, a tediously dedicated and loyal band of brothers, were under the stewardship of Rakhmetev, an ascetic and single-minded paragon of revolutionary piety who epitomised the 'hardness' considered a prerequisite of the committed militant. His portrayal was that of a rugged extremist who put his activism before all considerations. He was insensitive to the suffering of others and prepared to spill blood for political ends. Rakhmetev's influence on the puritanical Ulyanov is apparent in any appraisal of his later deeds. Vladimir became committed to the seizure of the state by a revolutionary vanguard while holding liberals and democrats in contempt. Chernyshevsky had shaped the fledging radical's stance long before he had ever read Marx.

Vladimir, who excelled at school and breezed through his exams, entered Kazan University. He rapidly became embroiled in radical student protest and, just as speedily, was expelled. It hardly mattered, he had already found his calling. The most significant activist of the period was Georgi Plekhanov. He had formed the Emancipation of Labour Group with Lev Deich, Pavel Axelrod and Vera Zasulich in 1883, and still ran the organisation from exile in Switzerland. A movement of agrarian socialism had taken firm root in the revolutionary culture of Russia. But Plekhanov argued that capitalism had already arrived there, and any activism had to acknowledge and embrace the bourgeois stage of development. They should look then, not to the peasantry, but to the urban working class. Naturally a bitter rift developed between agrarian and urban revolutionary organisations with both sides publishing scathing denunciations of the other. Vladimir, firmly in the urban camp, quickly joined a group in Kazan run by N. E. Fedoseev who was in touch with Plekhanov's party in exile. He also read widely and devoured books by the likes of David Ricardo, Charles Darwin, Friedrich Engels and, naturally, Karl Marx, who he quickly became obsessed by. His political outlook was increasingly informed by hatred and he came to detest not just the Romanovs but the aristocracy, the middle classes, the urban merchants and the landed gentry. As Service also put it at this point in his development 'although his revolutionary ideas were as yet unformed, the revolutionary commitment was already firm'.[9] Vladimir, like so many, was set in his beliefs before he even knew what his beliefs were. His intellectual outlook would be shaped to fit the mould of adolescent indignation that had preceded it and which would inform it for the remainder of his life.

In 1889 the family decamped 300 miles south to a village in the region of Samara. They had barely any contact with the large peasant community. Vladimir continued to educate himself but, as he studiously avoided the labouring classes of Russia, his revolutionary ideas were purely theoretical. When they moved to the town of Samara itself the young man was thrilled to be removed from the ignorant peasantry and to have access to a library and other 'educated' radicals. He joined a discussion group led by Alexei Sklyarenko, another dedicated socialist with romantic notions of terrorism, before gaining a certificate of qualification from St. Petersburg University in 1891. But, while qualified as a lawyer, his flirtation with the profession would be even briefer than that of Robespierre. That same year a famine hit which was widely blamed on the Tsar, but the young 'idealist' refused to help, coldly believing that such events were inevitable and would hasten the arrival of socialism. He even argued that aid should be denied to the starving peasantry as it would expedite the revolutionary crisis, suggesting that the famine thus 'played the role of a progressive factor'.[10] He also not only insisted that the peasantry pay his family their full due on land rents, deriving a substantial income even as they began to die of starvation around him, but sued his impoverished rural neighbours for damaging his family's estate. He indulged himself in such coldly acquisitive practices even while continuing to denounce 'gentry capitalism'.

Vladimir's compatriots had already noticed how he 'revelled in his rejection of concepts such as conscience, compassion and charity'.[11] That was how it appeared at any rate. In reality, as far as Ulyanov was concerned, anything that brought about the overthrow of the corrupt system was, by definition, a moral act. His growing adherence to Marxism meant he increasingly regarded historical progression and the triumph of socialism as inevitable. As such, the only considerations that motivated him were ones that would hasten the birth of the communist state. Such was his faith in his mission that all horrors could be justified in its creation.

In 1893, while his family headed for Moscow, the young radical relocated to St. Petersburg. He took a room in Yamskaya Street, near the library, and continued to study industrial and economic development. He had only ever flirted with a legal career, while continuing to be supported by his mother, and he avoided the capital's factory workers as assiduously as he had recoiled from the peasantry. Despite his lack of practical experience he began to churn out articles of his own, starting with 'New Economic Trends in Peasant Life'. Yet he also clashed with the likes of V.P. Vorontsov who not only refused to call for violent revolution but campaigned for economic and social betterment within the existing system. The chief exponent of this theory was Eduard Bernstein who argued that Russian peasant agriculture was too backward for capitalism to thrive there. Under his influence theorists like Kuskara and Pëtr Struve claimed that urban capitalism was not impoverishing the workers. They suggested that it was thus possible to reconcile it with socialism within a system of parliamentary democracy. Such heresy appalled the Marxists like Plekhanov who despised the concept of evolutionary, as opposed to revolutionary, socialism. Vladimir damned their lack of extremist ardour at a meeting in February 1894. Nadezhda Konstantin Krupskaya, another attendee, was struck by the intensity of his commitment. The pious couple would soon be united, perhaps more for their shared passion for politics than any genuinely romantic feelings.

It was in this period that Ulyanov came to admire the borderline psychotic Sergei Nechayev, particularly his wish to liquidate the whole Romanov line. Indeed, the intensity of Lenin's extremism was beginning to alarm some of his peers. Pëtr Struve and Mikhail Tugan-Baranovski were already expressing concern about Vladimir's inflexible view of Marxism as an unquestionable creed. They called him a secular 'believer' who refused to accept that *Capital* was less than perfect. Yet his combination of dogmatic rigidity, simmering hatred and proclivity for terrorism were only to worsen as the years progressed. He wrote a scathing attack on Struve and declared, contrary to his rival's prognosis, that Russia had entered the bourgeois-capitalist stage decades before. But, as others had noted, Vladimir had never travelled and had no real conception of what a modern industrial society like Britain or Germany was truly like. If he had, he would have realised just how backwards Russia really was.

It was purely coincidental that shortly afterwards he was given a passport and departed for Switzerland where he met Georgi Plekhanov in Geneva. Accustomed to living in material comfort, and taken by the beauty of the locale,

Vladimir contemplated renting an Alpine lodge for a spell but rejected the idea when discovering how much he would have to pay a maid. His concern for the working classes never extended to giving them a decent wage. On his return Vladimir continued to broaden his Marxist circle meeting Yuli Martov and Alexander Kremer. Through the latter he became active in the formation of the Union of Struggle for the Emancipation of the Working Class, getting involved with striking workers and direct proletarian action for the first time. But the rise of the Russian labour movement was the catalyst for the Okhrana to take an increased interest in activism and in December 1895 Vladimir was arrested and ultimately sentenced to Siberian exile.

He had become engaged to Nadezhda Krupskaya, or Nadya, as he came to call her, and his new fiancé was permitted to accompany him on his exile. Vladimir rented a spacious house and employed a fifteen year old serving girl while remaining free to write or stroll in the woods and gather wild mushrooms. He enjoyed a well-stocked library in captivity which allowed him to finish *The Development of Capitalism in Russia,* a work which referenced over 500 books and articles. It argued that Russia's economy was more than advanced enough to allow a full Marxist revolution to occur, suggesting that a socialist revolution could swiftly follow a bourgeois revolt against the Romanovs. In the massive work he also identified, for the first time, a wealthier strain of bourgeois peasants who he labelled *kulaki*: kulaks. He published further works, including a withering repudiation of Eduard Bernstein's theory that peaceful reform was preferable to revolution. Bernstein had argued that socialism was doomed to failure if it depended on capitalism bringing the economy to ruin first, and he was repulsed by the idea of violent revolution. But, for daring to challenge orthodox socialism, he was denounced as a 'revisionist'. Lenin transformed the tag into a label of abuse that would be employed by his direct followers, as well as those of Mao, to justify persecution and horror at unimaginable levels.

In the meantime he kept working, and Nadya secured a commission for him to translate Sidney and Beatrice Webb's work on English trade unionism. It was while serving his sentence that, on 10 July 1898, he agreed to marry her. Rumours that it was a marriage of political convenience have dogged the relationship ever since. Certainly there was little evidence of genuine warmth, from Vladimir at least. While passionate about ideology and his socialist heroes like Marx, he never showed any indication of being able to love anything else. Their relationship may be best summed up by their sleeping arrangements in St. Petersburg during the revolutionary turmoil of 1917. The pair slept in separate beds with a note pinned to the wall between them declaring 'Proletarians of all Countries Unite!' It was the perfect symbol of their priorities; political activism was all, human relationships and the enjoyment of life's pleasures were incidental. Nadya later affirmed that they rejected 'bourgeois' concepts of love as the focus of true Marxists was on working collaboratively for the revolution. Such a pious arrangement also allowed them to be self-righteous about the fact that they were rejecting religion, tradition and the submissive husband-wife relationship that was the norm in Russian society.

In 1900 Vladimir was released and, feeling himself under too much surveillance, opted for the life of an exile. His travels, as he liaised with other socialist groups, took him across much of the continent over the next two decades: Zurich, Munich, London, Paris, Sweden, Finland, Krakow and Bern. He had two main aims: the establishment of a political party and a newspaper. In 1901 Victor Chernov had founded the Party of Socialist-Revolutionaries (SR), an agrarian socialist organisation, but Vladimir's intention was to resurrect the rival Russian Social Democratic Labour Party (SD) which had held its first Congress in Minsk in 1898. On that occasion, a mere nine Marxists, including Pëtr Struve, had attended the meeting. They were promptly arrested afterwards, yet Ulyanov, despite the schism that had opened up between Struve and his faction, was determined to revive the movement. That pattern of enmities continued when Vladimir had a bitter falling out with Plekhanov as both sought to control the organisation's periodical. Nevertheless, the paper, called *Iskra* ('The Spark'), initially a monthly journal, rolled off the presses in December 1900. On its masthead it declared, with chilling accuracy, 'Out Of This Spark Will Come a Conflagration'.

In a blizzard of activity, between April 1901 and February 1902, the young militant also penned a substantial pamphlet that clarified his political manifesto. He named it *What Is To Be Done?* swiping the title of the Chernyshevsky book he had revered as a youth, and published it under the pseudonym 'Lenin'. The name stuck. He recommended a military style of organisation where the rank and file of the party obeyed the orders of the high command. In essence, Lenin, who never shed the patrician characteristics he developed as a young man, argued that the new socialist state could not operate without an *elite,* precisely that aspect of existing society he wanted to destroy. It was written by a man on a moral crusade. He was determined to slay the ogre of autocracy and repeatedly proclaimed the necessity of violent revolt while talking of 'rallying the troops'. In fact he advocated mass terror, urging that all Russian antagonisms 'be combined into a single gigantic torrent'.[12] But he criticised targeted assassinations, a tactic he deplored for its timidity. Lenin presented his case with the true faith of one convinced in the historical inevitability of his cause. But, like Marx, he reserved the bulk of his argument to pour bile on his philosophical peers. Lenin dismissed trade unionism as *bourgeois politics* which aims only at improving the workers' rights and material conditions rather than their revolutionary consciousness. The majority of the rambling and repetitive essay was a repudiation of 'philistines' like Bernstein and his followers. Lenin was adamant that he was utterly correct in his drive to violently overthrow autocracy and impose socialism, while Bernstein was simply wrong to agitate for a Burkean programme of political and economic reform. Yet, in reality, Bernstein's course resulted in spectacular progress for the working man, while Lenin's led to oppression, slavery, censorship, famine and murder on a colossal scale.

The Second Congress of the Social Democratic Party finally opened in Brussels on 17 July 1903. However, following prompt interference from the Belgian police, it relocated to London where it re-opened on 29 July. Despite its title it was effectively the first congress of an entirely new organisation. It is wholly typical that a meeting of those most committed to establishing a socialist utopia, one centred on the fraternity of a brotherhood of man, dissolved into acrimonious rancour before the delegates had even assumed their seats. The *Iskra* board had already succeeded in driving out the Jewish Bund before they spectacularly fell out with each other. Lenin wanted party membership restricted to active participants while Yuli Martov felt it should be open to workers who were sympathetic to their manifesto. The groups nearly came to blows over the issue and Lenin's faction, noted for, and proud of, their aggression and surliness, were dubbed the 'hards' - an epithet they wore as a badge of pride. Lenin's belligerence, unpleasantness and combativeness shocked many delegates even while thrilling others. He pushed for an elite central council and, winning the debate, rechristened his faction the Majoritarians (bol'sheviki) and Martov's clique the Minoritarians (men'sheviki). Plekhanov said privately that he detected something of the Robespierre about Lenin and, after some prevarication, slid over to Martov's bloc. The party had, in characteristic left-wing fashion, become bitterly and irreconcilably divided at its very first congress. The rift that had opened between Bolsheviks and Mensheviks would only widen as the years passed.

In May 1904 Lenin published *One Step Forward, Two Steps Back*, a robust, and deeply hypocritical, justification of his actions. He castigated his rivals and denounced the Mensheviks as 'traitors'. Ideologically the two camps were becoming ever more polarised. The Mensheviks were increasingly uneasy with Bolshevik calls for a violent rising and their use of armed robbery to fill their revolutionary coffers. The Bolsheviks perceived the Mensheviks' preference for democratic process, and their willingness to consider a settlement with the liberal bourgeoisie, as the most craven surrender to the established order. The Bolshevik party would, in contrast, submit to one will – Lenin's will. His intolerance to any deviation continued to reach new heights of fanaticism. Service refers to Lenin's 'unshakeable belief in the righteousness of his cause...He 'knew' he was correct and he would not back down in the face of criticism'.[13] He was a dictator in his personal life too and would explode in fury if contradicted. Obsessed with order, he lined up his pencils in perfectly formed rows while the other members of his household, terrified of disturbing him and incurring his wrath, crept around on tiptoes. His life was one of battles continually waged against any 'heretics' whose ideas failed to marry with his own. In 1915, in a letter to Inessa Armand, the French activist with whom he had a fling, he made these traits clear:

> 'This, then, is my destiny. One fighting campaign after another – against political imbecilities, vulgarities, opportunism etc. This has been going on since 1893. And this is the reason for the hatred shown by the philistines. Ah well, I still wouldn't swap this destiny for 'peace' with the philistines'.[14]

Figes noted how his single-mindedness resulted in him being consumed by a lust for power. 'Lenin was driven by an absolute faith in his historical destiny. He did not doubt for a moment, as he had once put it, that he was the man who was to wield the 'conductor's baton' in the party.'[15] His political ideology grew to be all-consuming. It turned into an obsession that overwhelmed all other considerations. His existence was Spartan, and he expressed no real interest in beauty, love or culture. He admitted he did not want to listen to Beethoven as it might make him want to pat people on the head instead of beat them. He was interested in culture and literature purely for their social and political utility. He did not smoke, hardly drank, and, as stated, his relationship with Nadya was more one of party leader and secretary than tender lovers. While he enjoyed a brief passion with Armand, he terminated the affair when he realised it was distracting him from his political purpose, his 'destiny', as he melodramatically put it.

Even as the Revolution of 1905 broke out Lenin refused to waver in his obsession with Menshevism. His priority, while his associates planned a third party Congress intending to bring the factions back together, was for the Bolsheviks to retain complete independence from their political rivals. His venom for the 'monstrous' Mensheviks remains quite shocking, especially considering the backdrop of war and revolution which might, one would think, have assumed priority. Yet he was more preoccupied with smashing the Mensheviks than the Romanovs. Lenin, having set up his own paper, *Vperëd* ('Forward'), now seethed with rage at all those involved with *Iskra*. In the event, when the Congress was called in London that spring, Plekhanov, Martov and the other leading Mensheviks, showing themselves to be every bit as petty as Lenin, refused to attend. Having wanted a Bolshevik Congress, Lenin got exactly what he desired. He mocked the Menshevik belief in a middle class revolution that protected civil rights, declaring their rivals had prostituted their Marxist principles. Lenin, with pseudo-religious zeal, regarded Menshevism as a 'heresy'. He praised socialist terrorism, as well as the Jacobins of the 1790s, and exhorted his colleagues to follow their example. This cry for 'mass terror', largely endorsed by his fellow Bolsheviks, fell on fertile soil. But while the Bolsheviks insisted on the necessity of a violent working class rising, mass terror and a dictatorship of the proletariat, the working classes were notable by their complete exclusion from the proceedings. It made little difference to the intensity of the feud. The warring factions were now effectively the Gironde and the Montagnards of revolutionary France, and the Mensheviks would pay the price for failing to heed the warnings of history.

Unlike a number of activists who had raced to Russia as soon as revolution ignited there in 1905, Lenin did not dare venture east until the Tsar issued his Manifesto in October. He hoped to stir up proletarian violence on his arrival and, like Marx, decried the Commune of 1871 for insufficient ruthlessness. Lenin was determined not to make the same mistake. He wrote to the Bolshevik Combat Committee to wail that 'I see with horror, for God's sake with real horror, that there has been talk about bombs *for more than a year* and yet not a single bomb has been made'.[16] He also recommended that workers arm themselves with kettles filled with boiling water, paving slabs and acid to hurl at police from the rooftops. But when the imperial throne reasserted its authority, Lenin quickly fled to Finland and then Paris. While there, not satisfied with his ongoing feud with the Mensheviks, he clashed bitterly with his chief rival for leadership of the Bolsheviks, Alexander Bogdanov. The loathing seemed entirely mutual. Lenin rallied a clique around himself and denounced Bogdanov, wrapping his vendetta in a cloak of ideological purity. He even produced a book, *Materialism and Empiriocriticism*, purely as a tool to use in his assault.

The conference organised by Bolsheviks in Prague was attended by only eighteen delegates, the majority of SDs heading for the rival Menshevik congress in Vienna. Among the most prominent of Lenin's acolytes in that period were Grigori Zinoviev, Nikolai Bukharin, Anatoli Lunacharski and Sergo Ordzhonikidze, the latter of whom was a ruthless, hard-line, explosive tempered and heavy drinking Georgian who particularly despised the compromising timidity of the Mensheviks. Lenin had, by this stage, become incredibly set in his mode of thought. He was an admirer of Hegel, Charles Darwin and Karl Kautsky, all thinkers with relatively rigid, pre-determined ideological frameworks, and he also approved of Machiavelli's justification of brutality in government. Yet, while he admired such scribes, he stuck to Marx and Engels with fanatical intensity. Later writers who introduced more nuance into social theory and the study of human nature and politics, like Nietzsche, Freud, Carlyle, Michels, Le Bon, Kierkegaard and Weber, were all dismissed. Kautsky, the German theoretician, was not long for Lenin's pantheon of heroes either. When WWI broke out, like most European socialists, he threw his support behind his nation. As far as Lenin was concerned, this was nothing more than an endorsement of militarism and imperialism. Kautsky had to be denounced.

Lenin, of course, ardently hoped for Russia's defeat and the subsequent collapse of the Romanov regime. He cheered the outbreak of the conflict, clapping his hands in delight at what he hoped would hasten the onset of European socialism. At the time Lenin lived in comfort and, as was his usual wont, all his needs were attended to by a maid on a meagre salary. From his safe little enclave in Switzerland he luxuriated in the chaos while millions of unfortunates were consumed by mud and slaughter. Yet despite believing in the inevitability of socialism, and the hope that global war might precipitate it, Lenin, along with the rest of the revolutionary class, was caught completely off guard when it happened. Shliapnikov, the leading Bolshevik in Petrograd, even at the height of the disturbances, was utterly dismissive, sneering 'What revolution? Give the workers a pound of bread and the movement will peter out'.[17] Lenin had argued in *What is to be Done?* that spontaneous revolutions could not occur without instruction from the intelligentsia. But his belief was revealed as a hollow theory. Revolution happened in Russia while all the revolutionaries were absent, in their comfortable, self-imposed exiles. This did not, quite naturally, put even the slightest dent in Lenin's political certainty.

This time, unlike in 1905, Lenin was determined not to wait. A deal was struck with the Germans who, hoping the Bolsheviks would undermine Russia's war effort, provided a secure train to ferry the revolutionaries, including Lenin and the likes of Karl Radek and Grigori Zinoviev, directly to Petrograd. On the journey Lenin learned that the Bolshevik Central Committee, led by Lev Kamenev and Joseph Stalin, had elected on supporting the Provisional Government, a decision which infuriated him. The party arrived at the Finland station shortly before midnight on 3 April 1917 where a sizeable delegation had been rounded up to meet them as a band played 'The Marseillaise'. Lenin roundly discouraged support for the Provisional Government and called on the throng to join him in bringing about the collapse of world capitalism. On the train he had drawn up a ten point manifesto called the *April Theses*. The document abandoned his notion for a bourgeois-democratic phase and called for an immediate socialist revolution. In the turmoil and uncertainty of revolutionary Russia it was Lenin's cast-iron conviction and determination that allowed him to seize the initiative, take full control of the Bolshevik movement, and aim it in the direction he alone desired. In reality, up to that point his position at the head of the party had been shaky, tenuous and frequently challenged; from that spring though it became virtually unassailable.

On 4 April Lenin went to the Tauride Palace, the grand building that previously housed the State Duma but was now home to the Provisional Government and the Petrograd Soviet. Other large parties had been permitted to congregate there and Lenin took the opportunity to unveil his April Theses to a delegation of Bolsheviks. He called for rule by the Soviets, the nationalisation of large scale industries and banks, the government seizure of all land and an end to the war.

Lenin, who believed that only a socialist administration could achieve these ends, saw his opportunity to seize the moment. He campaigned relentlessly, driving his message home and scorning any suggestion of compromise or co-operation with Mensheviks, Socialist-Revolutionaries or the Provisional Government. He was adamant on the need for a violent seizure of power to usher in a Marxist state, determined to push through the revolution at any cost. Robert Conquest described the process with memorable directness: 'In effect, Lenin saw that history was not behaving in accordance with Marxist theory, so he decided to force it to do so by subjective effort, like some phrenologist finding one of his subjects lacking the right bumps and producing them by clouting him on the head.'[18]

Lenin aimed to win the political backing of workers, peasants, sailors and soldiers and employed the time-worn divisive tactic of blaming bankers, industrialists and agricultural landlords for all Russia's woes. The rich, he declared, were 'parasites' who preyed on the masses. But what Lenin was really doing was denouncing any form of aspiration or deviation from his own political line. Such traits were to be brutally snuffed out. The hyperbolic rhetoric of the left, focused on blame, cocooned in hate, is indistinguishable from those who blame society's ills on immigrants or Jews, a fact of which they are blithely oblivious. It also neatly divided society into 'evil' bourgeoisie and 'virtuous' proletariat though such conclusions had no basis in fact at all.

Despite his oratorical posturing, Lenin disliked any proletariat activism not directed by the party. Yet the Bolsheviks' repeated calls of 'All power to the Soviets!' were finding more and more sympathetic ears among the workers. Such populist rallying cries were to prove more enticing and seductive to many than the cautious pragmatism expressed by any rival parties. While those of a measured disposition supported other groups, individuals of a more firey inclination increasingly turned to the Bolsheviks. Not only was their support growing, but it was comprised primarily of the sort of militant mob who would help to enforce their singularly violent vision. The continuation of the war also meant that more and more of the military were turning away from the Provisional Government and paying greater attention to Lenin whose party was alone in opposing the conflict. The radical sailors at the naval base on Kronstadt Island were particularly won over by his rhetoric. Lenin claimed that 'we, as an ideal, are against any coercion of people'.[19] He swore that he was about to create a society without oppression or exploitation. It would be a nation where the machinery of the state, designed to protect the interests of the ruling classes, would no longer be required. Such was his belief at any rate. But he could not have been more wrong. The reality would prove just as punitive towards the proletariat as it would against the elites, yet the appeal of his message was winning more and more converts. Yakov Sverdlov and Felix Dzerzhinsky rose in prominence in the ranks of Bolshevism while Kamenev,

Zinoviev and Stalin were proving themselves indispensable. The most significant new recruit though was from the ranks of the Mensheviks, the one who had frequently proven the most damaging thorn in the side of Bolshevism: Leon Trotsky.

He had been born Leiba Bronstein on 26 October 1879 at Yanovka in Kherson province, southern Ukraine. His father, David Bronstein, married to Aneta, was a successful and wealthy farmer who had expanded his agricultural operations through sheer hard graft. The soil of the Bronstein farm was fertile and the local railways connected the area to the bustling port of Odessa on the Black Sea. Business was good and at the family home the future revolutionary played croquet on the lawn as a boy. In his later years Trotsky was embarrassed about his affluent origins and tried to obscure them while also downplaying his Jewish heritage. Lenin did exactly the same. Trotsky was a highly intelligent child, indeed, something of an academic prodigy, and his illiterate father, not being a devout Jew, sent him to St. Paul's, the Christian school in Odessa. The fledgling intellectual received further encouragement from Moshe and Fanni Shpenster, the educated relatives who supported him through his school years.

Trotsky graduated to the Realschüle academy in 1895, just before his sixteenth birthday. This higher educational institute was situated in Nikolaev, halfway between Odessa and Yanovka, a quiet town where the authorities regularly dumped political trouble-makers after they had served their Siberian exile. Through a school-friend Trotsky joined the radical circle of the Czech dissident, Franz Shvigovski, eventually moving into his house. In that commune the broad cultural education he had been enjoying up to that point narrowed into an intense study of a particular economic and political outlook. He came to despise the system of government and his father's outlook and lifestyle, while still taking his money, naturally. In preference to the world around him, he committed to an untested theoretical model which provided a comfortably unifying analysis of society. As with all such radicals his mind was set by his mid-teens and he would stubbornly cleave to the same philosophy until his dying day. Trotsky was a fiercely intelligent, idealistic moralist, yet after his conversion to the cause, he would advocate all sorts of horrors in defence of those principles.

He read voraciously in that period, paying particular attention to the debating techniques of Schopenhauer. He also shed his Jewish heritage and met Alexandra Sokolovskaya, his first great love. Trotsky's group lived in a commune, immersed themselves in activism and produced a healthy dose of literature. Initially cynical about Marx, he was soon won over, but in January 1898 the group were noticed by the Okhrana and arrested. When Trotsky's mother visited him in prison and fretted over how he would get by as a revolutionary, he assured her that good people would help him out.[20] The inference was clear: revolutionaries were good people, any who opposed them were not. As such, the separate treatment to be meted out to both camps would be entirely justified. After nearly a year in prison, Trotsky learned he was to serve four years in Siberian exile. He swiftly married Alexandra so they could spend their confinement together.

He had ample leisure time there and, while the winters could be harsh, the summers were pleasant. As such, he was able to play a considerable amount of croquet at which he was fiercely competitive. Exiles were given a relatively generous government stipend and encouraged to seek employment. Many of them found jobs as tutors or librarians. Trotsky continued to broaden his reading and scoffed at Pëtr Struve's contention that activism should prioritise increased wages for the working classes. The couple bore two daughters while in exile. The second, born in 1902, coincided with the delivery of a bundle of papers which included copies of *Iskra* and Lenin's *What Is To Be Done?* The literature had an electrifying effect on Trotsky. While he had socialised with many radicals there his Siberian circle now seemed pathetically small and inconsequential. He saw in Lenin not just a kindred spirit but an intellect he yearned to engage with and, determined to join the revolutionaries, he decided to flee his exile without delay. Trotsky had no compunctions about abandoning his wife to look after two infant girls just as the Siberian winter was about to sweep in. The 'cause' was all.

It was on his escape that the young radical acquired the name of Trotsky for the first time. He reached Geneva safely but soon headed for London to introduce himself to Lenin. That historic meeting took place in October 1902 and Trotsky's talents as a writer and organiser were immediately obvious. It soon became apparent that he was a brilliant orator too. Trotsky shared Lenin's belief in a revolutionary vanguard and political terror and the two bonded immediately, quickly becoming friends. They would soon fall out bitterly, before their eventual reconciliation some fifteen years later, but for the duration they were united in the cause. At Lenin's bidding, Trotsky travelled to Marxist enclaves across Europe, making a dazzling impression everywhere he went. He drummed up support for the SDs' impending Congress and berated the SRs in numerous lengthy articles. In Paris he met Natalya Sedova, a graceful and stylish young militant and the pair were swiftly enraptured with each other. Alexandra was promptly and unceremoniously dumped, and Natalya would end up bearing him two sons. But his activism always came first and his relationship with his daughters, who he saw relatively fleetingly over the years, was to suffer. His eldest child, Zina, particularly idolised her father. As her mother had been unable to cope with both girls she had been packed off to live with Trotsky's sister. Years later she committed suicide with her troubled relationship with her father generally accepted as the principal cause. Trotsky blamed the tragedy on Stalin.

When the Congress that he had done so much to advertise took place, and descended into acrimonious rancour, he sided with the Mensheviks. That move opened a rift with Lenin which would not heal until the events of 1917. Trotsky wrote a series of withering attacks on the Bolsheviks and claimed that Lenin had become too preoccupied with an intellectual dictatorship. A true movement, he argued, needed to embrace independent proletarian activism such as strikes and protests - for a dictatorship of the party would swiftly become a dictatorship of the central committee succeeded by a dictatorship of the leader. His contention on this issue, one later paraphrased by Rosa Luxemburg, has been misinterpreted as a premonition of the future of the Russian state. In fact, he was referring strictly to party organisation and meant no such thing. Despite the venom of his attacks, Trotsky quickly became disillusioned with the Mensheviks too, despairing of their refusal to countenance violence. In believing that a true revolution must be wholly proletarian, he also grew uncomfortable with the Menshevik's sympathies for the bourgeoisie, who he despised.

When Russia erupted in protest in 1905 Trotsky, unlike Lenin, immediately rushed to St. Petersburg, declaring that the process of revolution would be a long and torturous one. He did not blanch about revolutionary violence and insisted on the formation of a Provisional Government to be followed by a Constituent Assembly. He threw himself into the St. Petersburg Soviet, loving the independence of being neither Bolshevik nor Menshevik, until he was finally arrested in December. In the wake of his incarceration, Trotsky declared, in somewhat Robespierrist and binary terms, 'On one side there is struggle, courage, truth, freedom... On the other – deviousness, baseness, slander, slavery... Citizens, make your choice'.[21] Trotsky was to be exiled for life, but was delighted to avoid a sentence of hard labour. He elected to flee again and made a daring escape, travelling hundreds of miles through snow and forest on a sleigh pulled by a team of reindeer, before being reunited with Natalya.

The pair headed to Vienna where Trotsky enjoyed his independence, no longer considering himself particularly aligned with either Bolsheviks or Mensheviks. He attempted to persuade them to unify though, in the process, became ever more alienated from both factions. Trotsky spent the time between the revolutions of 1905 and 1917 primarily occupied in journalism, with the radicals of that period mostly engaged in internecine, sectarian squabbling. This factional rancour would considerably worsen once they achieved power as, with the Jacobins in France and the ever splintering feuds in Marx's time, few people are worse at co-operating than socialists. It is perhaps the movement's habit of single-minded dogmatism and frenzied emotion that encourages hostility over compromise.

The irony of Trotsky's attempts to unite the SDs was not lost on his contemporaries who were only too aware of his fiery response to any contradiction. Such was particularly apparent in the post-1914 climate when he fell out spectacularly with Plekhanov, Alexander Potresov and Marian Melenevsky. During the war he repeatedly wrote of his revulsion for capitalism and its essentially militaristic nature while foreseeing a future of global unity under socialism. This was a remarkable conclusion as accord was nowhere to be found among the pathetically small group who loudly advocated it. As with Marx, it is almost impossible to understand how such a fine assortment of intellects all shared the same blind spot. It can only be explained by the nigh-on messianic faith such activists hold in their opinions, a belief so intense that it never wavers no matter how much evidence contradicts it.

Trotsky had been forced on his travels in his time in exile, and when revolution broke out in 1917 he was living in New York, enjoying an affluent middle class lifestyle. While the family dined in fine restaurants, their chauffer would patiently wait outside until his services were required. Trotsky's children, raised on his ideology of equality and his distaste for the servant / master relationship, always found this situation confusing. They wondered why the poor man was not invited to dine with them, but Trotsky was entirely blinkered to the discrepancies between the rhetoric and reality of his lifestyle.

On hearing news of events in Petrograd, the family set sail on 27 March and arrived on 4 May. The Mensheviks and SRs were giving the government tacit support, something that was anathema to Trotsky, while the Bolsheviks were denouncing capitalism which they predicted would lead Russia into social and economic ruin. They were now adamant about the necessity of a worker's government, the same manifesto that Trotsky had been recommending for years. This 'dictatorship of the proletariat' was the policy that now united them. In the heady excitement of that year the more extreme radicals were, if only briefly, to find a greater level of accord. Both Trotsky and Lenin agreed on the need to overthrow the Provisional Government and establish an administration based on the proletariat, agrarian reform and worker control of the factories. Capitalism, nationalism, imperialism and militarism must be resisted at all costs. Some Mensheviks still supported the war effort and this was one policy that Trotsky could not countenance. While many Bolsheviks were still bitter over the articles in which he had defamed them, Lenin realised the value such a brilliant political talent could bring to their cause. After initial hesitation, the Bolsheviks welcomed him with open arms.

Trotsky hoped to foment further revolution and spoke to the Kronstdat naval garrison to demand: 'I tell you heads must roll, blood must flow...The strength of the French Revolution was in the machine that made the enemies of the people shorter by a head. This is a fine device. We must have it in every city'.[22] Lenin, along with other Bolsheviks, had read widely on the French Revolution and admired Robespierre, the radical Jacobins, and the ruthless way they dealt with their enemies. He did not want to be too open about such concerns though and cautioned Trotsky over his public recommendation of the guillotine. But he too was determined on a violent upheaval, one that must come before the impending elections were held, and it was clear that he would not be squeamish about further brutality in its wake. Lenin had spent much of the summer a fugitive from the Provisional Government in Finland where he had gone to 'convalesce'. He returned in the autumn to lead the rising that would destroy it.

In the intervening period Kerensky had been forced to arm the radicals to save the regime from the Kornilov rising and Trotsky had become chairman of the Petrograd Soviet. The time was ripe. On the night of 24-5 October the forces of Bolshevism seized key points in the city to prepare for the seizure of power while Red Guards and their converts in the armed forces began to swarm onto the streets. Lenin and Trotsky went to the Petrograd Soviet which, since August, had moved to the Smolny Institute. Prior to 1917 the fine building, designed in the Classical Greek style by the Italian architect Quarenghi, had been home to the Society for the Upbringing of Well-Born Girls, now it would be the stage for the birthplace of the world's first socialist state. The two demagogues of Bolshevism harangued the deputies there. Trotsky taunted the Mensheviks and SRs, bellowing that 'you are pathetic individuals, you are bankrupt, your role is played out; go off to where you belong from now on, into the waste basket of history'.[23] Lenin was less abusive and rather more triumphalist declaring that

> 'we'll have a Soviet government as our own organ of power without any participation whatever by the bourgeoisie. The oppressed masses themselves will create their power. The old state apparatus will be destroyed at its roots and a new apparatus of administration will be created in the form of the soviet organisations'.[24]

Such idealistic rhetoric ushered in the most oppressive and brutal state the world had ever seen.

Even as they berated the deputies in the Soviet, the Bolshevik seizure of power had already begun. The battleship *Aurora* had slipped up the river Neva to a spot near the Winter Palace where its salvos were the signal for the rising to take place. It faced little opposition. Kerensky had already slunk away, and the few remaining bureaucrats were only defended by a skeleton force that quickly collapsed. Eisenstein's later rousing depiction of thousands storming the gates and a pitched battle taking place bears little relation to the reality of that day's events. That propaganda, like virtually all the subsequent material produced by Bolshevism, was a blatant lie. The proclamations they had made prior to the uprising had been equally mendacious. While they vocalised the ideal of Soviet power, and thus stood on a mandate of the direct self-rule of the people, this stated opposition to state authority was shredded as soon as they assumed control. Their slogan of 'All Power to the Soviets!' was a populist rallying cry; but their real intent was 'all power to the Party'. Soviets had spread throughout the land, but Lenin was determined they would be subordinated to Bolshevism. There was little interest in what the working man might want, just a determination to enforce the ideals of socialism. In *The Economics of the Transition Period* Nikolai Bukharin had commented on 'the manufacturing of Communist man out of the human material of the capitalist age'. In his personal copy of that book Lenin underlined the phrase and wrote 'exactly!'[25] in the margin. He and his peers would subvert every facet of the state in an effort to realise this ambition.

The Bolsheviks were finally to put nearly two centuries of confident theory to the test, but their conviction had been based on resentment and a miscalculation on how society operates. It was a bad combination. It would lead to the collapse of that society and a continual search for scapegoats to blame. The kind of regime they were determined to run became apparent from the outset. Lenin issued a Decree authorizing censorship on 26 October. It was swiftly followed by the creation of a Bureau of Propaganda and a Department of the Press. The previous Bolshevik campaigns for 'freedom of the press' were instantly forgotten - it was to be ruthlessly suppressed. Lenin advocated the banning of any rival parties' newspapers, the smashing of their printing presses and for their leaders to be arrested and beaten up. Trotsky called for an 'energetic purge' of the military and for the loyally communist Latvian riflemen to be drafted in to Petrograd for 'security'. Elections for Soviets tended to be carried out by a show of hands in front of an overwhelming and intimidating military presence. Secret ballots were unheard of. The subsequent Bolshevik dominance of such organisations was, in light of such tactics, hardly surprising. As soon as they had attained power the hard left had turned immediately to violence, limiting freedoms and the determination to strangle democracy.

Lenin had already decided on the necessity of a one-party state. His priority was ensuring that the Bolsheviks took control of the Petrograd Soviet and that the Mensheviks and SRs, having already been outmanoeuvred by the coup, were sidelined. Many Mensheviks and SRs had already walked out over the illegal seizure of power, a protest which only served to strengthen the Bolsheviks' position in the Soviet. A new instrument of government was formed with Lenin as its chairman; Trotsky suggested calling it the Council of People's Commissars which, by its Russian acronym, became known as Sovnarkom. Though it would eventually be eclipsed by the Politburo, which was established in January 1919, Lenin and his subordinates initially sought to concentrate all legislative power into its orbit. Lenin attempted to force through the postponement of the Constituent Assembly elections. He met opposition over this issue, as the Bolsheviks had been promising that only they could deliver the plebiscite, but there was to be unanimity over its subsequent suppression. Lenin also believed that, given the opportunity, the peasants would compete for the land in a capitalist scramble. So the state should focus on the establishment of socialist collective farms. The Bolsheviks called for the nationalisation of all elements of the economy and the obliteration of any trace of capitalist enterprise. But Lenin advised a more cautious approach, and while he approved of the state seizure of banks, mining, railways, the biggest factories and landed estates, he recommended they delay such measures with the rest of the economy. This was insufficient for the majority of the party who complained that it would leave 80% of the economy in capitalist hands.

Trotsky envisaged a plan in which the entirety of Russia's society and economy would be run like an army. It should consist of unquestioned central authority, with regiments of workers divided up and sent to carry out tasks the Central Committee deemed necessary for their grand plan. His society would thus be run like an ant colony in which the majority were merely mindless drones directed wherever their great leaders required. The concepts of freedom, individuality, initiative, creativity or joy played no part in his scheme. Communism would be imposed through coercion and compliance, while any questioning voices were to be ruthlessly crushed. He believed that socialism's ability to conscript workers gave it an advantage over capitalism. The economy would function more effectively with workers who were dragooned in by order of the state than ones who effectively had to be bribed by the promise of rewards. While the free market was a chaotic mess of strikes and disorder, the socialist economy promised smooth, compliant cohesion. In effect the Communists were to re-impose serfdom, all in the name of the workers, naturally. Warned that forced labour would be unproductive Trotsky replied that 'If this is so then you can put a cross over Socialism'.[26]

But while the party argued that they existed for the benefit of the workers, they were only tolerated so long as they benefitted the party. If the proles ever showed any resistance to the diktats of the communists the response would be immediate and utterly ruthless. Worker freedom would be crushed more effectively by communism than any other style of regime. Lenin and Trotsky were also diligent in subordinating the Trade Union movement to the state. As the party claimed to represent the workers' interests such organisations were considered unnecessary. More than this, as effectively capitalist associations, the leading Bolsheviks found them distasteful. Unions simply obstructed the smooth transition to socialism, itself a necessary precursor to the full implementation of the communist state.

The Bolsheviks believed that Russia's smallholding peasant farms were inefficient and, regardless, reeked of the market. They were too ideologically distasteful to tolerate. The new leaders were convinced that the future of Soviet agriculture lay in gigantic collective farms. In February 1919 they passed a Statute on Socialist Land Organisation which ruled that peasant farming was obsolete and allowed for the state seizure of vast tracts of land. It is a profound irony that the mass dragooning of the Russian worker, both rural and urban, in such a crudely impersonal manner, contributed to the spread of alienation at a far greater level than in any capitalist society. Collectivised farms tended to run at a loss and were dependent on state subsidies. Millions of peasants also began to be conscripted into forced labour regiments to collect harvests or to build roads and railways. The unmotivated staff were inefficient and their work was appallingly shoddy, faults which undermined the regime from the start. The economy, the availability and standard of goods, leisure and freedoms and the quality of life under the Soviets would prove so spectacularly inferior to that of America, its main capitalist rival, that the entire system ultimately crumbled under the weight of its internal contradictions.

But there was an aspect even more chilling than their attacks on the economy, freedom of expression and the concept of democracy. From the outset the regime was defined by its reliance on state-sanctioned terror. It is a stage that should have been predictable to anyone who had been paying attention. In 1908 Lenin criticised the 'excessive generosity' of the Paris Commune which 'should have *exterminated its enemies'*.[27] In the year that revolution broke, while some had called for the abolition of the death penalty, Lenin was without equivocation. 'Nonsense, how can you make a revolution without executions?...It is a mistake, impermissible, weakness, pacifist illusion'.[28] He now called for the summary executions of 'parasites' and vocalised 'one general aim: the *cleansing* of the Russian land of any harmful insects, swindler-fleas, wealthy bugs and so on and so on'.[29] In response to such rhetoric a secret police force was established, the Cheka, which was to act as the whip hand of the party. The brutality of this organisation, the forerunner of the KGB*, would become legendary. It was to exist outside the law and to focus on counter-revolution. By December 1917 the prisons were already so full of political inmates that common criminals began to be released. At the head of the organisation was Felix Dzerzhinsky who was of Polish descent but hailed from near Minsk in Belarus. Like many of his ilk, he was of aristocratic heritage and had known Trotsky on his Siberian exile. While there he liked to regale the other detainees with his poetry as they gathered around flickering campfires. Lenin had turned to him when looking for 'a staunch Jacobin' to run the organisation. The forty year old had spent his youth hoping to be a Jesuit priest and, despite abandoning religion, had lost none of his fanatical and extremist ardour, merely

* The organisation would change its name a dizzying number of times: Cheka (1917-22), GPU (1922-23), OGPU (1923-34), NKVD (1934-43), NKGB (1943-46), MGB (1946-53) MVD (1953-54) and KGB from that point on. For the purposes of a cohesive narrative, this book will limit its references to Cheka, NKVD and KGB.

transferring such qualities from religious to political persecution. Dzerzhinsky described his ideal agents as: 'determined, hard, dedicated comrades ready to do anything in defence of the Revolution. Do not think that I seek forms of revolutionary justice; we are not now in need of justice. It is war now – face to face, a fight to the finish. Life or death'.[30] He would find no shortage of suitable candidates.

Formed in November 1917, almost immediately after the seizure of power, the Cheka had recruited over 1,000 eager sadists by the following summer. The powers and responsibilities of the organisation were left deliberately vague, but Lenin's frequent calls for class war and his condemnation of bourgeois 'bloodsuckers' left little doubt over its primary targets. Indeed, the slogan 'Death to the Bourgeoisie!' was written on the walls of the Cheka's interrogation rooms. The organisation, endowed with virtually unlimited powers, became a state within a state. It could arrest and kill any political suspects, and its agents could act entirely at their own discretion. Evidence was considered unnecessary. The Bolsheviks were virtually unanimous on the need to violently suppress opposition to the Soviet government, like the regiments of Cossacks who were among its first targets.

The Cheka also proved pivotal in the suppression of the Constituent Assembly. Opposition hopes had rested with this legislature. It should be representative of the entire nation, while the Soviets only stood for the workers, peasants and soldiers. In the November elections the Bolsheviks polled just 24% and the idea of simply ignoring the result rapidly gained widespread acceptance in the party. Sovnarkom quickly backed Lenin's calls for the break-up of the Assembly and, naturally, all sorts of justifications were found for the repudiation of democracy. Laughingly they revolved around the allegedly unfair and undemocratic nature of the elections. It was agreed that when the delegates met at the Tauride Palace, they should be instructed to follow Sovnarkom's decrees. If they refused, they would be locked out. On 5 January 1918 Lenin attended the Constituent Assembly's first meeting. He and Sverdlov sat imperiously up in the position reserved for the Tsar's ministers when the Duma had met there. Viktor Chernov was repeatedly interrupted before being told the guards, who crowded the hall in intimidating numbers, wanted to go home. The building was locked behind them and never opened again. It was effectively the Bolsheviks second *coup d'état* in three months. Having used military force to drive out the deputies the Bolsheviks were branded as 'counter-revolutionaries' by the liberal Kadets. They responded by banning the party, declaring them 'enemies of the people', and arresting or shooting a number of their leaders. Power effectively rested with Sovnarkom and the Cheka.

There was, on the whole, a certain apathy about the demise of the Constituent Assembly, a sloth not shared by the fanatics who had dissolved it. None of their rivals could match the brutality, arrogance and intolerance of the

Bolsheviks. The particular mix of characteristics that enabled them to seize power was unique to the hard left and would propel them into the most brutal despotism in history. It ensured their success and would equally guarantee death or ruin for any who stood in their way. The Bolsheviks failed to improve the lot of the peasantry, but sought to court popularity by boasting how they had destroyed the rich. They reduced inequality, not by raising the conditions of the poor, but by eradicating the successful. This economic and class prejudice became endemic. It was used to justify all sorts of bigotry, and to excuse horrific violence. Class enemies were seen everywhere, not just the kulaks but the *burzhooi* as well; a term with obvious derivation from 'bourgeois' but one employed as a general form of abuse against anyone with even a whiff of privilege.

The casting of such villains was particularly useful as all the failures of the Bolsheviks' regime, like the severe bread shortages caused by their own misguided economic policies, could be blamed on speculators, hoarders, saboteurs, parasites and traitors. It was a perception continually reinforced by the socialist press who excoriated these 'enemies of the people'. One massive selling pamphlet that helped fan the flames of class hatred was *Spiders and Flies* by Wilhelm Liebknecht.

'The spiders are the masters, the money- grubbers, the exploiters, the gentry, the wealthy, and the priests, pimps and parasites of all types!...The flies are the unhappy workers, who must obey all those laws the capitalist happens to think up – must obey, for the poor man has not even a crumb of bread'.[31]

In reality the image presented by Liebknecht more closely resembled a communist society than a capitalist one. It also has to be understood that the rhetoric of class hatred was little more than a virtuous sounding mask the radicals used to justify their brutal treatment of anyone who crossed them.

Regardless, such propaganda was terrifically effective. In 1918 a factory worker proclaimed 'we should exterminate all the *burzhooi* so that the honest Russian people will be able to live more easily'.[32] Lenin himself went into rather more detail over such issues, relishing the chance to finally make his enemies pay. In December 1917 he called for a

'war to the death against the rich, the idlers and the parasites...[individual areas should develop unique policies for] cleansing the Russian land of all vermin, the bedbug rich and so on. In one place they will put into prison a dozen rich men, a dozen scoundrels, half a dozen workers who shirk on the job...In another place they will be put to cleaning latrines. In a third they will be given yellow tickets [such as prostitutes were given] after a term in prison so that everyone knows they are harmful and can keep an eye on them. In a fourth one out of every ten idlers will be shot. The more variety the better...for only practice can devise the best methods of struggle'.[33]

The Bolsheviks' certainty drove them into ever more draconian policies – a peculiar ruthlessness directed at smashing any hint of opposition. Lenin called the Kadets 'the political staff of the bourgeoisie' while Trotsky argued that, as the middle classes would fade from history anyway, the violence employed against them was for their own good. He declared 'There is nothing immoral in the proletariat finishing off a class that is collapsing; that is its right'.[34] It was nothing less than a declaration of war against an entire sector of society – an assertion that the extermination of a social class was a moral imperative. But the Bolsheviks, like the Jacobins that preceded them, swiftly turned on their fellows too, arresting numerous SR and Menshevik leaders as well as significant figures in the Peasant Soviet.

The royal family were also to become victims of the new regime with Lenin instrumental in determining their fate. The Tsar and his brood had been held since 30 April 1918 in the Ipatiev House in Yekaterinburg. Trotsky had initially favoured a show trial with himself as the prosecutor, but it was decided instead to simply remove them quietly. On 17 July they were dragged from their beds in the dead of night and marched down to the basement. Told that the house was under attack, and they were being moved for their own safety, they descended the darkened staircase dazed from sleep before being squeezed into a cramped cellar. In all eleven people were to be shot: the royal couple, their four beautiful young daughters, the frail and ailing thirteen year old Tsarevich, Alexei, and the family servants. It was intended to be a clinical procedure with each member of the family assigned their own assassin who was to finish them off swiftly and cleanly. Yet with personnel like Peter Ermakov, a particularly violent Chekist who had once sawn a man's head off during a bank robbery, such an outcome was always unlikely.

In a horribly bungled operation the room was blasted with gunfire and filled with cordite, dust and screams. It was a dreadful, chaotic scene. After nearly ten minutes of shooting Alexis and their youngest daughter Anastasia still showed signs of life before Ermakov, who had arrived half-drunk, attempted to finish them off with a frenzied bayonet assault. His commander, Yurovsky, pushed him aside and shot the young boy in the head. Just for good measure the revolutionaries then killed the family dog by driving a bayonet through it. As they were buried, acid was poured on the bodies to disguise their identities, but the killings were far from alone. On 12 June Nicholas's brother, Misha, had been marched into the woods with his secretary. There they were both shot and the bodies burned with paraffin, but not before the Cheka had pilfered Misha's watch. Just hours after the murders of the Tsar and his family, six other Romanovs who were held nearby, including the Grand Duke Sergei Mikhailovich, Alexandra's sister Ella and a nun who was accompanying them, were marched into the woods, beaten with rifle butts and flung into a flooded mine. Their killers then tossed down a number of grenades before finally setting a fire to finish them off.

But the majority of the Bolsheviks' victims came from rather lower down the social pecking order. Private trade in foodstuffs, which may have alleviated the worsening problem of supply, was ruthlessly suppressed when the state imposed a monopoly on food distribution. They ultimately hoped to replace the system of money with one of state rationing, but in the interim elected on aggressively expropriating grain from the peasantry. Trotsky had been made People's Commissar of Military Affairs and his Red Army were given the task of requisitioning. They were encouraged to be ruthless, for any peasants who were tardy in handing over their share were suspected of greed and hoarding. Such traitors deserved no pity. Lenin described hoarders as 'enemies of the people' and urged 'a merciless and terrorist defence and war against the peasant bourgeoisie holding on to grain supplies'.[35]

On 11 August 1918 Lenin sent a letter to the Bolsheviks in Penza to outline the policy:

'Comrades! The insurrection of five kulak districts should be *pitilessly* suppressed. The interests of the *whole* revolution require this because the last decisive battle with the kulaks is now under way *everywhere*. An example must be demonstrated.

1. Hang (and make sure that the hanging takes place *in full view of the people*) *no fewer than one hundred* known kulaks, rich men, bloodsuckers.
2. Publish their names.
3. Seize *all* their grain from them.
4. Designate hostages in accordance with yesterday's telegram.

Do it in such a fashion that for hundreds of kilometres around the people might see, tremble, know, shout: *they are strangling* and will strangle to death the bloodsucking kulaks.

Telegraph receipt and *implementation*.

Yours, Lenin.

Find some truly hard people.'[36]

Am I alone in thinking the truly chilling aspect of that note is the cheery 'Comrades!' that opens it? The human costs of such policies were appalling. Tibor Szamuely was involved in the collectivisation of 1919, hanging and shooting any peasant opposed to it. On one occasion he shot a Jewish schoolboy pleading for his father's life. Szamuely was rewarded for such diligence in 1936 when he disappeared into the maelstrom of the purges. A report of 19 February 1919 from Sir C. Eliot in Vladivostok to Earl Curzon detailed the seventy-one victims of the Bolsheviks in the Yekaterinburg area.

Two were thrown in a pit and had molten slag poured on them, seven were beheaded, several were ripped apart with various body parts torn off and heads smashed in before being partly skinned. Most were shot and bayoneted, some after being forced to dig their own graves.

In April 1918 Lenin had published a booklet called *The Current Tasks of Soviet Power*. He castigated any peasant or factory worker not pulling their weight and promised to 'punish them pitilessly'.[37] All Lenin's talk of obliterating oppression and coercion from society, and the principle of power to the workers, was hot air. He demanded complete subjugation to his interpretation of workers' freedom. Trotsky too supported the government's policy in grain requisitioning and Sovnarkom's directive outlawing private trade in foodstuffs. He saw no distinction between kulaks and merchants and was adamant that anyone caught hoarding should get ten years hard labour. Yet he was insistent that 'we want to create on this earth a real paradise for people'.[38] The Bolsheviks began to encounter resistance, particularly over the state grain trade monopoly. Calls increased to allow peasants to sell their excess produce on the open markets, but such a policy was in contravention of their principles, so the Bolsheviks would not budge. The consequence of their stubborn intransigence was the threat of economic collapse.

Yet while prepared to make war on their own people the party would, albeit reluctantly, agree peace with Germany. An armistice had been agreed almost as soon as they had overthrown the Provisional Government, and the Bolsheviks had dragged out negotiations for as long as they dared. Yet now, with the Central powers pushing for a response, a deal had to be agreed. The majority of the Bolsheviks favoured the waging of a revolutionary war against Germany, and Imperialism in general, before carrying the conflict further to spread socialism across the world. Such was their confidence that they assumed the implementation of socialism over Russia would be easy and its subsequent spread into Western Europe equally rapid. Lenin had previously called for exactly the policy of revolutionary war which the party's idealists still craved, yet he now realised it was an impossible course of action. He knew that a German invasion would sweep their revolutionary government aside and it was more sensible to focus on protecting what had already been won. But Lenin's realism came up against the brick wall of party idealism and it took all the skills at his disposal to batter it down.

It is startling to note that, as with the arguments over economic issues, Lenin was, in many ways, one of the least extreme of the revolutionaries. For the majority of them ideology trumped practicality any day. Lenin's pragmatism was phrased rather more brutally though. He justified his policy by exclaiming that 'The bourgeoisie has to be throttled and for that we need both hands free'.[39] Trotsky, who had sought a middle path, came round to Lenin's view and the Treaty of Brest-Litovsk was signed on 3 March 1918. It surrendered huge tracts of land including Ukraine, Poland, Finland and the Baltic states. Lenin's acceptance of the terms led to cries of 'Traitor!' and 'Judas!' from his own party.

But the peace terms agreed with Germany were, despite the protests of the rank and file, extremely timely. In March 1918 the government had relocated from Petrograd to Moscow and the party changed its name from the Bolsheviks to the Russian Communist Party. Yet, just as it appeared the new regime was becoming established, it faced the greatest threat to its existence yet. The forces opposed to communism rallied and a Civil War broke out in the summer of 1918 with the White Army, which hoped to overthrow the Bolsheviks, aided by detachments from Britain and France. Assailed from all fronts the regime's punitive approach reached previously untapped levels. Both the land war waged against the peasants and the Cheka's purges of political opposition went into overdrive. Trotsky, given effective stewardship of the Red Army, was to play a significant role in the campaign and left little doubt over how it was to be waged. In a telegram to Lenin dated 17 August 1918 he wrote:

> 'I consider it unacceptable to let steamers sail [the Volga] under a Red Cross flag. The receipt of grain will be interpreted by charlatans and fools as showing the possibility that agreement can be made and that civil war is unnecessary. The military motives are unknown to me. Air pilots and artillerymen have been ordered to bomb and set fire to the bourgeois districts of Kazan and then to Simbirsk and Samara. In these conditions a Red Cross caravan is inappropriate.'[40]

Trotsky's conduct during the war was controversial at the time and has remained so ever since. He had no compunction with shooting anyone in the Red Army whose dedication he questioned. He used Imperial officers in his forces but kept their family members hostage as security. He shot incompetent political commissars, decimated ineffective regiments, a brutal punishment unheard of since Roman times, and gave no preference to long-standing Bolsheviks. When Panteleev, a loyal party member, pulled his regiment from the fighting around Sviyazhsk, Trotsky ordered the whole lot of them shot. Some, who distrusted his recent conversion from Menshevism, feared he would emerge from the conflict as another Napoleon. Lenin could be just as brutal though. At the battle for Petrograd, he suggested that Trotsky should set up 30,000 men with machine guns to the rear of his forces to deal with any who fled the battlefield. But Trotsky himself, despite being guilty of quite startling brutality during the conflict, remained optimistic that war would soon be a thing of the past. Marx had taught that it was nothing but an imperial tool. When socialism had triumphed and ushered in a harmonious global society, then war would fade like the morning mist. The fact that his political brethren were the most un-comradely men one could meet had little impact on such wildly implausible fantasies. It was a common malady.

An additional spur to the Red Terror was the assassination attempt on Lenin on 30 August 1918. As he stepped out of his car he was shot in the shoulder and neck by Fanny Kaplan, effectively a Russian Corday. The Jewish woman, who was a former Anarchist before turning SR, was interrogated and shot by the Cheka. But the paranoia of the revolutionaries persuaded them she had been part of a massive conspiracy involving the SRs and the Imperial powers. Such fears were magnified as the attempt on Lenin's life came days after the assassination of Moisei Uritsky, the head of the Petrograd Cheka. Convinced they were surrounded by powerful enemies plotting their downfall they elected to wage implacable war on them. The Bolshevik press eagerly fanned the flames of such reprisals with the *Krasnaia Gazeta* proclaiming 'Without mercy, we will kill our enemies in scores of hundreds. Let them be thousands, let them drown themselves in their own blood. For the blood of Lenin and Uritsky let there be floods of bourgeois blood – more blood, as much as possible'.[41] Trotsky detested kulaks, merchants, capitalists and speculators as much as any other good Bolshevik, and was an enthusiastic advocate of the Red Terror being waged against thousands of upper and middle class citizens, many of whom were summarily shot. He left no illusions about the attitude of the Bolsheviks. 'We must put an end once and for all to the papist – Quaker babble about the sanctity of human life'.[42]

For suspected enemies of the regime there was to be no mercy and no escape. This became apparent early on when, taking exception to the anti-Soviet jokes of Bim-Bom the clown, the Cheka shot him on stage during a performance of the Moscow Circus. The killings and persecutions that followed often seemed completely arbitrary, there was no course of appeal, the prisons were far more crowded and brutal than under the Tsarist regime, and the types of torture employed by the revolutionaries reached new levels of barbarity. They would plunge the victim's hands in boiling water until their skin peeled off, saw their bones in half, roll naked suspects in barrels studded with hundreds of nails or crush their skulls by tightening a leather strap with an iron bolt around their head. They even attached metal cages containing rats to their torsos before heating the cage so the panicking rats chewed their way into the victim's guts to find refuge. Other favourites included burning prisoners alive or nailing them into a coffin with a corpse for company, tying them to planks and slowly pushing them into a furnace, gradually immersing them in boiling water, dousing them in freezing water until they became icy statues or raping, torturing or killing the suspect's loved ones in front of them.

The torturers were mostly young men who frequently laughed while carrying out their tasks, but women were involved too. Vera Grebennikova was reputed to have killed 700 victims in two months in Odessa while Rebecca Platinina-Maisel killed more than 100 in Archangel, including the entire family of her ex-husband, all of whom she had crucified. Tens of thousands were simply shot during the Civil War. In 1919 Lenin passed a note to Dzerzhinsky asking how many counter-revolutionaries were in Moscow's prisons. He scribbled 'about 1,500' on it and passed it back. Lenin casually drew a cross next to the number and 1,500 were killed that night. It later transpired that Lenin merely crossed the note to indicate he had read it. But Dzerzhinsky's reaction is a revealing insight on the punitive and arbitrary culture that dominated the regime, and Lenin, Stalin and Trotsky stood firmly behind the Cheka. Under the watch of the first of that trio it grew to number a quarter of a million dedicated members with a vast network of concentration camps.

The new converts to Bolshevism were, on the whole, not terribly advanced or nuanced thinkers, but the philosophy gave them a reassuring framework in which to live their lives. In dividing society into friends and foes, in giving them enemies to blame for the social injustices they had endured and in persuading them that their approach was both a moral imperative and a 'scientific' remedy, they would be prepared to follow where their party leaders pointed. Obedience to its diktats thus became necessary, and 'hardness' and 'discipline' could be justified in lieu of individual morality. The philosophy of Marxism gave the masses a reassuring ideology that salved their consciences, painted the world in simple to understand terms, absolved them of any pity for the victims of the regime and convinced them their actions had a *purpose*. As long as they persevered, and their opponents were removed, the socialist nirvana would eventually be realised. While the figures remain elusive, it is certain that several hundred thousand died at the hands of the Cheka in those few, short years; perhaps more than were killed in all the battles of the Civil War.

Lenin encouraged a culture of violence, robbery and looting. As Soviets spread through the provinces the locals were drilled in this message and some Kalmyks, wealthier peasants, were attacked by their neighbours who set fire to their farms and butchered their families, even cutting babies from the wombs of pregnant women. In Taganrog, an industrial town in the Don, Red Guards took fifty Kadets who had surrendered when promised an amnesty, bound their hands and feet and flung them in the blast furnaces of a large metal processing plant. In Evpataria, on the Crimean coast, the Soviet encouraged Bolshevik sailors to attack the bourgeoisie. Eight hundred had their arms and legs broken. Their shattered limbs were then tied above their heads before they were cast into the sea and drowned. Such massacres were sanctioned as official Bolshevik policy with decrees published to justify the violence. Huge fines were also imposed, and when the Cheka began arresting small traders and near destitute doctors and teachers, their propaganda persuaded them they must be hiding their wealth. Any who could not pay were summarily shot.

Similar levels of looting and terror were directed at the Church and, in some cases, entire monasteries were lined up and shot. Terrible carnage was wrought in Rostov by the Bolsheviks with hundreds of hostages shot, churches attacked and clergy executed. One priest had his nose and ears cut off in front of his parishioners at Easter Service. For good measure the Reds pulled his eyes out too. Lenin was dismayed at the vestiges of religion that lingered in the masses. When the summertime feast of St. Nicholas approached he declared 'It's stupid to be reconciled to the 'Nikolai' festival. We must get all the Chekas up on their feet and shoot people who don't turn up for work because of the 'Nikolai festival'[43] He recommended similar sanctions be employed at Christmas and the New Year. Such was the reality of the champion of the working man, the hero who would free them from the oppression of their capitalist masters.

Yet the Bolsheviks continued to give the impression that they represented the masses. The wealthy were forced to surrender their homes to the poor and engage in demeaning labour. But there were no economic benefits to such behaviour. It was a policy motivated by sheer spite which merely resulted in a crumbling economy and rocketing inflation. The consequences were again blamed on bourgeois elements and the violence against them ratcheted up another notch. Mob trials and lynching became commonplace, particularly as the economic crisis deepened and the belief took hold that the *burzhooi* were responsible. This type of vigilante 'justice' assumed an entirely class-based nature. The victims were primarily merchants, shopkeepers, employers, factory owners and any other figure with even a hint of authority.

The Bolsheviks quickly legitimised the practice by abolishing the old criminal justice system as a relic of the 'bourgeois order' and setting up People's Courts. These were presided over by twelve judges who were loyal to the party but had no legal experience. They arbitrated via their 'revolutionary conscience' alone. Convictions tended to be based on denunciations rather than evidence, which was not regarded as necessary. They were nothing more than mob courts - a crude precursor of the show trials which became a macabre art-form under Stalin. The detached and objective nature which must underpin any credible form of judicial procedure was replaced by hysteria, and sentences were usually determined by the social status of the suspects. In one court culpability was determined by an appraisal of the hands of the accused – soft hands meant that one was not a labourer and this was considered sufficient evidence to determine their guilt. Merchants could expect to face punitive retribution while those who had stolen from, or even murdered, the rich were treated much more leniently. In February 1918 Lenin had given such tribunals the authority to shoot suspects on the spot; ultimately though their role was taken over by the state police. Lastsis, one of the senior figures in the Cheka gave instructions to his staff asking them

'not to look for evidence as proof that the accused had acted or spoken against the Soviets. First you must ask him to what class he belongs, what his social origin is, his education and profession. These are the questions that must determine the fate of the accused. That is the meaning of the Red Terror'.[44]

The policy of requisitioning also increased significantly during the conflict against the Whites. Lenin had long felt that the Paris Commune collapsed because it failed to extend its power to the countryside and provoke a civil war. He was determined not to make the same mistakes. The Bolsheviks mistrusted the peasantry anyway. They were too close to the old regime, too preoccupied with private property, land ownership and free trade, too unsophisticated to be true revolutionary comrades. It was Lenin, after all, who had conveniently divided them into the poor peasants, who were the proletariats' allies, and the 'kulaks', the capitalist peasants who were to be their victims. Such a viewpoint was entirely fictitious, but it was a neat match for their ideology. When the peasant Soviets tried to get fair deals for their local populations they could simply be denounced as 'hoarders' by the state. Increasing levels of propaganda portrayed fat and greedy capitalist speculators sitting on veritable mountains of grain to stoke up resentment among the rest of the population. In the summer of 1918 Lenin made his intent clear:

'The kulaks are the rabid forces of the Soviet government...These blood-suckers have grown rich on the hunger of the people...These spiders have grown fat at the expense of the peasants ruined by the war, at the expense of the workers. These leeches have sucked the blood of the working people and grown richer as the workers in the cities and factories starved...Ruthless war on the kulaks! Death to all of them.'[45]

A 'Food Army' of militarised units with the power to seize grain by force was sent into the countryside. Fired up by Bolshevik propaganda, and filled with ideological zeal, the units behaved like bands of robbers and brigands, stealing seeds, guns, vodka and anything else they could lay their hands on. They frequently occupied villages and tortured residents until they got what they wanted. Peasants were stripped naked, whipped and killed, while rape was exceedingly common. When the peasants began to hide their grain the regime employed even more brutal methods which provoked numerous uprisings, frequently by the poorest peasants. These were mercilessly suppressed with whole villages wiped out and burned to the ground. The Bolsheviks then imposed Committees of the Rural Poor onto the peasant communes. Designed to divide communities between proletariat and bourgeois peasants, and to stoke up class war in the countryside they behaved even more appallingly than the requisitioning brigades. In the region of Saratov they seized private property and livestock, vandalised churches and brutally beat the populace. One peasant who could not pay was forced to watch while they raped his wife. Peasant uprising increased again before the committees, who had mostly pilfered grain for themselves, were eventually abolished. But the Bolsheviks just blamed the kulaks for the shortfall and extractions rose again. Instead of just grain, livestock and vegetables were added to the requisitioning list. An empty barn was regarded as evidence of a kulak hiding produce, so villages were to be cleared of stocks by any means necessary. The lines were drawn for the 'battle for grain' of spring 1919.

The ultimate consequences of these policies were appalling. In 1921-2 a terrible famine hit the Volga region. While it was true that there had been a drought, the most affected areas were those where grain seizures were most severe. The levels of requisitioning had stripped not just entire harvests from some regions but all supplies of seeds too. The policy was so thorough that the topsoil blew away leaving the region a dustbowl. The locals, frequently the poorest, were whipped and shot as 'kulaks' while peasants, who used to keep significant reserves, had turned to subsistence farming to prevent the Communists from stealing any excess harvest. It significantly worsened the crisis. When famine struck it hit the Don, Ukraine, Kazakhstan, the Urals and the Koma basin. It was swiftly accompanied by typhus and cholera. Starving peasants ate grass, weeds, leaves, moss, thatched roofs and tree-bark. They made flour from acorns, sawdust, clay and horse manure, as well as devouring rats, cats and dogs. People attempted to flee the worst hit areas, but the authorities had banned all transport to prevent the spread of disease and there were scenes of Biblical chaos at train stations. Cannibalism was rife: guards were posted on cemeteries and people feared going out at night less they be snatched by one of the roaming gangs out hunting for victims.

The government did little to help and tried to cover up the crisis. The press were banned from mentioning it, though Lenin did agree to let Gorky set up a private initiative to alleviate the situation. He also permitted foreign aid. Yet when America stepped in to help, Lenin closed the domestic programme and arrested those who had been involved. The US aid fed ten million people and provided sufficient seed to eventually avert the crisis. But the ingratitude of the Soviet regime was staggering. Trotsky was contemptuous of the help given by the American Relief Administration and spat that Herbert Hoover, the future US President in charge of the operation, was 'our most accursed enemy'.[46] It is doubtful the peasantry would have agreed. The Communists accused the Americans of spying and interfered with and hampered the relief efforts. It also transpired that they exported enormous quantities of cereals even while their own people starved in their millions.

Seven million orphans were created by the crisis and gangs of feral children who lived on begging, crime and prostitution swarmed through Russia's cities. Much of the countryside rose in armed revolt against the regime. These peasant militias were known as 'Greens', and their anger was understandable. The government had taken over their Soviets and begun to force them into collective farms. Their land had been appropriated by the state while the

Communists stole their food and threatened to starve them. Then they conscripted them to fight in the regime's wars, shooting 'shirkers' who rebelled against the draft in large numbers. The peasant reprisals were brutal: Communists were nailed to trees, drowned under the ice, burned alive or buried up to their necks and fed to dogs and rats. By March 1921 anarchy reigned in the countryside and the supply of provisions to the cities had all but dried up.

That spring also saw a series of urban strikes as industrial workers, fed up with food shortages and the lack of tangible improvements in their lives, rebelled against the regime. The Bolsheviks had brought the people destitution in lieu of liberation, and disillusionment with the 'workers' revolution' became rife. To combat the unrest, the Bolsheviks passed a Decree on Nationalisation which took management of the factories out of the hands of the Soviets or workers' organisations and handed it to the party. On more than one occasion the Cheka opened fire on striking labourers. Those behind the disputes were arrested and shot in large numbers while Mensheviks and SRs were denounced as 'counter-revolutionaries' and purged from the Soviets.

The nation was at crisis point and something had to give. The regime was hugely aided in this respect by the conclusion of the Civil War. It had been a bitter campaign with atrocities committed by both sides, but the Whites had failed to organise their effort around a coherent political ideology so were less effective at rallying support than their Red rivals. Anglo-French aid to the White cause also lacked true commitment. There was no real political unity behind the Allied intervention and, regardless, after four years of the Great War, they lacked the appetite for battle. While the peasant class had little love for the Bolshevik cause they feared a return to the old regime even more. The Bolsheviks were widely regarded as the lesser of two evils and could legitimately claim to be fighting for the Revolution. They had also appropriated its symbol, the red flag, for themselves. But once victory was secured Lenin and Trotsky realised the need for reform before the peasant rebellions and urban activism got out of hand.

Trotsky was perhaps the first to see that requisitioning was not working. He favoured full collectivisation as the solution to Russia's agricultural issues, but felt more time was required for its full implementation. In the meantime, peasants who produced a healthy surplus must be rewarded while industrial competition should be encouraged. It was a tacit realisation that socialism did not work, yet Trotsky would not admit as much. The Bolsheviks of course saw state ownership and control as the universal solution. They were repulsed by competitive trading or, even more unthinkably, rewarding the kulaks. But Lenin had come to a similar conclusion to Trotsky and at the Tenth Party Congress, which opened on 8 March 1921, he unveiled his New Economic Policy (NEP). He recommended giving material rewards to peasants who increased production in the hope it would motivate them to plant more sizeable crops. Once the peasants had handed over the produce mandated by the state they could trade any excess grain in the local markets. Requisitioning was also to be abolished. Lenin knew that it would be necessary to buy time to mould the utopian state, but he harboured no doubts that they would ultimately be successful. In a speech to the Youth League in 1920 he had declared that 'the generation of those who are now fifteen will see a Communist society, and will itself build that society'.[47]

The bulk of the party hoped for far more rapid results. As with his earlier suggestions designed to aid Russia's collapsing industrial sector, such as striking deals with western industrialists like Krupp Steel and the Nobel oil company, the pragmatic measures elicited howls of indignation from the party faithful. Members spluttered that he was doing nothing less than opening the back door to capitalism. They would rather see the peasants starve than admit any failings in their creed. The ideological purity of the party membership frequently exceeded that of Lenin, confronted as he was with the realities of government. The truth was that the revolution needed the market to save it, but Lenin's justifications for introducing the policy hardly endear him to the neutral reader:

'The peasant must do a bit of starving so as to relieve the factories and towns from complete starvation. On the level of the state in general this is an entirely understandable thing, but we're not counting on the exhausted, destitute peasant-owner understanding it. And we know you can't manage without compulsion, to which the devastated peasantry is reacting very strongly.'[48]

The Congress had taken place in the shadow of a massive peasant rising at Tambov in the Volga region, which Marshal Tukhachevsky had been sent to deal with. He had been instructed to show no quarter and the rebels wound up being gassed in their thousands. But what ultimately won the party over to the idea of reform was the mutiny at the Kronstadt naval base, a rising which shocked the delegates. The sailors, who had been the most loyal supporters of the regime in 1917, issued the following decree to justify their rising:

'By carrying out the October Revolution the working class had hoped to achieve its emancipation. But the result has been an even greater enslavement of human beings. The power of the monarchy, with its police and its gendarmerie, has passed into the hands of the Communist usurpers, who have given the people not freedom but the constant fear of torture by the Cheka, the horrors of which far exceed the rule of the gendarmerie under tsarism...But the worst and most criminal of all is the moral servitude which the Communists have also introduced: they have laid their hands on the inner world of the toiling people, forcing them to think in the way that they want. Through the state control of the trade unions they have chained the workers to their machines so that labour is no longer a source of joy but a new form of slavery. To the protests of the peasants, expressed in spontaneous uprisings, and those of the workers, whose living conditions have compelled them to strike, they have answered with mass executions and a bloodletting that exceeds even the tsarist generals.'[49]

One would think such powerful words might have made their targets take stock of their actions. Yet their subsequent deeds make it clear that was emphatically not the case. Such is the blessing conferred by true messianic faith one supposes. The Bolsheviks did at least realise the necessity of addressing the crisis though. The mutiny was crushed with pitiless brutality and, in the wake of its suppression, Zinoviev ordered another 500 rebels to be shot with a further 2,000 executed in the month following the rising. Thousands more were sent to concentration camps. In *Pravda* Lenin mendaciously claimed that the previously loyal sailors had been duped by agents of foreign capitalist powers. The Communists then turned to the peasant risings and snuffed them out, killing 15,000 and imprisoning 100,000 more. But while Lenin, and the shock of the Kronstadt mutiny, managed to convince the party membership of the necessity of change, they still championed the collectivist ideal and would support its return under Stalin. Lenin had calmed the party faithful by assuring them the measures were merely a stage on the way to the full implementation of socialism. NEP was rolled out across the nation which at least suggests that even the most dogmatically inflexible zealots can admit that change is occasionally necessary, even if the cost of such a realisation is appallingly high.

Their enthusiasm remained undimmed though and, having successfully crushed all internal opposition, they sought to impose their 'utopia' on the rest of humanity too. In March 1919 Lenin had established Comintern to allow the Bolsheviks to control foreign communist parties. It was also used to impress visitors with just how wonderful their regime was by organising trips for naive socialists to small Russian enclaves. Such communes bore as much resemblance to the rest of the nation as the similarly orchestrated excursions in North Korea have with the rest of that embittered state. But the gullible socialists of Western Europe wanted to believe, so they credulously lapped it up and spread the news of Russia's success to similarly blinkered idealists back home. The credulity of some of those visitors defies belief. In 1920 Ethel Snowden, who arrived in Moscow as a member of the British TUC and Labour Party delegation, was informed that the average Russian factory worker only earned enough in a month to feed his family for three days. She naively replied: 'Oh! How clever and frugal of the workers to live without any food for the other twenty-seven days of the month. How do they do it?'[50]

Lenin also used Comintern to denounce British imperialism even while plotting to bring the former satellites of the Russian empire back under the Bolshevik fold. This hypocrisy was particularly evident in the Ukraine where the Communists crushed the nationalist movement with a brutality that would have made the most cold-hearted imperialist blanch. At the First Congress of the Third International (Comintern) in the Kremlin on 2 March 1919 Lenin, oblivious to the contradictory nature of his proclamation, had declared of imperialism: 'This wild beast will perish and socialism will conquer throughout the world!'[51] By the Second Comintern Congress, held at the Smolny Institute from 19 July 1920, Lenin was ready to be more proactive. He disappointed Sylvia Pankhurst though, the feminist and communist whose mother had started the Suffragette movement. She bristled when Lenin suggested that Britain was not yet ready for socialism. Poland was another matter though. Lenin, in advocating for an invasion, penned a note to Trotsky's deputy, E.M. Skylanski which read: 'A beautiful plan. Finish it off *together* with Dzerzhinsky. Disguised as 'Greens' (we'll heap the blame on them afterwards) will advance 10-20 versts and hang the kulaks, priests, landed gentry. 100,000 rubles prize for each one of them that is hanged'.[52] Lenin and Trotsky expected the Polish workers to greet their armies as saviours and liberators. Instead they confronted them as the invaders they were and routed them.

Undaunted the leaders of the regime committed themselves to the regeneration of those already under their authority. To complete the task it would be necessary to control education and every aspect of the arts. Trotsky outlined their aim: 'The question of how to educate and regulate, of how to improve and complete the physical and spiritual construction of man, is a colossal problem which can only be conceived on the basis of Socialism...To produce a new, 'improved version' of man – that is the future task of Communism'.[53] He even had a template for what such a transformation would produce:

> 'Man will become incomparably stronger, more intelligent, more subtle. His body will be more harmonious, his movements more rhythmical, his voice more musical; the forms of daily existence will acquire a dynamic theatricality. The average human type will rise to the level of Aristotle, Goethe, Marx. It is above this ridge that new summits will rise.'[54]

But while they talked of wanting to 'educate' the populace, their real desire was to control and indoctrinate them. Lenin was reputed to have visited Ivan Pavlov and commented on how he hoped to condition man the way that eminent scientist had programmed dogs:

> 'I want the masses of Russia to follow a Communistic pattern of thinking and reacting. There was too much individualism in the Russia of the past. Communism does not tolerate individualistic tendencies. They are harmful. They interfere with our plans. We must abolish individualism...Man can be corrected. Man can be made what we want him to be.'[55]

The theories of the Communists and the Marxists had always pointed in this direction. For the Communists the ultimate ideal was the eradication of individuality. Man was never to be freed, he was to be remade in their own image. In the fantasy novels produced under the regime, like Bogdanov's *Red Star*, the paragon of Soviet virtue was a rational, committed collectivist who strove only for the greater good and subsumed himself in the service of the state. In his utopia, all citizens were clad in the same drab overalls, lived in identical housing and had their hair cut in a uniformly severe style. The desire to forge such bland, nightmarish societies was remarkably widespread and the intelligentsia saw no contradiction in imposing their values on the workers they claimed to represent even while stifling their freedom and independence. Under the Communists, culture was to serve a purely political purpose. Lenin, like Hitler, was profoundly conservative in his artistic tastes and both Soviet and Nazi regimes would make highly effective use of art, culture and cinema as tools of state propaganda and indoctrination. Lenin frequently wrote of the need for a 'cultural revolution'.

Lilina Zinoviev declared that 'We must make the young generation into a generation of Communists. Children, like soft wax, are very malleable and they should be moulded into good Communists'.[56] Education prioritised vocational training and the students' utility to the state, while Lenin also praised the work of F.W. Taylor who sought to condition workers into automatons. To Lenin this made them the ideal citizens. The Bolsheviks renewed their attacks on the Church and sought to replace the worship of God with worship of the state - closing the churches and slaughtering the clergy. Some citizens even began having Red weddings* with the ceremony taking place in front of a portrait of Lenin rather than an altar. By 1921 Lenin had ordered a new reign of terror with more churches closed and priests shot. In the famine of 1921-2, even though the Church threw itself into the task of famine relief, Lenin accused it of refusing to sell its gold to help the peasantry and used this as a pretext to purge it. He declared: 'we must now wage the most decisive and merciless war against the Black Hundred clergy and suppress its resistance with such cruelty that they will not forget it for decades to come...The more members of the reactionary bourgeoisie and clergy we manage to shoot the better'.[57] During the next two years over 7,000 clergy were killed including 3,500 nuns. The purges had themselves followed a massive programme of iconoclasms. But all their attempts to re-shape man were doomed to failure. In the summation of Orlando Figes:

'It was in many ways a utopian dream – one of the most ambitious in history – to believe that human nature could be changed by simply altering the social environment in which

---

* Not to be confused with Game of Thrones

people lived. Man cannot be transformed quite so easily: human nature moves more slowly than ruling ideologies or society. This is perhaps the one enduring moral lesson of the Russian Revolution – as it is indeed of the terrible history of this [the twentieth] century.'[58]

The attempts to impose new standards of morality in the population were especially ironic in light of the corruption of the party faithful. Exposed to temptation, the Communists quickly exhibited the same weaknesses, fallibilities and greed apparent in any other organisation. While they initially had modest salaries, party members took full advantage of the raft of freebies available to them. These included healthcare, maids, chauffeurs, cooks, food and clothing. Hungry workers soon began to resent those from the Soviets who suddenly acquired fine outfits, luxurious goods and swanky new cars. The Petrograd Provisions Department denied foodstuffs to the masses but sold them to black marketeers before gorging themselves on the profits. As money poured from the Soviets to the party, Stalin refused to 'spy on comrades', believing that political loyalty and the survival of the party eclipsed any concerns about the abuse of power. Socialist regimes removed the checks and balances that usually put a brake on such activities and, as one-party states, were singularly unaccountable. As such, they have frequently taken corruption to unprecedented heights.

The Bolsheviks were far more brazen than any Western government. They were not just an exclusive ruling elite who monopolised all bureaucratic posts and privileges, they were more like a mafia, one that dominated every aspect of public life, including the police and law courts. Their ranks had swelled immeasurably too. Between 1917 and 1921 the number of state employees rocketed from 576,000 to 2.6 million. While the economy stagnated and the workers suffered, bureaucracy flourished. Nepotism was just as rife as under the old regime too. Lenin made Krupskaya the Deputy Commissar for Education while Anna Ul'ianova, his sister, was appointed People's Commissar of Railways. Stalin was equally guilty of ensuring his supporters were handed prominent posts. As a result, a series of ruling dynasties, little different from the old aristocratic families in structure, came to dominate the state. During the Civil War they established restaurants reserved for party members. Within a short space of time they were also given higher salaries, chauffeured cars, first-class railway carriages, subsidised housing, foreign holidays, exclusive shops and hospitals along with rafts of other privileges. The Kremlin and the Petrograd Astoria, both reserved for the party elite, wallowed in caviar, champagne and obscene luxury, and the large numbers of service staff were ordered to treat party members with the sort of obsequious deference previously reserved for the nobility they now increasingly resembled. The likes of Zinoviev swanned from banquet to opera with a string of prostitutes in tow, all paid for by the workers, naturally. The top brass of the party appropriated the estates of the landed gentry for themselves, manning them with armies of servants. Trotsky took the luxurious accommodation of the Yusupovs while Stalin nestled into the ostentatious abode of a former oil baron.

Only Lenin refrained from such opulence. He lived in three Spartan rooms in the Kremlin. Like Robespierre, he had no interest in financial gain or, indeed, anything beyond his dedication to the cause. He was determined to project an image of ideological purity. Yet even he later succumbed. In 1921 he moved into the spacious grandeur of the Gorki mansion while a Rolls Royce was procured to ferry him around in grand style. The homes of the rest grew ever more stuffed with expensive items as their wives accumulated increasingly extravagant jewellery and wardrobes, and bribes became common political currency. These tastes endured too: during WWII, in the dreadful siege of Leningrad, while millions in the city starved and were reduced to eating dogs in the street or driven to cannibalism, the party members had ample provisions shipped in and gorged themselves on extravagant banquets. So much for Marx's forlorn hope that egalitarianism would reign in the society that followed his great revolution.

In 1922 Lenin, dissatisfied with the carnage that had been wrought against the Church, also called for show trials and mass executions of Mensheviks and SRs. It was as if he knew he was running out of time. On this occasion, the party faithful resisted his demands though sweeping new powers of censorship were unanimously agreed upon and the Cheka expelled numerous philosophers, scholars and writers. The leader's work had effectively been done though. The one-party state had been established: no rival agencies were allowed to operate, the Cheka rigorously policed the thought of the populace, the press was merely an organ of the state, the judiciary had no independence, the industrial economy and agricultural production increasingly came under party authority, aspiration and private enterprise were regarded as alien concepts, and terror lay in wait to be unleashed on a cowed populace. Lenin had created the ultimate totalitarian dictatorship. His successors would build upon the foundations he had laid. The costs of his achievement were enormous. Up to 1921 his regime had killed, through civil war, terror, famine and attendant disease, with the greater portion of the total coming in the appalling starvation that hit the Volga region, approximately ten million people.[59] Such figures were to be dwarfed in the coming decades.

The entire Soviet system and all its atrocities were built on the principle of whipping up and then maintaining class hatred. This single tenet, arrogantly regarded as a historical and scientific inevitability, was used to justify every suppressed freedom and murder committed over those bleak decades. From the start the Bolsheviks had enthusiastically taken up the mantle of Jacobinism while dismissing their liberal rivals as Girondins. In doing so the Russians ensured that, rather than attempting to draft an equitable constitution, any reforms they enacted were based on the same class enmities that had proven so disastrous in France. Revenge and social revolution were the great motivator, not political reform, and certainly not the freedom and welfare of the populace. In stifling the people's economic freedoms, their prospects, as well as their liberty, were significantly worsened.

After the murder of Nikolay Bogolepov, the Minister of Education, by a student named Karpevich in March 1901, Pëtr Struve had cautioned against the growing tide of activism. He argued that a revolution would be disastrous for Russia and recommended instead a period of social and political evolution akin to that of Western Europe; one in which workers' constitutional rights and material conditions could be improved within the framework of the capitalist system. The Bolsheviks, utterly convinced that their own path was correct, castigated his suggestion and roared with laughter at his naivety. The consequences of their miscalculation shattered the lives of millions. Commencing with fine principles, the revolutionaries had created the most appalling tyranny imaginable.

But nothing that happened had dented Lenin's certainty that he was creating the perfect state - no amount of war, famine, oppression, poverty, industrial and economic collapse or ever spiralling numbers of political incarcerations and murders would have persuaded him that he was doing anything other than establishing a workers' utopia. Lenin had arrived in Petrograd from seventeen years of exile and knew little of Russia or its people. He had been immersed in ideology, had barely ever worked and continued to draw an income from his mother's estate. According to Gorky, this ignorance of the gruelling nature of the proletariats' existence bred in him a 'pitiless contempt, worthy of a nobleman, for the lives of ordinary people...Life in all its complexity is unknown to Lenin. He does not know the ordinary people. He has never lived among them.'[60] He had a domineering attitude and a remarkable intolerance for dissent. His own wife described him, when engaged in clashes with political rivals, as being in a 'rage'. He seemed consumed with hatred and anger and cursed his opposition as 'blockheads', 'bastards', 'dirty scum', 'prostitutes', 'cunts', 'shits' and 'cretins'. Chernov wrote of him that

> 'Lenin possesses a devotion to the revolutionary cause which permeates his entire being. But to him the revolution is embodied in his person. Lenin possesses an outstanding mind, but it is a...*mind of one dimension* – more than that, a unilinear mind...He is a man of one-sided will and consequently a man with a stunned moral sensitivity.'[61]

He was all too characteristic of the type then.

On 25 May 1922 Lenin suffered a severe stroke. He recovered slowly, but on 10 March 1923 suffered a further massive stroke that incapacitated him. On 21

January 1924 he died. He had left no successor. The big beasts of the party, Trotsky, Stalin, Bukharin, Zinoviev and Kamenev, circled like sharks. Stalin had been dismissed by his rivals as a bureaucratic nonentity, a 'grey blur'. He would prove to be more of a Great White.

Stalin

Georgia had only become part of the Tsar's realm in 1859, following the capture of the Islamist rebel, Shamil, and Gori was still a small, rather backward town when Iosif Vissarinovich Dzughashvili, the boy who would grow up to put it on the map, was born there on 6 December 1878. His father Besarian, or 'Beso', was a cobbler, married to Ketevan 'Keke' Geladze. He was also a violent drunk who frequently beat both spouse and son in frightening alcohol-fuelled rages. Iosif's devout mother, a committed member of the Georgian Orthodox Church, hit the boy too, but her disciplinary spankings cannot be compared to the savage beatings he endured at the hands of his drunken father. She mostly, in contrast to her brutal husband, doted on him. Her tenderness would not be repaid.

Stalin's early years contrasted sharply with the genteel privilege of Lenin and Trotsky. Gori was a brutal, squalid environment and Iosif's family were crushingly poor. A bout of smallpox left the youngster with a badly pockmarked face, but his childhood acquaintances recalled him as confrontational, sly and ambitious. He was determined to be the leader of the local gang and would not rest until achieving his goal. The pecking order in Gori was decided by sometimes shockingly violent street fights, but in that rough, dog eat dog existence, Stalin's fortitude was such that he worked his way to the top of the pile. Many historians cite the hard experiences of his early life as playing a significant part in his later actions, and they undoubtedly influenced his adult personality. It is worth noting though that Robespierre's privileged upbringing and squeamish pacifism could not be further removed from Stalin's formative experiences. All they shared was an ideological similarity, yet both became tyrants of a singularly ruthless nature.

In 1888 young Iosif entered the Gori Spiritual School. His pious mother had ambitions for her son and his admission gave him an opportunity denied to the vast majority of boys in Gori: an education. Iosif's father, disapproving of Keke's ecclesiastical ambitions, dragged him out of the seminary and got him work in a shoe factory in Georgia's capital, Tbilisi, about fifty miles, or two days walk, from Gori. But Ketevan convinced the priests to persuade her husband to allow the boy back to school and Beso returned to Tbilisi where he disappeared down the bottle. He was never heard from again, descending into full-blown alcoholism and dying a few years later 'alone, unmourned and unloved', as one great writer might put it.

As his education developed Iosif became increasingly keen on poetry and Georgian literature, especially Alexander Qazbegi's *The Patricide*. The book told the story of Koba who lived a rugged, frontier life, eschewed the trappings of civilisation and commerce, and led a romantic rebellion against the Tsar. The book eulogised violence and revenge, portrayed the main protagonist as an honourable man, and cast all authority as inherently malevolent. While an idealised and naive tale it certainly influenced Stalin's later political inclinations. It had such a profound impact on the youngster that he even began referring to himself as Koba. The literary youngster completed his schooling with excellent grades. His report also commended him on his behaviour and in 1894, aged fifteen, he left for the Spiritual Seminary in Tbilisi.

The state capital, with a population of some 350,000, dwarfed little Gori which could boast no more than 20,000 inhabitants. The Seminary there was for boys regarded as academically able and aimed at a much higher level of schooling. The curriculum included mathematics, Greek, literature and history, but it was primarily geared towards preparing its students for the priesthood. This chapter of the boy's life would later prove a terrible embarrassment to the revolutionary who, like all his peers, grew into a militant atheist. Yet it was, nevertheless, a significant stage of his development. In fact, as the boys rebelled against its strict culture of hierarchical piety, the seminary inadvertently produced scores of revolutionary atheists. Having lost their religion the students sought elsewhere for meaning in their lives; they found it in Marx.

Bullock made some pertinent observations on how this period impacted the future dictator's thought processes:

> 'The fact that it was a Church education helped to form the mind of a man who was to become known for his dogmatism and propensity for seeing issues in absolute terms, in black and white. Anyone reading Stalin's speeches and writings will notice their catechistic structure, the use of question and answer, the reduction of complex questions to a set of simplified formulas, the quoting of texts to support his arguments...The continuity was strengthened by the same requirements of orthodoxy, the exclusion of doubt, the intolerance of dissent and the persecution of heretics in both systems.'[62]

Years later his daughter, Svetlana, said her father despised the priests at the seminary because they 'were intolerant, coarse, deceiving their flocks in order to hold them in obedience; that they intrigued, lied and as a rule possessed numerous faults and very few virtues'.[63] If ever a pot called the kettle black.

Iosif quickly became enamoured with socialist ideas and also enjoyed modest success with his poetry. In June 1895 a local journal, *Iveria*, published by Ilya Chavchavadze, printed the first of his poems to see the light of day: 'To the Moon'. Several more were published including 'Morning', a juvenile and rather nauseating ode to natural beauty and Georgian patriotism.

Morning

The rose's bud had blossomed out
Reaching out to touch the violet
The lily was waking up
And bending its head to the breeze

High in the clouds the lark
Was singing a chirruping hymn
While the joyful nightingale
With a gentle voice was saying

'Be full of blossom, oh lovely land
Rejoice Iverians' country
And you, oh Georgian, by studying
Bring joy to the motherland'

Robert Conquest has suggested, on the basis of such efforts, that 'a curious little volume might be made of the poems of Stalin, Mao and Ho Chi Minh, with illustrations by A. Hitler'.[64] Stalin spent a busy spell writing saccharine pieces for publication in the local socialist literature and later claimed his first exposure to Marx was in this period. He grew increasingly alienated from the authorities and obsessed with socialism while developing an interest in politics and economics. But as his militancy increased, his interest in poetry gradually waned.

This shift in his priorities is apparent from a school report of 28 September 1898. It recorded that the previously well behaved pupil 'is rude and disrespectful towards persons in authority and systematically fails to bow to one of the teachers'.[65] In May 1899 he walked out of the seminary without sitting his final exams. He had lost his faith but discovered a new religion. The diligence he had previously shown in his studies was transferred to a rigorous examination of socialist ideology, a subject that would obsess him for decades. Iosif worked briefly at the Physical Observatory, recording temperature and weather readings, and took up lodgings in a small flat. The cramped abode became a meeting point for a revolutionary group who resented the imperial order and craved radical change. Iosif adopted the rather unkempt fashions of his radical peers while reading in depth on the French Revolution and the Paris Commune of 1871. He also absorbed the work of Marx, Engels, Lassalle and

Plekhanov. He was particularly inspired when attending a talk on Marxism given by Lev Kamenev who, in 1936, would be consumed in his Terror. Iosif started to spread Marxist propaganda among the railway and factory workers in the area before, on the night of 21-22 March 1901, the Okhrana raided his workplace and several of his colleagues were arrested. He escaped capture, went on the run, and would lead the life of a fugitive for over fifteen years.

Iosif was never a great theorist but, having become affiliated with the Social Democrats, he began to excel in propaganda. He also proved capable of organising strikes and protests. In Batumi, on the Black Sea, an area dominated by oil barons, he began work at the Rothschild refinery shortly before it was partly consumed in a blaze. Iosif, suspected of arson, was incarcerated and served a spell in Siberian exile before escaping in 1904. The experience was hardly as forbidding as it sounds. Exile in the Tsarist system, where convicts were allowed to study, and given ample time and resources to do so, was akin to a dull holiday camp. Inmates socialised, read, had affairs, entertained visitors and lived in relative comfort on the allowance given them by the Tsar. Escape was easy, and having fled his bonds Iosif threw himself into activism in the wake of the 1905 Revolution, positioning himself in particular opposition to Anarchists, Social-Revolutionaries and Mensheviks. Of the latter he declared 'Against them any methods are good',[66] an indication of his future ruthlessness.

He met Lenin for the first time in December that year at the Bolshevik conference in Finland. They both declared no interest in taking part in the newly established Duma and reaffirmed their commitment to an armed uprising. But then the young activist was already showing a particular relish for the more brutal aspects of revolutionary agitation. On 16 July 1906 he married Ketevan Svaridze who presented him with a son, Yakob, the following year. After less than a year and a half of marriage, his wife died, possibly of tuberculosis. Iosif unceremoniously dumped Yakob with his in-laws. They also helped him with money so he could carry on his activism unencumbered by such concerns. Like all such radicals, his political ideology took priority over personal relationships. He had seen little of either his wife or child even before her premature demise, being otherwise engaged in militant activism, and Iosif would not see his son again for some fifteen years. But while fully committed to the Bolshevik cause he was well down the pecking order from Lenin, Plekhanov, Axelrod and Martov. He would remain relatively obscure for some considerable time. On 25 March 1908, as a result of his increasing activism, Iosif was again arrested by the Okhrana and imprisoned in Baku, though he was soon on the run once more. Years of incarceration, exile, escape and re-arrest followed.

Iosif's chief role in that period was organising armed robberies, principally from banks. It was the sort of behaviour he admired so much in Koba and, as it involved seizing the profits of capitalism to fund a party claiming dedication to the people, such criminality could, to those of a certain persuasion, be cast as altruism. That attitude served to exonerate the consciences of those taking part. Their self-image was close to the romantic fantasy of Robin Hood, but those on the business ends of their guns saw only the grubby reality of violent, pitiless bandits. The groups operated out of houses on Mount David in Tbilisi where Stalin's main accomplices were his old school-friend, Joseph Davrishevi and the Armenian Semën Ter-Petrosyou, who went by the name Kamo. It was not uncommon for them to throw bombs at the guards during the robberies or to resort to Mafioso style extortions from local businesses.

Their activities were frequently barbaric. On 26 June 1907 they carried out a particularly notorious raid in Tbilisi, or Tiflis, as it was known at the time. Stalin orchestrated a sizeable gang for the operation which had been authorised and approved by Lenin. They planned to attack the guarded carriages, which transported the bank's funds, just as the convoy entered the town's main square. Ten bombs were tossed at the police and the local Cossack contingent, tearing men and horses apart in a series of dreadful explosions. The gang followed up this indiscriminate slaughter by whipping out their concealed pistols before the dazed authorities could recover their senses. Under a hail of gunfire they plucked bags of cash from the wreckage before making good their escape.

The carriage with the main bulk of the booty had avoided the explosions and almost slipped away when one of the gang threw another bomb in its direction. It ripped the horse that was pulling it to pieces. Stalin's associate, Kamo, grabbed the sacks and heaved them into a small trailer attached to his horse before galloping away to a prearranged place of refuge. Yerevan Square was left a scene of carnage, littered with body parts and splashed with gore. The large number of bombs employed in a crowded square had killed and wounded scores of civilians. Fifty badly mangled survivors lay moaning and crying amid the smoke, severed limbs and charred and blood-spattered buildings of the plaza. Forty people had been killed.

Devotion to the cause meant that little sleep was lost over such massacres and life swiftly moved on. In 1912 Iosif became editor of the Bolshevik newspaper *Pravda* ('The Truth'), which made its debut on 22 April. In the same year he graduated to the Bolshevik Central Committee and adopted his famous moniker, dropping Dzughashvili for the punchier 'Stalin' – Man of Steel. Stalin and Lenin spent a period of time together in Krakow where Vladimir was impressed by the tough, working class demeanour of the Georgian. He saw him as the perfect archetype of the Bolshevik activist. But such attributes left him open to risk. On 23 February 1913 Stalin was arrested once more and exiled to Siberia.

This time it would be four years before he tasted liberty again, yet it proved a relatively comfortable experience. Stalin was put up by a local family and promptly got their thirteen year old daughter pregnant. After the child gave birth the shameless radical wasted no time in getting her pregnant again. While a sentence of hard labour was an option for such prisoners, Lenin and Trotsky had also enjoyed similarly cushy periods of incarceration. There is simply no comparison between the experience of those imprisoned by the Tsar and those sent to the gulag once Stalin took stewardship of the state. As with France, however bad things were under the old regime, they would become incomparably worse when the revolutionaries took over. Stalin was still in Siberian exile when Revolution hit in February 1917 and, on hearing that the monarchy had crumbled, he raced back to Petrograd.

He arrived on 12 March, just ten days after the abdication of Nicholas II, and was put up by a loyal Bolshevik family, Sergei and Olga Alliluev, a couple he had known for years. The Alliluevs, in true Bolshevik style, regularly let their young children fend for themselves when they were busy with revolutionary activity. Stalin settled in quickly and was somewhat taken by the family's daughter, Nadya. Though he was in his late thirties and she, at sixteen, was less than half his age, he lost no time in seducing her. On this occasion he would at least have the decency to marry the girl, though, in characteristic party fashion, she effectively became his secretary. She was a good loyal party girl, obviously; those of such an inclination only ever associate with people who share their outlook. They live in an insular little bubble, cocooned from contact with any whose opinions they may find disagreeable. The Bolsheviks were already developing into an exclusive class with close parallels to Russia's old aristocracy. Stalin, for instance, later befriended Dzerzhinsky's personal assistant Stanislaw Redens who married Nadya's sister, Anna, and became a leading figure in the Cheka. Upon arriving in Petrograd, Stalin and Kamenev quickly established themselves among the Bolshevik hierarchy until Lenin returned and seized full control of the party apparatus. Stalin immediately rallied behind him. By the end of the year he had become indispensable to the party bureaucracy. But it was really in the struggle against the Whites that he began to assert himself.

In the early stages of the Civil War Stalin was put in charge of grain procurement in the south around, ironically, Tsaritsyn, the metropolis on the Volga that would later bear his name. He showed his true colours by acting as a power-crazed lunatic, considering himself the superior of the Red Army commanders in the region and purging the middle classes wherever he could. He got Sergei Minin and Kliment Voroshilov to join him in forming a Military Council, a measure supported by Lenin, and Stalin quickly adopted the military-style clothing that would be his trademark for the rest of his life. His antipathy to Trotsky also solidified in this period and an opposition to the former Menshevik, the Revolution's 'Napoleon', began to coalesce around him. Having assumed a position of seniority in the area Stalin employed remarkable brutality and intimidation against the peasants, torching whole villages in a widespread policy of terror. He also practised severe discipline with Red Army conscripts, and was terribly profligate with their lives. He relied on numerical superiority while blithely indifferent to the sickening rate of casualties incurred by his tactics. Stalin saw treachery and conspiracies everywhere with any setbacks blamed on wreckers, saboteurs and counter-revolutionaries. In reality his own policies were creating ever greater inefficiencies, problems he then blamed on traitors to the regime.

By the time that Lenin was debilitated by a series of strokes Stalin had assumed the position of General Secretary of the Communist Party. The role was not quite as significant as it perhaps sounds. But it reflects the fact that he had become a senior figure in the organisation, a contender to succeed the great leader, even if he was regarded as an outsider at the time. Yet he was able to use the unassuming nature of his position to his advantage. Lenin had attempted to scupper Stalin's chances of succeeding him by criticising his brutality, but his efforts were half-hearted at best and terminated by illness. Besides, he had criticised Stalin's rivals too, chastising Trotsky, for instance, for his arrogance and ambition. Lenin had a regular habit of condemning others for traits he forgave in himself.

Stalin survived the leader's censure and, because he was largely regarded as a bureaucrat, was able to portray himself as a servant of the party, an image his more overtly ambitious competitors were unable to employ. The other contenders, to a man, considered Trotsky the greatest threat to their chances. It was their good fortune that his conceit and intellectual posturing had already alienated much of the party faithful. Those who wanted to level society respected only bland uniformity and anyone who stood out reminded them of the old elites. Trotsky's charisma, polemical flamboyance and beautifully tailored suits filled his peers with revulsion.

It is striking that 'individualist' was considered a particularly damning slander among Marxists. The admirable trait was, of course, conformity. Trotsky just stood out too much. To the Soviet 'Republicans' Stalin appeared to have Cato's modesty while Trotsky had the whiff of Caesar about him. Stalin had also worked assiduously on appointments and, as a result, the levers of power in the party were largely indebted to him. While Trotsky was the great orator, writer and theoretician, Stalin was the archetypal bureaucrat. In the Kafkaesque corridors of Soviet power he epitomised the more highly regarded qualities of industriousness and service to the state - one who had no time for glamour or ambition. So it appeared at any rate. But while the likes of Kamenev and Zinoviev considered him a mediocrity they could use to defeat Trotsky it was really Stalin who was using them. As the others jostled for position, he would show the patience of Tokugawa. Once the great orator was out of the way, it would be their turn.

Trotsky hardly helped his cause when he published *The New Course*, a criticism of party policy, particularly of NEP, even as the ailing Lenin lay dying.

A Left Opposition rallied round him, but Stalin, Bukharin, Kamenev and Zinoviev took the opportunity to unite against him. At the time of the NEP crisis Lenin had called for an end to factionalism. They were demands which would end in dictatorship, for they could be used to ruthlessly crush any deviation. Factionalism eventually became the greatest of crimes – a heresy from accepted scripture that demanded stern punishment for any apostate. Now Lenin's words were employed as a justification to isolate Trotsky. Kamenev and Zinoviev turned on him and accused him of starting a faction, a charge that could have been levelled at any one of them. Perceived as the party splitter, and disliked for his grandiosity, he was ruined. Kamenev and Zinoviev demanded his expulsion from the party but Stalin, wanting to appear moderate, prevented it. That could wait until later.

In January 1925 Trotsky, under increasing pressure, was forced out as Commissar for Military Affairs. He hoped to ward off accusations that he was a new Napoleon, but all he had done was effectively neutralise himself by cutting his ties with the Red Army. With their great rival isolated the other big beasts of the party began to manoeuvre against each-other. While the Politburo was initially led by Kamenev after Lenin's death, Stalin had been gradually building a faction around himself. Vyacheslav Molotov, Lazar Kaganovich, Kliment Voroshilov, Sergo Ordzhonikidze, Sergei Kirov and Semen Budyonny constituted the core of his support. All were renowned for their hardness and revolutionary commitment. Kamenev and Zinoviev made their move against Stalin and Bukharin in 1925, but in launching their attack at a time of weakness for the party the assault seemed treacherous. Stalin, in contrast, promised to provide stability. By the end of the year he and Bukharin controlled the Politburo and the Central Committee.

In April 1926 Trotsky, Zinoviev and Kamenev came together in a desperate bid to survive. They formed what was known as the United Opposition. Trotsky referred to his opponents as 'Thermidoreans'. The slur, in reference to those who had overthrown the tyranny of Robespierre and ended the Terror, was a common insult among Marxists. It is revealing of their mindset that they considered it a form of abuse. To be a Jacobin, by contrast, was a badge of pride. The triumvirate denounced Stalin and Bukharin who accused them of factionalism, purged their support and, in 1927, expelled them from the party. Stalin and Bukharin had stood on a platform of defending NEP. Within a year Stalin would destroy his ally, repudiate NEP and introduce his new economic vision for Russia. Stalinism was about to begin in earnest.

Socialists the world over have long tried to distance themselves from Stalin. He was, they claim, merely a brutal dictator who had no real interest in their manifesto. But, much as they may wish it were so, there is no truth in this claim at all. Stalin had based his campaign on adherence to party ideology and reverence for the legacy of Lenin. His rise and eventual regime depended on convincing the party membership of his rigid loyalty to the Marxist-Leninist line. He had moved quickly to establish these credentials. Within a month of the leader's death Petrograd had been renamed Leningrad even as his embalmed corpse, at Stalin's insistence and against the protests of his widow, was put on ghoulish display in Moscow. Following his death Lenin was portrayed as a Messiah and his political writing as the New Gospels. But if Christianity had surrendered to Communism, and Lenin was the new Christ, then the role of St. Paul would be adopted by Stalin. He busied himself with compiling Lenin's speeches and writing, expunging them of any contradictions or sections where the former leader had been proven wrong. He also made sure to draw parallels between his own written efforts and those of the founder of the Communist state. He further emphasised this role by publishing *The Foundations of Leninism* in 1924, an able compression of socialist ideas.

Stalin, while not a talented writer or the most advanced of ideological thinkers, had been an avid and committed student of socialist theory for some time. He always considered himself more of a practical revolutionary than a theoretician, but the role played a greater part in his revolutionary make-up than has often been assumed. Of all the Russian thinkers: Lenin, Trotsky and Bukharin included, it is Robert Service's judgement that 'Only Bogdanov can be categorised as an original thinker'.[67] Stalin, then, is far less removed from his intellectual peers, who effectively synthesised the ideas of others, than is frequently believed. He cannot be compared with Lenin for the depth of his ideological scrutiny and is certainly no match for Trotsky as a stylist (who is?), but he was a rigorous student of the genre nonetheless.

Stalin made sure he was well versed in socialist theory and was tutored in Hegel, Kant, Feuerbach, Fichte, Schelling, Plekhanov, Kautsky and Francis Bradley. Such tutoring was, admittedly, an attempt to paste over his own theoretical incompetence and, frequently, incomprehension, but his efforts to such ends cannot be faulted. His treatment of his teachers certainly can though. His chief tutors, Jan Sten and Ksenofontov were later shot, as was David Ryazonov after protracted and creative torture eventually persuaded I.I. Rubin to denounce him. Stalin, knowing the importance of theory to his position, wanted no witnesses to any chinks in his armour left walking around.

Their tutoring certainly paid dividends though. He became increasingly prolific in contributing articles to the socialist press relatively early in his career and, of course, his long-standing tenure as editor of *Pravda* should not be underestimated. Some felt that *Anarchism or Socialism*, published as early as 1906-7, was so accomplished that it must have been penned by another's hand. In 1913 he composed *Marxism and the National Question*, his most famous and perhaps most original work. It confirmed him as an authority on the issue and contributed to his later role in the formation of the USSR (Union of Soviet Socialist Republics). Ideologically Stalin followed Marx's template, as Lenin had done before him, fully endorsing the need for a violent revolution followed by brutal suppression. It was a path that would establish the 'proletarian dictatorship' by ruthlessly crushing the old propertied classes. All vestiges of the old society were to be eliminated and 'modernity' would reign while a centralised economy and command of production would prove far more efficient than wasteful capitalism. Stalin's commitment to these central principles was unswerving. It would remain firm until his death.

He had been clear about such tenets when, in October 1917, he published an article in *Pravda* which argued 'The existing government of landlords and capitalists must be replaced by a new government, a government of workers and peasants'.[68] Those same workers and peasants were to experience untapped levels of suffering when their defender assumed control of the state. But there is no denying the strength of Stalin's conviction to socialism, the cause to which he dedicated his life. He continued to agonise over ideology during the Civil War, poring over a copy of Lenin's *The State and Revolution* while on campaign and making detailed notes in the margins. But, not only was he well versed in socialist theory, it was vital for him to ensure that he was faithful to it too. It was what drove him and what his ambition relied upon. Stalin's rise to power depended on the fact that he could convince the membership of his unswerving loyalty to the party and his rigid, inflexible adherence to Marxist dogma. These were the traits they valued above all others. It was a culture that would see them support atrocities beyond compare.

He knew the best way to secure support was to give the party what it wanted. It was to that end that Stalin elected to overturn NEP and institute a policy of collectivised agriculture, one of the rocks upon which socialism was built. While it had been useful to express support for NEP in order to remove Trotsky, it became even more expedient to oppose it to win over the rank and file. The party faithful had never come to terms with Lenin's retreat from their socialist ideals, even though the crisis in the Volga that precipitated the *volte-face* had been catastrophic. There was also a lingering suspicion that Lenin had been insufficiently vigorous in his pursuit and prosecution of the kulak menace. The Bolsheviks were not motivated by reality or practical concerns, but by ideology alone. They would follow their sacred book – no matter the consequences - and to win their loyalty Stalin would return them to the theoretical purity they desired. The result would be famine on an altogether different scale.

Famine

The trigger for the shift in policy was a grain crisis at the beginning of 1928. In reality, it was little more than a temporary blip which could have been corrected with a sensible market adjustment. But the party turned to a radical and panicked overhaul instead. The shortfall was caused by the Soviet Union's endemic mismanagement of the economy and almost universal incompetence in financial matters. The Bolsheviks had focused on developing industry and provided few incentives for the peasants to increase their output. In warring on the kulaks, they had also eliminated the most efficient members of the rural workforce. The result was a sharp decline in grain production. But Stalin blamed the shortages on kulak hoarders and ordered a programme of requisitioning to address the situation. The use of brute force to seize grain which had been produced for profit would only worsen the crisis. It destroyed the motivation of the peasantry, though it convinced the party they had found a simple answer to the problem. Yet it simply never occurred to them to improve trading conditions. Their rural policies thus reveal the paradox at the heart of socialist thinking: While the Bolsheviks wanted to encourage agricultural production, their doctrinal position meant they automatically regarded peasants that rose to the challenge as enemies of the state.

The short term fix of requisitioning inspired Stalin to widen the policy, for he knew the move would placate the left of the party. The manifesto he hit upon was a three-pronged plan: Requisitioning was to be stepped up, agricultural production would be consolidated into giant collective farms, and the kulaks would be dealt with once and for all. He then planned to sell the grain overseas and use the revenue to finance a massive programme of industrialisation and militarisation. All manufacturing was also to be brought under the aegis of the state. The new policy line was announced in April 1929 as the First Five Year Plan. It was, in reality, not a plan at all but a series of targets with no real operational schedule for how the desired totals were to be achieved. Bukharin and the Right Oppositionists, who preferred sticking with NEP, prudently warned that Stalin's plan was likely to result in disaster. But the majority left of the party emphatically endorsed it. They had never been comfortable with the concessions made to the market and relished the opportunity to overturn them - to return to pure socialism while launching an attack on their class enemies into the bargain. Yet their idealism would be proven a hollow sham and Bukharin's predictions entirely correct.

The sliver of prosperity and liberty permitted under NEP had been welcomed by the populace. Order, and even a sense of tranquillity, had been restored to the nation. But the Five Year Plan would bring the state to its knees once more. Stalin's brief shift to the right had been an aberration in a lifetime's unswerving commitment to the radical left. It had allowed him to outmanoeuvre his rivals while maintaining allegiance to the Leninist line. But, as Lenin had always declared NEP to be a temporary measure, Stalin was able to shift camps again while maintaining his ideological purity. Having defeated the leaders of the party's left, Stalin swiftly adopted their policies to isolate Bukharin. He presented himself as the guardian of socialism and promised abundance and happiness for the Soviet citizens. The wealth of greedy factory owners, bankers and landlords was to be redistributed while Stalin's opponents were repeatedly tarred as 'capitalists' and 'kulak sympathisers' in *Pravda*. The tactic was tremendously successful. Over the second half of 1929 Bukharin was ousted from Comintern and the Politburo before his supporters were purged too. The bulk of the party were convinced their ideology was superior to that of commerce, and Stalin was eager to give them the opportunity to prove it. They grasped it with both hands.

Early efforts at collectivisation had fizzled with the introduction of NEP and by 1928 less than 2% of households were involved in them. Stalin believed the giant farms would make his state the richest granary in the world. But such enterprises had not emerged in capitalist economies and, while Stalin focused on imposing Marxist ideology on Soviet agriculture, no one suggested using better quality ploughs or more efficient forms of crop rotation. A state-owned economy and state-directed society was the aim, and if it was to be achieved by the implementation of force then so be it. Scores of agents, up to 30,000 of them, were sent to the Volga, Ukraine, Siberia and the Caucasus. Arbitrary targets were set and a policy of brutal requisitioning encouraged.

On 7 November 1929 Stalin, somewhat prematurely, announced the success of collectivisation, his progressive policy to which villages, even whole provinces, were said to be flocking. The plenum ratified his position and issued a decree on the need to radically overhaul agricultural production. In December a new Commissariat of Agriculture was established, headed by Yakovlev, that recommended complete collectivisation of the grain-producing areas within three years. Their mania was fuelled by the dizzying effects the Wall St. Crash had on the most dedicated zealots. Communists the world over celebrated the Depression even as it devastated the working classes – the very people they claimed to care about. Its apparent collapse persuaded them they had been right about capitalism all along. The time was now surely ripe to roll out full socialism. This enthusiasm was made apparent by Pyatakov in October 1929. He declared that 'We are obliged to adopt extreme rates of collectivization of agriculture [because of] the same tension with which we worked in the time of armed struggle with the class enemy. The heroic period of our socialist construction has arrived'.[69] There would be a terrible price to pay for this conviction.

The first victims of the party's rediscovered fanaticism were the kulaks. In May 1929 it was declared that a kulak farm was one that involved hired labour, machinery and commercial activities. It was a definition that applied to almost any smallholding in the state. Anyone judged to have taken in even temporary help or to own a single cow or horse was now deemed a vile capitalist and a legitimate target for persecution. The Bolsheviks were poised to attack not just the peasantry who were marginally less destitute than their peers, but also the most influential villagers - any who were hostile to, or even reluctant to embrace, the regime. Such elements were to be removed from the collective farm so they would not corrupt its socialist purity. But the policy merely erased the most efficient and productive farmers. The earlier 'crisis' had already been blamed on kulak 'hoarders' and hysterical class hatred had whipped up animosity against them. Now the party were largely united on the need for their 'removal'. But what began as a policy of deportations became far more brutal, and much of the impetus originated at grassroots level, like the Central Volga Party Committee that voted to expel them on 20 May 1929.

On 27 December 1929 Stalin announced the aim of 'the liquidation of the kulaks as a class'.[70] The policy was endorsed by the Politburo on 30 January 1930. Widespread class hatred was used to justify the mass expulsions to the rapidly mushrooming network of concentration camps in the most hostile and isolated areas of the vast state. But, despite all the rhetoric, the kulaks were far from wealthy. They were certainly significantly poorer than the government officials who were enthusiastically persecuting them. Yet the policy of de-kulakization gave the party a convenient target to blame for all the inefficiencies of their own policies. It also spread far further afield than those areas initially targeted for collectivisation. For this Stalin turned to Vyacheslav Molotov (The Hammer), the man who, in Simon Sebag Montefiore's judgement, was 'a stickler for Bolshevik theory and severity: the Robespierre of Stalin's court'.[71]

Molotov, with his heavyset physique and pug face, offset by glasses, carefully manicured moustache and tailored suits, appeared part academic, part retired boxer. He had divided the kulaks into three different classes which would be subject to separate treatment. Category III kulaks were to be used as slave labour in road construction, forestry and mining; those in category II were to be detained in camps while category I suspects were to be immediately eliminated. The families of category I members were to be deported. Molotov took personal responsibility for the death squads and concentration camps. Detachments of loyal party enforcers were drafted in to ensure the targets set by the Central Committee were met while any resistance was to be snuffed out. In the event, the party faithful set about the task so enthusiastically that such instructions seemed superfluous.

The original plan allowed for 1,065,000 families or 5 to 6 million individuals to be de-kulakised, but regional initiative swelled this number considerably. Official documents show that while the party recommended targeting 4-5% of farms, provincial enthusiasm frequently saw the number balloon to 20%. Most impartial research has concluded the minimum number of evictions to have totalled 10 million. Robert Conquest, who has studied the period closer than anyone and to whom I am indebted for the majority of evidence in this section, has suggested a figure of 13 million. But even these bald statistics fail to capture the horror of that period. Heads of households were rounded up and shot while their families were targeted for exile in the second wave of the programme. The numbers involved were already so vast that the NKVD found the task too much for them to handle and they turned to the party for support. Despite the excesses which could result in, for instance, fifteen out of nineteen farms being de-kulakised in Dnipropetrovsk province, a further series of deportations was ordered in February 1931. Word of the plan leaked and a million or more families fled, abandoning everything they owned. Some smashed their machinery or burned their property as a form of protest.

While party activists tended to support the policy, it was met with horror by the majority of the peasantry. The behaviour of the agents significantly heightened the incipient alarm felt in rural areas. Activists involved in the clearances, infused with class hatred, screamed 'kulak bastards' at the children and 'blood-suckers' at their parents. Their targets were also derided as 'parasites', 'vermin' and 'louses'. Few of the brutal agents doubted the truth of the verbal barbs they hurled and any who protested were ruthlessly beaten. A woman activist later justified her actions by claiming that 'they are not human beings. They are kulaks'.[72] Mikhail Sholokov dramatized the type of committed activist involved in the clearances. He recorded one agent's disgust at his partner's squeamishness over beating children. 'Snake!...How are you serving the revolution? Having pity on them? Yes...You could line up thousands of old men, women, and children and tell me they'd got to be crushed into the dust for the sake of the revolution, and I'd shoot them all down with a machine-gun'.[73] It was a portrayal supported by the testimony of Lev Kopelev who recalled that when carrying out his duties 'I emptied out the old folks' storage chests, stopping my ears to the children's crying and the women's wails...I was convinced I was accomplishing the great and necessary transformation of the countryside'.[74] But the version of events in *the History of the Communist Party* paints a somewhat different picture: 'the peasants chased the kulaks from the land, dekulakised them, took away their livestock and machinery, and requested the Soviet power to arrest and deport the kulaks'.[75] In reality the peasants were the targets of the persecution rather than its cheerleaders.

Every aspect of de-kulakisation was simply abominable: from the trumped-up charges that were levelled, the mass shootings, the appalling conditions of transportation, the state of the camps or labour sites they were shipped off to, and the sheer number of victims involved. Party organs admitted that the kulak clearances were largely aimed at potential enemies of the regime: White Army personnel, former police officers and the likes of gendarmes. But an examination of individual cases reveals the reality of their targets. One peasant who had served in the Red Army had two horses and a cow, sufficient evidence to single him out for punishment. He was charged crippling taxes which he could not pay and his property was seized and handed to an activist. Accused of owning fifty head of cattle, among numerous false allegations, he was sentenced to five years hard labour. Another was sent to clear snow off a railway line. When he returned, all his property was gone apart from a kettle. He was then arrested and deported to Siberia to join a logging gang. Another was ordered to pay tax on a quantity of grain over five times what his land could produce. He bought crops from elsewhere to cover the costs and was then arrested and exiled to Siberia for engaging in private trade. Yet another had all his property seized, including his children's clothes, bar what they were wearing. His children ended up begging, but activists seized whatever they were given. The man's whole family were evicted and died in exile. One peasant was deported because he had hired a girl for one month to help with the harvest while his son was serving in the Red Army. Another girl recalled how her father was brutally beaten before the family were violently kicked out of their home and herded onto cattle trucks. At a stop the girls were allowed to try and find milk for the baby, but when they returned the train had gone. Separated from her sister by an angry mob, she never saw her family again. Category I prisoners suffered even more. In Kiev, in the winter of 1929-30, between 70 and 120 were shot in the gaol every night. In Peltova prison, 36 inmates were crammed into cells built for seven, and daily rations were just 100 grammes of black bread. Around 30 prisoners died every day.

The transportation of those targeted evokes images of the Holocaust, only it was on a much larger scale, and the journeys were far longer. Vassily Grossman described the terrible sight as kulaks were driven from their homes in long processions, whipped and stumbling in the mud. Many died where they fell. 'The party activists didn't give a damn about them'.[76] Huge numbers were herded into cattle trucks and attached to trains which pulled 50 or 60 cars. Around 15-20% of those deported, chiefly children, died en route, a total of around three million victims before they even reached their destination. One account reports a pregnant woman giving birth while in transit. The baby died and the guards slung its corpse off the moving train. Many were transported by river and mass drownings were common. Upon arrival in Siberia many deportees were forced to fell trees and construct their own accommodation.

Food was scarce, usually a bowl of soup a day, and the death tolls were horrendous. All were swiftly put to work and expected to be able to feed themselves from the poor soil and hostile climate. Some worked so hard that they prospered and were thus deported again.

The mortality rates were appalling. Fifty families were sent to Sverdlovsk: In 1942 just five returned to report that all the others had died. A Ukrainian couple, their parents and nine children were sent off to the Solovetsky Islands. A nine year old boy found wandering the wilderness, who had endured a bullet in the leg, survived, but all twelve of the other family members had perished. In Tomsk, at a camp where 13,000 kulaks were held on meagre rations, 18-20 people died every day. Nearly 5,000 arrived at a camp in a Siberian forest in October 1931. Within six months only half remained. Scores of 'class criminals' who died in such dreadful conditions were children. Casualties were just as high in the projects organised by the Soviets themselves. In 1932 thousands were sent to mine gold at Magadan, one of the coldest parts of the entire state. When winter swept in not more than one in fifty, including the guards and dogs, survived. Over 170,000 slave labourers were drafted in to construct the 227 kilometre long Baltic – White Sea Canal. Some 25,000 of the prisoners died in a year and a half of the brutal construction project and, when completed, it was discovered the canal was not deep enough for the large vessels it had been built to accommodate.

Many party members had used the opportunity to settle scores. Countless numbers were denounced as kulaks on the basis of personal grudges, and a mountain of propaganda was churned out to justify the dreadful clearances. *Pravda* published reams of articles about the issue suggesting, in March 1930, that the wider peasantry recognised 'the need for the organization and development of collective farms, the need for the elimination of the kulaks as a class'.[77] Sergei Eisenstein made a propaganda film about the phenomenon that portrayed the kulak as 'fat, lazy, gluttonous, brutal, as scummy a creature as ever trod this earth'.[78] In reality of course if there ever was such a thing as a kulak, then he was an industrious, innovative spendthrift, the direct opposite of the caricatured stereotype.

The process of de-kulakisation was designed to remove troublesome elements who might interfere with the policy with which it went in tandem: collectivisation. The process of herding the peasantry into collective farms was an even bigger operation, and every bit as brutal. The Soviets were convinced the grain crisis would be solved by the practice as socialist farming was, in their rigid view, more efficient than capitalist husbandry. They also believed that uniting the peasantry in a class war against the kulaks would mobilise them to support both collectivisation and requisitioning. Their compliance would be unnecessary however as force and dogmatic hysteria were the true agents of the procedure. Those involved in ordering the measures felt sure the ends would justify the means. They were convinced that they were creating a socialist utopia, so any temporary suffering would ultimately be justified. Any perceived to be disrupting the process were deemed to deserve no mercy at all. Agents sent into the countryside were under strict instructions:

'You must assume your duties with a feeling of the strictest Party responsibility, without whimpering, without any rotten liberalism. Throw your bourgeois humanitarianism out of the window and act like Bolsheviks worthy of Comrade Stalin. Beat down the kulak agent wherever he raises his head. It's war – it's them or us! The last decayed remnant of capitalist farming must be wiped out at any cost!...Your job is to get the grain at any price. Pump it out of them, wherever it is hidden, in ovens, under beds, in cellars or buried away in back yards. Through you, the Party brigades, the villages must learn the meaning of Bolshevik firmness...*Don't be afraid of taking extreme measures*. The Party stands four-square behind you. Comrade Stalin expects it of you. It's a life-and-death struggle; better to do too much than not enough...This is no time for squeamishness or rotten sentimentality.'[79]

An activist named Grigorenko summed up the effectiveness of these commands years later:

'We were deceived because we wanted to be deceived. We believed so strongly in communism that we were prepared to accept any crime if it was glossed over with the least little bit of communist phraseology...Confronted by something unpleasant, we compelled ourselves to believe that it was an isolated phenomenon and that on the whole the country's state of affairs was just as the party described it...in other words, just as it was supposed to be according to communist theory.'[80]

Mikhail Sholokov also asserted how hatred of the kulaks was a strong motivating factor. The combination of ideological certainty and class informed loathing was as potent a cocktail as it has always been. The party faithful felt exempted from any true compassion for their victims because of the widespread acceptance of 'class enemies'. Vassily Grossman referred to the same issue, but also to a rather more mundane motivator. He admitted that there were 'those who believed the propaganda and who hated the parasites and were on the side of the poorest peasantry...But most of them were merely anxious to carry out instructions. They would have killed their own fathers and mothers simply in order to carry out instructions'.[81] Many, naturally, had severe reservations, but loyalty to the cause and the party line, as well as fear of the consequences of any refusal to participate, shepherded the reluctant into complying with the enthusiastic.

The party spread around the fiction that collectivisation was 'voluntary'. In reality, the peasants, Soviets, and many party members opposed it, but their feelings were irrelevant. The process was powered by a ruthless policy of state-enforced compunction. Ivan Deutscher was travelling in Russia when he met a highly ranked NKVD officer who told him: 'I am an old Bolshevik. I worked in the underground against the Tsar and then I fought in the Civil War. Did I do all that in order that I should now surround villages with machine-guns and order my men to fire indiscriminately into crowds of peasants? Oh, no, no, no!'[82] There is, however, no indication that he stopped. The concerns of such individuals were brushed aside, and those who spoke out against the policy frequently found themselves deported with the kulaks.

A peasant in a Sholokov novel vocalised the true feelings of many when complaining: 'You'll collect the grain, and then you'll load it into trains and send it abroad. You'll buy automobiles, so that Party men can ride around with their bobbed-hair women. We know what you want our grain for. We've lived to see equality all right'.[83] Rather than enthusiastically embracing socialism many felt they were reduced to a condition inferior to the serfdom endured by their grand-parents. But peasants who objected to collectivisation were simply arrested as 'enemies of the people'. The harsh treatment sparked ever greater and more widespread rebellions which were crushed with typical Bolshevik ruthlessness. In fact the situation grew so critical that it became apparent to even the top brass that something needed to be done. It was at this point that, in Martin Amis's words,

> 'Lenin accepted defeat, withdrawal and compromise. In other words, he accepted reality. Stalin did not. The peasantry no longer faced a frigid intellectual. It faced a passionate lowbrow whose personality was warping and crackling in the heat of power. He would not accept reality. He would break it.'[84]

Stalin's solution to the resistance was comprised of a three-pronged assault: propaganda, concession and ever more violent repression. On 2 March 1930 he wrote an article, 'Dizzy with success', which denounced the 'coercion', 'excesses' and 'distortions' of the collectivisation campaign he had insisted on. He suggested that peasants could leave the farms if they wanted to, but also gave allowance for small plots of private land within the communal areas as an inducement for them to join willingly. These measures were designed to quell the concerns of the majority, but those still opposed to the process were to be denounced as kulaks and deported. The second wave of expulsions which followed the brief impasse significantly outnumbered the first.

In December 1932 'internal passports' were introduced which prevented peasants from leaving the collective farm to work in the cities, adding yet another layer to the chains which shackled them with increasing force. In 1931 they began to seize meat too, yet every attempt the party made to increase production had the opposite effect. Peasants responded to the latest measures by killing and eating their cattle. Horses were frequently sold or set free under the assumption they would be replaced by tractors. Unfortunately, the promised vehicles were unavailable. Even when the tractors did finally begin to arrive, few people knew how to maintain them. As such the peasants were left with few sources of food and nothing to pull their ploughs.

The inhabitants of collective farms were labouring for the bureaucrats who tormented them rather than for themselves, but even without this factor they would have been considerably less efficient than more manageable holdings. Naturally, the authorities blamed everyone but themselves for the unsatisfactory levels of produce. Yet their greatest miscalculation was that grain production could be increased by party diktats rather than the market process. In three years, from the start of collectivisation, the state doubled the amount of grain it seized from the countryside. The government's requirements took precedence over the needs of the populace. Even at the best of times the peasants were left with starvation rations.

By 1934 nine-tenths of the arable farmland of the USSR was held in 240,000 collective farms which had replaced the 20 million family farms held prior to 1929. The produce of the giant farms was considered state property, and the penalties for anyone damaging or seizing goods were severe. There was to be no mercy shown to 'anti-Soviet elements'. The attack on the peasantry had gone hand in hand with an assault on the Church which was ruthlessly suppressed. Members of the clergy were frequently shot and exiled along with the kulaks. Churches and monasteries were closed and icons destroyed. Only one religion was to be permitted - that of socialism. The peasants were regarded as serving the needs of the state and their own desires, consolations or quality of life were practically immaterial. Vast numbers had lost any sense of autonomy, were herded into colossal enclosures, violently hounded for any scraps of food they may have concealed for themselves, and seen scores of their peers arrested and deported in the most barbaric conditions imaginable. But as hard as it was to conceive the situation for a significant part of the population was about to get immeasurably worse. The results of collectivisation were the displacement of tens of millions of peasants, the enslavement of tens of millions more and the virtual collapse of agricultural production. The storm clouds of a major disaster were gathering.

The Islamic lands of Uzbekistan, Turkmenistan, Tajikistan, Kyrgyzstan and Kazakhstan had been conquered by the Tsarist armies in the 18th and 19th centuries. Kazakhstan had a particularly nomadic culture and collectivisation there was especially costly. At least a million people died of starvation in just a handful of years while many more were dispossessed. Terrible famines broke out in several areas but, costly in human life though they were, they would prove small fry in comparison with events to the west of those embittered regions. The true catastrophe was to strike in the Ukraine as well as the Kuban, Don and Volga regions of the North Caucasus. It was an area larger than France and Germany combined that would be transformed, in Robert Conquest's unforgettable phrase, into 'one vast Belsen'.[85] Boris Pasternak also wrote memorably on the tragedy. 'What I saw could not be expressed in words. There was such inhuman, unimaginable misery, such a terrible disaster, that it began to seem almost abstract, it would not fit within the bounds of consciousness. I fell ill. For an entire year I could not write.'[86] If a writer of Pasternak's calibre could not find the words, then what chance for the rest of us? Yet try we must.

In the Ukraine the Soviets planned to attack not just the peasantry, but the nationalism that remained an active force there. A similar motivation would justify the assault on the Cossacks of the Don region. Lenin had always declared that 'The interests of socialism are above the interests of the right of nations to self-determination'.[87] This was entirely in keeping with pure Marxism which called for the dissolution of all divisions of class and nationality within society. Lenin considered nationalism to be part of the bourgeois stage of development. While it could be utilised as a force to be deployed against the imperial powers, it must ultimately be subsumed, or destroyed, in the socialist state.* Lenin's pragmatism had realised the necessity of accommodating Ukrainian nationalism, but the party purists had always resented it. Stalin would give them what they wanted again.

It was the determination to crush Ukrainian patriotism, despised as a deviation from socialism, which would be the principal cause of the horror to come. The twin policies of collectivisation and de-kulakisation hit the Ukraine hard in 1929-30. Yet, for Stalin, this was not enough to pacify the region. Arrests and show trials of any suspected of Ukrainian nationalism proliferated through those years. The suspects were initially drawn from the academic, clerical and professional classes, though the persecution of the intelligentsia was rapidly followed by an assault on the peasantry. Clearances of this nature were to be dressed up in the usual language of dogma. And while the purges in the countryside had already been extremely thorough, the Bolsheviks claimed that the class enemy remained a pervasive influence that was yet to be exterminated. The tactics employed throughout the rest of the state were to be practiced in the Ukraine, but to a far greater extent. As early as the summer

* Vestiges of Lenin's ideology can still be found on the left in the tendency of Labour's 'intelligentsia' like Christine Shawcross, Shami Chakrabarti and Diane Abbott to sneer at the nationalism of the plebs.

of 1930 one of the local activists declared: 'the peasant is adopting a new tactic. He refuses to reap the harvest. He wants the bread grain to die in order to choke the Soviet government with the bony hand of famine. But the enemy miscalculates. We will show him what famine is.'[88]

Unrealistic demands were made of the Ukraine which stripped it of most of its crop in 1932 and resulted in party purges when the province failed to provide its 'due'. In the first six months of that year *Pravda* castigated the Ukrainian authorities over their 'failures' on fifteen occasions before, in July, came the decision which would have truly calamitous consequences. Stalin demanded 7.7 million tons of grain from the region. The local authorities managed to get the amount reduced to 6.6 million tons, but this was still utterly unfeasible. The decree was swiftly followed by another, issued on 7 August 1932, which declared all produce of the collective to be state property. It provided the legal sanctions to back the confiscation of the peasants' grain. Vassily Grossman's assessment of this twin assault was stark: 'The decree required that the peasant of the Ukraine, the Don and the Kuban be put to death by starvation, put to death along with their little children'.[89]

Stanislav Kossiov reported on the already severe food shortages at the Third Ukrainian Communist Conference on 6-9 July 1932. He advised that the state's requirements could be met from other areas which had enjoyed a bumper harvest. His warnings were ignored. Molotov declared that criticisms of the plans and targets were 'anti-Bolshevik' and vowed there 'will be no concessions or vacillations in the problem of fulfilment of the task set by the Party and the Soviet government'.[90] Guard towers manned by activists armed with shotguns were positioned around farms to oversee the procurements. The requisitions in August alone virtually cleared the countryside, but by November only 41% of the demands had been met. Faced with such figures, the party determined to step up its efforts to wring every bit of grain it could from the region.

Stalin had moaned how the peasants, driven off their land, repatriated to the east, herded into collective farms, attacked with clubs and whips and starved in their millions, turned on the officials. It was, in his perception, a betrayal of the party and all that they were trying to do for the people. Such intransigence must be punished. The August Decree in particular would have severe consequences. Not only the produce of the collective farm, but all property, livestock and equipment was now regarded as belonging to the state. Anyone who transgressed the law would, if they were fortunate, have all their property confiscated and be sentenced to ten years in prison or a labour camp. If unlucky they would simply be shot. Even palming a few grains of wheat was considered a crime sufficient for the full weight of the law to swing into action. Soviet agents were instructed to show no mercy when enforcing the decrees and there were reports of peasants being shot for stealing two sheaves of corn. One man who canoodled with some girls in a barn was sentenced to ten years for disturbing the pigs. Another woman received a ten year stretch for collecting a hundred ears of ripening corn from her own plot two weeks after her husband had died of starvation. In one month, in Kharkov alone, 1,500 death sentences were carried out.

Brigades of armed thugs were sent out in gangs to find the supposedly hidden grain. By 1932 even these experienced trackers could find little evidence that any produce had been squirrelled away. Some baulked at what they were asked to do. One delegate reported back that he could make the mandated delivery of meat, but only if he used human corpses. Most however were compliant, and those who were not were simply liquidated and replaced with more reliable Bolsheviks. Any taking the side of the peasants were predictably accused of conspiring with class enemies. One collective chairman, who declared that his search had revealed not a speck of grain, was immediately denounced as the ringleader of the hoarders himself. Yet the agents of the state were usually well fed themselves. Their generously stocked pantries were kept securely guarded while starvation began to rage all around them.

The activists became inured to the violence, hunger and death that spread rapidly, and their behaviour grew ever more brutal as a consequence. They already believed they were serving a great cause and were deeply suspicious of the peasantry thought to be undermining the purity of socialism. The desensitising nature of their tasks exacerbated attitudes of this ilk, and a wilful cruelty was encouraged. In Kharsyn village a woman who was seven months pregnant was caught picking a few strands of wheat and was beaten so violently with a wooden board that she died. Another woman who had three children to feed, and whose husband had been arrested, was caught digging up a handful of potatoes at night. She was shot and her three children soon starved to death. Near Kiev, the head of the Soviet shot seven people he caught picking corn. Three of them were children of just fourteen and fifteen years old. Conditions got so bad that activists assumed anyone not obviously starving must be concealing food. Some brigade leaders transported dying individuals to the cemeteries to save them from making two trips and there are numerous accounts of emaciated children and elderly peasants lying among the corpses in mass graves for a period of several days.

One activist described the experience and his justifications:

'I heard the children...choking, coughing with screams. And I saw the looks of the men: frightened, pleading, hateful, dully impassive, extinguished with despair or flaring up with half-mad, daring ferocity. "Take it. Take everything away. There's still a pot of borscht on the stove. It's plain, got no meat. But it's got beets, taters 'n' cabbage. And it's salted! Better take it, comrade citizens! Here, hang on. I'll take off my shoes. They're patched and repatched, but maybe they'll have some use for our dear Soviet power." It was excruciating to see and hear all this. And even worse to take part in it...And I persuaded myself, explained to myself, I mustn't give in to debilitating pity. We were realizing historical necessity. We were performing our revolutionary duty. We were obtaining grain for the socialist fatherland. For the Five Year Plan. With the rest of my generation I firmly believed that the ends justified the means. Our great god was the universal triumph of Communism, and for the sake of that goal everything was permissible – to lie, to steal, to destroy hundreds of thousands and even millions of people, all those who were hindering our work or could hinder it, everyone who stood in the way. And to hesitate or doubt about all this was to give in to 'intellectual squeamishness' and 'stupid liberalism'...For I was convinced that I was accomplishing the great and necessary transformation of the countryside; that in days to come the people who lived there would be better off for it; that their distress and suffering were a result of their own ignorance or the machinations of the class enemy; that those who sent me – and I myself – knew better than the peasants how they should live.'[91]

Once such violence had become commonplace, as soon as the party activists were habituated to the practice of terror, it could be continued as a standard way of administering Soviet policy. The great famine surely paved the way for what was to follow.

As the requisitions continued to intensify and starvation took hold the peasantry tried desperately to hide a few scraps of food. They ate fat scraped from wooden casks and made bread, biscuits and porridge from ground-down bones or nettles and weeds. People ate horse manure, partly because it contained grains, and consumed dogs and cats which were boiled to make their sinewy flesh palatable. They devoured berries, mice, rats, tree bark, rotten potatoes and fungi. When some peasants dug acorns out of the snow to combine with potato peel to make a form of bread a corpulent party official sneered at the 'parasites' who would 'do anything to get out of working'. Yet, coupled with the vast quantities being sent off for export, the policies of the Soviet administration created sights the peasantry found almost unbearable. When the starving peasants became aware that grain was being stored nearby they rebelled, particularly when informed by older villagers about the help they had always received in times of want or famine under the Tsar. Local well-guarded granaries held stocks of 'state reserves' put aside for emergencies. To the Bolsheviks, the deaths of their own citizens, the workers their revolution was supposed to benefit, did not count as such a crisis. Soviet inefficiencies also meant that huge stockpiles of fodder were left piled up where they began to rot while batteries of NKVD men were posted around them to keep the starving peasantry at bay. Large potato stores rotted too and numerous accounts record that peasants who looted such supplies were either machine-gunned in the attempt or rounded up and shot later.

Peasants began to desert the worst affected areas of the Ukraine, but border guards prevented them from entering Russia or Romania, turning them away or shooting the more determined. By November, dissatisfied with the amount of grain leaving the region, the authorities decided to punish the locals by preventing goods from the towns entering the worst hit areas. By the end of the year the party had wrung 4.7 million tons of grain from the Ukraine or 71.8% of the target they had set. So as 1933 dawned a decision was taken to renew the assault on the Ukrainian farmers. At a joint meeting of the Politburo and Central Committee on 27 November 1932 Stalin blamed the shortfall on wrecking and sabotage by anti-Soviet elements as well as the un-Marxist approach of both collectives and representatives on the ground.

On 4 and 8 December *Pravda* called for a merciless struggle against the kulaks in the Ukraine, while on 7 January 1933 it published an editorial which declared that the Ukrainian Communist Party had allowed class enemies in the region to organise themselves. On 24 January 1933 the Ukrainian party were blamed with failing in their duties of grain collection and lambasted for 'lack of class vigilance'. Pavel Postyshev was given the task of rectifying the situation. He immediately made it clear that no food was to be given to the peasantry. Postyshev was shown statistics of grain production but dismissed them as 'false figures' provided by 'enemy elements'. Party members were purged and large numbers of vets, blamed for the decline in livestock, were shot. The entire staff of the Meteorological Office were also arrested. Over thirty civil servants were shot for various acts of 'sabotage' while huge numbers of new agents, primarily Russians, were drafted in. Not all the measures in the world though could produce grain from nothing, but still Stalin scoffed at reports that the area had been hit by famine. The Bolsheviks were so blinkered by ideology and hatred that they were blind to the true causes. Their adherence to dogma had left them with a severe case of tunnel vision. The costs of this obstinacy were to be catastrophic.

One of the worst criminals of the region was a native, Lazar Kaganovich, a Kievan Jew. He was a plump, balding bureaucrat, noted for his gregarious personality, but his joviality contrasted sharply with a merciless brutality, visibly evident in his cold eyes. Kaganovich was adamant that all the problems in the area resulted from issues of class struggle or kulak sabotage. But, unlike Stalin's unconvincing dismissals, Kaganovich could not claim ignorance of the issue. He had personally toured the famine-hit region yet expressed nothing but contempt for what he saw. While Kopelev was stunned by the amount of corpses he witnessed, Kaganovich remained unmoved and continued to order executions of hoarders. In the Kuban he commanded that fifteen whole villages be deported to Siberia. After a busy day persecuting the starving he would then gorge himself in the evenings, his appetite undiminished by the nature of his task.

Yet, as bad as the catastrophe had already been, death on an epic scale only truly began in March 1933. The desperate populace ate glue, shoes, earthworms, sparrows, bluebells, nettles, ants and dandelions. They ripped up fur and skins to make a kind of soup and clawed grass out of the ground to devour its roots. In some regions the lucky inhabitants could find and boil snails. Despite such desperate measures the epidemic of death multiplied alarmingly. Communities set aside wagons purely for ferrying bodies to the pits which served as mass graves and the carts overflowed with corpses. The remains were unceremoniously slung in holes or piled up away from the main dwelling areas. Horrifying accounts relate how scores of victims took months to die in agony while survivors were helpless to ease the suffering of their friends and families. Untold numbers lost their minds and senses before they finally perished. After one woman buried her four year old son, the brigades suspected they had found a grain pit. They attacked it with picks and spades until they dug the boy's body up before leaving the woman to rebury the child herself. Another former activist commented how

'The most terrifying sights were the little children with skeleton limbs dangling from balloon like abdomens. Starvation had wiped every trace of youth from their faces, turning them into tortured gargoyles...There is nothing more terrible for the mother than the sign of her emaciated, enfeebled children who through hunger have forgotten to smile...Everywhere we found men and women lying prone, their faces and bellies bloated, their eyes utterly expressionless.'[92]

That spring, just as famine tightened its grip like a vice, the laws against unlicensed movement came under severe restrictions. Peasants were banned from travelling on the railways or from any sort of industrial work. Some special projects like road or rail construction advertised for staff and fed their workers. But the locals were too weak to dig the amount required to earn the pittance of bread they so badly needed. Desperate peasants thronged the train stations anyway. Many died and bodies began to pile up by the tracks. When Arthur Koestler saw starving Ukrainian peasants in 1932 he recalled 'I was told that these were kulaks who had resisted the collectivisation of the land and I accepted the explanation; they were enemies of the people who preferred begging to work'.[93] But, despite the efforts of the authorities, many made it into the cities. Some even got hold of bread rations that had been diverted to the urban population even while denied to the rural workers. Many did not though. In the streets of Poltova and Kiev around 150 bodies were cleared away every morning. As people went about their everyday business starving peasants were strewn like autumn leaves through the streets. Most were ignored but some were helped. One witness in Kharkov reported seeing 'a woman swollen with hunger, lying in the Horse Market. Worms were literally eating her alive. A number of people placed small pieces of bread next to her, but the poor lady was already too close to death to eat them. She cried and asked for medical assistance, which no one gave'.[94] (Doctors had been banned from treating such cases).

Peasants were regularly cleared from the cities by the police too. On 27 May 1933 several thousand who had come to join the bread queues were herded onto trains and transported to a large pit far from the city where they were abandoned to die. The railways became a significant means of dealing with the problem. A train engineer in the Don region noted a mysterious locomotive of five to ten empty freight cars which headed for Rostov every morning. It returned hours later with the carriages locked. He took little notice until one day a fellow worker dragged him over and showed him that the coaches were stuffed with corpses. The NKVD had orchestrated the whole operation with great secrecy.

Those caught up in the crisis reacted to the famine in a variety of ways. As food ran out relationships disintegrated and families fought each-other for crumbs. Parents would even steal scraps from their children. Murder was not uncommon in such circumstances. In the village of Bilka, one Denys Ischenko killed his sister, brother-in-law and their sixteen year old daughter, as well as his friend Petro Korobeynyk, for a small sack of flour and a few loaves of bread. Others turned to cannibalism, cooked and ate their own children, were driven insane or committed suicide. Some of the cannibals waylaid strangers or set traps for children. Others were less predatory though. When one activist returned to the Ukraine from his placement in Siberia he found his village a ghost town. His younger brother was living on tree bark and hares he had managed to catch. But he told his sibling their mother had said they should eat her if she died.

While acts of this ilk sound appalling the true criminals of course were the party bureaucracy. Driven by virtue, their consciences remained untroubled while their stomachs stayed full. They still believed they were creating a utopia even though 'In the countryside, now, instead of growing fat on the loyally thrumming grain factories of which a German philosopher had fleetingly dreamed, the peasants were eating each other, and eating themselves'.[95] Stalin appeared not to care. Marx had said that agriculture should be collectivised, and so it was; he said that industry must come under the aegis of the state, and so it did.

The manner in which people reacted to and coped with the plight of their children varied too. Some, as stated, killed and ate them, but others sacrificed themselves for their progeny. In the Ukrainian deportations one testimony recounts how when the head of a family was arrested his wife hung herself. Some neighbours took in the couple's little boy. He slept on their stove at night and haunted his old house in the daytime though he had lost the ability to speak. One woman with six children had felt forced to let three of them die so the three brightest and strongest might survive. One local partisan, after seeing one of his offspring beaten to death for stealing vegetables, left his remaining four children with the local bureau which made no promises but managed to put them in a children's home. Two of them died immediately and a few days later their father hanged himself outside the district office. Some families sent their children away believing they may have a better chance of survival if allowed to roam, scavenge and beg. Some gangs were known to prey on these orphans but others, like the homeless children who occupied the Kharkov tractor plant, found security in numbers. They caught and cooked cats, dug potato peelings and fish heads out of rubbish tips, trapped birds and begged. Other abandoned youngsters formed into large feral gangs which stole or turned to prostitution to survive. The regime naturally blamed the plight of the children on the consequences of a 'kulak trick'.

The reality was different. In fact the authorities were rounding up large numbers of children who were then put into camps where they were left to die. Thousands perished in this manner and were buried in pits so shallow that dogs and wolves dug the carcasses up and feasted on them. Many were simply shot. Although a law legalising the execution of twelve year olds was not introduced until 7 April 1935 there are numerous accounts of mass shootings of children younger than that age both before and afterwards, like the seventy-six youths shot at the Lebedyn Children's Centre after consuming horsemeat. Other groups were drowned in barges on the Dnieper. Most died of hunger though. Of the seven million famine victims approximately three million were children while at least a million of the three million who died during de-kulakisation were also under eighteen. This figure of four million dead children does not account for the huge number who died in the camps or work projects.

Those who survived were often recruited into 'pioneer brigades' where they were brainwashed in the principles of class hatred. The pioneers then enthusiastically joined in the denunciation of starving peasants who had secreted away a few stalks of grain. Such individuals frequently grew up to become the most dedicated NKVD officers. It was depressingly common for these children to denounce relatives and many records indicate that pioneers had their own parents arrested. It was announced that Pavlik Morozov, a fourteen year old pioneer, had denounced his own father before being murdered by a group of peasants including his uncle. Morozov was transformed into a martyr by the regime and had a museum opened in his honour. In fact he had been killed by the NKVD who then executed thirty-seven peasants charged with being kulaks to cover up the crime.[96] More than one mother expressed thanks that her own children had died rather than being transformed into an ideological robot of the type that made up the ranks of pioneers.

Ukraine was left utterly devastated by the Bolsheviks' policies. Numerous accounts describe a vast area reduced to a barren wasteland: stripped of all vegetation, houses gone to ruin, fences and hedges ripped away and used for fuel. Just a few souls were left, wild-haired, emaciated and unresponsive individuals, their hollow, uncomprehending eyes staring blankly into space. Bodies were initially buried individually, then in pits, before finally being abandoned. Villagers recount seeing the corpses of neighbours who had collapsed in the fields being picked apart by ravens while those who died at home were devoured by rats. Others simply lay dead in the streets or under fences. Some testimonies recall the horror of seeing their dead friends consumed by maggots.

Many individual accounts survive from those who explored the region, and all were shocked by the terrible scenes that confronted them. These testimonies come from not just locals but foreign correspondents who reported on the calamity, as well as soldiers who traversed the region, often giving their rations to the starving multitudes while their officers turned a blind eye. One group of villagers reported that, when checking on their neighbours, they entered the house to find some inhabitants dead, others barely breathing. The family's daughter was gnawing on the leg of a table. When they approached her the girl tensed up and began to growl like a rabid animal. She never once glanced at the intruders though. Two locals who had moved to America returned to find their parents dead and their sister's face so deformed that it was unrecognisable. In the Kuban one activist entered a house to discover an old couple who had expired, the man's hand tenderly resting on his dead wife's head, while a younger man with long hair, who had gone quite mad, was engaged in a furious battle with some cats for possession of a half-eaten pigeon.

The Soviets eventually realised they must act to alleviate the situation. They arranged for seed and even food to be sent to the area while some medical centres were established too. Yet they remained utterly unapologetic and unrepentant about the crisis, and they still refused to accept their ideology was anything less than perfect. They also, unlike during Lenin's famine, blocked all attempts by the International Red Cross and any other foreign agencies to provide help. All shortages and problems were blamed on the usual suspects of kulak saboteurs, wreckers and capitalists. There was never to be any suggestion that they were remotely culpable. But while the Bolsheviks sneered at the laziness of the peasants and the greed of the kulaks the entire responsibility lay with their own policy line. The crisis had been caused almost wholly by the 44% rise in procurements during the period, however much the authorities attempted to pass the buck. Exports were a significant part of the problem, with up to five million tons a year sold abroad. But the grain reserves were even more responsible for the disaster. Numerous reports cite significant quantities of grain left to rot in the open while protected by guards and barbed wire fences. *Pravda*, which had fanned the flames of class war, made no mention of the famine and neither did any other publication in the state. The news blackout was total, but the Russian and Ukrainian press were full of reports of healthy, smiling peasants and the glory of collectivisation. Not only did the party apparatchiks blame the peasantry, but there was no sympathy at all. Indeed, they adopted a self-congratulatory tone. M.M. Khatayevich boasted to an activist about the 'triumph' from a Communist viewpoint.

'A ruthless struggle is going on between the peasantry and our regime. It's a struggle to the death. This year was a test of our strength and their endurance. It took a famine to show them who is master here. It has cost millions of lives, but the collective farm system is here to stay. We've won the war.'[97]

In June 1933 Kalinin lectured a congress of collective workers and claimed that 'Every farmer knows that people who are in trouble because of a lack of bread, are in that predicament not as the result of a poor harvest, but because they were lazy and refused to do an honest day's work'.[98] The peasants hoped the revolution would deliver their own plot of land and the autonomy to farm it. Instead, it had ripped such freedoms from their grasp and reduced them to a savagely brutal servitude far worse than that endured under the Tsars. The party that campaigned against the exploitation of labour had effectively enslaved 85% of the population. As part of establishing the most perfect human society they had committed mass murder comparable with any genocide in history. Yet, in the wake of these events, their consciences were as clean as can be.

Even after the famine there were widespread purges of any Ukrainian intelligentsia suspected of harbouring nationalistic sympathies. Around 2,000 academics, scientists and writers were shot. The Soviet farm system remained brutal for decades after the famine. And the collapse of incentives and peasant morale meant it was considerably less productive and efficient than the Tsarist system. Famine and cannibalism would return with sporadic regularity. On 14 April 1937 Vyshinsky wrote to Molotov about a number of instances of cannibalism in Cheliabinski in the Urals. One woman had eaten a four month old child, another shared an eight year old with her thirteen year old, while yet another woman ate her own three month old baby. In 1946-7 another terrible famine ravaged the Ukraine leaving over 800,000 dead. Yet the lessons appear never to have been learned, and decades later the *Large Soviet Encyclopaedia* still declared that 'hunger can only be overcome as a result of the socialist reconstruction of society'.[99]

The sacrifices that had been made to impose the monolithic failure were truly breath-taking. The total peasant dead from famine, de-kulakisation and death in labour camps was an eye-watering 14.5 million, well over double the amount killed in the Holocaust. It must additionally be pointed out that this is a conservative estimate. The suffering endured by the survivors, both the physical and mental scars they bore, is even harder to catalogue. It cannot be denied that the numbers who suffered serious effects from the calamity dwarf those who died in it. Yet there were other consequences too. A line had been crossed, and the widespread acceptance that any measures, any number of casualties, were justifiable in the advancement of their sacred cause meant other atrocities would swiftly follow. In *Into the Whirlwind* Evgenia Ginzburg described how NKVD officers were gradually dehumanised: 'Pace by pace. As they followed one routine directive after another, they climbed down the steps from the human condition to that of beasts'.[100] Having been suitably indoctrinated and conditioned, it would not be long before those 'beasts' were unleashed again.

Terror

Among the most famous images of Stalin's regime is the one with little Gelya Markizova pictured in the great dictator's warm embrace. The little girl had presented Stalin with a sizeable bouquet of flowers at a public function before being swept up into his arms. That iconic photograph captured the Soviet premier beaming with genuine warmth as Gelya tenderly wrapped her arms around his neck, the picture of childhood contentment. It appears the perfect endorsement of his rule, the benevolent leader communing with his happy and contented citizens. Yet, unsurprisingly, the heart-warming scene was shadowed by a dark secret. Shortly after the delightful image was recorded, one milked for all it was worth by the Soviet propaganda machine, Gelya's father was shot as a Trotskyite and Japanese mole in Stalin's Great Terror. Her mother was later arrested and deported to Kazakhstan where she was run over by a truck and killed. Gelya herself was subsequently shunned by her classmates, socially ostracised as the daughter of an enemy of the people. The numbers of those caught up in similar tragedies would reach dizzying levels.

There are some parallels between that picture of little Gelya and the Seventeenth Party Congress which met in Moscow in January 1934. It was another scene of joyous celebration, but the festive mood was equally fleeting and the epitaph decidedly grisly. The Party Congress was effectively the Olympics of Communism. Every four years or so an extravaganza was held that drew excited delegates, abuzz with anticipation, from across the empire. On this occasion they were in a particularly celebratory mood and the convention was dubbed 'The Congress of Victors'. Despite having presided over famine, deportations and a prison camp system of particularly brutal severity they slapped each-other on the back and cheerily toasted the 'triumphs' of the preceding four years. All that mattered to them was the grand success of their socialist ideals. Landowners and capitalists had been defeated, the farms collectivised and industry and the economy brought under the aegis of the state.

While they had fallen some way short of the targets set out in Stalin's Five Year Plan, there had still been significant growth in manufacturing, and this was sufficient to prompt gushing praise from all quarters. Molotov opened the Congress on 26 January by declaring 'Our country has become a country of mighty industry, a country of collectivisation, a country of victorious socialism'.[101] Zinoviev commended 'the struggle which Comrade Stalin conducted on an exclusively high level of principle, on an exclusively high theoretical level'.[102] Kirov added to the eulogies by declaring, with bitter irony, that 'Our successes are really tremendous. Damn it all...you just want to live and live – really, just look what's going on. It's a fact!'[103] The applause was deafening. If their consciences appeared untroubled it was because the delegates were so convinced of the moral justness and inevitability of their cause that any measures, any costs were thought worthwhile and all progress to that end was to be celebrated. Yet to visualise that scene should fill anyone with a sense of genuine morality with revulsion. A vast hall of plump, pink-faced, self-satisfied and comfortably attired communists applauded themselves for the nightmare they had presided over, the millions they had killed and the immeasurable suffering they had unleashed. It is no consolation to learn that of the 1,966 delegates in attendance that day, 1,108 were soon to be consumed by the Great Terror that would sweep the nation.*

The storm clouds began to gather when elections to the Central Committee produced a shocking result. Delegates were handed lists of names and instructed to cross out any candidates they opposed. Their returned forms automatically counted as votes for those who remained unmarked on their lists. Kirov was crossed off the fewest lists while the name with the greatest number of negative responses was Stalin. One needs little imagination to visualise the leader's reaction. Like most of his inclination, Stalin bristled over any disagreement and was contemptuous of democracy that failed to go his way. He began to see traitors everywhere. Stalin had received nearly 300 negative votes, though it was announced that he had got just three; Kirov had received only two, the same announcement declared he got four. Despite that shocking duplicity, one fact was undeniable: Kirov now presented a legitimate threat to Stalin himself. Having secured control of the party and the state he was loath to let a rival bask in the spotlight. He was also determined that it was he, and he alone, who could now push the state towards full socialism after

* Of the 130 members of the party's Central Committee at that Congress just 40 would survive the next four years.

such a promising, auspicious start. After establishing himself as unchallenged head of state by 1929, Stalin had immediately set about implementing socialism in the countryside. The result was famine and brutality of Biblical severity. Yet the nation still stubbornly refused to blossom into the workers' paradise their prophets had promised. It was clear then that further stern measures needed to be taken – this time with the industrial sector and the party hierarchy itself.

To this end, Stalin surrounded himself with a loyal cadre of supporters, all committed communists and hard men. His inner circle included Mikhail Kalinin, Lazar Kaganovich, Anastas Mikoyan, Sergo Ordzhonikidze, Vyacheslav Molotov, Valerian Kuibyshev and Kliment Voroshilov. The latter of these had been a close confidant of Stalin since the Civil War when a number of sources allege the pair had crammed their political rivals onto a barge before sinking it and drowning them all in the icy waters of the Volga. Despite such chilling testimony, Voroshilov was a ridiculous figure, as vain as he was perfidious. A smug and preening sycophant, his self-satisfied smirk was as permanent a feature of his visage as his methodically clipped Hitlerish moustache and carefully tousled hair. Voroshilov fancied himself something of a dandy and had a particular fondness for uniforms. He enjoying dressing grandly, festooning his chest with a vast array of medals and admiring himself while strutting up and down in front of a mirror. Born on 4 February 1881 in eastern Ukraine he had been a Bolshevik since 1905 and, faults apart, was renowned for his charm and affability. He fancied himself as a great military figure but only truly excelled in obstinacy. His ineptitude in martial affairs saw him preside over a string of disasters, but despite his uselessness and notorious stupidity, his loyalty to the inner circle was rewarded with continual promotion.

Such was par for the course in Soviet Russia which was as far from a meritocracy as it is possible to get. Voroshilov was to be complicit, as were many others, in what was to follow. It seems that ideas were percolating and gestating in the great dictator's head that year and Stalin's response to the Night of the Long Knives of 30 June 1934, in which Adolf Hitler wiped out his political opposition, was telling. Stalin gushed 'Did you hear what happened in Germany? Some fellow that Hitler! Splendid! That's a deed of some skill!'[104] One can almost see a light-bulb flick on above Stalin's head. He was, it seems, inspired. Hitler had shown the way, but it would take far more than the two hundred or so killed by Germany's dictator to sate Soviet appetites. As the poet Anna Akhmatova put it the 'vegetarian years' were over, 'the meat-eating years'[105] were about to begin.

It was just a few months later, after a plenum in Moscow on 28 November 1934, that Stalin personally escorted Kirov to the train station. Sergey had barely begun work back in Leningrad when, on 1 December, as he arrived at the Smolny Institute, his bodyguard, M.D. Borisov, lagged behind him. Some accounts suggest he was delayed by Chekists, others that the strapping officer was too unfit to keep up with the forty-eight year old pen-pushing commissar. The confusion, the possible complicity of the NKVD and the unconvincing second version justifiably raise suspicions about what followed. When Kirov ascended the stairs Leonid Nikolaev was waiting for him. He pressed himself against a wall to let his target pass and then shot him in the back of the head. Kirov was killed instantly. But Nikolaev's subsequent suicide attempt was foiled by those who rushed to the scene. Almost as soon as the investigation began news broke that Kirov's bodyguard, Borisov, had been killed in a car crash. Yet none of the other passengers had suffered even the mildest of injuries. Reports later emerged which suggest the NKVD had beaten him to death with iron bars. One hardly needs to be a conspiracy theorist to feel that events surrounding the killing do not quite stack up.

We will never know for certain who ordered Kirov's murder though it is far from beyond the realms of possibility that it was Stalin. Indeed, logically it can hardly have been anyone else. Regardless, there are so many deaths we *do* know he was responsible for that pinning culpability on him is practically immaterial. He certainly used the event to roll out a punitive programme in the state and its convenience in this regard cannot be overlooked. The murder would prove the catalyst for the Terror; it was employed as the spark to vindicate all that followed, though other justifications were quickly seized upon. The NKVD were immediately given increased powers to arrest, try and execute 'enemies of the people', defined by the top brass as 'not only one who commits sabotage, but one who doubts the rightness of the Party line.'[106] It was announced that Kirov had been killed as part of a wide-ranging anti-Soviet conspiracy. Such theories would excuse all the accusations to follow. At the head of this fictitious plot was Trotsky who, having being exiled in 1929, was alleged to be pulling the strings from overseas. In the Soviet mind, he became the ultimate, all-knowing, super-villain. Yet, in a deep irony, the policy line adopted by Stalin was effectively the same manifesto Trotsky had been recommending for years. Such inconvenient realities would be ignored in the blood-bath that was to follow and, regardless, the genuine motivations for the horror stem more from the ideological conviction of the perpetrators than such a shaky pretext.

The Soviets had absolute faith that their system was perfect. So the fact that it was failing, was riven with inefficiency and falling well short of production targets, could have only one explanation. Capitalist moles must be infiltrating the system to destroy it from within. The Terror would weed out the wreckers, saboteurs and traitors who were preventing full-blown socialism from developing. Anti-Socialist elements, Trotskyites and spies employed by the capitalist powers were to be unearthed and driven from the cultural sphere. And having decided on the problem they quickly arrived at the solution. A quick scan of the production figures was considered sufficient to calculate the number of wreckers in each region. Quotas, based on these estimates, were distributed to the provinces where local commissars were instructed to locate traitors. But, as is usual in such cases, the regional delegates far exceeded the figures they were given, for any failure to do so would have resulted in suspicion falling on them.

When seized, suspects were to be interrogated until they confessed. The use of torture to 'verify' accounts was made compulsory. Under such vigorous pressing detainees were expected to confess to not just their own guilt but the complicity of others as well. Once implicated, new suspects found themselves effectively defenceless against such accusations. Some high profile cases were to be given the honour of fabricated show trials, but the majority would simply be swallowed up by the camps or shot. The bureaucratically inclined Bolsheviks kept such rigorously detailed accounts and records of their crimes that not the slightest doubt remains about the scope of the atrocities committed under their rule. There are tens of millions of NKVD files that provide verbatim accounts of every stage of the charges and investigations they undertook. While huge efforts were made to conceal and whitewash the reality to outsiders, no attempts were made to distort the official record. We consequently learn, for example, that Kamenev's widow was shot for 'a counter-revolutionary conversation with a foreign diplomat'.[107] The numbers consumed by such flimsy allegations would prove breathtaking.

Ostensibly the individual in charge at the outset was Genrikh Yagoda, the man who had risen to become head of the NKVD in the years following the death of Dzerzhinsky. Yagoda's great legacy was the creation of the gulag though he is sometimes better known for his penchant for French wine, orchids and sex toys. But two other figures would rise to prominence during the Terror and become synonymous with it. Nikolai Yezhov, the man who succeeded Yagoda, would become one of the most notorious killers of all time. He was born in Lithuania in 1895 to a father employed as a forest warden, who also ran a brothel, and a mother who worked as a maid. The 'poison dwarf', who stood just under five feet tall, had a gentle, rather handsome face, but his piercingly intense eyes suggest a harder edge to his nature. It was not deceptive. He had joined the Red Army in 1919 and, despite his minimal education, his dedication saw him rise through the party hierarchy. He was hyperactive, bisexual and a hypochondriac, suffering from anxiety and numerous imaginary ailments. He was equally enthusiastic about constructing intricate model yachts and taking part in orgies, frequently with his wife, Yevgenia Feigenberg, who was also notorious for her promiscuity. Yezhov was a workaholic and unfailingly reliable. When given a task, one could depend on him completing it, though some complained he did not know when to stop. He was enormously popular, liked by many who met him, especially women, and was widely regarded as gentle and humane. Yezhov, a loving husband and doting father to his adopted daughter, Natasha, was renowned for his charm, energy and sense of humour. Others were less complimentary though. Many peer and Soviet accounts talk of his 'repellent personality', 'sadistic inclinations' and lack of 'any trace of conscience or moral principles'.[108] While some women found him enticing, many others were repelled and dreaded an encounter with him. But one thing is beyond dispute: he was about to embark on the career which would indelibly cast him as one of the great villains of world history.

Startlingly, despite the notoriety of Yezhov, the Terror threw up a figure with an even darker reputation. While many regional directors became infamous for their enthusiastic sadism, none could match the rigour and pure brutality of the Georgian, Lavrenti Beria. He has often been called Stalin's Himmler, and there was even a physical resemblance in the bespectacled, balding, weak chinned bureaucrats of enthusiastically sadistic tendencies. In reality though, Beria was significantly worse than the lord of the SS. While Himmler was personally squeamish, his Soviet counterpart took an active role in torture and murder, and drew unnatural pleasure from dishing out sadistic beatings. He was also infamous as a particularly violent serial rapist of young girls. The Soviet system threw up a significant number of perverse sexual deviants. Kalinin had a famous, and seemingly insatiable, proclivity for young ballerinas while Bulganin, Zinoviev and Khrushchev used their position to intimidate scores of young women into sleeping with them. Abel Yenukidze grew increasingly careless about his liaisons even as his lovers became ever younger. Eventually he was sleeping with girls aged between nine and eleven while paying off their mothers. But, even among such company Beria stands out as a particularly vile piece of work. In 1949 he was introduced to Lilya Drozhdova, a willowy beauty who was just fourteen years old. She was essentially pimped out to him by her own mother and was subsequently showered with expensive gifts. Her compliance may have saved her from a far worse fate. There are numerous tales of assaults carried out by Beria, or accounts like that of the actress Tatiana Okunevskaya. Having already been raped by him, she refused a second invitation to his home. Her reticence was rewarded with seven years in the gulag. In 2003 human remains were found in the basement of Beria's home, evidence that his depravity may have reached hitherto undiscovered depths.

Beria, who hailed from Sukumi in Abkhazia, Western Georgia, first came to visit Stalin at his summer house in 1931, already a committed and ambitious Chekist with his eyes on the prize. He was a protégé of Sergo Ordzhonikidze, but when his mentor was promoted to Moscow he ingratiated himself with the stylish, charming and popular Nestor Lakoba. It was in the summer of 1933 that he truly caught Stalin's eye. Clearing away undergrowth with an axe at the dictator's summer residence he informed Stalin that he could do a similar job on anything else that needed pruning. It was phrased as a joke though it was clear that he was deadly serious. Stalin saw in him the qualities he wanted though his wife, Nadya, found him repulsive for the same reasons. There is no doubt that the vegetarian Beria was intelligent and competent, being a trained architect, among other accomplishments. He could also be charming and was widely described as genial and an excellent father-in-law and grandfather. It was in sadism that he truly excelled though, and for which he will be long remembered. Beria was certainly the most sinister figure of the entire regime.

After Kirov's assassination the state swung into action with remarkable speed. A suspicious mind might almost think events had been planned in advance. Indeed, Simon Sebag Montefiore describes Stalin's reaction to Kirov's death as 'self-conscious and preplanned Thespianism'.[109] On the very same day as the shooting Stalin ordered Yenukidze to sign an emergency law. It decreed the trial of accused terrorists within ten days and their immediate sentence or execution afterwards. Right from the start Stalin had targets in his sights and ignored any evidence that did not implicate Zinoviev, Kamenev and the Right Opposition. But while he was prepared to let suspicion fall on such illustrious rivals, he would not move against them just yet. Stalin was still testing the waters, gauging the response to his actions. Just five days after Kirov's death sixty-six suspected terrorists were shot with another twenty-eight gunned down in Kiev on 8 December. On 28 and 29 December Nikolaev and fourteen co-defendants were tried and, on the law of 1 December, promptly shot. Their families were then shot as well. In total, 6,501 people were executed that month alone. Yezhov rooted out suspected terrorists, and the NKVD tortured prisoners into implicating Zinoviev and Kamenev who were both swiftly arrested. Waves of further arrests followed.

Among the first of the notable party members to be targeted was Yenukidze who, instead of deferring and giving all the credit to Stalin, was foolish enough to be honest about the role he had played in Baku. Lakoba and Beria had attempted to outdo each-other with the sycophantic nature of their accounts of Batumi, but Yenukidze was not so obsequious, or shrewd. Yezhov promptly uncovered a cell, with Yenukidze at its head, and 110 of his staff, librarians, maids and secretaries, were arrested for terrorist offences. Two were executed and the rest sent to the camps. Yenukidze was sacked, forced to publish a 'Correction of Errors', sent off to run a regional sanatorium, and vigorously denounced at a plenum by Yezhov and Beria. His arrest would follow soon enough. Yezhov accused Zinoviev and Kamenev of planning Kirov's murder and Yenukidze of facilitating the operation. Yenukidze attempted to blame Yagoda, but accusations of him aiding Troyskyites were quickly thrown back in his face. Like a feeding frenzy Mikoyan, Sergo, Voroshilov, Beria, Stalin and Kaganovich all joined in with virulent denunciations. The ghosts of the French Assembly hovered in the Kremlin as Saturn prepared to devour her children yet again. Yenukidze was expelled from the party. The measure would be temporary, but the culture of denunciation would prove rather more enduring.

There was a widespread belief that an Old Bolshevik would never confess without the application of significant pressure, so ever-worsening levels of suffering were introduced to the interrogation process. Stalin's instructions to the NKVD interrogators left little to the imagination: 'Mount your prisoner and do not dismount until they have confessed'.[110] They would follow his directions enthusiastically and, like a Grand National jockey in a desperate scramble for the finish line, they would not spare the whip. The torture employed during the Terror followed a series of set patterns but inventive sadists added numerous creative punishments. Officially physical torture was outlawed until 1937 when it became commonplace. In reality, it had been frequently employed prior to that date, but the most common form of pressing was known as 'the conveyor'. Under this system, a relay team of interrogators would swap places at regular intervals allowing them to harass a prisoner without pause for hours or even days. Suspects were denied sleep or food for as long as the process lasted. Three days was said to be as painful as any torture and it was widely believed that no one could resist this type of questioning for a week. The combination of sleep deprivation, threats and constant haranguing would eventually break most subjected to it. A number of the accused were forced to stand for periods of several days or more, though many testified that sitting for long periods, and being unable to shift weight from one foot to another, was even more painful. The Soviets later came up with the idea of removing the seats from the chairs. Any suspects who started to flag were revived by being slapped about the face or doused with freezing water. One victim, after enduring days of questioning, was sent to a cell to 'rest'. The room was partly submerged in water and he was forced to stand with it lapping against his shins for fourteen hours. A schoolteacher, Fatimat Agnayeva, was pressed continually for eight days and then hung by her hair from a hook in her cell where she died.

Confessions gained as a result of such measures could be withdrawn, so for high profile cases the interrogation frequently lasted several months. It would utterly break the victim's resistance. Suspects were kept continuously cold, dragged from their beds after just fifteen minutes rest and disorientated by blazing lights. The confusion, powerlessness, hunger and freezing conditions eventually reduced them to a husk. The families of prominent figures were frequently taken hostage with threats that they would be harmed. Confessions usually followed. The Decree of 7 April 1935 which allowed the state to execute children as young as twelve, a piece of administration supported by Molotov, Khrushchev, Bulganin and Yagoda, was influential in this regard, and Yezhov recommended that it was displayed prominently as a reminder to those under questioning. Suspects often had their spouses or other family members tortured in their presence. Stanislav Kossior, who had resisted creative torture with great bravery, finally cracked when his gaolers raped his sixteen year old daughter in front of him.

As arrests continued to multiply it became necessary to secure speedier confessions. So violence became an ever more frequent part of interrogation. Sandbags were slammed into suspects' stomachs, a process that could, and frequently did, prove fatal. Interrogators forced their victims to stand for several hours against the wall while on tiptoes, an agonising process that broke nearly everyone. Prisoners had their wrists and feet bound behind their backs before being hoisted in the air on a pulley, or had their hands repeatedly slammed in doors. Others were submerged in ice-cold water or had wet cloth wrapped around their heads. As the material dried it shrank, constricting their skulls and causing terrific pain. Many were simply beaten by thuggish recruits, with this sort of torture proving especially common in the provinces. Some had their legs broken, toenails ripped out or their genitals crushed. It was not unheard of for suspects to be beaten so hard that their eyes popped out. Instances of detainees being beaten to death were terrifyingly common. Such fatalities were usually recorded as having suffered heart attacks. The standard weapon for these assaults was a chair leg, though hands and feet were stamped on too and the likes of pincers employed in numerous locations. The beatings frequently depended on what was to hand or on the sadistic imaginations of those engaged in the process.

Torture was justified because the Soviets claimed the bourgeois powers used it against socialist suspects so they must retaliate in kind. In official terms it was described as 'an exception applicable to known and obstinate enemies of the people, as a method both justifiable and appropriate'.[111] Few resisted torture, and it was usually scaled up until it became so unbearable that those subjected to it cracked and confessed. Some accounts recall subjects stubbornly enduring beatings but breaking when having their faces submerged in a bucket of spit or after their interrogators urinated on their heads, an activity that became quite common practice. In exceptionally rare cases the accused resisted all methods of torture. This simply meant that, rather than being publicly tried, they were quietly shot in a remote location.

By 1936 Stalin felt secure enough to move against the party's big beasts and Zinoviev and Kamenev were dragged from their cells and subjected to further questioning. More arrests followed. An old associate of Trotsky, Valentin Olberg, was vigorously 'questioned' by the NKVD. After the ordeal, he admitted that Trotsky had been involved in Kirov's murder. His 'confession' was followed by yet another spate of arrests which continued to proliferate through the spring of 1936. The regime then hit upon the idea of holding show trials with Zinoviev and Kamenev lined up as the first sacrificial lambs. Ostensibly Yagoda was in charge but it was really Yezhov who was pulling the strings. The old friends of Zinoviev and Kamenev were arrested to ensure their compliance and Yezhov promised to spare the other witnesses' lives providing they testified against the two main defendants. When one of Yagoda's Chekists, Mironov, confided that he was unsure if Kamenev would confess, Stalin quizzed him: 'Do you know how much our State weighs with all the factories, machines, the army with all the armaments and the navy?...can one man withstand the pressure of that astronomical weight?...Don't come to report to me until you have in this briefcase the confession of Kamenev.'[112]

The pair were psychologically rather than physically tortured. Yezhov, for instance, promised to shoot Kamenev's son. They were deprived of sleep, harangued and threatened relentlessly. They finally let the Politburo know that they would confess if it could be guaranteed that there would be no executions. Yet when Yagoda dragged them to the Politburo, the cabinet were absent. Only Stalin, Voroshilov and Yezhov were there to preside over their fate. Voroshilov had already revealed the depth of his judicial impartiality. Having read the witness condemnations of the pair, he fumed: 'these bad people...all typical representatives of *petit bourgeois* with the face of Trotsky...are finished people...This scum must be liquidated absolutely...we need to be sure the NKVD starts the purge properly'.[113] In front of their judges, the accused asked for guarantees that they would not be harmed. Stalin coldly informed them that this was really a trial of Trotsky and what's more 'we are old Bolsheviks, disciples and followers of Lenin and we don't want to shed the blood of Old Bolsheviks, no matter how grave their past sins'.[114] Zinoviev and Kamenev, only too familiar with the fate of the Old Cordeliers, really should have known better than to be gulled by such assurances. They admitted their guilt as long as their families were to be protected and there were to be no executions. Stalin responded that 'That goes without saying'.[115]

Now that the verdicts had been agreed the trial could go ahead and the scripts were prepared. It was announced that a monolithic conspiracy dubbed the 'United Trotskyite – Zinoviete Centre' had designs on assassinating Stalin, Voroshilov, Kaganovich, Kirov, Sergo, Zhdanov and others. The trial opened on 19 August attended primarily by NKVD staff, with a generous smattering of foreign correspondents. Yagoda made himself available to proceedings from a comfortable annexe. Three judges presided over affairs with Vasily Ulrikh, like a great corpulent slug resplendent in scarlet, assuming a position of regal magnificence in the centre. But the real star of the show was the prosecutor, Andrei Vyshinsky, whose indignant venom would become notorious. Vyshinsky was a particularly odious presence; a bespectacled bureaucrat who was a crawling worm to his superiors but a bullying tyrant to his subordinates. He relished the sniffing out, prosecution and shooting of suspects connected to the entirely fictitious Trotskyite conspiracy the regime imagined itself assailed by.

Sixteen defendants were on trial in total and all of them, thanks to the ministrations they had suffered at the hands of the NKVD, were mere shells of the men they had been before. Errors proliferated. The NKVD claimed that Trotsky's son had ordered the Kirov hit from a Danish hotel. But it was discovered that the hotel had been demolished in 1917. Few journalists noticed and the court glossed over such hiccups even as Vyshinksy announced that he was already investigating cases against Karl Radek, Bukharin, Rykov and Tomsky. They must have quailed with fear. Tomsky alone seemed to perceive what was coming and promptly shot himself. Demian Bedny published the poem 'No Mercy' to whip up hysteria about the verdicts even as *Pravda's* headline blared 'Crush the Loathsome Creatures! The Mad Dogs Must Be Shot!'[116] Vyshinsky agreed: 'These mad dogs of capitalism tried to tear limb from limb the best of our Soviet land. I demand that these mad dogs should be shot – every one of them!'[117] The judges concurred with the prevailing sentiment – death it was.

The executions were carried out on 25 August. Zinoviev screamed and begged for mercy while Kamenev snapped at him to show a bit of dignity. Yezhov and Yagoda were in attendance, accompanied by the enthusiastically bloodthirsty Voroshilov, while the squeamish Vyshinsky made excuses and sent an underling. Even as the verdicts were carried out, Stalin, who had promised them mercy, was sunning himself on the beach at Sochi. The hand on the trigger belonged to Vasily Blokhin, a thickset, dark-haired Chekist of dour countenance who would personally kill thousands. So great was his number of victims that many regard him as the man who has personally killed more people than any other figure in history. Both victims were despatched with a gunshot to the back of the head before the bullets were dug out of their skulls and handed to Yagoda as macabre mementoes. The bodies were then burned. On hearing the news Nikolai Bukharin commented 'I am so glad they have been shot like dogs'.[118] When his own turn came two years later, Bukharin, in less celebratory mood, would write forty-three letters to Stalin from his cell begging for his life. None were answered. Later that day the leading lights of the party acted out Zinoviev's undignified end for Stalin while they all roared with laughter. Hate can make callous demons of us all. But the loathing the Communists had allowed themselves to feel for capitalists and Trotskyites was only just beginning to be released. This first great trial had set a precedent and laid out the template. Now it could be rolled out across the state on such a vast scale that it would engulf every walk of life from Kiev to Vladivostok and beyond.

A week after the executions of Zinoviev and Kamenev, Stalin instructed Yagoda to choose and shoot 5,000 of the oppositionists already interned in camps. From that point on, shootings of groups of forty or so occurred once or twice a week, with only children aged eleven or under exempted. Having reneged on their promise not to shoot the esteemed pair the Soviets had little compunction in turning on the family members they had pledged to spare too. Kamenev's wife had been arrested on 19 March 1935 and exiled. In January 1938 she was tried again and shot in the autumn of 1941. His eldest son, Alexander, was arrested in August 1936, sentenced in May 1937, and shot in

July 1939. His younger son was sent to an NKVD children's home and had his name changed. Three of his brothers were shot and a large number of other relatives, including three sisters, were sent to the labour camps. Zinoviev's son, Stefan, was shot in 1937.

It was not long before the interrogators began to aim their sights on other notable targets. On 8 September 1936 Bukharin was summoned to the Central Committee and accused of being involved in a plot to murder Stalin. When he protested his innocence Kaganovich exploded that he was lying and ordered the 'whore' to be dragged to the cells. He was swiftly released on Stalin's orders, but his time would come. On 30 September Stalin officially replaced Yagoda with Yezhov who was promoted to People's Commissar of Internal Affairs. Thus discredited Yagoda was a marked man, and he too would fall victim in due course. Much of the intrigues of the remainder of that year though centred around Georgia which Beria was happily purging. On 11 August Beria had set the tone when he shot the Armenian First Secretary in his office. By the time he was finished 425 of the 644 delegates to the Georgian Party Congress had been shot or despatched to the gulag. In the Georgian purges which followed Budu Mdivani, speaking from a position of authority, responded to his interrogator by spitting: 'You are telling me that Stalin has promised to spare the lives of Old Bolsheviks! I have known Stalin for thirty years. Stalin won't rest until he had butchered all of us, beginning with the unweaned baby and ending with the blind great-grandmother'.[119] For such accurate impertinence he was savagely beaten and swapped between lengthy spells in two cells – one freezing cold, the other suffocatingly hot. He was dragged out half-dead and threatened that his wife, four sons and daughter would all be killed, threats which were soon carried out. Mdivani was finally shot himself.

Another founder of the republic, Mamia Orakhelashvili, had his eyes gouged out in front of his wife, but Beria reserved his true energies for his old mentor. On 27 December, after much badgering, Nestor Lakoba agreed to go to dinner at Beria's residence having relented only after Lavrenti's mother pleaded with him to attend. Lakoba felt sick shortly afterwards and was dead within hours. He had been poisoned. It is not known if Beria's mother was in on the plot or if the ambitious brute had duped her as well. Beria had the organs removed from Lakoba's body and then burned the corpse. He then personally tortured Lakoba's family, driving his widow mad by putting a large snake in her cell. Beria then tortured her to death in front of her fourteen year old son before beating his former benefactor's children to death as well. This case was far from unique. In the provinces local magnates were arranging trials for 'wreckers' to cover up their own inefficiencies and then using them as an excuse to bump off their rivals and enemies. Beria was the most unsettling and well-chronicled of this type, but he was far from alone. Shortly before murdering Lakoba he had arrested Papulia Ordzhonikidze, Sergo's older brother, while Sergo's Deputy

Commissar, Yury Pyatakov, was targeted as the next in line for the show trial treatment. The net was being widened.

On 29 November 1936 Vyshinsky ordered measures designed to crack down on the imaginary crimes of sabotage and counter-revolutionary activism in the manufacturing sector. In fact, all the inefficiencies and accidents had resulted from pressure from the top which demanded the expansion of industry at an unfeasible and unsustainable pace. Despite the truth of the situation, it became an accepted fact within party circles that Siberia was riddled with wreckers. It was concluded that all the accidents in Pyatakov's region were the result of deliberate sabotage. He was blamed for orchestrating the whole scheme. Evidence and charges were fabricated and confessions duly obtained. In truth, the archives reveal that the accused had warned the party of the dangers long before they even conceived the trial; and that similar accidents continued to happen for years after the saboteurs had all been removed. Pyatakov's wife had been arrested in July over her links with Trotsky before Yezhov informed Yury that he was being relieved of his post and charged with complicity. Pyatakov offered to shoot all the other suspects, including his wife, to prove his innocence. Yezhov laughed at his suggestion. Pyatakov's confession of being a saboteur was sent to Sergo even as the NKVD began rounding up Ordzhonikidze's advisers. The arrest of a relative was a test of loyalty, so when Ordzhonikidze then appealed to save his brother, Papulia, he effectively doomed both of them. Putting personal interests above those of the party invited only scorn.

The investigations in that period also implicated Bukharin. He wrote numerous letters to his good friend Voroshilov, who snubbed them. By December Yezhov had gathered evidence against Bukharin, Rykov, Radek, Pyatakov and around 200 others who were alleged to be members of the Azov – Black Sea wing of the Trotskyite centre. Another 300 were fingered in Georgia and 400 more in Leningrad. Pyatakov and Radek were to be tried speedily while Bukharin and Rykov were left to stew and sweat for some considerable time. Yezhov read out the charge that Pyatakov had described the workers as a 'herd of sheep', an accusation that could be levelled at every leading Bolshevik since 1917, if not before. But the Plenum exploded in fury. One member spluttered 'That's how low this vicious Fascist agent, this degenerate Communist has sunk, God knows what else! These swine must be strangled!'[120] Stalin arranged for a showdown between Bukharin and Pyatakov in front of the Politburo, but the latter had been through the NKVD's wringer and looked like a whipped dog. Sergo, concerned, asked him if his testimony was voluntary. But Voroshilov denounced Pyatakov as a 'swine', a 'pig' and a 'son of a bitch'. Before it had even begun, Stalin was dictating the summation of the case to Vyshinsky.

The trial opened on 23 January 1937 with the net immediately widened to incorporate thousands of potential victims. The Terror was about to begin in earnest. Radek, having memorised his lines, outlined several different levels of Trotskyites as well as those who had aided them in ignorance. As Simon Sebag Montefiore put it 'Those without blind faith were to die'.[121] The trial was a farce. It was alleged that Pyatakov had flown to Oslo in 1935 and been briefed on the whole plan of sabotage by Trotsky, who was working with Rudolph Hess. But the Norwegian authorities immediately made it clear that no such flight had entered their airspace. The prosecution also alleged that an innocuous prang was an attempt on Molotov's life, with the driver of the car prepared to sacrifice himself for the evil mastermind of the scheme: Trotsky. Yet Vyshinsky still boasted that the case had been proven with a rigour entirely absent from bourgeois courts. It is astonishing that such ludicrous evidence was devoured by Western journalists and then widely decreed part of a sound judicial process.

On 29 January Pyatakov and thirteen others were sentenced to death. Radek got ten years. Soviet propaganda whipped the people up into a frenzy and, despite temperatures of -27^{0}C, some 200,000 thronged the streets of Moscow crying out that the court's verdict was the people's verdict. They screamed for the blood of the Judas-Trotsky. Maria Svanidze's diary was illustrative of how people were swept up in the paranoia, hate and blood-lust: 'These moral monsters deserved their end...How could we so blindly trust this band of scoundrels.'[122] The inefficiencies and the rushed nature of the Soviet economy meant that, for those persuaded by the hype, there was no end of evidence that Trotskyite wreckers were everywhere. Sergo Ordzhonikidze had been promised that Pyatakov would not be executed. He now suggested that, since the saboteurs had been arrested, life could return to normal. The hostile response he got made it clear that he was swimming against the tide. Sergo's opposition to the purges identified him as an enemy of the regime and a marked man, and Stalin ordered the NKVD to search his rooms. After arguing with Stalin, who mocked him, Sergo appeared in a fraught state and, on 18 February 1937, sensing all too well which way the wind was blowing, he shot himself. The papers were ordered to report that he had died of a heart attack. The fate of the old Georgian effectively cowed others who may have considered voicing concerns. With no effective opposition left, the next two years were to be a relentless cavalcade of slaughter.

With the assault against the party already in full swing Stalin turned on the army. Kaganovich, Voroshilov and Budyonny had been encouraging Stalin to purge their 'enemies' in the Red Army for some time. Their main target was Tukhachevsky, one of the great pioneers of modern, industrialised warfare. He had developed methods of using aircraft, tanks and artillery in concert so successfully that the Nazis utilised them in their Blitzkrieg tactics in WWII. His command of contemporary ordinance was remarkable, but his confidence and ability rankled with a party membership defined chiefly by pettiness and their need for others to show deference. Tukhachevsky was not the sort to pander to their insecurities. On 15 June *Pravda* published Voroshilov's report declaring that the military, including members of the top brass, was riddled with anti-Socialist and Trotskyite elements. Tukhachevsky was linked to Trotsky, Bukharin, Rykov, Yagoda and Yenukidze. Among the main charges facing the group of traitors was their failure to take Warsaw in the Polish invasion of 1920. In reality, the operation had failed because Stalin and Budyonny, in charge of the southern flank, had refused to support Tukhachevsky's assault from the north of the city. Stalin had been filled with bitterness towards his far more capable military rival ever since. He thirsted for the opportunity to avenge the stain on his reputation and heap the blame for his failures on the Marshal.

After he was incarcerated in Moscow, Yezhov and Voroshilov arrested most of the rest of the high command. Vyshinsky recommended torture and the nature of the blood spatters on Tukhachevsky's confession, which was streaked with 'flying' blood, offer compelling testimony to the violence of his interrogation. Under such pressure he admitted that 'Rightist' elements in the military had conspired with Nazi Germany to overthrow the regime and assassinate Stalin. Tukhachevsky's associates were then tortured and implicated in the imaginary plot too. Mikoyan and Kaganovich were persuaded by the 'evidence' of this wide-ranging collusion with German Fascism and Stalin himself appeared genuinely shocked when declaring 'It's incredible but it's a fact, they admit it'.[123] The leading military lights, presumably knowing which side their bread was buttered, colluded with the fiction. Marshal Yegorov, whose own wife was under suspicion, snarled for 'All these traitors to be wiped off the face of the earth as the most hostile enemies and disgusting scum'.[124] Molotov, Kaganovich, Voroshilov and Vyshinsky all joined in the denunciations in front of an enthusiastically applauding throng: 'Our government will exterminate such people...For this traitor, bastard and shit, there is only one punishment – execution'.[125]

At their trial on 11 June 1937 the judges were the fellow Marshals of the accused. All were sentenced to death the same day. Tukhachevsky's wife, daughter, mother, sisters and brothers were then arrested. His wife and both brothers were killed, three sisters sent to the camps and his young daughter, Svetlana, was placed in a home for children of 'enemies of the people'. She was sent to a camp at the age of seventeen. His mother and remaining sister died in exile. But the judges of the Marshals quailed too and one of them, Belov, later said 'Tomorrow I'll be put in the same place'.[126] He was. All the judges, with the exception of Budyonny, Shaposhnikov and Ulrikh, were later shot. Budyonny stood out among the figures in the court that day. He was another of Stalin's loyal cronies and one of his incompetent officers who would survive the purges. Famous for his preference for cavalry charges over the tank he had all the appearance of an anachronistic relic of the Tsarist era. The sharp-dressing Budyonny possessed something of the élan of one of Charles I's Cavaliers and was instantly recognisable by his heroically flamboyant moustache. Yet even he did not escape unscathed and his wife was later arrested.

Voroshilov carried out another enormous purge and arrested 40,000 members of the armed forces by 29 November 1938. Three of the five marshals, fifteen of the sixteen commanders, sixty of the sixty-seven corps commanders, and all seventeen commissars were shot. The consequences of such root and branch purging were most apparent in the later Winter War against Finland. Put in charge of the operation, the useless Voroshilov sent wave after wave of infantrymen, armed with rifles, rather than 'wasteful' machine-guns, up the centre against the strongest section of the Finnish line. The losses were horrifying, and the bloody nose that Finland gave to the Soviets encouraged Hitler into believing he could conquer Russia with ease. Stubborn though Finnish resistance was Tukhachevsky, had he still been in place, would undoubtedly have employed Russia's vast superiority in ordinance in flank attacks that would have blasted their defences to pieces with brutal efficiency. It was more through luck than judgement that the state retained such capable men as Chuikov, Vasilevsky, Rokossovsky, Koniev and, especially, Zhukov, undoubtedly the most able commander of WWII. That slice of fortune enabled Russia to eventually triumph over Nazi Germany.

On 2 July 1937 the Terror was officially rolled out across the state as the Politburo ordered local secretaries to arrest and shoot elements hostile to the Soviet regime. The slaughter was just another process, like the Five Year Plan, that would usher in the workers' utopia. Lists were sent out to the regions which quickly filled their quotas and asked permission to prosecute ever greater numbers. The centre was only too happy to comply and the figures kept rising: thousands, tens of thousands, hundreds of thousands and even more were to die. And the totals sent to the camps would dwarf those executed. As more saboteurs and anti-Soviet elements had to be found the victims were drawn from ever-widening sectors of Soviet society: party members, policemen, engineers, proletariats, academics, artists, doctors, ethnic groups including Poles, Germans and Koreans and members of religions like Baptists, Jehovah's Witnesses, Buddhists, Muslims and priests; all were swept up in the maelstrom. The relatives of people selected for execution were to be deported too, and entire families were killed and tortured, children orphaned, shattered survivors left shell-shocked while the bodies continued piling up.

Any friends or relatives of those arrested, if not incarcerated themselves, were subsequently shunned by their acquaintances as 'enemies of the people' and frequently lost their jobs, homes and possessions. Virtually all were completely innocent of any wrongdoing whatsoever. If any were actually guilty of any seditious behaviour, then it was pure coincidence rather than evidence of any astute judgement or efficient intelligence work by the state. The centre and the regions were equally complicit in the carnage, and the number of those involved in the atrocities rivals the number of victims. Hundreds of thousands of officials either ordered or carried out the murders. Apart from those later engulfed in the Terror themselves, not one ever faced a legitimate trial for the crimes they had committed. And Stalin was unrepentant:

'Who's going to remember all this riffraff in ten or twenty years time? No one. Who remembers the names of the *boyars* Ivan the Terrible got rid of? No one...The people had to know he was getting rid of all his enemies. In the end, they all got what they deserved...Ivan killed too few *boyars*. He should have killed them all to create a strong state.'[127]

Stalin himself was as active as the regional commissars and on one day alone, 12 November 1938, he signed 3,167 death warrants. Molotov, Kaganovich, Voroshilov, Zhdanov and Mikoyan were just as busy. Stalin and Molotov colluded in personally ordering 39,000 deaths. The belief that they were creating the perfect state, that those who obstructed them truly deserved their fates, led to a terrible cheapening of the value of life. Yezhov went on record to suggest that 'if during this operation, an extra thousand people will be shot, that is not such a big deal'.[128] It was targeted slaughter, political and ideological genocide. A massacre designed to eradicate an entire social class, to expunge those who deviated from the party line. Hate and certainty combined to convince them of the benefits of removing the 'Other'.

It was in this period, as the prisons swelled to bursting point, that torture became ever more brutal and commonplace. The Soviet gaols made the feared Peter and Paul fortress of the Tsarist regime rather resemble a Butlin's holiday camp of the 1950s, a symbol of happier and more innocent times. Overcrowding was horrendous. One Kharkov prison, designed to house 800 inmates, was stuffed with 12,000 prisoners in 1937. In Zhitomir, 160 men had been crammed into a cell built for eight and, as a result, five or six died every day. The overcrowded institutions were filthy and unhygienic, and many accounts focus on the unbearable smell. Any sort of games, frivolity or even loud speech were ruthlessly suppressed. The cells, the prisons, the inmates' clothes and even the food were saturated with damp and mould. On top of such appalling conditions, inmates had to endure the soundtrack of the screams of those being tortured. Prisoners were forced to listen to this dreadful racket day and night knowing that it was often their friends being subjected to the sadistic treatment, and that their own turn would inevitably come.

Three of the five great prisons in Moscow – the Lubyanka, Lefortovo and Butyrka, were for political prisoners only. The Lefortovo was also the favoured location for the torture of suspects, but the Lubyanka, just a few minutes' walk from the Kremlin, was the most significant and famous by far. The grand edifice was used as the headquarters of the NKVD, but a significant section of the building was given over to act as holding cells. The hastily constructed execution block to the rear of the Lubyanka helped speed up the efficiency of the whole process considerably. Just as it had in France in the 1790s the state targeted the innocent; the Soviets though did it on a far grander scale. Practically anyone who had ever been abroad was in the camps by 1940 including the majority of the nation's sporting stars who were regarded as 'loathsome counter-revolutionary degenerates'. An opera singer who had danced with the Japanese ambassador also found herself incarcerated as a result. In 1937 an engineer received a parcel from a friend in Poland containing shoes, crayons and a couple of dolls. He was shot while his friend, who had received nothing, got ten years in a concentration camp. One woman was sentenced to ten years for remarking that Tukhachevsky was handsome. Another man got three years for smiling in sympathy as some dockers regaled each-other with anti-Soviet anecdotes. Trials, which followed the trumped-up charges, were perfunctory. Evgenia Ginzburg recounted how her trial at the Collegium was done and dusted within two minutes. On average, death sentences accounted for around ten per cent of those incarcerated, but the rates were significantly higher in that institution. Between 1 October 1936 and 30 September 1938 the Collegium alone heard 36,157 cases, sentencing 30,514 of those accused to death and 5,643 to imprisonment. Not one individual in that period was acquitted.

Families were increasingly targeted. When Aleksandr Karin and his wife were shot, Yezhov ensured that their thirteen year old daughter was turned out onto the streets. Months later, an emaciated shadow of her former self with nothing of the child remaining, she was forced by the Pioneers to denounce her parents as spies and endorse their execution in front of a large, baying audience. On 5 July 1937 the Politburo ordered the NKVD to incarcerate the wives of all condemned traitors for between five and eight years and to put their children into 'state protection'. Initially 18,000 wives and 25,000 children were removed. Yezhov then announced that children over the age of three could be imprisoned. Around a million children were confined to state-run orphanages and did not see their mothers for twenty years. Budyonny's wife, Olga, had been flirting with Bolshoi singers and Polish diplomats. For those high crimes she would suffer. Stalin said to the cavalryman 'we won't let anyone, even a wife, compromise you in the Party and the State'.[129] She was sentenced to ten years and driven insane by the solitary confinement. With such esteemed members of the Soviet hierarchy targeted it is no surprise the party ranks were decimated. Even Nikolai Krylenko, the People's Commissar of Justice, who had signed innumerable death warrants himself, was shot. Almost no one was safe, no one but Stalin.

Thousands of party members had the power of life and death over practically anyone they chose. Many were consumed as a result of personal vendettas but, as an unavoidable consequence of the nature of the Terror, a huge number of the perpetrators were the most committed socialists who were removing those they genuinely believed were impeding their political dream. The widening climate of suspicion saw Soviet society grow increasingly accusative even as the likes of courtesy and tolerance became almost unknown. The culture thus created encouraged the baser human instincts, and the paranoid nature of their philosophising allowed the Bolsheviks to see plots everywhere. As a result, denunciations spread like wildfire. It has been reasonably estimated that one in every five people was an NKVD informer. Workers denounced their colleagues, residents denounced their neighbours and friends of victims denounced those who had persecuted them. Once the finger had been pointed at a suspect the assumption of guilt was almost impossible to shake off. In such an atmosphere it was out of the question to query the official state line or locate other critics of the regime. Individuals denounced their friends, relatives and colleagues who had been targeted and frequently claimed their former association had only been motivated by a desire to unmask their peer as a mole. As a consequence, all societal associations within the state dissolved and all that remained was loyalty to the party.

The chief denunciator was Polia Nikolaenko of Kiev who sent some 8,000 people to their deaths. When her potential victims began turning on her she wrote to Stalin: 'I was, am and will be devoted to the Party and the Great Leader. You helped me to find Truth. STALIN'S TRUTH IS STRONG'.[130] She was eventually discredited, but Stalin protected her. At the heart of it all was Yezhov who worked a gruelling schedule, supervising interrogations and beatings every day. He was involved in the arrest, torture and killing of scores of friends, including his 'godfather' Moskvin and the man's unfortunate wife, a couple who Yezhov had socialised with for years. He could spend all night chatting to an old comrade, then order them shot in the morning. *Pravda* sang his praises calling him 'an unyielding Bolshevik who without getting up from his desk, night and day, is unravelling and cutting the threads of the Fascist conspiracy'.[131]

The figures continued to spiral across the state. Khrushchev was given a quota of 50,000 for Moscow – he had 55,741 shot, and then requested permission to shoot another 2,000 ex-kulaks. Of the thirty-eight Secretaries in the area he shot thirty-five. When Stalin complained it was too many, Khrushchev despairingly protested that there were many more that needed to be liquidated. But he later had the evidence of his complicity in the killings destroyed. In Askabad they were given a quota of 6,277. They shot 13,259 in total. The local magnates the Terror was supposed to target used it to eradicate their enemies and protect their friends. But it was now only a matter of time until a second wave of terror dealt with those entrenched local elites. Stalin's loyal henchmen were to be sent into the provinces to purge the purgers – Zhdanov, Mikoyan, Kaganovich and Molotov were charged with carrying out the task and finding wreckers to blame for the inefficiencies of Soviet industrialisation.

Two stand out among this second wave – Andrei Andreyev and Georgi Malenkov. Andreyev went to Saratov in the Volga where he embarked on a frenzy of arrests and shootings in the local tractor industry. He travelled on to Kuibyshev and beyond leaving a bloody trail in his wake wherever he went. Malenkov, who was sent to Armenia with Mikoyan and Belarus with Yezhov, may have killed as many as 150,000 people. He was fat, pasty and sweaty, with greasy, lank black hair plastered to his forehead. Central casting would no doubt recommend him to play a predatory paedophile clad in a dirty overcoat and lurking by a playground. He more than lived up to the sinister, unsettling impression suggested by such a role. The enthusiastic cleaners of provincial enclaves, who descended on rural Russia like the Four Horsemen of the Apocalypse, often got mixed messages from the centre. Pavel Postyshev had massacred the bureaucracy in Kuibyshev in an effort to prove his loyalty and dedication. Summoned to the Plenum in January 1938 he was to pay for killing the 'wrong people'. Yet, shortly after criticising him for his excesses, Stalin signed a quota for 48,000 more victims. In February 1938, Yezhov and Khrushchev went to purge Kiev and made 106,119 arrests. The bloodletting began, but this time Khrushchev was praised for his 'merciless uprooting of Enemies'.[132]

On 2 March 1938, a few months after the shooting of Yenukidze on 20 December 1937, the third great show trial began. It prosecuted Bukharin, Rykov and Yagoda along with many others. Bukharin had written to Stalin from his prison cell to plead 'Koba, why is my death necessary for you?' Did Stalin chuckle malevolently to himself on receipt of that note, or did he review it with icy disdain? We can only speculate. What we do know is that no reply was sent, and no mercy was shown. When Bukharin refused to implicate himself the way Kamenev and Zinoviev had done Mikoyan sneered, with impenetrable Soviet logic, 'If you won't confess you're just proving you're a Fascist hireling'.[133] Threats to shoot his wife and children soon changed Bukharin's mind. It is striking that such tactics still worked despite the fact that every family member promised clemency before had subsequently shared their relatives' fates. Krestinsky protested his innocence from the stand. But the court had destroyed the evidence which might exonerate him. Following a lengthy recess, a bedraggled looking Krestinsky withdrew the statement and confessed his guilt. Some observers felt the change in him so striking they believed he had been replaced by an actor.

Yezhov, when denouncing Yagoda, declared he had been a German spy since 1907. He also accused his predecessor of attempting to poison him by spraying mercury onto his curtains. After Yagoda had been arrested a search of his premises revealed a vast collection of female clothing, though whether he wore the items or merely collected them as trophies is unknown. Under interrogation Yagoda had fingered Rykov, Yenukidze and Marshal Tukhachevsky, before confessing to the murder of Kirov and the poisoning of Maxim Gorky who had conveniently died of natural causes in 1936. Sharangovich was more compliant than many on the stand and freely confessed to poisoning huge numbers of pigs and horses. He also took full responsibility for all the problems caused by collectivisation in Belarus, thus conveniently exonerating the party of any blame in the disaster. A cynical mind might suggest such outcomes were the purpose of the entire enterprise. Having thus exonerated the state the witnesses cleared the ground for Stalin to blame the 'foul-smelling heap of human garbage' while lamenting that 'with our riches and abundance of products, there is a shortage first of one thing, then of another. It is these traitors who are responsible for it'.[134]

Vyshinsky's summation left no doubt as to the motivations for the proceedings:

'Our people are demanding one thing: crush the accursed reptile! Time will pass. The graves of the hateful traitors will grow over with weeds and thistles...Over the road cleared of the last scum and filth of the past, we, our people, with our beloved leader and teacher, the great Stalin, at our head will march as before onwards and onwards, towards Communism!'[135]

The accused were dragged away while Bukharin's wife, along with Rykov's spouse and daughter, were arrested and sentenced to twenty years hard labour. Astonishingly Anna Bukharina and Natalya Rykova both survived their ordeals. Yagoda's parents and sister were exiled and his brother-in-law and father-in-law were shot. Both his parents died in the camps. Yezhov also made it clear that the net of persecution was to be considerably widened: 'There will be some innocent victims in this fight against Fascist agents. We are launching a major attack on the Enemy...Better that ten innocent people should suffer than one spy get away. When you chop wood, chips fly'.[136]

Yet the treatment meted out to Postyshev and Yagoda had signalled a warning: the central authorities would be prepared to blame those prosecuting the Terror in order to deflect culpability from themselves. The torturers, who largely believed the trumped-up charges they hurled at innocents, were tortured in their turn and in all 20,000 NKVD men fell victim themselves. The new crop of recruits considered any display of human sympathy for, or humanity to, their victims to be a concession to bourgeois attitudes and a betrayal of the glorious class struggle. But, of all the old breed, there was one figure more vulnerable than anyone else. Through 1938 Stalin began to order the execution of Yezhov's protégés before informing him he required new assistance in running the operation. It became clear that he was grooming Yezhov's successor when Beria was officially appointed First Deputy of the NKVD on 22 August 1938. The pair initially turned their attention to the far east where the army had thus far escaped the purges. Another frenzy of killings would not save him though.

Yezhov was already falling out of favour when news of the sexual exploits of his promiscuous wife reached the prudish Stalin. When Yevgenia's best friend, Zinaida Glinkina, was arrested, she knew what was coming and took a lethal dose of poison. Even as she died, late that November 1938, Yezhov was at the Politburo being savaged by Beria and Malenkov. On 23 November he was grilled by Stalin, Molotov and Voroshilov. He was removed from the NKVD and, accused of espionage, would suffer the same fate he had inflicted on so many others. He was isolated, his former friends abandoned him, and he was to die for a crime he had not committed. It was perhaps one of the few events in that dreadful period in which a macabre form of justice can be said to have taken place. He wailed that his friends 'turned their backs upon me as if I was plague-ridden...I never realised the depth of meanness of all these people'.[137] As Oscar Wilde once quipped 'one would have to have a heart of stone not to laugh'.

On 25 November Beria was appointed Commissar of the NKVD. It was to be a busy debut. On the day that Beria started his new position Stalin and Molotov authorised 3,176 executions. His cronies were then drafted in to wipe out Yezhov's faction. Henchmen like Shalva Tsereteli and Bogdan Kobulov were particularly renowned for their brutality, but their boss kept an active hand in proceedings. Beria interrogated Bukharin's attractive twenty-four year old widow, Anna Lavina, flirting with her before taunting her. She was ripped away from her young son and spent twenty years in the camps. Between 24 February and 16 March 1939 Beria presided over the executions of 413 important prisoners including Marshal Yegorov and ex-Politburo members Kossior, Postyshev and Chubar. Then, quite suddenly, Stalin and Beria decided to curtail the Terror. Perhaps they realised that if they carried on there would be no one left. At any rate, the state had been suitably cowed by the carnage inflicted on it over the preceding two-plus years.

All the excesses were blamed on Yezhov who, on 10 April 1939, after several months in limbo, was finally arrested. He was denounced by his fellow murderers like Malenkov who were promoted even as he fell. But the clearing up would still take some considerable time. On 16 January 1940 Stalin signed 346 death warrants. They had been incarcerated by Yezhov's regime, now they were liquidated, but not before some prolonged and energetic torture by Beria and Kobulov. Beria beat R.I. Eikhe relentlessly and gouged out one of his eyes. When he still would not confess to being a spy he was shot anyway. On 2 February the trial of Yezhov was held in Ulrikh's office. He was accused of being a spy for Poland, England and Japan as well as conspiring to assassinate Stalin.

At his execution, which, took place the very next day, Yezhov collapsed twice and had to be dragged into the compound to be shot. Stalin derided him as 'scum...a rat who killed many innocent people'.[138]

While the Great Terror was over, no one doubted that, with Beria now at the helm, terror as a *practice* would continue. Torture and killing were still very much on the menu, even if the appetite for bloodshed had diminished. Beria ordered Kobulov to mercilessly beat and torture the foreign press officer Yevgeni Gnedin, while Tsereteli was ordered to kill the Soviet Ambassador to China and his wife in a car crash. Others who thought they had survived the Terror were about to discover they were mistaken; Stalin was about to turn on their wives. Beria began investigating Polina Molotova, the wife of Vyacheslav Molotov, who ran a perfume empire. He claimed to find 'saboteurs' among her employees, but she escaped, for now. Bronka Poskrebysheva, the wife of Alexander Poskrebyshev, had been foolish enough to petition for the release of her brother, Metalikov. Beria had previously groped Bronka and when she had slapped him commented that he would not forget it. On 27 April 1939 she called Beria to ask about her brother, and he invited her over to discuss it. She was never seen again, and it emerged that she had been shot two years later. Anastas Mikoyan's two sons were sent to the gulag while Mikhail Kalinin's wife was beaten unconscious under the personal supervision of Beria before being sent to the camps as well.

On 5 May 1940 Kira Kulik, the beautiful wife of one of Stalin's useless commanders in the Finnish War, was bundled into a car in Moscow, driven to the Lubyanka, and tortured by Beria. After suffering their treatment for a month she was shot through the head by Blokhin. Kobulov arrived late and complained that they had not waited for him. Her husband was never told. He considered her missing and continued searching for her for twelve years. Molotov's wife survived until after the war when Stalin's increasing anti-Semitism and paranoia towards doctors took a firm grasp of his faculties. Molotov was ordered to divorce her and on 21 January 1949 Polina was arrested along with her doctor, secretaries and sisters. A sister and brother of hers would both die in prison. Polina herself was sentenced to five years in exile. Allegiance to the party and the cause trumped even marital vows in the minds of committed socialists, or for those who simply wanted to survive. Molotov did, just.

Another wave of atrocities took place during and after the war. Just as the conflict was about to begin Stalin arrested Boris Vannikov, one of his chief armaments experts, and Mikhail Kaganovich, the brother of Lazar. The charges were related to inefficiencies in the air force and Vannikov suffered brutal torture. Pavel Rychayov, from the air-force high command, was also arrested and shot while several other victims implicated Mikhail Kaganovich. Stalin decided that he was an agent of Hitler, even though he was Jewish. Mikhail, under investigation, knew what was coming so shot himself to save his family. But few events better illustrate Soviet stubbornness, their subsequent, inevitable blunders, and a conviction resistant to even the most serious of errors, than the eventual outbreak of hostilities.

On 21 June 1941 Beria, sick of what he called an avalanche of misinformation about German intentions, ordered the recall of the Soviet minister in Berlin while promising to 'grind him to dust'[139] in the gulag. He also reported to Stalin 'My people and I, Iosif Vissarinovich Stalin, remember your wise prediction: Hitler will not attack in 1941!'[140] Shortly after his confident declaration, just after midnight on 22 June 1941, a Communist labourer from Berlin, Alfred Liskov, swam across the Pruth to inform the Soviets that the Nazis had been given the order to invade. As a reward for risking his life to deliver such vital news, Stalin demanded he be shot for 'disinformation'. Less than two hours after issuing the execution order a German army of over three million men smashed across the border and annihilated the Soviet defences. Stalin then ordered that Dmitri Pavlov, his Western Front Commander, be shot, despite the fact that the crisis had resulted entirely from his own dreadful errors. When Nikolai Baibakov was given responsibility for the Caucasus he was informed that if the oilfields fell into German hands he would be shot; and if they were destroyed to prevent them falling into German hands, he would still be shot.

The Terror was reignited during the conflict. A total of 994,000 servicemen were condemned and 157,000 shot. As Russian personnel retreated, the NKVD tossed grenades into the prisons they abandoned. On 3 October 1941 Beria executed 157 high profile inmates like Olga Kameneva, Trotsky's sister and Kamenev's widow. On 28 October another twenty-five were shot including the air ace Rychagov. In all 4,905 prisoners were killed in just eight days. But one of the most notorious acts of the regime had already taken place earlier in the war. In April and May 1940 some 22,000 captured Polish personnel were killed in the region around the forests of Katyn. The executions took under a month to complete and were carried out by Blokhin and two other NKVD officers in a soundproof hut with padded walls. It was an attempt to wipe out the Polish officer class along with various other counter-revolutionary 'undesirables'. Merkulov and Kobulov presided and similar massacres swiftly followed in Latvia, Estonia and Lithuania where tens of thousands were gunned down. Many mass burial sites were later discovered: at Vinnitsa 9,000 bodies were unearthed, 50,000 were uncovered between Vladivostok and Khabarovsk, 46,000 near Leningrad and 50,000 close to Minsk.

Beria used the gulag's 1.7 million slave labourers to build Stalin's weapons and railways. It is estimated that 930,000 of them died. In 1943 Beria arrested 931,544 people in territory 'liberated' by the Soviet advance. In early 1944 another 800,000 men were deported from Chechnya and Kalmyk. In all, Beria transported 1.5 million people from the territories with approximately 530,000 dying en route or on arrival at the camps. New decrees issued during the war also proved costly with Order No. 270 declaring that anyone failing to fulfil their military duties would be summarily executed. The legislation would reap a terrible harvest after the war. In 1942, as a reaction to Lend-Lease, a new crime, 'praise of American technology', was added to the USSR's legal code. One could be sent to the gulag for nothing more than complimenting an American jeep. But despite such measures Stalin was, at least, an able war-time leader. He re-opened the churches, oversaw a phenomenally successful armaments programme, listened to his generals and performed a great service to his people when making a grand public appearance in Moscow even as the Nazis were at the gates of the city. His stewardship was a significant factor in the Soviet victory over Hitler's forces. Yet the persecution continued after the conflict ended.

Even as the Soviet Union basked in the glow of its remarkable triumph, another massive wave of arrests in 1946-7 targeted Jews, Army officers and those released to aid in the struggle against Nazism. Soldiers who had been captured by the Germans were also sent to the camps and there were numerous cases of indomitable men who had survived Auschwitz being sent to the gulag following their 'liberation'. On 2 March 1946, disappointed at the performance of the air-force in the war, Stalin had Air Marshal Novikov and Aircraft Production Minister, Shakhurin, arrested and tortured, though the real boss of aircraft production was Malenkov. Stalin used the men he was grooming from the next generation to handle the case. He relied on Victor Abakumov, who he promoted to Minister of State Security, and Andrei Zhdanov, the dapper and moustachioed commissar who, as the husband of Svetlana, was his son-in-law. Zhdanov, whose sharp suits, slick hair and ready smile made him resemble the comic relief in a Cary Grant movie, was not quite so gregarious as he seemed. Abakumov, for his part, was just as sadistic as Beria but considerably less intelligent. The latter wanted Novikov and Shakhura both shot. Stalin ordered them sentenced to between seven and ten years hard labour instead. There was no suggestion that the old tyrant was mellowing with age though; during the Doctors Plot, which marked the last thrash of the tail of his regime, he had famously commanded his interrogators to 'beat, beat and beat again'.

There are manifold reasons why terror played such a consistent part of Stalin's regime. The chief cause was hostility for any opinion that deviated from the ideals of socialism, an antipathy significantly magnified by the excessive faith of those converted to the ideology. This incipient anger is heightened as the idealism of the left results in unrealistic hopes. When expectation turns to frustration, venom is directed at those believed to be thwarting the socialist dawn. And, because hatred is at the core of far-left activism, the recourse to violence was instinctive and immediate. Stalin's regime is the ultimate expression of this characteristic, yet the blame lies not with the malevolent forces of capitalism, but with the left's own ideological framework: on a philosophy based on erroneous assumptions about human nature and economic development. The result is a system guaranteed to fail, one that can only be maintained by the application of force. There are mountains of evidence supporting this contention, though it has little impact on the certainty of the faithful. The justifications given for the Terror, while demonstrably false, were widely believed with an unshakable conviction by huge swathes of the state.

Events were chiefly driven by the fact the Soviets knew, without a shred of doubt, that Marxism was scientifically perfect. This led them to the conclusion that any inefficiencies in the system must be the fault of wreckers, saboteurs and traitors. As these people were interfering with the imposition of the ideal society, they could be removed without compunction. Their extermination was, in fact, a moral imperative. The reality of course was that in destroying incentives, in removing competition and the profit motive from the economy and allowing the state to assume control of all industry, the Soviets had created all the problems besetting to the economy and quality of production themselves. Others were to pay the price for their own arrogance and incompetence though, and millions suffered the most appalling fates as a consequence. It is a similar story with all those accused of being Nazi agents. Not only were all innocent of the charges levelled against them, but the authorities had actually been colluding with the Nazi hierarchy themselves all along. And as soon as the Terror had finished, the minute he stopped killing Fascist collaborators and German spies, Stalin made a pact with Hitler. As part of that accord he swept up 570 German Communists from Moscow's prisons and handed them to the Gestapo.

Despite such obvious falsehoods though there remains the possibility that the accusers believed their justifications. One supposes they must have, however ludicrous they sound to us now. For those most committed, it was the piety of their convictions that propelled the paragons of morality into carnage. Natasha Andreyeva, the daughter of Andrei, 'believed absolutely' that the NKVD only arrested enemies and said 'My father believed wreckers and Fifth Columnists were destroying our State and had to be destroyed. My mother was utterly convinced. We prepared for war'.[141] Stalin himself had, in 1937, voiced personal reasons for the coming slaughter that was to decimate the party. Chastising the Old Bolsheviks about to face the state's wrath he lamented that 'Maybe it can be explained by the fact that you lost faith'.[142] It is a quote that neatly encapsulates the religious frenzy which informed the killings. For the hatred of their enemies, and the determination to drive through their agenda at any cost, were driven by messianic absolutism.

In Robert Conquest's analysis, Bolshevism 'had become, in the most classical way, an example of a sect, a fanaticism'.[143] Simon Sebag Montefiore is another who noted the psychological similarities between the devout members of religion and socialism:

'The Bolsheviks were atheists but they were hardly secular politicians in the conventional sense: they stooped to kill from the smugness of the highest moral eminence. Bolshevism may not have been a religion, but it was close enough...They would die and kill for their faith in the inevitable progress towards human betterment, making sacrifices of their own families with a fervour only seen in the religious slaughters and martyrdoms of the Middle Ages – and the Middle East'. [144]

A cynical veteran Communist emphasised this mindset when commenting that a Bolshevik was 'someone who had absolute faith in the Party no matter what...A person with the ability to adapt his morality and conscience in such a way that he can unreservedly accept the dogma that the Party is never wrong – even though it's wrong all the time'.[145]

Santayana's definition of the fanatic is that 'he redoubles his efforts while forgetting his aims. He doesn't want to think or to know. He just wants to *believe.*'[146] It is a view ratified by a victim of the purges. He analysed an NKVD officer known for his charm and gentle nature who, nevertheless, gained a fearsome reputation for barbarity:

'What would a Prygov say if he were required to defend himself in a court of law? He would not, we believe, refer to superior orders, but to the teachings of Marxism and Leninism as he understood them. Prygov was as loyal and obedient as an S.S. man. But his faith was founded on a conviction that it fully accorded with the demands of reason and conscience. He was fully convinced that this was no blind faith, but was founded on science and logic. He was brutal because the general line required him to be brutal. The general line, so long as it accorded with the fundamental tenets of Marxism, was everything to him. Without the allegedly scientific foundation of the general line, which was the backbone of his faith, all the instructions of the Party authorities would have lost their significance for him. He was convinced of the logical and ethical correctness of his Marxist principles, and on this conviction his faith depended.'[147]

This tendency was one compounded by the drive to conformity. The Soviets hoped to extinguish any kind of deviation from the party line. And it led the faithful to flock like sheep and partake in the maelstrom of condemnation, torture and murder that engulfed the USSR. This is not to suggest that there is any unanimity of thought on the left at all. The relentless factional squabbling that has continually riven the movement clearly shows this not to be the case. But there is undoubtedly a *desire* to impose a blanket viewpoint, and the result of this impulse is the hostility to dissent that has defined the left for centuries. The Bolshevik party members regarded those who existed outside their own circle with the same contempt that southern planters in the early USA viewed their slaves. They exhibited the same double standards of compassion for their own and contempt for 'the other'. While they maintained humanist values within their community, this perception allowed them to treat outsiders with callous brutality.

In *Pravda* on 21 August 1936, during the trial of Zinoviev and Kamenev, Pyatakov published a manifesto which contrasted the purity of Bolshevik motives with the vulgar morality of the people they were persecuting:

> 'One cannot find the words to fully express one's indignation and disgust. These people have lost the last semblance of humanity. They must be destroyed like carrion which is polluting the pure, bracing air of the land of the Soviets; dangerous carrion which may cause the death of our leaders, and has already caused the death of one of the best people in our land – the wonderful comrade and leader S.M. Kirov.'[148]

The expression of such sentiments did not, of course, save Pyatakov from sharing the fate of the accused. These traits acted cyclically. The herd instinct reinforced the advocates' faith in their views which further cemented the bonds between and reliance on their colleagues. The activists' commitment to the cause became so total that they could not bring themselves to question their actions even as the bodies started piling up. But then the climate of the USSR meant that promotion would always be reserved for those who excelled in flattery, obsequiousness, submission and brutality. These are not the qualities on which successful states are built.

Yet the top brass and intellectual elite were utterly blind to such consequences. In 1936 Bukharin remarked that 'one is saved by a faith that development is always going forward. It is like a stream that is running to the shore. If one leans out of the stream, one is ejected completely'.[149] In 1924 Trotsky had stated: 'None of us desires or is able to dispute the will of the Party. Clearly, the Party is always right...We can only be right with and by the Party, for history has provided no other way of being in the right'.[150] It was Pyatakov again though who, in 1928, perhaps best summarised this aspect of their mentality. 'A true Bolshevik has submerged his personality in the collectivity of the Party...In order to become one with this great Party, he would fuse himself with it, abandon his own personality, so that there was no particle left inside him which did not belong to the Party.'[151] Bullock summed up this mindset as 'a common ideology based upon what was believed to be a scientifically proven set of propositions about history and society, with the same degree of certainty for the converted as the doctrines of the Catholic Church'.[152]

Stalin himself lived a comfortably relaxed existence through the whole period of famine and terror. He and his family flitted between their Kremlin flat and a dacha at Zubalovo that had previously belonged to an industrialist. Stalin presumably found that ironic rather than hypocritical. The Stalin brood, who later relocated to a grand dwelling at Kuntsevo, lived a comfortably bourgeois existence there and generously entertained a string of guests. The family also took long summer holidays in the state dachas on the Black Sea where Stalin was particularly fond of Sochi. While staying at one of his summer residences he liked to play billiards, read on the veranda or potter about the garden, pruning the roses or weeding the flowerbeds. He also held frequent dinner parties with his commissars. These could be rowdy affairs with pranks, singing, dancing and wrestling. Stalin liked to test his guests, plying them with alcohol, while he remained sober, to see how they might blab once their inhibitions had been loosened. We can only speculate on just how uncomfortable such evenings were for everyone except Uncle Joe.

But, despite the idyllic surroundings, the leader's own family were far from exempt from his capriciousness and brutality. Stalin had at least two illegitimate sons who were both abandoned without a backwards glance though later forced to sign confidentiality agreements by his secret police. Yakov, his son from his first marriage, was ignored for fifteen years and then, after their reconciliation, relentlessly bullied. When Yakov tried to commit suicide, but failed in the attempt, his unsympathetic father grumbled that he couldn't even get that right. After he was later captured by the Nazis during WWII, Stalin refused a prisoner exchange and, believing his son had betrayed him, had his wife arrested. Yakov's later successful suicide in captivity finally earned him some grudging respect from the old man. But it was Stalin's in-laws who suffered particularly badly. The family of his first wife Kato, soon felt his wrath. Her brother, Alyosha Svanidze and his wife Maria were both arrested, as was his sister Mariko. All of them were executed in 1941. Alyosha had been told he would be released if he recanted his crimes. He testily responded that he could not recant to something he had not done. He then spat in his interrogator's face and snarled 'Tell Stalin that's my answer to him'. Stalin's second wife, Nadya, was neglected in favour of party commitments. She enrolled anonymously in the Industrial Academy in Moscow where she became aware of the famine under his regime. It is believed that such revelations may have contributed to her actions in 1932. The fragile and troubled woman retreated to her rooms in the Kremlin and, taking a pistol, shot herself through the chest. *Pravda*, with typical mendacity, reported her death as being from appendicitis. Stalin's reaction to her suicide was more of anger and self-pity than remorse.

The Alliluyev clan were naturally aggrieved. They felt her husband had been culpable in Nadya's demise, but they wisely held their tongues. It would do them no good. In the late 1940s the Alliluyevs were encouraged to write a memoir to add to the growing library of publications about Stalin. Anna took to the task and included some sentimental touches that humanised the dictator, like reminiscing about the time Stalin had dozed off while smoking his pipe and burnt his bedsheets. As a result, she was arrested and sentenced to ten years hard labour for defaming him. Just for good measure he threw her sister-in-law, Zhenya, in gaol too. They would remain incarcerated until after his death. Still not satisfied Stalin ordered Anna's husband, Stanislas Redens, to be shot. The cumulative effect of such persecution drove Anna insane. Nadya's brother, Pavel, was almost certainly poisoned and his wife was sentenced to ten years. As for Stalin's formidable mother, Keke, he had little to do with her. If he did visit her it was as a photo opportunity for *Pravda*, and when she died in 1937, Stalin didn't even attend the funeral. The one family member he had been close to was his daughter Svetlana, but this changed as she became more independent. When the teenager started an affair, Stalin had the man sent to the gulag. He was, admittedly, a married womaniser in his forties. Perhaps the man's taste in adolescents reminded Stalin of himself. When Svetlana protested 'But I love him!' Stalin slapped her twice across the face, hard. Their relationship never recovered.

But for all the killing that had gone on in those terrible years, the one death that Stalin desired above all others was Trotsky. Always Trotsky. His great nemesis had been despatched first to Kazakhstan, then deported to Turkey. From there he had fled to Mexico where he found refuge in Coyoacán, on the outskirts of Mexico City. Initially he had been freely loaned accommodation at the Blue House by the artist Frida Kahlo, with whom he had an affair, before eventually moving to another address nearby. He found many allies on his long exile and his sympathetic supporters included H.G. Wells, George Bernard Shaw, John Maynard Keynes, H.L. Mencken and the Bishop of Birmingham. He had remained a thorn in Stalin's side penning a stream of withering critiques of the Stalinist regime. But in truth his ideological make-up was built on entirely the same principles: the forced implementation of socialist economic policies; sweeping use of censorship and propaganda; strident intolerance for any dissent to the Marxist line; the use of revolutionary violence; and undisguised loathing for a variety of social classes. He avidly supported the single-party terror-state and it is hard to imagine that a Trotsky run USSR would have been markedly different to those of Stalin or Lenin.

Trotsky was strongly opposed to drinking and swearing and was something of a prude in personal matters, but two associates of his had remarked on the failings in his character. Max Eastman commented on his lack of 'a feeling for others as individuals' while Alfred Rosmer responded 'That's quite true. He has no humanity. It's entirely absent from him'.[153] During his exile, the movement of the left had become riven between Trotskyites and 'mainstream' communists. Yet, even at the conferences organised by Trotsky's supporters, the incessant bickering and irreparable factional rifts were just as bitter as ever.

In his absence Trotsky's relatives were rounded up and prosecuted. In 1937 his youngest son, Sergei, was shot in the Terror and his first wife sent into exile. Alexandra's relationship with Trotsky had effectively begun in Siberia; it was where he callously dumped her with their two daughters. It was also where, because of her association with him, she died in 1938, consumed by the incomparable horror of the gulag. Trotsky himself had been part of the culture that had introduced the concept of exterminating the relatives of 'enemies of the people' during the Civil War, so he could hardly complain, though he did. On 20 August 1940 Stalin's agents finally caught up with him. Ramón Mercader, a former lieutenant in the Spanish Republican Army, inveigled his way into Trotsky's confidence, isolated Stalin's old foe and then, when his back was turned, plunged an ice pick into his skull. In the photos taken afterwards, as the great revolutionary lay dying in hospital, his head resembles a slowly deflating football.

The Soviet press reported that 'the little Judas' had been the loyal servant of the ruling classes in the capitalist countries for decades. He had, it was claimed, infiltrated the Bolsheviks to assassinate Lenin and Stalin and had vigorously worked to further the interests of Tsar, landlords and capitalists. He was a Menshevik counter-revolutionary who had betrayed the Red Army and had been employed in the foreign intelligence services of Britain, Japan, Germany and France for over twenty years. The creativity of the Soviet propaganda machine was ever Russia's greatest cultural avenue in those years. All the lies and all the horror had little effect on the faithful though. Just weeks before his death Trotsky had proudly declared that 'My faith in the communist future of humanity is no less ardent and is even firmer today than it was in the days of my youth'.[154]

The closing of minds, the narrowing of potential and the corruption of idealistic virtue is an almost inevitable consequence of putting on the mental straitjacket of committed left-wing activism. The intelligent may be even more prone to such effects as they are adept at constructing ever more persuasive arguments to justify their continued allegiance. Trotsky was a luminous talent in so many ways and his story, even prior to his violent death, was one of tragedy. A tragedy of an immense intellect that became shackled by stubborn dogmatism, of a moral crusade that was consequently expressed through brutal authoritarianism and of so much potential that ended up squandered through forced isolation and a squalid murder. The left has no end of such tragedies of tarnished potential to offer, though few tales can match the mythic qualities of Trotsky's life. And of his death.

Trotsky was one of the last victims of the Terror; he would be a long way from one of the last victims of the regime. Untold numbers suffered in that period, and the quantities of those incarcerated is nigh on incalculable. In 1938 alone there were approximately 4.5 million arrests. Conservative estimates suggest that at least a million were executed in that two year long frenzy of denunciation and murder, though some estimates put the total considerably higher. The truly sobering thought though is the realisation that those who were shot may have been the lucky ones.

Gulag

Martin Amis, in his singularly lucid fashion, perhaps summed it up best: 'Your chair is never softer, your study never warmer, your prospect of the evening meal never more secure than when you read about the gulag: the epic agony of the gulag.'[155] The Soviets had been arresting and deporting 'politicals' from almost the moment they had assumed power. Their hunger to find ever more victims on which to pin the blame for their errors saw the system rapidly mushroom into a vast complex that reached the very fringes of their disparate domains. The charges, such as Anti-Soviet Agitation, Counter-Revolutionary Thought, Diversionism and Socially Harmful Element were ambiguous enough to be applied to practically any scenario, though evidence was frequently just invented anyway. The Bolsheviks had, they believed, sound reasons for focusing on political rather than common criminals. They claimed that all crime resulted from the exploitation of the masses and that under their system criminality would simply wither and die. The likes of petty burglars were consequently seen as their allies against class enemies who constituted the real threat to society. Political inmates were regarded as 'enemies of the people', as less than human. As such, no treatment was considered too dehumanising, or too cruel.

The principal chronicler of the gulag is Aleksandr Solzhenitsyn. He had been born in Stavropol Krai, just north of Georgia, on 11 December 1918 and grew into a committed communist. He served with distinction in the Red Army in WWII but, as the conflict drew to its conclusion, he was arrested for some thinly veiled criticism of Stalin in a letter sent to a school-friend. He was subsequently imprisoned from 1945-53 and began writing on his release. In the brief thaw after the Stalinist years he was allowed to publish his seminal novel on camp life, *One Day in the Life of Ivan Denisovich,* in 1962, but the repression in the years that followed saw the book banned and led to his expulsion. He published *The Gulag Archipelago,* his authoritative study on the phenomenon, in exile in

America in 1974. Solzhenitsyn identified three significant waves when prisoners were swept into the gulag: 1929-30, during de-kulakisation, 1937-8, the years of the Terror, and 1944-6, which targeted entire nations. But whatever the scale of these surges there was a continuous flow to the camps that lasted from the Bolshevik seizure of power until years after Stalin's death. Politicals were arrested almost immediately, then those returning from the front after the First World War, then rivals in the Civil War followed by any who were resistant to requisitioning. Once set in motion this train never stopped running, and the circles kept widening: rebellious Kronstadt sailors, members of religious orders, historians. The experience of those caught up in the system followed a familiar pattern: arrest, incarceration, interrogation, sentencing, transport and exile to a forced labour camp in a hostile and remote location.

The sort of charges frequently levelled were ludicrous and would be hilarious were the consequences not so dire. One woman was sentenced for taking a pencil from her workplace. She had pocketed it so that her son could do his homework as, under the miracle of the Soviet economy, she was unable to afford one. Others were sentenced for telling an anti-party joke or for having pointed out some imperfection of the state in which they lived. The code called for the death penalty for anyone who could be considered a 'diversionist'. One student complained that his lecturer frequently cited Marx and Lenin, but never Stalin. The teacher disappeared immediately and was never seen again. Solzhenitsyn also recounted the famous story of the district party conference in Moscow Province which called for a tribute to Comrade Stalin. After eleven exhausting minutes of continuous applause the director of the paper factory sat down, with everyone else following his lead immediately. The director was arrested the same day. Aleksandr Lebed was ten minutes late for his factory shift on two occasions. He was sentenced to five years in the gulag as a result. This was the reality of the worker's paradise. The process of arrest could be brutal and heartless too. One woman, convinced by the NKVD that she would only be a few minutes, abandoned her three month old child to talk to them. She did not return for ten years. Inoshin, a railway engineer, was mourning a dead child when they came for him. The NKVD men took the corpse which was, in local tradition, lying peacefully in state in his flat, and casually dumped it on the floor so they could search the coffin. When they were done they left the tiny body sprawled on the carpet.

There was little thought for relatives either. Family members were left in the dark and could queue for five days just to ask for information. Frequently they were dismissed with no answer or told that 'no correspondence' was permitted with the prisoner they had enquired about. This curt response usually meant the man had been shot. Once in the custody of the NKVD, suspects were treated to their characteristic levels of hospitality and 'questioning'. There was terrible overcrowding in the cells and prisoners were humiliated in numerous ways. In the morning they were forced to use a toilet, which was no more than a hole in the ground, while long, angry and impatient queues abused them. Solzhenitsyn described new forms of torture that followed such indignities: skulls constricted by iron bars, suspects trussed up almost naked and left for swarms of ants and bedbugs to feed on them, iron bars heated over a primus oven before being forced into their anal cavities. Torturers spat into prisoners' open mouths or poured salt water down their throats, leaving them parched for days. At the opposite end of the scale they would, on occasion, fill suspects with water to bursting point. Other times they scraped the skin off a suspect's back before rubbing in turpentine or shoved needles under people's fingernails. Some were dragged around by their hair or beards. They took Richard Ohola, who had helped suppress the Kronstadt revolt, and used pliers to suspend him by his moustache for ten minutes on each side. Others were stripped from the waist down and laid on the floor with their legs spread and held firmly apart. Their gaolers then stamped on their genitals with great hobnail boots.

The punishment cells also introduced creative levels of suffering. Some prisoners were kept in pits, ten feet deep and open to the elements. The pit was the suspect's cell and toilet. Rations were just three ounces of bread and a glass of water a day. Lieutenant Chulponyev, a heavyweight boxer whose body swarmed with lice after just ten days, was imprisoned in such a pit for a month. In the notorious punishment block of the Lubyanka the guards in the corridors, which were 'warmed' by working radiators, wore thick fur coats and boots. In the unheated punishment cells the prisoners were stripped to their underwear, denied shoes, and left for five days, getting a single bowl of gruel on the third day. On some occasions they would keep an inmate locked up for six days instead of the usual five. If the prisoner asked why they had not been let out, they would get twenty days for insubordination. Others, even teenage girls, were arrested and kept barefoot in cells, their feet submerged in freezing water.

Some of the punishments employed in such institutions were remarkably inventive. Chebotareyev was interrogated fiercely and regularly beaten while deprived of food and sleep for 72 hours. He was then given a fine meal and a carafe of wine. He ate the food but was not a drinker so refused the wine. After finishing his meal he was handed a confession which admitted he had colluded with Japanese agents. He refused to sign it and was beaten again before being dragged away. Blaginin, who had been arrested with him, got the same treatment. He, however, gulped down the wine and woozily signed the confession. He was promptly shot for espionage. The Soviets even employed a comfy chair as part of their interrogation techniques. It was not as pleasant as it sounds. Suspects, who had been deprived of sleep for an extended period, were moved to a sofa where the questioning continued. In the comfy chair it was even more difficult to resist drifting off, but if their eyes began to close they were savagely beaten. Solzhenitsyn also recounts tales of how the Cheka fed live prisoners to the zoo animals. The accounts cannot be verified, but he does wonder how the wildlife survived the famine years if the stories were not true. 'This is the precise line the Shakespearean evildoer could not cross. But the evildoer with ideology does cross it, and his eyes remain dry and clear'.[156]

After the purgatory of prison came the hell of transport. Herded into cattle trucks, regularly beaten by guards with mallets, kept in unsanitary conditions, the convicts froze during winter and boiled in the summer. Prisoners died by the score while being transported to the camps. Two types of trains were used for transport. Stolypin wagons were ex third-class carriages with the seats ripped out and wooden bunks fitted in their stead. There were no toilet facilities on the trains and prisoners were crammed in behind iron bars and constantly watched. The other type of transport was cattle trucks, large empty spaces which usually had holes cut in the floor for use as a toilet. Food was scarce, 300 grams of bread a day or a two kilogram lump designed to last a journey of thirty-four days. Those in the trucks would get one cup of water a day if they were lucky, even in summer. One convict recalls being given water just three times in a twenty-eight day journey with the train periodically called to a halt so the guards could sling the corpses out. Nina Gagen-Torn recalls her train being parked for four days. In the summer heat the metal container began to bake like an oven while the prisoners lay in their own excrement. The guards abused and taunted them for days before finally relenting and allowing them a drink. Journeys to the east could take forty-seven days, and inmates arrived with scurvy and diarrhoea if they were lucky, typhus and dysentery if they were not.

One train, SK950, destined for Komsomolsk, epitomised the horror of the transports. The journey had taken sixty days, twenty-four of which had seen the train idling in sidings due to poor organisation. Compartments designed for a maximum of eighteen people were stuffed with forty-eight individuals. Wagons were unheated, water supplies were inadequate and the prisoners were given nothing but frozen bread. For one ten day stretch they had nothing to eat at all. Of 1,291 passengers fifty-three had died and 401 were hospitalised with pneumonia and frostbite. Corpses had been left in the carriages for extended periods and the survivors swarmed with lice. Another grim tale, recounted by Mariya Sandratskaya, records sixty-five nursing mothers with sixty-five babies transported in appalling conditions in a pair of cattle trucks for eighteen days. The babies' nappies turned green with filth. Two of the mothers slit their own throats with broken glass while another was driven insane. On arrival at the camp, two more women attempted suicide while another hurled her baby at an NKVD officer.

Many, assigned to the most remote camps, would stumble from the trains to discover they had a torturous sea journey to endure as well. Battered cargo ships waited to transport them past Japan to far-flung locales like Kolyma. That destination, in the far northeast of Siberia, may have been the most inhospitable of all. The journey could take three months by train to Vladivostok, then a long and rough passage by sea would follow. The ship's 'cargo' was to be kept secret so when, for instance, the *Indigirka* was crippled by a reef off Hokkaido in 1939, the crew elected to let the prisoners drown in the hold rather than seek aid. Over 1,000 perished. But there are worse tales than this. In 1933 the *Dzhurma* sailed too late and got stuck in the winter ice. It was stuffed with 12,000 prisoners. Trapped in the freezing conditions as supplies ran out, they all suffered a lingering death.

On the transports it was standard practice for prisoners to be kept locked in the hold which soon swam with the vomit of sea-sick passengers. Food and water were either flung in or lowered in a bucket, forcing the prisoners to fight over the scraps they were given. Criminals tormented the politicals on the crossings, spitting and urinating on them from the top bunks. They also set about other prisoners, beating, robbing, even killing them. Men and women were supposed to be kept separate, but guards could be bribed and gang rape was common. Orderly queues could form giving the victims no respite and some women were literally raped to death. Sometimes men simply broke down the partitions that divided them, as on the crossing to Kolyma in 1942 described by Janusz Bardach, a Polish teenager. Gangs of men attacked the women in packs, several at a time, holding and beating them and ripping their clothes off as their victims struggled desperately. When all the women had been violated, with many lying dead, they turned on adolescent boys. It seemed an eternity before the guards eventually turned hoses on the criminals to bring their rampage to an end.

It was after ordeals such as these that the convicts finally arrived at the camps, or at the deserted and hostile environments in which they would have to build their own prison. Initially a rather ad hoc affair the Soviet concentration camp system had spread rapidly. There were already eighty-four separate camps in 1921, and by its peak it developed into a system of 476 separate camp complexes with thousands of individual camps. The gulag really began to move into gear from 1923 after the establishment of the prison at the monastery on the Solovetsky Islands in the White Sea. That was the institution that proved the model for all that followed. In the first year of its existence Naftaly Frenkel, a Jew born in 1883 in Haifa, then part of the Ottoman Empire, was sentenced to ten years hard labour for profiteering. Frenkel had already become a millionaire from the timber trade and his entrepreneurial spirit did not rest in confinement.

He wrote a detailed report on how to improve camp efficiency and his recommendations were sent to Genrikh Yagoda. Suitably impressed by what he read Yagoda had Frenkel released in November 1924. He was running the economy department of the camp network by September 1925. His reforms transformed the system into a viable and profitable enterprise, even if the cost was worse conditions and increasingly meagre rations. He divided the inmates into three categories, those capable of heavy work, those limited to light work, and invalids. Each were given specific rations with invalids getting half the amount of food as those assigned to heavy labour. Rations ranged from 800 grams of bread and eighty grams of meat down to 400 grams of bread and forty of meat. Taken over the entire duration of camp history these meagre portions would grow to look exceedingly generous. Weak prisoners, starved of food, tended to perish quite quickly. This saved supplies and costs which were reserved for more productive labourers. Prisoners were set demanding targets in punishing work like road building and clearing trees. If capable of labour, they would be fed enough to stay alive – if not, they would be considered 'waste' and left to die. The Soviets, in focusing on economic efficiency, would make the vilest bloodthirsty capitalists seem like the most generous of benefactors in comparison.

It was in 1929, when Stalin introduced the Five Year Plan, that the gulag multiplied alarmingly. Article 58, which defined counter-revolutionary crimes, was expanded to incorporate a wide range of new offences. People could be arrested for a 'negative attitude' to any aspect of the regime as well as sympathy for Trotsky or any kind of friendliness shown to the United States. The pace of change demanded of an industrial base not built to accommodate such rapid growth led to a spike in mistakes and accidents; this, in turn, resulted in a huge increase in those arrested as 'wreckers' and 'saboteurs'. Coinciding with the hordes being sent east as a result of 'de-kulakisation', for resisting collectivisation or for stealing a handful of corn to feed their starving children, the camp network mushroomed spectacularly. All those exiled were to toil in service of Stalin's dream of industrial expansion. Yagoda, who played a pivotal role, was particularly enthusiastic about the massive programme of camps in the north. Coal, gas, oil and wood, abundant in Siberia, were all required in vast quantities for the Five Year Plan, while roads, railways and canals were needed to facilitate the expansion of industry. Geologists had also recently discovered gold in the hostile and distant region of Kolyma. The gold mined there would be used to purchase foreign technology and machinery. Mining, logging and construction were to be the chief duties of those sent to toil as slave labourers.

The NKVD were given responsibility for the giant concentration camp network which went under the new acronym: GULAG. Frenkel's system was to be employed throughout the camps while he was placed in charge of the construction of the Baltic – White Sea canal. The expansion that took place meant that by 1930 the population of the camps was 300,000. By 1934, just as the Terror was about to begin, it was a million. Loyalty to one's state rather than socialism was considered a crime by the Bolsheviks so vast quantities of Poles, Ukrainians, Latvians and others were arrested for nationalist inclinations.

From 1937 the numbers deliberately worked to death or simply killed rose sharply. The camps remained deadlier, more brutal places, for another fifteen years, and the idealised literature that had praised their redemptive qualities ceased to appear. The camps were not to be mentioned now; they were to vanish. Yet, even as they faded from sight they continued to grow, and the prison population had topped two million by the time Beria was put in charge. He would make them more brutal, more efficient and more productive still.

As the camp system expanded groups of exiles were sent out to increasingly remote locations. At the transit camps the prisoners were hemmed in behind imposing barbed-wire fences and left to the mercy of the elements. And mercy is not a quality for which the Russian winter is renowned. Eventually, tents and crude shelters were added which provided a degree of warmth and cover, but these original settlers faced a dreadful ordeal. On the island of Nazino in the Ob river, 6,114 people were sent out in such terrible conditions that between thirty-five and forty of them died every day during transport. They arrived at Nazino starving and freezing with no food, tools or provisions. They were unable to even light fires and 295 died on the first day alone. On the fifth day a meagre ration of flour arrived which, in starving desperation, they tried to mix with river water in their hats. Within three months over 4,000 were dead. Those who had survived had done so by eating the flesh of their fallen comrades.

There are hundreds, if not thousands, of similarly bleak stories scattered throughout the vast empire. Solzhenitsyn describes a much later camp where former Russian officers, who swarmed with lice, gnawed the bones of dead horses, baked patties from potato peelings and smoked horse manure. Arrival at a completed camp was a marginally less grim experience. The gates of Auschwitz famously bore the legend 'Work Sets You Free', and the earlier Soviet camps were adorned with similarly uplifting slogans. Over the entrance to one of the Kolyma camps a large sign, decorated with a rainbow, declared 'Labour in the USSR is a Matter of Honesty, Glory, Valour and Heroism!' Another in Solovetsky proclaimed 'With an Iron Fist We Will Lead Humanity to Happiness!' Well, at least that one was *half* right.

On arrival at the camps prisoners were washed and shaved to remove the lice from their journeys. Their heads were kept cropped for the duration of their stay. They were then dressed and sorted into various work categories. The cursory health checks involved in this process resembled a slave market with prisoners roughly handled like the disposable commodity they were. With thousands of individual camps the size and specific conditions could vary dramatically. It has to be conceded though that for the inmates they ranged from appalling all the way to unbearable. The layout of the gulag was almost as uniform as a Roman military camp: rows of barracks, with stores and other buildings at the centre, laid out in a square or rectangle behind a tall barbed-wire fence. Armed guards in wooden watchtowers scanned the interior while guard dogs patrolled the perimeter.

Inside the barracks there was usually a crude stove for heat and a bucket as a latrine. Beds were overcrowded wooden bunks. Prisoners frequently slept on bare planks, but sometimes bunks were equipped with a crude straw mattress. The likes of sheets and blankets were rare in the extreme, but decidedly common were the bedbugs. Oleg Volkov recalled his horror at the insects that swarmed across him on arrival at the Solovetsky camp. He dashed outside only to be enveloped in clouds of mosquitoes. The barracks were freezing in winter and all inmates recall the disgusting smell which persisted all year round. The stench was a combination of mildewed clothes, sweat and faeces. The overcrowding caused significant tension and, in the unhygienic conditions, lice proliferated.

Prisoners were fed twice a day on watery soup, universally regarded as disgusting. It was usually peppered with cabbage and potatoes with sometimes pig fat or fish heads flung in. The camp system worked assiduously to calculate the absolute minimum amount of sustenance required to maintain productivity. Maximum rations were 550 grams of bread and 15 grams of meat, but these were cut significantly for anyone who failed to hit their quota. To put this in some perspective the brutal Japanese POW camps on the River Kwai, which have a deservedly fearsome reputation, provided 700 grams of rice, 600 of vegetables, 100 of meat, 20 of sugar, 20 of salt and 5 of oil, a feast of unimaginable abundance to an inmate of the gulag. To supplement their diet some camps made inmates drink a revolting brew made by steaming pine needles. In periods of shortage, especially during the war, they ate nothing at all. The bread was appalling, but ubiquitous and highly valued. It was a camp tradition that anyone caught stealing another's bread was to be killed. Prisoners usually had to share crude, handmade bowls and spoons. Inmates had learned to urinate in their hoods or boots for added warmth. Others urinated into the food bowls that were shared between them and refused to use their water ration to rinse it out. The tensions that arose worsened an already unbearable situation, and months of living in such conditions could destroy an individual's physical and mental well-being for decades.

Convicts were kept under strict regimes. They were marched to their place of work every day under the watchful eye of a contingent of armed guards and dogs. Even one day off a month was relatively rare. In some camps prisoners only got one rest day every three months. This day of 'rest' was often spent on camp maintenance or cleaning. When horses started to collapse through exhaustion regulations were introduced to prevent them from being overworked. But no legislation was ever passed to apply the same principle to human labour. The most common types of camp work were coal mining, nickel mining, road and railway building, logging, digging canals and digging peat, but inmates were also involved in fishing, farming, urban construction and factory work. They even helped run nuclear power plants and made children's toys. Every aspect of the Soviet economy was dependent on slave labour. Norms were set – the area of trees to be felled, the weight of coal or rock to be dug out, or the length and depth of ditches to be dug. But provided only the crudest of implements, malnourished and unused to such heavy labour many fell pathetically short of their targets and had their meagre rations cut as a penalty. As a result they were even less likely to fill their quota the following day.

Already weakened, the workers had to cope with Arctic conditions in the winter and mud and mosquitoes in the summer. Winters were unimaginably cold with temperatures dropping to minus 50 and below. When storms swept in a rope was passed from man to man to hold onto as they trudged back to the camp. Sometimes a prisoner would stumble and lose their grip on the line. Their bodies were not found until spring, usually fewer than a hundred yards from the route of the work detail. The brutality of the guards and working conditions are strikingly recorded in the account of Bernard Grzywacz, a Pole who endured the horror of the mines at Vorkuta.

'We had a quota we had to fulfil, and what food we got depended on how far we met it. In more than eleven years I never met it once. Fights broke out. We were all starving. The lucky ones got jobs on the surface. The guards decided who was too weak to go down the mines by getting us to strip and face the walls: the ones whose buttocks were shrivelled with starvation were kept above ground. In snow storms we had to link arms for the walk back to barracks, and hold on to a rope. Any man who fell out was shot. If he didn't die then, he soon did, from the cold. The guards had a way of testing if anyone was feigning by bashing their skulls in with a sledgehammer.'[157]

Soviet inefficiency continued to dog projects too. In 1947 it was decided to build a railway connecting the Ob River to Vorkuta. But persistent problems plagued the poorly conceived scheme. By 1953 the railway stretched 500 kilometres from one direction and 200 km from the other. The line was extremely shoddy, and work had not even begun on the port it was designed to serve. It had cost 40 billion roubles and tens of thousands of lives. But after Stalin's death the project was simply abandoned. It joined a slew of other monumental failures. The conditions for the workers who toiled in such modernist schemes were practically medieval. Work was done by hand – loggers were denied chainsaws, tractors or any other mechanised means of moving felled trees, while miners and those digging canals worked with nothing but picks, shovels and wheelbarrows. Regulation clothing was often in short supply too, even though one pair of underpants was supposed to last a minimum of nine months. It was not unusual to only have enough boots for half the inmates at a camp with the remainder improvising footwear from tree bark, scraps of cloth and old tires fastened together with string. The wearers of such leaky garments frequently suffered frostbite. Workers were forced to toil without breaks after being force-marched a few miles. And the targets were crippling. One Kolyma camp demanded 28,800 pounds be mined every day. Many who failed to fill their quotas were forced to work until midnight under spotlights. They then slogged back to the camp to consume some gruel before being sent straight back out to work again.

Conditions at Kolyma were arguably worse than anywhere. The inmates ate moss, which was the staple diet of the local reindeer, while some devoured the week old corpse of a horse which swarmed with flies and maggots. They even ate a bucket of grease that had been brought in to lubricate the wheels of wagons. Prisoners toiled in freezing temperatures but were barred from lighting fires to warm themselves. Any who lagged behind while they trudged to work were savagely beaten with clubs and mauled by dogs. When the temperature dropped below minus sixty, work was supposed to be cancelled, but it was frequently not recorded and the prisoners were sent out anyway. Many froze to death while the stragglers were shot. Injuries were common, and with malnourished labourers forced into such gruelling tasks in terrible conditions the fatality rates kept rising. Some became so desperate they mutilated themselves to escape from the labour. They rubbed acid in their eyes or wrapped a damp cloth around their foot for a day to induce frostbite. Some were even seen to nail their testicles to a bench or stump. Others cut off their own hands or feet with an axe to excuse them from labour. The commanding Chekist at Solovetsky, Vanka Potapov, kept the grisly trophies in a large pile of some 400 dismembered body parts that he proudly showed off to visitors.

Despite the reality of camp life the authorities also subjected their inmates to a relentless stream of propaganda. For the Soviets, forced labour was just another aspect of the 're-education' they considered an integral part of their regime. It was for their own good and both they and the collective would benefit in the long run. Solzhenitsyn reminds us that the Soviets were just following their ideological imperative. After all, Marx had suggested the only way of reforming prisoners was through productive labour,[158] something else the German knew nothing about. Solzhenitsyn also argued that Marx and Engels's belief in the dictatorship of the proletariat made the army, police and camps of the Soviet regime inevitable. The new state must rely on compulsion, and compulsion could only be achieved by force.

Realities of this nature differed wildly from the image the Soviets wished to project though. The propaganda depicted 'the types one meets in the offices of interrogators as chivalrous guardians of truth and humanitarianism, as our loving fathers. We are exposed to lectures on everything under the sun – and even herded in to listen to them.'[159] Perhaps they felt that work quotas were not met and camp inefficiencies were so rife because the inmates were not true socialists. A healthy dose of propaganda would rectify the issue. Vladimir Bukovsky spat that 'In our camp, you were expected not only to be a slave labourer, but to sing and smile while you worked as well. They didn't just want to oppress us: they wanted us to thank them for it'.[160] The sort of lectures delivered on the superiority of socialism also assumed anyone from outside the Soviet Union must be deeply ignorant, as one Polish inmate recalled of his tutor. 'He imparted such truths as these with unshakeable confidence in our complete lack of knowledge, for how could we, brought up in a bourgeois state, expect to have the advantage of even the most elementary education?'[161] Inmates, who had been bombarded with Soviet propaganda, expressed similar attitudes to foreigners. Antoni Ekart, another Pole interred in the system, recalled the utter disbelief he met from the camp intellectuals when he told them that he, a factory worker in the West, owned six or seven suits. 'You Lie!' they spat at him. Others laughed at the claim of John Noble, a US citizen picked up in Dresden, that American workers drove their own cars.

The propaganda was a joke to many. But some party members were so devoted they kept their faith even when brutalised by the regime they defended. Solzhenitsyn records the reaction of such individuals who would whisper to each-other

> 'It's our duty to support Soviet interrogation. It's a combat situation. We ourselves are to blame. We were too softhearted; and now look at all the rot that has multiplied in the country. There is a vicious secret war going on. Even here we are surrounded by enemies. Just listen to what they are saying! The Party is not obliged to account for what it does to every single one of us – to explain the whys and wherefores'.[162]

Yet some of these committed politicals got a rude awakening. Olga Adamova-Sliozberg pleaded for a lighter workload for her brigade of party members. The camp commandant retorted that when the party had thrown his children onto the street after accusing him of being a kulak they declared it was the Soviet law. He gruffly told Olga 'So there you are, you can stick to your Soviet law and dig nine metres of mud a day'.[163] Nikolai Adamovich Vilenchik though, even after serving seventeen years, declared 'We believed in the Party – and we were *not mistaken*!'[164] Such is the nature of ideological certainty. Marx had been proven wrong in every forecast he made, and the socialist state he inspired was a failure too – a punitive disaster that crushed rather than liberated the workers. But none of this made any difference to them. They wanted to believe – and so they did. For evidence is always powerless when confronted with faith. Solzhenitsyn had his own explanation as to how they remained oblivious even in the light of such realities: 'They needed ideological arguments in order to hold on to a sense of their own rightness – otherwise insanity was not far off'.[165]

Yet they remained uncomprehending about the true nature of the regime and their undeniable complicity in its terrible crimes.

The camp guards could act with kindness, as some did, and they were certainly under no compunction to be severe, but the vast majority were excessively brutal. The diary of Ivan Chistyakov chillingly records how a guard could descend from poetic ebullience to sullen indifference in a startlingly brief period of time. He developed a callous lack of empathy and it was not long before he was unmoved when discovering a heap of murdered inmates. 'If someone gets on your nerves, you take a shot at them, you just leave them where they fell'. Such behaviour was the natural consequence of instilling a pathological hatred of non-conformists into society. Relentless propaganda had conditioned the guards into despising their charges as something less than human. It is hardly surprising that they acted on it. Anne Applebaum describes their behaviour as 'unthinking, stupid, lazy cruelty, of the sort that might be shown to cattle or sheep'.[166] The prisoners were derided as 'swine', 'saboteurs', 'traitors', 'dogs' and 'fascists'. Even Jews and party members who had fought against the Nazis were labelled 'fascists'. Camp commanders, by punishing the malefactors who opposed the glorious future, tended to regard themselves as playing a vital role in the socialist transformation of the country. As such, their barbaric treatment of prisoners was considered entirely honourable. It was an attitude that regarded greater brutality as inherently moral. Inmates were simply an expendable commodity, ones who had impeded the socialist utopia, and thus deserved to labour to help realise it.

The subsequently callous treatment spread through the system like a virus. In Ustvymlag the commandant, Tarasyuk, discovered a large number of prisoners had been put on increased rations by the camp doctor to counter the effects of pellagra, a disease caused by protein deficiency and starvation. He ordered their rations to be cut immediately and all 246 died within a month. Scores of accounts also record that those who collapsed while working or being marched through the woods were summarily shot in huge numbers. In Angus Macqueen's superb three hour long 1999 documentary on the gulag a number of ex-camp guards were interviewed - and all remained resolutely unapologetic. They explained their actions by claiming that everyone behaved in the same manner and the state had persuaded them their charges were evil, subversive elements who deserved what they got. Remarkably, every one of them fell back on the very same justification that Stalin himself had employed – that Peter the Great had killed and tortured as well, and they too were simply following the accepted standards of the day. Their fury was reserved for the likes of Yeltsin and the capitalists who had risen to prominence in the decade since the collapse of the Soviet Union. When switching to that subject blasé indifference was suddenly transformed into animated indignation. This is how humanity works – people need to rationalise their actions, so arguments can always be found to excuse past misdemeanours. As a consequence, they became completely blinded to the despicable nature of their crimes. The disparity in the interviews with the guards and those with their broken and tear-stained former prisoners was startling, yet they simply could not admit to the horrific nature of their actions.

The camps, just like the prisons, had punishment cells. Any sort of resistance to camp rules or work requirements would earn an inmate a spell in isolation, as would adhering to any form of religious observation. Punishment cells in the camps were cold, dark and damp. Broken window panes were not replaced and inmates were stripped to their underwear even as snow swirled around them. They frequently had little more than a concrete breeze block as a seat. At Kuranakh-Sala the cell was a sodden log frame where the temperature was recorded as minus 58. At other locations the cell was just a hole dug in the ground. Aino Kuusinen recalled a special punishment block built for a group of nuns in Potma. Their agonised screams could be heard throughout the camp when they were regularly stripped and beaten, yet nothing made them surrender their rituals. Eventually they were dragged out into the woods and shot. Kuusinen also recounted another group of religious women. They refused to wear numbered clothing, so their gaolers burned the numbers into their flesh instead and forced them to attend the roll call naked. Another pious sect refused to handle anything from the Soviet 'Anti-Christ'. Told they would only be fed if they filled in the appropriate forms they all starved to death instead. The next shipment of prisoners discovered their bones which had been picked clean by carrion. In the punishment cells the rations were smaller and the food worse; the bread even blacker and harder, the soup more watery still. Janusz Bardach described his cell as being ankle deep in water with wet and mouldy walls. The sodden bench was crumbling and the cold and damp penetrated to his very bones. He had been stripped to his underwear and it was impossible to lie down. Even to sit, he was forced to lean on the slimy walls.

In some locations punishment cells were constructed without a floor. The convict would be forced to perch on a series of logs the thickness of a man's arm which had been positioned vertically in the base of the cell. Keeping balance was notoriously difficult and any slip would elicit a violent beating. Some were tied naked to trees in the summer where swarms of mosquitoes would feast on them, or were harnessed to horses by their ankles. Riders would then gallop the steed through the forests until their 'passenger' stopped screaming. They were locked naked in unheated bell towers with their arms and legs tied behind their backs or were forced to sit on poles for eighteen hours with weights strapped to their ankles. Others were given rotten meat to eat or were forced to walk nearly naked for two miles in freezing conditions. The Solovetsky punishment cells, in the cellars of the church, were so fearsome that almost none who were sent there came out alive. At one camp on those islands, scattered across the bitter White Sea, the prisoners who failed to meet their work targets were forced to spend the night in the woods. Around 150 of them froze to death. But many selected for punishment were simply killed – shot in the back of the head in the usual Soviet fashion. In the camps though, such killings were frequently done in public, a practice all the more effective at cowing the remaining inmates.

As if the ministrations of the camp guards were not enough the political prisoners were relentlessly abused by the criminals who were turned against them as unofficial enforcers. Already introduced to their charms on the long journeys to camp the criminal class, or *urkas,* were given a position superior to that of the 'enemies of the people'. They took full advantage of their new status in the pecking order. It perfectly fitted the Soviet idea of using one class to purge another. The *urkas* were wild and uninhibited, strolling around naked and openly copulating, masturbating or defecating in public. They would frequently descend on the politicals in gangs and beat, rape or rob them, even smashing out gold teeth with hammers. They sometimes got their women to assist them in raping nuns, a practice they appeared to particularly enjoy. It was not unknown for them to drown their victims in the toilets for refusing to hand over food parcels. The *urkas* were liberally covered in tattoos and Solzhenitsyn describes seeing criminals decorated with eagles, radiant sun logos, large hammers, hearts, fornicating couples, sexual organs, masturbating monkeys and portraits of Lenin and Stalin.

The criminals had their own rigid hierarchy and code and any that transgressed it risked having an eye put out by a gang leader expertly wielding a pick. In more serious cases the punishment was death. They were also obsessed with card games, though they frequently bet other people's possessions on the outcome. On some occasions they bet for each-other's eyes. In one criminal card game they bet on a young boy who the winner raped. Their victim later committed suicide. These bets could backfire though. One *urka* bet a political's suit on the turn of a card, but the man was transferred to another camp the same day. As a penalty for forfeiting the bet the criminal had three fingers lopped off his left hand. Another had an enormous penis tattooed across his cheek after losing a game. He then grabbed a hot poker and pushed it into his face, erasing the offending mark but scarring him for life.

In some ways women's camp experiences were preferable to men's, in others they were worse. Women subsisted better on the rations and were less prone to the illnesses and disease that afflicted male inmates. More adept at sewing and repairing their garments they were better clad and also far likelier to get more generous rations or preferential treatment on the work details. But such concessions were usually gained by surrendering sexual favours. Despite initial distaste with the idea most capitulated fairly rapidly. Any who resisted soon realised the alternative was worse. Lev Razgon, when visiting a camp, recalled how he gave his meal to a girl who reminded him of his daughter. When she had finished she stood up and removed her clothing, responding to his confusion by saying 'People don't feed me without it'.[167] There was plenty of resentment from the women who were not picked out for such treatment though. They seethed with jealousy and often violently attacked their 'luckier' sisters.

Rape was a regular feature of the camps and many accounts cite habituated victims offering no resistance when seized. But others did. One woman on the White Sea canal refused to give in to the demands of a guard so he handed her over to a group of *urkas* who gang-raped her and pulled out her gold teeth. The camp chief was a serial rapist himself so she had no one to complain to. When one sixteen year old girl attempted to hide from her brutal guards they set the dogs on her. The savage mauling left her with terrible injuries. All the unrestrained sexual activity meant that babies were born in the camps as well. Pregnant women and nursing mothers were frequently arrested with their offspring which further swelled the camps' population of minors. One woman was sent down when eight months pregnant and, after enduring the usual gruelling journey, she gave birth to a dead baby. In the waves of de-kulakisation, ethnic clearances and political purges, hundreds of thousands of very young children were sent off to the camps. Some women deliberately got pregnant while incarcerated in order to ease their workload and increase their rations, happily sleeping with their gaolers to this end. Others attempted abortions to spare the child the suffering of camp life.

Hava Volovich left a vivid memoir which recalled the experience of child-rearing in a camp. She would brush off the bed bugs that fell from the walls like sand before leaving her infant in the care of old women. But they would steal the child's food while she was sent out to work. Despite the horrors of camp life she was as much consumed by the mothering instinct as any other woman. The tenderness of her account, and her desperate attempts to provide for her daughter, are genuinely touching. Transferred to a maternity camp her daughter was given to the 'care' of nurses who treated their charges appallingly. She faded quickly and died at sixteen months, already a hollow shell. Her naked body was casually tossed into the morgue along with all the adult victims of the regime. This heart-wrenching tale is compounded when one learns that the guilt-ridden but blameless mother described her act of giving birth as 'the worst crime there is'.[168]

Official Soviet propaganda painted a rather different picture:

> 'The sun shines in their Stalinist fatherland. The nation is filled with love for the leaders and our wonderful children are happy just as the whole young country is happy. Here, in wide and warm beds, sleep the new citizens of our country. Having eaten, they sleep sweetly and are certainly dreaming happy dreams.'[169]

In truth, as they did nothing to aid camp efficiency, children tended to be kept in the coldest, most dilapidated accommodation the camps had to offer. Nursery jobs usually went to 'trusties', largely criminals who had no regard for their responsibility, or their charges. The scale of the problem was vast. In 1949 alone a camp census listed 503,000 women of whom 9,300 were pregnant while 23,790 nursed infant children. Few would survive their bleak childhood. Those that did were usually sent to harsh state-run orphanages or work camps where they were bombarded with Soviet propaganda.

At the bottom of the camp hierarchy were the living dead, those who were referred to as 'goners' or 'shit-eaters'. These were the inmates who had effectively been driven mad with starvation and the brutality they faced on a daily basis. They had lost all humanity – all except the survival instinct. Individuals in such advanced stages of starvation, and all its attendant diseases, bore physical scars too. They developed skin sores which soon grew into huge boils that leaked pus while their teeth loosened and fell out. Their eyesight diminished and their legs swelled up horribly. In their addled state they frequently raved, thrashed about the camps or crouched, screaming, in corners. They lost control of their bowels and carried their stench around with them, becoming caked in diarrhoea. They fell on anything they could eat: birds, rats, piles of rotting rubbish. They hung around camps like ghosts, hovering in the mess hall for scraps before swooping on any bowl left with a few dregs of soup. Inevitably the bowl would get knocked to the floor in their struggles and they would dive to the ground to slurp up any sustenance they could before it drained away.

These inmates fought for kitchen scraps with a savage intensity. They hung around the kitchen door and rubbish tips to fall on any potato peelings or fish bones that might be thrown out. Some were even known to plunge into the latrine after some meagre form of sustenance. They were furtive, wide-eyed animals who lived to survive and eke out a bare existence on instinct and desperation. They were non-responsive to any who spoke to, or even hit them, often curling up into a ball until their tormentor had moved on. These desperate individuals were emaciated spectres whose soul and spirit had faded away long before their wracked bodies expired. The majority of inmates felt no sympathy for the shit-eaters though, just contempt.

When not haunted by the goners the camps were haunted by death, and death stalked the camps at all times. Dysentery, pneumonia, frostbite, starvation, hypothermia, injuries sustained at work. All consumed inmates in vast numbers. Conditions in Solovetsky were so bad that it is estimated that in 1925-6 a quarter of the inmates, some 1,500 people, died of typhus, starvation and dysentery. Records show that in 1929-30, when the complex had swelled considerably, there were 25,552 cases of typhus alone. Solzhenitsyn testifies to how people could drop dead in all manner of circumstances: mid-sentence, while walking, working, sitting, lying down, eating. The dead were taken out at night in carts. An NKVD officer smashed their skulls in with a pickaxe to ensure no one got out alive. Their bodies were then flung in a pit. The Russian landscape is littered with such mass graves and many remain as yet undiscovered.

Survival in circumstances like these frequently depended on ruthless self-preservation. It was brutality that reigned in the camps, particularly with the criminals who despised the goners and politicals. People barged the half-blind, infirm and elderly out of food queues. One *urka* boasted of encountering a Western scientist eating a fishtail. He punched him so hard in the throat the university lecturer vomited and died the next day. 'Serves him right!'[170] he sneered. Shalamov testified that in the camps there was little more eloquent than 'a rifle butt, a punch in the teeth'.[171] The title of Janusz Bardach's memoir gives another indication of how prisoners acted to survive in such conditions: *Man is Wolf to Man.* While in the prisons the strong had often helped the weak, in the camps they preyed on them. It was a dog eat dog existence, a desperate struggle for survival where people were as far removed from the ideals of socialism as possible. The camp system turned people against each-other at all levels though many survived by becoming 'trusties', effectively camp collaborators. They received superior clothing and rations for helping to subjugate the others, and survival rates among the trusties were markedly higher.

The camps were geared towards production rather than death, so they *did* have hospitals to nurse the sick back to work. Some were superbly equipped with caring staff. Others were ramshackle affairs, like grimy barracks, where criminals stabbed doctors to death for a shot of opium. Many of the lesser hospitals were simply run by unqualified and clueless trusties or criminals. The facilities were under tremendous pressure to return people to work, so few stayed for any duration in either case. Some survived the camps by keeping themselves occupied. They wrote poems or music and those who produced such compositions, along with actors and storytellers, were much revered in the gulag. Any who could entertain or impress the others were likely to be protected, like the film star Tatyana Okunevskaya and the footballer Nikolai Starostin who came to resemble camp royalty.

With the distances involved and the fact that most camps were in vast areas bereft of civilisation, but patrolled by guards, escape from the permanent camps was virtually impossible.* Kolyma, for instance, was four times the size of France, a vast area scattered with camps where temperatures drop to -70c. It is estimated that two million people died there. Astonishingly some did break loose, but the numbers were pitifully few, unlike in the Tsar's day when freedom was just a dashing sleigh ride away. The majority of escapees were criminals rather than politicals, and it was a relatively common tactic for two such individuals to plan an escape and invite a third to join them. He would be their meal on the long journey ahead. It was not unheard of for the bodies of runaways who had been caught and shot to be displayed above the camp gates. Other facilities simply left corpses strewn in the no man's land by the wire for a month. One wonders if Stalin ever reflected on the difference between his own prison system and that of the Tsar's – with its well-stocked libraries, pantries stuffed with food, convivial company, croquet on the lawn, ease of escape and ready availability of nubile teenagers. One can be sure that, even if he did, he still felt himself morally superior to the leaders he had replaced.

During the war the camp system grew even harsher and more punitive. With the increasing brutality of the regime and crippling food shortages fatalities in the camps shot up. Conservative estimates suggest some two million inmates died during the conflict. Approximately 10,000 were shot, largely for insufficient effort, while during the retreat the NKVD machine-gunned 4,000 political prisoners in Lvov and over 10,000 more in various Baltic and regional locations. In the panicked attempt to evacuate the remaining prisoners to the east, countless more suffocated to death in over-packed train carriages or fell victim to German bombs. Others were simply abandoned or forced to march on foot. Those unable to make the journey were shot. One NKVD officer, marching from a prison in west Ukraine, had all 954 of his charges gunned down.

The Soviets used the war to deport 'foreigners' and vast trains of Crimean Tartars, Volga Germans, Poles, Finns and Lithuanians were herded off to the east. Upwards of three million were exiled to a bleak and uncertain future. Vast numbers of POWs swelled the camp population even more though most were simply herded into open spaces and left to die behind the wire. A total of four million prisoners were taken in the war. Mortality rates are hard to ascertain, though they were certainly terribly high. The influx to the camps coincided with a huge exodus as millions of convicts were given amnesties and drafted into the Red Army. They were primarily herded into penal battalions who were ordered to charge across minefields. During the war the American Vice-President, Henry Wallace, visited Kolyma. He was informed that it was populated by free workers and was convinced by such tales, as well as by the party members drafted in to

---

* The temporary ones were another matter and desertions of the chaotic road, rail and canal projects were far more common.

act as miners. The industrial supplies and boots that America subsequently sent in their Lend-Lease programme were predominantly employed in the Soviet slave labour camps and, regardless, arrived after Russia had already turned the Nazi tide.

As they 'liberated' Europe and unearthed evidence of Nazi horrors the NKVD constructed eleven concentration camps of their own in East Germany, one of them thrown up right over the ruins of Buchenwald. These were built, not for Nazi war criminals, but doctors, lawyers, journalists, teachers, businessmen and judges. They were designed to break the German bourgeoisie. It is believed that 240,000 passed through the camps with more than a third, 95,000 of them, perishing. Similar camps were set up in Hungary, Czechoslovakia, Romania and Bulgaria while Stalin continued to indulge himself in fruitless vanity projects like the Danube – Black Sea canal which is believed to have claimed 200,000 lives and to have been as useless as its northern counterpart. The camp system was exported too, to China and North Korea where it is believed some 200,000 are still imprisoned for contact with foreigners and disrespect of the government. Around 400,000 are said to have died in internment in that small state alone.

There was another massive surge in arrests after the war and in 1947, in an echo of the Nuremberg Laws, the state banned marriages between Soviet citizens and foreigners. Further waves of arrests followed in 1948-9, with hundreds of thousands of recently released inmates slung back in the gulag again. Many saw their families incarcerated too for good measure. The camp system reached its peak in the early 1950s with close to three million inmates but slowly declined from that point on. The gulag was gradually abandoned, not through any sudden recourse to humanity, but because it had begun to cost more to police it than it benefitted the ever creaking Soviet economy.

The later years of the system witnessed a number of rebellions which were brutally put down. Red Army personnel crushed rebels under the tracks of their tanks and bayoneted survivors where they lay. The brief thaw under Khrushchev, which allowed for the publication of *Ivan Denisovich,* was reversed by the reactionary regimes of Brezhnev and his successors and the Soviets were still gaoling 'dissidents' in significant numbers in the 1970s and '80s. A further twist to the system saw them sending inmates to psychiatric hospitals instead, brutal institutions in which mercy was in short supply. Resistance to socialism was officially re-diagnosed as a severe psychological condition. The recasting of criticism of the Soviet Union as a mental illness was a startling new low. It is almost as if the authorities had concluded that anyone who resisted or denied Soviet perfection must be insane. Treatment focused on drugs, restraint and electric shocks rather than rehabilitation. The system became even worse under the KGB hard-man Yuri Andropov before eventually breaking with the accession of the reformist Mikhail Gorbachev. He finally decided to pardon political prisoners and in 1987 the gulag ended, having lasted nearly the entire duration of the Soviet Union itself.

Western societies have attempted to live on the principle that virtue is rewarded and vice is punished – yet, in the Soviet example, vice was rewarded and virtue punished. The defective system warped its citizens into repellent behaviour in expectation of impossible results. Every failure merely stiffened their resolve and added another layer to their brutality. Solzhenitsyn has his own theories as to how and why this happened.

'To do evil a human being must first of all believe that what he's doing is good, or else that it's a well-considered act in conformity with natural law. Fortunately, it is in the nature of the human being to seek a *justification* for his actions...Ideology – that is what gives evildoing its long-sought justification...That was how the agents of the Inquisition fortified their wills: by invoking Christianity; the conquerors of foreign lands, by extolling the grandeur of their Motherland; the colonizers, by civilization; the Nazis by race; and the Jacobins (early and late), by equality, brotherhood and the happiness of future generations.'[172]

Martin Amis agrees and concluded that 'Ideology brings about a disastrous fusion: that of violence and righteousness – a savagery without stain'.[173] Solzhenitsyn went on to compare Soviet Russia unfavourably with that of the Tsars, informing us that from seven attempts on Alexander II's life only five people were executed. 'If just *one* such attempt had been made on Stalin, how many millions of lives would it have cost us?'[174] Solzhenitsyn also reminds us that almost immediately after his brother was executed for attempting to assassinate Tsar Alexander III, Lenin entered the Imperial University in Kazan. Under the Bolsheviks, his entire family and social circle would have been tortured and shot. Indeed, it is difficult to think of *any* regime which compares with that of the Soviets. Their slave system was every bit as bad as America's enslavement of Africans a century and more before, if not worse. There were benevolent families and plantation owners who treated their charges relatively well. The same could not be said about the camp commandants. Soviet slavery was based on lines of alleged ideology rather than race, but this aspect only served to make it even more arbitrary. The entire nation effectively lived in a state of bondage with the threat of even worse slavery hanging over their heads at all times.

Anne Applebaum has a bleak but accurate outlook when forecasting that

'our ability to debase and destroy and dehumanise our fellow men has been – and will be – repeated again and again: our transformation of our neighbours into 'enemies', our reduction of our opponents to lice or vermin or poisonous weeds, our re-invention of our victims as lower, lesser or evil beings, worthy only of incarceration or expulsion or death'.[175]

The contemporary left are vocalising sentiments eerily familiar to these right now, and that refusal to learn from the past, that obstinacy was also apparent in the furious reaction of some to Solzhenitsyn's criticisms of the camps. In the 1960s Anna Zakharova, the wife of an NKVD officer, was scathing about Ivan Denisovich for

'having such an attitude to the Soviet people, [he] hopes for nothing but the sick bay in order somehow to get out of redeeming his guilt, the wrong he did to his motherland, through toil...And why exactly should a person try to avoid physical labour and show scorn for it? After all, for us labour is the foundation of the Soviet system'.[176]

We will never know the exact figures of those who passed through the camps, and we are even less certain of the number of fatalities. One thing is beyond dispute though: the numbers are bewildering, and yet even they do not account for the suffering of those left behind. Wives widowed, children orphaned, parents dying in despair, families obliterated, swathes of society ostracised as friends or relatives of 'enemies of the people'. The amount of lives blighted by the camps utterly dwarfs the number of inmates, and those figures are staggering. Anne Applebaum's exhaustive study puts the total of gulag inmates and exiled labourers at approaching 29 million. Official figures admit to some 3 million dead. But, as the camp authorities were reluctant to report fatalities, the true figure is certainly much higher. It is not unreasonable to assume that 5-7 million is a far more likely estimate. The actual total may be higher still.

Legacy

It must be conceded that the Soviet Union was, in many ways, a spectacular success. It achieved astonishing modernisation and progress, becoming an industrial powerhouse in a startlingly brief period of time; it defeated the formidable menace of Nazi Germany in WWII; it developed nuclear technology and became a world superpower, the only real rival to the USA, and it even competed with, and for a considerable while led, America in the space race. These are all remarkable achievements, and many advocates of socialism still use them to defend the system. The cost, however, was phenomenal. Russia's industrial expansion was financed by the sale of grain which contributed to a famine that killed perhaps 8 million people. It was also built on the backs of slave labour with up to 29 million more incarcerated, millions of whom perished in appalling circumstances. More than this Russia's meteoric industrialisation, lauded in many left-wing circles, came some two centuries after the process had begun in Britain. So it was inevitable that it would be comparatively rapid. The regime was also supported by suffocating oppression, censorship and propaganda. There were very few real freedoms, no elections for any party other than the Communists and no plurality of opinion was permitted. The Soviets crushed any who deviated from their version of socialism, whether they were political, religious or nationalistic in their inclination. They even, like the Jacobins before them, persecuted those who were merely apathetic about the party line.

The government relied on terror to subjugate the masses, and the resources of the state were diverted to ensure its success in specific areas to the detriment of others. As a result, the cost of Soviet modernisation was felt by its citizens whose quality of life was abominable. Maria Svanidze had, in terms familiar to millions under the regime, complained in her diary 'Why have the prices flown upwards 100% while nothing is in the shops?'[177] The people endured not just the violence, the brainwashing and the censorship, they constantly struggled to get even a loaf of bread. Shortages of this nature were endemic. It was said at one point that there was not a single light-bulb or bar of soap to be got in the whole of Moscow; so much for the workers' paradise. In fact, the Soviet economy was worse off in the '80s than it had been in 1914. Stalin's own daughter, Svetlana Alliluyeva, remarked that her grandfather, a skilled labourer in Petrograd, had lived in a four room apartment – 'as much as a Soviet professor could dream of today'.[178] Alec Nove's authoritative *Economic History of the USSR* described Stalinism as 'the culmination of the most precipitous peace-time decline in living standards known in recorded history'.[179]

The hunger and shortages, which were the norm, frequently had even more disastrous results. They prompted Martin Amis to conclude, in a barb that targets the wider philosophy rather than merely the Soviet example, 'Famine belongs to the Communist tetrarchy – the other three elements being terror, slavery and, of course, failure, monotonous and incorrigible failure'.[180] To that list he might have added 'deception' as all such states have been built on a wilful and dramatic distortion of the truth. The Soviets' reliance on pathological mendacity permeated every aspect of life in their state. We can look, for instance, at the massive programme of sport they backed in a determined effort to prove the superiority of socialism. But, prepared to give their idealism a nudge, they pumped their athletes full of performance-enhancing drugs to ensure that reality matched their ideology. The Soviets faked show trials, doctored photographs, invented tales of Nazi collusion, rewrote history and produced reams of fantastical propaganda. The regime's continual recourse to lying and cheating has deservedly drawn the acerbic attention of Orwell, Koestler, Conquest, Solzhenitsyn and a raft of others. Under socialism, demoralised workers were guilty of increasingly shoddy standards, and a culture of pathological deceit had developed to paste over the cracks. The eventual result was Chernobyl, a disaster which undermined the whole system. The true costs will never be known, but perhaps 100,000 died from the fallout.

Stalin though believed himself to preside over the socialism he had been converted to as a teenager. Capitalists had been driven out and the state controlled the economy. Politically only those sympathetic to such Marxist principles were permitted to operate. Landlords and private land ownership had been crushed with the state sharing 'equally' the bounty of the collectivised communes. But Russia had been the fourth greatest industrial power even prior to the Revolution, so suggestions of the 'miracle' of its manufacturing base having bloomed from nothing were wide of the mark. And, while its industry had expanded significantly under the Bolsheviks, it was at the cost of the nation's culture, its freedoms, and its soul. Meiji Japan had gone through a far greater level of industrial growth than Soviet Russia, with none of the costs, simply by encouraging a more efficient and less wasteful system that rewarded and motivated those who took part in it. Stalin, by contrast, had removed scores of the most efficient farmers and engineers and severely de-motivated the remainder.

It is also ironic that a state constructed on the recommendations of Marx significantly worsened the alienation he had hoped to erase. Solzhenitsyn categorised life in Soviet Russia as consisting of constant fear, servitude, secrecy and mistrust, universal ignorance, squealing, betrayal, corruption, cruelty, slave psychology and endless lies. One citizen subjected to it lamented how 'the fear which it instilled in our minds and souls still puts people's consciousness in chains and paralyzes it...All of this generated constant fear of authority, alienated the human being from the state and made relations between them abnormal'.[181] It had become a hard, cold, profoundly suspicious and accusative nation.

Lyubov Vailievna's diary on 22 October 1937, the day of the vote for Stalin's new constitution, offers a fascinating snapshot of life behind the Iron Curtain:

> 'I woke up about three and couldn't get back asleep until after five...Suddenly I heard a burst of gunfire. And then another, ten minutes later. The shooting continued in bursts...until just after five...That is what they call an election campaign. And our consciousness is so deadened that sensations just slide across its hard, glossy surface, leaving no impression. To spend all night hearing living people, undoubtedly innocent people, being shot to death and not lose your mind. And afterwards, just to fall asleep, to go on sleeping as though nothing had happened. How terrible...'[182]

When her daughter Irinia returned from school she declared that her teachers had told her 'there are mass arrests going on right now. We need to rid ourselves of undesirable elements before the election!'[183] But when Lyubov went to vote she found that, instead of offering a choice, the ballot had a single name on it, and it was already marked. She laughed uncontrollably like a child. Stalin later addressed delegates to brag about those same elections, boldly announcing that 'Never before in the world have there been such genuinely free and genuinely democratic elections, never! History knows no other example.'[184]

Many of the apologists of the regime praise its level of education, yet this too is something of a hollow claim. The achievements of the Soviet Union make it clear that the standard of education in science was relatively high, but it too was hardly immune from political interference. Weissburg, the eminent physicist of the Kharkov institute, recorded the enormous investment the state had made in science in general and physics in particular, but also lamented the number of his co-workers who had been arrested. Two of his esteemed colleagues, Shubnikov and Obremov, were incarcerated and put to work digging canals which transformed them, in Weissburg's phrase, into 'expensive navvies';[185] incompetent ones too. The renowned Biology professor, I.J. Agol, was shot and even Sergei Korolev, the genius behind the Soviet's fledgling space programme, was sent to Kolyma.

It was even worse in the Humanities, or, indeed, any subject prone to political interpretation. Historians were considered especially dangerous and were among the first to be targeted in the Terror. Stalin himself had worked in concert with Andrei Zhdanov to create the official view of history so that it tallied with socialist 'realism'. The subject was to be based less on evidence and more on party decrees. Stalin made it clear that 'one must sometimes correct history'.[186] As a result, education in that sector consisted of propagating an intricate tissue of lies. The study of literature was similarly affected while purges of those with un-Soviet ideas and nationalist leanings continued in schools and universities in the Ukraine for decades after the famine.

The measures taken to restrict education hampered the industrial growth that the Bolsheviks were so keen on encouraging. Specialists from the pre-revolutionary period were hounded from their jobs, including up to 60% of teachers, and the university system practically collapsed until 1934. Students who were the scion of the old class were expelled. By 1930 only half of Soviet engineers had adequate training while just 11.4% had higher education. When the brilliant engineer Peter Palchinsky pointed out the flaws in the Dnieper Dam project he was arrested and shot. Natasha Andreyeva, the daughter of Andrei, gives clear evidence of the sort of indoctrination that Soviet education focused on: 'We *knew* as children the first thing to be done was to make people strong, to make a New Man, and educate the people'.[187] [emphasis by the author] Education is supposed to impart an inquisitive questioning rather than the sort of blind acceptance evident in such sentiments. That good old socialist certainty had been instilled into the obedient masses from cradle to grave. But the consequences of embedding this ideology into the minds of the citizenry were dreadful. Nadezhda Mandelstam, the wife of the poet, testified that 'Every new killing was excused on the grounds that we were building a remarkable "new" world'.[188]

After Stalin's death the situation certainly improved. The Politburo acted in concert to deny the brutal Beria any chance of assuming leadership, arresting and shooting him to prevent any continuation of Stalin's terror, and the regimes of Khrushchev and his successors were, in comparison with what had gone before, decidedly moderate. Yet such can partly be explained by the efforts of their notorious predecessor. William Rufus could afford to be an easy-going, party-loving monarch largely because the brutal reign of his father, William the Bastard, had cowed the nation into submission and snuffed out any hint of rebellion. So it was with Stalin. Khrushchev, who in 1948 had arranged for the arrest and deportation of a further million people from the Ukraine, a crime comparable with the height of de-kulakisation, was also up to his neck in the Stalinist Terror or, in his own words, 'up to the elbows in blood'. His successors subsequently returned the Soviet Union to an increasingly repressive state. Life in Russia in the years after 1953 was still a stifling experience for the majority and, when challenged, the regime was as ruthless as ever in crushing dissent in Hungary, Poland and Prague. The Soviet Union remained economically backwards and politically and culturally repressed, and the KGB were an ever-present threat.

The cultural restrictions begun in Lenin's reign and tightened under Stalin were never truly relaxed. Russia had a great artistic tradition: Pushkin, Tolstoy, Dostoyevsky, Mussorgsky, Diaghilev, Repin, Rimsky-Korsakov, Turgenev, Gogol, Chekhov and Tchaikovsky had lit up the nineteenth century. But under the repressive regime of the Bolsheviks this rich well of talent all but dried up. Art was to be rigorously controlled and only that which followed the party line or sang the praises of the regime was permitted. Satire and cultural freedom died a death in Communist Russia. For Stalin and the Soviet hierarchy, culture existed primarily to reinforce people's faith in and reliance on the state; anything else was anathema.

It was a climate that led to the advancement of figures like Lev Mekhlis who was made editor of *Pravda* in 1930. Mekhlis was a particularly fanatical Communist, raising his child as a New Man, with a portrait of Lenin in his cot, and recording the child's socialist development in a journal. He was, in many ways, the Marat of Bolshevism, preaching a puritanical morality while practising unbridled brutality in the Civil War, Terror and at the front in WWII. When a gigantic stash of German pornography was found during the war the prudish Mekhlis wrote a booklet denouncing Hitler's corruption of his troops. He printed 11 million copies of this widely derided pamphlet. It was a peculiar use of valuable resources during the conflict, yet the cultural life of the nation was placed in the hands of such characters.

All areas of the arts came under the Soviet aegis. While Boris Shumiatsky nominally ran the film board it was really Stalin who was in control. He appointed directors and screenwriters, doctored scripts and even songs, and personally oversaw every film before it was released. Censorship was rigorously enforced and all productions had to toe the party line. When a film, *The Young Guard*, was released after the war Stalin, who had not checked the script, was furious. The movie depicted a group of adolescents active behind Nazi lines. In doing so, it gave credit to those acting on their own initiative rather than portraying the party rallying the populace and saving them from Hitler's invasion. Such interpretations were unthinkable, and actors could fall victim to the dictator's brutality as much as any other profession. Solomon Mikhoels, a significant star, was murdered on Stalin's orders – drugged, clubbed over the head and shot. His body was then dumped in the snow and run over with a truck to give the authorities the cover story that he had died in a tragic accident.

Music, shorn of ideology or any 'incorrect' social or political views, was the one exception to this rigorous censorship. Hence the continuing success of Shostakovich and Prokofiev, though they too had to tread carefully and follow the directives of the party. Rachmaninov fled to America almost as soon as the Bolsheviks assumed power. Stravinsky had absconded to Western Europe even prior to that before joining his compatriot in the 1940s. Art was similarly subverted and many of Russia's greatest painters were dragooned into rendering saccharine endorsements of the regime. Much artistic output was dedicated to the evils of capitalism and the inevitability of the world-wide triumph of socialism. Some even depicted the workers of England as impoverished third-world citizens in comparison to their Soviet peers. There was little space to explore creative expression, and truly experimental artists like Kandinsky and Chagall were forced to live and work abroad. The Soviets were aided in such attempts by external agencies too. A group on the extreme left, Proletkult, which boasted 400,000 members, aimed at the cultural destruction of the old world, with the movement's poet Vladimir Kirillov, boasting that 'In the name of our tomorrow we will burn Raphael; Destroy the museum, and trample over art'.[189]

Books were also heavily constrained, despite the fact that Stalin had been immersed in literature all his life and never lost his passion for it. But it was because he was an aficionado of the genre that he knew how powerful a tool it could be in service of the state. Fiction lagged a long way behind Marxist dogma in Stalin's list of priorities. As much as he admired great writing, he had no hesitation in perverting it. He believed that literature had found its true calling in serving the socialist ideal. His appreciation for the form resulted in occasional leniency with authors, but there were limits to his magnanimity and the culture in which they could operate was still suffocatingly limited. Writers like Mikhail Bulgakov were tolerated, though kept on a short leash, but true masterpieces like Pasternak's *Doctor Zhivago* or Grossman's *Life and Fate* could only be published abroad. Ayn Rand, horrified by communism, also fled Russia in 1926 and composed her monumental paeans to competition, ambition and creativity in America.

Those who remained behind largely regretted their tardiness. Bulgakov wrote the idolatrous *Batumi* about Stalin's early life, but the dictator still suppressed it and would not allow it to be performed. The author subsequently wrote his anti-Stalin masterpiece *The Master and Margarita* in secret. Vladimir Mayakovsky, the great writer and poet, had been a true believer, a supporter of socialist realism, the futurist manifesto, the Communist Party and Lenin. Yet he ended up committing suicide by shooting himself in the chest in 1930. Boris Pasternak was preserved though the great poet Osip Mandelstam went to the gulag where he perished. Boris Pilniak was shot in 1938, and Isaac Babel shared his fate in 1940.

Maxim Gorky, the talisman of the nation's left, returned to Russia, but he became something of a lapdog, an emasculated apologist for the regime. It was the only way he would be permitted even the pretence of liberty. Stalin said of him that 'Gorky's a vain man. We must bind him with cables to the Party'.[190] Bind him they did. Gorky was reduced to commenting on the liquidation of the kulaks in *Pravda* where, in a sad echo of Hébert, he croaked that 'If the enemy does not surrender, he must be exterminated'.[191] He also described the concentration camps and slave labour projects as 'great work'.[192] Gorky had visited Solovetsky and wrote a travelogue which lingered on the beauty of the islands and the attractiveness of the accommodation there. He described comfortable cells with crisp bed sheets and flowers in vases by the windows, clearly attempting to make capitalist institutions appear primitive in comparison. Gorky depicted burly workers with healthy complexions dressed in clean linen and sturdy boots. He scoffed at the suggestion that there were any political prisoners among the incarcerated. The tainted work concluded by marvelling at how the happy inmates were transformed from criminals into productive and enthusiastic members of a socialist society.

Gorky also led a thirty-six writer collective in composing a paean to the chaotic and blood-soaked Baltic-White Sea canal. It too focused on the redemptive effect the labour had on the workers, altering them, in Anne Applebaum's phrase, into *Homo Sovieticus*. There was little mention of the brutal, primitive nature of the work, the inefficiency of labour or the shoddy standard of the completed project, and certainly none of the tens of thousands of lives it had cost. The portrayal instead focused on how those engaged in their tasks had undergone a conversion of religious intensity that cleansed their souls. Soviet literature and culture ever linked the individual's morality and sense of contentment with their utility to the state. To the Bolshevik mind such concepts were indivisible.

On 26 October 1932 fifty notable writers were invited to Gorky's mansion. There the author stood mute while Stalin informed them that writers were 'engineers of human souls'.[193] Their job was to persuade the populace of the 'truth' of the socialist promised-land. But of the 700 authors who met at the First Congress of the Union of Soviet Writers in 1934, only fifty would survive to attend the second meeting in 1954. The Party Congress admitted that 600 writers had been sent to the camps, though Solzhenitsyn claimed the figure was much higher. As a result of Stalin's continual interference, one could count the great works of literature produced through the entire duration of Soviet rule on the fingers of one thumb. The remaining authors, such as they were, were put at the service of the party, like the talentless hack Demian Bedny who in 1936 produced the poem 'No Mercy', or D. Dzhambul who two years later penned one called 'Annihilate'. The priorities of the state were apparent in such sentiments. Many of the surviving writers simply closed their eyes and minds to what was going on. Years later Surkov ruminated that 'I have seen my friends, writers, disappear before my eyes, but at the time I believed it necessary, demanded by the Revolution'.[194]

The strictures that afflicted literature were felt in every avenue of the arts. In 1939 Vsevolod Meyerhold, a significant figure in Russian theatre, wrote 'I, for one, find the work of our theatres pitiful and terrifying...Go to Moscow theatres and look at the colourless, boring productions which are all alike and differ only in their degree of worthlessness...In your effort to eradicate formalism, you have destroyed art!'[195] For airing such divisive opinions he was arrested and tortured. Meyerhold, a frail sixty-five year old man, was beaten about the spine, the back of the legs and the soles of his feet with a heavy rubber truncheon with such force that he felt as if boiling water was being poured on him. His torturer also urinated in his mouth. After enduring such indignities for a fortnight he was shot. A few days after his arrest his young wife, the actress Zinaida Raikh, was discovered murdered at their home. She had been stabbed seventeen times before having her eyes gouged out.

Having removed 'subversive' elements the Soviet Union was more than ever under the heel of an ideological elite, one with access to goods and services denied the rest of society, and one which had appropriated the residences, dachas, chauffeurs, maids, tutors and chefs of the old regime. The ruling class were a tiny, exclusive oligarchy whose conceit and hypocrisy were boundless. Utterly convinced of their superior intelligence and morality, they possessed an entitlement about their position that put the Divine Right of Kings to shame.

They strutted about like self-satisfied peacocks, taking the finest things in life while brutalising, starving and murdering the masses who lived in fear of their whims. The state now controlled, bar the rump of the Orthodox Church, every single aspect of the lives of the oppressed masses they lorded it over.

The people's existence was one of bondage, fear and penury, with no opportunity for social advancement, financial improvement or even the consolations of rich cultural diversity. Instead, they were continually hectored by pious propaganda. Citizens in the Soviet Union existed purely to serve the state and to think what they were told to think. Any deviation, individuality or creativity was considered a terrible crime and was met with the severest of penalties. The concepts of leisure and the pursuit of the finer things in life were alien; the suggestion of travel or free and open enquiry utterly forbidden. And the regime was supported on an enormous number of lies, deceptions that were repeatedly driven home on a populace who were starved of the truth. The results of failing to meet human needs merely resulted in corruption on an epic scale, at every level of society. If the populace could not gain remuneration by lawful avenues, then they would do so via illegitimate means. Russia is still reaping the legacy of this culture today.

The effects were felt beyond the borders of the USSR too. Stalin backed both Mao Zedong in China and Kim Il Sung in North Korea and also sanctioned communist aggression against South Korea. The benefits of capitalism though should have been obvious in the post WWII landscape, even as communism began to spread further across the globe. Japan and West Germany had been crushed in the war but, by embracing the free market and liberal democracy, both bounced back rapidly and became remarkable success stories. The 'victorious' nations of Russia, China and Eastern Europe had decades of poverty and oppression to look forward to. The Bolsheviks had effectively seized control of a state that was attempting to grope its way towards freedom and prosperity and transformed it into a monolithic slave empire, a prison camp nearly three times the size of the continental USA, a despotism of oppression and murder beyond the imagination of even the most wildly creative dystopian novelist. Had the story of Russia in the twentieth century been released as fiction it would have been dismissed as implausible bunkum; though it would also have been devoured as a relentlessly gripping and morbidly fascinating psychodrama.

Yet the higher ranks of Soviet personnel were, on the whole, educated, moral people who were friendly and caring in their private lives and retained a variety of interests and zest for life. Their attachment to politics was greater than average, but otherwise they were relentlessly normal. In different circumstances they would have led ordinary, productive lives, been affable friends and neighbours and restrained from committing acts of violence. The daughter-in-law of the talented Beria even claimed of him that 'In another era, he would have been so different. If he'd been born in America he would have risen to something like Chairman of General Motors'.[196] But the fact that there was nothing remarkable about them illustrates how just about anyone can be guilty of such atrocities. All they require is sufficient moral certainty and for events to turn in their favour. But this realisation simply makes their deeds even more terrifying. And the justifications given for the Jacobins cannot be applied to the Soviets. Their brutality was committed not from a position that was threatened, but from one of unassailable strength. From that lofty perch they showed themselves to be guilty of not just monstrous arrogance, intolerance, and brutality, but also a complete submission to an utterly baseless ideology and quite jaw-dropping hypocrisy.

By the post-war period the Bolsheviks behaved just like the imperialists they had derided for so long. They decked themselves out in ever more ostentatious displays of their rank and prestige, wearing uniforms dripping with elaborate gold braid epaulettes and bedecked with row upon row of medals awarded for increasingly banal achievements. They had themselves immortalised in life-size oil paintings, attempting to adopt an air of grandeur while sitting astride noble steeds. They gorged themselves on caviar and champagne, living in grand style at a number of luxurious addresses while an army of chauffeurs ferried them around in a fleet of prestige cars. And they employed squadrons of servants to trail around after them as they closed their ranks into an ever more exclusive caste centred on nepotism and personal favours. At the top of it all Stalin, for instance, repeatedly promoted his debauched, alcoholic and useless son, Vasily, to ever more prestigious offices in the nation's military. Despite such resemblances though, they were more unaccountable, and certainly more ruthless, than perhaps any royal house or aristocratic oligarchy the world has known.

On his rise, Stalin had proven that no one could match his ruthlessness. But it is the left's culture of denunciation and attack that encourages the success of such characters. The Georgian was certainly an aberration, but even without him the USSR would have been a repressive, totalitarian and impoverished state where quality of life and individual freedoms were crushed. However unusual he was, Stalin had millions of mundane enablers. The regime was, after all, powered by the certainty in which left-wing ideology was held, a widespread hatred of the 'enemy', and the resultant desire to censor information and punish malefactors. The movement has a tendency for an excessive adherence to doctrine, as well as a desire to monopolise the political and cultural sphere. And hostility is ever directed at any perceived to bar the way to socialism's 'promised land'. As such, it will always prove attractive to dreamers, to those who lean towards idealism over pragmatic realism. In culture and the arts, such people can be inspirational. In politics, in the theatre of the possible, they can prove decidedly dangerous.

In the Soviet example, allegiance to the party and the ideal led millions into complicity with the Stalinist atrocities, and most were convinced their actions were eminently justified. They were, of course, sincere in their beliefs. They could not have acted as they did otherwise, and it is hardly surprising that, after successfully overthrowing the state, this certainty hardened into megalomania. They genuinely believed the repressive measures they employed would be unnecessary in the utopia to follow. Of course, such conviction only made their violence more indispensable, made it, in fact, a moral imperative. They had been persuaded that their brutality would create a paradise on earth, a faith comparable with the culture of martyrdom in fundamentalist Islam. But their aim was more than restructuring society, it was in remodelling humanity. In Glover's analysis 'When the end is as large as changing human nature, all necessary means may seem acceptable...The belief system included a commitment that the end was so good that absolutely nothing should be allowed to stand in the way of the most efficient means to reaching it'.[197] The faith in their mission was so strong that this contention was still held by Lazar Kaganovich years after Stalin's death:

'you must think of humanity as one great body, but one that requires constant surgery. Need I remind you that surgery cannot be performed without cutting membranes, without destroying tissues, without the spilling of blood? Thus, we must destroy whatever is superfluous. These are unpleasant acts, granted, but we do not find any of this immoral. You see, all acts that further history and socialism are moral acts.'[198]

Stalin was equally adamant about this process. In 1932 Lady Astor visited Moscow and brazenly asked him 'how long will you keep killing people?' Considering her naïve, he brusquely replied that the process would continue as long as was 'necessary'[199] to establish the communist society. The great leader considered himself a man of virtue too and this quality, and his conception of morality, are evident in the notes he made in his personal copy of the 1939 edition of Lenin's *Materialism and Empiriocriticism.* The tome is liberally sprinkled with notes of enthusiastic agreement with the author and, peculiarly, the loving way he had repeatedly written out Lenin's name in Latin script. But the most interesting addition was the set of lists he wrote on the flypaper at the end of the book:

'NB! If a Person is:
1) strong (spiritually)
2) active
3) intelligent (or capable)
then he is a *good* person regardless of any other 'vices'

1) weakness

2) laziness
3) stupidity
are the only thing *(sic)* that can be called vices'[200]

For Stalin then, it was dedication to the cause that defined morality and hesitation, vacillation or doubt were to be despised. In the mind of the committed radical, ideology can trump morality and humanity because, to the extremist, such concepts are synonymous. Stalin believed everything he did that was designed to ensure the triumph of socialism was a virtuous act, no matter how appalling his deeds appear to us now. He slept easy because to him decency and despotism were indistinguishable when carried out in the name of the great cause.

It is for the same reason that when the modern-day activist pours violent scorn or abuse on their opponents, or smashes up someone else's property not only is their conscience untroubled, it is actually *replenished*. We saw this when the activist group 'Class War' attacked a small family business in Shoreditch in September 2015. An enraged mob descended on the premises while actually brandishing flaming torches and terrifying the customers inside, including children. They daubed 'scum' across the glass panes of the establishment and smashed the windows of adjacent properties. Yet they felt charged with the virtue of their actions. So did Kelsey, the young Minnesota woman we met in the introduction who went a step further and actually launched a physical assault on a young man. Such activists are depressingly common and, make no mistake, in clement circumstances they would be acting as enforcers for the likes of Stalin with little hesitation.

Stalin's view of Marxism, in his own words, was that 'the revolutionary proletariat alone is destined by History to liberate mankind and bring the world happiness' though it would take much 'trial and suffering and change' to attain 'scientifically proven socialism'. This could only come about as a result of 'the class struggle: Marxism *is* the masses whose liberation is the catalyst for the freedom of the individual...Many storms, many torrents of blood' would define 'the struggle to end oppression'.[201] It is all there: the utopian conviction of a moral, sin-free and glorious future in which all share liberty and equality; the unshakeable certainty in the ideology that will bring the perfect society to fruition, and the belief in the necessity of struggle and, ultimately, violence, for which justifications could always be found. The results of such measures would, after all, make all those sacrifices worthwhile. But one aspect eternally absent from the radical's ambition is the opinions of others. It is not an issue that ever seems to have occurred to them. Stalin always believed he was freeing the workers; if only they had the sense to see it. It was a faith that never left him. In 1950 he published *Marxism and the Problems of Linguistics*. While he had abandoned his support for Esperanto, he reasserted his belief that communism would ultimately cover the world and a single language would unite the people. All that he had been through, all the murders and calamities he had overseen had not dented his faith in the justness of his cause or the inevitability of its triumph.

It is not surprising that Stalin should have blinded himself to the faults of his regime. But what is still difficult to comprehend is how so many others in the West, who really should have known better, were supportive of his rule for such a long time. The day after Stalin's death, on 6 March 1953, the *Daily Worker* in London published a saccharine cartoon that mourned his passing while celebrating 'his work and teaching'. The image depicted sobbing proletariats congregating in front of vast industrial projects while a gigantic figure of Stalin loomed over the scene, posing like Napoleon while imbued with the serenity and dignity of the Dalai Lama. Such was the credulity of Britain's left.

Plenty of evidence had existed prior to that date which should have warned against such sentiments. On 6 October 1939 a cartoon published in the *Daily Telegraph* showed Stalin dancing and joking with Death, while the incomparable David Low had been tossing barbs at the dictator for decades. Plenty of other information on the reality of Stalin's regime had been in circulation for years. There were protests in the West about the Soviet forced-labour camps as early as 1931 while accounts which captured the true nature of collectivisation and famine were also freely available. The show trials of 1936-8 were open to Western journalists, most of whom credulously lapped up what they were served as the real deal.

The Soviet Decree of 7 April 1935, which allowed for twelve year olds to be tried as adults and then executed, was also common knowledge, but the French Communist Party argued this merely proved how quickly children matured under socialism. Eugene Lyons had been a true believer. But he was disillusioned when discovering the reality and published a scathing and meticulously researched analysis of the Stalinist regime in the *New English Weekly* of 9 June 1938. *Darkness at Noon*, Arthur Koestler's savage indictment of Stalin's trials, went to print in 1940, while George Orwell famously lampooned the Soviet state in *Animal Farm* and *Nineteen Eighty Four*, fictional allegories which were also published in the forties. Yet when the latter condemned Stalinism he was widely attacked on the left for his lack of solidarity. Friedrich Hayek had composed *The Road to Serfdom*, a devastating, and wholly accurate analysis of socialism's inevitable failures in 1943, while six notable authors dismantled communism's abject faults in *The God That Failed* in 1950. The NKVD man, Walter Krivitsky, and Boris Bazhanov, who had worked in Stalin's secretarial entourage, both defected and wrote widely on the truth of the regime and the repellent dictator at its head. But many remained committed supporters even after *The Origins of Totalitarianism,* Hannah Arendt's unsparing exposé of Soviet crimes, was published in 1951.

With so much available evidence Stalin's apologists could not possibly cite ignorance as an excuse, yet the Soviet regime found a remarkable number of champions in the West. Among the most dedicated of such individuals were Sidney and Beatrice Webb, leaders of the Fabian Society and founders of the London School of Economics. They were also key figures in the rise of the Labour party with Sidney, an active MP, securing a cabinet position under Ramsay MacDonald. In 1935 they published *Soviet Communism: A New Civilization?* a study which consisted of 1,200 pages of rigorously detailed apologies for every aspect of Stalin's regime. The whole volume simply regurgitated Soviet propaganda, which the Webbs uncritically accepted as fact, and praised 'the sense of freedom and equality'[202] which they believed defined the USSR. It counts as perhaps the most spectacularly worthless piece of academia ever produced. For the second edition they jubilantly, and prematurely, removed the question mark from the title. But many other respected academics shared their enthusiasm. E.H. Carr, the Cambridge don, worked on his fourteen volume apologia for the Soviet Union from 1946 until his death in 1982 while C.P. Snow, active in the Labour party, remained a committed Stalinist his entire life. J.D. Bernal, the British physicist, even suggested that critics of the Soviet system 'should be silenced'.[203]

The period of the famine was one especially awash with the sort of revisionist, distorted hogwash to which the left seems especially susceptible. Numerous reports of the disaster had appeared in a wide range of Western publications, both in Europe and America, but they were largely dismissed as lies of the right-wing press. When Gareth Jones, a former secretary of Lloyd George, reported the truth of events in the *Manchester Guardian* on 30 March 1933 he was subjected to bitter libel from the likes of Walter Duranty. Yet the evidence was irrefutable. On 6 March 1935 the *Chicago American* covered the famine on its front page with gruesome photographs supporting the article. By that stage, the US House of Representatives had already passed and printed a memorandum on the disaster on 28 May 1934. Malcolm Muggeridge had also made a detailed report in the *Fortnightly Review* on 1 May 1933. He described how

'On a recent visit to the Northern Caucasus and the Ukraine, I saw something of the battle that is going on between the government and the peasants. The battlefield is as desolate as in any war and stretches wider; stretches over a large part of Russia. On the one side, millions of starving peasants, their bodies often swollen from lack of food; on the other, soldier members of the GPU carrying out the instructions of the dictatorship of the proletariat. They had gone over the country like a swarm of locusts and taken away everything edible; they had shot or exiled thousands of peasants, sometimes whole villages; they had reduced some of the most fertile land in the world to a melancholy desert.'[204]

Despite such compelling and overwhelming evidence the majority of the left simply shut their eyes to it and continued with their furious denials. Sidney and Beatrice Webb dismissed Muggeridge as a foolish and misguided youth. Western Soviet sympathisers, unable to face the truth, even angrily denounced the testimonies of famine survivors. They were aided in such delusions by the Soviet regime itself. The Bolsheviks declared that reports of the famine in the western press were lies invented by the capitalist powers which were jealous of socialism's success. Apologists in Europe and America lapped up such reports. The influential French radical leader, Edouard Herriot, was given a carefully guided tour of the Ukraine. He announced in *Pravda* on 13 September 1933 that stories of famine in the region were simply lies of the bourgeois press. Vassily Grossman was contemptuous of the statesman's visit, especially when learning of Herriot's admiration for the diet of chicken soup and cutlets served to the youngsters he had met. On the neighbouring farm the children were desperately scrambling in the dirt for earthworms to devour.

Martin Amis identified H.G. Wells, George Bernard Shaw and Sidney and Beatrice Webb as 'the century's four most extravagant dupes of the USSR'.[205] Together with John Maynard Keynes and others they founded *The New Statesman*, a Labour weekly, just prior to the outbreak of WWI. That achingly left-wing periodical still laughingly, and rather pompously, proclaims its commitment to 'Free thinking since 1913' on its cover. That is, in the usual leftist vernacular, free thinking within incredibly narrow parameters. Wells had met Stalin in 1934 and commented that he had 'never met a man more candid, fair and honest'. It explained 'his remarkable ascendancy over the country since no one is afraid of him and everyone trusts him'.[206] Shaw visited while famine was ravaging the state and reported that the Russians were uncommonly well fed. He added that 'I did not see a single under-nourished person in Russia [and that] in the USSR, unlike Britain, there was freedom of religion'.[207]

Sir John Maynard Keynes justified the actions of the regime as they were fighting 'a war against an enemy class'.[208] Sidney and Beatrice Webb, whose magnum opus was reissued in 1937, right at the worst point of Soviet rule, vocalised the same distaste for the peasantry that the Bolsheviks did, writing of their greed, cunning, drunkenness and sloth. They heartily endorsed the project that would transform them 'into public spirited co-operators, working upon a prescribed plan for the common product to be equitably shared among themselves'.[209] The Webbs fully supported the brutal process of de-kulakisation and concluded that 'strong must have been the faith and resolute the will of the men who, in the interest of what seemed to them the public good, could take so momentous a decision'.[210] They refused point-blank to accept reports of famine and were adamant that any shortages resulted from the intransigence and vandalism of the kulaks and peasantry. They also claimed that de-kulakisation resulted from peasant tribunals and that communities were, on the basis of their judgements, asking the state to evict those trying to impede the collectivisation they were desperate to embrace. The Webbs argued that such courts were 'more seriously judicial, more balanced in their discussion, than any court trial I have attended in America'.[211]

The favourite source of this deluded couple was the aforementioned Walter Duranty, the Moscow correspondent of the *New York Times*. He was certainly the most notorious apologist of the period. It was Duranty, an admirer of Stalin, who in 1932 published Red Square in the *New York Times*. The article enduringly, and rather callously, coined the phrase that 'you can't make an omelette without breaking eggs'.[212] Duranty well knew the truth of the famine, but he brazenly lied to keep socialism's image pristine. He first issued flat out denials and then, when it was covered in depth by fellow correspondents in his own paper, declared on 23 August 1933 that all such reports were 'an exaggeration or malignant propaganda'.[213] Despite this he eventually admitted that three million had died, a total he brushed off as he didn't consider it excessive. When Duranty was later given a guided tour of the region he recanted, dismissing such a total as wildly excessive. He then ridiculed Muggeridge as a fabricator of falsehood. Duranty's mendacious reports were seized upon by sympathisers in the West, and the subsequent cheerleading of the regime continued for decades. Malcolm Muggeridge called him 'the greatest liar of any journalist I have met in fifty years of journalism'.[214]

Yet this despicable liar, this enabler of genocide, was feted by the leftists of the day. In 1932, Duranty was awarded the Pulitzer Prize for 'dispassionate, interpretive reporting of the news from Russia'. It went on to extol his 'scholarship, profundity, impartiality, sound judgement and exceptional clarity'. At a pro-USSR banquet at the Waldorf Astoria, crammed with New York's smug left, no one received anything approaching the level of thunderous applause as that accorded to Duranty. And the same pro-Communist dupes who swallowed the Duranty line viciously attacked the likes of Muggeridge for decades. Nothing blinkers the eyes to evidence or corrupts the soul quite like ideology does. It resulted in falsification and propaganda being corrupted into 'scholarship'. Hollywood happily colluded in the charade too, releasing tripe like *North Star* in the late forties, a film which outstripped the most blatant Soviet propaganda in its depiction of an idealised collective farm.

It was the same story when it came to the show trials and the Great Terror. Despite compelling evidence in the West about the scale of the killings, the camps and the transparent falsity of the court cases, with Trotsky's and Professor Dewey's exhaustive Commission standing out as especially persuasive testimonies, the majority of sympathetic opinion in Europe and

North America closed their minds and eyes to the evidence again. The playwright Bertolt Brecht told Sidney Hook that 'The more innocent they are, the more they deserve to die',[215]a comment he uttered even while writing a play condemning the same features of Nazi Germany.* The Liberal *Manchester Guardian* and the press of the Labour party were openly critical of the trials, but even such sympathetic voices did little to affect the opinions of those who wished to believe.

The majority verdict sided with the Soviets including the *New Statesman* which concluded that 'there had undoubtedly been much plotting in the U.S.S.R.'[216] The eminent British pro-Communist lawyer, Pritt, writing his autobiography in 1966, long after Khrushchev had revealed the truth of events, *still* held 'a Socialist belief that a Socialist state would not try people unless there was a strong case against them'.[217] There really is no reasoning with faith. Walter Duranty, of course, stuck his oar in. He repeatedly defended the Soviet version of events in the *New York Times* and wrote of the trials that 'no one who heard [them]...could doubt for a moment that what they said was true'.[218] Professor Owen Lattimore eulogised the clear 'democracy' of the trials while Sir Bernard Pares, in his *History of Russia*, argued that the cases, crimes and evidence presented were all entirely genuine. Professor Harold Laski praised Vyshinski as 'an ideal Minister of Justice'.[219] People's opinions were unaffected by the evidence – they were dependent purely on belief, on which side their bread was buttered prior to events. Those invested in socialism simply believed the Soviet line and dismissed all truthful accounts as fabrications.

But Jean-Paul Sartre went even further. He argued that evidence of the Soviet slave camp system should be ignored even if it were true as such admissions would dent the aspirations of the French proletariat. George Bernard Shaw commented on the purges that 'We cannot afford to give ourselves moral airs when our most enterprising neighbour (the USSR) humanely and judiciously liquidates a handful of exploiters and speculators to make the world safe for honest men'.[220] The left even conspired to silence or discredit those who had been in the camps or had direct evidence of the purges. Smears of this nature proliferated in France, which was a hotbed of Communist agitation. Victor Kravchenko, who had written *I Choose Freedom*, came under a particularly bitter and sustained attack. The French Communist journal *Les Lettres françaises* published an article by a source which claimed Kravchenko's work was faked. But the editor, Claude Morgan, was later forced to admit that he had actually invented the source and lied to try and defame Kravchenko. At the subsequent trial, the Communists denounced testimony from camp survivors and in opposition put up witnesses like the Dean of Canterbury who testified

---

* Brecht's former mistress, the actress Carola Neher, was later arrested in Russia and was never heard from again.

that the Soviet Union was a beacon of liberty. Kravchenko won his case and posterity has proven his work to be of an unimpeachable standard of accuracy. But the verdict made little difference. The French intelligentsia continued to denounce the writer and any other critics of the Soviet regime. Pierre Daix, the editor-in-chief of *Les Lettres Françaises* composed poetic defences of the liberating effect of the gulag while Pat Sloan, the British Communist, described Soviet imprisonment as 'an almost enjoyable experience'.[221] In 1966 Sloan claimed that 'Among most writers on the U.S.S.R. in the 1930s, I have least to be ashamed of, or to wish to withdraw'.[222]

The tipping point in such delusions was 1956 - the year that Khrushchev revealed Stalin's crimes and denounced him. It was also when he showed the regime had lost little of its appetite for violent suppression when, mere months after his moralistic grandstanding, the Hungarians protested against his oppressive regime. Stalin's successor sent in the tanks to crush them pitilessly. It was, for many, a wake-up call. Kingsley Amis, previously a Communist, 'in common with the overwhelming majority of intellectuals everywhere',[223] abandoned the movement in the wake of the Hungarian rising and was scathing about any who remained. The British Communist Party suffered a raft of defections, particularly after it emerged it had deliberately misled the reporters of the *Daily Worker* about events in Hungary.

That was the same year that Bertrand Russell published *Why I am Not a Communist*, a brilliant essay which witheringly dismantled the ideology's case brick by brick. He opposed Marx for two reasons 'one, that he was muddle-headed; and the other, that his thinking was almost entirely inspired by hatred...his chief desire was to see his enemies punished, and he cared little what happened to his friends in the process'. He further added that 'I am completely at a loss to understand how it came about that some people who are both humane and intelligent could find something to admire in the vast slave camp produced by Stalin'. Yet many retained their belief beyond that year and such was their stubbornness that their faith would long endure.

In the 1960s and '70s while Soviet Russia was still largely excused, the populist protest movement focused on the Vietnam War. Yet they ignored the part played by the Soviets in inflaming that conflict. Martin Amis noted 'the wildly peergroup-competitive but definitely unfakeable emoting and self-laceration of the crowds outside the American Embassy in Grosvenor Square, where they gathered in their tens of thousands'.[224] My, how the movement has changed. John Kenneth Galbraith, a Harvard economist active in the Democratic party, was still commending the economic development of the Soviet Union in 1985, when it was on the very brink of collapse. When Ota Šik, economic minister in Alexander Dubček's Czechoslovakia attempted to set him straight on the realities of fiscal Marxism, Galbraith simply dismissed him.

Rather unbelievably there are supporters of more recent vintage too. Andrew Murray had been a significant British Communist for years before joining Jeremy Corbyn's Labour Party as their election campaign chief in 2016. He had gone on record as abhorring 'the hack propagandists [who] abominate the name of Stalin beyond all others'. Remarkably Murray had also spoken on behalf of the Communist Party of Britain to state that 'Our Party has already made its basic position of solidarity with the People's Republic of Korea quite clear'. In the year 2000 the so-called New Communist Party of Britain established a website which published a remarkable essay by one Andy Brooks. It presented a view of the twentieth century through the most distorted lens imaginable. He eulogised the likes of Lenin, Stalin, Mao, Kim Il Sung, Ho Chi Minh and Fidel Castro while lamenting how they had been 'subjected to denigration and abuse by the hired hands of the bourgeois media...Trotskyites and revisionists'. The reason for the hatred levelled at Stalin was apparently because 'the Soviet Union was the hope of working people across the world'. He continued to claim that

'The colossal achievements of the Soviet Union led by Stalin was living proof of the validity of the socialist system...While the economies of the imperialist world crashed and burned the people of the Soviet Union saw their living standards rise twelvefold. While the imperialists prepared for another world war, against themselves and eventually against the USSR, the Soviet Union worked tirelessly for collective security and peace'.

Brooks wholesale accepted the Stalinist version of the show trials, asserted confidently that Kirov was 'shot dead by an agent of the Trotskyite opposition' and dismissed any suggestion of atrocities committed under the regime. I could go on, but I'm sure you get the idea. It really is an eye-popping essay that is well worth a read, a frankly hilarious diversion, though for all the wrong reasons.

In an article in *The Guardian*, on 16 February 2006, Seumas Milne also made some extraordinary claims. He lamented the 'rewriting of history' which had resulted in negative portrayals of Stalin and Mao and suggested that 'For all its brutalities and failures, Communism in the Soviet Union, eastern Europe and elsewhere delivered rapid industrialisation, mass education, job security and huge advances in social and gender equality. It encompassed genuine idealism and commitment'. Milne subsequently suspended his journalistic career and rose to become the director of communications for Jeremy Corbyn's Labour party. He was also alleged, in true Stalinist fashion, to have doctored the speech of Clive Lewis at the 2016 Labour Conference and helped arrange for the demotion of the man many had tipped as a challenger to Corbyn's leadership. Try to imagine that the Tory party had secured the services of a press officer who not only beseeched us to stop wittering on about the dreadful massacres that had happened under Hitler and to focus instead on the generous old age pensions he had introduced, the wonders he performed with the economy, the vast improvements in employment that had happened under his regime, the deserved privileges he had arranged for mothers and the marvellous youth groups he had established. Picture him then censoring the speeches of Conservative MPs and arranging for those who deviated from the party line to be purged from the ranks. All hell would break loose, but when exactly that happens with Labour, yet again, there is not a murmur of dissent.

The wholesale hatred Milne has for the West is palpable in numerous articles he has penned which repeatedly lament the 'revisionism' which has given Stalin and Mao such poor reputations. He also compares Western civilisation's record in colonialism unfavourably with that of the East's Communist regimes. While it is undeniable that imperialism has been responsible for a swathe of atrocities, with the rule in the Belgian Congo standing out as a particularly vile example, this is still a most contentious point. But as Milne insists on attempting to persuade us of the positive aspects of the Chinese and Soviet systems, then we must examine the *benefits* of Western civilisation too. We have free speech, an autonomous press, liberty to travel, and a vibrant culture with minimal censorship and propaganda. We enjoy a successful economy and well-stocked shops, regular elections which offer a choice between a number of political parties, as well as, crucially, the rule of law. The Stalinist and Maoist regimes offered none of these. One wishes to grab individuals like Milne by the lapels and ask him that if the Soviet Union was such a triumph, then why did it collapse in ignominious failure?

Solzhenitsyn certainly had an eloquent response to the whining of fools like Milne. If the suffering they had endured was insufficient 'Is it not still more dreadful that we are now being told, thirty years later, "Don't talk about it!"?'[225] Western societies are far from perfect, particularly their track record in foreign policy, yet they are infinitely superior to the socialist states such individuals defend. They are superior in rights, prosperity, infrastructure, services, freedoms and quality of life; this really shouldn't be a discussion anymore. Life in America in the twentieth century was an infinitely preferable experience to that endured east of the Iron Curtain. The US did have, it is true, its own distasteful witch-hunt against communism, particularly in the 1950s when 'un-American thought' was rigorously policed. It was in many ways as repressive and resistant to free political discourse as the USSR was in those dark days. One thing cannot be denied however: the body-count in America's persecution of the politically incorrect was decidedly lower than that of any communist regime. Paradoxical though it sounds, it was far better to be a communist in McCarthy's America than in Stalin's Russia.

Yet the loyalty of the converts still endures. Every year, at the May Day Parade in London, some 20-30,000 march. They still proudly loft their hammer and sickle flags while waving large portraits of Stalin, Lenin, Marx and others. Their banners echo the same rhetoric that defined much of the 20th century in those failed states, and Labour grandees like Jeremy Corbyn and John McDonnell can be relied on to attend and address the faithful. We shall leave the last word though to perhaps the most notorious of all the Soviet apologists. Still widely read and lauded in left-wing circles, the Marxist historian Eric Hobsbawm wrote, shortly before his death in 2012, that capitalism crushed the integrity of artists and intellectuals. Considering the track record of socialist states that was a remarkable conclusion, but it pales into insignificance next to the sentiments Hobsbawm aired when interviewed by Michael Ignatieff on 'The Late Show' on 24 October 1994. He started off with the same old doom-laden Manichean certainties which justified his membership of the Communist party by arguing that 'You didn't have the option. You see, either there was going to be a future or there wasn't going to be a future and this was the only thing that offered an acceptable future'. He seemed oblivious to the fact that the 'future' was just fine without communism. But Ignatieff then asked him if it would have made a difference to his commitment to the party if he had known through the 1930s just how many people were dying as a result of the regime and he responded, shockingly, 'Probably not'. Pressing him further his interlocutor asked 'had the radiant tomorrow actually been created, the loss of fifteen, twenty million people might have been justified?' Hobsbawm's response was immediate: 'Yes'.[226]

Chapter 4
The Nazi Quandary

'I am a Socialist, and a very different kind of Socialist from your rich friend, Count Reventlow. I was once an ordinary working-man. I would not allow my chauffer to eat worse than I eat myself.'

Adolf Hitler in conversation with Otto Strasser. 21 May 1930

It is a well-known fact that Hitler and the Nazis were of the 'Far-Right'. This assertion, repeated endlessly in the decades since WWII, is taken as given and rarely, if ever, questioned, certainly by the left who use it as a cudgel to demonstrate the superior virtue of their movement. Yet it is a view that should be challenged, and any serious interrogation of the evidence makes it clear that the case is far less black and white than is widely assumed. The phrase 'right-wing', in modern parlance, has become generally, and lazily, associated with racism. Yet this belief has come to dominate primarily because Hitler has long been viewed as the flag bearer, the face of the movement. As a consequence, stereotyped and insulting assumptions are thrown around, but they bear little relation to the reality of conservatism which is a far more moderate and less divisive movement. Those of the right tend to value freedom, age-old liberties, minimal state interference, and the elasticity of the free market. To be right-wing can also be taken to be of a conservative disposition, to have a somewhat sluggish reticence towards change, certainly towards change for its own sake. As such, there is far greater tolerance for established ruling elites than on the left and a strong inclination towards economic liberalism. It is, as a consequence, virtually inconceivable that someone of a right-wing disposition would rail against capitalism. This resistance to change, this reverence for society as it stands, can be manifested in a more cautious attitude towards immigration, and it is undeniable that at the extremes of the movement this inclination is expressed in overtly racist terms. But to suggest that this aspect defines the philosophy is a gross error. It is a *far* rarer phenomenon on the right than the animus towards bankers or Tories is on the left.

But to return to the issue at hand, was Hitler right-wing? Well, he was undeniably culturally conservative in many ways. Hitler's taste in art, music and architecture was profoundly traditional. He found modern art distasteful, even decadent, and he *loathed* jazz. He also revered figures like Frederick the Great and Otto von Bismarck, men who practically epitomise the privileged elites that many feel define the historical right. Yet the same allegations could be levelled at Stalin whose taste in art, music and architecture was every bit as conservative as the Führer's. He too lionised the titans of Russia's past, in particular Ivan the Terrible and Peter the Great, yet no one would consider calling Stalin right-wing. Hitler has also been criticised for taking money from capitalists, but then so did Lenin and, regardless, the number of businessmen who made donations to the Nazi party has been wildly exaggerated.

As for the rest of Hitler's manifesto, there is little that seems even remotely right-wing. He loathed capitalism, despised the aristocratic elites of German society, as well as the bourgeois class, and, in contradiction to what is widely believed, he hated Christianity too. It was, after all, founded by a Jew. Hitler blamed the collapse of the great Ancient Empires, which he revered, on Christianity's rise. He joined a movement called the German *Labour* Party and it was that segment of the population that his programme was primarily designed to benefit. The talk that attracted Hitler to the DAP was given by Gottfried Feder, who was well known for attempting to ingratiate himself with the Socialist-Revolutionaries who briefly transformed Munich into a Soviet-style commune. The subject of that speech was on 'How and by what means is capitalism to be eliminated?' Hitler was won over by his attack on the increasing power of banks, corporations and department stores.

The 25 Point Programme of the Nazis, which was issued on 24 February 1920, called for equality, rent controls, the nationalisation of large commercial concerns, profit sharing in heavy industries, old-age pensions, start-up schemes for small businesses, land reform and proscriptions on usury. After winning power, Hitler introduced generous benefits for mothers and the elderly while enthusiastically adopting the robustly left-wing fiscal policies of John Maynard Keynes. That famed economist advocated a planned economy, and believed that by 2029 people would be working sixteen hours a week while filling the rest of their time attending poetry recitals and listening to string quartets. It was a quaintly inaccurate forecast that perfectly epitomises the Bloomsbury group. Hitler's hatred of the Jews, his most famous trait, was largely inspired by his aversion to capitalism, banking, corporations and large department stores, all of which were considered synonymous with Judaism. It was an inclination he shared with the greater body of publicly expressed socialist thought over the previous century and a half, for socialists had long regarded Jews as members of a privileged elite. The Nazis were also radical eco-warriors who opposed animal cruelty, passed environmental protection laws and clean air acts, banned smoking on public transport decades before anyone else and recommended organic farming, rural living and vegetarianism. Rudolf Hess, Hitler's deputy, championed homeopathy and herbal remedies.

From this ideological base, Hitler moulded a society virtually indistinguishable from the extreme left-wing states that preceded and followed it, particularly those of Stalin and Mao. Nazi Germany was a single-party state that dissolved trade unions, banned opposition parties, closed down any representative parliamentary bodies and called a halt to elections. The judicial process was elbowed aside in favour of government diktats. They took full control of the nation's press, education and media, produced blizzards of propaganda to shore up the regime and brought all professional and social clubs and activities under the aegis of the party. The state also took a leading role in the economic development of the nation. In fact, the overall direction of the economy in Nazi Germany was primarily determined by centralized planning. The Nazis prioritised social engineering and advanced a narrow coda of acceptable thought and behaviour while using a brutal secret police force and network of concentration camps to deal with any troublesome elements, liquidating those they considered a threat to their position. There was a strong emphasis on indoctrinating and subjugating the youth, before weaponising them in defence of the regime, and the Church was severely repressed. The workers and rural labourers were eulogised while scorn was poured on the 'parasites' of capitalism. The state's actions were euphemistically dressed up as 'cleansing' with their victims referred to as 'cattle', 'lice' or 'vermin'. Indeed, the Nazis considered themselves to be stout, working class folk standing up to an elite mired in greed and corruption, rather like nearly every leftist organisation there has ever been.

The entire machinery of the state was directed towards advancing a narrow political ideology while attacking a relatively small sector of the populace, an assault largely justified on economic grounds. Nazi Germany relied on complete subservience to and reverence for the party and, in particular, the leader. The central tenets of conservatism are small government and the free market, with all the liberties that programme entails. The prevailing belief on the right is that the state should serve the individual. But Hitler preferred big government and a state-controlled economy, with all the restrictions inherent in that manifesto.

In his collectivist interpretation, individuals existed to serve the needs of the state. The totalitarian states of Russia, China and Germany are virtual mirrors of each-other in practically every manner that counts. It thus seems ludicrous to consider Hitler even *remotely* right-wing, never mind to boldly position him as the embodiment of the 'Far-Right'. His true affiliation warrants a more thorough investigation then. For an uncritical acceptance of the Nazis as a far-right movement cannot be substantiated with even a rudimentary appraisal of the evidence.

The crimes of National Socialism are certainly the most well chronicled and widely known in the annals of human history. People who know little about Stalin, and nothing at all about Mao or Pol Pot, know all about Hitler and the Holocaust. Yet few are aware that the Nazis saw themselves as a moral movement rather like every other branch of socialism. They believed that they possessed a rare virtue and were fully justified in attacking the degenerate strain that corrupted their society. Their approach would sweep aside the vibrancy of Weimar culture where expressionistic art, jazz bands, wild transvestite club nights and astonishing new modes of design like the Bauhaus had thrived. But the puritans of National Socialism were confident in their superiority over such 'distractions'. Even the SS, those most complicit in the eventual atrocities, believed they were engaged in a heroic task to save the nation from a genuine threat. Even as their duties became increasingly grim, they grew ever more persuaded of their position as a moral elite. The worse their role got, the more it confirmed their sworn vow of honour, loyalty, courage and commitment to the cause. The SS truly believed it made them more virtuous than those engaged in less demanding work. They also prided themselves on the efficient and humane way in which they went about their duties without unduly alarming or injuring their charges. It was, for instance, made clear to them that under no circumstances were they to steal from those under their 'care'. This too assured them that their behaviour was eminently virtuous.

In Romania, when the locals set about the Jewish population with enthusiastic brutality, the SS troops were appalled by their bloodlust. By comparison, their methodical approach assured them they occupied a moral plateau far above that of the Romanian death squads. But despite their 'civilised' approach they still believed they had a 'moral right' to exterminate the Jews. In Jonathan Glover's analysis 'The more horrible the acts the SS committed, the more they were able to think of themselves as showing heroism, remaining morally pure themselves at the same time as overcoming revulsion against atrocities in order to obey the commands of duty'.[1] The SS were indoctrinated with the idea that, as they were obeying a 'higher law', they had a just imperative to carry out their grisly missions. If their duty called on them to massacre women and children, they followed their orders without question. It was an attitude that led to a wildly distorted perception of priorities. One SS man bemoaned the terrible waste in uniforms that he witnessed and tutted 'It is hard to believe something like this could happen here'.[2] The 'here' in question, the location where he despaired of such a 'waste', was Auschwitz.

The same paradox was true of the 'Lord of the SS', Heinrich Himmler, the man Hannah Arendt concluded was the Nazi 'most gifted at solving problems of conscience'.[3] He was a slight, unassuming character, a doting father who addressed his love letters to 'Bunny'. Most accounts from those who met him record a charming, fun loving and humorous man who enjoyed dancing, laughing and slapping his thighs in merriment, a picture far removed from the one he conjures in people's minds today. When speaking to the SS about the things they had seen and done Himmler commended their resolve. 'To have endured this and, at the same time, to have remained a decent person...has made us tough, and is a glorious chapter that has not and will not be spoken of'. Himmler had swiped the slogan 'My Honour is my Loyalty' from one of Hitler's speeches and bestowed it on the SS before emphasising the historic nature of their task. It was Himmler who emphasised the virtues of comradeship, obedience, loyalty, courage, discipline and honesty to which his troops should adhere. The fact that their role was difficult to bear only increased their conviction that they were taking part in a moral crusade. A successful applicant for the SS was required to be a 'good and decent person' who could supply two character references. And Himmler reminded them that 'I expect kindness. See yourself as helpers not dictators'.

Yet, as ever, decency and morality could be subverted should the sacred cause demand it. Himmler had found justifications for transgressing accepted norms early in his career and on 11 October 1936 he defended the Nazi's absorption of the police force and the expansion of the Gestapo as a matter of moral expediency.

> 'I basically did that which my conscience and common sense told me was right. The fact that others were bemoaning 'violation of the law' was completely immaterial when the life and death of the German people were at stake...In fact by what we did we laid the foundations for a new code of law, the law of destiny of the German people'.[4]

Himmler allowed himself to believe the moral purity of his mission was so irreproachable that any subversion of legality or bourgeois morality was justifiable. He was following a 'higher law', a conviction that would allow him to swerve any contemporary standards of procedure or decency. Yet as late as 1940 he still sought Jewish repatriation to Africa as the solution to the 'problem'. He argued that 'one rejects the Bolshevik method of physical extermination of a people out of inner conviction as un-German and impossible'.[5] But when given the order he would soon find appropriate justifications to carry out the task.

However, while he rationalised his duties, Himmler does not appear to have been personally cruel or sadistic. He regarded himself as 'not a bloodthirsty man, and not one who takes pleasure in difficult duties'. On 15 August 1941 he witnessed the shooting of 200 Jews at Minsk and was so rattled by the experience he nearly collapsed. Yet he was a zealous administrator and seems to have absorbed Hitler's bizarre racial theories as some kind of incontrovertible truth. These qualities allowed him to rise to the very pinnacle of the Nazi state and he doesn't appear to have lost any sleep over the pivotal role he played in the deportation and extermination of millions of human beings. The man behind those horrors was a complex mess of contradictions and bizarre beliefs. Himmler was obsessed by natural, holistic remedies, insisted that every concentration camp should have its own herb garden, was fanatically opposed to hunting and any form of animal cruelty, rigorously measured skulls to determine the optimum 'Aryan' cranium and was a student of runes. He brought his love of pseudo-mysticism and pseudo-science into the SS which became ever more saturated with ritual while believing their increasing hardness was a necessary shield in the cause of defending the purity of German blood.

In the wake of Reinhard Heydrich's assassination, Adolf Eichmann became chief facilitator of the Holocaust. The evidence unearthed at his trial revealed his conscience to be similarly untroubled. The peculiar nature of Eichmann's moral compass became clear when one of the young police officers assigned to guard him handed him a copy of *Lolita*. Visibly annoyed he thrust it back two days later muttering that it was 'Quite an unwholesome book'.[6] Despite this the psychologists who examined Eichmann ruled him to be 'normal', though one of them memorably concluded he was 'More normal, at any rate, than I am after having examined him'.[7] But Eichmann, like Himmler, was not personally cruel. It is clear from the accounts of his trial that he was no calculating killer, no monster. In personal terms his greatest crime was to slap the face of Dr. Josef Löwenherz, head of the Viennese Jewish community. It was an impulsive act that troubled his conscience even years later. But he was less affected by ensuring the trains kept running to the camps.

His story is illustrative of how normal, decent people can commit abominable crimes when circumstances, or justifications, allow it. Those who believe their long term goals are virtuous can always pardon short term 'excesses'. Eichmann epitomised what Hannah Arendt referred to as 'the banality of evil'. Indeed he was a moderate sort who, before being swept up in events in the 1940s, had never vocalised the sort of hatred so common on the left. It was he who effectively created the stereotype of one who is 'only following orders'. His defence rested on the fact that he was obeying not just orders but the law. He claimed that his duties had been acts of state and thus exempt from criminal proceedings. More than this, while he was aware of what was taking place and had visited Treblinka and Auschwitz, claiming the sight shocked him to the core, he was involved merely in transportation and played no part in the killing at all. As 'Eichmann told it, the most potent factor in the soothing of his conscience was the simple fact that he could see no one, no one at all, who actually was against the Final Solution.'[8] It is the same culture of compliance that enables the modern activist to spout hatred about Tories, bankers and capitalists. Indeed, for them to be utterly baffled on the rare occasion they face criticism for their own hate speech.

This culture resulted in Eichmann's conscience being so clear that he repeatedly referred to feeling 'elation'. But there was a stark difference between his pristine self-image and the grubby reality of the cold, bureaucratic angel of death. Indeed 'he would have had a bad conscience only if he had not done what he had been ordered to do – to ship millions of men, women, and children to their death with great zeal and meticulous care'.[9] He could rationalise his actions just as all those discussed in these pages had done before him. All those who followed would do the same. But the court was unsympathetic to such sentiments and concluded that Eichmann did not follow orders, he gave them. The judges' verdict on him was powerfully eloquent:

> 'just as you supported and carried out a policy of not wanting to share the earth with the Jewish people and the people of a number of other nations – as though you and your superiors had any right to determine who should and who should not inhabit the world – we find that no one, that is, no member of the human race, can be expected to want to share the earth with you. That is the reason, and the only reason, you must hang.'[10]

Yet Hitler too regarded himself as a wholly virtuous man. His motivation sprang from how the Jews violated his sense of morality and decency. He perceived them as being responsible for prostitution and pornography as well as 'degenerate' art, music and wider culture. He displayed the same prim reserve that Eichmann had done, calling prostitution a 'moral plague' while demanding that 'Theatre, art, literature, cinema, press, posters and window displays must be cleansed of all manifestations of our rotting world and placed in the service of a moral, political and cultural idea'.[11] In fact Hitler was so puritanical that he didn't touch alcohol or tobacco, or even drink coffee. It is shocking that such prudishness could come from individuals with so much blood on their hands, but as twisted as it sounds, Hitler's hatred of the Jews was founded on this sense of rectitude. He found their culture so offensive that he was sure it corrupted the morality on which a successful society depended, and he believed so strongly about the threat they posed that his hatred grew to enormous depths.

Hitler's belief in the moral justness of his cause was so total that he held it right to the end. Even as he sheltered in the bunker while Berlin was bombed into ruins, and the full scale of the Holocaust he had commanded became clear, he could declare that 'we have lanced the Jewish abscess; and the world of the future will be eternally grateful to us'.[12] He truly felt he had acted for the benefit of humanity and expected praise rather than condemnation for what he had done. It was a belief informed by the sort of conviction held by all the other demagogues in these pages. When von Richtofen met Hitler as it was all unravelling in 1944 he concluded that 'one can't help feeling this is a man blindly following his summons, walking unhesitatingly along the path prescribed to him without the slightest doubt as to its rightness and the final outcome'.[13] Years earlier Molotov had a similar impression of him, describing Hitler as 'very smug...and vain. He was clever but narrow-minded and obtuse because of his egotism and the absurdity of his primordial idea'.[14] It was an analysis almost indistinguishable from that which Chernov had made of Lenin. Hitler was driven by the certainty, religious in its intensity, that he was a 'Man of Destiny'. 'His was a closed mind impervious to argument or doubt. It was thanks to this, the assurance that he possessed the key to history'[15] that he would persevere, take extraordinary risks, and be willing to journey to such terrible darkness, resolute in the belief that he was ridding the world of evil.

Much of this conviction was centred on Hitler's faith in the historical and philosophical justifications for his racial theories. The Nazis had been utterly persuaded in the accuracy of the *Protocols of the Elders of Zion*, the laughable Russian forgery which became a sort of Bible in their movement. But there was another text, a far older one, that they held in even greater esteem. This work, considered practically a sacred document to the movement, was Tacitus' *Germania*. Naturally, Tacitus considered the courage and dignity of the simple people who lived east of the Rhine superior to the greed, decadence and ostentation of Rome. He regarded the Germans as 'natives of the soil and extremely little affected by immigration or friendly intercourse with other nations...For myself I accept the view that the peoples of Germany have never been tainted by intermarriage with other peoples, and stand out as a nation peculiar, pure and unique of its kind'. The image presented in those pages would prove irresistibly attractive to Nazism, particularly Himmler, who having absorbed Tacitus, was persuaded of 'How great, how morally pure our ancestors were'. The Nazis regarded the musings of Tacitus, a man who had never even been to Germany and whose views on the topic were distorted by an all-consuming bias, as an oracle of indisputable truth. The Teutonic Myth espoused in his writing became the basis for their movement. It also informed their hostility to Judaism which was increasingly perceived as a threat to the national 'purity' they hoped to guard. This belief would be taken to extraordinary lengths by Nazism. The *Germania* became so revered in their culture that, even as the tide turned against them in WWII, Heinrich Himmler diverted some SS units to search for an original text of the book at a critical period during the conflict in Italy.

The embers of this strident nationalism were kept alive in the nineteenth century by Johann Gottlieb Fichte whose philosophy focused on strengthening the national consciousness of the German people. But Fichte had a number of ideological peers, and the most noteworthy of the breed was undoubtedly Friedrich Nietzsche. He primarily hoped to destroy Judaeo-Christian morality as he considered the virtue of the faithful, based on the promise of eternal reward, distastefully self-centred. He also considered religion to be marred by its long history of persecution. What was needed was an entirely new aspirational morality. Yet Nietzsche's philosophy developed from this starting point to effectively advocate pure selfishness in his conception of 'will to power'. He influenced Nazism in other ways too, suggesting that Christianity was a conspiracy by Jews in a slave revolt against their Roman masters. Hitler also noted Nietzsche's observation that 'Men believe in the truth of all that is seen to be strongly believed in', something he would employ to devastating effect in his later speeches. This twisted interpretation of his writing meant the Nazis, like the Soviets before them, valued hardness. They saw compassion for those who obstructed their utopian dream as a weakness. Their unshakeable certainty in the moral justness of their cause and their revulsion for the avaricious 'insects' they hoped to eradicate mirrored each other too.

Hitler frequently cited Schopenhauer as one of the greatest thinkers mankind had produced. In 1818 the philosopher had produced *The World as Will and Representation*. Hitler quoted him at length, admired his theories on the power of human will, and was particularly struck by the philosopher's belief that the Jew is 'The Great Master of Lies'. Hegel also inspired the movement, especially his belief in 'heroic leadership' and a progressing series of historical epochs. Yet, in the Führer's interpretation, history was recast as a series of struggles between different races. In these tussles, the superior race would end up dominating the inferior ones. The Nazi leader believed he lived at a critical point in human history. He was certain that capitalism was sick and in terminal decline. Much of this process was the fault of Jewish financiers who sought to subvert the great nations, plunge them into wars, and establish political and financial control over them by manipulating the market and the press. The time was thus ripe for the implementation of his particular form of socialism.

Immanuel Kant was yet another inspiration for the Nazis, particularly his belief in following rational rules which should be obeyed out of a sense of duty.

The Königsberg philosopher, who had helped shape the views of both Hegel and Nietzsche, argued that expressing sympathy for others was a mere inclination which had little moral value in relation to societal obligations. Kant's voice proved most influential to Eichmann, Himmler and the SS in the '40s, but the Nazis did not have to look to the past to find philosophical justifications for their ideology - for they gained an influential cheerleader after coming to power too. Martin Heidegger, the world-renowned philosopher with a seat at the University of Freiburg, openly supported the movement and freely advocated anti-Semitism. After joining the party he argued that 'The much lauded "academic freedom" will be expelled from the German university; for this freedom was not genuine because it was only negative'.[16] He even agitated for lecturers and students who did not subscribe to National Socialism to be removed.

Beyond these philosophical justifications, the Nazis felt they had a scientific basis for their beliefs too, for eugenics was a popularly held and widespread view at the time. Hitler was particularly influenced by the work of the German botanist Erwin Baur who had published the *Principles of Human Heredity and Race Hygiene* in 1921. The range of apparent academic support for their manifesto assured the Nazis they occupied an intellectual and moral high ground that their rivals could not challenge. Hitler's adherence to the theories of the day allowed him to forward his views on the racial inferiority of the Jews as being supported by 'the science'. The followers of National Socialism thus perceived their movement to be purely scientific and free from dogma, one with an indisputably empirical basis. It was a rigidly deterministic viewpoint that would propel them into unimaginable horror.

Yet the Führer's own book, *Mein Kampf*, was more influential on the Nazi ranks than all of this academia. The hefty tome was written early in Hitler's career, during his incarceration after the abortive Munich Putsch of 1923, and the ideas contained in its pages are ones he adhered to for the remainder of his life. It ultimately sold in prodigious quantities though, having been forced to wade through it, the current writer would be willing to wager the majority of people who bought it never actually read it, or certainly never finished it. Its message though was one distilled through the Führer's speeches in far crisper and more memorable form, and by the late '30s there can have been few people in Germany who were unaware of their leader's manifesto. Elements of his writing are far from the left-wing agenda, like his belief that monarchy can be an effective form of government as the personnel are held to account more effectively than when responsibility is dispersed through the democratic system; but the spine of his argument has a markedly radical slant.

Hitler was profoundly affected by the poverty he endured while living in Vienna and his main focus, at least in the early stages of the book, was on the social problem and the 'poverty trap'. He was repulsed by inequality and informed his readers that the gulf separating the manual worker from the bourgeoisie 'is often deeper than people think'.[17] Addressing this disparity became the driving force of his political activism. The solution would lie, as it so often does, in attacking privilege, though his meandering ruminations would lead him to some conclusions which diverged sharply from mainstream left-wing thought. There are shades of Orwell though in the sections where Hitler declared the only way to study this social problem was to experience it. Yet, unlike his Eton educated counterpart, his immersion in poverty was genuine and he was not remotely sure he would escape. Orwell did so deliberately and relatively briefly, always secure in the knowledge that he would return to his comfortably bourgeois existence. But, while he lived among the poor and experienced their conditions, he never truly shared their despair. Hitler did.

Hitler believed that cultural differences between the classes arose from the contrasting circumstances into which they were born. He concluded that 'the end of all social activity [must]...be a means to find a way of eliminating the fundamental deficiencies in our economic and cultural life – deficiencies which necessarily bring about the degradation of the individual or at least lead him towards such degradation.'[18] He admitted to having despised the Habsburg regime in his youth and was initially drawn to the Social Democrats whose manifesto focused on improving conditions for the working classes. Yet when he began to ask questions and raise concerns over their rigid outlook the representatives of the left responded with remarkable intolerance. They threatened to throw him from the scaffolding and chased him off the building site on which he worked.

'I now realised the meaning and purpose of those brutal orders which prohibited the reading of all books and newspapers that were not 'red' and at the same time demanded that only the 'red' meetings should be attended. In the clear light of brutal reality I was able to see what must have been the inevitable consequences of that intolerant teaching.'[19]

Hitler began to realise that the agencies of the far-left did not truly have the concerns of the working class at heart. They used the Trade Union movement for their own political ends rather than to benefit the workers, aspiring to keep the proletariat down so they would look to them for leadership. If the labourers ever achieved a significant rise in their living standards then they would not require their representatives any more 'for there was a danger that if these masses once felt content they could no longer be employed as mere passive material in the political struggle'.[20]

Hitler's hatred of inequality and his distaste with established elites ultimately led him to latch on to a scapegoat to blame for society's ills. He slowly came to the conclusion that a widespread conspiracy was responsible for propagating division and it controlled the press, the financial sector and the Marxist movement, all with the intent of advancing its own interests. He believed that conspiracy to be orchestrated, naturally, by the Jews. The point at which he expressed this realisation is perhaps the most memorable section of his writing:

'Was there any shady undertaking, any form of foulness, especially in cultural life, in which at least one Jew did not participate? On putting the probing knife carefully to that kind of abscess one immediately discovered, like a maggot in a putrescent body, a little Jew who was often blinded by the sudden light'.[21]

He admitted to having taken a considerable time to have reached this conclusion. Hitler was initially repelled by the anti-Semitism of the Austrian press and opposed the idea of attacking people of a different faith 'on grounds of human tolerance'. Slowly though he began to notice just how different the Jews were. Hitler was finally persuaded of their malevolent intent by 'the activities of a certain section of the Jews themselves. A great movement, called Zionism, arose among them. Its aim was to assert the national character of Judaism; and the movement was strongly represented in Vienna'.[22]

Having latched on to this idea he began to detect evidence for it all around him. Hitler saw every type of smutty literature and all decadent theatrical performances as the handiwork of Jews. He also perceived their press as praising Jewish authors while being critical of Germans. Hitler regarded the Marxists and Social Democrats as havens for Judaism and believed that Jews were primarily responsible for prostitution and the white slave trade. His antipathy was largely inspired by his belief that they constituted a privileged class in Germany at the time, one which had no concern for the interests of normal, working people. He was also clear on the need to lump all the elements his movement opposed into one homogenous mass

'it will be necessary to block them all together as forming one solid front, so that the mass of followers in a popular movement may see only one common enemy against whom they have to fight. Such uniformity intensifies their belief in the justice of their own cause and strengthens their feelings of hostility towards the opponent.'[23]

For all his frequently demented ravings, Hitler had an undeniably firm grasp of human psychology and this tactic, consciously or not, is still employed by the radical left. They continue to lump bankers, capitalists, Tories and Zionists into a convenient collective they can scream hate at. But it is a lazy form of virtue. It is, after all, difficult to rouse oneself to do something productive. But to sit about and boost one's ego by lording it over others is simplicity itself, and Hitler was acutely aware of this. When reading *Mein Kampf* one is also struck by the utter conviction the author had in his moral integrity and superior virtue. He perceived greed, corruption, decadence and larceny all around him. While his prejudices differ somewhat from those of the contemporary left, the tone is almost eerily similar at times.

These parallels continue. Germany's cultural decline was largely blamed on 'Jewish bankers' and 'the slow elimination of the personal control of vested interests and the gradual transference of the whole economic structure into the hands of joint stock companies'. Hitler lamented the impact of 'money-grabbing capitalism' and despaired how the German State Railways are 'now to be turned over to international capitalists'.[24] His solution to such issues was 'to make sure that capital remained subservient to the State and...to safeguard the social rights of the workers',[25] hardly views which sound particularly right-wing. He criticised the 'commercialization' of the German nation and the suggestion that commerce was the most effective method of reviving the nation's fortunes. He compared this view unfavourably with that of their most significant neighbour as 'France was restoring public education on a humanitarian basis, thus doing away with the idea that national life is dependent on commerce rather than on ideal values'.[26] Hitler was adamant that the state should take direct responsibility for both education and the press to help influence the masses. He referred to freedom of the press as a 'will-o'-the-wisp' and concluded 'with ruthless determination the State must keep control of this instrument of popular education and place it at the service of the State and the Nation'.[27]

All these policies were aimed at arresting the moral decline of the German nation and the building of a virtuous society where the likes of syphilis, venereal disease and prostitution were eradicated. The sort of cultural decadence Hitler bristled against also faces opposition from the right, if one thinks of the *Daily Mail* for instance, but it rarely meets true *political* opposition. And while the right rarely hopes for culture and education to be used for political ends, that goal has been a frequent aspiration of the left. Yet one fact is undeniable: Hitler epitomised the fusion of hatred and moral superiority so typical of the left – the same ingredients behind all the atrocities covered in these volumes.

His motivations for his antipathy on the Jews also have a decidedly leftist leaning. The Jew, he claimed, had historically advanced his 'commercial interests' since Biblical times, specialising in exploitation while thriving off the toil of others. They effectively acted as a 'parasite' on the societies in which they lived. Hitler claimed that 'Only with the entrance of the Jew did that feeling of estrangement between employers and employees begin which led at a later date to the political class-struggle'.[28] It all sounds so terribly familiar. It was because of the role of the Jew as a merchant, banker, landlord, newspaper mogul and capitalist that Hitler justified the series of historical pogroms as a legitimate reaction against their greed and mercantile activities. To Hitler the story of the Jew through the ages was, remarkably, one of 'privilege'. He even claimed that 'after a little while he began to twist things around, so as to make it appear that it was he who had always been wronged, and vice versa. There were really some particularly foolish people who could not help pitying this poor unfortunate creature of a Jew'.[29]

Hitler genuinely believed that, through Freemasonry, the Jew grew to control governments, the press, the stock-exchange, banking and international high finance. This conspiracy resulted in them pulling the strings behind the scenes and directing international policies on a worldwide scale. The key players in this globe-spanning plot were the Rothschilds. Hitler believed they exerted a malign influence in practically every sphere of human experience, whether cultural, social, political or mercantile. Sadly these demented ideas still exert a firm grip on the left's lunatic fringe and, as more such individuals discover each-other online, deranged views of a Rothschild backed Zionist conspiracy are becoming more commonplace again. For Hitler though, this cabal lay at the heart of the inequality he campaigned against. The rise of the Jew meant the small artisan worker disappeared. The factory labourer who took his place was effectively disinherited and unable to provide for his old age. This left the German suffering from alienation. It is ironic, given such a view, that Hitler believed Marxism to be the final attempt by the Jew to secure complete political control of the world. It aimed, according to his addled brain, to overthrow democracy and institute the dictatorship of the proletariat which would enable the Jew to rule by brute force.

Yet Hitler was equally clear on his distaste for the elitist system of Weimar Germany and his intent to destroy it from within, and he made it plain that his movement was geared towards the disenfranchised rather than the winners in life. His party 'was not meant to be an organization for contented and satisfied people, but was meant to gather in all those who were suffering from profound anxiety and could find no peace, those who were unhappy and discontented'.[30] Given his insights into psychology it is also worth quoting his perception of the ideal activist, a conclusion which largely tallies with the modern radical:

> 'The future of a movement is determined by the devotion, and even intolerance, with which its members fight for their cause. They must feel convinced that their cause alone is just, and they must carry it through to success, as against other similar organizations in the same field...The greatness of every powerful organization which embodies a creative idea lies in the spirit of religious devotion and intolerance with which it stands out against all others, because it has an ardent faith in its own right. If an idea is right in itself...then it is invincible and persecution will only add to its internal struggle.'[31]

Hitler's ideology was shaped by his aversion to the 'foreign oppressor' who had waged war against Germany before emasculating and humiliating the nation. As such his temper was very much the mindset of one who sides with the underdog against a privileged elite. Indeed, he loathed both the dynastic regime which had preceded the war and the 'bourgeois statesmen' who had risen to prominence in its wake. Hitler's hatred of the Jews was also informed by his belief that they occupied a preeminent position among the ruling elite. So it was an animus with entirely leftist origins. But then, as we shall see, contemporary anti-Semitism has primarily socialist roots too. Hitler was, in essence, merely continuing a proud tradition. But his was a philosophy distorted by being viewed through the prism of extreme nationalism as well as one consumed with a juvenile enthusiasm for war.

As such, despite the abundance of evidence presented here, it must be conceded that those of a left-wing persuasion would not truly recognise themselves or their movement were they to scrutinise *Mein Kampf*. But neither would those of a right-wing bent, and that is the issue. To label Hitler as right-wing is to severely distort the man's ideology and priorities. He repeatedly stated that it was not fiscal matters that motivated him but racial concerns. His ideal state, which controlled the education and breeding of the population, also bears strong similarities to that extolled by Plato and his successors. Still, Hitler must be analysed primarily in the light of his extraordinary xenophobia and not by any affiliation to a societal or economic philosophy which could legitimately be identified as either left or right, despite his knack for combining the worst aspects of both movements. But if he was not quite *purely* left-wing the evidence suggests he inclined rather more in that direction than he did to the right.

In its autobiographical sections, *Mein Kampf*, in the way it romanticised Hitler's struggle from poverty against the privileged establishment, is notoriously unreliable, even if it offers a fascinating insight into the psyche of the author. Yet he proved himself utterly sincere on the views he expressed on dismantling the Weimar Republic, providing full employment for the working man, Lebensraum, war in the east and the persecution of the Jews. We must conclude then that he was equally honest about the rest of his manifesto and the decidedly leftist slant to his worldview. Many on the left base their belief that Hitler was right-wing on the German leader's oft-stated opposition to Marxism. Yet, just as Sunni have eternally warred against Shia, internecine rivalry has defined left-wing activism since its inception. The Montagnards in France feuded bitterly with Brissotins, Cordeliers, Enragés, sans-culottes and each-other; the Bolsheviks in Russia turned mercilessly on Mensheviks, Socialist Revolutionaries, Trotskyites, Ukrainian Communists and themselves, and the old sage himself, Marx, relentlessly sniped at Moses Hess, Bruno Bauer, Mikhail Bakunin, Pierre-Joseph Proudhon, Ludwig Feuerbach, Wilhelm Weitling, Max Stirner, Karl Grün, Gottfried Kinkel, Andreas Gottschalk, August Willich, Karl

Vogt, Ferdinand Lassalle and Karl Schapper. There was barely a left-wing radical in the period that he didn't consider an enemy. The next volume will show this trait remained just as prevalent through the leftist regimes in China, Cambodia and Vietnam. The fact that one is in opposition to a leftist clique is no evidence at all that one is right-wing. Those who dismiss this issue might also, if they pondered it even briefly, realise why Hitler opposed the recommendations of the *Jewish* Karl Marx, despite sharing both his prejudices and motivations. The same principle explains Hitler's distaste for the wider movement which, in the likes of Lenin, Trotsky, Rosa Luxemburg, Yagoda and Kaganovich, had a markedly Jewish personnel.

Indeed, we may suggest the antagonism between National Socialism and Bolshevism originated less from an ideological disparity than their pursuit of the same slice of the electorate. Jonah Goldberg memorably argued that 'the battle between Nazis and the communists was a case of two dogs fighting for the same bone'.[32] It is no coincidence, after all, that the Swastika is displayed on a red flag. Hitler estimated that almost half the 2,000 strong audience at his first big speech, at the Hofbrau Haus in Munich on 24 February 1920, was comprised of communists. By the time he had stepped down from the lectern they had all been converted to the cause, a neat illustration of the crossover appeal between the movements. The Führer confirmed to Rauschning that communists were to be welcomed into the Nazi ranks. He was also clear that 'The petit bourgeois Social Democrat and the trade union boss will never make a National Socialist, but the Communist always will'.[33]

In examining the parallels between Nazism and the Soviet state, the ease of this cross-pollination becomes clear. Both based their policy line on attacking privileged elites while focusing on economically socialist principles, though the Nazis, who continued to permit private enterprise when it was subordinated to the interests of the state, were not quite as extreme as the Soviets in this regard. Both eulogised the proletariat while pouring scorn on the 'parasites' of capitalism and both produced rafts of propaganda which depicted workers breaking free from their chains or toiling contentedly in sunny meadows while, no doubt, singing hymns to the state and the great leader responsible for such abundance.

Just as in Russia, the majority of Germany's greatest cultural talents resultantly chose exile over the artistic handcuffs imposed by their leaders, while the Nazi practice of book burning was emulated on a considerably widened scale in Maoist China. A large part of Nazi propaganda also emphasized the greater level of equality and social mobility in Hitler's Germany, particularly in the workplace and the armed forces. Yet ultimately, both Hitler and Stalin believed the development of a state was dependent on politics rather than economics. Bullock has also noted how both movements 'shared an insistence on the importance of winning the support of the masses with an equal insistence on the inability of the masses to organize themselves. For both Nazis and Communists they were a resource to be mobilized, not a membership to be represented'.[34]

There were numerous similarities between the two leaders as well. Both Hitler and Stalin were provincials who the more refined members of the political class felt they could manipulate to their advantage. Those elites were, in both instances, very much mistaken, but the ways in which they viewed themselves and were regarded by others have notable parallels. Bullock's exhaustive study concluded that both men 'saw themselves, not as tyrants or evil men, but as leaders prepared to devote their entire lives to a higher cause, and entitled to call on others to do the same, so releasing in themselves and in those who accepted their claim a perverted moral energy and self-confidence'.[35] Hitler praised the hardness of the Soviets and repaid the compliments Stalin had given him: 'Stalin, too, must command our unconditional respect. In his own way he is a hell of a fellow! He knows his models, Genghiz Khan and the others, very well'.[36] Both men relied on the adversarial school of politics still so dominant on the left today: the greedy, scheming scapegoat, whether Tory, Zionist, Jew or Kulak, who is still the preferred bogeyman of leftist activism. They also ultimately created societies geared towards the creation of a 'New Man', a phrase liberally employed under both regimes.

The ways those states mirrored each-other have already been listed but their greatest divergence might be that, though Stalin's persecution had a primarily theoretical basis, Hitler's was both ideological *and* biological. In principle though, they were cut from the same cloth. 'Substitute 'class' for 'race'...and Stalin would have found little to disagree with'[37] in Hitler's Germany. Both sought to improve society by driving out those who did not fit while advancing a narrow definition of the ideal citizen, and both would end up exterminating those who did not measure up. For the Communists it was philosophical imperfections that were to be expunged, for the Nazis it was primarily physical imperfections. For the Bolsheviks the reliance was on propaganda, censorship and brainwashing, for the Nazis it was sterilisation, eugenics and euthanasia as well. It has been claimed that the Communists preached social justice and equality while the Nazi doctrine was one of racism and the power of will, that the intent of the Bolsheviks was good while that of Hitler was bad. But these claims are untrue. Both societies were based on the destruction of cultures which they despised, both were mired in resentment, assaulted privilege, valued community over independence, believed themselves to be agents of historical inevitability and were characterised through the strong crushing the weak. As we shall see in the next volume, every word of this section is equally true of Mao's China.

Hitler's chief resistance to Marxism, apart from believing it conspired to forge a Jewish world dictatorship, was its opposition to nationalism. But this aspect also helps explain Nazism's extraordinary appeal. For while the Soviets claimed to represent the workers, the suggestion that they cared as much about labourers beyond their borders diluted their message. For the Nazis, the fact that their appeal focused solely on German workers *magnified* it. These claims created a sense of unity among the populace and significantly increased their support. It really felt like the Nazis valued them as people rather than focusing on some vague philosophical ideal. More than this, while Nazi appeals relied partly on the promise of a new economic system designed to benefit the workers their message proved more attractive than that of the Communists, for it also responded to the specific nationalist resentments that had festered in the wake of WWI, Versailles and Germany's subsequent economic collapse.

The other attractions of the movement are quite obvious and foremost among them were the assets of their party leader. His military service had made a significant impact on both his manifesto and personality for it was in the army that he developed the bold decisiveness which would serve him so well in the political arena. Hitler considered himself an artistic genius who had been diverted into politics and he certainly brought a keen eye that gave the Nazis a flamboyance, visual flair and sense of theatre, qualities that made them stand out from their political rivals. The epic scale Hitler brought to the movement was very much influenced by his love of Wagnerian opera but was also inspired by his enthusiasm for Ancient Rome. And he adopted the fasces, eagles, architecture, cult of the leader and grandiose spectacle that the Caesars had employed to such enduring effect.

As much as he considered himself an artist though his real gift was in public speaking, at which he was electrifyingly brilliant. From the beginning, Hitler was a master in rousing his audience and sought to appeal to the emotions rather than reason or intellect. He was conscious of keeping his message clear and repeatedly driving his points home in a performance that kept building to a fever pitch of intensity. Few in history could match his ability to rouse the passions of his audience while conveying ideas with such liquid clarity. He was also remarkably progressive in the way he embraced modern technology, becoming a pioneer in the use of cinema, radio, the motor car and aeroplanes in political campaigning. The Nazis subsequently became masters of propaganda, a field in which they grew ever more sophisticated. This too was designed to appeal directly to the emotions of their audience and was so effective that both contemporary cinema and advertising frequently employ tropes originated by the Nazis. Even the Olympics still use the revolutionary techniques employed by Hitler to transform that event from a sports meeting into the significant cultural event it remains today.

Hitler was also influenced by the success of Mussolini's movement, with the march on Rome in 1922 inspiring his own Munich Putsch. However, Arendt makes it clear that 'The Nazis knew well enough that they had more in common with Stalin's version of Communism than with Italian Fascism'.[38] It was widely accepted at the time though that Fascism had also emerged from the revolutionary left. Its members marched under red flags on May Day and its mandate centred on the state control of industry, collectivism, high tariffs and workers' councils. The main theorists of Italian fascism were Alfredo Rocco and Giovanni Gentile, a pair of Marxists who also culled ideas from Hegel, Saint-Simon, Nietzsche and Sorel. Gentile believed that individual liberalism and capitalism were responsible for a rise in alienation and the collapse of social obligations. He promised a genuine freedom denied under those systems. Fascism was designed to embrace all of social life, restoring societal cohesion and transforming a selfish culture into one of public service. But Rocco and Gentile's truly radical innovation was to reject the international revolution by employing the pre-existing administrative structure of the nation-state. The focus was to be on syndicalism, an economic programme which allowed the state to co-opt any large industries or corporations. They believed that such institutions should benefit the nation rather than the business owners. The resultant system permitted private enterprise but only under total government control and regulation. While small businesses were to be left alone, major concerns like car manufacturers or construction companies must end up part-owned, and significantly controlled, by the state. The result was a nationalist and economically statist philosophy that took its name from the Roman fasces, the bundle of sticks that could be broken individually but was far stronger when united.

In Italy the movement was led by the charismatic and bombastic Benito Mussolini, a prominent member of the Italian Socialist Party and enthusiastic supporter of the Communist International. Mussolini, named after three revolutionary heroes, was born to Alessandro, a committed socialist and member of Marx's First International. Benito embarked on a career as a left-wing journalist before falling in with a group of Bolsheviks and radicals in Switzerland. It has long been speculated that he mingled with Lenin while he was there. He founded a paper called *Class War*, the journal of the Italian Socialist Party's extremist wing, and declared that 'I am and shall remain a socialist and my convictions will never change! They are bred into my very bones'.[39] He was a committed Red who had helped organise the communist revolutions that swept through Europe in 1917 before forming his new organisation on more nationalistic lines. Indeed, Mussolini had cited Georges

Sorel, the radical Marxist and class war enthusiast, as the true prophet of his movement. His Fascist manifesto called for a minimum wage, workers' representation in government, the repeal of noble titles, swingeing progressive taxation to squeeze the rich, the expansion of the franchise, a sweeping programme of nationalisation and provision for the schooling of the proletariat. Even his final days were spent colluding with socialists and communists while still denouncing the bourgeoisie. When sentenced to death his compatriot Bonabacci, a friend of Lenin's, cried out 'Long live Mussolini! Long live socialism!'[40]

His thuggish Blackshirts inspired the Nazi movement's Brownshirts, and those of the British Union of Fascists too, while Italy's syndicalist financial line was later adopted in Germany, providing the basis for both Volkswagen and the Autobahn. Hitler allowed private ownership, just as Mussolini did, but that independence was conditional on it serving the needs of the state. Big business was also compelled to finance the healthcare, maternity leave, pensions and rent controls introduced under the Nazis. What they eventually constructed was a command economy known as *Befehlswirtschaft*. Under this system centralised planning replaced the market. Buyers and sellers were no longer permitted to base their economic activities on the laws of supply and demand. Instead, the state regulated production quotas, allocated resources, decided who produced what and where, and set the prices for materials, goods and services. Hitler employed the centrist, robustly left-wing fiscal agenda of John Maynard Keynes in establishing sizeable state-sponsored programmes to kick start the economy. The Nazis also introduced universal healthcare, rent controls, price controls and a minimum wage. The bonds between the ideologies were such that in 1934 Hitler gloated to an enthusiastic Mussolini that 'Capitalism has run its course'.[41] In its financial basis, as in so many other aspects, Nazi Germany was the antithesis of right-wing values.

Given their message, populist policies, vivid appeals and strong, charismatic leadership, it is little wonder that the Nazis began to accrue considerable working class support in Germany. The party's voters were initially drawn from the proletarian class, and it inspired little bourgeois or aristocratic interest. As the movement grew, two distinct groups emerged within its ranks. One was centred in Munich and sought to represent the likes of artisans and lower middle class shopkeepers. The north was dominated by a much larger youth movement that focused on hostility to big corporations, department stores and finance capital. It called for a revolution in social reform and an appeal to the working man. But the groups were united in favouring dictatorship over democracy and by a rabid anti-Semitism. The most prominent figure in the northern faction was Gregor Strasser who gathered a clique around himself that included his brother Otto as well as Heinrich Himmler and Joseph Goebbels. Their National Socialism focused on anti-capitalism and demanded the nationalisation of heavy industry, profit-sharing and land reform. Strasser wrote that 'We National Socialists are enemies, deadly enemies, of the present capitalist system with its exploitation of the economically weak...and we are resolved under all circumstances to destroy this system'.[42] Goebbels also attacked 'the money pigs of capitalist democracy'.[43] Goebbels had initially been attracted to Bolshevism while Julius Streicher had started out in the German Socialist party. He only joined the Nazis after seeing Hitler speak and ended up running their paper, *Der Stürmer*.

Hitler did not fully commit to the northern faction's programme, but he did not repudiate it either. This 'party within a party' became so influential that he was forced to see off a challenge to his leadership and authority from Strasser and subsequently felt compelled to put Strasser and Goebbels in charge of propaganda, an indication of the significance of their manifesto. It was a part of the movement that never really went away and even when he provoked WWII the Führer did so by employing the vernacular of class war, characterising the fight against Britain as one 'between those who have been through the Adolf Hitler schools and those who have been at Eton'.

The Nazis, knowing their audience and appeals, opened up 'cells' in working class institutions, effectively their own form of trade unions, and agitated for and supported strikes. Hitler hoped to unify Germany by eradicating class differences and at the conclusion of his speeches he would call to 'workers, blue collar or white!' But, ever the pragmatist, Hitler, who knew his party needed votes before they could exercise influence, looked for any avenue to exploit. He tried to court businesses by focusing on his determination to defeat Marxism and restore German fortunes, but had little success. The 1928 election produced a disappointing return for the Nazis but showed a surprising level of support in the countryside which Hitler quickly exploited. But it was the re-focus of attacks on big business in 1929-33 that gave the decisive boost to their electoral success. Many have suggested that the Nazi movement was heavily financed by the capitalist purse prior to 1933. But this is a largely false claim with little evidence to support it.

The economic growth of the latter part of the Weimar period meant that few were receptive to the Nazi message in the late '20s, but the financial meltdown that hit Germany in the wake of the Wall Street Crash saw a massive spike in their appeal. The period of the Depression was ideal ground for the sort of irrational fears and hysterical beliefs that Hitler specialised in and his constant focus on 'Germans' transcended the class boundaries that limited Communist appeal. The party began to accrue considerable lower-middle class support while his image of a dynamic leader who would replace the failed committees and coalitions of Weimar Germany was also politically seductive. Hitler was always vague in his specific policies, he could more effectively keep the loyalty of the party faithful that way, but he repeatedly denounced 'the system' and spoke of his desire to destroy it. For the Nazis were, at their very core, an anti-establishment revolutionary movement.

Hitler had, in the wake of the abortive Munich Putsch, always been clear that he was determined to gain power by legal means but sought to rip up the constitution once he had done so. In the Leipzig trial of 1930 he made it plain that 'The constitution only marks out the arena of battle, not the goal. We enter the legal agencies and in that way will make our party the determining factor. However, once we possess the constitutional power we will mould the state into the shape we hold to be suitable'.[44] In fact, Hitler had been clear about this intention since at least 1923 when declaring in *Mein Kampf* that any participation in parliamentary democracy was 'only for the purpose of destroying this institution from within'.[45] Goebbels had voiced similar sentiments in 1928 when he wrote an article warning that 'We go into the Reichstag in order to acquire the weapons of democracy from its arsenal. We become Reichstag deputies in order to paralyse the Weimar democracy with its own assistance'.[46]

Yet to do so he first needed a parliamentary majority, and by the 1930s it had become apparent that Hitler was attempting to find a compromise that would give his party the broadest possible appeal. To this end he made clear his intent to rein in the extreme left of the party. Otto Strasser, Gregor's younger brother, maintained an independent radical line which particularly irritated Hitler. On 21 May 1930 they met in an attempt to reconcile their differences. Strasser criticised the leader by declaring 'You want to strangle the social revolution, for the sake of legality and your new collaboration with the bourgeois parties of the right'.[47] It was the worst insult one Nazi could hurl at another. Hitler reassured him of his commitment to socialism, but when Strasser asked him if he would work with Krupp Steel if he came to power, Hitler replied: 'Of course I should leave it alone. Do you think that I should be so mad as to destroy Germany's economy? Only if people should fail to act in the interests of the nation then – and only then – would the State intervene. But for that you do not need an expropriation...you need only a strong State.'[48] Having failed to reach an accord, Otto was turned out of the party and politically abandoned by his brother.

Despite this schism the Nazi message still focused on anti-capitalist rhetoric, a line that proved increasingly persuasive as the Depression tightened its grip. They were also seen as being the only party who could truly stand up to the Communists, and with the spectre of Bolshevism looming ever larger, and rumours from Russia growing ever more alarming, the image was a significant asset to the Nazi cause. The combination of these factors, and the ever-deepening crisis in Germany, saw the Nazis swept to power in 1933. Hitler swiftly made good on his promises and dismantled the constitution before establishing an effective dictatorship. But to consolidate his rule it was essential for the Führer to deal with the radical elements in his own party. Gregor Strasser was driven from the ranks in 1933, but the real purge would have to wait until the following year.

Ernst Röhm, the head of the SA, was set on using his Brownshirts for 'completing the National Socialist revolution' and dismissed any who resisted such calls as 'bourgeois simpletons'.[49] The radicalism and rebelliousness of the SA posed a threat to Hitler's authority, but their manifesto of working class agitation against privileged elites, entirely leftist in its origin, had sat comfortably in the Nazi movement. Hitler hoped to find the balance between such conflicting interests and reconcile both radical and conservative thought with Nazism. Röhm, for his part, sneered at the manner in which Hitler conciliated and colluded with the establishment, but his idealism put him at loggerheads with the Führer who had a far more realistic approach to government. The real issue though was how the thuggish behaviour of the Brownshirts offended the sense of decency and respect for order of most middle class Germans. Hitler's true focus was on strength, unity and Germany's industrial and military might. As such, civil strife threatened to disrupt his plans. Hitler, whose loyalty had to be to the army, was hardly reassured by Röhm's declaration that the SA were 'the destiny of Germany'.[50]

A conspiracy of a planned violent overthrow was concocted and, on 30 June 1934, in what became famous as the Night of the Long Knives, those alleged to be at its head were shot. Perhaps 200 were killed including Röhm, Gregor Strasser, von Schleicher and von Kahr. All were considered more of a threat than the conservative elements who Hitler despised but was confident he could control. Germany's new dictator was open about his responsibility for the event and was widely acclaimed for his boldness, patriotism and commitment to order. The fact that he had turned on the combustible elements in his own organisation gave the impression that he prioritised Germany and its military over his personal interests. Just a few weeks later von Hindenburg died and the offices of Chancellor and President were combined in the shape of the Führer. The collapse of the SA allowed for the rise of the SS, a far more disciplined force, committed to Hitler and destined for historical infamy.

Hitler's appeals prior to 1933 were obvious, even though his manifesto of dismantling the Weimar Republic, repudiating Versailles, cancelling reparation payments, rebuilding the German army into a formidable force, reversing the nation's dramatic economic decline and embarking on a massive programme of job creation, appeared an impossible dream. When, after finally being appointed Chancellor, he achieved all his objectives in a remarkably short period of time he must have appeared, to many Germans at least, like some sort of saviour. It must surely have become easier for moderate Germans, who had endured two disastrous decades, to gloss over the unsavoury aspects of his regime. But even as his support continued to grow Hitler's next concern, having dealt with the radical wing of his own party, was in handling the conservative elements whose support would help him realise his ambitions. Hitler needed to tread carefully on this issue. Even after his purges hostility to big business continued to enjoy widespread support in the party's ranks, while the distrust of large department stores and consumer co-operatives was synonymous with the anti-Semitism at the party's heart. Goebbels had made this issue transparent when declaring that 'As socialists, we are opponents of the Jews, because we see in the Hebrews the incarnation of capitalism, of the misuse of the nation's goods'.

But Hitler's programme prioritised militarism alongside unity and racial purity. So Germany's industrial class were as essential for his plans as the proletariat. With re-armament and the restoration of German prestige among his top priorities he settled on an economic model that effectively adopted fiscal policies from both left and right. Large state-driven operations were introduced while private enterprise was encouraged to flourish alongside them. The mixed economy adopted by the Nazis meant that, in peacetime, their state was considerably more efficient and productive in the manufacturing and financial sectors, and also significantly less punitive, than the Soviet Union.

But while Germany's new leader was willing to reach an accommodation with the established elites, he was equally keen that such an agreement would not be permanent. To this end he resisted pressure for the Enabling Law to be replaced by a new constitution, and when he felt his regime was sufficiently established he severed the ties that had helped cement it in the first place. For while Hitler had no hesitation in using them for his own benefit, as a tool with which he could advance his radical agenda, he had nothing but distaste for the traditional ruling classes, though he did admire entrepreneurs like Porsche and the Junkers family, the aviation magnates. Private enterprise was encouraged as long as it served the state, but the Nazis also confiscated a number of prosperous assets, particularly in Austria and Czechoslovakia, with the Rothschilds and Skoda among their principal victims. In the event though, Germany's economic turnaround was primarily sparked by Hitler's massive state-sponsored programme of re-armament, thus hitting two of his principal targets with a single stroke.

The Führer got the chance to test the effectiveness of his re-armament programme in the Spanish Civil War of 1936-9. In many ways the dress rehearsal for WWII, it was perceived at the time as being a straightforward clash between right and left. It is not quite so simple. Franco's regime bore many similarities to Italian Fascism, even if it relied heavily on allegiance to the Church and Spain's traditional ruling elites. It had also, up to that point, been widely accepted that Hitler was a socialist, even if he was considered an undesirable and uninvited guest by many of that persuasion. Yet the change in perception to viewing him as right, and Stalin as left, was a dramatic one. George Watson's conclusion is that this 'sudden shift of view has not been explained, and perhaps cannot be explained, except on grounds of argumentative convenience. A single binary opposition like cops-and-robbers or cowboys-and-Indians is always satisfying.'[51] In reality, that shift in perception arose as a result of Stalinist propaganda. Uncle Joe took to casting all his opponents as 'fascists', even Trotsky who was accused of plotting a 'fascist coup'. The radical leftists who had flocked to his banner simply recast all their rivals as 'right-wing'. It was a baseless definition that stuck in the public consciousness and remains as robust as it was decades ago, yet it is a complete misrepresentation of actual events. Years later Hitler even told Albert Speer that if the Spanish Civil War began again he would side with the idealistic Reds rather than the reactionary Catholicism of Franco. Perhaps subsequent events had forced a sharp change of mind.

At the time though Hitler gave his backing to the Nationalists but his chief priority was in prolonging the conflict rather than ensuring a speedy and emphatic victory for their cause. After all, the longer the war dragged on, the more it distracted the other European powers from his re-armament. Stalin provided much military help too, but the deciding factor was the inevitable lack of unity in the Soviet-backed Republican camp. The leftists expended nearly as much energy fighting each-other as they did their opponents, shooting thousands of members of their own side, while Franco's cause was far more united and effective. The victor's regime proved undeniably distasteful, but atrocities were committed by both sides, and no one can know what would have happened had the Republicans triumphed instead. Considering the track record of far-left regimes, it is easy to imagine that it may have been even worse.

Much of the Republicans' hostility focused on their opposition to religion and their anti-Catholic manifesto. As the war progressed they destroyed countless churches and even exhumed, exposed and mocked the bodies of nuns, priests and monks. They also murdered a further 6,000 members of the clergy, perhaps the grisliest ecumenical slaughter since the St. Bartholomew's Day Massacre. Republican death squads went on to butcher some 55,000 civilians in total, though even more decisive were the repeated and bloody purges carried out within their ranks. When they had taken Barcelona the leftists gave an indication of Spain's future should they triumph. Red banners were draped everywhere while revolutionary songs and slogans blared out of loudspeakers. A certain mode of dress, behaviour and speech was expected, and conformity was demanded. All the churches were gutted or destroyed, and massive bonfires built of their art and treasures. There was no private property, all businesses had been collectivised, all cars commandeered, and the press subjected to strict censorship. There were terrible shortages and long queues for bread. The radicals brimmed with certainty that they were right about everything, yet they were divided into some fifteen different factions. Suspicions about traitors reached such a manic intensity that an oppressive shroud hung over the city, and debate was abandoned in favour of denunciation.

The Communists particularly turned on POUM (Workers' Party of Marxist Unification) – a quasi-Trotskyite organisation. Trotskyists were accused of being Fascists in the pay of Franco and Hitler, lies which were repeated throughout the communist press. The *Daily Worker* was particularly enthusiastic in its denunciations while the *New Statesman* refused to print George Orwell's articles on Spain. They feared the accuracy of his reports might undermine the socialist cause. Thousands of suspects were slung in gaols by the secret police and huge numbers disappeared or were shot. The purges in Spain happened at the same time as those in Russia, and under the same pretext. But, despite the sordid reality, the conflict excited the enthusiasm of intellectuals across Europe as a 'just war'. While the Nationalists were the aggressors, starting the war against the democratically elected Republic, it is rarely so cut and dried. Civil conflicts, removed from the distasteful connotations of international and imperialist wars are frequently subject to such simplistic revisionism by left-wing academia. The net result was that a significant number of idealists journeyed to Spain to join in the fighting. It would, for example, be almost impossible to find a more thoughtful, decent and humanitarian representative of the left than Orwell, yet he too, before becoming disenchanted with the violent divisions of the Republican cause, set off for Spain to shoot enemies he had dehumanised as 'Fascists'.

Hitler's regime, which grew in authority between 1933 and 1939, was established in the same period that Stalin exerted an ever firmer grip of his own state. But the use of terror during peacetime in Nazi Germany was, in comparison to the Soviet example, virtually non-existent. Even as late as 1937 just 7,500 had passed through the German camps – a total that bears little relation to the 29 million imprisoned under Stalin. The death toll of the Nazi system peaked at an absolute maximum of 2,000 prior to the outbreak of WWII. While this is extraordinarily high when compared to most states, it is paltry in comparison to most socialist states. Even with the Jews, while the propaganda machine was ramped up to encourage hatred of the 'vermin', the actual persecution of them as a minority was relatively slight prior to 1939. Such observations are advanced, not to defend the abhorrent Nazi regime in any way, but to offer some perspective between that infamous state and those of a more overtly left-wing origin.

It all changed in the 1940s of course and the crimes committed in that decade have a well-deserved reputation as perhaps the darkest period in history. It really all started years before that though with that all-consuming hatred expressed by the advocates of National Socialism, and the casual acceptance of it by wider society. That is how it always begins – with pathological resentment on the one hand and a tepid indifference, a lack of opposition on the other. It was that loathing, tacitly encouraged, condoned or ignored, that created the Holocaust, and the same culture facilitated the cruelty of the camps. It was an animus, let us not forget, informed by a hatred of bankers, capitalists, Zionists and newspaper moguls, for when hatred is directed at the 'strong' who will leap to their defence? But this is its result, and as long as this enmity endures there remains the possibility that such horrors will surface once more.

That culture of hatred took root, and from that foundation the Holocaust was allowed to gain momentum. It happened gradually, incrementally, and the population of Germany, blinded by the tacit acceptance of the hate that was nurtured in the nation's breast, sleepwalked into it in stages. In 1933 Jews were barred from jobs in teaching, the civil service and in journalism, the sort of careers where they may be able to influence the opinions of others. The persecution increased in 1935 when the Nuremberg Laws prohibited Jews from marrying or having sexual relations with German citizens, but it was not until 1937, and Kristallnacht, that widespread violence was employed for the first time. It would still take a further five years, and the experience of the greatest war in human history, before the Holocaust began in earnest though, and all of this came only after years of propaganda had, drop by drop, turned the majority population more and more against the minority in their midst. It must also be remembered that the Nazis had engendered remarkable economic benefits and worked miracles on the pride of the nation, after decades of defeat, depression and appalling privation. The temptation to turn a blind eye to the distasteful aspects of the regime must have been high.

Even as late as 1939 the policy line with regard to the Jewish 'problem' still prioritised resettlement, with Madagascar selected as the most likely target. The difficulties of logistics and financing such an operation made its realisation unlikely and the outbreak of war made it impossible. But the annexation of Poland meant the Nazis could now resettle the Jews on their doorstep. With the onset of war attitudes to life and death suffered an abrupt readjustment; and prioritising the Jewish refugees for food and adequate medical care over the German people and, particularly, the Wehrmacht, became increasingly difficult to justify. In consequence, mortality rates in the Jewish ghettoes began to rocket. The escalation of the conflict following the launch of Operation Barbarossa in 1941, and the extermination squads employed in the east, resulted in opposition to the Holocaust, which was finally rolled out in 1942, being relatively minimal. By the time hostilities reached sickening new levels in the war against Russia, the acceptance of Jewish life as comparatively cheap had been incrementally established in German society for a number of years.

But then the twin policies of sterilisation and euthanasia, established nearly a decade before the gas chambers opened, had significantly eroded attitudes to life and death long before that period, and the gradual acceptance of such ideas certainly smoothed the progression to the Holocaust. This agenda, though it is little known today after an almost complete historical whitewash, also had its roots in the left and enjoyed broad support among the ranks of the socialist intelligentsia. There was widespread agreement that to make the perfect society it would be necessary to weed out 'undesirable' elements. After all, it was said, feckless people bred more than the accomplished and they would pollute the gene pool were their numbers not rigorously controlled. The idea, once arrived at, resulted in a series of increasingly alarming suggestions. In 1933 George Bernard Shaw, the luvvies' socialist champion of the day, had written extensively on the benefits of socialists killing anyone not useful to the nation. He primarily meant capitalists, who were irredeemable, but was also enthusiastic about extending the policy to anyone considered a burden on the state. He considered the suggestion 'quite reasonable and very necessary' and hoped 'to discover a humane gas that will kill instantly and painlessly: in short a gentlemanly gas – deadly by all means, but humane, not cruel'.[52]

Shaw and Beatrice Webb, with whom he was in correspondence, agreed that ethnic cleansing and the extermination of the unfit were essential parts of the socialist programme. Both she, and her husband Sidney, did not just favour the liquidation of 'enemies of the people', they also sneered at the 'squeamishness' of those opposed to such measures. Beatrice would hardly have protested when, in a letter to her on 6 February 1938, Shaw defended 'the right of States to make eugenic experiments by weeding out any strains that they think undesirable'.[53] The support for this manifesto was so widespread on the left that in 1931 the *New Statesman* despaired of the 'most intransigent opponents of eugenics [as being]...amongst those who cling to the individualist views of parenthood and family economics'.[54] The same article proudly noted how those who championed the elimination of the genetically weak were a who's who of Britain's leading social democratic intellectuals like the Webbs, John Maynard Keynes and 'even' the *Manchester Guardian*. Bertrand Russell had also, rather more moderately, proposed that the state issue colour-coded procreation tickets to prevent the dilution of the elite's gene pool. Virginia Woolf was just as enthusiastic about socialist euthanasia. Her diary entry of 9 January 1915 recorded her thoughts on seeing a number of mentally handicapped people, concluding that 'It was perfectly horrible. They should certainly be killed'.[55]

The Fabian Society, the British socialist organisation that effectively gave birth to the Labour party, also supported eugenics and the forced sterilisation of society's undesirables. The list of those who shared this goal is long indeed. William Beveridge, the progressive liberal whose report served as the basis for the welfare state introduced under Labour after WWII, was a keen eugenicist, as was Julian Huxley. Marie Stopes, the birth control pioneer, advocated the policy, as did Margaret Sanger, her even more lauded and 'problematic' American contemporary. Sanger, a committed socialist from a young age, was not just a eugenicist but an outspoken racist too. Her 'Negro Project' sought to limit population growth in 'inferior stocks' of the black population. *Birth Control Review*, the magazine she edited, published numerous articles on Germany's programme and printed pieces by a number of significant Nazis, including Ernst Rüdin, Hitler's director of sterilisation and founder of the Nazi Society for Racial Hygiene.

Justice Holmes, the progressive judge, and Democratic President Woodrow Wilson were both keen American eugenicists, as were Theodore Roosevelt, Alexander Graham Bell and the scientists at the Carnegie Institution. But G.K. Chesterton was subjected to heaps of derision for opposing the policy held by nearly all 'thinking people'. From 1907, thirty-two American states passed sterilisation laws and over 60,000 US citizens were sterilised. Canada and much of Europe followed suit. Many of the programmes were predicated on grounds of race, and the majority had commenced long before Hitler came to power in 1933. Euthanasia and sterilisation were so popular on the left that they were even practised by Swedish Democrats up until the 1950s. The policies adopted by the Nazis thus had widespread support among progressive intellectuals. The mainstream acceptance of these ideas certainly encouraged Hitler in putting them into practice.

The full truth of the matter is even more shocking though; for socialism had long advocated not just these nauseating policies but had also crossed the line into recommending genocide. George Watson's remarkable study, *The Lost Literature of Socialism*, is particularly informative on this topic. His conclusion, after exhaustive research, is that 'In the European century that began in the 1840s, from Engels's article of 1849 down to the death of Hitler, everyone who advocated genocide called himself a socialist, and no exception has been found'.[56] In the article that he refers to, published in Marx's *Neue Rheinische Zeitung* in January 1849, Engels, in writing on the Hungarian War, had called for the extermination of small nations and recommended the liquidation of Serbs,

Slavs, Basques, Bretons and Scottish Highlanders. He regarded such races as embodying counter-revolution that threatened the socialist future and claimed the 'next world war will result in the disappearance from the face of the earth not only of reactionary classes and dynasties, but also of entire reactionary peoples. And that, too, is a step forward.'[57]

H.G. Wells also supported socialist and ethic genocide, as did his Californian equivalent, Jack London, the overt racist who persuaded boxing champion James J. Jeffries to come out of retirement to 'wipe the golden smile off the face of that nigger' Jack Johnson and save the white race. Wells wrote *Anticipations of the Reaction of Mechanical and Scientific Progress Upon Human Life and Thought* in 1902. Like most progressive thinkers of the day he was adamant that if a new order was to be created then the lowest, most unproductive classes needed to be culled. For him, this vision rested on largely racial lines.

'And how will the new republic treat the inferior races? How will it deal with...those swarms of black, and brown, and dirty-white, and yellow people, who do not come into the needs of the new efficiency? Well, the world is not a charitable institution and I take it they will have to go. The whole tenor and meaning of the world, as I see it, is that they have to go...it is their portion to die out and disappear'.

By Hitler's time then, the association between socialism and genocide was universally understood and widely recommended. There was no real doubt about whether Hitler was a socialist either. Harold Nicolson was among the first students of Fascism and concluded of Nazism that 'it is certainly a socialist experiment in that it destroys individuality'.[58] He judged it to be a kind of militarised socialism while Julian Huxley, the half-brother of Aldous, concluded that Fascism was 'a short cut towards the unified Socialist state which should be our goal'.[59] A 'short cut' it may have been, and there were fears that it could give socialism a bad name, but no contemporary suggested that the movement was conservative or right-wing in any way. The leftist German poet Horst Wessel, an avid supporter of Nazism who was christened a 'Socialist Christ' by Goebbels, would certainly have agreed. In *The Lion and the Unicorn* (1941) George Orwell, who harboured no doubt that Nazi Germany was economically socialist, argued that the speedy collapse of France the previous year demonstrated that competition was inefficient and that socialism was superior to capitalism. The event proved to him that 'A planned economy is stronger than a planless one'.[60] The West, he argued, should learn from Hitler's example that planning works and the chaotic scramble of the free market does not. Orwell further claimed that any who argued that the Nazis were not socialists were simply in denial of an incontrovertible truth.

It was Germany that had led the way in socialism from around 1830-1920, so its influence on Nazism is hardly surprising. Indeed the movement had evolved from the socialist doctrines of Fichte, Lassalle, Paul Lensch and Oswald Spengler, as well as Johann Plenge, an admirer of the utopian idealism of H.G. Wells. He argued that, in order to succeed, socialism must become a form of power politics. Drieu la Rochelle, the noted writer and intellectual, switched his allegiance from Communism to Fascism as he perceived the latter a better bet for imposing the international socialism he craved, while Max Eastman, W.H. Chamberlain, Peter Drucker and F.A. Voight all concluded the essentially identical nature of Fascism and Communism in the 1930s. Friedrich Hayek had done the same in devastating fashion and concluded that 'Few are ready to recognise that the rise of Fascism and Nazism was not a reaction against the socialist trends of the preceding period, but a necessary outcome of those tendencies'.[61] He also poured scorn on the already growing idea that Nazism came from the right. That concept had developed from a rift between rival socialist factions with the losing side tarring the other, as they always do, as right-wing fascists.

But while numerous academics foresaw the dangers of collectivism these conclusions are not entirely satisfactory. While Hitler took a class-based approach during his political rise his outlook was predominantly nationalist, and if his later state was based on social planning his approaches to agencies on both left and right reveal the truth about the Nazi regime. The reality is that it was not truly of either wing. While ideologically he certainly leaned very much more left than right, what primarily motivated Hitler was racism, a pathological xenophobia that over-rode all other considerations. To this end he would adopt any pragmatic course that would help to implement his deranged schemes. As his particular brand of anti-Semitism had primarily economic origins he commenced from a purely leftist point of view. But, despite his megalomania and a loathing of the Jews that bordered on insanity, Hitler was no dummy. He was also not handcuffed by the rigid ideology of the Communist states. As such, when he approached power he realised how the agencies of the right, Germany's aristocratic and manufacturing elite, would be useful in helping realise his ambitions. They could help establish the financial, industrial and military platform on which all his other dreams depended. So his stance shifted, he was able to absorb and utilise Germany's existing mercantile and social structures to roll out his ideological model across the nation. It was his maxim, after all, that it was necessary to 'evolve or die'. Evolve he did, and the hard left of his own party, constrained by ideological and inflexible dogmatism, were to pay the price by not following his lead and failing to adapt.

Yet, while he was willing to crush the extreme left-wing of his party, the debt he owed to the ideology was undeniable. Hitler's socialism was economically radical while, in his veneration of the *Germania*, he lionised a noble past that had been corrupted and degraded by capitalism into a selfish and avaricious state. There is nothing of Burke in Hitler's musings, but there is an awful lot of Rousseau, Paine and Marx. Like those writers he looked back to a flinty ideal where virtue and courage reigned, one that predated property and civilisation. He was also influenced by Darwin, and Marx again, in believing that society could be scientifically planned, objective knowledge was a bourgeois illusion, democracy was an optimistic phase whose time was up, and entire species could be dispensed with if they conflicted with the demands of history. Hitler confessed to Hermann Rauschning in 1933 that 'I have learnt a great deal from Marx',[62] while also concluding that their differences were more tactical than ideological. He declared 'I have put into practice what those peddlers and pen-pushers have timidly begun'.[63]

His socialism diverged from the Soviet example as, rather than dividing the German state through civil strife and the expropriation of property, Hitler sought to unite and strengthen it. The later alliance between the two powers, while largely a marriage of convenience, also suggests there was still some remnant of empathy between them, even allowing for the ultimate savagery of the Nazi invasion. C.P. Snow, the novelist and Soviet sympathiser, demurred on the Nazi-Soviet Pact that 'Two political sophisticates were always likely to get together'.[64] Even when war between them became inevitable Goebbels excitedly recorded his hopes for the invasion in his diary on 16 June 1941. There would be no return to the Tsars after Bolshevism was overthrown; *true* socialism would take its place.

It had widely been felt that their pact would allow socialism to bleed capitalism white, a result that appeared to many on the left as a most desirable scenario. While some despaired of the turn of events the Dean of Canterbury welcomed the news while G.D.H. Cole, the Oxford professor, wrote in the *New Statesman* that since all morality is class morality it was 'justifiable and necessary for the proletariat to use any method, and to take any action, that would help it to victory over its class enemies'.[65] Both states were to follow this advice to its inevitable end and, following the signing of the accord, the Nazis learned much from their more experienced partners. It is widely believed that the Soviet massacre at Katyn, and other atrocities like the shooting of 5,000 Polish officers in Smolensk in April 1940, may have inspired the later policy of mass shootings adopted by the Nazis. In his memoirs, Pjotr Grigorenko also claims that the Soviets were killing people with exhaust fumes some ten years before the Nazis employed the technique as a precursor to the gas chambers. Rudolf Höss wrote his own account, *Commandant of Auschwitz*, and recalled just how impressed the Nazis had been with the Soviet camp system. He was also clear on how much it influenced their approach in dealing with the Jews.

The reasons why the Holocaust happened, or was allowed to happen, can largely be found in basic human psychology. There were many of course who willingly partook in the genocide because they were persuaded that the Jews truly deserved their fate, that they were a malign influence on society who fully merited the widespread hatred directed at them. Dr. Fritz Klein, in light of his profession, was asked to explain his actions at Auschwitz. He responded: 'Of course I am a doctor and I want to preserve life. And out of respect for human life, I would remove a gangrenous appendix from a diseased body. The Jew is the gangrenous appendix in the body of mankind'.[66] This is where hatred leads and Klein, like so many others, expressed no doubt that his actions were entirely moral and justified. Glover cited the importance that this sort of conviction played in the horrors of the 1940s. 'The belief system was central to Nazism...The beliefs motivated the repression of human responses and the erosion of people's previous moral identity. A new moral identity grew round acceptance of Nazi beliefs'.[67] Hitler spoke with religious reverence about this trait when declaring that 'It is our faith in our nation that has made us little people great, that has made us poor people rich, that has made us wavering, fearful, timid people brave and confident'.[68] Nazism was, in many ways, a religious movement rather than a political one. It relied on ritual, spectacle and reverential awe. It aspired to create mankind anew and called on its followers to unite and have pure faith in the justness of their cause.

The resultant herd mentality plays a pivotal role in human psychology. It too is a vital factor in understanding events in Nazi Germany. The majority of individuals find it difficult to deviate either from behaviour that most other people are engaged in or from what they feel is expected of them at any given time. It is a trait that explains not just the willing complicity of so many, but also the hate-filled rhetoric and regular mob violence of the contemporary movement. This herd mentality remains prevalent on the left where people love to gather in large crowds to protest some alleged injustice or other. Feeling oneself part of a movement is immensely empowering. Yet that feeling of strength and unity can all too quickly turn sour. For people feel entitled to unleash their violent instincts when part of a group – an impulse they restrain when acting individually. R. Niebuhr concluded that there is 'an increasing tendency among modern men to imagine themselves ethical because they have delegated their views to larger and larger groups'. Hayek argued that 'To act on behalf of a group seems to free people of many of the moral restraints which control their behaviour as individuals within the group'.[69]

This sort of compliance, a significant feature of the human psyche, has been scrutinised by numerous behavioural psychologists. Derren Brown has conducted tests, devised by Stanley Milgram, in which, when instructed to do so by a man in a white coat with a clipboard, people will believe that they are administering electric shocks to an individual who screams in pain whenever they press a button. Normal, decent members of the public carry on with the process until it appears they have killed the victim. In another experiment, which took less than an hour, Brown persuaded ordinary people to apparently push a man to his death from the roof of a tall building because the people around them encouraged them to do so. Adolf Eichmann, remember, offered the justification that everybody else was involved in the same process as the cornerstone of his defence. This compliance, this kind of social acceptance is key. In an interview with Gitta Sereny in 1971, Franz Stangl, the commandant of Treblinka, explained that the guards 'became conditioned to performing horrible tasks, so long as the horrors were sanctioned and encouraged and so long as the victims meant nothing to them 'personally' and could be thought of as outside the human race'.[70]

What also strikes when examining accounts from the period is the sheer mundanity of those involved. The psychologist Robert Jay Lipton, when commenting on Nazi horrors, warned that 'ordinary people can commit demonic acts'. Zygmunt Bauman concluded that 'The most frightening news brought about by the Holocaust and what we learned of its perpetrators was not the likelihood that 'this' could be done to us, but the idea that we could do it'.[71] Jonathan Glover also stressed how 'Hitler addressed psychological needs going beyond materialism and economics. People need a system of beliefs to make sense of the world and sometimes the most helpful system is a simple one'.[72]

This conditioning can prove extremely pervasive, especially in adolescent minds. In the '70s and '80s Jim Keegstra, a Christian teacher in Eckville, Alberta, Canada, indoctrinated his students in anti-Semitism and an appreciation for Nazism. Keegstra had decided that in denying Christ was God the Jews were calling God a liar, so he 'educated' his students in the Jewish-world conspiracy. One of his pupils dutifully wrote that 'Hitler was one of the most successful people in the world ever to go against the Jews. If people would have been listening, he could have rid the world of the Jews for ever. It's funny how people never want to hear the truth'. Keegstra had added the comment 'But the Jews control the press, mass media and the propaganda'. Others believed that Jews had assassinated Lincoln and travelled around in large gangs bashing in children's heads, raping and drowning women and disembowelling men before leaving them to bleed to death. A student felt 'In my opinion, this must come to a dead halt...We must get rid of every Jew in existence so we may live in peace and freedom'.[73] After Keegstra was sacked his replacement found his brainwashed students rejected the evidence of the death camps and any theories that contradicted his views as part of a conspiracy. Remarkably, almost identical sentiments about a 'Zionist press' remain common on the hard left today.

Anti-Semitism and the Left

It would be tempting, and at least partly true, to argue that the modern left has nothing in common with Nazism. As much as it is based in bigotry, and as widespread are its declarations of hate, the contemporary left does not tend towards racism. Its prejudices are of a different hue. However, if one scratches the surface, it quickly becomes clear that the connections are rather more than skin deep. The reality is that the modern strain of anti-Semitism, quite distinct from the religious prejudice directed against 'evil Jews' that dominated in the Middle Ages, originated around the same time as socialism. It has been inextricably bound up with it ever since. Both phenomena were born in the late eighteenth century, blooming during the French Revolution, when suspicions arose over dubious relations between Jewish finance and nation states. In the hysteria of that period conspiracy theories about the evil machinations of the super-rich were enthusiastically devoured. These shadowy tales gripped the imagination. The rumours quickly coalesced into a popular view that a Rothschild backed conspiracy pulled the strings of government and finance behind the scenes.

Having emerged first in France these tall tales soon gained a foothold in the wider cultural psyche where they have never really gone away. They spread quickly from France to Germany so Hitler, in spouting the bile that filled the pages of *Mein Kampf*, was maintaining an identifiably left-wing tradition, even if the racial undertones which informed his worldview added a relatively new dimension to that characteristically economic strain of prejudice. Worryingly, the belief in a powerful clique of Zionists and financiers, who manipulate the press and subvert governments, is resurgent on the left once more. It is a story that has lasted since the late eighteenth century and survives today in a form instantly recognisable as the same prejudice spouted by Marx and Hitler, one that shows no signs of abating at all.

Among the 'pioneers' of the first wave of anti-Semitic French leftists was Charles Fourier. He was one of the true founders of socialism, and regarded trade, which he associated with the Jews, as 'the source of all evil'. In his perfect socialist society communities were to be divided into *phalansteries* of 1,620 individuals, micro-communes where Jews were to be dragooned in to do the menial farm work and manual labour, rather like the Spartans' slave population of Helots. David Aberbach argues that for Fourier 'the Jews were the leprosy of society, unalterably dishonest, unworthy of French citizenship'.[74] But other

French socialists, like Jules Michelet and Pierre-Joseph Proudhon, were equally robust anti-Semites. Michelet, the pre-eminent nineteenth century French historian, wrote widely in the 1830s and '40s expressing his hatred for the Jewish economic elite, particularly the Rothschild family. Yet Proudhon went even further, suggesting that Jews should be 'exterminated'.[75] Hatred of materialism, widespread in French socialism during and after the Revolution, associated Judaism, and financiers like the Rothschilds, with the capitalism they opposed. The reality, as ever, diverged sharply from the hysterical paranoia. Aberbach's exhaustive study reveals that the vast majority of capitalists at the time were Christians and that over 60% of French Jews died as paupers.

The ideas persisted though, and in 1853 the French writer Joseph Arthur, Comte de Gabineau, produced an *Essay on the Inequality of the Human Races* which enshrined this cultural hatred in racial terms. He recast the difference between the Jew and the Gentile as one that was less doctrinal and more biological. Having become embedded in France this anti-Semitic branch of socialism, and particularly its new more overtly racist strain, quickly spread to Germany. Johann Gottlieb Fichte, among the major theorists of modern liberalism, formulated his most significant theories from around 1797. Anti-Semitism formed an integral component of his philosophy, and the majority of his socialist brethren, like the rabidly anti-Semitic Karl Dühring, proved sympathetic to such views. Bruno Bauer argued that Europe's future lay in a struggle between the inferior Slavic people and the superior Germanic race. He claimed that Jews were alien to Germany and should be barred from citizenship.

Karl Marx, as we have seen, broadly shared the opinions of his socialist peers. From August 1842 he eagerly devoured all the anti-Semitic articles of Hermes, the editor of the *Kölnische Zeitung*, who advocated a system of apartheid in Germany. Marx had been furnished with these essays by Oppenheim and in November, his appetite for such fare apparently un-sated, he also read the anti-Semitic tracts published by Bruno Bauer in Ruge's *Deutsche Jahrbücher*. In a letter to Engels in 1862 Marx commented on Ferdinand Lassalle that

'he stems from the Negroes who joined the march of Moses out of Egypt. (If his mother or grandmother on his father's side did not mate with a nigger). Now this combination of Jewry and Germanism with the negroid basic substance must bring a peculiar product. The pushiness of this lad is also nigger-like'.[76]

The more evidence of this nature that is unearthed the less surprising it seems that Hitler, who grew up in the wake of this culture, developed such twisted opinions. Marx shared with Hitler a hatred of Russians and Slavs, people he believed were inferior, while desiring a war of conquest between Germany and Russia. As Hitler later freely admitted, he did indeed learn much from Marx. But the culture of Jewish socialists who denounced their own kind was not restricted to Marx. It was part of a long tradition that included Heine, Boerne and Karl Kraus too, all outspoken anti-Semites.

By the nineteenth century it had become an accepted maxim that a Jewish secret society had either ruled or aspired to rule the world since antiquity. Around the time of the 1848 revolutions it was widely suggested that war in Europe was waged purely on the whims of the house of Rothschild. If they decreed that conflict was financially injurious to their interests then it would not happen. Mikhail Bakunin was another icon of the left persuaded in the truth of the Rothschild myth. He believed they controlled global events behind the scenes and declaimed on 'This whole Jewish world which constitutes a single exploiting sect, a sect of bloodsucker people, a collective parasite, voracious, organised in itself, not only across the frontiers of states but even across all the differences of political opinion'.[77] Views of this ilk were so pervasive that they influenced historians like J.A Hobson who in 1905 declared 'Does any one seriously suppose that a great war could be undertaken by any European state, or a great state loan subscribed, if the House of Rothschild and its connexions set their face against it?''[78]

In Germany and Austria the rise in anti-Semitism, which would prove so crucial in informing Nazism, was accelerated by the crash of 1873. Just as in 2008 the blame was placed on bankers and finance capital. Conspiracy theories about the shady activities of Jewish financiers rose sharply after the recession of 1873 and a hatred of bankers and Jews, widely viewed as parasites exploiting decent working people, became widespread. An influential spur in this belief was *The Way to Victory of Germanism over Judaism*, the 1879 book by Wilhelm Marr, a German atheist and radical leftist. Marr's tome, which first coined the phrase 'anti-Semitism', was an attempt to ground hatred of Jews in the progressive language of eugenics. The mania subsequently took a firm grip of the middle class leftist movement.

In Austria the decidedly left-wing German Liberal Party, under the leadership of Georg Ritter von Schoenerer, rallied support on a primarily anti-Semitic manifesto. His party had a particularly strong following in the universities where it was pivotal in forming the first student organisations. Both the student unions and the labour movement enthusiastically supported his opposition to the Rothschilds. They also admired his determination to wrest the train companies from their sphere of influence by nationalising the railways. Over 40,000 leftist agitators signed his petition which effectively proved the catalyst for modern anti-Semitism in Austria. Arendt was clear that Schoenerer 'was sincere beyond doubt...but developed quickly that Pan-German ideology which was to influence Nazism more deeply than any other German brand of antisemitism'.[79] It was on the left that these views proliferated. Ruth Fischer, the co-founder of the Austrian Communist Party, demanded action to 'Kick down the Jewish capitalists, hang them from the lampposts, and stamp upon them'.[80] The Christian-Socials under Karl Lueger, following a bitter contest for primacy with the socialist workers' movement, became another influential force in Austrian socialism. They helped keep the state's tradition for anti-Semitism alive. It was because of that tradition that in August 1920 Hitler declared to the NSDAP that 'if we are socialists, then we must definitely be anti-semites...How, as a socialist, can you not be an anti-semite?'[81] The assertion of that viewpoint won him thunderous applause.

In France, while there were conservative elements who defended the Jews, the radicals all but universally denounced them as the financial agents of the aristocracy. Anti-Semitic attitudes were wrapped up with anticlericalism, which still prevailed, and nineteenth century French socialism clung fervently to these traditions, at least until the shock of the Dreyfus Affair finally began to soften such ingrained attitudes. The prejudice was inspired by the usual hatred of bankers and Rothschilds and when, during the 1848 Revolution, Toussenel published *The Jews, Kings of the Era*, its acerbic sentiments were acclaimed across the left-wing press. But after that rebellion was crushed the next twenty years, under the autocratic right-wing rule of Napoleon III, proved an era of prosperity and security for the Jewish population of France, a return to the civic rights and opportunities they had enjoyed under Bonaparte.

The culture of anti-Semitism returned in a torrent following the collapse of his rule and the Communards' rising of 1871, and was still prevalent when the Dreyfus Affair broke in 1894. The scandal began when a Jewish officer of the French General Staff, Alfred Dreyfus, was accused of treason and collusion with Germany. The subsequent trial, itself a significant catalyst in sparking the movement of Zionism, polarised France. Initially the socialist and radical press, which was wholly anti-Jew, was particularly hostile. But as the case came to be seen as more of a *cause-célèbre*, a cudgel with which to beat the establishment, elements of the radical movement gradually shifted to the Dreyfus corner. Sections of the left still branded Dreyfus as 'the class enemy', but critics and supporters of the wronged officer could be found on both sides of the political divide. It must be conceded though that the two men who eventually proved to be his principal cheerleaders, Émile Zola and Georges Clemenceau, were of the left. It was the moment when the tide finally started to turn, especially when it was eventually revealed that all the evidence against Dreyfus had been fabricated by his superior officers, though that was not discovered until nearly a decade after he had been ruined by the allegations. It was this affair, and the baying French mobs it inspired, that persuaded Theodor Herzl to found the Zionist movement aimed at forging a safe haven for the world's Jews. Yet the first Zionist Congress of 1897 was still widely viewed as evidence of a Jewish world conspiracy. But while the Dreyfus incident had a remarkable effect on quelling anti-Semitism in France, it still persisted. Louis-Ferdinand Céline, a French left-wing writer of the 1930s, published tracts in 1938 calling for the extermination of the Jews as a race. Despite his appalling views contemporary left-wing figures like Will Self have continued to speak in Céline's defence, calling him ultimately 'triumphant'.

Despite the shift in public opinion, hatred of the Jews stubbornly clung on across the globe. In America the Populist leader, Tom Watson, an attorney and left-wing journalist, began his career in the 1890s as a defender of the rural poor who staunchly opposed banking and big business. Yet by 1914 his vision had morphed into one that was deeply anti-Semitic and characterised by some particularly vicious rhetoric. He was an outspoken opponent of 'Jewish money' while growing ever closer to the Socialist Party of America. In 1915 he whipped up a mob to lynch the Jewish factory foreman Leo Frank who had been wrongly accused of murdering an Irish girl. Father Charles Coughlin, a left-wing anti-capitalist demagogue and staunch supporter of FDR, was another influential conspiracy theorist and anti-Semite. But though his noxious views were common knowledge, he was regarded by establishment liberals as being 'on the side of the angels'.[82]

The left in Britain had proven stubborn too. In 1910-11, striking miners in Wales, urged on by their trade union bosses, attacked Jewish businesses in what was christened the 'Tredegar pogrom'. The likes of Virginia Woolf, Beatrice Webb and Vita Sackville-West of the Bloomsbury Set were still expressing disparaging sentiments about the Jews in the early twentieth century while Aldous Huxley, another left-leaning writer who flirted with their group, was frequently scathing about the Jews. He even christened the most unpleasant character in *Brave New World* 'Morgana Rothschild'. Sidney Webb had defended eugenics and predicted that a failure to follow the policy would result 'in this country gradually falling to the Irish and the Jews'.[83] The 1930s also saw the foundation of the British Union of Fascists under the former Labour MP Oswald Mosley. That movement, cemented in anti-Semitism, looked ridiculous to the inhabitants of the isle and provoked widespread derision. Many on the left though were attracted to his populist socialist message which opposed governments they claimed were in thrall to the wealthy few while demanding action over the housing conditions of the nation's poor. Moseley's calls for 'the conscious control and direction of human resources for human needs' still sound familiar today. It must be conceded though that the Labour party also played a significant role in rallying opposition to Britain's own anti-Semitic demagogue.

Yet, remarkably, sections of the left persisted in unsympathetic attitudes to Judaism after WWII. The plague even returned in the land that had been scarred by the Holocaust. The Polish Communist Party acted to expel the Jews from their territory, and when Christopher Hitchens visited some time later, a discussion with Jacek Kurón revealed the depths of anti-Semitism in the party's ranks.

'He showed me a violently Jew-hating letter...this time by hand, confessing that the first missive had been dictated to him in a police station! This showed a real sickness in the Communist system, not just because of the use of bigotry as a provocation, but because anti-Semitism had historically always been used by the Polish right wing against the Reds.'[84]

Rajani Palme Dutt, a major theorist of the Communist Party of Great Britain, gave indications of the opposition to Zionism that was to come when issuing a statement on Palestine in April 1947. He believed that the prospect of an Israeli state diverted Jewish people from 'the real solution of the problem of anti-Semitism, which is along the lines of democratic and full equality of rights in the countries in which they live'.[85] Unsurprisingly, in the wake of the ovens, demands to Jews that they should assimilate did not go down terribly well, but his comments seem excessively moderate in comparison to what followed in Russia. In his later years the increasingly anti-Semitic Stalin perceived a worldwide Zionist and capitalist conspiracy centred on a Wall Street that was infested with Jews. He also believed that 'Zionist agents of American imperialism' were responsible for decadence like modern art.

The mania of Stalin's later years began with paranoia over the independence of Tito's Yugoslavia which had thrown off the Nazis without any help from Moscow. Tito was quickly cast as an enemy in the mould of Trotsky and calls spread for a purge of his supporters across Eastern Europe. In September 1949 László Rajk, a veteran communist and the Hungarian Interior Minister, was put on a show trial in Budapest with seven others. In an echo of the Moscow tribunals of the '30s they enthusiastically confessed to being fascist spies and American agents before being shot. Worse soon followed in Czechoslovakia when Otto Sling and the General Secretary of the party, Rudolf Slánsky, were arrested with twelve others and charged with colluding with Tito and Western intelligence. The majority of those accused were Jewish and the trial, which began on 20 November 1952, took place just as Stalin's new hatred for Israel as an American vassal was becoming a mania. The charge of 'Zionist-Titoist-Western agent!' became an increasingly common one. All the Czech suspects publicly admitted their guilt and were hanged shortly afterwards. Arthur London, who survived the experience, recalled his interrogation at the hands of Major Smola who screamed 'We'll get rid of you and your filthy race. You're all the same. Not everything Hitler did was right, but he destroyed the Jews and he was right about that. Too many of you escaped the gas chamber. We'll finish what he started'.[86]

Stalin also grew to distrust the medical profession, as he considered it riddled with Jews, and launched violent purges against Soviet doctors. In the period of the 'Doctor's Plot' *Pravda* declared that the guilty parties, bought and paid for by American intelligence, were part of 'the international Jewish bourgeois-nationalist organisation called 'Joint'. The filthy face of this Zionist spy organisation, covering up their vicious actions under the mask of kindness, is now completely revealed'.[87] Had a stroke not abruptly ended Stalin's regime his pogrom against the Jews was likely to be as bloody as any unleashed while he was in power. He even planned to deport the entire Jewish population of the USSR to Siberia. But then this is the same man who had promised Ribbentrop, Nazi Germany's Foreign Minister, that he would remove Jews from all senior posts as soon as Gentile replacements could be found.

Yet contemporary anti-Semitism outlasted even that great ogre. The Soviets continued to persecute Jews while Communist agencies in France, Britain and across Europe dutifully echoed their sentiments. They also denounced any who raised objections as Zionist shills. Pat Sloan of the British Communist Party defended the purge and in *Labour Monthly* claimed that

> 'the Soviet Government did, in fact, nip a conspiracy in the bud. The recent announcement of the doctors' plot discovered in Moscow has so far run true to form...So let the Press shriek 'fantastic' and 'frame-up' and 'anti-Semitism'. We've had it all before. But the facts will show, as they have shown before, that drastic steps must sometimes be taken by a Socialist state against capitalist conspirators and their tools.'[88]

In the same issue Andrew Rothstein wrote an article to give a Jewish endorsement of the latest Soviet atrocity. He argued that the working class movement had never been welcomed by 'petty Jewish capitalists' who had now found an advantageous force in Zionism. He even claimed they had collaborated with the Nazis before throwing their lot in with America – effectively the highest bidder for their services. As a result

> 'Jewish millionaires in the USA took over in practice the leadership of the world Zionist organization. Hence when a plot involving Zionists was uncovered, neither it nor the shrieks of those determined to deny it was at all surprising...The Zionist leaders of this and other countries have rushed into the press to attack the Soviet Union for arresting a few degenerate middle-class professional men whom thwarted class hatred of socialism (thwarted Zionism for some) had led into terrorist attacks on behalf of Wall Street...[There is] but one road to safety...the victory of working-class internationalism over bourgeois materialism and Zionist racialism'.[89]

The ink had barely dried on Rothstein's rant before Stalin died and the Soviet authorities declared the Doctors Plot to be a fabrication, blaming the whole farrago on Beria. Yet those who had defended it so loudly barely blinked. There was a new enemy for the left to focus on.

Israel quickly became an ideological battleground during the Cold War. The lies churned out by Soviet propaganda were eagerly devoured and the belief that Zionists operated to further American interests gradually gained a foothold in mainstream left-wing thought. The reality was that such claims had their roots securely planted in the paranoid imaginings of the Soviets. Yet the truth had little impact, and the belief took a firm hold following the Six-Day War of 1967. Perry Anderson, the firebrand radical who edited *New Left Review* published a scathing piece on the figures who had 'captured' British intellectual life in 1968. It may be a coincidence that his targets – Wittgenstein, Berlin, Popper, Namier, Gombich, Klein at al, were Jewish, but it seems unlikely. Jean-Paul Sartre was even more outspoken, and loudly justified the murder of eleven Israeli athletes at the Munich Olympics in 1972. As the mainstream turned against Judaism once more the extremes of the left became more overt in their anti-Semitism, even going so far as to echo Nazi rhetoric. On 15 December 1977 the Marxist leader, Ulrike Meinhof, praised the Holocaust in the *Frankfurter Allgemeine Zeitnung*, arguing that Jews were capitalists who deserved to be gassed. She believed that Germans supported her Red Army terror group *because* of their anti-Semitism, yet she remained a heroine to the radical left.

The line between anti-Zionism and anti-Semitism has become increasingly blurred. But the claims that Zionism is an organ of American imperialism, the allusions between the movement and Nazi Germany, the belief that Israel is a terrorist state, and the contention that Zionism has a controlling hand in markets, industry and the media, all originated in Soviet propaganda. As with the distorted perception of Fascism, the reason the left hates Israel today is largely because Stalin told them to nearly a century ago. Stalin's Cold War policy in the Middle East also encouraged the left's noxious marriage with Fundamental Islam. That partnership was epitomised in Ken Livingstone's decision to invite Sheikh Yusuf al-Qaradawi to City Hall. After they warmly embraced Livingstone announced that Yusuf was 'a leading progressive voice' within Islam. Yet the man he praised has openly supported terrorism against Israel, the murder of gays and violence against women.* This should come as no surprise, for extremist Islam has a long history of violent anti-Semitism. In *Eichmann in Jerusalem* Hannah Arendt recounted how the Arab countries

---

* Livingstone dismissed Andrew Anthony's criticism of Qaradawi as Zionist propaganda. Yet the journalist had plucked his evidence directly from the cleric's own website.

'had openly offered refuge to hundreds of [Nazi war criminals]. The Grand Mufti's connections with the Nazis during the war were no secret; he had hoped they would help him in the implementation of some "final solution" in the Near East. Hence, newspapers in Damascus and Beirut, in Cairo and Jordan, did not hide their sympathy for Eichmann or their regret that he "had not finished the job".'[90]

Recent events in Turkey show the trait remains alive and well. In the summer of 2017 Recep Erdogan's increasingly backwards regime banned schoolchildren from being taught about evolution. Two newspaper columnists quickly chimed in with their support. One argued that Charles Darwin was 'a big-nosed Jew who enjoyed the company of monkeys' while another suggested that evolution was true, but only to the extent that monkeys were descended from Jews who were being punished for their sins. Holocaust survivor Marceline Loridan-Ivens claimed that anti-Semitism was as bad in France in 2017 as it was in the 1940s, a rise she, and many others, have linked to the large numbers of Islamic migrants. For it was when the radical fringes of Islam and the left united over the Palestinian issue that the sickness of anti-Semitism began to go mainstream once more.

It is not necessary to detour into a long explanation of the unfortunate conflict between Israel and Palestine. Both sides have a claim to that land and it is hoped that some accord can be found. But to blame the Israelis for all the wrongs of the war simply because they have proven the stronger side is not a rational reaction to events, particularly when much of the aggression has originated from the Arab and Palestinian quarter. Israel is a democratic state that gives full rights to all its citizens, Jewish or Palestinian, arguably the only such nation in the Middle East, and the occupation of Palestinian territories only occurred after frequent attacks from its neighbours. It has offered to withdraw when peace is achieved, but this hope has continually floundered with Arab refusals to recognise its right to exist. In fact, Hamas not only rejects a two-state solution, it has repeatedly called for the murder of all Jews worldwide. The left largely fails to acknowledge this though and has, once again, refused to admit their allies may be at fault.

The union between extremist Islam and the radical left was effectively cemented in the summer of 1967. The Arab nations were startled by the ease with which Israel dispatched them after they attacked it that June. And the thumping they received made it increasingly difficult to view the Jews as victims. The Arabs, despite their role as aggressors, came to believe they were the targets of a plot supported by American might to keep them in subjection, a view encouraged by Soviet propaganda. As they already shared this interpretation, the left quickly bought into the fiction. The convenient trope of dispossession and oppression took hold.

There is plenty of evidence that makes cleaving to that view particularly easy. It is, after all, undeniable that there is much suffering among the Palestinian population and the actions of the Israeli government can be criticised in numerous ways. But the situation there is far more complex than is generally assumed. It is clear, for instance, that the greater part of the racist rhetoric, and the majority of the violence, has originated in the Palestinian camp. A perusal of the Israeli Declaration of Independence and the Charter of Hamas offers genuine clarity on this issue. The former promises complete equality and freedom for people of all nationalities and religions while hoping for peace with their Arab neighbours; the latter utterly rejects peace while calling for death to the Jews.

Ultimately, it is difficult to escape the conclusion that the current crisis lies in the fact that, three years after the Holocaust, the Arab nations of the Middle East tried to wipe the Jews from the face of the earth once more. And they haven't really stopped trying since. It is also pertinent to note that there are three million Palestinian Arabs resident in Israel, who all enjoy full rights, but there is not one Israeli Jew in Palestine. If there was they would almost certainly be lynched. When Egypt foreswore violence against the Jewish state the entire Sinai Peninsula, an oil-rich region three times the size of Israel, was returned to them immediately. An equivalent declaration from Palestine would likely achieve similar results with the occupied territories.* Yet, as with so many other subjects, the left have picked their side and, as a result, objectivity seems beyond them. They will simply find justifications for one side while screaming hate at the other.

There are few more eloquent expressions of this approach than *The Hidden History of Zionism*, a remarkable tract that can be regarded as the bastard offspring of the *Protocols*. It was published in 1988 by Ralph Schoenman, a radical American leftist so extreme that he may be considered borderline deranged. His 'analysis' gives a grossly distorted account of 'barbarous' Zionists and noble Palestinian resistance. He accuses Zionists of colluding with Nazis in the Holocaust while planning nothing less than the complete eradication of the Palestinian people. There are frequent insinuations on the Machiavellian

---

* Even as I write repulsion over the antics of ISIS, disillusion with the hijacking of the Arab Spring by the likes of the Muslim Brotherhood and anxiety over the intentions of Fundamentalist Iran has seen opinion among moderate Sunni Arabs begin to shift. There has been a swing away from Islamism and cautious overtures are being made towards Israel. The radicals are naturally furious about this and will resist it. But there is at least a chance that moderation may conquer extremism in the Middle East and that conflict might finally give way to peace and co-operation. That wish may be wildly optimistic, but we can still fervently hope for some light at the end of the tunnel for that embattled region.

schemes of 'Jewish capitalists, and Rothschild plantation managers'. Yet while Israel is accused of fomenting genocide there is no mention of Palestinian aggression or inflammatory Arab rhetoric. He also ignores the attacks by Jordan, Egypt, Iraq, Syria and Lebanon, as well as the volunteers who poured in from Morocco, Yemen, Pakistan, Sudan and Saudi Arabia. By the later sections the mask has slipped and his ire is directed away from Zionists and pointed squarely at the Jews, and by the end his political leanings are laid bare.

'As the Zionist state is at once a species of capitalist class rule and an extension of U.S. imperial power in the region, the struggle against Zionism becomes, programmatically, a struggle for a socialist Palestine and, as the dawn follows the long night, a struggle for a socialist Arab East...from the Mediterranean to the Persian Gulf, from the Brook of Egypt to the Euphrates...and beyond.'[91]

The implication is clear. The only solution to the crisis of the Middle East is to cleanse the entire area of Jews. The character assassination of Schoenman penned by David Horowitz in *Radical Son* is highly recommended. The delusional, anti-Semitic ravings of the *Hidden History* are best avoided.

One may suggest that, in siding with extremist Islam against the only true democracy in the region, the left have picked the wrong side, but such pleas will also fall on deaf ears. The end result is that 'Zionist' has become one of the movement's ubiquitous slurs. And the hate expressed for anyone suspected of harbouring Zionist sympathies is startling. That includes, of course, the majority of Jews. Those who subscribe to this view frequently argue that anti-Zionism is not anti-Semitism, that they simply oppose the actions of the state. But this is a ludicrous suggestion. Anti-Zionism is, by definition, not a criticism of Israeli policy. It is a repudiation of the Jewish state's right to exist. No one is anti – any other country, no one questions whether, say, Saudi Arabia is still viable. The anti-Zionists claim is to seriously argue that everyone in the world should be allowed a state: Pakistanis, the Irish, Thais, Arabs, Palestinians and Germans should all be allowed a state, so should Zimbabweans, Peruvians, Scots and Icelanders; everyone except the Jews. More than this, their solution to the crisis in the Middle East is to kick the Jews out. For the holder of such views to claim they are not anti-Semitic is a remarkable leap of logic even if they are, on the whole, generally expressed by individuals whose grasp of the Arab-Israeli War is tenuous at best. The reality is that Zionism is simply a movement for Jewish self-determination and cultural renaissance. It recognises that Jews are a nation like any other and are thus deserving of the same rights as any other established group. This seems eminently reasonable. In writing in the *Financial Times* in February 2016, Simon Schama was entirely correct to state that 'anti-Semitism has not been caused by Zionism; it is precisely the other way around. Israel was caused by the centuries-long dehumanisation of the Jews'.[92]

The opponents of Zionism also claim that, by labelling them anti-Semitic, their rivals are merely attempting to shut down criticism of Israel; yet the truth is very different. If one listens to their rhetoric it is clear that measured objections to the occupation are rare in the extreme. What predominates is blind hatred, directed at a caricatured stereotype, and informed by a belief that a powerful Jewish lobby pulls the strings of the media and manipulates the financial and political spheres. It is essential to allow rational critiques of Israel. But this does not rule out a distinction being drawn between such an approach and the increasingly vocal rants of rather more bigoted individuals. It is also pertinent to point out that Israel, the only Jewish state in the world, draws a level of ire incomparable with any other, whether North Korea, Russia, Syria, Nigeria, Saudi Arabia, Venezuela or elsewhere. As Ruth Wisse observed 'What a relief to have a Jewish state on hand to represent the world's worst criminal! Without it, activist students might have to worry about Iran, or jihadist beheadings, or mass female enslavement in Africa, about all of which, to my knowledge, scarcely a tear has been shed or a nickel raised'.[93]

The peculiarity of singling out Israel raises serious concerns about, not just the issues that get a free pass from the left, but whether the attacks are informed by genuine compassion or rather less well informed spite. For the closer one moves to the extremes of the movement the more volatile this hatred is, and the greater the frequency with which one hears about conspiracies of the 'Zionist press' and the Rothschilds. More than that, they feel safe in their hatred; righteous and unashamed. Secure in the belief that the people who caution them on their excesses are the ones with something to hide. As one studies this worrying phenomenon in greater depth it becomes ever clearer that the world's oldest prejudice is very much alive and well, and that the same lies that armed the left for centuries, and informed Hitler's insane worldview, remain part of our cultural capital.

The left's tendency to believe that racism can only spring from a combination of prejudice and power also prevents a clear analysis of the issue. As long as they remain persuaded that hatred of the Jews is inspired by their position of strength then anti-Semitism is not regarded as racism at all but as resistance. It is a position exacerbated by the belief that Israel has been both created and propped up by the West, hatred of which is all but ubiquitous. It is the same mindset that blames the West for Islamic terror today. One would hope that events since 9/11 might have made it clear to the left that they have picked the wrong side. But the attacks on Israel have only increased in intensity. And those barbs are tossed by people who sit in complete safety and security while lecturing Israelis on how they should behave. One imagines that if those same liberals were subjected to rockets raining down on them from Scotland or Canada they would expect their governments to stamp on it pretty quickly. But reason appears to have little impact on the ardour of the faithful. Israel is surrounded by astonishingly aggressive neighbours that have attacked it and called for its destruction for seventy years. It has consequently learned the only thing those neighbours understand is a significant display of force. The fact that the Jewish people have drawn such a firm line in the sand also has to be understood in light of the two millennia of persecution they faced prior to 1948 and the terrible events of the Shoah which drew that long period to a close. Who then has the right to judge?

The result of all this rationalising means that anti-Semitism has effectively, if unconsciously, become another of the long list of prejudices considered acceptable on the left. The bigotry that helped define the movement for the nineteenth century before being abandoned by the mainstream left in the twentieth century has returned with a vengeance. That much was apparent in the '60s in the often outspoken anti-Semitism of the Black Panthers, the revolutionary Maoist organisation that sought to overthrow 'the system' and establish a socialist government. As part of their commitment to world socialism they blindly followed the example of the Soviets and Chinese in supporting the Arabs against the Israelis. On 30 August 1969 the *Black Panther* periodical printed an article entitled 'Zionism + Imperialism = Fascism'. The group also published a poem called 'Jew-Land' which bragged you 'Couldn't kill the Jews too soon' and 'I won't rest until the Jews are dead'.[94] Stokely Carmichael, the socialist radical, and his Student Nonviolent Coordinating Committee (SNCC) shared this outlook. He expelled all the Jews from his movement in 1966 and the following year lent enthusiastic support to the Arab invasion of Israel. Gore Vidal, the darling of progressives everywhere, also spent decades spouting anti-Semitic tropes.

This rising tide of anti-Semitism has become commonplace among radicals, but is particularly virulent in universities on both sides of the Atlantic. Significant incidents, including violent attacks, have been reported at campuses as diverse as upstate New York, Temple University, Oberlin College in Ohio, Cornell and UC Irvine. In Boston police had to protect a rally for Israel from a pro-Palestinian mob that threatened violence while screaming 'Jews back to Birkenau!' At the University of California a sizeable meeting was arranged in early 2015 to demand the institution agree to a boycott on Israel. A large and unruly crowd, waving Palestinian flags, heckled Jewish students and chanted 'Allahu Akbar' throughout the proceedings. Following the meeting Azka Fayyaz, a member of the UC Davis student senate posted on Facebook that 'Hamas & Sharia law have taken over UC Davis...Israel will fall insha'Allah'.[95] The next day a Jewish organisation at the university had two large swastikas daubed on its fraternity house.

At Berkeley an experiment was filmed that sought to gauge student reactions. It began with a young man waving around a large ISIS flag while denouncing American imperialism. Students either ignored him or gave tacit support, wishing him 'good luck', nodding while saying 'right' or raising their fists in a gesture of solidarity. He was only rebuked when he lit a cigarette and was told 'you can't smoke on campus'. But when he started to wave an Israeli flag he was immediately attacked. 'Israel is a thief in the day and a thief in the night. Hamas is the greatest'. One man passing by repeatedly shouted 'Fuck Israel' while a woman declared 'All of Israel are killers'. Dozens abused him or gave him the finger as they passed. Another young man screamed 'that flag you wave is the psychological genocide of this planet'. Such distorted views are, sadly, rife across the American college system.

A similar culture is developing in the UK. In January 2016 the student Israel society at King's College, London planned to host a speech by Ami Ayalon, a peace activist who champions a two-state solution, a concept repeatedly rejected by Palestinian activism. But the KCL Action Palestine group showed zero tolerance for free speech and an indecent taste for violence. A large mob attacked the meeting, hurling chairs and smashing windows. Esther Endfield, from the KCL Israel Society, wrote 'When did it become so unsafe in one of the global universities in the world that we can no longer hold an event without being scared of our safety?' She invited the Action Palestine group to a discussion to talk freely about the issues which divide them. But the invitation was declined. The resistance to free speech in academia and the recourse to violence is growing in both English speaking lands, as is the rising tide of violent opposition to Israel.

In Britain this appeared confirmed by the election of Malia Bouattia as the president of the NUS. Her attitude was apparent in her dismissal of the University of Birmingham as 'something of a Zionist outpost'. Bouattia's frequent criticism of 'mainstream Zionist-led media outlets'[96] is also alarming, particularly to those who have read the *Protocols of the Elders of Zion* or *Mein Kampf*, which she was effectively quoting. When Malia claims, as she has, that 'non-violent protest' is not enough, it also sends out a chilling message. And when advocating 'resistance' rather than 'peace talks' the implication seems quite clear. The fact that she is a Muslim may or may not be relevant in shaping her opinions, but one might question why Malia thinks it is fine for there to be dozens of Muslim and Arab states, many of which are a considerable size, but not a single one for the Jews. The entirety of Jewish land is a paltry 8,000 square miles, the size of Wales, while the Islamic world covers nearly 12,000,000 square miles, well over three times the size of Canada. Yet individuals like Bouattia only question the right of the former to exist.

In December 2016 a cross bench peer, Baroness Ruth Deech, issued a report commissioned after a sharp increase in verbal and physical attacks on Jewish students. She warned that many institutions were not tackling anti-Semitism and were becoming 'no-go zones for Jewish students'. Certain universities were singled out for Jews to avoid and these included Manchester, Southampton, Exeter, Oxford and others. But it was SOAS (the School of Oriental and African Studies in London), which emphatically topped the list. One talk at SOAS, in which a Palestinian activist had described Israel as a 'racist' state and 'a fascist endeavour', was under investigation, while more trouble followed when the institute's director, Baroness Valerie Amos, elected to meet Mark Regev, Israel's new ambassador to Britain. When the student body found out, a Facebook group quickly materialised with messages calling Regev 'an abhorrent racist' and asking 'Who the hell meets a vile Zionist terrorist who defends the mass murder of children?' An angry mob descended on Amos's office screaming obscenities and threats. Nate Reidy, the Student Union's trans and gender-identity officer, tweeted 'Will be around later on to fuck shit up', presumably oblivious to the fact that Israel is unique in the Middle East in its tolerance of homosexuality, pansexuality and gender identity. SOAS has become so notorious, with some feeling this shift has occurred since becoming a heavily Islamic dominated institution, that it is now frequently referred to as the 'School of Anti-Semitism'.

Eric Pickles, the former Conservative Party chairman, spoke out in the same week to praise Baroness Deech's courage and to caution that he had long held the same concerns. He also criticised the 'cowardice' of the institutions that had allowed the culture to proliferate. The Baroness wondered if the large number of Saudi Arabian donations to British institutions might have played a role, though the allegation was strenuously denied by all the universities. Professor Anthony Glees seemed to ratify her findings though. He talked openly about the growing militancy and 'feeling of menace' when giving talks on campus. Glees blamed the internet and the rise of 'self-absorption' encouraged by social media. He was alarmed at the amount of aggressive heckling which threatened free speech. The terrorist expert claimed that anyone challenging left-wing views would automatically be 'shouted down'. When he questioned whether protestors had a right to prevent the Israeli ambassador from speaking at universities, he was abused as 'white, male, colonialist, Zionist and racist'[97] and was ultimately driven from the stage. While he welcomed debate, he reported feeling decidedly threatened and concluded those who abused him had 'closed minds'.

Numerous accounts shed light on the student perspective too. On 6 May 2017 Robbie Travers, a somewhat marginal and decidedly moderate internet personality, announced his retirement from social media after some terrifying attacks. Travers was a student at Edinburgh University and a political commentator for the Gatestone Institute. He also campaigned against anti-Semitism while being a reasonable, but outspoken, critic of fundamentalist Islam. On 4 May that year some left-wing activists posted a lengthy thread on Reddit with numerous pictures of Robbie with his family and friends going about their daily business. All had clearly been tailed and subversively photographed. The thread also revealed the addresses of several of those targeted by the group. A slew of comments called Robbie a 'Jew' or 'Zio' who needed to be hurt, killed or 'thrown in the oven, like the other six million'. There was much talk of 'holocausting' and 'Jo Coxing' both he and his relatives. Travers withdrew from the internet out of concerns for the safety of his loved ones. He eventually felt safe enough to return when the guilty parties were arrested, having, after all, left public evidence of their intent. But he soon commented again about 'the campaign of intimidation, hatred and bile by my classmates'.

Similar claims emerged from Oxford University's Labour Club when Alex Chalmers resigned as co-chairman after claiming that a large proportion of members 'have some kind of problem with Jews'. He commented on how 'Zio' was a common slur while the song 'Rockets over Tel Aviv' was a frequent refrain. Some students had laughed at the assassination of Yitzhak Rabin. When Chalmers challenged them that Rabin had made significant efforts towards peace and worked with the Palestinian leadership on producing the Oslo accords they sniffed 'Who cares? He was a Zionist'.[98] Another mob from the Labour club even arranged to get together and scream 'Filthy Zionist!' at a Jewish student whenever they saw her. Baroness Royall later led an inquiry into the club which concluded that abuse of Jews and a nascent anti-Semitism were significant issues. But the Labour party only issued a heavily redacted summary of the report. It led to claims that they were attempting to suppress its findings, particularly after the Jewish Chronicle obtained the transcript and published it in full.

For more examples of the rising hatred of Zionism among radicals one need only peruse the internet. It is not necessary to regurgitate that bile here. Some cases are unintentionally amusing though, like the Gay Pride march through Chicago in June 2017. The organisers banned a group of Jewish participants when they had the temerity to turn up with a rainbow flag decorated with a Star of David. Not terribly inclusive of them, and one suspects their show of solidarity with the Palestinians might not be reciprocated. There is much evidence too among the cultural doyens of the left, like the French film director and devout Marxist, Jean-Luc Godard, who called a producer 'a filthy Jew' and defended the Palestinian massacre of eleven Israeli athletes at the Munich Olympics. He also asserted that Israel was a cancer on the map of the Middle

East. That other arch propagandist of the left, Ken Loach, loudly denounced Radiohead for the high crime of agreeing to play a concert in Tel Aviv. Loach also praised *Perdition*, a play by Jim Allen which cast Jews as demons who were culpable for the Holocaust. But the most pressing issue in recent years has been the rise of anti-Israeli sentiments in the parliamentary Labour party itself, a quite startling tale that unfolded while evidence was being gathered for this section. The furore was such that it eventually drew condemnation from grandees like Gordon Brown, Ed Balls, Tony Blair, David Blunkett, Chuka Umunna, John Woodcock and Tom Watson. The scale of the problem was apparent when Watson called for action against anti-Semitism in the party and Twitter lit up with some 50,000 Labour supporters demanding his removal.

At the Labour Party conference in September 2015 the shadow foreign secretary, Hilary Benn, spoke at receptions for both the Labour Friends of Israel (LFI) and the Labour Friends of Palestine and the Middle East (LFPME). At both events he delivered roughly the same speech. It focused on the appalling effects of the conflict on both Israeli and Palestinian children and the necessity for negotiation and compromise from both sides. The LFI gave an enthusiastic response to his address, but the LFPME reacted furiously. Benn was loudly and angrily heckled while one audience member screamed that 'this isn't about peace, this is about justice'. That comment received wild applause while Benn was denounced as a 'disgrace' who should be sacked immediately. But the demands for 'justice' at the expense of 'peace' reveal why Palestinian activism remains so problematic, for justice really means retribution. The fact that these scenes happened in September 2015 is highly revealing about recent developments in the Labour party. That was the same month that Jeremy Corbyn was elected leader.

Corbyn seems a decent enough sort, if rather vain and not terribly bright, but he appears blind to the faults in his ideology and the terrible defects in those he regards as allies. He is a man who for decades ingratiated himself with the worst aspects of Palestinian and Islamic extremism, one who has a 'softly softly' approach to ISIS and who has called the genocidal lunatics of Hamas and Hezbollah his 'friends'. He has spoken at countless events with the flags of those organisations fluttering in the breeze, and has invited anti-Semitic demagogues and Holocaust deniers into Parliament on numerous occasions. Remarkably, he compared Marwan Barghouti, a convicted terrorist accused of plotting a series of suicide bombings in Israel, to Nelson Mandela, calling him 'an iconic figure for ordinary Palestinians'. He also described Raed Salah as an 'honoured citizen', despite the fact that the notorious hate preacher and anti-Semite had called Jews 'monkeys' and 'bacteria'. Corbyn leapt to the defence of Steven

Sizer, a conspiracy theorist who has blamed the Jews for 9/11. He defended Ibrahim Hewitt, a Palestinian activist who had penned a widely distributed pamphlet crammed with rampant homophobia, recommendations on the servile status of women and demands that adulterers and apostates be stoned to death. Corbyn claimed he was someone he had grown to know 'extremely well, and I consider him to be a very good friend'. He also greeted Azzam Tamini, who called suicide bombing 'a noble cause' that he would willingly take part in for God, and described the speeches of Hasam Badrau, Khalid Mashaal and Abdul Aziz Umar, all senior figures in Hamas, as 'electrifying'.

Corbyn liaised with Leila Khaled, who had blown up and hijacked a number of planes. When the terrorists who had killed 600 Israelis, many of them children, were released in a prisoner exchange, he called them his 'brothers', even questioning whether there was a 'serious case' against them. Just a month before being elected leader, it emerged that he had accepted £2,000 from Ibrahim Hamami, a Hamas sympathiser who applauded the stabbing of Jews. He also welcomed Dyab Abou Jahjah to a Stop the War meeting attended by the Hezbollah MP Hussein el-Hajj. The Belgian activist had talked of his hatred of homosexuals, joy at 9-11, and described the death of every American, British or Dutch soldier as a 'victory'. Jajah, who claimed that Europe has made 'the cult of the Holocaust and Jew-worshipping its alternative religion' recalled meeting the Labour leader on numerous occasions and spoke warmly of him as 'a political friend'. Corbyn had even campaigned for the release of Jawad Botmeh and Samar Alami, the men convicted for bombing London's Israeli embassy in 1994. After his profile increased he distanced himself from such comments, but he never retracted them, nor apologised for them, and neither did he criticise such groups in any way. He also remained cold to any Israeli and Jewish groups which sent feelers in his direction. With such a man at the helm it was not surprising that violently radical sentiments bubbled through the ranks at an alarming rate.

Some of the views that emerged were absolutely startling. The Luton Labour Councillor Aysegul Gurbuz claimed that Hitler was the 'greatest man in history' and that Iran should develop nuclear weapons to 'wipe Israel off the map'. Vicki Kirby, a parliamentary candidate and Vice-chair of Labour's Woking branch, tweeted that Hitler was a 'Zionist God' and that Jews had 'big noses'. Hers was an especially damaging revelation as she had already been suspended for anti-Semitic rants before being swiftly re-admitted. Another Labour activist let back after a suspension was Gerry Downing. The member of Socialist Fight excused ISIS, demanded that the perpetrators of 9/11 'must never be condemned', and tweeted that 'Marxists must address the Jewish question'. A number of similar tweets followed, one suggesting that 'Zionism is in the vanguard of injecting

Muslim hatred into Western politics'. He then expanded on such sentiments by declaring that

> 'The role Zionists have played in the attempted witch-hunt against Jeremy Corbyn's Labour leadership campaign is glaringly obvious...Since the dawning of the period of neo-liberal capitalism in the 1970s, elements of the Jewish-Zionist bourgeoisie, from Milton Friedman to Henry Kissinger to the pro-Israel ideologues of the War on Terror, have played a vanguard role for the capitalist offensive against the workers.'

Downing subsequently appeared on the BBC's Daily Politics show with Andrew Neil to clarify his position. After making it clear that he believed his sort of radical agitation was at home in Jeremy Corbyn's Labour party, he continued to ramble incoherently about the conspiracy of Zionist millionaires and billionaires who exerted 'overwhelming political authority' within the ruling classes of Europe and America.

The day after Islamists attacked Brussels, Bob Campbell, a Labour activist from Middlesbrough, put up a lengthy post on Facebook which claimed that 'ISIS is run by Israel'. He later suggested that the reason ISIS had not attacked Israel was 'because the dog doesn't bite its own tail'. He then posted an image of the Israeli Prime Minister Benjamin Netanyahu hung from a tree alongside another entitled 'Holocaust the sequel...Please stop Israel'.[99] Khadim Hussain, a Labour Councillor and the former Lord Mayor of Bradford posted similar sentiments arguing 'There is no doubt who created the so called ISIS and who is arming those vile terrorists!...Greater Israel, courtesy of ISIS.' He also moaned that the death of millions of Africans during the colonial era is not taught in schools while 'Your school education system only tells you about Anne Frank and the six million Zionists that were killed by Hitler'. In truth, the colonisation of India and the Atlantic slave trade are both on the national curriculum. Beinazir Lasharie, a Kensington Councillor, shared similar sentiments when posting 'Many people know who was behind 9/11 and also who is behind Isis. I've nothing against Jews...just sharing it!' Grahame Morris, the Communities spokesman and friend of Jeremy Corbyn, posted an image of an Israeli flag with the caption 'Nazis in my village, do you see the flag they fly'.[100] The Easington MP then made it clear that he wants British Jews who serve in the Israeli defence force to be treated as terrorists. Mr. Morris also agreed to host an event chaired by Sameh Habeeb who not only published an article by a Holocaust denier on Holocaust Memorial day but also founded the *Palestinian Telegraph* which printed claims that Israeli soldiers had joined the earthquake relief work in Haiti purely to harvest and devour organs from the corpses of the victims.

Sami Ramadani, an academic described by Corbyn as a 'fascinating, great friend' said that criticism of Corbyn's leadership and claims of anti-Semitism in the party came from 'Zionist mouthpieces' and were 'led by backers of Israel to undermine Jeremy Corbyn's support for Palestine'. Josh Simons, who worked as an adviser for Corbyn, also testified that Seumas Milne had a 'rant' at him about Israel and quizzed him about his family background. Simons said that Milne had 'at least a blind spot with anti-Semitism and at worst a wilful disregard for it'.[101] It soon emerged that the former journalist had links with the PLO dating back to his student days in 1976 and had long appeared sympathetic to Fatah, Hamas and the Iranian regime. Milne had also made comments at a London rally in 2009 that Britain owed Palestine because 'this crime began 90 years ago, when Palestine was promised by a British government to *another people'*.[102] [Emphasis, mine] Ilyas Aziz, yet another culpable Labour councillor, shared multiple anti-Semitic images about the Rothschilds, made comparisons between Israeli actions and the Nazi genocide, suggested that all Israelis should be deported to America, as 'it's big enough', and repeated the 'blood libel' slurs about Gaza. These latter stories centre around the allegation that Jews consumed the blood of Gentile and Christian children during religious rituals, a neat way of insinuating that they are not just metaphorical bloodsuckers but literal ones too. Ali Milani, the Labour candidate for Uxbridge, had posted sneering insinuations about alleged parsimony when commenting 'Nah, you won't mate. It'll cost you a pound #jew'. He also questioned Israel's right to exist and denounced Piers Morgan as a Zionist.

These kind of sentiments even came from those close to the Labour leader. The Momentum organiser Jackie Walker took to the internet to comment that black people still face oppression in a way that Jews don't, before going on to state that 'Jews were the chief financiers of the slave trade'. Joss MacDonald, a chief Labour speechwriter and a key aide of Corbyn, posted a number of comments accusing Israel of being an 'apartheid' state that was committing 'genocide' while using the Holocaust as an excuse to cover its crimes. Andy Slack, meanwhile, a big Corbynista, Momentum supporter and Palestine activist, posted an image on an extreme Jew-obsessed American website of a stereotypical hook-nosed Jew rubbing his hands next to a Star of David which dripped with blood. The caption accompanying the image declared 'The modern state of Israel was created by the Rothschilds, not God, and what they are doing to the Palestinian people now is EXACTLY what they intend for the whole world'.

Naz Shah, MP for Bradford West, was another who called for the mass transportation of Jews to the US while comparing Israel's policies with those of Nazi Germany. She was also photographed at numerous protests calling for boycotts on Israeli products, which many campaigners claim will only deepen the well of mistrust between Israel and Palestine - a suspicion that must be overcome for progress to be made in the region. Shah was also photographed bringing her two daughters, aged ten and seven, to a Free Palestine protest at a McDonald's. Once there the group shouted 'Allahu Akbar', smeared ketchup around the premises and disrupted customers by playing dead while draped in Palestinian flags. Huseyin Abduharr Ali, the secretary of Stroud Green Labour, had publicly declared his 'love' for Hezbollah, compared Israel to ISIS and claimed Hollywood is Zionist propaganda. Salma Yaqoob described Israel as a 'pig' and posted scores of rants against Zionists while Apsana Begum called Tony Blair a peddler of Zionist propaganda. When Sadiq Khan, the former MP for Tooting, became Labour's new Mayor of London, a sizeable group of his Islamic supporters paraded through the streets carrying a large banner declaring their congratulations for defeating his rival for the job, the 'millionaire Jew Zac Goldsmith'. *

The most notable, certainly the most famous, of those caught up in the controversy was Ken Livingstone, the charismatic former Mayor of London and head of the Greater London Council (GLC). He had blithely announced that Adolf Hitler had supported Zionism and when confronted about his remarks, remained unapologetic. Livingstone had gleaned the information from the largely discredited book, *Zionism in the Age of Dictators*, by the American Marxist Lenni Brenner. The study, written by a political activist rather than an academic, is widely dismissed as a virulently anti-Israeli rant and is considered notoriously unreliable. But it was seized upon by those who shared its sentiments. In 1983 *The Labour Herald,* the paper edited by Livingstone, printed a review of Brenner's book which said that Jewish leaders shamelessly 'used the sympathy stirred up...after the Holocaust for their own devious ends'. Livingstone, despite the certainty with which he clung to his unpleasant position was, of course, completely wrong about the Nazi leader. Hitler, far from supporting the movement, had made his views on Zionism quite clear in *Mein Kampf* when declaring that 'They have not the slightest intention of building up a Jewish State in Palestine so as to live in it. What they are really aiming at is to establish a control organization for their international swindling and cheating'.[103]

If Livingstone had claimed that *Eichmann* had supported Zionism, he would have been technically correct, but he still wouldn't have had a point. Livingstone clearly intended to draw a parallel between Zionists and Hitler, to suggest that one who favoured the Jewish state in Israel was, in some way, as bad as the Nazis. The implication is ludicrous. The Jews supported Zionism because it gave them the prospect of a safe refuge, a haven from the incessant persecution that had assailed them for millennia. The Nazis who supported it

---

* The reader can decide for themselves on the relevance of the extraordinarily high percentage of Islamic figures on this list.

did so because it presented an opportunity to get the Jews they despised so much out of their country while protecting the purity of German blood. Drawing any kind of connection between such contrasting motivations is absurd. The Israeli ambassador to Britain, Mark Regev, responded with disgust to Livingstone's insinuations. He was 'Not sure which is worse, deliberately distorting Hitler's goals or accusing his Jewish victims of being his partners'.[104]

The prevalence of such views under Corbyn should not be too surprising. After all, long before he rose to the stewardship of the party, friends of his, like the sinister George Galloway, were gleefully announcing that Bradford was now an 'Israel-free zone'. Jewish Labour MPs were soon subjected to considerable abuse from their fellow politicians and Momentum staffers. Ruth Smeeth, for one, was abused as 'a fucking traitor' and 'a yid cunt'. One Corbynista penned a thousand word essay detailing how he planned to kill her. Luciana Berger was sent caricatured pictures of herself as a greedy hook-nosed Jew as well as images of the yellow star that Jews were forced to wear by the Nazis. She was also called a 'pig', a 'fugly kike cow', received rape and death threats, and was told to 'move to Israel, you don't belong in Europe...It's only going to get worse'. Both women claim to have been sent thousands of such abusive messages from party members and supporters. John Mann, another Labour MP, received torrents of abuse. He was called a 'Zionist shill', denounced for taking '30 shekels to betray his own kin' from the 'Jewish lobby purse strings' and received numerous threats of violence from left-wing activists. All three were subject to such abuse simply because they had dared to criticise the prevalence of anti-Semitic sentiment in the party.

It would be easy to dismiss such evidence as isolated incidents, despite the plethora of examples. But John McTernan cited an example in the *Spectator* which suggested it may be more widespread than commonly assumed. Addressing the Tottenham Labour party he reported that antipathy towards a Jewish state was all but unanimous, as was, remarkably, support for the late Soviet one, and this in June 2016. When the comedian turned Labour activist Eddie Izzard called for the party to address the issue of anti-Semitism on his Facebook page it provoked a large number of responses from his Labour supporting followers. Just six expressed support for his sentiments while seventy-two angry posts denied there was any anti-Semitism in Labour at all, brushed the whole thing off as a hoax manufactured by the Tories and the *Daily Mail* to undermine Corbyn, expressed support for all the vile comments that had been made or crassly abused Izzard himself for even raising the topic.

Regardless, with the clamour about the issue growing the Labour leadership had to be seen to act, and so they did, even though Corbyn refused to accept the party had a problem with anti-Semitism. Some members facing allegations were suspended and Shami Chakrabarti was put in control of an 'independent' enquiry into the issue. Her conclusions, which were widely condemned as a 'whitewash', exonerated Labour of any wrongdoing. Even as the results of the enquiry were announced Chakrabarti, full of earnest self-regard, sat next to Corbyn and calmly passed him the answers to journalists' questions so that he could rabbit the appropriate responses. But at that press launch one of Labour's few surviving Jewish MPs, Ruth Smeeth, was heckled by a Momentum member about being a shill of the right-wing press. She left in tears. Corbyn made no intervention and appeared not to care.

Remarkably, almost immediately after her enquiry was done, Chakrabarti joined the party herself and was promptly rewarded for her services with a peerage on the personal recommendation of Jeremy Corbyn. As if that was not enough, she was then appointed to the post of Shadow Attorney General. These appointments cast a long shadow over her role and supposed impartiality, but the Labour leader had hardly covered himself in glory either. When speaking at the launch of her investigation Corbyn had declared that all forms of racism must be stamped out, and that most Jews were no more responsible for the actions of Israel than Muslims were for those of ISIS, thus drawing exactly the same allusions himself that a raft of his own party members had been suspended for.

Following the cover-up the majority of the suspensions were quietly rescinded. George McManus, who had claimed that Tom Watson was a 'Judas' who had taken 'Jewish money', returned to the fold. Vicki Kirby was appointed an aide to the senior Unite figure, Jennie Formby, while the likes of Naz Shah returned to her seat in the House of Commons as though nothing had happened. As for the Oxford University Labour Club it was clear, so Baroness Royall concluded, that not only had anti-Semitic attacks taken place, but that disciplinary action was warranted. Instead the Labour NEC dropped all charges against the accused. Had the Tories behaved in this manner, by ignoring racism in the party and rewarding their squalid accomplice with a peerage, then sections of the left would doubtless have rioted, working themselves into a self-righteous fury while screaming for justice. Whitehall would be in flames and Trafalgar Square would have run red with blood. As it is the whole squalid farrago elicited no more than an apathetic shrug, followed by a precipitous rise in support for Labour, particularly among the young. Stephen Pollard of the *Telegraph* concluded that 'The message it sent was clear: Labour regards the rights of Jew-haters to attack Jews as more important than the rights of its Jewish members to be free from attack'.[105] Pollard made frequent comments in his column on the significant rise in online anti-Semitic abuse. He also recorded the hundreds of abusive messages received daily by himself and other Jews. These missives accuse them of controlling finance and the media, cast disgusting aspersions about the rampant Jewish abuse of children, and promise gruesome death in a myriad of inventive ways.

Following such a feeble response from the party's top brass similar abuse, rather predictably it has to be said, returned with a flourish barely a year later. During the election campaign of 2017 Andrew Percy, the Conservative MP for Brigg and Goole was attacked in the street as 'Zionist scum' by a self-confessed Corbyn supporter. His staff were spat on. Zac Goldsmith, the 'millionaire Jew', also reported abuse while Sheryll Murray, another Tory MP and member of the Conservative Friends of Israel, had Swastikas carved into her campaign posters. Messages on social media even urged people to 'burn the witch' and 'stab the cunt'. An unidentified man urinated in the doorway to her office while screaming obscene abuse at the security camera. When a Labour motion in Haringey attempted to endorse the UN's condemnation of anti-Semitism the meeting erupted in protests and a Jewish councillor was spat on. Joe Goldberg and Natan Doron, two Jewish Labour councillors in Haringey reported repeated abuse from Corbyn supporting Momentum members. And the unofficial Labour Party page on Facebook was deluged with comments after PM Teresa May described herself as a 'proud supporter of Israel'. Lynne Gillard claimed that Mrs. May, the daughter of an Anglican vicar, and her husband were both Jews who had communed with the Chief Rabbi in Downing Street after her election victory. Kim Marie added 'you don't get anywhere in British politics unless you...are Jewish. It is that bad here now. Weird isn't it, the Jews now acting like the Nazis?' Jacky Cox fumed at the cosy and profitable shadowy relationship between Britain and a Jewish state that John Anderson described as 'satanic'.[106]

It is little surprise then that at the Labour Party conference in Brighton in September 2017 the controversy flared up yet again. A healthily attended and enthusiastic meeting chaired by Naomi Wimbourne-Idrissi was characterised by incidents like Michael Kalamanovitz's demand that the Jewish Labour Movement and Labour Friends of Israel both be expelled from the party, a suggestion that was heartily applauded. Miko Pelo, who had also recommended an open discussion on Holocaust denial, claimed the meeting was about free speech before immediately proposing that 'It's about the limits of tolerance: we don't invite the Nazis and give them an hour to explain why they are right; we do not invite apartheid South Africa racists to explain why apartheid was good for the blacks, and in the same way we do not invite Zionists – it's a very similar kind of thing'.[107] It was additionally claimed that the pro-Israel lobby was attempting to prevent Corbyn from becoming PM. The Labour Party Marxists even circulated a leaflet which quoted Reinhard Heydrich while comparing Zionists to Nazis.

Worried moderates made the scale of this strain quite clear: Labour MP John Mann claimed 200 members had forwarded him a link to a US white supremacist site which supported Ken Livingstone's absurd claims about Zionism while John Cryer, the chairman of the Parliamentary Labour Party, described how he had seen tweets from party members which were 'redolent of the 1930s'. They made his hair stand on end. More than one wag pointed out that the slogan plastered all over the conference – 'Labour: For the Many, Not the Few', might have been made more accurate by altering the first letter of the last word to a 'J'. Despite the numerous calls for action from his own party, when Corbyn made his keynote speech at the conference just days later he made no reference to the controversy at all – though he did make a pointed observation on the 'oppression' of the Palestinian people. Shami Chakrabarti, whose seedy cover-up looks worse every day, stayed equally mute on the matter.

But the treatment of those charged with racism was very different when the boot was on the other foot. When Robbie Travers mocked ISIS he was subjected to an investigation by Edinburgh University. It was alleged that by posting such comments he had made Islamic and minority students feel 'threatened' and 'unsafe' though, conversely, when he reported that some students at the university had been using 'Zio' as a racist slur he was dismissed for attempting to spread lies about anti-Semitism. He also recounted how thirteen of his Jewish friends were leaving the UK for Israel as they no longer felt safe in the increasingly hostile climate. Though the charges were ultimately dropped, Travers was only cleared after a lengthy and expensive legal process. The woman who had accused him faced no censure at all. It was also claimed that Edinburgh University had been informed that students from their Communist Society had declared that gassing was 'too good' for Jews while calling for 'death to all Israelis', 'death to Israel' and encouraging the 'annihilation of Zionists'. The leader of the society was also on record as having planned trips to Israel to deliberately harm 'Zionists'. Yet this time the administrators felt no need to investigate, never mind prosecute.

Trevor Phillips and the Labour MP Sarah Champion fell victim to the same sort of inconsistency. Phillips, one of the most reasonable and decent commentators of the day, had made some mild and incontestable remarks about Islam. But while many vile anti-Semites lingered in the party for years, he was suspended immediately. Champion had aired an impassioned plea about the spiralling number of cases involving the abuse of young girls by large numbers of men in places like Rotherham and Newcastle. She suggested that cases of this nature would keep happening unless we were honest about the nature of the crimes; that they involved gangs of 'predominantly Pakistani, Muslim men', and that this salient fact must be confronted to help us prevent a repeat of the rising tide of rape. Unlike the cases involving anti-Semitism, there was no 'suspension', no 'investigation', just an ultimatum. Champion was curtly informed that she could either quit or be sacked. She resigned. When Amina Lone spoke in Champion's defence she was unceremoniously booted out of Manchester City Council and barred from the following year's election. Naz Shah, sitting comfortably back in the Commons after her brief sabbatical, had pressured Corbyn to act on Champion's comments before compounding the situation by reposting a tweet from a fake Owen Jones account. It read 'Those abused girls in Rotherham and elsewhere just need to shut their mouths. For the good of diversity'. No disciplinary action was forthcoming. In fact, remarkably, Shah was speedily promoted to Shadow Minister for Equality to replace the ousted Champion.

Corbyn again made his allegiances clear in November that year when snubbing an invitation to attend a dinner with Benjamin Netanyahu before immediately accepting a similar offer from MEND – Muslim Engagement and Development. The director of the latter organisation is one Azad Ali, a man who has frequently spoken of his distaste for democracy and a desire to see Sharia implemented in the UK. Ali has also freely admitted his 'love' for Anwar al-Awlaki, an Al-Qaeda recruiter who was one of his 'favourite' speakers, and who defended Hamas while approving of clerics who call for the murder of British soldiers. It came as little surprise when it emerged that Corbyn had spent years as a paid shill of Iranian television. He had even continued to take their money and spout propaganda after Ofcom had withdrawn the licence of Press TV for torturing an interviewee.

In March 2018 a large number of Labour members were suspended when it emerged that a significant number of anti-Semitic comments had been posted on a closed Palestine Live group on Facebook. The leader of the opposition had briefly been a member of the group. It was also suggested that Corbyn and Elleane Green, the Palestine Live founder, were close friends who had organised a number of events together. Green had posted numerous comments and articles claiming that Israelis dealt in a black market of murdered children, that both 9-11 and the Paris attacks had been arranged by Israeli intelligence to provoke Western assaults on the Middle East, that the Rothschilds were attempting to impose a 'New World Order' and that 'no friend of Israel' should be allowed to stand as an MP.

That story had broken in the very same month that the issue finally provoked a response. On 26 March, a huge protest was arranged by Britain's Jewish community in Parliament Square. They called on the Labour leader to properly tackle the anti-Semitism polluting his party. That issue was compounded when it emerged that Corbyn had been supportive of a deeply anti-Semitic mural which depicted a group of stereotypically hook-nosed Jewish bankers playing Monopoly on a board perched on the backs of black slaves and the oppressed poor. An Illuminati symbol loomed over the picture. When howls of protest erupted from his own party members Corbyn finally agreed that anti-Semitism existed in 'pockets' in the party. He conceded that it was time to try and forge links with the Jewish community, yet he accepted no culpability. Considering the balance of evidence, one wonders how sincere the 'apology' was and what genuine changes would result from the declared shift in policy.

Most remained robustly unconvinced, and these fears seemed confirmed when Corbyn's next port of call was to attend an event organised by Jewdas, a far-left group which claimed that accusations of anti-Semitism in Labour were part of a plot by Tories and right-wingers. On its Twitter page the group also described Israel as 'a steaming pile of sewage which needs to be properly disposed of'. Jewdas had been highly critical of a number of senior Jews and aspects of Judaism and, with Corbyn in attendance, the members erupted into chants of 'fuck capitalism!' and 'fuck the Tories!' The organisers of the Parliament Square protest were also roundly booed. His response to the protest then, by immediately turning to an Israeli hating organisation, showed his true colours. The cynics were proven correct, yet the leadership continued to deny there was a problem and refused to address the issue.

The controversy continued on 1 April when a massive exposé in the Sunday Times unearthed over 2,000 hate-filled rants by Corbyn supporters on five internet groups that the leader himself had joined. The pages, with names like 'We Support Jeremy Corbyn', 'We Trust and Support Jeremy Corbyn's Labour', 'Jeremy Corbyn Leads us to Victory' and 'I'm Backing Jeremy Corbyn for Prime Minister' were awash with all the usual bile. One comment, revealed in a police report, referred to 'Jew scum' and concluded 'Adolph *(sic)* you should have finished the job'. Apart from Corbyn himself, and John McDonnell, twelve other senior advisors of the pair were also members and regular posters on the pages. Among them was James Meadway, McDonnell's economics adviser, who was also a member of a group called 'The Witch is Dead!', a page dedicated to celebrating Margaret Thatcher's death while promoting violence against Tory MPs. Worse followed when it emerged that Christine Shawcroft, who had been charged with eliminating anti-Semitism from the party, had defended a vile post by Alan Bull which mocked the Holocaust and claimed it was a hoax. Even as she stepped down, she was still protesting that the story of anti-Semitism in Labour was a plot contrived by their political opponents. It had been 'stirred up to attack Jeremy, as we all know'. *The Guardian* was also in denial, highlighting a letter from forty-two 'senior academics' suggesting that the whole sorry saga had been cooked up by sloppy journalism. However, it soon emerged that the letter's signatories were primarily employed in the media departments of second rate universities, as well as being journalists for *The Guardian* and the *New Statesman*. It is also undeniable that the majority of the evidence originated, not from journalism, but straight from the horse's mouth, and that most complaints came from Labour insiders.

It even emerged that Corbyn had described counter-protestors who screamed hatred for Israel at the Parliament Square marchers as 'good people'. That comment came in an interview with the paper *Jewish News* which described his responses as 'not good enough'. Corbyn also met with Jewish leaders. But they were left exasperated by the summit and fumed that they 'got nothing from the meeting, not a thing'. When the Labour leader was asked why he had not tackled the issue of anti-Semitism with the same passion that he'd demonstrated over the Windrush debacle, he simply shrugged before nominating Kate Osamor, who had signed a pledge in support of Ken Livingstone, Jackie Walker and others charged with anti-Semitism, for a peerage. In the wake of all the furore, the Labour Party of Israel severed ties with its British counterpart until it addressed the issue, a move which prompted Corbyn to complain that 'I wish they would read Shami Chakrabarti's report'.

With such a blinkered view it was hardly surprising that Corbyn soon appeared at the May Day rally in London. While there he gave a rousing speech in front of hundreds of Soviet flags and banners bearing heroic images of Stalin, renowned as an anti-Semitic mass murderer. The very next day Emily Thornberry was present at a speech in which the Palestinian President Mahmoud Abbas claimed that the Jews deserved the centuries of persecution they had faced, including the Holocaust, because of their 'social role related to usury and banks'. But Thornberry wrote a gushing report of the event. Corbyn even had the sheer gall to demand that the Tories launch an inquiry into 'Islamophobia' in their own party, despite being unable to produce a shred of evidence to support his complaints. He then promptly celebrated the end of Ramadan in June 2018 with Fadi El-Itani, who has frequently compared Zionists to Nazis and accused Israel of being guilty of their own 'Holocaust'.

In September Momentum invited the British anti-Israeli activist Ewa Jasiewica to speak at an event attached to the Labour party conference. Yet, not only was she outspoken in her views, the artist had actually defaced the memorial of the Warsaw ghetto by scrawling 'Free Gaza and Palestine' across it. Ash Sarkar even spoke up to defend the desecration. Jasiewicz at least had the decency to apologise later. Sarkar never did. When the new Labour charter was finally unveiled it was roundly criticised for failing to comply with the recommendations of the International Holocaust Remembrance Alliance (IHRA) thus effectively permitting comparisons between Israelis and Nazis and allowing Israel's very existence to be condemned as a racist endeavour.

Britain's Jewish community united in condemning the move, with the Chief Rabbi claiming that it showed 'unprecedented contempt'. But their stance provoked some even more remarkable responses. Mary Lockhart, a Fife councillor, suggested that all the criticism had been orchestrated by Mossad to undermine Corbyn's electoral chances. Damien Enticott, another councillor based in Bognor Regis, posted articles and videos which called Jews 'parasites' and claimed they were paedophiles who drank the blood of children and deserved execution. Peter Willsman, one of the so-called 'JC9', the key Corbyn supporters on the National Executive Committee (NEC), Labour's ruling body, was recorded in a stunning outburst at a meeting attended by the leader. He claimed there was no anti-Semitism in the party, despite having attended meetings at which a number of cases had been heard, and that all counter claims had been 'falsified on social media' by 'Jewish...Trump fanatics'. When others attempted to counter his rant Willsman, who had led the group which defended Ken Livingstone over his comments linking Hitler and Zionism, screeched that he would 'not be lectured'. Corbyn made no attempt to intervene, and no disciplinary action was forthcoming.* In contrast, when MP Margaret Hodge rebuked the leader as 'anti-Semitic and a racist', she was cautioned that she faced extreme sanction and the disciplinary process began in less than a day, something the party had not managed in two years of Ken Livingstone's suspension. The threat was soon withdrawn, following the receipt of a seven page document from Mrs. Hodge's lawyers. But when Ian Austin denounced the failure to tackle anti-Semitism as a 'bloody disgrace' that risked the party becoming a 'sewer' he too was subjected to an official investigation. It left the leadership open to the allegation that while keen to persecute the critics of anti-Semitism, they continued to be lenient with those guilty of it.

But worse was to follow. Several photos promptly emerged of Corbyn doing the salute of the anti-Semitic Muslim Brotherhood and laying a wreath while praying at the graves of Salah Khalef, Fakhri al-Omari, Hayel Abdel-Hamid and Atef Bseiso, the leaders of Black September, the terrorist offshoot of the PLO which had murdered eleven Israeli athletes at the 1972 Munich Olympics and committed a number of other bloody atrocities.† The group had been supplied with weapons by German neo-Nazis, who saw them as allies in their war against the Jews. But Mossad finally tracked down and assassinated the leadership in 1991-2. The ceremony in Tunisia was attended not just by Corbyn but also Fatima Bernawi, who had planted a bomb at an Israeli cinema, and Maher al-

* Willsman was finally suspended a year later after claiming the Israeli Embassy had manufactured the whole crisis in a bid to discredit Jeremy Corbyn.

† Shaul Ladany, a Holocaust survivor and speedwalker, who was on the Israeli team at that Olympics, went public following the revelations about Corbyn. Ladany had seen his pride on returning to German soil as an Olympian turn to horror when he witnessed the attack and overheard the terrorists exclaim that 'The Jews are not human'. When he saw Corbyn lay a wreath in honour of the men who had masterminded it he was filled with anger and revulsion.

Taher, the leader of the Popular Front for the Liberation of Palestine (PFLP) who went on to murder a British rabbi a month later.

Dennis Skinner, another Labour MP, attempted to slander the reportage as lies because the Munich terrorists were buried in Libya – but none of the reports had claimed otherwise. All were clear that Corbyn's wreath was laid at the graves of the men who *planned* that abomination, not those who carried it out. Yet in just a matter of days Skinner's lies had received 26,000 likes, were shared 19,000 times and garnered nearly 2,000 approving and gloating comments from people who had clearly never read the articles in question. Corbyn's effort to heal relations amounted to the publication of a brief essay which was dismissed by the *Jewish Chronicle*. It tweeted 'So Corbyn's great move is a piece in the Guardian saying our worries are overheated rhetoric and all would be well if only we could just talk. And not a word of contrition about anything except process. He really is shameless'. Hamas, in contrast, released a statement declaring that 'we salute Jeremy Corbyn's supportive positions to the Palestinians'. At Labour's conference in Liverpool the following month the entire hall was awash with hundreds of Palestinian flags. It was a defiant show of contempt which sent a clear message - the party had learned nothing.

One almost wants to laugh, especially after Yasmin Alibhai-Brown argued that the fake issue of anti-Semitism in Labour was detracting from the very real threat of active Nazis. Unfortunately, she made that claim in response to a photo of a reunion of the cast of *'Allo 'Allo*, the 1980s comedy set in occupied France. This farcical motif continued when leaders met to discuss the crisis in the party. A Corbyn supporter positioned himself outside the meeting while playing the Monty Python theme on a glockenspiel. It seemed very apt, but to those on the receiving end it was far less amusing. A number of Labour MPs who joined the protest in Parliament Square were subjected to torrents of abuse and threats. They were also warned that they could face de-selection. Len McCluskey, the head of Unite and a key ally of Corbyn, condemned the 'hostility' of Britain's Jewish community and chillingly warned that anyone who had criticised the leader over the issue 'can expect to be held to account'. Ken Loach, the far-left filmmaker, allegedly spoke to a rally to recommend that critics be kicked out of the party.

Ruth Smeeth and Luciana Berger went public with the full catalogue of abusive emails and threatening phone calls that had flooded into their offices. Both women were called 'Zionazi', 'parasite', 'Tory cunts', 'Jewish shills' and were told to 'hang' or 'kill' themselves by hundreds of Labour members who repeated claims that conspiracies about the Jewish New World Order were 'absolutely true'. Sarah Champion reported that she too had received numerous death threats, while Margaret Hodge was denounced as a 'traitor', 'stupid bitch' and 'Blairite scab'. Others wrote 'She is clearly in the pocket of the Zionists' and 'I wonder how many pieces of silver Israel paid her to spread her lies'. The Corbyn supporting paper, *The Word*, splashed a large picture of Hodge across its front page under the headline 'The Enemy Within' while in an interview in the *Sunday Times* she claimed that 'most of the nastiest abuse has come from the far left. It's worse than I got from the BNP'. Emily Benn, granddaughter of the iconic Labour MP Tony, also went public with her displeasure and was slammed as 'a disgusting, lying, little Tory mouthpiece'. Ray Ellis claimed her grandfather would be spinning in his grave while George Galloway suggested she probably had 'a mental health issue'. Joan Ryan was sent scribbled messages from self-confessed Corbyn supporters who expressed the wish that she be raped and set on fire. One called her a 'Jew whore' who should be 'shoved right back in the ovens'.*

Lord Levy, a Labour peer, had spoken out about the crisis and was sent an email in response from Fred Milani, a far-left supporter of the new regime. It read

> 'I see that you dare to criticise the Labour leader. Who the hell are you to comment on Jeremy Corbyn? You are just another Jewish pig bloodsucker living on taxpayers' money. What are you doing in this country anyway? Why don't you piss off to Israel? We don't need Jewish bastards like you in this country.'

When the police contacted him about the issue, Milani accused the force of merely acting on the behest of the Jewish state. Laura Kuenssberg, the BBC's political editor, even had to have a bodyguard at the Labour conference after receiving an avalanche of death and rape threats. John Mann also made further revelations about the hard left's response. Mann is not Jewish, but the Labour MP had spoken out against anti-Semitism in the party. As a result, he was sent a dead bird in the post, and his wife and daughters received numerous threats of rape and violence. Tracy Ann Oberman, the *Eastenders* actress, also quit the party after torrents of anti-Semitic abuse. Labour supporters denounced her as a rich Jew who avoided tax in her castle in the Dordogne, despite the fact that she has never been to the Dordogne. Undeterred, they also made sneering comments about her family dying in the Holocaust. Even Rachel Riley, the delightful television presenter, was inundated with abuse after speaking out against the racism infecting the party. Bob James, a Labour member in North Wales, accused her of 'prostituting her religion' for '30 pieces of silver', but he was far from alone. Thousands of Labour supporters sent her messages describing her as a 'rat' or 'vermin', deliberately employing Nazi terminology, while many others made vile reference to the Holocaust.

---

* When Ryan abandoned the Labour party in despair over the issue Chris Williamson gloated how he had played the Kool and the Gang hit 'Celebration', outside her office.

The crisis became so severe that the party began to splinter. When attempts were made to deselect Luciana Berger over her perceived disloyalty in opposing anti-Semitism she resigned along with Chukka Umunna, Angela Smith and five others. Just days later, Ian Austin and Joan Ryan quit too - the former declared that he was 'ashamed' of his party and blamed Corbyn for 'creating a culture of extremism and intolerance'. When Austin, who was raised by a couple of Holocaust survivors, stood up to condemn anti-Semitism in the Commons he was heckled by Corbyn's comrades. Three peers, Lords Triesman, Darzi and Turnberg also resigned the whip over the scandal. Lord Triesman said anti-Semites were shielded while loyal party members were slung out unceremoniously. He directly accused Corbyn and his inner circle of anti-Semitism and described the party as 'institutionally anti-Semitic'. John Mann also quit the party because it had been 'hijacked' by anti-Semites, while Louise Ellman, chairman of Labour Friends of Israel, walked out just weeks after hard left activists had attempted to oust her on the eve of Yom Kippur.

Yet the response of the top brass remained feeble. Jennie Formby, the party's general secretary, dismissingly claimed that it was 'impossible' to deal with the issue, even as it emerged that just twelve of the near 15,000 reported cases had resulted in any affirmative action. In April 2019 the *Sunday Times* printed a damning report on Labour's failure to act. It revealed that members who had posted comments like 'Heil Hitler', 'Fuck the Jews' and 'Jews are the problem' had faced no disciplinary measures more than a year after being investigated. Dozens of serious complaints had simply been dismissed. Many felt that Jackie Walker had only been expelled when the Equality and Human Rights Commission (EHRC) announced it planned to investigate the party. Prior to that declaration no action had been taken against Walker for three years.

Others slipped entirely through the net. Pam Bromley, a Lancashire councillor, had posted a string of conspiracy theories about the Rothschilds, complained about 'Jewish' media attacks and even suggested that Theresa May was behind the Manchester bombing. But she was simply readmitted and quickly went on the warpath again, arguing that the 'vicious thugs who make some of these allegations...should be prosecuted. We need to go on the offensive'.[108] She also argued that Emily Thornberry would not be an appropriate leader as she supported the Labour Friends of Israel. But she gave her blessing to Chris Williamson instead, a man suspended for making anti-Semitic remarks. Sian Bloor, a union official and party member, was also let off after blaming 'Jewish Israelis' for 9-11 and claiming that 'Zionists control world events'. The *Jewish Chronicle* revealed that Rachel Abbotts had been voted in as a councillor in Derbyshire long after she had been reported for sharing material blaming the outbreak of WWII on Jewish aggression against Germany. Sara Reeves, a candidate for Windsor and Maidenhead, blamed 9-11 on the 'neocons and the new world order', boasted about reading *Mein Kampf* to 'travel to a place of knowledge' and posted an image of a bloated pig stamped with the star of David and the word 'Rothschild'. A number of piglets decorated with the logos of the CIA, al-Qaeda, Boko Haram and Israel suckled at its teats. Reeves claimed the suckling pigs included 'the Jews...so it's not an anti-semitic post'.[109] At the time of writing she remained a Labour party member. In June 2019 Lisa Forbes was elected MP for Peterborough despite approving of articles which claimed that Islamic extremists were created by Mossad and the CIA and suggesting that Theresa May had a 'Zionist Slave Master's agenda'. She had also boasted about enjoying a thread which asked why Palestinians didn't just stab more Jews. Barry Gardiner argued that she should be 'forgiven' and she enjoyed the full backing of the party.

Much of the top brass remained resistant to any counter measures. Some went even further. It emerged that Maria Carroll, a Corbyn ally, had given advice on how to beat charges of anti-Semitism in a secret Facebook group. Those counselled included Alan Bull, who called the Holocaust a 'hoax', claimed the Israelis had murdered Princess Diana and dismissed Tony Blair's New Labour as a 'Mossad front', Mollie Collins, who also claimed the Holocaust was faked and argued that the Rotshchilds shot down Malaysia airliner MH370, and Sue Grant who screamed Hitler's camps were 'not DEATH CAMPS!!!' before comparing Israeli Jews to the Nazis.[110] When Tom Watson announced that he would be launching an independent examination of the issue Jennie Formby publicly dismissed the move as 'inappropriate'. Chris Williamson, a key Corbyn aide, addressed a meeting of Momentum and was even more dismissive, claiming the party had already been 'too apologetic' over the issue. The assembled members nodded in agreement and heartily applauded his sentiments. He also booked a room in Parliament to screen a film which suggested it was not the Jews who were the subject of a witch-hunt, but the Labour MPs who had been charged with anti-Semitism.* Williamson later claimed that 'dark forces' were influencing the media to hype the issue while Ken Livingstone, who argued that 'It's not anti-Semitic to hate the Jews of Israel',[111] dismissed it all as a right-wing, capitalist plot to undermine the leftist regime. Indeed, the idea that it was all lies by the right wing-press spread like wildfire through the culture of the left. It seems, yet again, that nothing has been learned in the near century since the Stalinist horrors.

It was widely reported that Corbyn had not tackled the problem because he felt 'too upset' at being criticised over it. Yet just days later Corbyn and Abbot

---

* Williamson had also spoken in the House of Commons to defend Colonel Pedro Banos. The Spanish author had written a demented book claiming the Rothschilds controlled the world economy and Israel was complicit in the assassination of JFK.

immediately began arguing in favour of clemency and 'support' for Shamima Begum, a member of ISIS who still defended the Manchester attack as a justifiable retaliation and claimed to feel nothing when seeing piles of decapitated heads. The message was clear. An indifference to Jewish interests coupled with a defence of the vilest of anti-Semites seems ingrained in the psyche of the hard left. As a result, the abuse continued without pause. Margaret Hodge publicly slammed the party for doing nothing about the threats she had received, including one which urged Hezbollah to kill her, while in October 2018 Rod Liddle reported in the *Telegraph* how four young Jews were barred from attending a speech given by John McDonnell in North London. No clear reason was given, though when asked why only Jews appeared to be excluded, a Labour member on the door declared that it was because they were 'aggressive people'. The film of her tirade spread quickly. It was even alleged that another Corbyn supporter had attempted to set fire to a protestor who had draped himself in the Israeli flag.

Any attempts to heal the rifts proved equally disastrous. Heather Mendick, a loyal supporter, was employed by Corbyn to rebuild the party's relationship with the Jewish community. Yet the hard-line member of Momentum had made claims that anti-Semitism was being 'weaponised against the Left' while dismissing calls for Labour to adopt the IHRA recommendations. She had also shown considerable loyalty to Chris Williamson and Pete Willsman, two of the most notorious names to emerge from the scandal. Corbyn also appointed Laura Murray, the daughter of Andrew Murray, one of his best friends and closest aides, to investigate complaints of anti-Semitism. But Murray had not only posted comments declaring 'please no bourgeoisie on my profile', despite living in a £1.3 million house paid for when the family sold their £50 million Picasso to the Qatari royal family, it was also alleged that she had sent abusive messages to Rachel Riley after the TV presenter stood up to oppose anti-Semitism.

Some of Corbyn's closest allies were even revealed to have moved to block sanctions from being imposed on those facing allegations. When the activist Kayla Bibby posted a picture of a face-hugging alien with the Star of David on its back sucking the life out of the Statue of Liberty she commented that it was 'The most accurate photo I've seen all year!' But Thomas Gardiner stepped in to prevent her suspension, a move compounded when she shared an image of both father and son in the Presidential Bush family and commented '100 per cent Jew Tools'. Seumas Milne, Andrew Murray and John McDonnell are also charged with blocking action against Glyn Secker and Rebecca Gordon-Nesbitt, both accused of posting dubious material and joining troublesome groups. Laura Murray overruled a recommendation that Patricia Sheeran be suspended after alleging links between Israel and ISIS. In an email exchange which included

Seumas Milne and Andrew Murray, a recommendation had come from Jeremy Corbyn's office that 'you investigate without suspension'. It was further alleged that Corbyn himself had made moves to block the suspension of Chris Williamson and he outright refused to sack Richard Burgon when he was forced to admit to a string of controversial comments. Indeed, Williamson's suspension was quickly lifted and he returned as the party whip, a move that provoked accusations of favouritism and caused great frustration among those hoping to address the crisis. The *Sunday Times* printed a lengthy report which showed how Corbyn's office had interfered in over a hundred cases. Yet the leadership team claimed it had made no intervention in the process at all, assertions that seemed to have been proven false when all the new evidence emerged.

These allegations were at the heart of a *Panorama* documentary which aired in July 2019. It was a searing investigation and numerous insiders stepped forward to condemn both the anti-Semitism they had seen and the leadership's apparent attempts to cover it up. Corbyn was shown speaking on Iran's Press TV after a number of Egyptian soldiers were killed in a terror attack. Even the authorities in Cairo confirmed the atrocity had been carried out by Jihadis. But Corbyn slithered into his seat to point the finger elsewhere, insinuating that 'I suspect the hand of Israel in this whole process'. Another Press TV clip was soon dug up with Corbyn complaining that the BBC had committed bias by suggesting 'that Israel has a right to exist'. This was aired in the nation presided over by Ali Khamanei who, shortly afterwards, threatened that 'The Zionist regime is a true cancer tumour on this region that should be cut off. And it definitely will be cut off.' It also emerged the Labour leader had written a foreword for a reissue of J.A. Hobson's 1905 book on Imperialism which argued that Europe's banks and press were controlled by Jews. Hobson claimed they pulled the strings of states while the Rothschild backed conspiracy was bent on war and world domination. It was effectively the same interpretation that informed *Mein Kampf* and it has long been assumed that Hitler read, and was inspired by, Hobson's work. Yet Corbyn called it 'brilliant', a 'great tome' and essentially 'correct'.

The party's top brass responded by yet again denying that there was a problem, thus ensuring that no real action would be taken. They dismissed *Panorama*'s investigations as 'biased' and threatened legal action against those who had voiced criticisms. They were simply cast as disaffected employees who had a grudge against the leader.* It is the routine response from the hard left:

---

* In the event it was the whistleblowers who sued the party. Labour lost the case and conceded they had made defamatory and false allegations against the litigants. They were forced to apologise 'unreservedly' to the former members they had bullied and were hit with a substantial six figure sum for damages. Yet Corbyn, unapologetic and still in denial, immediately put out a statement which voiced damning opposition to the

deny any wrongdoing while blaming traitors within. So the party exploded in rebellion against the leadership once more. Sixty-seven Labour peers signed a full page advert in the *Guardian* which accused Corbyn of 'allowing anti-Semitism to grow in our party'. A total of 200 MPs, peers and staffers lodged formal complaints while a number of prominent British Jews, including Simons Schama and Sebag Montefiore, published a letter which referred to 'a pool of poison in the party's soul'. A similar letter followed just weeks later. Twenty-four prominent figures like Simon Callow, Trevor Phillips, Tom Holland, Antony Beevor, Joanna Lumley and John le Carré denounced Corbyn and the anti-Semitism he had allowed to flourish. The GMB trade union passed a motion condemning Labour's 'toxic culture' while Baroness Hayter compared Corbyn's 'bunker mentality' to the 'last days of Hitler'. She was immediately sacked, which rather proved her point, and showed Corbyn cared rather more for his own hurt feelings than those of Labour's Jews. Tom Watson again pledged to fight the disease, a move which prompted a scathing attack from Corbyn loyalists like Diane Abbott and Len McCluskey. Momentum's Jon Lansman began proceedings for the NEC to abolish Watson's position in the party. The attempt, which hoped to side-line Watson without putting the issue to a vote, ultimately fell short but only just. Yet, exhausted from the fight, Watson resigned his post just weeks after the failed coup.

Even as the crisis continued to swirl the Labour frontbencher Fabian Hamilton arranged a Westminster meeting with Yahya Al-Saud, a Jordanian MP who has praised Palestinian terrorism and described Israel as a 'Jewish tumour'. The saga ran right to the swansong of Corbyn's leadership. In the disastrous 2019 election campaign that saw Corbynism demolished at the polls, thousands of Labour supporters, who would identify themselves as 'anti-racists', poured out bile to defend, justify or brush off the racism that continued to mar the party. Quizzed several times during the campaign, the leader consistently refused calls to apologise for his movement's anti-Semitism. The party then selected the far-left activist Kierin Offlands to star on a number of their campaign leaflets, but his old Twitter posts were resurrected, and they told the usual story. He sneered that Israeli soldiers were 'stormtroopers', claimed Zionists and Nazis were effectively the same and concluded by 'Remembering I need to hate Israeli Jews and people who think the State of Israel was / is a good idea'.

Even before the dust had started to settle the Jewish Labour Movement (JLM) submitted a dossier to the EHRC. It claimed that abuse had continued to rise

---

verdict. He then promptly formed an internet friendship with Grime artist Wiley who had commented that 'Jewish people...make me sick' and retweeted a post from Kekman which read that 'I'm so sick of fucking Jews...You are the most vile people in the history of humanity.'

over the preceding year and cited numerous shocking examples. Labour members were reported as calling for 'the extermination of every Jew on the planet', deriding Jews as a viral infection that needed to be 'eliminated' or dismissing them as 'bent-nose manipulative liars'. Another claimed the Red Sea was the 'ideal destination' to get rid of the Jews 'who are a cancer on us all'. There was 'no need for gas chambers anyway – gas is so expensive and we need it in England'. One called for the 'complete extinction of all Jews' while another councillor was told he was 'licking the bum of Jews for money'. Mariatu Conteh, accused of making that remark, had also put up a post suggesting Israel wanted to conquer 'the gentile world and establish our Jewish new world order'.

Others claimed that 'Hitler was right', criticism of Ken Livingstone was part of a 'Jewish conspiracy' and that Jews were 'subhuman' and should be forced to eat bacon. Prostitution was blamed on the Jews while another councillor was told to 'go home and count your money'. David Cooper of Nottinghamshire went even further. The report claimed he posted a rant demanding 'I call for the complete annihilation and extermination of every Jew on the planet. The Jew is worse than Black Death, worse than ebola virus. The Jew represents pure evil. We need to eliminate this infection.' Hundreds of other cases highlighted Holocaust denial and continuing claims about the Rothschild conspiracy of world domination. The majority of cases had either not been dealt with or were brushed off with no further action taken. The JLM concluded that Labour

> 'promotes known anti-Semites to positions of power; does not take action (and in fact subverts action) against those guilty of abhorrent anti-Semitism; victimises those that speak out against anti-Semitism; fails to protect Jewish members from anti-Semitism; allows Jewish MPs to be hounded out of their political home; and derides the issue of anti-Semitism to the extent that its very existence within the party is denied.'[112]

On the day before going to the polls a noisy contingent of Corbynites taunted a group protesting about anti-Semitism. They jeered 'From the river to the sea, Palestine will be free' - the words of Hamas, a clarion call to eradicate the state of Israel and exterminate its people. In April 2020 an internal report was released. It absolved the leadership of any wrongdoing and wittered on for 860 pages about the 'factional hostility' directed at the party's leader. That's right. It was Jeremy who was the victim all along.

When the EHRC report was published it largely ratified all the concerns. It criticised Shami Chakraharti's whitewash and concluded that Labour had indeed 'breached the Equality Act 2010'. They were guilty of 'unlawful acts of harassment and discrimination' and of 'political interference in anti-Semitism complaints'. Labour members were found guilty of 'Antisemitic conduct' while the leadership were held accountable for 'serious failings'. They were judged to have meddled in and attempted to cover up at least twenty-three separate cases. The report highlighted 'multiple failures' and an 'inadequate' system for resolving them. They concluded that there was a culture in the Labour party which 'at best, did not do enough to prevent antisemitism and, at worst, could be seen to accept it'. Despite their party's conviction for unequivocal racism, thousands of Corbynites immediately took to Twitter to deny or gloss over the findings, and to pledge their unswerving support for their erstwhile leader. Corbyn himself claimed that 'the problem was...dramatically overstated for political reasons by our opponents inside and outside the party, as well as by much of the media.' He even brazenly concluded that those smears 'hurt Jewish people'. Pam Bromley, who had been cited in the report, admitted that she had not read it before dismissing it as a 'circus' and a 'farce'.

The disease appears to be spreading to the American left too with Ilhan Omar, the Somali-American Democratic representative from Minnesota tweeting sentiments like 'Israel has hypnotised the world, may Allah awaken the people and help them see the evil doings of Israel'. She recently compounded the issue by arguing that Israeli influence in US policymaking was 'all about the Benjamins baby',* insinuating the malign influence of Jewish money. Peculiarly, she does not appear to have much to say on the oil-rich Gulf states who have spent millions on lobbying the Senate. Rashida Tlaib, a congresswoman from Detroit, and a daughter of Palestinian immigrants, also caused a storm when commenting on a picture of Kamala Harris posing with the Israeli PM Benjamin Netanyahu. She tweeted 'Hoping you are still part of the resistance to racism against ALL people. This picture says otherwise'. Tlaib had also joined an Instagram group on the Palestinian cause which compared Jews to rats and suggested that Israelis had carried out 9/11. In August 2019 Omar and Tlaib posted a cartoon that showed them being silenced by Donald Trump and Benjamin Netanyahu whose arms formed the Israeli flag. The drawing was the work of a notoriously anti-Semitic Holocaust denier from Iran, and to make the message clear a large Star of David was slapped across the middle of the image. More worryingly, both managed to deflect accusations of anti-Semitism as just more evidence of 'Islamophobia' while appearing sympathetic towards Al Qaeda and ISIS. Their rhetoric allowed Black Lives Matter to win widespread support even while expressing increasingly anti-Semitic views.

Bernie Sanders suggested the attacks on both women were a way of 'stifling' legitimate criticism of Israeli policy while Alexandria Ocasio-Cortez moved to defend Omar too. A resolution designed to tackle anti-Semitism was speedily side-tracked into a resolution against 'anti-Semitism, Islamophobia, racism and other forms of bigotry', neatly deflecting the blame for those who 'weaponise hate' onto white supremacists. It will likely be used as a shield to allow

---

* Benjamins is ghetto slang for dollars.

defamations of the world's only Jewish state to continue unabated. Worrying sentiments continue to spread through American universities while concerns have also been raised about activists like Linda Sarsour. Many on the American left are acutely aware that criticising Israel and the support it gets from the US is a guaranteed way of attracting progressive support. The Democrats appear to be copying the Labour template to the letter, and the party's support of Palestinian causes looks like allowing the rhetoric to continue unchallenged.

There are obvious consequences to all this inflamed rhetoric. Sheryll Murray, when interviewed about her experiences in the *Daily Mail*, was crystal clear about how threatened she had felt. 'Momentum and that hard-Left movement are personalising it. I genuinely feel there's a small step from normalising violent language to normalising actual violence. If you tolerate this, you start to feel other things are acceptable. It moves from damaging buildings to damaging people'.[113] She is entirely correct to voice such fears. All who bear witness to evidence of the Holocaust are appalled by it. But what preceded the death camps were the years of demonization, the conspiracy theories about pernicious Jewish influence and the blasé acceptance of that abuse. Before the jackboots came the huddled talk of Zionists and Rothschilds, of rumours of the power of Jewish money, media and political influence. That was the culture that paved the way to Auschwitz, the hatred that made the gas chambers possible. It is a hatred that is being ramped up once more no matter how much the likes of Jeremy Corbyn deny it. The wheel keeps turning, and we are in danger of coming full circle again.

The tragedy of this tale and the enduring situation is twofold. Not only does the hatred for Judaism yet endure, but the safe haven that the Jews sought proved a mirage too. When finally securing their state they simply faced persecution from the scores of radicals among their Islamic neighbours, ones who have persuaded vast swathes of the left to join them in their crusade and thus effectively return to the anti-Semitism in which their movement found its roots. In his column in the *Sunday Times* on 2 September 2018, Dominic Lawson cited a chilling example of this trait when reprinting a message a Corbyn supporter and senior charge nurse in A & E had tweeted to a Jew. 'Before I block you I will say that if Jews like yourself get Jeremy unseated, with Jeremy so popular and you get us subjected to more Tory rule, the so-called anti-semitism you think you see will be nothing to what you will see'. Harpreet Singh, the head of maths at Sandye Place Academy in Bedfordshire, also posted that 'every sane person is anti-Semitic' and 'of course we hate the Jews'. He continued 'God bless Jeremy Corbyn. He is a modern day saint. And I mean it. If one of your loved ones was at the mercy of Israel, you would feel his morality, his conviction and his commitment to The Truth'. The tale appears to be opening a new chapter, and the left are defending the new generation of genocidal lunatics while continuing to denounce the West. If and when a new Hitler arises, he will inevitably come from their ranks again.

Post Script

Over the first half of the century, up to the death of Stalin in 1953, the rise of socialism, in both its Russian and German variants, resulted in modern slavery and catastrophic loss of life. Yet it was still widely celebrated by the liberal intelligentsia. In the next volume we will examine how that enthusiasm saw its crimes spread across the globe in the latter half of the twentieth century, and of how its revival threatens us today. For a hundred years after socialism gained the ascendancy, and despite the horrors it presaged, the ideology has flourished into fashion once more. Its influence is now largely cultural and social rather than economic or political, but it remains a threat and is inflicting serious damage on the social fabric of the areas where it has taken root. It will take a significant effort for it to loosen its grip.

Acknowledgements

I am indebted to Aidan O'Keeffe, Catherine Lee and Paidraig McNally for their assistance with the text. I would also like to extend thanks to Charlotte Elliston, Vladmimir Mikheev, Graham Hobbs, Candice Butler and Nicholas Hill for helping with sources and feedback, and Neil Hart and Matt Bates for their work on the cover and website.

For full Bibliography and Index go to:

www.okpublishing.co.uk

Notes

Introduction

[1] Brooker, Charlie. *David Cameron is Like a Hollow Easter Egg* (2 April 2007) Guardian online
[2] Delingpole,Ivo. *How Eton Works* (26 September, 2015) Spectator Life, London;p.29
[3] Harman, Harriet. *Diary* (14 November 2015) Spectator, London;p.11
[4] http://entertainment.guardianoffers.co.uk/i-dd-rm001189-xac/nye-bevan-vermin-quote/?utm_source=merchandising&utm_medium=labour&utm_campaign=nye%20bevan%20vermin
[5] Cited in Conquest, Robert. *Dragons of Expectation* (2005) London;p.30
[6] Cited in Pendlebury, Richard. 'A Lifetime of Poison.' *Daily Mail* (30 April 2016) p.13
[7] Conquest, Robert. *Reflections on a Ravaged Century* (1999) London;p.137
[8] Ryan, Alan. *On Politics* (2012) London;p.914
[9] Hardman, Isabel. 'Labour's Lost Thinker' *Spectator* (19 September 2015) London;p.18
[10] Burke, Edmund. *Reflections on the Revolution in France* (2004) London;p.181

Chapter 1 – Liberty, Equality, Fraternity

[1] Diderot, Denis. *Oeuvres*, vol 5 *Correspondance*;pp.537-538
[2] Letter from Denis Diderot to Sophie Volland, 8 October 1768. In Denis Diderot, *Oeuvres,* vol 5, *Correspondance* (Paris: Laffont, 1997) p.895
[3] Young, Arthur. *Travels in France* (1905) London;p.27
[4] Young, Arthur. *Travels in France* (1905) London;pp.45-6, 61-2, 67, 132-3, 254-5
[5] Schama, Simon. *Citizens* (2004) London;p.122
[6] Moorehead, Caroline. *Dancing to the Precipice* (2010) London;p.59
[7] Marquise de la Tour Du Pin. *Memoirs* (1999) London;p.72
[8] Marquise de la Tour Du Pin. *Memoirs* (1999) London;p.139
[9] Schama, Simon. *Citizens* (2004) London;p.186
[10] Schama, Simon. *Citizens* (2004) London;p.259
[11] Scurr, Ruth. *Fatal Purity* (2007) London;p.79
[12] Schama, Simon. *Citizens* (2004) London;p.256
[13] Marquise de la Tour Du Pin. *Memoirs* (1999) London;p.104
[14] McPhee, Peter. *Robespierre. A Revolutionary Life* (2013) New Haven;p.32
[15] Matrat, Jean. *Robespierre, or the Tyranny of the Majority* (1975) London;p.37
[16] Matrat, Jean. *Robespierre, or the Tyranny of the Majority* (1975) London;p.31
[17] Matrat, Jean. *Robespierre, or the Tyranny of the Majority* (1975) London;p.39

[18] McPhee, Peter. *Robespierre. A Revolutionary Life* (2013) New Haven;p.xvii
[19] McPhee, Peter. *Robespierre. A Revolutionary Life* (2013) New Haven;p.xvii
[20] Matrat, Jean. *Robespierre, or the Tyranny of the Majority* (1975) London;p.51
[21] Hibbert, Christopher. *The French Revolution* (1980) London;p.62
[22] Schama, Simon. *Citizens* (2004) London;p.377
[23] Schama, Simon. *Citizens* (2004) London;p.378
[24] Schama, Simon. *Citizens* (2004) London;p.378
[25] Schama, Simon. *Citizens* (2004) London;p.344
[26] McPhee, Peter. *Robespierre. A Revolutionary Life* (2013) New Haven, Connecticut;p.66
[27] McPhee, Peter. *Robespierre. A Revolutionary Life* (2013) New Haven, Connecticut;p.68
[28] McPhee, Peter. *Robespierre. A Revolutionary Life* (2013) New Haven, Connecticut;p.68
[29] Marquise de la Tour Du Pin. *Memoirs* (1999) London;p.113
[30] Young, Arthur. *Travels in France* (1905) London;p.226
[31] Young, Arthur. *Travels in France* (1905) London;p.210
[32] Matrat, Jean. *Robespierre, or the Tyranny of the Majority* (1975) London;p.63
[33] C.J.Fox to R.Fitzpatrick, 30 July 1789, BL Add Mss 47580,fol.139
[34] 5 February 1790, *Parliamentary History,* Vol. XXVIII;p.351
[35] Young, Arthur. *Travels in France* (1905) London;p.323
[36] Zamoyski, Adam. *Holy Madness* (1999) London;p.99
[37] Price, Richard. *A Discourse on the Love of our Country* (4 November, 1789) www.constitution.org
[38] O'Brien, Conor Cruise. *Edmund Burke* (2002) London;p.206
[39] Zamoyski, Adam. *Holy Madness* (1999) London;p.75
[40] Schama, Simon. *Citizens* (2004)London;p.375
[41] Madame de la Tour du Pin. *Memoirs* (1999) London;p.125
[42] Marquise de la Tour Du Pin. *Memoirs* (1999) London;p.134
[43] Tackett, Timothy. *The Coming of the Terror in the French Revolution* (2015) Cambridge, Mass;p.63
[44] Hibbert, Christopher. *The French Revolution* (1980) London;p.140
[45] Schama, Simon. *Citizens* (2004) London;p.59
[46] Israel, Jonathan. *Revolutionary Ideas* (2014) Princeton, New Jersey;p.89
[47] Tackett, Timothy. *The Coming of the Terror in the French Revolution* (2015) Cambridge, Mass;p.122
[48] Cited in Tackett, Timothy. *The Coming of the Terror in the French Revolution* (2015) Cambridge, Mass;p.127
[49] Tackett, Timothy. *The Coming of the Terror in the French Revolution* (2015) Cambridge, Mass;p.137
[50] Sagan, Eli. *Citizens and Cannibals* (2001) Lanham, Maryland;p.327
[51] Sagan, Eli. *Citizens and Cannibals* (2001) Lanham, Maryland;p.331
[52] Tackett, Timothy. *The Coming of the Terror in the French Revolution* (2015) Cambridge, Mass;p.140

[53] Tackett, Timothy. *The Coming of the Terror in the French Revolution* (2015) Cambridge, Mass;p.140
[54] Marquise de la Tour Du Pin. *Memoirs* (1999) London;p.145
[55] Tackett, Timothy. *The Coming of the Terror in the French Revolution* (2015) Cambridge, Mass;p.140
[56] Tackett, Timothy. *The Coming of the Terror in the French Revolution* (2015) Cambridge, Mass;p.141
[57] Tackett, Timothy. *The Coming of the Terror in the French Revolution* (2015) Cambridge, Mass;p.141
[58] Scurr, Ruth. *Fatal Purity* (2007) London;pp.137-8
[59] Matrat, Jean. *Robespierre. A Revolutionary Life* (2013) New Haven;p.75
[60] McPhee, Peter. *Robespierre. A Revolutionary Life* (2013) New Haven;p.75
[61] McPhee, Peter. *Robespierre. A Revolutionary Life* (2013) New Haven;p.88
[62] McPhee, Peter. *Robespierre. A Revolutionary Life* (2013) New Haven;p.42
[63] Zamoyski, Adam. *Holy Madness* (1999) London;p.115
[64] McPhee, Peter. *Robespierre. A Revolutionary Life* (2013) New Haven;p.89
[65] Israel, Jonathan. *Revolutionary Ideas* (2014) Princeton, New Jersey;p.407
[66] Israel, Jonathan. *Revolutionary Ideas* (2014) Princeton, New Jersey;pp.44-5
[67] Israel, Jonathan. *Revolutionary Ideas* (2014) Princeton, New Jersey;p.335
[68] Israel, Jonathan. *Revolutionary Ideas* (2014) Princeton, New Jersey;p.286
[69] Saga, Eli. *Citizens and Cannibals* (2001) Lanham, Maryland;p.427
[70] De Tocqueville, Alexis. *The European Revolution* (1968) London;p.116
[71] Sagan, Eli. *Citizens and Cannibals* (2014) Lanham, Maryland;p.37
[72] Scurr, Ruth. *Fatal Purity* (2007) London;p.142
[73] Sagan, Eli. *Citizens and Cannibals* (2001) Lanham, Maryland;p.140
[74] Sagan, Eli. *Citizens and Cannibals* (2001) Lanham, Maryland;p.139
[75] Scurr, Ruth. *Fatal Purity* (2007) London;p.173
[76] Tackett, Timothy. *The Coming of the Terror in the French Revolution* (2015) Cambridge, Mass;p.111
[77] Israel, Jonathan. *Revolutionary Ideas* (2014) Princeton, New Jersey;p.204
[78] Tackett, Timothy. *The Coming of the Terror in the French Revolution* (2015) Cambridge, Mass;p.89
[79] Tackett, Timothy. *The Coming of the Terror in the French Revolution* (2015) Cambridge, Mas;p.154
[80] Cited in Israel, Jonathan. *Revolutionary Ideas* (2014) Princeton;p.304
[81] Tackett, Timothy. *The Coming of the Terror in the French Revolution* (2015) Cambridge, Mass;p.174
[82] Andress, David. *The Terror* (2006) London;p.84
[83] Young, Arthur. *The Example of France, a Warning to Britain* (1793) London;p.4
[84] Moorehead, Caroline. *Dancing to the Precipice* (2010) London;pp.151-2
[85] McPhee, Peter. *Robespierre. A Revolutionary Life* (2013) New Haven, Connecticut;p.126
[86] Sagan, Eli. *Citizens and Cannibals* (2001) Lanham, Maryland;p.297
[87] Cited in Israel, Jonathan. *Revolutionary Ideas* (2014) Princeton;p.430
[88] Schama, Simon. *Citizens* (2004) London;p.532

[89] Schama, Simon. *Citizens* (2004) London;p.532
[90] Andress, David. *The Terror* (2006) London;pp.93-4
[91] Scurr, Ruth. *Fatal Purity* (2007) London;p.216
[92] Scurr, Ruth. *Fatal Purity* (2007) London;p.216
[93] Scurr, Ruth. *Fatal Purity* (2007) London;p.216
[94] Scurr, Ruth. *Fatal Purity* (2007) London;p.216
[95] McPhee, Peter. *Robespierre. A Revolutionary Life* (2013) New Haven, Connecticut;p.138
[96] McPhee, Peter. *Robespierre. A Revolutionary Life* (2013) New Haven, Connecticut;p.138
[97] McPhee, Peter. *Robespierre. A Revolutionary Life* (2013) New Haven, Connecticut;p.127
[98] Tackett, Timothy. *The Coming of the Terror in the French Revolution* (2015) Harvard;p.228
[99]Tackett, Timothy. *The Coming of the Terror in the French Revolution* (2015) Harvard;p.231
[100] Tackett, Timothy. *The Coming of the Terror in the French Revolution* (2015) Harvard;p.231
[101] Schama, Simon. *Citizens* (2004) London;p.557
[102] Scurr, Ruth. *Fatal Purity* (2007) London;p.221
[103] McPhee, Peter. *Robespierre. A Revolutionary Life* (2013) New Haven, Connecticut;p.142
[104] Schama, Simon. *Citizens* (2004) London;p.566
[105] Andress, David. *The Terror* (2006) London;p.150
[106] Schama, Simon. *Citizens* (2004) London;p.599
[107] Cited in Matrat, Jean. *Robespierre* (1975) London;p.210
[108] Schama, Simon. *Citizens* (2004) London;p.601
[109] Schama, Simon. *Citizens* (2004) London;p.605
[110] Sagan, Eli. *Citizens and Cannibals* (2001) Lanham, Maryland;pp.265-6
[111] Sagan, Eli. *Citizens and Cannibals* (2001) Lanham, Maryland;p.273
[112] Sagan, Eli. *Citizens and Cannibals* (2001) Lanham, Maryland;p.266
[113] Schama, Simon. *Citizens* (2004) London;p.608
[114] Israel, Jonathan. *Revolutionary Ideas* (2014) Princeton, New Jersey;p.459
[115] Scurr, Ruth. *Fatal Purity* (2007) London;p.241
[116] Scurr, Ruth. *Fatal Purity* (2007) London;p.239
[117] Israel, Jonathan. *Revolutionary Ideas* (2014) Princeton, New Jersey;p.455
[118] Schama, Simon. *Citizens* (2004) London;p.623
[119] Scurr, Ruth. *Fatal Purity* (2007) London;p.258
[120] Tackett, Timothy. *The Coming of the Terror in the French Revolution* (2015) Harvard;p.303
[121] Schama, Simon. *Citizens* (2004) London;p.640
[122] Tackett, Timothy. *The Coming of the Terror in the French Revolution* (2015) Harvard;p.299
[123] McPhee, Peter. *Robespiere. A Revolutionary Life* (2013) London;p.165
[124] Schama, Simon. *Citizens* (2004) London;p.672

[125] Scurr, Ruth. *Fatal Purity* (2007) London;p.259
[126]Scurr, Ruth. *Fatal Purity* (2007) London;p.259
[127] Cited in Andress, David. *The Terror* (2006) London;p.288
[128] Andress, David. *The Terror* (2006) London;p.228
[129] Israel, Jonathan. *Revolutionary Ideas* (2014) Princeton, New Jersey;p.509
[130] Cited in Andress, David. *The Terror* (2006) London;p.224
[131] Andress, David. *The Terror* (2006) London;p.225
[132] Andress, David. *The Terror* (2006) London;p.224
[133] Schama, Simon. *Citizens* (2004) London;p.666
[134] Andress, David. *The Terror* (2006) London;p.249
[135] Schama, Simon. *Citizens* (2004) London;p.659
[136] Schama, Simon. *Citizens* (2004) London;p.660
[137] Scurr, Ruth. *Fatal Purity* (2007) London;p.262
[138] McPhee, Peter. *Robespierre, A Revolutionary Life* (2013) New Haven, Connecticut;p.179
[139] McPhee, Peter. *Robespierre, A Revolutionary Life* (2013) New Haven, Connecticut;p.181
[140] Sagan, Eli. *Citizens and Cannibals* (2001) Lanham, Maryland;p.269
[141] Scurr, Ruth. *Fatal Purity* (2007) London;p.275
[142] McPhee, Peter. *Robespierre. A Revolutionary Life* (2013) New Haven, Connecticut;p.183
[143] Mantel, Hilary. *A Place of Greater Safety* (2010) London;pp.770-1
[144] Scurr, Ruth. *Fatal Purity* (2007) London;p.285
[145] Andress, David. *The Terror* (2006) London;p.276
[146] Andress, David. *The Terror* (2006) London;p.310
[147] Sagan, Eli. *Citizens and Cannibals* (2001) Lanham, Maryland;p.182
[148] McPhee, Peter. *Robespierre. A Revolutionary Life* (2013) New Haven, Connecticut;p.195
[149] Andress, David. *The Terror* (2006) London;p.278
[150] Andress, David. *The Terror* (2006) London;pp.295-6
[151] Andress, David. *The Terror* (2006) London;p.310
[152] Scurr, Ruth. *Fatal Purity* (2007) London;p.279
[153] McPhee, Peter. *Robespierre. A Revolutionary Life* (2013) New Haven, Connecticut;p.214
[154] Saga, Eli. *Citizens and Cannibals* (2001) Lanham, Maryland;p.485
[155] McPhee, Peter. *Robespiere. A Revolutionary Life* (2013) New Haven, Connecticut;p.217
[156] Israel, Jonathan. *Revolutionary Ideas* (2014) Princeton, New Jersey;p.674
[157] Sagan, Eli. *Citizens and Cannibals* (2001) Lanham, Maryland;p.499
[158] Cited in Schama, Simon. *Citizens* (2004) London;p.549
[159] Cited in Schama, Simon. *Citizens* (2004) London;p.665
[160] Sagan, Eli. *Citizens and Cannibals* (2001) Lanham, Maryland;p.50
[161] Sagan, Eli. *Citizens and Cannibals* (2001) Lanham, Maryland;p.65
[162] Schama, Simon. *Citizens* (2004) London;p.727
[163] Sagan, Eli. *Citizens and Cannibals* (2001) Lanham, Maryland;p.538

Chapter 2 – The Philosophy of Revolution

[1]Magee, Bryan. *The Story of Philosophy* (1998)London;p.129
[2] Russell, Bertrand. *A History of Western Philosophy* (1984) London;p.660
[3] Rousseau, Jean-Jacques. *Confessions* (2000) Oxford;p.7
[4] Rousseau, Jean-Jacques. *Confessions* (2000) Oxford;p.19
[5] Rousseau, Jean-Jacques. *Confessions* (2000) Oxford;p.395
[6] Rousseau, Jean-Jacques. *Confessions* (2000) Oxford;p.321
[7] Rousseau, Jean-Jacques. *Discourse on the Arts and Sciences* (2014) Adelaide;p.nn
[8] Rousseau, Jean-Jacques. *Confessions* (2000) Oxford;p.541
[9] Rousseau, Jean-Jacques. *A Discourse on Inequality* (1984) London;p.83
[10] Rousseau, Jean-Jacques. *A Discourse on Inequality* (1984) London;p.84
[11] Rousseau, Jean-Jacques. *A Discourse on Inequality* (1984) London;p.85
[12] Zamoyski, Adam. *Holy Madness* (1999) London;p.10
[13] Rousseau, Jean-Jacques. *A Discourse on Inequality* (1984) London;p.123
[14] Tacitus. *The Annals of Imperial Rome* (1977) Harmondsworth;p.132
[15] Rousseau, Jean-Jacques. *A Discourse on Inequality* (1984) London;p.116
[16] Rousseau, Jean-Jacques. *Discourse on the Arts and Sciences* (2014) Adelaide;p.nn
[17] Cited in Zamoyski, Adam. *Holy Madness* (1999) London;p.3
[18] Rousseau, Jean-Jacques. *A Discourse on Inequality* (1984) London;p.58
[19] Rousseau, Jean-Jacques. *Confessions* (2000) Oxford;p.401
[20] Damrosch, Leo. *Jean-Jacques Rousseau* (2007) New York;p.264
[21] Rousseau, Jean-Jacques. *Confessions* (2000) Oxford;p.439
[22] Rousseau, Jean-Jacques. *Confessions* (2000) Oxford;p.440
[23] Rousseau, Jean-Jacques. *Confessions* (2000) Oxford;p.441
[24] Rousseau, Jean-Jacques. *Confessions* (2000) Oxford;p.441
[25] Rousseau, Jean-Jacques. *Confessions* (2000) Oxford;p.442
[26] Rousseau, Jean-Jacques. *Confessions* (2000) Oxford;p.465
[27] Rousseau, Jean-Jacques. *Confessions* (2000) Oxford;p.470
[28] Rousseau, Jean-Jacques. *Confessions* (2000) Oxford;p.484
[29] Damrosch, Leo. *Jean-Jacques Rousseau* (2007) New York;p.299
[30] Damrosch, Leo. *Jean-Jacques Rousseau* (2007) New York;p.304
[31] Rousseau, Jean-Jacques. *Confessions* (2000) Oxford;p.535
[32] Rousseau, Jean-Jacques. *Émile* (2015) USA;p.3
[33] Rousseau, Jean-Jacques. *Émile* (2015) USA;p.9
[34] Rousseau, Jean-Jacques. *Confessions* (2000) Oxford;p.335
[35] Damrosch, Leo. *Jean-Jacques Rousseau* (2007) New York;p.193
[36] Ryan, Alan. *On Politics* (2012) London;p.533
[37] Rousseau, Jean-Jacques. *Confessions* (2000) Oxford;p.348
[38] Rousseau, Jean-Jacques. *Confessions* (2000) Oxford;p.348
[39] Rousseau, Jean-Jacques. *Émile* (2015) USA;p.49
[40] Rousseau, Jean-Jacques. *Émile* (2015) USA;p.61
[41] Rousseau, Jean-Jacques. *Émile* (2015) USA;p.18
[42] Rousseau, Jean-Jacques. *Émile* (2015) USA;p.79

[43] Rousseau, Jean-Jacques. *Émile* (2015) USA;p.98
[44] Blom, Philipp. *Wicked Company* (2011) London;p.xvii
[45] Zamoyski, Adam. *Holy Madness* (1999) London;p.65
[46] Zamoyski, Adam. *Holy Madness* (1999) London;p.72
[47] Rousseau, Jean-Jacques. *Émile* (2015) USA;p.94
[48] Rousseau, Jean-Jacques. *Émile* (2015) USA;p.101
[49] Rousseau, Jean-Jacques. *The Social Contract* (1994) Oxford;p.45
[50] Damrosch, Leo. *Jean-Jacques Rousseau* (2007) New York;p.350
[51] Rousseau, Jean-Jacques. *The Social Contract* (1994) Oxford;p.67
[52] Rousseau, Jean-Jacques. *The Social Contract* (1994) Oxford;p.75
[53] Rousseau, Jean-Jacques. *The Social Contract* (1994) Oxford;pp.76-7
[54] Rousseau, Jean-Jacques. *The Social Contract* (1994) Oxford;p.167
[55] Rousseau, Jean-Jacques. *The Social Contract* (1994) Oxford;p.14
[56] Rousseau, Jean-Jacques. *Émile* (2015) USA;p.5
[57] Rousseau, Jean-Jacques. *The Social Contract* (1994) Oxford;p.156
[58] Rousseau, Jean-Jacques. *A Discourse on Inequality* (1984) London;pp.115-6
[59] Blom, Philipp. *Wicked Company* (2011) London;p.210
[60] Berlin, Isaiah. *Freedom and its Betrayal* (2003)London;p.47
[61] Rousseau, Jean-Jacques. *Confessions* (2000) Oxford;p.568
[62] Russell, Bertrand. *A History of Western Philosophy* (1984) London;p.665
[63] Damrosch, Leo. *Jean-Jacques Rousseau* (2007) New York;p.420
[64] Damrosch, Leo. *Jean-Jacques Rousseau* (2007) New York;p.426
[65] Damrosch, Leo. *Jean-Jacques Rousseau* (2007) New York;p.424
[66] Russell, Bertrand. *A History of Western Philosophy* (1984) London;p.653
[67] Russell, Bertrand. *A History of Western Philosophy* (1984) London;p.651
[68] Russell, Bertrand. *A History of Western Philosophy* (1984) London;p.656
[69] Rousseau, Jean-Jacques. *Confessions* (2000) Oxford;p.404
[70] Damrosch, Leo. *Jean-Jacques Rousseau* (2007) New York;p.241
[71] Ryan, Alan. *On Politics* (2012) London;p.537
[72] Berlin, Isaiah. *Freedom and its Betrayal* (2003) London;p.41
[73]O'Brien, Conor Cruise *Edmund Burke* (2002) London;p.151
[74] Keane, John. *Tom Paine. A Political Life* (2009) London;p.8
[75] Paine, Thomas. *Rights of Man Part II* (February, 1792) In *Rights of Man, Common Sense and Other Political Writings* (2008) Oxford;p.271
[76] Paine, Thomas. *Rights of Man* (March, 1791) In *Rights of Man, Common Sense and Other Political Writings* (2008) Oxford;pp.108-9
[77] Keane, John. *Tom Paine. A Political Life* (2009) London;pp.12-4
[78] Keane, John. *Tom Paine. A Political Life* (2009) London;p.189
[79] Macpherson, C.B. *Burke* (1980) Oxford;p.52
[80] Burke, Edmund. *Reflections on the Revolution in France* (November, 1790) This edition – 2004. London;p.141
[81] O'Brien, Conor Cruise. *Edmund Burke* (2002) London;pp.49-50
[82] O'Brien, Conor Cruise. *Edmund Burke* (2002) London;p.138
[83] O'Brien, Conor Cruise. *Edmund Burke* (2002) London;p.1
[84] Prior, James. *Life of the Right Honourable Edmund Burke* (1854) London;p.1

[85] Fennessy, R.R. *Burke, Paine and the Rights of Man. A Difference of Political Opinion* (1963) The Hague;p.52
[86] Fennessy, R.R. *Burke, Paine and the Rights of Man. A Difference of Political Opinion* (1963) The Hague;pp.12-3
[87] Keane, John. *Tom Paine. A Political Life* (2009) London;p.20-4
[88] Levin, Yuval. *The Great Debate. Edmund Burke, Thomas Paine and the Birth of Left and Right* (2014) New York;p.12
[89] Fennessy, R.R. *Burke, Paine and the Rights of Man. A Difference of Political Opinion* (1963) The Hague;p.53
[90] Keane, John. *Tom Paine. A Political Life* (2009) London;p.48
[91] O'Brien, Conor Cruise. *Edmund Burke* (2002) London;p.16
[92] Keane, John. *Tom Paine. A Political Life* (2009) London;p.51
[93] Fennessy, R.R. *Burke, Paine and the Rights of Man. A Difference of Political Opinion* (1963) The Hague;p.19
[94] Cited in Keane, John. *Tom Paine. A Political Life* (2009) London;p.437
[95] Fennessy, R.R. *Burke, Paine and the Rights of Man. A Difference of Political Opinion* (1963) The Hague;p.19
[96] Cited in Keane, John. *Tom Paine. A Political Life* (2009) London;p.206
[97] Fennessy, R.R. *Burke, Paine and the Rights of Man. A Difference of Political Opinion* (1963) The Hague;p.19
[98] Burke, Edmund. *Observations on a Late Publication Intitled the Present State of the Nation* (1769) socserv2.socsci_mcmaster.ca/econ/ugcm/3ll3/burke/works01.pdf
[99] Burke, Edmund. *A Philosophical Enquiry into the Origin of our Ideas of the Sublime and Beautiful* (1756) http://www.gutenberg.org/files/15043/15043-h/15043-h.htm#A_PHILOSOPHICAL_INQUIRY;p.130
[100] Burke, Edmund. *A Philosophical Enquiry into the Origin of our Ideas of the Sublime and Beautiful* (1756) http://www.gutenberg.org/files/15043/15043-h/15043-h.htm#A_PHILOSOPHICAL_INQUIRY;p.144
[101] Burke, Edmund. *Letter to a Noble Lord* (1796) http://www.ourcivilisation.com/smartboard/shop/burkee/tolord
[102] Paine, Thomas. *Rights of Man* (March, 1791) In *Rights of Man, Common Sense and Other Political Writings* (2008) Oxford;pp.100-1
[103] Burke, Edmund. *Reflections on the Revolution in France* (November, 1790) This edition – 2004. London;p.376
[104] Paine, Thomas. *The Age of Reason* (October, 1795) This edition – 2004. New York;p.63
[105] Paine, Thomas. *The Age of Reason* (October, 1795) This edition – 2004. New York;p.56
[106] Keane, John. *Tom Paine. A Political Life* (2009) London;p.45
[107] Keane, John. *Tom Paine. A Political Life* (2009) London;p.61
[108] Fennessy, R.R. *Burke, Paine and the Rights of Man. A Difference of Political Opinion* (1963) The Hague;p.31
[109] Paine, Thomas. *The Age of Reason* (October, 1795) This edition – 2004. New York;p.45

[110] Paine, Thomas. *Rights of Man* (March, 1791) In *Rights of Man, Common Sense and Other Political Writings* (2008) Oxford;pp.116-7

[111]Macpherson, C.B. *Burke* (1980) Oxford;p.59

[112] Burke, Edmund. *A Philosophical Enquiry into the Origin of our Ideas of the Sublime and Beautiful* (1756) http://www.gutenberg.org/files/15043/15043-h/15043-h.htm#A_PHILOSOPHICAL_INQUIRY;p.208

[113] Kirk, Russell. *Burke and Natural Rights* (1951) http://www.kirkcenter.org/index.php/detail/burke-natural-rights-1951/

[114] Levin, Yuval. *The Great Debate. Edmund Burke, Thomas Paine and the Birth of Left and Right* (2014) New York;p.45

[115] Burke, Edmund. *Reflections on the Revolution in France* (November, 1790) This edition – 2004. London;p.276

[116] Keane, John. *Tom Paine. A Political Life* (2009) London;p.61

[117] Paine, Thomas. *Agrarian Law* (1797) In *Rights of Man, Common Sense and Other Political Writings* (2008) Oxford;p.416

[118] Burke, Edmund. *Reflections on the Revolution in France* (November, 1790) This edition – 2004. London;p.152

[119] Cited in Levin, Yuval. *The Great Debate. Edmund Burke, Thomas Paine and the Birth of Left and Right* (2014) New York;p.45

[120] Levin, Yuval. *The Great Debate. Edmund Burke, Thomas Paine and the Birth of Left and Right* (2014) New York;p.54

[121] Burke, Edmund. *A Letter to a Member of the National Assembly* (1791) http://www.gutenberg.org/files/15700/15700-h/15700-h.htm#MEMBER_OF_THE_NATIONAL_ASSEMBLY;p.nn

[122] Paine, Thomas. *Rights of Man* (March, 1791) In *Rights of Man, Common Sense and Other Political Writings* (2008) Oxford;p.145

[123] Paine, Thomas. *Rights of Man* (March, 1791) In *Rights of Man, Common Sense and Other Political Writings* (2008) Oxford;p.145

[124] Norman, Jesse. *Edmund Burke. Philosopher, Politician, Prophet* (2013) London;p.198

[125] Levin, Yuval. *The Great Debate. Edmund Burke, Thomas Paine and the Birth of Left and Right* (2014) New York;p.11

[126] Burke, Edmund. *Reflections on the Revolution in France* (November, 1790) This edition – 2004. London;pp.119-20

[127] Burke, Edmund. *Letter to Charles Jean François Depont* (November, 1789) http://oll.libertyfund.org/titles/burke-further-reflections-on-the-french-revolution;pp.7-8

[128] Burke, Peter. *The Fortunes of the Courtier* (19995) Cambridge;pp.128 & 163-78

[129] Paine, Thomas. *Rights of Man* (March, 1791) In *Rights of Man, Common Sense and Other Political Writings* (2008) Oxford;p.134

[130] Paine, Thomas. *Rights of Man Part II* (February, 1792) In *Rights of Man, Common Sense and Other Political Writings* (2008) Oxford;p.228

[131] Burke, Edmund. *An Appeal From the New to the Old Whigs* (August, 1791) http://archive.orgh/details/appealfromnewtoo00burkiala;pp.107-8

[132] Burke, Edmund. *Reflections on the Revolution in France* (November, 1790) This edition – 2004. London;p.138
[133] Burke, Edmund. *Reflections on the Revolution in France* (November, 1790) This edition – 2004. London;p.139
[134] Burke, Edmund. *Reflections on the Revolution in France* (November, 1790) This edition – 2004. London;pp.128-30 & 134
[135]Burke, Edmund. *Reflections on the Revolution in France* (November, 1790) This edition – 2004. London;p.94
[136] Paine, Thomas. *Common Sense* (January, 1776) In *Rights of Man, Common Sense and Other Political Writings* (2008) Oxford;p.9
[137] Burke, Edmund. *Reflections on the Revolution in France* (November, 1790) This edition – 2004. London;p.342
[138] Burke, Edmund. *Letters on a Regicide Peace* (1796) http://oll.libertyfund.org/titles/burke-select-works-of-demund-burke-vol-3;p.56
[139] Burke, Edmund. *An Appeal From the New to the Old Whigs* (August, 1791) http://archive.orgh/details/appealfromnewtoo00burkiala;p.138
[140]Burke, Edmund. *Letter to a Noble Lord* (1796) http://www.ourcivilisation.com/smartboard/shop/burkee/tolord;p.nn
[141] Paine, Thomas. *Rights of Man Part II* (February, 1792) In *Rights of Man, Common Sense and Other Political Writings* (2008) Oxford;p.291
[142] Cited in Keane, John. *Tom Paine. A Political Life* (2009) London;p.125
[143] Paine, Thomas. *Rights of Man* (March, 1791) pp.125-8, & *Rights of Man Part II* (February, 1792) pp.212 & 220-1 In *Rights of Man, Common Sense and Other Political Writings* (2008) Oxford
[144] Burke, Edmund. *Reflections on the Revolution in France* (November, 1790) This edition – 2004. London;pp.373-4
[145] Burke, Edmund. *Reflections on the Revolution in France* (November, 1790) This edition – 2004. London;p.279
[146] Paine, Thomas. *Rights of Man* (March, 1791) In *Rights of Man, Common Sense and Other Political Writings* (2008) Oxford;p.176
[147] Paine, Thomas. *Rights of Man Part II* (February, 1792) In *Rights of Man, Common Sense and Other Political Writings* (2008) Oxford;pp.290-311
[148] Paine, Thomas. *Agrarian Justice* (1797) In *Rights of Man, Common Sense and Other Political Writings* (2008) Oxford,;pp.416-20
[149] Paine, Thomas. *Agrarian Justice* (1797) In *Rights of Man, Common Sense and Other Political Writings* (2008) Oxford;pp.431-2
[150] Paine, Thomas. *Rights of Man Part II* (February, 1792) In *Rights of Man, Common Sense and Other Political Writings* (2008) Oxford;p.266
[151]Paine, Thomas. *Agrarian Law* (1797) In *Rights of Man, Common Sense and Other Political Writings* (2008) Oxford;p.425
[152] Paine, Thomas. *Rights of Man Part II* (February, 1792) In *Rights of Man, Common Sense and Other Political Writings* (2008) Oxford;p.320
[153] Keane, John. *Tom Paine. A Political Life* (2009) London;p.97
[154] Burke, Edmund. *Letter to a Noble Lord* (1797) http://www.ourcivilisation.com/smartboard/shop/burkee/tolord; p.nn

[155] Burke, Edmund. *Reflections on the Revolution in France* (November, 1790) This edition – 2004. London;pp.138 & 144
[156] Paine, Thomas. *Rights of Man* (March, 1791) In *Rights of Man, Common Sense and Other Political Writings* (2008) Oxford;p.135
[157] Paine, Thomas. *Rights of Man Part II* (February, 1792) In *Rights of Man, Common Sense and Other Political Writings* (2008) Oxford;p.212
[158] Burke, Edmund. *A Letter to a Member of the National Assembly* (1791) http://www.gutenberg.org/files/15700/15700-h/15700-h.htm#MEMBER_OF_THE_NATIONAL_ASSEMBLY;p.nn
[159]Keane, John. *Tom Paine. A Political Life* (2009) London;p.163
[160] Keane, John. *Tom Paine. A Political Life* (2009) London;p.348
[161] Thompson, E.P. *The Making of the English Working Class* (1991) London;p.80
[162] Mori, Jennifer. *William Pitt and the French Revolution* (1997) Edinburgh;p.93
[163] Keane, John. *Tom Paine. A Political Life* (2009) London;pp.102-3
[164] Hitchens, Christopher. *Thomas Paine's Rights of Man* (2006) London;p.137
[165] Keane, John. *Tom Paine. A Political Life* (2009) London;pp.438-41
[166] Cited in Hague, William. *William Pitt the Younger* (2005) London;p.374
[167] Paine, Thomas. *Letter to the People of France and the French Armies on the Event of the 18th Fructidor* (1797) Paris;p.27
[168] Burke, Edmund. *Speech on Moving his Resolutions for Conciliation With the Colonies* (22 March, 1775) http://www.gutenberg.org/files/151998/15198-h/15198-h.htm#CONCILIATION_WITH_THE_COLONIES;p.nn
[169] Fennessy, R.R. *Burke, Paine and the Rights of Man. A Difference of Political Opinion* (1963) The Hague;p.167
[170] Paine, Thomas. *The Age of Reason* (October, 1795) This edition – 2004. New York;p.72
[171] Cited in Sperber, Jonathan. *Karl Marx. A Nineteenth Century Life.* (2013) London;p.32
[172] Berlin, Isaiah. *Karl Marx* (1995) London. Introduction;p.ix
[173] Berlin, Isaiah. *Karl Marx* (1995) London;p.28
[174] Cited in Sperber, Jonathan. *Karl Marx. A Nineteenth Century Life.* (2013) London;p.52
[175] Cited in Kamenka, Eugene (editor) *The Portable Karl Marx* (1983) London;p.17
[176] Cited in Kamenka, Eugene (editor) *The Portable Karl Marx* (1983) London;p.20
[177] Sperber, Jonathan. *Karl Marx. A Nineteenth Century Life.* (2013) London;p.63
[178] Sperber, Jonathan. *Karl Marx. A Nineteenth Century Life.* (2013) London;p.68
[179] McLellan, David. *Karl Marx. His Life and Thought* (1976) St. Albans;p.55
[180] Cited in Kamenka, Eugene (editor) *The Portable Karl Marx* (1983) London;p.22
[181] Berlin, Isaiah. *Karl Marx* (1995) London;p.55
[182] Cited in Kamenka, Eugene (editor) *The Portable Karl Marx* (1983) London;p.114
[183] Cited in Wheen, Francis. *Karl Marx* (2000) London;p.56
[184] Sperber, Jonathan. *Karl Marx. A Nineteenth Century Life.* (2013) London;p.123
[185] Cited in Kamenka, Eugene (editor) *The Portable Karl Marx* (1983) London;p.147
[186] Cited in Kamenka, Eugene (editor) *The Portable Karl Marx* (1983) London;p.150
[187] McLellan, David. *Karl Marx. His Life and Thought* (1976) St. Albans;p.133

[188] Cited in Kamenka, Eugene (editor) *The Portable Karl Marx* (1983) London;p.158
[189] Cited in McLellan, David. *Karl Marx. His Life and Thought* (1976) St. Albans;p.167
[190] Cited in McLellan, David. *Karl Marx. His Life and Thought* (1976) St. Albans;p.170
[191] Wheen, Francis. *Karl Marx* (2000) London;p.103
[192] Cited in Kamenka, Eugene (editor) *The Portable Karl Marx* (1983) London;p.174
[193] Cited in Wheen, Francis. *Karl Marx* (2000) London;p.108
[194] Sperber, Jonathan. *Karl Marx. A Nineteenth Century Life.* (2013) London;p.182
[195] Cited in Wheen, Francis. *Karl Marx* (2000) London;p.106
[196] Cited in Wheen, Francis. *Karl Marx* (2000) London;p.96
[197] Marx, Karl. *The Communist Manifesto* (2015) London;p.1
[198] Marx, Karl. *The Communist Manifesto* (2015) London;p.52
[199] Marx, Karl. *The Communist Manifesto* (2015) London;p.1
[200] Marx, Karl. *The Communist Manifesto* (2015) London;p.2
[201] Marx, Karl. *The Communist Manifesto* (2015) London;p.5
[202] Marx, Karl. *The Communist Manifesto* (2015) London;p.6
[203] Marx, Karl. *The Communist Manifesto* (2015) London;p.20
[204] Marx, Karl. *The Communist Manifesto* (2015) London;p.35
[205] Marx, Karl. *The Communist Manifesto* (2015) London;p.52
[206] Sperber, Jonathan. *Karl Marx. A Nineteenth Century Life.* (2013) London;pp.210-11
[207] Sperber, Jonathan. *Karl Marx. A Nineteenth Century Life.* (2013) London;p.225
[208] Cited in Kamenka, Eugene (editor) *The Portable Karl Marx* (1983) London;p.270
[209] Cited in McLellan, David. *Karl Marx. His Life and Thought* (1976) St. Albans;p.200
[210] Berlin, Isaiah. *Karl Marx* (1995) London;p.128
[211] Cited in Sperber, Jonathan. *Karl Marx. A Nineteenth Century Life.* (2013) London;p.250
[212] Cited in Kamenka, Eugene (editor) *The Portable Karl Marx* (1983) London;p.245
[213]Cited in Sperber, Jonathan. *Karl Marx. A Nineteenth Century Life.* (2013) London;p.252
[214] Cited in McLellan, David. *Karl Marx. His Life and Thought* (1976) St. Albans;p.213
[215] Cited in McLellan, David. *Karl Marx. His Life and Thought* (1976) St. Albans;p.217
[216] Sperber, Jonathan. *Karl Marx. A Nineteenth Century Life.* (2013) London;p.267
[217]Cited in Sperber, Jonathan. *Karl Marx. A Nineteenth Century Life.* (2013) London;p.268
[218] Cited in Sperber, Jonathan. *Karl Marx. A Nineteenth Century Life.* (2013) London;p.269
[219] Cited in Sperber, Jonathan. *Karl Marx. A Nineteenth Century Life.* (2013) London;p.493
[220] Cited in McLellan, David. *Karl Marx* (1976) St. Albans;p.76
[221] Cited in Wheen, Francis. *Karl Marx* (2000) London;p.186
[222] Cited in Wheen, Francis. *Karl Marx* (2000) London;p.198
[223] Cited in Wheen, Francis. *Karl Marx* (2000) London;p.198
[224] Cited in Wheen, Francis. *Karl Marx* (2000) London;p.202
[225] Ryan, Alan. *On Politics* (2012) London;p.578
[226] Cited in Ryan, Alan. *On Politics* (2012) London;p.591

[227] Cited in Sperber, Jonathan. *Karl Marx. A Nineteenth Century Life.* (2013) London;p.292
[228] Cited in Wheen, Francis. *Karl Marx* (2000) London;p.208
[229] Cited in Wheen, Francis. *Karl Marx* (2000) London;p.226
[230] Cited in Wheen, Francis. *Karl Marx* (2000) London;p.225
[231] Wheen, Francis. *Karl Marx* (2000) London;p.247
[232] Wheen, Francis. *Karl Marx* (2000) London;p.250
[233]Cited in Wheen, Francis. *Karl Marx* (2000) London;p.263
[234] Wheen, Francis. *Karl Marx* (2000) London;p.268
[235] McLellan, David. *Karl Marx* (1976) St. Albans;pp.365-6
[236] Wheen, Francis. *Karl Marx* (2000) London;p.315
[237] Wheen, Francis. *Karl Marx* (2000) London;p.315
[238] Cited in Berlin, Isaiah. *Karl Marx* (1995) London;pp.78-9
[239] Cited in Wheen, Francis. *Karl Marx* (2000) London;p.321
[240] Cited in Wheen, Francis. *Karl Marx* (2000) London;p.321
[241] Cited in Sperber, Jonathan. *Karl Marx. A Nineteenth Century Life.* (2013) London;p.375
[242] Cited in Wheen, Francis. *Karl Marx* (2000) London;p.326
[243] Cited in Sperber, Jonathan. *Karl Marx. A Nineteenth Century Life.* (2013) London;p.381
[244] Cited in McLellan, David. *Karl Marx* (1976) St. Albans;p.392
[245] Cited in Wheen, Francis. *Karl Marx* (2000) London;p.328
[246] Cited in Sperber, Jonathan. *Karl Marx. A Nineteenth Century Life.* (2013) London;p.394
[247] Cited in McLellan, David. *Karl Marx* (1976) St. Albans;p.455
[248] Cited in Wheen, Francis. *Karl Marx* (2000) London;p.336
[249] Cited in Wheen, Francis. *Karl Marx* (2000) London;p.103
[250] Cited in Kamenka, Eugene (editor) *The Portable Karl Marx* (1983) London;p.23
[251] Cited in Wheen, Francis. *Karl Marx* (2000) London;p.64
[252] Cited in Kamenka, Eugene (editor) *The Portable Karl Marx* (1983) London;p.26
[253] Cited in Wheen, Francis. *Karl Marx* (2000) London;p.240
[254] Cited in McLellan, David. *Karl Marx* (1976) St. Albans;p.453
[255] Cited in Kamenka, Eugene (editor) *The Portable Karl Marx* (1983) London;p.53
[256] Cited in Kamenka, Eugene (editor) *The Portable Karl Marx* (1983) London;p.250
[257] Cited in Moore, Charles. *Margaret Thatcher: Volume Two* (2015) London;p.22
[258] Cited in McLellan, David. *Karl Marx* (1976) St. Albans;p.441
[259] Cited in Kamenka, Eugene (editor) *The Portable Karl Marx* (1983) London;p.557
[260] Cited in Kamenka, Eugene (editor) *The Portable Karl Marx* (1983) London;p.557
[261] Cited in McLellan, David. *Karl Marx* (1976) St. Albans;p.441
[262] Cited in McLellan, David. *Karl Marx* (1976) St. Albans;p.441
[263] Cited in McLellan, David. *Karl Marx* (1976) St. Albans;p.442
[264] Cited in McLellan, David. *Karl Marx. His Life and Thought* (1976) St. Albans;p.439
[265] Cited in Wheen, Francis. *Karl Marx* (2000) London;p.358
[266] Cited in Kamenka, Eugene (editor) *The Portable Karl Marx* (1983) London;p.71

Chapter 3 – The Soviet Nightmare

[1] Cited in Figes, Orlando. *A People's Tragedy* (1997) London;p.87
[2] Cited in Figes, Orlando. *A People's Tragedy* (1997) London;p.102
[3] Figes, Orlando. *A People's Tragedy* (1997) London;pp.125-7
[4] Cited in Figes, Orlando. *A People's Tragedy* (1997) London;p.132
[5] Cited in Figes, Orlando. *A People's Tragedy* (1997) London;p.139
[6] Horowitz, David. *Radical Son* (1997) New York;p.55
[7] Figes, Orlando. *A People's Tragedy* (1997) London;p.27
[8] Amis, Martin. Kob*a the Dread* (2002) London;p.27
[9] Service, Robert. *Lenin* (2010) London;p.73
[10] Cited in Service, Robert. *Lenin* (2010) London;p.88
[11] Cited in Service, Robert. *Lenin* (2010) London;p.81
[12] Lenin, Vladimir. *What is to be Done?* (1902)via internet;p.47
[13] Service, Robert. *Lenin* (2010) London;p.159
[14] Cited in Service, Robert. *Lenin* (2010) London;p.229
[15] Figes, Orlando. *A People's Tragedy* (1997) London;p.390
[16] Cited in Service, Robert. *Lenin* (2010) London;p.177
[17] Cited in Figes, Orlando. *A People's Tragedy* (1997) London;p.311
[18] Conquest, Robert. *Reflections on a Ravaged Century* (1999) London;pp.54-5
[19] Cited in Service, Robert. *Lenin* (2010) London;p.273
[20] Service, Robert. *Trotsky* (2010) London;p.54
[21] Cited in Service, Robert. *Trotsky* (2010) London;p.99
[22] Cited in Service, Robert. *Trotsky* (2010) London;p.172
[23] Cited in Service, Robert. *Trotsky* (2010) London;p.187
[24] Cited in Service, Robert. *Lenin* (2010) London;p.309
[25] Cited in Glover, Jonathan. *Humanity* (1999) London;p.254
[26] Cited in Figes, Orlando. *A People's Tragedy* (1997) London;p.723
[27] Cited in Glover, Jonathan. *Humanity* (1999) London;p.255
[28] Cited in Glover, Jonathan. *Humanity* (1999) London;p.255
[29] Cited in Glover, Jonathan. *Humanity* (1999) London;p.258
[30] Cited in Figes, Orlando. *A People's Tragedy* (1997) London;pp.510-11
[31] Cited in Figes, Orlando. *A People's Tragedy* (1997) London;p.524
[32] Cited in Figes, Orlando. *A People's Tragedy* (1997) London;p.524
[33] Cited in Figes, Orlando. *A People's Tragedy* (1997) London;pp.524-5
[34] Cited in Figes, Orlando. *A People's Tragedy* (1997) London;p.510
[35] Cited in Service, Robert. *Lenin* (2010) London;p.358
[36] Cited in Service, Robert. *Lenin* (2010) London;p.365
[37] Cited in Service, Robert. *Lenin* (2010) London;p.350
[38] Cited in Service, Robert. *Trotsky* (2010) London;p.221
[39] Cited in Figes, Orlando. *A People's Tragedy* (1997) London;p.544
[40] Cited in Service, Robert. *Trotsky* (2010) London;p.223
[41] Cited in Figes, Orlando. *A People's Tragedy* (1997) London;p.630
[42] Cited in Figes, Orlando. *A People's Tragedy* (1997) London;p.641
[43] Cited in Service, Robert. *Lenin* (2010) London;p.395

[44] Cited in Figes, Orlando. *A People's Tragedy* (1997) London;pp.534-5
[45] Cited in Figes, Orlando. *A People's Tragedy* (1997) London;p.618
[46] Cited in Service, Robert. *Trotsky* (2010) London;p.290
[47] Cited in Jisheng, Yang. *Tombstone* (2012) London;p.88
[48] Cited in Service, Robert. *Lenin* (2010) London;p.426
[49] Cited in Figes, Orlando. *A People's Tragedy* (1997) London;pp.763-4
[50] Cited in Figes, Orlando. *A People's Tragedy* (1997) London;p.605
[51] Cited in Service, Robert. *Lenin* (2010) London;p.390
[52] Cited in Service, Robert. *Lenin* (2010) London;p.411
[53] Cited in Figes, Orlando. *A People's Tragedy* (1997) London;p.734
[54] Cited in Service, Robert. *Trotsky* (2010) London;p.311
[55] Cited in Figes, Orlando. *A People's Tragedy* (1997) London;pp.732-3
[56] Cited in Figes, Orlando. *A People's Tragedy* (1997) London;p.743
[57] Cited in Figes, Orlando. *A People's Tragedy* (1997) London;p.749
[58] Figes, Orlando. *A People's Tragedy* (1997) London;p.751
[59] Figes, Orlando. *A People's Tragedy* (1997) London;p.773
[60] Cited in Figes, Orlando. *A People's Tragedy* (1997) London;p.386
[61] Cited in Figes, Orlando. *A People's Tragedy* (1997) London;p.391
[62] Bullock, Alan. *Hitler and Stalin* (1998) London;pp.13-6
[63] Cited in Bullock, Alan. *Hitler and Stalin* (1998) London;p.14
[64] Conquest, Robert. *Reflections on a Ravaged Century* (1999) London;p.208
[65] Cited in Service, Robert. *Stalin* (2010) London;p.41
[66] Cited in Service, Robert. *Stalin* (2010) London;p.59
[67] Service, Robert. *Stalin* (2010) London;p.92
[68] Service, Robert. *Stalin* (2010) London;p.144
[69] Cited in Conquest, Robert. *The Harvest of Sorrow* (2002) London;p.111
[70] Cited in Conquest, Robert. *The Harvest of Sorrow* (2002) London;p.117
[71] Sebag Montefiore, Simon. *Stalin. The Court of the Red Tsar* (2004) London;p.40
[72] Cited in Conquest, Robert. *The Harvest of Sorrow* (2002) London;p.129
[73] Cited in Conquest, Robert. *The Harvest of Sorrow* (2002) London;p.130
[74] Cited in Sebag Montefiore, Simon. *Stalin. The Court of the Red Tsar* (2004) London;p.48
[75] Cited in Conquest, Robert. *The Harvest of Sorrow* (2002) London;p.128
[76] Cited in Conquest, Robert. *The Harvest of Sorrow* (2002) London;p.137
[77] Cited in Conquest, Robert. *The Harvest of Sorrow* (2002) London;p.133
[78] Cited in Conquest, Robert. *The Harvest of Sorrow* (2002) London;p.133
[79] Cited in Conquest, Robert. *The Harvest of Sorrow* (2002) London;pp.147-8
[80] Cited in Conquest, Robert. *The Harvest of Sorrow* (2002) London;p.148
[81] Cited in Conquest, Robert. *The Harvest of Sorrow* (2002) London;p.148
[82] Cited in Conquest, Robert. *The Harvest of Sorrow* (2002) London;p.157
[83] Cited in Conquest, Robert. *The Harvest of Sorrow* (2002) London;p.152
[84] Amis, Martin. *Koba the Dread* (2002) London;p.127
[85] Conquest, Robert. *The Harvest of Sorrow* (2002) London;p.3
[86] Cited in Conquest, Robert. *The Harvest of Sorrow* (2002) London;p.10
[87] Cited in Conquest, Robert. *The Harvest of Sorrow* (2002) London;p.25

[88] Cited in Conquest, Robert. *The Harvest of Sorrow* (2002) London;p.221
[89] Cited in Conquest, Robert. *The Harvest of Sorrow* (2002) London;p.225
[90] Cited in Conquest, Robert. *The Harvest of Sorrow* (2002) London;p.223
[91] Cited in Conquest, Robert. *The Harvest of Sorrow* (2002) London;pp.232-3
[92] Cited in Conquest, Robert. *The Harvest of Sorrow* (2002) London;p.245
[93] Cited in Crossman, Richard (ed.) *The God That Failed* (1965) New York;p.53
[94] Cited in Conquest, Robert. *The Harvest of Sorrow* (2002) London;pp.248-9
[95] Amis, Martin. *Koba the Dread* (2002) London;p.134
[96] Figes, Orlando. *Natasha's Dance* (2003) London;p.478
[97] Cited in Conquest, Robert. *The Harvest of Sorrow* (2002) London;p.261
[98] Cited in Conquest, Robert. *The Harvest of Sorrow* (2002) London;p.261
[99] Cited in Conquest, Robert. *The Harvest of Sorrow* (2002) London;p.346
[100] Cited in Conquest, Robert. *The Harvest of Sorrow* (2002) London;p.344
[101] Cited in Sebag Montefiore, Simon. *Stalin. The Court of the Red Tsar* (2004) London;p.132
[102] Cited in Amis, Martin. *Koba the Dread* (2002) London;p.152
[103] Cited in Sebag Montefiore, Simon. *Stalin. The Court of the Red Tsar* (2004) London;p.132
[104] Cited in Sebag Montefiore, Simon. *Stalin. The Court of the Red Tsar* (2004) London;p.134
[105] Cited in Sebag Montefiore, Simon. *Stalin. The Court of the Red Tsar* (2004) London;p.134
[106] Cited in Applebaum, Anne. *Gulag* (2004) London; p.111
[107] Cited in Conquest, Robert. *The Great Terror* (2008)London;p.xv
[108] Cited in Conquest, Robert. *The Great Terror* (2008) London;pp.14-15
[109] Sebag Montefiore, Simon. *Stalin. The Court of the Red Tsar* (2004) London;p.152
[110] Cited in Sebag Montefiore, Simon. *Stalin. The Court of the Red Tsar* (2004) London;p.190
[111] Cited in Conquest, Robert. *The Great Terror* (2008) London;p.122
[112] Cited in Sebag Montefiore, Simon. *Stalin. The Court of the Red Tsar* (2004) London;p.190
[113] Cited in Sebag Montefiore, Simon. *Stalin. The Court of the Red Tsar* (2004) London;p.192
[114] Cited in Sebag Montefiore, Simon. *Stalin. The Court of the Red Tsar* (2004) London;p.193
[115] Cited in Sebag Montefiore, Simon. *Stalin. The Court of the Red Tsar* (2004) London;p.193
[116] Cited in Sebag Montefiore, Simon. *Stalin. The Court of the Red Tsar* (2004) London;p.197
[117] Cited in Sebag Montefiore, Simon. *Stalin. The Court of the Red Tsar* (2004) London;p.197
[118] Cited in Amis, Martin. *Koba the Dread* (2002) London;p.115
[119] Cited in Conquest, Robert. *The Great Terror* (2008)London;p.225
[120] Cited in Sebag Montefiore, Simon. *Stalin. The Court of the Red Tsar* (2004) London;p.210

[121] Sebag Montefiore, Simon. *Stalin. The Court of the Red Tsar* (2004) London;p.214
[122] Cited in Sebag Montefiore, Simon. *Stalin. The Court of the Red Tsar* (2004) London;pp.214-5
[123] Cited in Sebag Montefiore, Simon. *Stalin. The Court of the Red Tsar* (2004) London;p.227
[124] Cited in Sebag Montefiore, Simon. *Stalin. The Court of the Red Tsar* (2004) London;p.228
[125] Cited in Sebag Montefiore, Simon. *Stalin. The Court of the Red Tsar* (2004) London;p.229
[126] Cited in Sebag Montefiore, Simon. *Stalin. The Court of the Red Tsar* (2004) London;p.229
[127] Cited in Sebag Montefiore, Simon. *Stalin. The Court of the Red Tsar* (2004) London;p.236
[128] Cited in Sebag Montefiore, Simon. *Stalin. The Court of the Red Tsar* (2004) London;pp.234-5
[129] Cited in Sebag Montefiore, Simon. *Stalin. The Court of the Red Tsar* (2004) London;p.245
[130] Cited in Sebag Montefiore, Simon. *Stalin. The Court of the Red Tsar* (2004) London;p.255
[131] Cited in Sebag Montefiore, Simon. *Stalin. The Court of the Red Tsar* (2004) London;p.242
[132] Cited in Sebag Montefiore, Simon. *Stalin. The Court of the Red Tsar* (2004) London;p.277
[133] Cited in Sebag Montefiore, Simon. *Stalin. The Court of the Red Tsar* (2004) London;p.219
[134] Cited in Conquest, Robert. *The Great Terror* (2008) London;pp.390-1
[135] Cited in Conquest, Robert. *The Great Terror* (2008) London;p.391
[136] Cited in Sebag Montefiore, Simon. *Stalin. The Court of the Red Tsar* (2004) London;p.222
[137] Cited in Sebag Montefiore, Simon. *Stalin. The Court of the Red Tsar* (2004) London;p.290
[138] Cited in Sebag Montefiore, Simon. *Stalin. The Court of the Red Tsar* (2004) London;p.332
[139] Cited in Amis, Martin. *Koba the Dread* (2002) London;p.196
[140] Cited in Amis, Martin. *Koba the Dread* (2002) London;p.176
[141] Cited in Sebag Montefiore, Simon. *Stalin. The Court of the Red Tsar* (2004) London;p.264
[142] Cited in Sebag Montefiore, Simon. *Stalin. The Court of the Red Tsar* (2004) London;p.213
[143] Cited in Conquest, Robert. *The Great Terror* (2008)London;p.7
[144] Sebag Montefiore, Simon. *Stalin. The Court of the Red Tsar* (2004) London;p.88
[145] Cited in Sebag Montefiore, Simon. *Stalin. The Court of the Red Tsar* (2004) London;p.89
[146] Amis, Martin. *Koba the Dread* (2002) London;p.178
[147] Cited in Conquest, Robert. *The Great Terror* (2008)London;p.446

[148] Cited in Conquest, Robert. *The Great Terror* (2008)London;p.99
[149] Cited in Conquest, Robert. *The Great Terror* (2008)London;p.112
[150] Cited in Conquest, Robert. *The Great Terror* (2008)London;p.112
[151] Cited in Bullock, Alan. *Hitler and Stalin* (1998) London;p.554
[152] Bullock, Alan. *Hitler and Stalin* (1998) London;p.457
[153] Cited in Service, Robert. *Trotsky* (2010) London; p.334
[154] Cited in Service, Robert. *Trotsky* (2010) London; p.485
[155] Amis, Martin. *Koba the Dread* (2002) London;p.59
[156] Solzhenitsyn, Aleksander. *The Gulag Archipelago* (2003) London;p.78
[157] Glover, Jonathan. *Humanity* (1999) London;p.240
[158] Solzhenitsyn, Aleksander. *The Gulag Archipelago* (2003) London;p.214
[159] Solzhenitsyn, Aleksander. *The Gulag Archipelago* (2003) London;p.56
[160] Cited in Applebaum, Anne. *Gulag* (2004) London;p.228
[161] Cited in Applebaum, Anne. *Gulag* (2004) London;p.226
[162] Solzhenitsyn, Aleksander. *The Gulag Archipelago* (2003) London;p.62
[163] Cited in Applebaum, Anne. *Gulag* (2004) London;p.328
[164] Cited in Solzhenitsyn, Aleksander. *The Gulag Archipelago* (2003) London;p.243
[165] Cited in Solzhenitsyn, Aleksander. *The Gulag Archipelago* (2003) London;p.244
[166] Applebaum, Anne. *Gulag* (2004) London;p.256
[167] Cited in Applebaum, Anne. *Gulag* (2004) London;p.153
[168] Cited in Applebaum, Anne. *Gulag* (2004) London;p.296
[169] Cited in Applebaum, Anne. *Gulag* (2004) London;p.296
[170] Cited in Applebaum, Anne. *Gulag* (2004) London;p.320
[171] Cited in Applebaum, Anne. *Gulag* (2004) London;p.320
[172] Solzhenitsyn, Aleksander. *The Gulag Archipelago* (2003) London;pp.77-8
[173] Amis, Martin. *Koba the Dread* (2002) London;p.86
[174] Solzhenitsyn, Aleksander. *The Gulag Archipelago* (2003) London;p.349
[175] Applebaum, Anne. *Gulag* (2004) London;p.514
[176] Cited in Applebaum, Anne. *Gulag* (2004) London;p.323
[177] Cited in Sebag Montefiore, Simon. *Stalin. The Court of the Red Tsar* (2004) London;p.236
[178] Cited in Conquest, Robert. *The Dragons of Expectation* (2005) London;p.154
[179] Cited in Amis, Martin. *Koba the Dread* (2002) London;p.150
[180] Amis, Martin. *Koba the Dread* (2002) London;p.30
[181] Cited in Conquest, Robert. *The Great Terror* (2008) London;p.488
[182] Cited in Amis, Martin. *Koba the Dread* (2002) London;p.189
[183] Cited in Amis, Martin. *Koba the Dread* (2002) London;pp.190-1
[184] Cited in Amis, Martin. *Koba the Dread* (2002) London;pp.191-2
[185] Cited in Conquest, Robert. *The Great Terror* (2008) London;p.331
[186] Cited in Sebag Montefiore, Simon. *Stalin. The Court of the Red Tsar* (2004) London;p.142
[187] Cited in Sebag Montefiore, Simon. *Stalin. The Court of the Red Tsar* (2004) London;p.262
[188] Cited in Sebag Montefiore, Simon. *Stalin. The Court of the Red Tsar* (2004) London;p.88

[189] Cited in Figes, Orlando. *Natasha's Dance* (2003) London;p.450
[190] Cited in Sebag Montefiore, Simon. *Stalin. The Court of the Red Tsar* (2004) London;p.97
[191] Cited in Sebag Montefiore, Simon. *Stalin. The Court of the Red Tsar* (2004) London;p.98
[192] Cited in Sebag Montefiore, Simon. *Stalin. The Court of the Red Tsar* (2004) London;p.98
[193] Cited in Sebag Montefiore, Simon. *Stalin. The Court of the Red Tsar* (2004) London;p.99
[194] Cited in Conquest, Robert. *The Great Terror* (2008)London;p.306
[195] Cited in Amis, Martin. *Koba the Dread* (2002) London;p.16
[196] Cited in Sebag Montefiore, Simon. *Stalin. The Court of the Red Tsar* (2004) London;p.522
[197] Glover, Jonathan. *Humanity* (1999) London;p.255
[198] Cited in Glover, Jonathan. *Humanity* (1999) London;p.256
[199] Cited in Glover, Jonathan. *Humanity* (1999) London;p.252
[200] Cited in Service, Robert. *Stalin* (2010) London;pp.341-2
[201] Cited in Sebag Montefiore, Simon. *Young Stalin* (2008) London;p.66
[202] Cited in Conquest, Robert. *The Great Terror* (2008) London;p.viii
[203] Cited in Conquest, Robert. *The Dragons of Expectation* (2005) London;p.146
[204] Cited in Conquest, Robert. *The Harvest of Sorrow* (2002) London;p.260
[205] Amis, Martin. *Koba the Dread* (2002) London;p.21
[206] Cited in Amis, Martin. *Koba the Dread* (2002) London;p.21
[207] Cited in Conquest, Robert. *The Harvest of Sorrow* (2002) London;p.316
[208] Cited in Conquest, Robert. *The Harvest of Sorrow* (2002) London;p.316
[209] Cited in Conquest, Robert. *The Harvest of Sorrow* (2002) London;p.317
[210] Cited in Conquest, Robert. *The Harvest of Sorrow* (2002) London;p.317
[211] Cited in Conquest, Robert. *The Harvest of Sorrow* (2002) London;p.318
[212] Cited in Glover, Jonathan. *Humanity* (1999) London;p.255
[213] Cited in Conquest, Robert. *The Harvest of Sorrow* (2002) London;p.319
[214] Cited in Conquest, Robert. *The Harvest of Sorrow* (2002) London;p.320
[215] Cited in Conquest, Robert. *The Great Terror* (2008)London;p.465
[216] Cited in Conquest, Robert. *The Great Terror* (2008)London;p.467
[217] Cited in Conquest, Robert. *The Great Terror* (2008)London;p.467
[218] Cited in Conquest, Robert. *The Great Terror* (2008)London;p.468
[219] Cited in Conquest, Robert. *The Great Terror* (2008)London;p.469
[220] Cited in Service, Robert. *Comrades* (2008) London; p.206
[221] Cited in Conquest, Robert. *The Great Terror* (2008)London;p.474
[222] Cited in Conquest, Robert. *The Great Terror* (2008)London;p.475
[223] Amis, Martin. *Koba the Dread* (2002) London;p.8
[224] Amis, Martin. *Koba the Dread* (2002) London;p.11
[225] Solzhenitsyn, Aleksandr. *The Gulag Archipelago* (2003) London;p.40
[226] Cited in Conquest, Robert. *Reflections on a Ravaged Century* (1999) London; pp.10-11

Chapter 4 – The Nazi Quandary

[1] Glover, Jonathan. *Humanity* (1999) London;p.358
[2] Cited in Glover, Jonathan. *Humanity* (1999) London;p.359
[3] Arendt, Hannah. *Eichmann in Jeruslaem* (2006) London;p.105
[4] Cited in Bullock, Alan. *Hitler and Stalin. Parallel Lives* (1998) London;p.496
[5] Cited in Bullock, Alan. *Hitler and Stalin. Parallel Lives* (1998) London;p.716
[6] Cited in Arendt, Hannah. *Eichmann in Jerusalem* (2006) London;p.49.
[7] Cited in Arendt, Hannah. *Eichmann in Jerusalem* (2006) London;p.25
[8] Arendt, Hannah. *Eichmann in Jerusalem* (2006) London;p.116
[9] Arendt, Hannah. *Eichmann in Jerusalem* (2006) London;p.25
[10] Cited in Arendt, Hannah. *Eichmann in Jerusalem* (2006) London;p.279
[11] Cited in Glover, Jonathan. *Humanity* (1999) London;p.356
[12] Cited in Bullock, Alan. *Hitler and Stalin. Parallel Lives* (1998) London;p.649
[13] Cited in Bullock, Alan. *Hitler and Stalin. Parallel Lives* (1998) London;p.910
[14] Cited in Sebag-Montefiore, Simon. *Stalin. The Court of the Red Tsar* (2004) London;p.345
[15] Bullock, Alan. *Hitler and Stalin. Parallel Lives* (1998) London;p.158
[16] Cited in Glover, Jonathan. *Humanity* (1999) London;p.369
[17] Hitler, Adolf. *Mein Kampf* (2017) Mumbai;p.33
[18] Hitler, Adolf. *Mein Kampf* (2017) Mumbai;p.39
[19] Hitler, Adolf. *Mein Kampf* (2017) Mumbai;p.50
[20] Hitler, Adolf. *Mein Kampf* (2017) Mumbai;p.56
[21] Hitler, Adolf. *Mein Kampf* (2017) Mumbai;p.63
[22] Hitler, Adolf. *Mein Kampf* (2017) Mumbai;p.62
[23] Hitler, Adolf. *Mein Kampf* (2017) Mumbai;p.118
[24] Hitler, Adolf. *Mein Kampf* (2017) Mumbai;p.216
[25] Hitler, Adolf. *Mein Kampf* (2017) Mumbai;p.193
[26] Hitler, Adolf. *Mein Kampf* (2017) Mumbai;p.216
[27] Hitler, Adolf. *Mein Kampf* (2017) Mumbai;p.221
[28] Hitler, Adolf. *Mein Kampf* (2017) Mumbai;p.285
[29] Hitler, Adolf. *Mein Kampf* (2017) Mumbai;p.284
[30] Hitler, Adolf. *Mein Kampf* (2017) Mumbai;p.300
[31] Hitler, Adolf. *Mein Kampf* (2017) Mumbai;pp.318-9
[32] Goldberg, Jonah. *Liberal Fascism* (2007) London;p.72
[33] Cited in Watson, George. *The Lost Literature of Socialism* (2010) Cambridge;p.75
[34] Bullock, Alan. *Hitler and Stalin. Parallel Lives* (1998) London;p.84
[35] Bullock, Alan. *Hitler and Stalin. Parallel Lives* (1998) London;p.388
[36] Cited in Glover, Jonathan. *Humanity* (1999) London;p.344
[37] Bullock, Alan. *Hitler and Stalin. Parallel Lives* (1998) London;p.766
[38] Arendt, Hannah. *Eichmann in Jerusalem* (2006) London;p.176
[39] Cited in Goldberg, Jonah. *Liberal Fascism* (2007) London;p.44
[40] Cited in Goldberg, Jonah. *Liberal Fascism* (2007) London;p.52
[41] Cited in Hannan, Daniel. *How we Invented Freedom & Why it Matters* (2013) London;p.53

[42] Cited in Bullock, Alan. *Hitler and Stalin. Parallel Lives* (1998) London;p.168
[43] Cited in Bullock, Alan. *Hitler and Stalin. Parallel Lives* (1998) London;p.168
[44] Cited in Bullock, Alan. *Hitler and Stalin. Parallel Lives* (1998) London;p.274
[45] Hitler, Adolf. *Mein Kampf* (2017) Mumbai;p.313
[46] Cited in Bullock, Alan. *Hitler and Stalin. Parallel Lives* (1998) London;p.381
[47] Cited in Bullock, Alan. *Hitler and Stalin. Parallel Lives* (1998) London;p.184
[48] Cited in Bullock, Alan. *Hitler and Stalin. Parallel Lives* (1998) London;p.185
[49] Cited in Bullock, Alan. *Hitler and Stalin. Parallel Lives* (1998) London;p.365
[50] Cited in Bullock, Alan. *Hitler and Stalin. Parallel Lives* (1998) London;p.368
[51] Watson, George. *The Lost Literature of Socialism* (2010) Cambridge;p.83
[52] Cited in Watson, George. *The Lost Literature of Socialism* (2010) Cambridge;pp.97-8
[53] Cited in Watson, George. *The Lost Literature of Socialism* (2010) Cambridge;p.98
[54] Cited in Lawson, Dominic. 'A Reminder: 'The Uneducated' Protest us From Brilliant Idiots.' *Sunday Times* (12 February 2017)
[55] Cited in Watson, George. *The Lost Literature of Socialism* (2010) Cambridge;p.98
[56] Watson, George. *The Lost Literature of Socialism* (2010) Cambridge;p.82
[57] Engels, Freidrich. 'The Magyar Struggle'. In *Neue Rheinische Zeitung* No. 194. 13 January 1849
[58] Cited in Watson, George. *The Lost Literature of Socialism* (2010) Cambridge;p.82
[59] Cited in Watson, George. *The Lost Literature of Socialism* (2010) Cambridge;p.83
[60] Cited in Watson, George. *The Lost Literature of Socialism* (2010) Cambridge;p.90
[61] Hayek, Friedrcih. *The Road to Serfdom* (2001) Abingdon, Oxfordshire;p.4
[62] Cited in Watson, George. *The Lost Literature of Socialism* (2010) Cambridge;p.74
[63] Cited in Watson, George. *The Lost Literature of Socialism* (2010) Cambridge;p.74
[64] Cited in Watson, George. *The Lost Literature of Socialism* (2010) Cambridge;p.87
[65] Cited in Watson, George. *The Lost Literature of Socialism* (2010) Cambridge;p.88
[66] Cited in Glover, Jonathan. *Humanity* (1999) London;p.325
[67] Glover, Jonathan. *Humanity* (1999) London;p.360
[68] Cited in Glover, Jonathan. *Humanity* (1999) London;p.329
[69] Hayek, Friedrich. *The Road to Serfdom* (2001) Abingdon, Oxfordshire;p.146
[70] Cited in Chandler, David. *Voices From S-21* (2000) Chiang Mai, Thailand;p.146
[71] Cited in Chandler, David. *Voices From S-21* (2000) Chiang Mai, Thailand;p.154
[72] Glover, Jonathan. *Humanity* (1999) London;p.361
[73] Cited in Glover, Jonathan. *Humanity* (1999) London;p.363
[74] Cited in Aberbach, David. *The European Jews* (2012) London;p.28
[75] Cited in Aberbach, David. *The European Jews* (2012) London;p.28
[76] Cited in Sperber, Jonathan. *Karl Marx* (2013) New York;p.411
[77] Cited in Wheen, Francis. *Karl Marx* (2000) London;p.340
[78] Cited in Arendt, Hannah. *The Origins of Totalitarianism* (1994) New York;p.24
[79] Arendt, Hannah. *The Origins of Totalitarianism* (1994) New York;p.43
[80] Cited in Goldberg, Jonah. *Liberal Fascism* (2007) London;p.76
[81] Cited in Watson, George. *The Lost Literature of Socialism* (2010) Cambridge;p.82
[82] Cited in Goldberg, Jonah. *Liberal Fascism* (2007) London;p.18
[83] Cited in Goldberg, Jonah. *Liberal Fascism* (2007) London;p.249
[84] Hitchens, Christopher. *Hitch-22* (2011) London;p.190

[85] Cited in Palmer, Jamie. 'The Holocaust, the Left, and the Return of Hate.' http://www.thetower.org/article/the-holocaust-the-left-and-the-return-of-hate/
[86] Cited in Aaronovitch, David. *Party Animals* (2017) London;p.249
[87] Cited in Aaronovitch, David. *Party Animals* (2017) London;p.250
[88] Cited in Aaronovitch, David. *Party Animals* (2017) London;p.251
[89] Cited in Aaronovitch, David. *Party Animals* (2017) London;p.252
[90] Arendt, Hannah. *Eichmann in Jerusalem* (2006) London;pp.12-3
[91] Schoenman, Ralph. *The Hidden History of Zionism* (1988) http://takingaimnow.com/hhz/ch02.htm
[92] Schama, Simon. 'The Left's Problem With the Jews has a Long and Miserable History.' *Financial Times* (19 February 2016) p.nn
[93] Wisse, Ruth. 'Anti-Semitism Goes to School.' https://mosaicmagazine.com/essay/2015/05/anti-semitism-goes-to-school/ (22 July 2017)
[94] Wolfe, Tom. *Radical Chic* (2009) New York; p.73
[95] Jessica Chasmar. The Washington Times http://www.washingtontimes.com/news/2015/feb/3/university-of-california-students-chant-allahu-akbr/
[96] Weisfield, Hannah. 'What Hope the Fight Against Anti-Semitism?' http://www.theguardian.com/commentisfree/2016/apr/22/antisemitism-malia-bouattia-nus-muslim-anti-zionist
[97] Harding, Eleanor. 'Left Wing hate mobs' http://www.dailymail.co.uk/news/article-3338867/Universities-dominated-Left-wing-hate-mobs-Professor-says-free-speech-stifled-challenging-views[-shouted-down.html (30 November 2015)
[98] Chalmers, Alex. 'Anti-Semitism, Anti-Zionism, Oxford and Me.' http://www.newstatesman.com/politics/staggers/2016/03/most-important-election-next-five-years-isnt-country-its-unite (15 March 2016)
[99] Will Worley 'Campbell Denies Suspension' http://www.independent.co.uk/news/uk/politics/labour-suspends-member-who-thinks-isis-israeli-conspiracy-a6956551.html (30 March 2016)
[100] Peev, Gerri. 'Corbyn's Great Pals' http://www.dailymail.co.uk/news/article-3728588/Storm-Corbyn-s-great-pals-compare-Israel-ISIS-terrorists-Row-Labour-anti-Semitism-grows-comments-two-ministers.html (8 August 2016)
[101] Peev, Gerri. 'Corbyn's Great Pals' http://www.dailymail.co.uk/news/article-3728588/Storm-Corbyn-s-great-pals-compare-Israel-ISIS-terrorists-Row-Labour-anti-Semitism-grows-comments-two-ministers.html (8 August 2016)
[102] Cited in Groves, Jason. 'Now Expel Ken For Hitler Row, Corbyn Told.' *Daily Mail* (30 April 2016) p.12
[103] Cited in Hitler, Adolf. *Mein Kampf* (2017) Mumbai;p.295
[104] Cited in Swinford, Steven. 'Livingstone Cut Loose.' *Daily Telegraph* (29 April 2016) p.3
[105] Pollard, Stephen. 'Social Media Makes Jew-Hating So Easy.' *Daily Telegraph* (8 February 2017) p.16
[106] Doyle, Jack. 'Anti-Semitic Abuse Rife on Pro-Labour Web Form' *Daily Mail* (20 September 2017) p.2

[107] Martin, Daniel. 'Shame of Anti-Semites.' *Daily Mail* (26 September 2017) p.6
[108] Kerbaj, Richard. 'Vile Anti-Semitic Taunts.' *Sunday Times* (7 April 2019) pp.14-5
[109] Kerbaj, Richard. 'Vile Anti-Semitic Taunts.' *Sunday Times* (7 April 2019) pp.14-5
[110] Rose, David. 'Holocaust Deniers Given Secret Advice.' *Mail on Sunday* (17 November 2019) p.22
[111] Owen, Glen. 'Livingstone Blames it all on 'Ghastly Blairites'.' *Mail on Sunday* (31 March 2019) p.4
[112] Jewish Labour Movement. Submission to the EHRC. *Daily Telegraph* (6 December 2019) p.1
[113] Hardy, Frances. 'How Can This be Happening Here?' *Daily Mail* (1 July 2017) p.15

Printed in Great Britain
by Amazon

54477497R00274